The South American Table

The South American Table

THE FLAVOR AND SOUL OF
AUTHENTIC HOME COOKING FROM
PATAGONIA TO RIO DE JANEIRO,
WITH 450 RECIPES

Maria Baez Kijac

Foreword by Charlie Trotter

THE HARVARD COMMON PRESS | BOSTON, MASSACHUSETTS

The Harvard Common Press
535 Albany Street
Boston, Massachusetts 02118
www.harvardcommonpress.com

PRINTED IN THE UNITED STATES OF AMERICA

PRINTED ON ACID-FREE PAPER

LIBRARY OF CONGRESS CATALOGING-IN-PUBLICATION DATA

Kijac, Maria Baez.
   The South American table : the flavor and soul of authentic home cooking from Patagonia to Rio de Janeiro, with 450 recipes / Maria Baez Kijac.
      p. cm.
Includes bibliographical references and index.
   ISBN 1-55832-248-5 (hc : alk. paper) — ISBN 1-55832-249-3 (pbk : alk. paper)
   1. Cookery, Latin American. 2. Cookery—South America. 3. South America—Social life and customs. I. Title.
   TX716.A1K55 2003
   641.598—dc21   2003011100

Special bulk-order discounts are available on this and other Harvard Common Press books. Companies and organizations may purchase books for premiums or resale, or may arrange a custom edition, by contacting the Marketing Director at the address above.

Cover design by Night & Day Design
Cover photograph by Alexandra Grablewski
Interior design by Richard Oriolo

10 9 8 7 6 5 4 3 2 1

TO MY DECEASED PARENTS,
ALONSO BÁEZ CHÁVEZ AND MARÍA LUISA CARRERA DE BÁEZ,
WHO TAUGHT ME THE VALUES THAT MADE ME
THE PERSON I AM TODAY

AND TO MY DECEASED HUSBAND,
PETER KIJAC, WHO HAS BEEN THE INSPIRATION
FOR THIS BOOK

Contents

Foreword

A S EAGER COOKS AND GOURMETS around the United States seek to learn ever more about cuisines from around the world, there is one area in particular that remains largely untapped—the foods of South America. Maria Baez Kijac goes a long way in remedying that problem for us with the publication of *The South American Table*. This glorious work is a literal love note to the beauties and pleasures of the foods of South America. The pages within are absolutely packed with history, geography, anecdotes, and, of course, tremendous recipes. Each preparation is introduced with pertinent cooking information or an insightful story that makes the actual preparation of the dish just that much more special.

In my own cuisine, I covet ideas from around the world, and I can enthusiastically say that I have thoroughly mined these pages and discovered many gems. The *Sopa de Quinua con Chancho* (Quinoa Soup with Pork), for example, is a preparation that is simultaneously exotic and earthy, with the elegant flavors of cumin and annatto subtly perfuming the dish. Also, the *Calabi Matutero* (Chicken with Okra and Cabbage), which was originally made with goat, is extremely light and delicate, yet it has tremendous depth of flavor. Additionally, I'm quite fond of the *Librillo en Salsa Mani* (Tripe in Peanut Sauce). This unique preparation, with its satiny peanut essence, will forever change the way you think about tripe. And for sheer sensual delight, go straight for the *Cuscuz de Tapioca* (Tapioca and Coconut Cake). You will be sneaking bites of this when no one is looking.

Best of all, this book contains exclusively recipes that are straightforward and unintimidating, approachable for any level of experience in the kitchen. Plus, you will discover, as I have, that the foods of South America are quite healthy, relying on fresh seasonal produce and deemphasizing the use of cream and butter. Furthermore, if *The South American Table* whets your appetite to learn more, then you can refer to the stunningly extensive bibliography in the rear of the book.

One's appreciation for the utter depth of information contained here will grow with each visit into these pages. We all owe Maria Baez Kijac a hearty salutation of "Three cheers!" for her prodigious accomplishment, for with *The South American Table*, she has delivered a masterpiece.

Charlie Trotter

Acknowledgments

THE SOUTH AMERICAN TABLE WOULD not have been possible without my husband's encouragement and belief that I should write this book. His passion for excellence in food and scholarship made him a wonderful partner, and his collaboration was invaluable. After he passed on, my daughters, Patty, Carol, and Stephanie, took over, and it was their love and encouragement that made me continue with the book. The last few months of finishing *The South American Table* were made easier with their help—testing, editing, and doing anything that was needed to make my job less difficult. I will be forever grateful to them for taking time off from their busy lives to help me.

During my 15 years of research, many wonderful and generous people in North and South America have touched this book in so many ways. I will always remember with fondness the years I belonged to gourmet and cooking groups on the North Shore of Chicago. These groups provided me with an outlet for my growing curiosity about the cuisines of the world. At the time, I didn't realize that these experiences would be vital to my understanding of the South American table. There wasn't a food, no matter how complicated, that we wouldn't dare to tackle. It was with these groups that I first encountered the Brazilian *feijoada*, and I'll never forget our first attempt to make chocolates. While we prepared wonderful dinners from around the world, we also got together to make jelly, candy, and hors d'oeuvres. These memories will remain with me forever. However, the most important thing I made was friends: Ann Hill and Dave Gutkneth, Connie and Jack Kindswater, Janet and Joe MacGowen, Elaine and Hoyt Matthews, Susan and Dave Spears, Lois and Harrison Steans, Jessica and Ron Tesarik, and Lynn and Mike Zarimba.

When I started this project, the biggest challenge I had was finding sources for good recipes. South American cookbooks were hard to come by, but it was amazing that soon after I began, my family and friends were able to provide me with an enormous amount of resources. As many of them traveled throughout South America, they sent me books and recipes from the countries they visited. My special thanks go to my sisters, Fina Waterston and Ximena Báez, and my brother Polo Báez for providing me with books and with recipes they collected from friends. They were always ready to help with whatever kind of research I needed.

All of us who use the computer for writing books know how much we depend on it. After my husband's death, I found myself lost around the computer. Debbie Allen was the angel who came to my rescue. It was Debbie, with her incredible patience and understanding, who made me lose my fear of the computer. She quickly anticipated my needs and set up directories and everything else needed to complete this book. She was always ready to guide me whenever I needed help. Debbie, I will be forever grateful for your help.

After Debbie moved to California, my brother Edgar Báez and my son-in-law Tim Shanahan took over, installing software, teaching me how to use a new computer, and coming to fix whatever needed fixing. I don't know how I could have finished this book without their help.

I would also like to thank some special friends, whom I consider my extended family: June and Bob Doench, Chris and Jim Miller, and Jane and Ted Schulte. They have encouraged me and given me their support, especially after my husband's death. Their love and care pulled me through some very difficult times. They will always have a special place in my heart.

When I think back and remember the times I wanted to give up on the project, I had some other friends who reminded me of the importance of sharing my culture and the treasures of the South American table. These people include Henry and Millie Rucker, Dr. Julia Gorelik, and Dr. Pieter Van Heule. My deepest thanks go to each of them.

I also want to thank my friend and colleague Elaine Gonzalez for all the years of friendship and the wonderful times we have had traveling, studying Mexican cuisine, and going to the International Association of Culinary Professionals (IACP) annual meetings. To my friend Judy Eberlin, thank you for your encouragement and for coming week after week to help me test the tamales and empanadas, and to my friend Barbara Johnson, thank you for volunteering with the testing of many desserts. Thank you to Barbara Palinkas and Diane Hugh for their help and support, and to Dr. Emma Ottolenghi, whom I met in Washington, D.C., and who generously offered to send me some out-of-print books on Bolivian cooking. They were invaluable in my research. Emma, thank you so very much for trusting me with those precious books.

There were many South American friends who were vital to my research. It was a lucky day for me when my Colombian friend Margarita Patmore moved next door. She and her mother, Sol Name, introduced me to the foods of their country and showed me how to prepare different specialties. Sol was very helpful, always bringing books from Colombia and Venezuela that helped identify ingredients with scientific names and pictures. Martin Patmore, whose job took him to South American often, was always ready to look for more cookbooks to bring back to me. Many thanks to all of them for putting up with me so many Sunday mornings, when I invited myself over to eat Margarita's special *arepas* and sip a cup of their delicious Colombian coffee.

My Ecuadorian friend Irma Oppenheimer was always introducing me to her South American friends, hoping they could help me with my research. Helena Chapellín Wilson was one of Irma's friends who came from a family of gifted cooks. She herself is an accomplished cook and a wonderful, generous friend, who came to my house to show me the intricacies of *hallaca* (tamale) making. Thank you, Helena, for the family recipes you shared with me. Thank you, Irma, for your help and your very gracious Bolivian mother, who gladly shared with me her knowledge of the cuisine of her country. The *chuño* from Bolivia was a great help with my testing.

I don't have enough words to thank my Chilean friend Kika Keefe and her husband, Howard, for all the years of friendship and generosity and for inviting me to Chile anytime I needed to go. Kika opened her recipe files to me and showed me the foods that were important to her cuisine. She took me to the coast so that I could become acquainted with the fabulous seafood there and had her cook prepare what is most typical of Chile. Kika's friends were as gracious as she and invited us to taste their wonderful specialties.

My Uruguayan friend Yvonne Miles was my consultant extraordinaire. It is hard to find books on Uruguayan cuisine because it is primarily European and has very little indigenous influence. It was a revelation for me every time Yvonne shared her family recipes. They clearly showed their European roots, but I could always find the South American touch. Her pasta dishes and crepes have become favorites of mine. Yvonne took me to different places in Uruguay, from the fashionable resort of Punta del Este, where I could see how the wealthy entertained, to the north, where I learned about the eating and drinking habits of the people who live in the country. Many thanks, Yvonne, for the wonderful experiences you gave me and the terrific recipes your family and friends contributed to this book.

So many of my South American friends were especially kind in helping me to identify ingredients and providing me with books, recipes, and advice. Thanks to them all for their help and years of friendship. In alphabetical order, they are: Olga Lozano, Conchita Luckesi, Ana María Montoya, Carmen Ochoa, Doris Rucci, Betty Russo, Coca Skok, Mary Jane Terán, Gloria Walters, and Loreto Willes. And thanks also to two of my cousins in Ecuador,

Gladys Almeida de Franco and Lucy de Almeida, and to my Brazilian friend and colleague Teresa Corcao, who all graciously contributed their very special recipes.

There is one friend I have saved for last. About eight years ago, I met Margarida Nogueira at the IACP convention in San Francisco. Margarida is one of the foremost food professionals in Rio de Janeiro. We became close friends, and her expertise on the foods of Brazil has been of utmost importance to me in my writing on Brazil. Margarida is one of the most generous people I have ever met. She was always ready to do research for me and send me the latest books and any recipe I requested—as well as many that she felt were important to Brazilian cuisine. With the IACP and Slow Food organizations, Margarida and I have traveled together to many cities and countries, but most meaningful to me was our time together in Brazil, Portugal, and Italy. These trips were very helpful in my understanding of those countries' foods and the origin of many Brazilian specialties. Margarida shared many recipes from her family and friends, and her generous contributions are seen throughout this book.

The last person to come aboard to help me with this book was Cynthia Clampitt. Cynthia wears many hats, and she always made time to help me with whatever I needed— writing, editing, formatting, testing. Having somebody of Cynthia's talent was extremely helpful to me. Writing a book is a lonely task, and Cynthia was always willing to discuss problems that would arise as the book progressed. Thank you, Cynthia, not only for your help but your professionalism and for giving me the sense that I wasn't alone.

These acknowledgments would not be complete without mentioning the Vernon Area Library. Over many years of research, it has been an important resource to help me find unusual books from libraries across the country. Whenever I went in with an unusual request, the librarians were ready to help me, using every means at their disposal to find the answers. Thank you, thank you.

This book would not have become a reality without my agent, Lisa Ekus. I received a contract in less than two months thanks to Lisa's incredible passion and dedication. I'll always be grateful to Lisa for her support and for getting The Harvard Common Press to publish my book. My editor, Pamela Hoenig, has been a blessing from the beginning. She immediately immersed herself in the book and captured the essence of it. Pam saw what was needed to cultivate this book and was always there by phone to guide me and give me whatever time was necessary to finish the book. Her cheerfulness, enthusiasm, and superb editing are present throughout this book. From the bottom of my heart, thank you, Pam.

Bruce Shaw is an extraordinary publisher, and his high standards and positive energy filter down to his staff, which includes managing editor Valerie Cimino, the marketing department, and my terrific copyeditor, Barbara Jatkola. I thank them all for their continued faith and dedication to this project, for they have made this a wonderful experience for me.

There were so many people who were instrumental in the completion of this book, and all deserve my gratitude. If I have omitted any names in error, please forgive me and know that it wasn't intentional. I hope that everyone who reads this book will appreciate these people's contributions.

Three books have been particularly helpful in my research on the foods of the Andes; I could not have identified so many ingredients without them. They are *America's First Cuisines* by Sophie D. Coe, *Lost Crops of the Incas* by the National Research Council, and *El Pan de América* by Eduardo Estrella. *The Masters and the Slaves* by Gilberto Freyre was tremendously helpful with the foods of Brazil.

My deepest thanks also go to Elisabeth Ortiz, who 30 years ago wrote her pioneering work *The Book of Latin American Cooking*, the most comprehensive book to date on the foods of Latin America.

Preface

LIKE MANY SOUTH AMERICANS, I come from a large, extended, Catholic family. My heritage is a mixture of Spanish, Indian, and, according to my father, some Portuguese. Growing up in Quito, Ecuador, I was surrounded by a loving family who cherished spending time together. Unlike many women who grew up in South American families during my time, I had parents who strongly encouraged their daughters to pursue a higher education, creative thinking, and independence.

The holidays were very special times for my family and me. Memories of the commotion and excitement of preparing for the holidays are still vivid in my mind. My parents and relatives thrived on fussing over the preparation of foods specific to each holiday. My mother and aunts were accomplished cooks, and each mastered the preparation of breads, tamales, and pastries.

Mealtimes represented a daily celebration of life. A great deal of care was taken not only in preparing the daily menus but in creating just the right ambiance as well. Our dinner table was the backdrop for fresh flowers, crisp linens, savory foods, and lively conversations. The dishes we prepared varied from continental to creole. The conversation also varied, and I often wonder whether it was the food that enhanced the conversation or the conversation that enhanced the food.

The enjoyment of good food draws people together in a way that nothing else does. It is one of the few commonalities shared by people the world over. Cultural, religious, even political differences seem to be more readily set aside when sharing a meal. We Americans, with our never-ending curiosity, love varied foods, as witnessed by the huge number of ethnic restaurants in this country. The love of good food, however, is universal. It is this universal aspect of food, this connecting with others when we share food, that delights me.

There were several reasons I felt prompted to put this book together—reasons that are connected to who and what I am, to my life, and to my heritage. As a child growing up in Ecuador, I learned to know and appreciate the wholesomeness of South American food. With maturity, this appreciation turned into a conviction about the importance of this cuisine. My conviction and my husband Peter's passion for food influenced me to pursue culinary arts through formal studies of French, Spanish, Mexican, and other international cuisines. It is Peter whom I have to thank for encouraging me to do my first Latin cookbook, *Cooking with a Latin Beat*. After that book, I came to realize more and more that South American cuisine is in a class of its own. In many ways, while giving us something new, it is also closer to the foods we Americans like to eat regularly, more familiar and almost comforting. It is also certainly very much in tune with our contemporary beliefs in striving for well-balanced, healthy, tasty, and relatively easy-to-prepare foods.

South American cuisine still remains one of the world's best-kept secrets. Paradoxically, although South America gave the Old World a wealth of foodstuffs, it has done almost nothing to export its great cooking. South American cooking is not just the cooking of the Indians, or the Africans, or the Spaniards or Portuguese. Rather, it is a magnificent blend of virtually all the cuisines of the world with the foods and traditions of the continent's indigenous peoples. The variety of dishes and flavors that ultimately resulted from this mixture, along with the improvisations of native cooks, make for a unique cuisine that I believe is unsurpassed in the world. This book covers only the 10 Latin countries that were colonized by Spain and Portugal, even though the three Guianas and the Malvinas (Falkland Islands) are certainly part of South America.

It has been said that to understand a particular cuisine, one must understand the land from which it comes—its history and geography and its people. Understanding South American cuisine would be somehow incomplete without at least a general understanding of South American people and their psyches. I have attempted to provide some background in the first three chapters: The Geography of South America, The Pre-Columbian Civilizations of South America, and the A Brief History of South American Cooking. It is important to understand that although a common Hispanic heritage permeates Latin America, South Americans are quick to borrow from other nationalities when they see fit. This includes foods, traditions, and techniques from France, England, China, Italy, the United States, and many other countries, all of which have had an impact on the social and cultural climate of South America.

South Americans remain, above all else, individuals. They prefer to do things their own way. They take pride in family and home, and they are extremely hospitable. *Mi casa es su casa* (My home is your home) and *La casa es chica, pero el corazón es grande* (My home is small, but my heart is big) are expressions often heard by visitors. *La familia* (the family) is the focal point of South American life, as is the table around which the family gathers for their meals or to entertain friends and relatives. At mealtime, all the members of the family congregate around the table not just to partake of the food but also to share the events of the day. The family meal is a very important part of South Americans' lives. Families are close-knit, and members keep in constant touch with one another. Children usually live at home until they get married, and very often even after they are married. It is not uncommon for a couple to stay with one set of parents until they have saved enough money to move out on their own. South Americans are passionate about life, and they embrace all aspects of it. They take what comes, whether it is joyful or sad, accepting it all as part of life.

Music is woven into the fabric of South American culture. It is at the core of our being. It is with music that we express our joys, struggles, and longings. The music and dance of South America are glorious expressions of the people who settled here. They speak of the homes left behind and of experiences and struggles in the new land. It was out of this cultural diversity, and out of these experiences, that the regional music was born—the *zamba* in Brazil, the *cumbia* in Colombia, the *salsa* in Venezuela, and the *tango* in Argentina and Uruguay. It is to the sound of this music that people dance until the early hours of the morning, celebrating life.

I wrote this book with music in my heart and can attest to its importance. The Mexican writer Carlos Fuentes wrote in his book *Inez* that music is "the midpoint between nature and God." Whether this is true for all people, I cannot say, but it is certainly true for South Americans. For us, music and food go hand in hand—there can never be a large gathering without music, whether that gathering is an Argentine *asado* (barbecue), the killing of a pig in the Andes, a Peruvian *pachamanca* (cookout), or the Chilean *curanto* (a clambake-like feast that traces its roots to the Mapuches, one of the few indigenous people to successfully resist Spanish inroads during the colonial period). We love to sing or dance to the beat of the *tango* or *cumbia* or to listen to the mostly sad music of the Indians of the Andean highlands, to the *joropos* (music of the plains) of the *llanos* of Venezuela, and to the joyful African tunes.

South American cooking, like Italian and Chinese, is a tasty cuisine that stresses the use of fresh ingredients, uses little meat and lots of seafood, and is relatively inexpensive. It is also wholesome and is good for everyday meals as well as for entertaining. It is a comfortable cuisine that doesn't intimidate. And it is being discovered across the United States. South American salsas are all the rage with chips and veggies. One-pot meals are perfect for today's lifestyles, and South America has a wealth of them, ready to be incorporated into busy schedules. Tamales and empanadas are here to stay and have become standard items in supermarkets. Rice dishes will become as popular as pasta dishes. *Batidos*, drinks made with fresh fruit and either milk or water, are appearing more and more, as are ice creams made with exotic tropical fruits. The time has come for South American food to take its rightful place among the cuisines of the world.

Writing this book has been a labor of love. As a Chinese poet and cookbook author once wrote, "So much planning and hard thinking go with the preparation of each dish that one may say I serve it with my whole soul." Indeed, so much planning, thinking, and work has gone into researching, writing, testing recipes, and living the life that has brought me to this point that I can honestly say that I have poured my whole heart and soul into this book. I serve it to you with pride and joy.

The Geography of
South America

B<small>EFORE BEGINNING A BOOK THAT</small> encompasses the cooking of an entire continent, it helps to understand the terrain. South America often surprises people, as the continent is larger and more diverse than many imagine. (It is also farther east than most think—the west coast of South America actually lies almost due south of the U.S. East Coast.) Chile's Atacama Desert is one of the driest places on earth, with some parts going as long as 20 years without rain. On the other hand, Chocó, in western Colombia, has some of the world's wettest weather. Patagonia, in southern Argentina, has glaciers and snowy, windswept peaks, while the Amazon region is famous for its lush tropical rain forest. The Andes, one of the planet's great mountain ranges, are largely volcanic.

South America stretches about 4,750 miles from the northernmost part of Colombia to the southernmost tip of Chile, reaching from the warm, gentle waters of the Caribbean into the icy seas surrounding Antarctica. It is approximately 3,000 miles across at its widest point. The highest point, Argentina's Mount Aconcagua, is 22,831 feet above sea level. The lowest point, also in Argentina, is the Valdés Peninsula, on the Atlantic coast, which is 131 feet below sea level. Because of its size and position, South America has almost every kind of climate, and it is also a land of incredible beauty.

The astonishing diversity of landforms and latitudes has had a tremendous impact on the development of everything in South America, from plants and animals to civilization and cuisine. The Andes mountains, the Amazon River, and the great grasslands that sweep down the continent's center have had the most noticeable, and the most legendary, influence. But every terrain and climate zone has contributed something to the cultures and economies of the continent.

South America can be roughly divided into three major regions: the Andes, the highlands, and the central plains or lowlands. The central plains are diverse, ranging from rain forest to grasslands to thorn forest.

The Andes

THE ANDES ARE THE HIGHEST mountains in the Western Hemisphere and the longest mountain chain in the world. Running down South America's west coast through seven countries, they are the continent's spine. Although the Himalayas may have the tallest peaks in the world, the Andes have the most peaks over 10,000 feet. Formidable in their altitude, ruggedness, and occasional explosiveness, these mountains gave rise to South America's most important and sophisticated early cultures. The Andes also are home to the potato, one of the most important foods South America has contributed to the world.

The Andes are a complex series of ranges and plateaus. They are still growing, through both volcanic activity and the movements of tectonic plates. Although earthquakes and eruptions are among the many hardships the region's inhabitants must endure, the lava flows add richness to the soil, and the resulting geological changes have occurred at a slow enough pace that stable climate zones and ecosystems have developed around them.

There are significant differences between the lower levels of the Andes and those higher up. The area at the base of the mountains is known as the *tierra caliente*, or hot land. This is where the lowland rain forest grows. It is also a region of rich farmland, where bananas, sugar cane, and cacao are cultivated.

The next level up the mountains is the *tierra templada*, or temperate land. This region has cooler weather and more evergreens than the *tierra caliente*. It is ideally suited to the growing of *arabica* coffee beans, the classic "mountain-grown" coffee.

The highest habitable region of the Andes is the *tierra fría*, or cold land. Here the cloud forest gives way to small farms and terraces, where farmers have raised food crops such as potatoes and quinoa for centuries. Andean condors soar among the rugged cliffs. The peaks and crags above the *tierra fría* are inhospitable and almost always covered with snow.

Between two mountain ranges in the Andes, the Cordillera Oriental and Cordillera Occidental, is a high plateau region known as the Altiplano, or high plains. The Altiplano is a region, mostly in Peru and Bolivia, where indigenous peoples still live much as they always have, raising potatoes, herding camels, and paddling reed canoes on Lake Titicaca. This region is about 500 miles long, 80 miles wide, and 12,000 feet above sea level, and it is one of the highest heavily populated areas in the world. The region is cool, dry, and occasionally bleak but also rich in minerals. South America's indigenous camels, vicuñas, llamas, alpacas, and wild guanacos, though important throughout the Andes, are abundant here.

The Highlands

THE GUIANA HIGHLANDS IN THE north and the Brazilian Highlands in the east make up more than one-third of South America's landmass. High hills and deep valleys make travel through the highlands difficult. However, time and water have carved these regions into glorious plateaus and formations.

The Guiana Highlands lie in the south and east of Venezuela, take up about half of the country, and are almost uninhabited. They are home to Angel Falls, the world's tallest waterfall, and are also the location of the *tepuis*, remote sandstone mesas that few people have explored. The *tepuis* have never been farmed, grazed, or inhabited by humans. Because so many of the animals and plants that have survived here have become extinct elsewhere, scientists once hoped that they would find dinosaurs on the *tepuis*.

In the center of Brazil are the Brazilian Highlands, called the Planalto. These highlands, which are larger than the Guiana Highlands, sweep downward from high to low elevation from Brazil into Paraguay and Argentina in the south and Venezuela in the north. Located in the Brazilian Highlands is one of South America's major tourist attractions, Iguaçu Falls. At this falls, which is shared by Brazil and Argentina, the Iguaçu River plunges over the edge of the Brazilian plateau. The drop is 240 feet, which makes Iguaçu Falls about 50 percent taller than Niagara Falls. *Iguaçu* is a native name that means "great waters."

The Pantanal is a vast, low-altitude floodplain located within the Upper Paraguay River basin, in the northernmost part of the Paraguay River. This floodplain is home to many unique flora and fauna. The Pantanal and Upper Paraguay River basin also extend into Bolivia and Paraguay, but about 80 percent of the floodplain is in west-central Brazil, in the states of Mato Grosso and Mato Grosso do Sul.

The Central Plains

Rivers and Basins

THE AMAZON IS A GIANT river that snakes across almost the entire width of the continent, draining an immense basin. At 4,000 miles long, it is second in length to the Nile but first in the volume of water carried. The Amazon discharges an average of 7 million cubic feet of water per second into the Atlantic. Fresh water can be drawn from the ocean miles from the spot where the Amazon pours forth its vast floods, and the mud carried out to sea is still and visible 62 miles from shore. In places, the Amazon is so wide that standing on the bank, one cannot see the far side of the river.

The Amazon is more than just a river; it is part of an entire system of rivers that drains the vast Amazon basin. There are three major river systems in South America: Amazon, Orinoco, and Río de la Plata. Together, these three systems drain the vast interior lowland. In addition to containing a huge network of streams and rivers, the Amazon basin is the site of the world's largest rain forest. This is a region of rich diversity in both plants and animals. It is also a place where boundaries are difficult to establish, because flooding rivers can spread for miles through the trees, blending river and forest in ways that make life in the basin different from anywhere else on earth.

The Orinoco River, along with its system of feeder streams and drainage basin, is the northernmost of South America's major river systems. It travels from Colombia across Venezuela, with tributaries that both water and drain this region's broad grasslands, called the *llanos*.

The Río de la Plata is south of the Amazon, with its mouth forming the border between Uruguay and Argentina. The major tributaries of this system are the Paraguay, Paraná, and Uruguay Rivers.

South America has a few impressive lakes. Lake Titicaca, which sits at an altitude of 12,500 feet and straddles the border between Bolivia and Peru, is notable for being the highest navigable lake in the world. Lake Maracaibo, in northwestern Venezuela, is another important lake. In southern Chile, the Región de los Lagos, or Lake District, stretches south 1,000 miles and contains 12 lakes, many snowcapped volcanoes, beautiful landscapes, and hardwood forests. But lakes in general are relatively unimportant on this continent. The waterways that have shaped South America, and that still play a vital role, are the rivers. Today they supply fish, provide transportation, and make irrigation possible, just as they have for millennia.

Grasslands

SOUTH AMERICA'S BROAD, FERTILE GRASSLANDS had a huge impact on the success of introduced animals. These vast prairies made it possible for cattle, sheep, and horses to thrive. Each region has a different name for its grassland region, but the largest and most important regions are the *llanos* in the north, primarily in Venezuela and Colombia, and the *pampas* in Argentina, Uruguay, and southern Brazil. These are the areas that have given rise to lifestyles that center on raising cattle, and it is here that the culture of South America's cowboys (called *llaneros* in the *llanos* and *gauchos* in the *pampas*) developed.

The *llanos* lie just east of the Andes and make up a region twice the size of Nevada. Here, where the Orinoco River flows, there are birds, capybaras (large rodents that inhabit the lakes and streams), and jaguars. But most of all, there are cattle. Poor soil makes growing crops difficult, but cattle thrive. When the wet season floods the area, the myriad birds that flock to the *llanos* help draw tourists as well. Although ecotourism will never replace cattle in the region's economy, it is contributing to both the economy and people's interest in protecting wild animals.

The *pampas* spreads west from the coastal city of Buenos Aires, fanning out through the Río de la Plata river system. This region is primarily grasslands, broken up by only a few hills and sand dunes. Like the *llanos* to the north, it is important cattle-raising land. The *pampas* is home to numerous large cattle ranches, known in Spanish as *estancias*. However, unlike the *llanos*, the *pampas* also is good for agriculture, with wheat being the most common crop. Much indigenous wildlife, including burrowing owls, great flocks of flamingos, and even an occasional armadillo, can be seen in this region.

Other Regions

THE REMAINING CENTRAL PLAINS REGIONS are diverse and often extreme: They include the following:

- Deserts, such as the Atacama in Chile

- Frozen tundra in the far south, one of the most forbidding places in the world

- Forests of thorny shrubs and trees, such as those in the Gran Chaco in Paraguay, with names such as *quebracho*, or ax breaker

The Gran Chaco

The Gran Chaco is a large plain that covers parts of northern Argentina, southern Bolivia, and the Paraguayan Chaco. It has evolved over thousands of years as a result of the dumping of silt by rivers coming down from the Andes. The Chaco covers about two-thirds of Paraguay, but only a small portion of the country's population lives here. The High Chaco in the northwest, with little rainfall and covered with dense scrub forest and cacti, has been called "The Green Hell"; hardly anyone can survive here, but it is rich in wildlife. The southern part of Paraguay, called the Low Chaco, is a swampy land, full of tall palm trees called *carandai*. This area is mostly used for cattle ranching. The Middle Chaco is mostly an inhospitable area, where people depend on forestry to make a living. It is here where the red *quebracho*, or ax breaker, trees grow. Besides supplying one of the hardest woods available, these trees are a good source of tannin, which is used in tanning leather. The Mennonites settled here to practice farming.

- The Yungas region of Bolivia—deep tropical valleys located on the eastern side of the Andes

- The *selva*, including the tropical rain forest of the Amazon basin, known as the low *selva*, with lush vegetation and forest; and the eastern slopes of the Andes, called *montaña* or high *selva*, with dense vegetation and mostly covered by mist and clouds

South America also has some famous islands, such as the Galapágos Islands, located about 600 miles off the coast of Ecuador. It was in these islands that Charles Darwin formulated his famous theory of the evolution of the species. There are 13 major islands and 3 smaller ones in the archipelago. Only 5 of the islands are inhabited. Much of the wildlife here is unique to the Galapágos.

West of the Chilean mainland are a number of islands that belong to Chile, among them the Juan Fernández Islands. Daniel Defoe's famous novel *Robinson Crusoe* was inspired by the adventures of Alexander Selkirk, who was shipwrecked on one of these islands. The largest lobsters in South America live in this area. Another famous island is Easter Island, discovered on Easter Sunday by Dutch explorers and well known for its huge stone statues.

The Pre-Columbian Civilizations
of South America

A SMALL BUT ELEGANT MUSEUM ATOP the Banco Central in Quito, Ecuador, contains a surprising collection of ancient artifacts collected during archaeological excavations in the region. Among the finds on display is a set of statues believed to date from as early as 9000 B.C. The statues are remarkable because they portray individuals with unmistakably Oriental facial features. I observed them, wondering about their creation—and their creators. How did the statues get here? Who made them or brought them? According to one theory, a small group of Asians crossed the Bering Strait via a land bridge from Siberia to Alaska during the last ice age, some 12,000 to 30,000 years ago. Were the figures carried by those original travelers to South America? Or were they made here, near Quito, by the descendants of that first band?

Historians theorize that migrating tribes found their way through North and Central America down to the tip of South America. Most archaeologists estimate that descendants of the earliest of these migrants had reached Tierra del Fuego, off the southernmost tip of South America, by 9000 B.C. These first people settled throughout the Americas and eventually produced a considerable variety of civilizations, due to the tremendous diversity of environmental conditions.

Some of these migrating groups settled in the highlands, while others went to the lowlands. As the population in each region grew, groups became organized into more complex societies. Some of these groups formed advanced tribes and even remarkable civilizations, such as the Incas, while others remained seminomadic and still inhabit remote areas of the Amazon jungle today.

If South America's numerous cultures arose from one source, they took dramatically different directions once they arrived on the continent. Their languages, in particular, varied greatly across the continent and even within regions. Four principal Indian cultural regions are generally recognized in South America—Circum-Caribbean, Andean, Tropical Forest, and Marginal—although each of these regions contains numerous subdivisions.

The early inhabitants were mainly hunters and gatherers, but by 7000 to 5000 B.C., they were occasionally turning to cultivation. I imagine that after thousands of years of nomadic life, some members of the groups observed that plants grew in places where seeds had fallen to the ground, thus leading them to simple farming.

The first indigenous plants to be domesticated were probably squash and peppers. Maize, or corn, seems to have been domesticated between 4000 and 3000 B.C. in Peru, and from there it spread to other areas. Then manioc (also called yuca or cassava; page 296) and potatoes were added to the native larder, though in different regions. In South America, the conversion to a truly agricultural society (rather than a nomadic society with a few domesticated plants) probably began around 2000 to 1000 B.C., depending on the region, although some groups have remained hunter-gatherers even up to recent times.

With the domestication of plants, people needed to find ways to make foods more edible. Some foods contained toxic substances that had to be removed before eating. Others had strong fibers that made them difficult to chew. In the beginning, people used baskets or animal skins to boil water. They did so by heating stones in a fire and dropping them in the water, using some kind of tongs to remove the stones. Cooking directly over a fire was probably the first method of cooking meat and other foods, even though people at that time mostly ate raw meat, as recorded by early chroniclers. They also used leaves to wrap foods, especially fish and ground corn, to be cooked over a fire.

The Indians used stones and shells to grate or grind foods, such as manioc (yuca), cereals, and *ajíes* (hot peppers). Eventually, they developed cooking utensils made of stone, wood, clay, and fibers, which provided the means of preparing and serving a variety of foods. One of the first utensils was made out of a gourd, the fruit of the calabash tree. Once the flesh was removed from the gourd, the empty half shell was put in the sun to dry. Then it was ready to undergo a complicated process to make it ready not only for serving food but also for decorating and painting. These gourds became works of art and the symbols of many regions. People took pride in making these beautiful gourds, which were used to serve water, drinks, corn and manioc mushes, and other foods.

Research shows that Andean farmers not only grew domesticated plants but also cross-bred wild plants with domesticated ones, which added to the genetic diversity of many plants. The achievements in plant husbandry and agriculture of some of these groups rank above those of the civilizations of other continents during the same time periods.

Despite differences in language, culture, and location, the tribes grew remarkably similar foods—basically starchy roots and whatever could be gathered or caught. In the Amazon, the starchy root was manioc (yuca), which was the staple of the local diet. This was supplemented by fruits, nuts, and whatever else could be gathered in the area. People in this region also hunted for tapirs, monkeys, rodents, and a variety of other animals. Fish were always available in the rivers, streams, and lakes. The Indians of the highlands were more advanced in farming. There the starchy roots were potatoes and sweet potatoes, but farmers also grew beans, corn, squash, other tubers, and seeds.

The size of the Indian population living in South America at the time of the European arrival in the late 1400s and early 1500s is unknown. The indigenous peoples lived in small, widely dispersed groups. They had little contact with one another, except in the form of trade and occasional battles. Hence groups had little knowledge of the size of groups not in their immediate vicinity, and there were no written records of population. Almost everything we know about the early peoples of South America comes from the accounts of the Europeans who had first contact with them and from the ongoing research of archaeologists.

The first Indians the Spaniards found in South America were the Arawaks, who lived in the western part of the Caribbean coast of Venezuela, and the Caribs, who inhabited the eastern part of the coast of Venezuela and the Caribbean coast of Colombia. (The Arawaks had also spread to the interior of the Brazil's Amazon region.) Both tribes lived by gathering wild plants, hunting, fishing, and farming. They cultivated tobacco, corn, cotton, manioc (yuca), and fruits. Descendants of these tribes still live in the Orinoco delta (northeastern Venezuela) and the rain forest of south-central Venezuela, bordering Brazil.

The Guajiro Indians lived in the desert-like area of the eastern Guajira Peninsula, along the Gulf of Venezuela, in the northernmost part of the country. Because of the scarcity of water, these Indians were seminomadic. They primarily cultivated corn, and when the Spaniards brought cattle, they took to them immediately and became herdsmen. They traded animals for textiles and foodstuffs. The Quiriques lived in the region east of Lake Maracaibo, in northwestern Venezuela. They fiercely resisted the Spaniards and eventually were nearly annihilated. Also in Venezuela were the seminomadic Chaqués, who lived in the highlands during the rainy season and moved to the plains during the dry season. They grew manioc (yuca), sweet potatoes, beans, and squash.

The Timote Indians inhabited the Andes. Like the Incas, but on a smaller scale, they cut irrigated terraces into the mountain slopes to grow potatoes and corn. They also cultivated cotton, tobacco, cacao beans, other beans, squash, sweet potatoes, manioc (yuca), and fruit trees. They used tobacco as medicine and cacao to make drinks.

The Indians who lived in what is now Colombia were as varied as the country's terrain, which ranges from mountains to Caribbean coast to Amazon rain forest. They all spoke different languages and had lifestyles that ranged from nomadic to farming. The Tairomas flourished in the northeastern highlands on the Caribbean coast. They were among the more advanced Indian civilizations. Researchers believe that about 250,000 people lived in one community, building large stone buildings and using gold, emeralds, and other semi-precious stones (which were abundant in the area) to make magnificent ornaments to decorate these buildings. The Muiscas (called Chibchas by the Spaniards) were the most advanced civilization in Colombia. They lived in many areas of the plateaus and slopes of the Andes, especially in Boyacá and Cundinamarca (where Bogotá is today). They mined gold and emeralds, with which they made exquisite ornaments, as well as salt. They lived at the crossroads of commerce and traded these items with other peoples, such as the Caribs, Arawaks, and Quechuas. This is the tribe that became famous because of El Dorado, literally "the gilded man." When the Spaniards arrived in what is now Venezuela, an Indian told them about a man, probably the chief of a tribe, whose body was covered with gold dust. The Spaniards set out to find him. Soon "El Dorado" also came to refer to the kingdom of riches where this man was believed to live. Despite intense searching, the Spaniards never found the mythical man or kingdom. Another important tribe in Colombia was the Quimbayás, who still live in some parts of eastern Colombia. The Yaguas of the Amazon jungle still live in huts built on stilts, and the Motilóns live in the forest and resist contact with the outside world.

Some historians speculate that Ecuador may be the birthplace of South American civilization. Artifacts found from the Valdivia culture indicate that it might be related to ancient Asian cultures. Valdivia pottery resembles ancient Japanese pottery, and as mentioned earlier, statues found in excavations here have Oriental features. Aside from this speculation, it has been very difficult for historians to learn about the beginning of Ecuadorian civilization. Historian Federico González Suárez believes that four peoples occupied the highlands of Ecuador before the arrival of the Spaniards: the Punis, Puruhaes, Cañaris, and Caras. The Caras, who conquered the Quitus, a very important tribe, are considered to be the oldest inhabitants of what is known today as the province of Pichincha, where Quito, the capital of Ecuador, is located. The Cañaris inhabited the southern part of Ecuador and fiercely resisted Inca invaders. In fact, it took the Incas many years to subdue them. It was only after the Inca emperor Tupac Yupanki fathered a son, Huayna Cápac, by a Cañari princess that he succeeded. Huayna Cápac led his people north, but it took him many years and a marriage to another Ecuadorian princess, Paccha, to subdue this part of the country. Atahualpa was born from this marriage and later became the Inca emperor of Ecuador. This created two different civilizations, the Peruvian Quechuas and the indigenous Ecuadorians. The Incas were never fully accepted by the Ecuadorian Indians.

The Salasaca and Saraguro Indians of central Ecuador are descendants of the relocated Inca colonists. The Otavalos, who live in the province of Imbabura, north of Quito, were farmers and weavers. Several groups of Indians live in the Amazon rain forest of eastern Ecuador. Some of these peoples, such as the Colorados, paint their bodies with dyes made from annatto seeds. The Jívaros, Shuars, Huaoranis (better known as Aucas), Tetetes, Secoyas, and lowland Quechuas are the most widely known tribes. Their diets were very much like that of the Amazonian Indians mentioned earlier. It is believed that by the thirteenth century, Ecuador was populated by many cultures that were mainly farmers, growing the typical staples (corn, squash, beans, and hot peppers). They also grew quinoa, amaranth, more than 300 varieties of potatoes, and several other tubers. They lived mostly in villages scattered on the mountain slopes and in the valleys of the Andes.

Although the Inca civilization is the best known in South America, it was the last of several advanced pre-Columbian cultures. It is believed that the first inhabitants of Peru lived in caves. The oldest cave known to have been inhabited is Pikimachay, in the department of Ayacucho, south of Lima. The human remains found there may date back to 15,000 B.C. The inhabitants of these caves were probably nomadic hunters and gatherers. Around 3500 B.C., small groups started congregating mainly along the coast, where they could supplement their diets by fishing and hunting for deer and other game. Eventually, they became farmers, and there is new evidence that cotton, hot peppers, beans, squash, corn, *lucuma* (a tuber), quinoa, and amaranth were cultivated in the Ayacucho basin before 3000 B.C.

Many civilizations predated the Incas by a few centuries. Archaeologists believe that the Chavín culture, which developed on the coast between 1200 and 800 B.C., was the oldest and most important pre-Columbian culture. The Chavín culture is credited with developing not only agriculture but also weaving, pottery, and architecture.

The Moches lived in the coastal valleys of Moche and Lambayeque from about A.D. 100 to 800. They lived by fishing in the Pacific Ocean and farming in the desert, as they were skilled at building canals and aqueducts for irrigation. El Niño caused flooding every few years, which devastated the Moches' adobe buildings. Also, sand from the desert frequently covered their cities, crops, and irrigation canals. Eventually, the Moches got tired of rebuilding their cities and moved inland. It is very possible that climatic conditions were one of the factors that eventually caused their disappearance. After the Moches disappeared, most of Peru came under the influence of the Huaris, whose center was near the city of Ayacucho.

The Chimú culture probably began around A.D. 900 and flourished north of Lima, where they built Chan Chan, their capital. The Chimús developed new techniques for working with copper and creating pottery, and they built towns around irrigated areas. South of Lima were the Nazcas, who etched giant animal shapes into the desert—the famous Nazca lines. The Chinchas, another tribe of great importance, flourished along the southern coast of Peru. They were adept at seafaring and were great fishermen and sailors. Unfortunately, they disappeared a few years after the conquest.

Living in the Peruvian Andes were the region's two most important tribes: the Quechuas and Aymaras. The Quechuas were the larger and more advanced of the two groups, but both became part of the Inca Empire. The Aymaras lived in southern Peru, near Lake Titicaca, which lies on the border between Peru and Bolivia. The Aymaras of Peru belonged to a larger group of Bolivian Aymaras. The Peruvian Aymaras had trouble growing food because of the harsh weather of the highlands. The Bolivian Aymaras fared better because of the irrigation methods developed by the Tiahuanaco culture. (It is not known which group arose first, the Aymaras or the Tiahuanacos.) These methods allowed the Aymaras to grow more crops, such as vegetables, beans, corn, and potatoes.

The origin of the Incas is obscure and surrounded by legends, most of which are more mythical than historical. According to one legend, the Incas were of divine origin, sent by the sun god. Manco Cápac and his sister/wife Mamma Ocllo, the first children of the sun, were sent to earth to act as liaisons between the sun god and the people. They supposedly emerged from Lake Titicaca and, using a golden rod, found a place to establish the Inca Empire. The Incas settled in what now is Cuzco, in southern Peru, in the early fifteenth century. In less than 100 years, this relatively unknown culture subdued several ethnic groups and began to conquer neighboring civilizations, starting from the coast and high-lands of Peru. Eventually, their empire extended from northern Ecuador to northern Chile and Bolivia, all the way to Mendoza in west-central Argentina. The empire was called the Tahuantín-suyu, or Four Corners of the World, and comprised 12 million to 15 million people, who spoke at least 20 languages and gave absolute obedience to the Inca, or supreme leader. The Inca took care of his subjects, who were safeguarded against famine and other natural disasters. The first Inca, Pachacuti, was a dynamic leader and manager of the empire. He devised many ways to unify the many different ethnic groups he conquered. He made Quechua the official language of the empire (although the Aymaras kept their own language). The Inca moved whole *ayllus* (communities) to settle in conquered areas and organized them into *marcas* (tribes), without changing their ways and yet instilling a sense of unity and pride in their common cultural and religious values.

Although most crops grown in the region had been domesticated and developed by earlier tribes, it was the Incas who brought them to new heights of development and spread them throughout the empire. At the time of the conquest, the Incas had domesticated about 70 crop species, and their rulers had accumulated supplies in their warehouses to feed their people for at least three years. Amazingly, without the wheel or animals for plowing, the Incas developed complex systems of irrigation and terracing unparalleled in other parts of the world.

Unlike the primitive peoples, who had diets based mainly on meat, the Incas had a mostly vegetarian diet. Along with corn and beans, they ate potatoes and other tubers, peppers, tomatoes, and squash to achieve a balanced diet. They did not use much salt to prepare their foods, perhaps because of its scarcity in many areas. Instead, they used hot peppers, called *ajíes*, to flavor their food. Peppers came in two basic kinds—hot and mild, and they could be yellow, green, or red. In Peru, Bolivia, Ecuador, and Colombia, pungent local herbs, such as *paico* and *quilquiña*, also were used to season foods. In general, however, condiments were scarce, and the Indians depended instead on clay pots for flavoring foods. Clay pots are ideal for cooking because once properly cured, they retain and intensify flavors. Another essential element was an appreciation of and respect for the humble ingredients of dishes and the work involved in preparing them, along with pride in the cooks' efforts.

The Incas had tremendous respect for the earth, and their culture revolved around agriculture. As a result, anything to do with farming was considered holy and religious. The Incas revered corn and quinoa as life-giving foods. According to legends, each planting season began with the Inca rulers planting the first grains with a golden spade. At harvest time, they held thanksgiving festivals to celebrate the successful season. Traditionally, to show gratitude, celebrants would spill a little of their first drink of *chicha de jora* (a fermented corn drink) on the ground for Pacha-Mama, or Mother Earth.

The first Inca historian, Garcilaso de la Vega, in his book *Comentarios Reales* (1609), gives a detailed account of the foods that sustained the Indians before the conquest. He classifies them into two categories: foods that grow above the ground and foods that grow below the ground. Among the first is *zara*, which is the Inca name for corn and has been called the bread of the Indians. Vega explains in detail the different ways in which it was prepared (toasted, boiled, or made into *chicha*). Other important foods grown above the ground were the grains quinoa, *kiwicha* (amaranth), and kaniwa, as well as lupini and other beans, peppers, squash, and a variety of fruits. Foods grown underground included potatoes, *oca*, *ullucos*, and peanuts.

Several tribes, such as the Nahua, Matsés, and Jíbaros, lived in the Amazon basin of Peru, as well as in the Ecuadorian and Brazilian Amazon. The Yaguas, also known as the Campas, still live in the *montaña*, on the east side of the Andes. The men hunt for deer, wild pigs, otters, and fish. The women do the farming, growing yuca and coca. The Shipibos, Piros, and Conibos also lived in this region.

In the highlands of Bolivia, as in Peru, the two most important groups were the Quechuas and Aymaras. The Aymaras lived around Lake Titicaca and in the province of La Paz, and there is evidence that some of them also reached southern Peru and northern Chile. The Quechuas were concentrated in the southern part of the Bolivian highlands. The Aymaras may have arrived at Lake Titicaca as early as 400 B.C. As mentioned earlier, they were farmers who grew potatoes, quinoa, squash, beans, corn, and peppers. Fishing was also important to them.

Historians believe that the powerful culture that developed at Tiahuanaco, 13 miles south of Lake Titicaca, arose between A.D. 500 and 800. The influence of this culture spread as far north as Ecuador. Not much is known about the Tiahuanacos, except that they developed advanced methods of irrigation. Recent excavations have shown evidence of a system of raised fields designed to protect crops from the salty waters of Lake Titicaca and to retain their heat during the cold Altiplano nights. It also appears that Tiahuanaco was the center of widespread trade. At its height, Tiahuanaco had a population of about 20,000 people, but after 300 to 400 years, the culture fell into decline. It probably disappeared around A.D. 1200.

Another Bolivian tribe was the Chipayas, who lived in the most inhospitable area of the Altiplano and survived by keeping llamas, hunting, and farming. Some early Bolivian cultures still survive. The Kallawayas came from the eastern shore of Lake Titicaca and lived a nomadic life. According to some legends, they are the direct descendants of the Tiahuanacos. They are gifted healers, and although they are nomadic, they also farm. The Sirionos, who are part of the Guarani group, live in the tropical forest of Bolivia. The men use bows and arrows to fish and hunt monkeys, armadillos, and tortoises. They also gather food from the surrounding forest. The Guarayos and Chiquitanos, who live in the low plains and tropical forest, generally survive on what the forest provides.

Not much is known about the tribes that populated Chile prior to the conquest. The Atacameños and Diaguitas lived in the oases of the north and knew something about irrigation. They grew potatoes, corn, and beans and kept llamas for wool. These groups were more organized than the Araucanians, who lived in the south and were the largest group of Indians in Chile at the time of the conquest, numbering about 500,000. The Araucanians comprised several scattered tribes and lacked a central government. Among these tribes were the Mapuches, Huilliches, and Pehuenches, who were related in race and language. They were seminomadic peoples who fiercely and successfully fought the Incas, and later the Spaniards, for many years to protect their land. Eventually, they succumbed, if not to the Spaniards' swords, then to their diseases, or they were absorbed into the Spanish culture through intermarriage. This is why Chile has one of the most homogeneous races in South America. The Mapuches who were not exterminated or integrated live on *reducciones* (reservations) in central-south Chile, where they have kept their language and culture intact. Most of the smaller tribes no longer exist. Today, in the northern part of Chile, the Aymaras live on the Andes, and the Huilliches live in small villages in the southern archipelago of Chiloé.

As in the rest of South America, Argentina's native tribes consisted of small bands of about 20 nomadic hunters or farmers. At the time of the conquest, dozens of tribes lived in the mountains, valleys, deserts, grasslands, and jungles. The Puelches and Quirandús lived in the western and eastern *pampas* and used the *boleadoras* (a long, heavy cord with a heavy ball at the end) to hunt small game such as partridge, armadillos, hares, small deer, and guanacos. They also gathered wild plants and fruits. The Guarani Indians, who lived along the northern part of the Paraná River, were farmers growing squash, melons, and sweet potatoes. In the northwestern provinces were the Diaguitas, who also lived in northern Chile. They raised llamas, vicuñas, and guanacos, from which they got wool as well as food. They also raised rheas, the region's great, flightless birds, and grew corn. From the pods of the carob trees they made a fermented drink like *chicha*. In the western provinces lived the Huarpes, who built extensive canals to irrigate their fields. These canals are still in use in many areas, especially in Mendoza. The Comechingones lived in what is today the province of Córdoba. They were farmers, cultivating corn, and ate the fruit of the *algarroba* tree. They also herded llamas.

In the seventeenth and eighteenth centuries, due to wars with the Spaniards, the Chilean Mapuches moved to what is now Argentina, joined other tribes, and became the Huilliches and Pehuenches. The basic food of the Pehuenches was *piñones*, seeds from the araucaria tree. They ate them raw, toasted, boiled, or made into flour, and they also exported them to tribes that roamed the *pampas*. The Puelches were nomads who lived in the eastern and western *pampas*.

The southern region of the continent, now known as Patagonia, was inhabited by the powerfully built Tehuelches. They wore few clothes in spite of the cold and used fire to keep warm, even when they were navigating in their canoes. Today these Indians raise sheep. The Chiriguanos lived in Tierra del Fuego, the southernmost part of Argentina. The Yagáns, or Yámanas, lived on the southern coast of Tierra del Fuego; today there are only a few left. The Onas also lived there, in small groups, and hunted guanacos. They are extinct.

In Paraguay, the major indigenous group was the Guaranis, who probably lived there for thousands of years. They occupied a large area extending from what is now Buenos Aires to Asunción, in Paraguay, and were organized in small villages of about 100 to 300 people. They were seminomadic and lived by hunting, fishing, gathering, and farming. Their staples were manioc (yuca) and corn, but they also grew squash, pumpkins, papayas, and peanuts. They gathered honey and palm nuts and hunted for deer and tapirs. When the soil in the region was exhausted, they moved to another area in the forest.

Other groups of Indians, such as the Macás, lived in the Chaco, a region of south-central South America. The environment there is hostile, but there is an abundance of wild-life. These Indians were seminomadic, hunting for deer, tapirs, giant anteaters, armadillos, capybaras, and rheas. They also practiced gathering and a little farming. The Indians who lived along the banks of the Paraná River gathered and cured *yerba maté*, which is used to make a bitter tea and is still very popular in the area. They fished using wooden hooks. The *surubí*, which lives in the Paraguay and Paraná Rivers, is the most popular fish in Paraguay. The *caimán* (alligator) is also found and hunted in these rivers. About 40,000 Indians, representing 17 tribes speaking 5 different languages, still live in this region.

Because of the isolation of Paraguay, the Spaniards decided to adapt to the life of the Indians, and many of the Indians became their kinsmen under the *encomienda* system, which allowed them to have about 20 Indians working for them. The Guaranis accepted the Spaniards and offered each one up to 20 wives. The result was a large population of mestizos, who became the majority. Paraguay is the only country in South America that has two official languages, Spanish and Guarani.

Uruguay had very few Indian cultures. The first inhabitants of Uruguay were hunters and gatherers, dating from about 11,000 B.C. When the Spaniards arrived in Uruguay, there were numerous ethnic groups related to the Tupi-Guaranis, such as the Charrúas, Bohanes, Chanas, Guenoas, and Yaros. The Charrúas were the most important group, and the ones who resisted the colonizers the most.

Indigenous peoples throughout the Americas identified, and occasionally domesticated, edible plants. Although many Indians remained hunter-gatherers, even to recent times, they developed sophisticated techniques for processing plant foods, including some that were poisonous without processing. One example is cassava (yuca), which is of major importance in the diets of the Amazonian peoples. These Indians figured out how to remove the poisonous prussic acid from the cassava roots. This was a labor-intensive task, usually performed by women and children. They peeled the roots with shells and used special stones to grate the flesh into a pulp. This pulp was put into a *tapitim* or *tipití*, a cylindrical basket woven with natural fibers and measuring about 10 feet long (still used today by some tribes), which was suspended from poles. A heavy weight was attached to the lower end to pull on the basket, thus squeezing out the poisonous liquid. Sometimes warriors used this liquid as the basis for *curare*, a poison put on arrows to kill the enemy. To get rid of the poison, the liquid, called *tucupí*, had to be boiled. The grated root was lightly toasted in a clay pot until all the moisture was gone. The result was a coarse white meal called *farina* or *farinha de mandioca* (manioc meal), depending on the region.

In the region that became Brazil, the rain forest had a huge impact on the foods available and how they were processed. Here, as elsewhere in the Amazon, cassava (yuca) was important. Called *manihot* in this region, it was made into *farinha*, bread, pastry, fermented preserves, and beverages. From the forest came Brazil nuts and cashews. Foods were wrapped in palm leaves for cooking. Turtles and huge fish were pulled from the Amazon River and roasted over coals, as they still are today. Other than a few ingredients and techniques, however, these more primitive tribes contributed less to the developing cuisine of South America than did the more sophisticated agricultural tribes to the north and west.

Before the arrival of the Portuguese, as many as 2 million to 3 million Indians may have been living in what it is now Brazil. Most of them were very primitive. Today about 220,000 Indians still live as their ancestors did in the Amazon basin. The Portuguese, for practical reasons, divided the indigenous peoples into two main groups: the Tupi-Guaranis and the Tupayas. The Tupis were dominant in the central basin and all the way south to the Río de la Plata. This group was made up of many tribes, including the Tupinambas, Tabanas, and Carijos. The Tupayas were situated more toward the interior, and the most important of those tribes were the Cauris and Aymaras. All of the Tupaya tribes spoke different languages that bore little resemblance to that of the Tupis. The Arawaks and Yanomamos lived in the interior, close to Venezuela. All of these groups were either hunter-gatherers or farmers and fishermen. The Tupis were the most important tribe in Brazil, and the ones the Portuguese first encountered. They showed the Portuguese how to survive on their foods and later taught the Portuguese women how to prepare these foods. Even so, the Portuguese eventually subjected the Indians to slavery, and after many years they either died or fled into the jungle. Some of them intermarried with Portuguese and Africans. The Tupis were instrumental in shaping Brazilian culinary culture, as we will see in the next chapter.

A Brief History of South American Cooking

THE FIFTEENTH CENTURY MARKED THE beginning of the European Age of Discovery. Before Christopher Columbus embarked on his historic voyage in 1492, most Europeans still held the belief inherited from ancient geographers that Europe, Africa, and Asia were situated on a central mass of land surrounded by oceans. They knew that the earth was round and had actually calculated its circumference with surprising accuracy, but they had concluded that the Ocean Sea stretched from the western shores of Europe to the eastern shores of China.

Europeans had long been importing goods from Asia—especially silks and spices—usually through Arab traders who controlled the land and sea routes running east from North Africa. Many hoped to find a way to cut out the middleman and find a direct route to China, which had been known as Cathay since Marco Polo's return to Italy in 1295. Toward the end of the fifteenth century, the Portuguese were quite active in their sea explorations. Capitalism began to rise in Europe, along with a greater demand for gold. Going around the tip of Africa to reach Asia was difficult, primarily because the sailors lost sight of familiar stars used for navigation, but also because Arab traders controlled the sea routes once the ships reached the other side of the continent.

The desire for alternate routes to the vast markets and valuable spices of eastern Asia continued to intensify. In 1492, Spain finally ended the centuries-long occupation of their country by the Moors. With all its soldiers and resources now freed up, Spain turned to pursuits other than war. The need for trade and money, reinforced by a growing rivalry with neighboring Portugal, convinced Ferdinand and Isabella, the monarchs of Castile and Aragon, to commission and finance the first voyage of Christopher Columbus. Columbus believed that the earth was smaller than previous measurements had indicated and calculated that he could reach Cathay before onboard stores of food and fresh water ran out. The object was to go westward across the Ocean Sea and discover a direct route to Cathay. But it was not just the desire for trade and wealth that spurred Columbus and other explorers on. The Spanish and Portuguese monarchies also hoped to bring more of the world under the "civilizing" influences of Catholicism. (By the way, Columbus was wrong—the earth was as big as others thought. However, because he struck land where he predicted China would be, he always believed that he had reached some unexplored part of Asia. It was Amerigo Vespucci, a navigator on Columbus's voyage, who concluded during later explorations that this great landmass was not part of Asia but was in fact a new continent. Because of his astonishing conclusion, along with his extensive exploration of the coast of South America, the new land was called America, although the name originally applied only to South America. Columbus, though incorrect in his assumption, is still acknowledged as one of the world's great navigators. He not only reached the New World but also returned to Europe, and then made three more trips to the Caribbean and, eventually, South America.)

The meeting of Old World and New World (however old it may have been) began a new era in culinary history. Few aspects of this Age of Discovery had as lasting an impact on people's lives as the explosive movement around the world of foodstuffs. The plants that had sustained the Americas became staples elsewhere, and the culinary mainstays of Europe and Asia flooded into the Americas.

Although Columbus could not possibly have realized that he had set in motion forces that were going to change the world forever, he did immediately recognize the value of the new foods he was encountering (which included flying ants and iguanas—this was an adventurous diner), as well as the potential of the cotton, spices, and unusual woods to which he was introduced by the inhabitants of the islands on which he'd landed. Sweet potatoes and hot peppers were among the treasures Columbus took back to Europe with him. When he returned to Hispaniola on his second voyage, he brought cuttings and seeds for such Old World favorites as wheat, chickpeas, onions, garlic, cauliflower, Brussels sprouts, beets, radishes, spinach, lettuce, melons, oranges, grapefruits, lemons, peaches, pears, apricots, almonds, sugar cane, cherries, and figs. The exchange had begun.

Many of the Old World plants (which had their origins in Asia and Africa as much as in Europe) adapted quickly to their new home. Sugar cane, in particular, grew incredibly well, becoming one of the staples of the islands' economies. But Columbus brought more than plants. He also brought cattle, pigs, sheep, goats, and chickens, which quickly multiplied, thanks to the rich grass and other vegetation (and which quickly replaced dogs, at that time one of only two forms of domesticated livestock—the other being turkeys—in much of Central America). The horse, too, made its first appearance in the New World in the company of Spanish explorers—but as transportation rather than food.

In his book *Food, Conquest, and Colonization in Sixteenth-Century Spanish America*, John C. Super writes that before long, the 1,000 head of criollo cattle introduced by Spanish explorers had become vast herds grazing on the seemingly endless pastures. Within one generation, livestock threatened to overrun some of the Caribbean islands.

But the impact of these explorers on the New World truly began to be felt only when the Spaniards reached the mainland. When Columbus landed on continental South America while exploring the Orinoco delta in what is now Venezuela, during his third voyage in 1498, the colossal food exchange began in earnest. As Zvi Dor-Ner notes in *Columbus and the Age of Discovery*, "The third voyage of Christopher Columbus marked the beginning of the phenomenon called the Columbian Exchange—the movement of people, cultures, and ideas motivated by the dynamic transfer of plants and animals, and even poisons, between two hitherto isolated worlds. This exchange would grow into a world-wide movement, in which whole populations either expanded remarkably within their homelands, or left those lands behind in mass migrations."

From the American cornucopia, maize, or corn, traveled to Europe and potatoes to Ireland, Russia, and later Nepal. To Asia and the islands of the Pacific went sweet potatoes, hot peppers, and pineapples. Hot peppers and peanuts became an integral part of Indian cuisine. The sweet potato became a staple of the Chinese diet, as did hot peppers, which also were adopted into Korean cooking. To Africa went corn, manioc (yuca), sweet potatoes, peanuts (called groundnuts in Africa), pineapples, and other fruits. European cuisines were enriched by chocolate, vanilla, squash, lima beans, green beans, red and green peppers, potatoes, tomatoes, turkey, and tapioca, to name some of the most prominent contributions.

Although all of these foods had a huge impact, the New World's most important contribution the global larder was probably corn. "If maize were the only gift the American Indian ever presented to the world," wrote Alfred W. Crosby in *The Columbian Exchange*, "he would deserve undying gratitude, for it has become one of the most important of all foods for men and their livestock." Father Joseph de Acosta was the first to call it "the bread of the Indians." In fact, corn has become the third most important food crop in the world after wheat and rice.

Because the most important grain in any society was called "corn," maize was soon identified as "Indian corn," the most important grain of the new land. In time, in North America, the word *corn* came to mean maize. In South America, maize goes by many names, mostly reflecting regional Indian terms for the grain. Today corn occupies an important place in the world not only as a source of food for humans and livestock but in industry as well. It is made into cereals, oil, flour, syrup, food coloring, glucose, animal feed, beer, medicine, even fuel for cars, as well as many other manufactured products, from adhesives to embalming fluid.

The Indians of the tropics made a bread from the bitter cassava (yuca), which is easy to grow and can be kept for a year or more. In fact, cassava played a major role in the conquest because it could be prepared in large quantities, it was cheap, and it kept well. The Portuguese took it to Africa, where it became a staple food. Cassava fed African slaves during the long journey to the New World. The Spaniards introduced cassava to the Philippines and Southeast Asia, and today it continues to be a major ingredient in the diets of peoples throughout the tropics.

Farther inland, in the cooler climates, other foods were discovered. Potatoes were a staple food among Andean peoples. They grew in temperate zones, at altitudes that ranged from sea level to 10,000 feet. Potatoes produced more food per acre than wheat and other grains. Food historian Reay Tannahill calls it "one of the world's most popular, comforting and conforming of foods." However, although early explorers were quick to recognize the potato's potential for feeding the masses back in Europe, not everyone accepted it immediately. In England, it was considered a delicacy that only rich people could afford, because of the outrageous prices of the initially limited stock. But in much of Europe, the potato was thought to be poisonous. This is not really as odd as it may sound. The potato is a member of the nightshade family and as such has poisonous relatives. And if potatoes are eaten green, they are indeed poisonous. In many places, the use of force or trickery was necessary to overcome people's concerns about the potato. Not until the second half of the eighteenth century did the potato receive wide acceptance in Europe.

Another great contribution to world cuisines was the tomato. At one time, Europeans and North Americans worried that it, too, might be poisonous (it also is a member of the nightshade family). However, the tomato was accepted early on as a medicine to treat diarrhea, liver and gallbladder disease, and digestive disorders. Today, the tomato enjoys tremendous popularity throughout the world. It is a key element of many cuisines and an indispensable ingredient in sauces, salads, and garnishes. Hot peppers, beans, and squash, which along with corn were staples of the Indian diet, also have become staples of many societies around the world.

The culinary richness of the Americas never ceased to amaze the conquistadors. Wherever they went, they were astonished by the variety of foodstuffs they found. Some early chroniclers wrote about the abundance of the land and the quantity of game and fowl to be found wherever they went. Deer and rabbits were so plentiful that young boys could catch them easily just by using sticks. There was also abundant small game, such as quail and turtledoves. The rivers and streams teemed with fish, and the sea provided an incredible variety of fish and shellfish.

Pedro Cieza de León, one of many early explorers to write about their discoveries in the New World, tells of his journey from Panama to Peru in the middle of the sixteenth century in *La Crónica del Perú*. He describes everything he saw, from the flora and fauna of each region he visited to the costumes of the people he encountered. He writes about the palm tree that produces the sweet white fruits called *palmitos* (hearts of palm), then relates how some Spaniards consumed enormous quantities of the delicacy, washing it down with water. This caused the *palmitos* to swell, and many of the diners died as a result. Cieza also writes about the *algarroba*—a tree similar to the Spanish carob tree, but of a different family—that produces fruit used to make flour. He describes a spice called *ishpingo*, which tastes much like cinnamon and looks like star anise. The natives used it to make a tea that cured stomachaches, as well as for flavoring foods. He also writes about the numerous unusual fruits that grew in abundance, including the avocado and pineapple, as well as myriad fruits that even today are rarely available outside South America.

At the time of the conquest, the diet of South America's natives was mainly plant based, with occasional fish or wild game. The indigenous peoples seem not to have developed an outstanding cuisine, such as the Mexican Indians did. None of the chroniclers of that time left a detailed account of the food served at the court of the Incas, as Father Sahagún did with the Aztecs. One of the few accounts of what the Inca leaders were served is recorded in the book *Atahualpa* (1939) by the Ecuadorian historian Benjamín Carrión. He describes the banquet that the Inca Huayna Cápac was offered in Tumipamba, the first stronghold of the Incas in the southern province of Ecuador. The menu consisted of *cuyes* (guinea pigs) roasted on large wooden forks, birds, deer, great quantities of cooked corn, and *chicha añeja* (a fermented drink made from germinated corn and aged in clay vessels). This was very simple indeed, compared to the feasts given by the Aztecs.

The Indians had not domesticated many animals, but they did excel in domesticating plant foods. Inca agriculture, for example, was highly developed, because the Incas were great experimenters. They experimented with habitat, yield, hybrids, and growing time. They dried meat, potatoes, and other root vegetables to avoid famine. They knew how to extract the poison from bitter cassava (yuca) to make a meal. They also knew that planting corn, squash, and beans together would achieve optimum results, because corn provides shade and support for the delicate beans, squash provides ground cover for moisture retention and minimal soil erosion, and beans regenerate the soil, providing the nitrogen needed by the other plants. To enrich the soil further, the Incas used guano (seabird droppings), a nutrient-rich fertilizer. (The richest guano, found off the coast of Peru, helped replenish many depleted soils in Europe after the conquest.) The Incas also used anchovy heads as fertilizer, a practice still followed today.

The Incas also had folk wisdom about dietary needs that has been confirmed by modern research. They knew how to combine plant foods to make up for the lack of protein and other nutrients in corn. When corn was introduced overseas without the benefit of this knowledge, there were terrible outbreaks of pellagra, a niacin-deficiency disease. In addition, the technique of soaking dried corn in water with lime or ashes to peel and soften the corn has been shown to add calcium to the corn.

Although some indigenous specialties, such as dog, guinea pig, and fish gravel (a coarse fishmeal) did not appeal to European settlers, they accepted many other Indian foods. They also brought with them animals and foodstuffs that were familiar and more to their liking. Sometimes this was not just a matter of taste. Without the requisite skills for processing some of the plants, there were too many unknown, and potentially lethal, options among the foods of this new land. The following foods—all of which would survive both the sea voyage and the first months in the new land—normally accompanied the immigrants:

400 pounds of crackers
2 barrels of flour weighing 700 pounds
8 kegs of wine, at 25 pounds each
2 barrels of dried broad beans and garbanzos [chickpeas], 100 pounds each
4 jugs of olive oil, 25 pounds each
6 jugs of vinegar, 25 pounds each
25 pounds of rice
50 pounds of dried fish and bacon
12½ pounds of soap
Onions, olives, garlic, dried figs, raisins, and almonds

The ease with which European animals and plants adapted to their new environment helped speed up colonization. Unlike the Pilgrims of North America, who brought their wives with them, the Spaniards didn't bring women from home and instead depended on Indian women to prepare their foods. These creative women used their own foods and techniques, as well as the foods the Spaniards brought, to create new dishes that would be acceptable to Europeans, thus giving birth to the creole cuisine of South America.

The Indians quickly adopted European animal foods, and pigs and chickens became part of Indian households. Unfortunately, for many Indians the greater variety of foodstuffs did not represent an improvement in lifestyle. Although the Catholic Church and the mission system protected many natives, those who did not benefit from their care often were subjected to slavery or servitude and had to do with whatever food they received from their masters. The Indians who worked in the mines survived 12-hour days with just a small portion of potatoes and coca leaves.

The Spaniards almost wiped out the highly nutritious grain amaranth because it was associated with native religious practices that the Spaniards considered barbaric. Quinoa seems to have been dismissed entirely and was replaced with wheat and other cereals of inferior nutritional value.

The Spaniards introduced to the New World a wide range of new ingredients, techniques, and culinary customs, just as the Moors had done in Spain over the preceding centuries. In her book *Spanish Cooking*, Pepita Aris writes about the Spaniards' respect for ingredients, which, together with an innate good sense and good taste, had resulted "in a cuisine that is straightforward, but extremely tasty." And that was the mark that the Spaniards left on the cuisine of the New World. The first settlers came from Andalusia, and their heritage is still very strong in the Andean countries. They brought oranges and olives, spices such as cumin and saffron, and the use of nuts and olive oil in cooking, which they inherited from the Moors. *Tapas* were invented in Andalusia, and variations of them can be found in every South American country, including empanadas, *pinchos* (small shish kebabs), croquettes, and *escabeches* (pickled foods), to name just a few. Soon after this first influx, people from Extremadura and other parts of Spain also immigrated to South America. They all left their mark on the cuisine and culture. For example, the influence of the Basques, who settled in Chile, Argentina, and Uruguay, is reflected in the penchant there for using fruits in savory dishes.

The Portuguese also were arriving in South America during this period, claiming and settling along the east coast. They started their exploration in the 1500s, not long after their rivals in Spain had discovered the continent. Their influence is seen most in Brazil, where the Portuguese language is spoken and Portuguese customs and foods blended with myriad other influences to shape the region. The Dutch and French settled in other parts of South America, but they were not major players in the region.

The Portuguese experience was different from the Spanish. In the first place, the Portuguese had no problem adapting to the tropical climate, because they were more pre-disposed to the tropics than the Spaniards. In his classic work *The Masters and the Slaves*, Gilberto Freyre attributes the Portuguese success to their ability to blend in, intermarrying with the local peoples "wherever they might settle, in Africa or in America." Freyre notes that "no colonizing people in modern times has exceeded or so much as equaled the Portuguese in this regard." The Portuguese quickly took Indian wives and embraced many Indian foods, such as cassava (yuca), which became a very important part of their diet. They brought their own foods, too, including sugar cane, *bacalhau* (salt cod), olives, sausages, wine for cooking, and the widespread use of eggs, cloves, cinnamon, and sugar, which the Portu-guese inherited from the Moors. They also brought dishes such as *cozidos* (stews), *cuscuz* (couscous), codfish cakes, and pork with clams.

The Portuguese soon realized that the forest was extremely important as a source of food and that the Indians living there would have to teach them how those foods were processed. The Tupi-Guarani Indians had been growing cassava for about 5,000 years in the Amazon forest of Brazil, Colombia, and Venezuela. This root was the bread of the natives in those areas, and the Portuguese quickly adopted it in all its forms, almost to the exclusion of the wheat they brought with them. They loved the freshly made cassava bread, and many believed it to be more nourishing and digestible than wheat bread. (Ironically, cassava is nutritionally inferior to wheat.) Cassava became the basis of the Portuguese diet, and today it is part of the daily diet of millions of people in Brazil. In some areas of Venezuela and Colombia, cassava bread is consumed more than cornbread or wheat bread. (The Spanish experience on the other side of the continent was the opposite, in that the Indians were the ones who adopted rice in place of the more nutritious native grains.)

Later on, when Portuguese women started to arrive, Indian women taught them how to make all sorts of delicate confections with the cassava. They also taught them the process of fermentation, which was used to prepare some of their delicacies. For example, they prepared wonderful preserves and the *carimã* cakes that have nourished Brazilian children for generations. The *beijú* (cassava pastry) was another specialty from which the natives developed a whole line of modern specialties. The *caribé* is made from *beijú-acú*, a round bread baked in the oven, then soaked in water until it is reduced to a paste. By adding more water to this paste, the natives made a drink called *mingau*. No wonder Freyre writes that "the national cuisine would have remained impoverished and its individuality would have been profoundly affected if these delicacies of native origin had not survived, for they give flavor to the Brazilian diet that neither Lusitanian dishes nor African cookery could supply." But he also notes that "it was in the kitchen of the Big Houses [plantation homes] that many of these confections lost their regional and exclusively Indian character to become truly Brazilian."

The natives of Amazonia contributed the famous fish *pirarucú*, which in northern Brazil is sometimes more important than salt cod or beef jerky. The turtle is another important food of the region, because of the variety of its uses. Brazilians use the meat, as well as the innards, in a number of unusual dishes. They also use turtle fat for cooking. Today turtles are raised in sizes that range from the size of a hand to three to four feet in diameter. The Indians had many uses for corn as well. Fresh corn was ground to make *pamuna*, which was wrapped in cornhusks. Today this dish is called *pamonhas*, and the corn is mixed with coconut and sugar and steamed like a tamale, a contribution of Brazil's African cooks. Another Indian specialty is *canjica*, originally called *acanijic*, which has become a national dish. It is made with cracked dried corn or fresh corn, coconut, sugar, and cinnamon. The Indians contributed the practice of using leaves to wrap foods for cooking and hot peppers to season foods, which the African slaves embraced wholeheartedly.

The African influence was of paramount importance in the development of Brazilian cuisine. The slave trade started in 1538 and lasted through the nineteenth century. Most of the slaves that came were from the west coast of Africa (present-day Senegal, Nigeria, and Angola). By the time the slaves gained independence nearly 400 years later, about 10 million Africans had arrived in Hispanic America. The greatest concentration of slaves was in Portuguese lands—the Caribbean and Brazil. Large areas became Africanized. Because so many slaves lived together on the big sugar and coffee plantations, they became almost like towns. Therefore, Africans in Brazil were able to keep their culture and traditions largely intact. They brought with them their music, dance, religious practices, and foods, all of which have become very important parts of Brazilian culture.

Because the climate of Brazil is very similar to that of West Africa, the slaves were able to grow some of their familiar foods. Many slaves tended small gardens, which supplied vegetables for their own needs. Sometimes they even had a surplus to sell. At a symposium titled "Good as Gold: Foods the Americas Gave the World," Professor Lydia Pulsipher, a cultural geographer, said that of all immigrants, the Africans were probably the ones that understood the environment best, because with the little spare time that was allotted to them, they managed to grow gardens and raise small animals. They were very successful as food producers.

In Brazil, as elsewhere, while many slaves worked in the fields or mines, others worked as servants and cooks, eventually becoming masters of their owners' kitchens. At first the Africans used their own techniques to prepare local ingredients, but later they also incorporated foods brought from their homeland, such as yams, okra, coconuts, ginger, sorghum, millet, and greens, to reproduce familiar dishes and flavors. They introduced the use of *dendê* (palm oil) and the generous addition of heat to their foods. (In Africa, this heat was supplied by a ginger known as *melegueta*, or grains of paradise, but the New World hot pepper readily played the same role. Both *dendê* and heat are indispensable elements of Bahian cooking. (Bahia is a region of Brazil.) This blending of influences extended to all available ingredients. For example, *molhada*, a Brazilian confection, combines native cassava (yuca) with coconut (Africa), cinnamon (Asia), and salt (Europe), all wrapped in a banana leaf (Africa). The Africans also changed Portuguese dishes by adding or substituting ingredients they liked better. To the *frigideira* (frittata), for instance, they added coconut milk and replaced olive oil with *dendê* and shellfish with codfish. Yet some Portuguese dishes remained intact, such as the *rabada* (oxtail stew) of the northeast and the famous *caldo verde* (kale and potato soup).

Northeastern Brazil (Bahia, Pernambuco, and Maranhão) is the stronghold of Afro-Brazilian cooking, which is most evident in Bahia. In Bahia, music and religion are very important, and they are always intertwined with food. African Brazilians blended their traditional religion with Catholicism, resulting in the Candomblé religion. One of the most important religious ceremonies is the preparation of ritual foods to feed the gods. *Bobó* (shrimp with yuca sauce), *acarajé* (black-eyed pea fritters), and *efó* (dried shrimp, fish, and spinach) are some of the descendants of these ritual dishes. Brazil's northeast is also the home of *carne seca* (beef jerky), and in the streets of Bahia, it is still possible to find some of the old confections, descendants of those made by the African women who once worked in the "Big Houses" on the plantations. It was on the plantations and in the convents that sweets and many other specialties of Brazil were developed: *beijos* (kisses), *sequilhos* and *sonhos* (doughnuts), and coconut and nut confections. In general, though, the daily diet of the masses now consists primarily of rice, beans, beef jerky, and manioc meal.

Spanish South America did not import as many slaves as did Brazil, because the Spaniards used Indian slaves, who were cheaper to obtain and better suited to work in the highlands. Only when the Indians had been decimated by brutal working conditions and Old World diseases did the Spaniards start importing African slaves, mainly to work on the lowland plantations. Most of the slaves brought over by the Spaniards came from the coast of East Africa (present-day Tanzania, Mozambique, and Madagascar). Because the slaves were not as concentrated in Spanish areas of South America as in Brazil and the Caribbean, they intermingled with the Indians and whites, producing a new race called *pardo*. In these regions, African culture was not preserved to the extent it was in Brazil. However, some of their customs, foods, and music survived. The African-influenced cooking of the coasts of Venezuela, Ecuador, Colombia, and northern Peru is different from that of the Bahia region of Brazil. Plantain casseroles; soups made with plantains, meat or seafood, and cassava (yuca) or other tubers; and unusual tamales and empanadas made with plantain dough are all very popular. The Africans in this region, like those in Brazil, used coconut milk and peanuts to season their specialties, both sweet and savory. They also used generous amounts of peanuts, coconut, and white or dark sugar to make a variety of confections.

Immigration to South America was slow during the first century after the conquest, but by 1800 Europeans were arriving by the millions. In the late nineteenth century, about 1 million Spaniards settled in Argentina and 500,000 in Brazil. A large number of Spaniards also settled in Uruguay and Chile. More than 1 million Portuguese came to Brazil, while others settled in Argentina. The largest number of immigrants during this period came from Italy. Brazil received more than 1.2 million Italian immigrants and Argentina more than 2.5 million. Italians also made the journey to Chile and Peru and were the dominant immigrant group in Uruguay. Other immigrants came from Germany, England, France, and the Slavic countries. These diverse populations had a profound influence on the native cuisine and helped fuel the creation of the *cocina criolla* (creole cuisine), as we will see in the recipes throughout this book.

The first German immigrants arrived in Brazil in 1824 and settled in Rio Grande do Sul. Other Germans settled in São Paulo, Santa Catarina, and Paraná. Most of the Germans who came in the beginning were farmers, laborers, and craftsmen. They retained their language and customs and made little effort to integrate. Outside Brazil, the largest concentrations of German immigrants were in Argentina, Chile, and Paraguay, as well as to a lesser extent in Venezuela and Colombia. About 100,000 Germans entered Argentina in the early twentieth century and settled primarily in Buenos Aires, with the rest scattered throughout the country. Some of the German and Swiss immigrants who came to Argentina settled in southern Patagonia and started the tourism trade by building chalets resembling those back home. No wonder San Carlos de Bariloche (a famous resort in northern Patagonia, bordering Chile) has been called the "Switzerland of Argentina."

The Welsh immigrants to Argentina settled along the Chubut River, close to the Atlantic coast, in an area that boasts fabulous marine wildlife (penguins, sea lions, whales, and more). This was an ideal place for tourists to visit, so the Welsh opened their homes and started offering their famous Welsh tea, accompanied by cakes developed by local housewives using native ingredients. The Germans followed suit and developed recipes for new cakes and sweets to sell to tourists.

Religion

Most South Americans practice the Roman Catholic religion, although in recent years evangelists have made tremendous strides in spreading the Protestant faith. In Brazil, Candomblé and Macumba are the two main religions introduced by West African slaves. Both have been affected by outside influences, especially Macumba, which is practiced mostly in Rio de Janeiro and combines West and South African beliefs with the European philosophy of spiritualism and the belief that the living can communicate with the spirits of the dead.

The main center for Candomblé is in Bahia, where there was the largest concentration of African slaves. To appease their Portuguese masters, the slaves changed the names of their gods. For example, the sea goddess, Iemanjá, who is the mother of all *orixás* (gods and goddesses), became Mary, the mother of Jesus. The main Candomblé ritual has to do with feeding special foods to the gods to gain their favor. These specialties are prepared by a group of priestesses who are known to be excellent cooks. The priestesses carefully follow tradition, for they fear that they might displease the gods if they do not. The ceremonies take several hours, with offerings, playing of drums, and dancing. Emotions build as the rhythm of the drums increases and the dancing becomes frenzied. Candomblé followers believe that everyone has an *orixá* to guide and protect him or her. In Bahia and Rio de Janeiro, millions of Brazilians go to the beach on New Year's Day to pay homage to Iemanjá. They bring offerings such as flowers, perfume, and fruit in hopes of securing the gods' protection in the new year.

The eclectic cuisine of Patagonia reflects the diversity of the region's settlers. Thus restaurants offer not only the famous Patagonian lamb barbecue, but also smoked trout, wild boar *pâté*, and jams and preserves made with the wonderful berries the area has to offer. These specialties are now found in gourmet shops, restaurants, and supermarkets for tourists to take home as souvenirs.

The Germans' major achievement was the popularization of their favorite drink, beer. In the southern part of Chile, in the city of Valdivia where many Germans settled, there is a beer museum in a bar that offers typical dishes to go with the beer. And in southern Brazil, the Germans hold an annual Oktoberfest in Blumenau and other towns. People come from all over Brazil, and even from Argentina, for the celebrations and food.

In the early nineteenth century, a group of about 370 German farmers, doctors, teachers, and artisans from the Black Forest settled in an isolated area near Caracas, Venezuela, called Colonia Tovar. This group remained isolated for 80 years, building Bavarian-style houses, intermarrying, and keeping the language and customs they had brought with them. Eventually, Colonia Tovar became a tourist attraction, offering authentic German food and dancing. Sausage and sauerkraut, sauerbraten, cakes, and jams are just a few of the specialties that attract people to this place.

The French immigrated mainly to Argentina, Brazil, and Uruguay. They exerted a tremendous influence on the industrial and cultural development of South America. The English immigrated mainly to Argentina and Uruguay, both of which have a strong English tradition. A small number of English also settled in Brazil.

The Russians, Yugoslavs, Poles, and Lithuanians who came to South America settled mainly in Brazil and Argentina, although some Yugoslavs also went to Chile. All of them left their mark on the creole cuisine.

The Chinese were the first Asians to arrive in Peru, in 1850, to work in the guano pits on the islands off the coast. Eventually, more than 100,000 Chinese came to work mainly on the plantations and in cotton fields, as well as on the railroads. They went on to open Chifa (Chinese) restaurants and to work in retailing.

After slavery was abolished in Brazil in 1888, coffee production costs rose, and cheaper labor was needed. In 1908, 165 Japanese families came to work on Brazil's coffee plantations. After their contracts were fulfilled, they moved mainly to São Paulo. More Japanese came in the ensuing years to work in agriculture, as merchants, and in industry. The biggest concentration of Brazil's Japanese population is in São Paulo, followed by Paraná and Mato Grosso. After World War II, many Japanese went to Paraguay, where they worked in farming, growing mainly soybeans.

Lebanese, Arabs, and Jews arrived in smaller numbers. Many of the Jews were from Portugal, where they had accepted imposed conversion to Catholicism and later left to escape the horror of the Inquisition. When the converted Jews, called Cristãos Novos, arrived in Brazil, they adopted new surnames, usually after trees or animals, such as Nogueira (walnut tree), Oliveira (olive tree), Pereira (pear tree), Coelho (rabbit), Raposo (weasel), and Leão (lion). Like the Sephardic Jews, who also left Portugal during or after the Inquisition, they brought with them their traditions and eating habits, which were integrated with the native cuisines, but they tended to stay in their own communities.

All these immigrants brought with them their customs and their foods, which, together with the native cultures and foods, fueled the creation of the creole cuisine. Members of the upper classes traveled to Europe and brought back recipes for special dishes, which they gave to their native cooks to adapt. Italians left an indelible mark on the cooking of Argentina, Chile, and Uruguay; Germans on that of Venezuela, Chile, and southern Brazil. Colombia has a rich and varied cuisine with strong Indian, African, and European roots. Peru, Ecuador, and Bolivia display their Inca roots, but with a Spanish flair. The cuisine of Brazil is a result of the marriage of Indian, Portuguese, and African influences. The further exchange of dishes among the countries of South America has added even more variety to this potpourri of foods. In general, however, many of these influences have been relatively superficial, affecting mainly the appearance, forms, and techniques of South American cuisine. The core of the cuisine remains stubbornly Hispanic (both Spanish and Portuguese).

I have found that on a very basic level, the one element that holds the cuisines of South America together is the Hispanic *sofrito*, an onion-based flavoring or sauce. This is the basis of almost every savory specialty in South American cuisine. A parallel for this connecting element may be seen in the comments of Copeland Marks, who writes in his book on Sephardic cooking, "Cooking styles, like handicrafts, identify ethnic cultures wherever they may be. In searching for a common fact in these exotic [Sephardic] cuisines, I found *Kashrut* [kosher cooking] as the thread that held them all together. Otherwise every community was different depending on geography and climate."

In addition, although Old World dishes were adopted in the New World, new dishes also arose. Creole cuisine produced the quintessential South American specialty—the tamale. No other specialty reflects the marriage of the Indian and European civilizations more than the tamale, which has become the mainstay of Christmas celebrations in most of South America.

As South American countries began gaining their independence, English influence began creeping into the cuisine, especially in the continent's southern countries. To the coffee that had already been imported from Africa (and that was flourishing), the English added beer, wine, and tea. They also introduced the practice of a morning tea break and a more substantial afternoon tea. The custom of having tea at 4:00 P.M. spread throughout South America and is still a favorite way to entertain friends, either at home or at a restaurant.

Around 1850, French cuisine became increasingly influential, especially among the elite. The legacy of French food being served for elegant receptions is still alive. But the French influence also spread among the middle classes, as can be seen in the often-used béchamel sauce, puff pastry, crepes, and vegetable puddings, to name just a few dishes. European pastries are still the favorite sweets of South Americans.

The Chinese also have left their mark in every country, as Chinese restaurants can be found in all the major cities. In addition, by the end of the nineteenth century, the United States began to influence South America's eating habits, and this influence continued to grow throughout the twentieth century. Hamburgers, hot dogs, pizza, roasted chicken, cheesecake, and soft drinks have become very popular in the past century.

Amazing as it may seem, the exchange continues, and the foods of South America are being discovered again. It is sad to note that some of the indigenous foods that fed the Andean peoples for 3,000 years have either disappeared or are about to, largely as a result of the introduction of Western crops. Fortunately, some of the colorful and nutritious ancient crops domesticated from wild relatives high in the Andes, such as quinoa, amaranth, *oca*, and *ullucos* are becoming the focus of worldwide attention. The scientific community is studying them for their nutritional value and looking for new ways to use them more widely, both in the Andes and in high mountain areas around the world. Quechua, the language of the native Andean Indians, has a phrase, *pacha kuti*, which refers to a periodic turn in the direction of the earth, a reversal in history and time. Perhaps this age-old concept will prove itself in a return to the crops of the ancients as well.

"Columbus arrived in the New World in 1492, but America has yet to be discovered," wrote Jack Weatherford in his wonderful book *Indian Givers*. After hundreds of years of stagnation, the revolution of food that the conquest sparked continues on a scale that is hard to comprehend. South Americans' eating habits are changing rapidly thanks to modern methods of communication and transportation. Indian gardens are still contributing numerous previously undiscovered foodstuffs to the world larder. Scientists are busy studying similar harsh, high-altitude habitats in the world to introduce nutritious Indian crops to areas where hunger and malnutrition are problems. In fact, they have successfully transplanted quinoa, amaranth, and a variety of other crops to other areas of the world. This movement of crops to new locations is combined with increasing interest in Latin America's culture, history, and foods.

Bebidas

BEVERAGES

SOUTH AMERICA HAS A WONDERFUL assortment of delicious beverages, thanks to the double blessing of a tremendous variety of climates and an immensely diverse population. The range of climates, from tropical to alpine, permits the growing of a wide array of fruits, grains, and other plants, both introduced and indigenous, that can be used to create a delightful assortment of libations. To German immigrants, we owe the wonderful beers that are made in just about every South American country. To the French, Italians, Spaniards, Portuguese, and Germans, we are indebted for our great wines, which are now produced in, and exported from, Chile, Argentina, Uruguay, and Brazil. There is also *aguardiente* from the Andean countries, the rums of Venezuela, *cachaça* from Brazil, and *pisco* from Peru, Chile, and Bolivia. From the Indians come the *chichas*, beverages that can be served freshly made or (far more commonly) fermented. Old ideas and new, indigenous ingredients and adopted, are blended into cocktails, punches, sangrias, *refrescos*, and more throughout South America.

Brazilians are practically religious about celebrating Sundays and holidays with *una bebidinha* (a little drink) accompanied by *de tira-gostos* (hors d'oeuvres). Ice-cold beer or *batidas*, made with *cachaça* and a variety of fruits or coconut, are served with simple snacks such as roasted peanuts or cashews, hard-cooked eggs, fried sausages, and shrimp on skewers. The important thing for Brazilians is to share these moments with friends and relatives.

For the South American family, fruit drinks are an integral part of daily life. Unfortunately, with the introduction of soft drinks, their consumption has decreased. The traditional *jugos* (fruit drinks), now share space on the table with bottles of Coca-Cola. What a pity, for these fabulous fruit drinks are not only delicious but highly nutritious. Made with fresh, sun-ripened fruits, they provide important vitamins and other nutrients needed for good health. It remains to be seen what impact this change will have on the population.

Pisco Sour		*Batido de Chocolate*	
Pisco Brandy Cocktail	35	Chocolate Milk Shake	45
Yunqueño		*Batido de Frutas*	
Bolivian Pisco Cocktail	35	Fruit Milk Shake	45
Coctel de Tumbo		*Batido con Leche y Agua*	
Banana Passion Fruit Cocktail	35	Drink with Milk and Water	45
Chilcano de Pisco		*Sorbete de Tomate de Arbol*	
Pisco Cocktail	36	Tamarillo Fruit Drink	46
Caipirinha		*Sorbete de Quinua*	
Cachaça Sour	36	Quinoa Fruit Drink	46
Batida de Coco		*Canelazo*	
Coconut Cocktail	37	Cinnamon Tea	47
Batida de Maracujá ou Abacaxi		*Vino Caliente*	
Passion Fruit or Pineapple Cocktail	37	Hot Wine Drink	47
Ponche de Ron		*Chucula/Masato*	
Rum Punch	38	Ripe Plantain and Milk Drink	48
Sangría		*Api de Quinua*	
Wine Punch	38	Hot Quinoa Drink	48
Sangría con Oporto		*Chocolate con Leche para las Once*	
Wine Punch with Port	39	Hot Chocolate with Milk for Eleven o'Clock	50
Ponche de Champagne con Jugo de Maracuyá		*Chocolate con Leche de Coco*	
Champagne Punch with Passion Fruit Juice	39	Hot Chocolate with Coconut Milk	50
Chicha de Jora		*Chocolate à Brasileira*	
Corn Drink	43	Hot Chocolate Brazilian Style	51
Jugo		*Cafezinho*	
Fruit Drink	44	Brazilian Coffee	52
Chicha o Jugo de Tamarindo			
Tamarind Drink	44		

South American Spirits

Aguardiente: Roughly translated as "spirits" or "liquor," *aguardiente* was probably one of the first spirits distilled from the sugar cane brought to South America by the Spaniards and Portuguese. In some of the Andean countries, this fiery drink is almost pure alcohol, and it is the cheapest and most popular drink of the poor and lower classes. From colonial days to relatively recent times, *aguardiente* was not carefully distilled and had a bad reputation—roughly equivalent to "moonshine" or "white lightning" in the United States. Now, however, it is often distilled with controls for quality and alcohol level, and high-quality *aguardiente* is finding a wider audience. It shares the same name of a potent and popular spirit made in Spain that is distilled from the skins and seeds of grapes— like the *grapa* (grappa) in Uruguay, also a potent spirit and popular drink of the masses. In Spain, there is a saying that a glass of *aguardiente* requires three men—one to drink it and two to carry him home. The name *aguardiente* is also applied to any spirit made by distilling fermented sugar cane and water, such as *cachaça*, white rum, and *pisco*.

Cachaça: In Brazil, *aguardiente* is called *cachaça*, which has become the second most consumed drink after beer. The production of *cachaça* started in 1532, when a Portuguese colonist brought some cuttings of sugar cane from Madeira. Unlike rum, which is distilled from molasses, *cachaça* is distilled directly from the fermented sugar cane juice. Most *cachaças* and other Andean *aguardientes* are not aged, just filtered before bottling, and as a result they are almost pure alcohol. These are the *cachaças* that are used in mixed drinks. Aged *cachaças* are usually served straight over ice.

Pisco: *Pisco* is a brandy made from pink *moscatel* (muscat) grapes, which grow in Peru, Chile, and Bolivia. The name of this *aguardiente* comes from the region of Pisco, in southern Peru, where the grapes used to make this spirit are grown. *Pisco* was originally called *aguardiente de Pisco*. According to chroniclers, the word *pisco* means "birds" in Quechua, and the Indians called this region Pisko because of the variety of birds found along the coast. The first grapes, called *quebranta*, arrived in Peru from the Canary Islands in 1532, after the Spaniards were in control of the Inca Empire. In the beginning, monks produced *aguardiente* exclusively from the grapes they had brought. By 1613, however, "*aguardiente* brandy" was produced out of the muscat grapes grown in the Pisco region.

Rum: Venezuela is the largest producer of rum in South America, producing white, golden, and dark rums. The barrel-aged golden and dark rums have achieved world recognition for their quality. Whether the rum is made from sugar cane juice or molasses and water, it is fermented by adding yeast and aged anywhere from one to several days, or even weeks for the better varieties. Lighter rums are usually blended and filtered through charcoal. Heavier rums are usually distilled in pots and aged in oak barrels. The final color is determined by adding caramel (which is made from sugar) in varying amounts. Good rum is widely used throughout South America to flavor desserts and in a variety of cocktails and punches.

Pisco Sour

PISCO BRANDY COCKTAIL *Serves 2*

In Chile, Peru, and Bolivia, the classic *pisco sour* is made with lemon juice, *pisco*, and egg whites, although personal and regional tastes introduce variations on the theme. Some use sugar syrup instead of granulated sugar. Some Peruvians throw the ice in a blender for a few seconds and add a sprinkling of cinnamon before serving.

Many other popular drinks also include *pisco*. In Chile, they make *pichuncho* with equal amounts of *pisco* and dry vermouth, and *piscola* with equal amounts of *pisco* and Coca-Cola. In Bolivia, they make the *Yunqueño* (recipe follows) with *pisco* and orange juice.

A Chilean gathering would not be complete without *pisco sours*. Because Chilean lemons are a little different from ours, some people prefer to use limes. I think that this drink tastes more like the Chilean version when made with fresh lemon juice.

> ¼ **cup** *pisco*
> **3 tablespoons fresh lemon juice**
> **2 tablespoons sugar, or more to taste**
> **1 large egg white**
> **1½ cups ice cubes**

Place all the ingredients in a cocktail shaker and shake vigorously. Add more sugar to taste, if desired. Strain into a shallow champagne glass and serve immediately.

Yunqueño

BOLIVIAN PISCO COCKTAIL *Serves 4*

The *yunqueño* is a Bolivian variation of the classic *Pisco Sour* (above). The drink takes its name from the Yungas region of La Paz, Bolivia, where it was invented. In this region, oranges are plentiful, as are tangerines, and *yunqueños* are sometimes made with tangerine juice as an alternative. Singani is the most popular brand of *pisco*. The original *yunqueño* was served straight up; now most people serve it over crushed ice in cocktail glasses.

> **1½ cups fresh orange juice**
> **1 tablespoon sugar**
> **1 cup Singani (***pisco***)**
> **2 drops angostura bitters**

Mix the orange juice and sugar together in a cocktail shaker or blender. Add the *pisco* and bitters and shake or process until well blended. Serve immediately.

Coctel de Tumbo

BANANA PASSION FRUIT COCKTAIL *Serves 4*

The flavor of the banana passion fruit is suggested, though not quite captured, by its English name. This tropical fruit grows abundantly in the departments of Cochabamba and Tarija, Bolivia. It is recommended that no ice be used in this drink because it would mask the wonderful fragrance of the fruit. The pulp is available frozen in 14-ounce packages in some Latin American markets.

> **1 cup thawed frozen banana passion fruit pulp**
> ½ **cup Singani (***pisco***)**
> **2 tablespoons sugar**

Combine all the ingredients in a blender. Serve in martini glasses.

Chilcano de Pisco

PISCO COCKTAIL *Serves 4*

This Peruvian cocktail is another way to serve *pisco*.

> **2 cups ginger ale**
> **⅓ cup *pisco***
> **1 tablespoon fresh lemon juice**
> **2 drops angostura bitters (optional)**
> **Crushed ice**
> **4 lemon slices or wedges for garnish**

In a glass jar, mix together the ginger ale, *pisco*, lemon juice, and bitters (if using). Serve in tall glasses filled with the crushed ice. Garnish each glass with a lemon slice.

Caipirinha

CACHAÇA SOUR *Serves 1*

This classic Brazilian drink is potent and delicious, and lately it has become very popular around the world. *Cachaça* is a raw, clear spirit distilled from sugar cane juice, rather than from molasses, like most rums. *Caipirinhas* are called *caipiroskas* when made with rum and *caipirissimas* when made with vodka. My Brazilian friend Margarida Nogueira makes a delicious *caipirinha*. Here are the steps she says you must follow to get a perfect drink. The lime can be cut ahead of time, covered, and refrigerated until needed, but it must be crushed just before serving.

> **1 lime, cut into ½-inch-thick wedges, then into ½-inch pieces**
> **1 teaspoon sugar, or more to taste**
> **¼ cup *cachaça* (vodka for a *caipiroska* or white rum for a *caipirissima*)**
> **Ice cubes or shaved ice**

Remove the white part of the membrane from the center of the lime pieces (it can give the drink a bitter taste). Place the pieces, pulp side up, in a mixing jar, add the sugar, and crush the pieces with a pestle. Add a little *cachaça* and crush the lime again. Add the rest of the *cachaça* and mix well. Add more sugar to taste, if desired. Serve in a cocktail glass filled with ice.

Batidas
"BEATEN" DRINKS

MY FRIEND MARGARIDA NOGUEIRA SAYS *batida* means "beaten," and *batidas* are just as popular in Brazil as caipirinhas—and more practical to prepare for groups of people. She sent me the recipes for the most popular ones, which are made with *cachaça* and coconut milk or fruit juices, such as passion fruit pulp, lime juice, or pineapple juice. Sugar is added to taste, as is the *cachaça*, depending on whether you want a weak or strong drink. The *batida* is "beaten" in a blender and kept refrigerated. To serve, add some crushed ice to a small wineglass and pour in some of the *batida*.

Batida de Coco

COCONUT COCKTAIL *Serves 6*

This is one of the most popular cocktails in Brazil, where coconut is a favorite ingredient in many drinks and sweets.

1 cup well-stirred canned unsweetened coconut milk

1 cup water

Sugar to taste

¾ cup *cachaça* or white rum

Crushed ice

Place all the ingredients except the ice in a blender and process until smooth. For a weaker drink, process in the blender with some crushed ice. To serve, add some crushed ice to a small wineglass and pour in some of the *batida*.

Batida de Maracujá ou Abacaxi

PASSION FRUIT OR PINEAPPLE COCKTAIL *Serves 4*

This is a great drink to serve with a *feijoada* (bean stew), because it can be made ahead and in large quantities, unlike the *caipirinha*, which has to be prepared just before serving.

¾ cup thawed frozen passion fruit pulp or pineapple juice

¼ cup water

½ cup *cachaça*, or more to taste

1 tablespoon sugar, or more to taste

Crushed ice

Put all ingredients except the ice in a blender and process for a few seconds. Add more sugar to taste, if desired. Serve in a small wineglass over crushed ice.

VARIATION This *batida* is not too strong. If you want a more potent drink, add more *cachaça*.

I N   T H E   P A S T ,   S O U T H   A M E R I C A N S , especially women, enjoyed punches made with a variety of spirits and fruit juices. In the past few years, however, the custom of serving punches at parties has declined, except at weddings, christenings, and showers, and punch is generally being replaced by wine, though some of us still prepare punches occasionally.

Ponche de Ron

RUM PUNCH *Serves 12*

Rum, especially white rum, has played an important role in Venezuela, and not necessarily for the good. In the interior, it is called *caña* (rum) or *caña blanca* (white rum). In the countryside, rum is consumed in such quantities that it has been called the curse of the masses. But in the cities, aged rum is used to make all sorts of cocktails and punches.

> 1 cup fresh lime juice
> ½ cup sugar
> 6 tablespoons grenadine syrup
> 2 cups light or dark rum
> ½ cup hulled and sliced strawberries
> One 1-liter bottle club soda or seltzer, chilled
> Ice cubes (optional)

1. In a large pitcher, combine the lime juice, sugar, grenadine syrup, and rum, stirring until the sugar is dissolved. Add the strawberries, cover, and refrigerate.

2. Right before serving, stir in the club soda. Serve in cocktail glasses, over ice, if desired.

Sangría

WINE PUNCH *Serves 8 to 10*

This popular Spanish drink, which Latin Americans have heartily embraced, is traditionally made with a mixture of wine, citrus juices, and club soda.

Sangría comes from the word *sangre* (blood) because of the color of the wine. The Spanish version uses a full-bodied red wine (preferably Rioja), orange liqueur, and sometimes brandy. A South American Cabernet Sauvignon is a good substitute for the Rioja. It is a refreshing summertime drink.

> One 750 ml bottle full-bodied dry red wine
> ½ cup fresh lemon juice
> ½ cup fresh orange juice
> ¼ cup sugar, or more to taste
> ¼ cup orange liqueur
> ¼ cup brandy (optional)
> 1 small lemon, thinly sliced and seeded
> 1 small orange, thinly sliced and seeded, if necessary
> Peaches, apples, or strawberries, or a combination, peeled, pitted, cored, or hulled, as necessary, and cut up
> 2 cups club soda, seltzer, or sparkling water
> Ice cubes

1. In a large pitcher, combine the wine, lemon juice, orange juice, sugar, orange liqueur, and brandy (if using). Mix well. Add more sugar to taste, if desired. Add the fruit, cover, and refrigerate for several hours or overnight.

2. Just before serving, add the club soda. Serve in cocktail glasses, each with 2 ice cubes and some of the fruit.

N O T E **Some versions of *sangría* use only wine, no liqueur or brandy. Either way, it is a delightful drink.**

Sangría con Oporto

WINE PUNCH WITH PORT *Serves 4*

I love this variation of classic *sangría* that I learned from a wine distributor. Because the ingredients are used in equal portions, you can easily increase the amounts to make this punch for a party.

> 1 cup fruity port
> 1 cup full-bodied dry red wine (preferably Rioja)
> 1 cup hulled and sliced strawberries
> 1 cup fresh orange juice
> Ice cubes
> 4 orange slices, seeded, if necessary

1. In a glass jar fitted with a cover, mix together the port and wine, then add the strawberries and refrigerate overnight.

2. Before serving, add the orange juice and mix well. Serve in cocktail glasses, each with 2 ice cubes and a few strawberries. Float an orange slice on top.

Ponche de Champagne con Jugo de Maracuyá

CHAMPAGNE PUNCH WITH PASSION FRUIT JUICE
Serves 12 to 14

To celebrate New Year's, there is no better choice than a delicious champagne punch, especially for the ladies. This punch is typical of those served in the countries where passion fruit or banana passion fruit are cultivated.

> Two 6-ounce cans frozen orange juice concentrate, thawed
> 1 cup thawed frozen passion fruit or banana passion fruit pulp
> ¼ cup sugar
> Two 750 ml bottles champagne

1. Mix the juices and sugar together well and freeze in ice cube trays.

2. Thirty minutes before serving, unmold the frozen juice cubes into a punch bowl. Just before serving, add the champagne to the bowl and serve in fluted glasses.

VARIATION Use ginger ale instead of champagne for a nonalcoholic version.

South American Wines

South America, according to *The Oxford Companion to Wine*, is the world's second-largest producer of wine after Europe. Argentina is the largest producer, followed by Chile and Brazil. Uruguay also produces good wines, especially rosé, but on a much smaller scale than the larger countries. The geographical diversity of some of the major wine-producing countries not only provides the ideal terrain and climate but also acts as a barrier to harmful diseases from abroad. Argentina's and Chile's grapes are free of downy mildew and phylloxera, which have destroyed many vineyards in Europe.

The first vines were planted in Peru, right after the conquistadors took hold of the Inca Empire in 1532. The Spanish missionary Juan Cidrón supposedly brought the first vines to Argentina in 1556, to plant in what is now the province of Mendoza. But the first vineyard on record was planted in 1557 in Santiago del Estero. The grape variety was probably Criolla, known as País in Chile and Mission in California. By the sixteenth century, the vines were well established, providing wine for local consumption, but wine production started to flourish only in the late eighteenth century.

Most of Argentina's vineyards are located in the west and north of the country. The grapes seem to thrive in dry valleys, where irrigation is provided by runoff from the Andes. The Andes also insulate the vineyards from the moist, cool air blowing off the Pacific Ocean. Because of the high altitude, the vineyards are warm during the day and cool at night.

Argentina has large regions with diverse climatic conditions, which makes it possible to grow different types of grapes. Important regions are the Cuyo (Mendoza and San Juan), Andean northwest (Salta and La Rioja), and south, in northern Patagonia, around Río Negro. Good-quality white wines, such as Chardonnay and Sémillon, are produced in the south. But the most important province is Mendoza, where Malbec, Argentina's most prestigious wine, is produced. The Malbec grape is a black grape native to France. It grows on the eastern slopes of the low mountains of the Andes. In Argentina, this grape yields complex, superbly balanced red wines that age well. Malbec is excellent with chicken, lamb, and dishes made with red wine that do not require the tannic astringency of Cabernet Sauvignon. It is a wonderful alternative to Merlot. Other varietals produced in Argentina are Chardonnay, Sauvignon Blanc, Merlot, Syrah, and Cabernet, to name just a few. Argentina has become the fourth- or fifth-largest producer of wine in the world.

It is believed that missionaries introduced the first vines to Chile to make wine for sacramental use. In 1551, the Spaniard Francisco de Aguirre founded the first large plantation in the well-watered valley around Copiapó, 500 miles north of Santiago. Later, the Spanish found better winegrowing regions in the south and moved to the Central Valley. It was not until 1851 that Chilean farmers imported the first quality vine cuttings from France's Bordeaux region. Among the imported vines were Cabernet Sauvignon, Merlot, and Carménère, which were planted in the

Maipo Valley. Until the end of the twentieth century, the most successful wines produced were Cabernet Sauvignon and Sauvignon Blanc. Now Merlot and Chardonnay are the most popular wines. Also in the late twentieth century, big corporations started replacing family-owned vineyards as the primary producers in Chile. In addition, Chileans have formed partnerships with well-known wine producers from France, Spain, and the United States, which have provided the technology for producing wine on a large scale.

Another important region in the Central Valley is the Rapel, which grows mostly red grapes that produce wonderful, full-bodied red wines. Rothschild has an important stake in the Los Vascos Winery in this area. Also found here are the Santa Rita Winery and Undurraga Winery.

Most of Chile's wines come from the Aconcagua and Maipo regions. The Aconcagua region is close to Santiago, the capital, and consists of two different subregions—one warm, the Aconcagua Valley, famous for its Cabernet, and one cold, the Casablanca Valley, whose name is usually associated with white wines. The credit for producing some of the best white wines in this area goes to winemaker Pablo Morandé. Chardonnay and Sauvignon Blanc are the main wines produced here. South of Santiago is Maule, where País is the most common grape. Bío-Bío, in the southern part of Chile, is one of the most extensive wine regions, planted with varieties of red grapes, especially País and muscat. The red wine produced here is generally consumed in Chile.

Uruguay's wine industry is the fourth largest in South America, and Uruguay is second only to Argentina in wine consumption. When the Basques immigrated to Uruguay beginning in 1870, they started the wine industry with the superior French grape called Tannat, renamed Harriague after one of the pioneers of Uruguayan viticulture. When the original vines were destroyed by disease, they were replaced with new Tannat vines imported from France, and thereafter the grapes were called by their original name. About 90 percent of Uruguayan wine is produced in the southern coastal departments of Canelones, San José, and Montevideo.

In Brazil, the Portuguese planted the first vines in the state of São Paulo around 1532. The Jesuits introduced Spanish vines in Rio Grande do Sul in 1626. But it was not until 1840, when the hybrid Isabella vine was introduced, that winegrowers achieved success. Widespread viticulture was established only in the late nineteenth century with the arrival of Italian immigrants, who settled in the Sierra Gaucha region, in the northeast of Rio Grande do Sul, and introduced new varieties of grapes, such as Barbera, Moscato, and Trebbiano. Marketable, high-quality wines did not appear until the late twentieth century, when winemaking companies such as Martini & Rossi and Moët & Chandon introduced modern equipment to Brazil.

Today most high-end restaurants in North America offer some South American wines. It is likely that the number of imports from South America will increase and North Americans will be able to choose from a wider range of vintages produced in a greater number of countries.

Chichas

CHICHA IS A HIGHLY ESTEEMED drink among South American Indians. Preparing a good *chicha* is considered an art, and many cooks take great pains to produce the best drink they can. *Chicha* can be prepared from many seeds, roots, or fruits, such as quinoa, peanuts, grapes, *oca* (page 427), and the berries of the *mulli* tree (pink peppercorns; page 429). *Chichas* made from pink peppercorns are considered a delicacy and are stronger than *chichas* made from corn.

In the tropical areas where yuca is a staple, *chichas* are made from *yuca brava* (bitter yuca) after the poisonous acid is removed. There are two methods of preparation. The yuca is grated and chewed to start fermentation, or the liquid obtained from the yuca is boiled, distilled, and then fermented.

Chicha de jora, made from corn, is without a doubt the favorite of the Indians. It played an important role in the life of the Incas, not only as a source of nourishment (the Indians drank *chicha* instead of water as a source of energy) but also in ritual and religious practices. The *chicha de jora* made for the Inca rulers was supposed to be very special because it was aged for a month.

Chicha de jora is made from a special kind of corn called *maíz jora* (the Indians called it *sora*), which is corn that has been buried for a few days until it develops sprouts. *Jora* is also available ground, called *harina de jora*. Different countries use different kinds of *jora*, which comes in various colors—white, yellow, red, and blue. In Ecuador, white *jora* is preferred, whereas in Peru and Bolivia, white and blue *jora* are used. In the Venezuelan Andes, *chicha* is made with corn *masa* (dough), *salvado* (wheat bran), and *miel de papelón* (syrup made from water and *panela*, molded brown sugar), which is used in many popular dishes. *Chicha de jora* is ready to use the day after it is made, but most people prefer to let it age for a few days to allow it to develop its full flavor. In Venezuela, unfermented *chicha* is called *chicha boba* (weak *chicha*) and fermented *chicha* is called *chicha fuerte* (strong *chicha*). Once it starts fermenting, *chicha* has a pleasant taste and can cause inebriation. *Chicha de jora* is available in the United States in South American groceries.

Another popular drink is *chicha de arroz* (rice), of which there are many variations, even within the same country. Some are served the same day they are made, and others are fermented for one or two days. Venezuelans use *guarapo* (see below) and distilled water to make *chicha*. In Bolivia, I found a version called *chicha para Carnaval*. South Americans celebrate Carnival, the period just before Lent, with many specialties prepared only for these festivities. The Bolivian version of *chicha* calls for three grains—barley, rice, and quinoa—along with a tablespoon of toasted sesame seeds. For seasonings, Bolivians use anise, black pepper, and fennel—rather unusual seasonings for a *chicha*.

People in Venezuela and the northern part of the Colombian Andes make another type of drink called *guarapo*. In Venezuela, it is made with water, pineapple peel, and *papelón* (*panela*). In Colombia, fresh lemon juice is preferred, and the *guarapo* is served mostly without fermenting. Venezuelans attribute all kinds of healing qualities to *guarapo*, especially for ailments concerning the stomach. It is considered the wine of the masses, and at one time it was perhaps more popular than *chicha* made with corn or other grains.

42 *The South American Table*

Sidewalk Cafés

 Throughout South America, sidewalk cafés are very popular, especially in the Andes. In the southern countries, which have four seasons, it is not possible to have open-air cafés year-round. But whenever possible, people congregate in these restaurants at all hours of the day, whether it is to have a cup of *tinto* (espresso) and visit with friends or relatives, or just to quench one's thirst with a large glass of freshly made *jugo de frutas* (fruit juice). These restaurants also offer appetizers or full meals.

Chicha de Jora

CORN DRINK *Serves 8*

The spices used to make this and other *chichas* vary from country to country. Bolivians often use anise in addition to the spices used here. The classic sweetener is *chancaca* or *panela*, but dark brown sugar works well as a substitute. *Maíz jora* is available in most Latin American, Peruvian, and Ecuadorian groceries. Dried orange leaves can be found in Mexican markets. Myrtle, a plant indigenous to Ecuador, has a sweet-sour taste; look for it in Ecuadorian markets, although it is not commonly available in the United States.

8 cups water

1 cup finely chopped *panela* or firmly packed dark brown sugar

4 cinnamon sticks

4 cloves

4 allspice berries

1 *ishpingo* (page 424; optional)

6 ounces *maíz jora*

3 fresh or dried orange leaves

2 sprigs myrtle (optional)

Peel of 1 pineapple cut about ½ inch thick

1 teaspoon pure vanilla extract

Sugar

1. In a large nonreactive pot, combine the water, *panela*, cinnamon, cloves, allspice, and *ishpingo* (if using). Bring to a boil over medium heat, stirring occasionally, until the *panela* is dissolved. Add the *maíz jora*, reduce the heat to low, and simmer for 30 minutes.

2. Remove from the heat and add the orange leaves and myrtle (if using). Cover and let cool to lukewarm. Transfer to a large plastic or glass jar and add the juice from the pineapple peel, twisting the peel to extract the juice. Some cooks add the entire peel to help with the fermentation (if so, the peel has to be scrubbed clean with a brush). Cover with a clean kitchen towel and let ferment for 2 to 5 days in a dark, warm spot. A thick layer of foam will appear on the surface when the *chicha* has fermented. Keep in mind that the longer it sits, the higher the alcohol content will be.

3. When ready, strain the *chicha* through a strainer lined with cheesecloth. Stir in the vanilla and sugar to taste. Refrigerate before serving in tall glasses.

NOTE **South American cooks use the same *maíz jora* to make 2 batches of *chicha*, recycling what's left in the strainer.**

Refrescos

REFRESCO IS THE TERM USED for all cold, nonalcoholic beverages. *Refrescos* include *jugos*, *sorbetes*, *licuados*, and *batidos*. *Jugos* are fruit juice drinks that can be made from any fruit, water, and sugar. In most South American homes, they are served for breakfast and lunch but may appear at any time during the day. *Sorbetes*, *licuados*, and *batidos* are generally made with milk and sometimes with ice cream. In Colombia and some other countries, you may find *refrescos* called *chichas*, a term that usually refers to a fermented drink (pages 42–43) but is also used for some unfermented beverages. There are so many *refrescos*, and the names change so much from country to country, that it is often hard to know what is being offered, but it will always be refreshing. When making a *refresco*, make sure the fruit is very ripe for optimum taste. When the fruit is ripe and sweet, very little extra sweetener is necessary.

Jugo

FRUIT DRINK *Serves 2*

South Americans always start the day with a glass of freshly made *jugo*. The type of fruit varies with the country and what is available. In my family, the favorite was *naranjilla* juice. Good hotels throughout South America offer a variety of juices for breakfast, but I always think with longing of the beautiful breakfast buffets served in Rio, where a wide selection of tropical fruits and juices is available.

> 1 cup diced fruit (such as pineapple, papaya, or berries, peeled, seeded, pitted, or hulled, as necessary)
> Juice of 1 lemon or lime
> 1 cup water
> 2 tablespoons sugar, or more to taste
> ½ cup crushed ice

Place all the ingredients in a blender and process until smooth. Add more sugar to taste, if desired. Refrigerate, if you wish, before serving in tall glasses.

Chicha o Jugo de Tamarindo

TAMARIND DRINK *Serves 4 to 6*

One of Colombia's most beloved drinks, this is also popular in other South American countries.

> One 14-ounce package frozen tamarind pulp
> 4 cups water
> ½ cup sugar, or more to taste

Place all the ingredients in a blender and process until smooth. Add more sugar to taste, if desired. Serve chilled.

NOTE To use frozen tamarind pulp, just break it into small pieces to put in the blender.

Batidos y Sorbetes

MILK SHAKES

BATIDOS ARE VERY POPULAR DRINKS throughout South America. They are usually made with milk, milk and water, cream, or ice cream, plus flavorings, especially chocolate or fruit. These beverages also are called *sorbetes* and are known as *licuados* in some regions.

Batido de Chocolate

CHOCOLATE MILK SHAKE *Serves 2*

Always popular with young people, this is a rich and satisfying milk shake.

- **1 cup milk**
- **½ cup whipping cream**
- **2 tablespoons Dutch-processed unsweetened cocoa powder**
- **1 tablespoon sugar, or more to taste**
- **½ teaspoon pure vanilla extract**
- **½ cup crushed ice**

Place all the ingredients in a blender and process until smooth. Add more sugar to taste, if desired. Serve immediately—it should be very cold.

Batido de Frutas

FRUIT MILK SHAKE *Serves 2*

Milk shakes can be made with just about any fruit. Try some of the more exotic fruits, such as *guanábana* (soursop), available frozen in South American groceries.

- **1 cup milk**
- **½ cup vanilla ice cream**
- **1 cup chopped fruit (such as strawberries, raspberries, mangoes, or peaches, or a combination, hulled, peeled, seeded, or pitted, as necessary)**
- **Sugar to taste**
- **1 cup crushed ice**

Place all the ingredients in a blender and process until smooth. Taste for sugar and serve immediately—it should be very cold.

Batido con Leche y Agua

DRINK WITH MILK AND WATER *Serves 6*

This *batido* has become quite popular in the United States. It is hard to resist, especially if made with passion fruit, banana passion fruit, *guanábana* (soursop), or Andean blackberries.

- **One 14-ounce package frozen tropical fruit pulp (such as cherimoya, *zapote*, *badea*, guava, or banana passion fruit)**
- **4 cups combination of milk and water, whatever ratio pleases you**
- **2 cups crushed ice**
- **Sugar**
- **Ground cinnamon for dusting (optional)**

Place the pulp, milk, water, and ice in a blender and process just to combine. Add sugar to taste and process again until smooth. Serve very cold in tall glasses, dusted with cinnamon, if desired.

Sorbete de Tomate de Arbol

TAMARILLO FRUIT DRINK *Serves 6*

Tamarillos, also called tree tomatoes, are native to Colombia and Ecuador and are now also grown in New Zealand. They have a tart, fragrant flavor all their own.

> **8 large ripe but firm yellow or red tamarillos or one 14-ounce package frozen tamarillo pulp**
>
> **4 cups milk**
>
> **½ cup sugar, or more to taste**
>
> **1 cup crushed ice**

1. If using fresh tamarillos, place them in boiling water and cook for 1 minute. Drain, saving 1 cup of the cooking water. Peel the tamarillos and place in a blender with a little of the reserved cooking water. Process until smooth. Strain through a fine-mesh sieve and return to the blender. If using frozen tamarillo pulp, break into small pieces and put in the blender.

2. Add the remaining ingredients and process until smooth. Add more sugar to taste, if desired. Serve immediately in tall glasses.

Sorbete de Quinua

QUINOA FRUIT DRINK *Serves 6*

The combination of grains and fruits is very popular in some Andean countries. The indigenous peoples used ground corn, quinoa, and amaranth to make porridges, which were flavored with local fruits. After the conquest, the Spaniards introduced other grains and spices to make the *come y bebe* (eat and drink) type of drink, such as the Chilean *Mote con Huesillos* (page 382). This is another such drink.

> **1 cup cooked quinoa (page 327) or amaranth (page 328)**
>
> **1 pint strawberries, hulled and chopped**
>
> **4 cups milk**
>
> **¼ cup sugar, or more to taste**

Place the quinoa, strawberries, and 1 cup of the milk in a blender and process until smooth. Add the remaining 3 cups milk and the sugar and process for a few seconds until blended. Add more sugar to taste, if desired. Chill well and serve in tall glasses.

Bebidas Calientes
HOT BEVERAGES

HOT DRINKS ARE AS COMMON as cold ones in South America. Coffee, even though it is not indigenous to the New World, has become not only a popular beverage but also an important cash crop in some regions, and the names of some Latin American countries have become almost synonymous with good coffee. Another adopted drink, tea, was brought by the English and French and is mainly reserved for afternoon tea parties, a popular South American tradition. A variety of herbal teas are offered in restaurants along with the traditional black teas.

Of the plants indigenous to the Americas, few are better known than the cacao tree, from which we get chocolate. Hot chocolate made with processed cacao beans was extremely popular in colonial times. More recently, however, hot chocolate is increasingly being replaced by coffee.

Maté, made from the dried leaves of an indigenous South American holly plant, is best known as the drink of the *gauchos*, although it also is popular among millions of Argentines, Uruguayans, Paraguayans, and people from southern Brazil. South America's Indian legacy also is reflected in some unusual hot drinks made with toasted ground grains.

Canelazo

CINNAMON TEA *Serves 4*

Canelazo is one of the oldest and most comforting drinks from the Andes. It is served at home and in the streets during many holidays, especially Christmas. There is nothing better on a cold night than a steaming cup of *canelazo* spiked with rum. This drink has survived for generations.

One year, when I was spending Christmas in Quito, I was invited for tea and a viewing of an old-fashioned Nacimiento (Nativity). It was a very special treat, and it took me back to my childhood, when we all fussed fixing the Nativity and waiting for friends and neighbors to drop by to sing *villancicos* (Christmas songs) and partake of refreshments afterward. *Canelazo* was always ready to warm up the guests before they headed home. When made with *naranjilla*, a fruit indigenous to Ecuador and Colombia, it is called *naranjillazo*. The original spike was *aguardiente*, which is still used by some.

  4 cups water
  ½ cup sugar, or more to taste
  8 cinnamon sticks
  Juice of 1 lemon
  1 cup thawed frozen *naranjilla* pulp
    (optional)
  Rum

1. Combine the water, sugar, cinnamon, and lemon juice in a medium-size saucepan and bring to a boil over medium heat. Reduce the heat to low and simmer, uncovered, until the water has developed a strong cinnamon flavor, about 15 minutes. Add the *naranjilla* pulp, if using, and simmer for 5 minutes more. Add more sugar to taste, if desired.

2. Strain, pour into mugs, and add rum to taste. Serve immediately.

Vino Caliente

HOT WINE DRINK *Serves 4*

This is a popular comfort drink for the cold winter nights typical of the Andes. The aroma of wine simmering with fragrant spices is absolutely irresistible. It warms the heart and the stomach.

  2 cups water
  ¼ cup sugar
  4 cinnamon sticks
  4 cloves
  4 thin lemon slices
  4 thin orange slices
  4 cups dry red wine

1. Place the water, sugar, cinnamon sticks, and cloves in a medium-size nonreactive saucepan. Slowly bring to a boil, stirring until the sugar has dissolved. Reduce the heat to low and simmer for 10 minutes.

2. Remove from the heat, cover, and let stand for 5 minutes. Add the lemon and orange slices and wine. Return to the heat, bring to a boil, reduce the heat to low, and simmer for 5 minutes.

3. Remove from the heat, strain, and serve at once in coffee cups.

Chucula/Masato

RIPE PLANTAIN AND MILK DRINK *Serves 2*

This delicious and nourishing drink is very popular in the coastal region of Ecuador. It goes by the name *chucula* in the southern states and *masato* in the north. It is especially attractive to people on sugar-free diets, because the very ripe plantain provides enough sweetness without the addition of sugar. Most Ecuadorians, however, like their drinks very sweet and use *panela* or regular sugar to sweeten it. Any kind of ripe banana can be used to make this drink; the little *niño* bananas will give it an even silkier texture. The consistency is like that of a milk shake. It can be made even thicker to serve as a dessert, topped with freshly beaten meringue. Very often people add shredded white cheese, such as Muenster, at the end and cook until melted.

> 1 very ripe (black) plantain
> 1 cinnamon stick
> 1 cup milk
> ¼ teaspoon pure vanilla extract
> Finely chopped *panela* or dark brown sugar
> (optional)

1. Peel the plantain and cut into ½-inch-thick slices, removing any black spots. Place in a medium-size nonreactive saucepan along with the cinnamon stick and water to cover. Bring to a boil, reduce the heat to low, and simmer, covered, until very soft, about 20 minutes.

2. Discard the cinnamon and transfer the plantains with the cooking liquid to a blender. Add the milk and vanilla and process until smooth. Taste; if more sweetness is desired, add *panela* to taste and pulse to mix well.

3. Serve warm or at room temperature. This drink tastes best when made just before serving.

Api de Quinua

HOT QUINOA DRINK *Serves 2 to 3*

Also known as *mazamorra de quinua*, this drink is a breakfast specialty in Bolivia. It is one of the best-loved comfort foods of the Altiplano. *Api* is usually flavored with cinnamon, but pineapple or dried apples may be used instead.

> 3 cups milk
> 2 cups cooked quinoa (page 327)
> ¼ cup sugar
> 1 cinnamon stick
> ¼ teaspoon pure vanilla extract
> Ground cinnamon for sprinkling

1. In a 2-quart saucepan, combine the milk, quinoa, sugar, and cinnamon stick. Bring to a boil over low heat, reduce the heat to the lowest possible setting, and partially cover. Simmer, stirring occasionally, until thickened, about 15 minutes.

2. Remove the cinnamon stick and serve hot in a cup, sprinkled with the cinnamon.

Chocolate Caliente

HOT CHOCOLATE

CHOCOLATE IS ONE OF THE most fascinating of all the foods the South American Indians gave to the world. The cacao tree originated in the Americas, probably in the basins of the Orinoco and Amazon Rivers, where most species of wild cacao are still found. Cacao grows there in the shady tropical forest, protected from the strong sun. The natives of these areas ate only the delicious white pulp that surrounds the seeds and discarded the precious beans. Wild cacao must have spread from Amazonia to other regions and probably was domesticated in Central America.

When the Spaniards arrived in what is now Mexico, they found the Mayas and Aztecs using cacao beans to make a drink that was so special that it was served to the emperor in gold goblets. It was believed to be an aphrodisiac, which is why the emperor drank so much of it. This unsweetened drink was made with toasted ground cacao beans, hot or cold water, and spices, such as *achiote* (annatto) or ground dried hot peppers. It was accessible only to the ruling class and nobility because cacao beans were so costly. (They were, in fact, used as currency by both the Aztecs and the Mayas, and the Aztecs even found a way to counterfeit them.)

The name of the drink, *xocoatl*, may be related to Quetzalcoatl, who was, at a time long predating the Aztecs, associated with vegetation and rain and was believed to have taught the people how to grow and use cacao. The Nahuatl word for the cacao tree is *cuauhcacahuatl*. Our word for processed cacao, *chocolate*, derives from the Aztec *xocoatl*, which probably meant "bitter drink." The botanist Linnaeus named the cacao tree *Theobroma cacao*. *Theobroma* is Greek for "food for the gods."

At the beginning of the conquest, the Spaniards found *xocoatl* unpalatable. In addition to the fact that it combined cacao with odd spices (and no sugar), it was prepared by beating it to a foamy consistency, and some Spaniards found the foam especially distasteful. By 1591, some Guatemalan women had created tablets that could be dissolved in hot water and sweetened with sugar to make a chocolate drink. Only then did the Spaniards take a serious interest in chocolate, and in 1631 they brought some cacao beans back to Spain. There they began making elaborate mixtures of cacao beans, sugar, spices, almonds, and hazelnuts, all ground together to make a paste that was eventually exported to other countries in Europe. Even so, it was not until 1828 that C. J. Van Houten developed a process for making cocoa powder for drinks and cacao butter for solid chocolate.

The chocolate drink we know today became a fashionable drink in Europe in the seventeenth century. When this sweetened European creation returned to the land of cacao's birth a few years later, it quickly became the traditional drink of the Andean countries. In Bogotá, Colombia, the chocolate drink *santafereño* was made by dissolving an unsweetened chocolate paste in hot milk or water and adding sugar. It was usually served after 5:00 P.M. with either tamales or an assortment of sweets, such as *almojábanas*, *colaciones*, or tortes. In Venezuela, hot chocolate, usually sweetened with *panela*, was served at the end of every meal and was enjoyed by people at every level of society. The upper classes would serve hot chocolate, along with various sweets and glasses of Venezuelan rum, during afternoon get-togethers. In the Andean countries, hot chocolate became an indispensable accompaniment to tamales around the holidays.

The cacao that was used in Mexico and Europe in the 1600s came from Soconusco in Mexico and from Guatemala. When production there fell and prices rose, other countries started providing large quantities of cacao. Guayaquil, the main port in Ecuador, had large plantations of wild cacao called *forastero*. By the end of the eighteenth century, about 40 percent of the cacao was coming from Guayaquil, mainly because the plantations there could provide large quantities at cheap prices. It was called *cacao de los pobres* (cacao of the poor). The quality of this cacao was not comparable to that from Soconusco or the Venezuelan variety called *criollo*, preferred by the colonial elite, but for the first time in history, cacao was accessible to the masses.

Venezuela also was involved in the early cacao trade. By the 1700s, everyone wanted chocolate, and trade was in the hands of an ever-widening circle of entrepreneurs. The Dutch, and later the Basques, got involved in exporting cacao from Venezuela. As Spain tried to gain a complete monopoly on cacao there, it became increasingly repressive in its rule. It is possible that the escalating brutality was a factor in firing Venezuela's independence movement in the early 1800s.

There are many ways of preparing hot chocolate. The only common denominator is that it should be thick and foamy. According to one saying, "For a cup of chocolate to be perfect, it must be hot, sweet, thick, and made by the hands of a woman." Unfortunately, in recent years hot chocolate has lost some of its glamour, and coffee and tea seem to be replacing this lovely drink in South America.

Chocolate con Leche para las Once

HOT CHOCOLATE WITH MILK
FOR ELEVEN O'CLOCK *Serves 4 to 6*

The name is taken from the time of day when this drink is usually served in Chile.

> 4 cups milk
>
> ¼ cup sugar
>
> 3 ounces unsweetened chocolate, cut into small pieces
>
> 1 strip orange or lemon zest
>
> 1 clove
>
> Pinch of freshly grated nutmeg
>
> 1 large egg white (optional)

Place the milk, sugar, chocolate, zest, clove, and nutmeg in a 4-quart saucepan and bring almost to a boil over low heat, stirring until the chocolate is melted. Remove from the heat, discard the zest and clove, and beat with an electric mixer or whisk until foamy. If using the egg white, beat in a small bowl with a little of the hot chocolate until foamy. Stir the mixture into the pot, beating constantly. Serve hot, making sure each cup has some foam.

VARIATIONS In Ecuador, this is made with a cinnamon stick instead of the zest. Two egg whites are beaten with ¼ cup sugar until stiff peaks form. This *espumilla* (meringue) is spooned on top of each cup of hot chocolate.

In Ecuador and Colombia, small cubes of fresh white cheese are added to cups of hot chocolate. The cheese softens with the heat and provides a wonderful contrast. Do not use cheese that becomes too stringy when softened, because it may cause choking. Brick cheese is a good choice.

For a richer and thicker chocolate, use 1 ounce chocolate per 1 cup milk. Add sugar to taste. In some countries, the milk is diluted with water.

Chocolate con Leche de Coco

HOT CHOCOLATE WITH
COCONUT MILK *Serves 4 to 6*

Hot chocolate with coconut milk is popular in the Pacific coast towns, where coconuts are plentiful.

> 3 cups milk
>
> 4 ounces unsweetened chocolate, cut into small pieces
>
> 1 cup well-stirred canned unsweetened coconut milk
>
> ¼ cup sugar

In a heavy 4-quart saucepan, combine 2 cups of the milk and the chocolate. Cook over low heat,

Chocolate Casero HOMEMADE CHOCOLATE

 This ancient way of preparing chocolate tablets is still practiced in some remote villages. After the cacao beans are removed from the pod, they are dried in the sun for a few days, then carefully toasted in an aluminum or cast-iron skillet, peeled, and ground in a heated grinding stone, called a *metate* in Mexico. The stone that is used to grind corn is also used to grind cacao beans. This three-legged stone has a curved surface and is heated underneath by a fire. First the beans are ground alone, then they are ground again with sugar or *panela*, until the mixture forms a soft dough that is shaped into small balls or spread on a mat to dry. Sometimes cinnamon, cloves, cilantro, or seeds from hot peppers are added during the second grinding. The dried dough is cut into small bars, which can be stored in a tin and used anytime to make hot chocolate.

stirring, until the chocolate has melted. Remove from the heat and beat with an electric mixer or whisk until foamy. Add the remaining 1 cup milk, the coconut milk, and sugar and simmer over medium-low heat, beating all the time, until very hot and foamy. Serve immediately.

Chocolate à Brasileira

HOT CHOCOLATE BRAZILIAN STYLE *Serves 4 to 6*

Because Brazil lies almost entirely in the tropics, the weather is pretty hot even in the cooler months. Hence cold drinks are generally preferred, and chocolate drinks may be served either hot or cold. Having enjoyed rich hot chocolate with espresso in Turin, Italy, I imagine that the addition of coffee to this drink comes from the Italians.

> **1 cup strong brewed coffee**
> **4 ounces semisweet chocolate, cut into small pieces**
> **3 cups milk**
> **3 tablespoons sugar**
> **Whipped cream for garnish (optional)**

In a 4-quart nonreactive saucepan, bring the coffee to a boil. Remove from the heat, add the chocolate, and stir until melted. Stir in the milk and sugar and simmer over low heat, beating with a whisk until very hot and foamy. Serve hot or cold, with a dollop of whipped cream, if desired.

Café COFFEE

VERY FEW NAMES OF FOOD or drink evoke images of South America as much as coffee. However, contrary to popular belief, coffee is not indigenous to America. It came from Africa, via Arabia and Europe, in the eighteenth century. Venezuela, Colombia, Ecuador, and Brazil are South America's biggest producers of coffee, which is consumed in great quantities throughout the continent. Unfortunately, the best beans are exported, and the coffee in most of the coffee-producing countries is of a lower grade.

Many years ago in South America, it was customary to roast the beans at home and grind them as needed. Today instant coffee has taken over in Ecuador, Peru, and Chile, although espresso, a very strong coffee, is beginning to make a comeback. In Argentina, a delicious espresso is found everywhere and any time of the day. It is served in demitasse cups with a twist of lemon, a glass of mineral water or orange juice, and some sweets, such as a piece of chocolate or a cookie.

In Brazil, the beloved *cafezinho* is a way of life, very much as it is in Argentina. It is similar to espresso, or *tinto*, and also served in demitasse cups. Colombians prepare their coffee the same way. Ecuadorians have special pots in which they make an "essence" of coffee that is then added to boiling water or milk and served for breakfast. It is served in demitasse cups.

In Brazil, Colombia, and other countries, coffee is brewed in flannel funnels, which are available in some South American groceries. The water is heated almost to the boiling point but not boiled.

Cafezinho

BRAZILIAN COFFEE *Serves 4*

This is the coffee Brazilians indulge in all day and night, at home and away from home. Making a good cup of coffee is considered an art in Brazil. Many cooks insist that the water should be brought only to 205°F, just below the boiling point.

> 2 cups cold water
> ¼ cup ground Brazilian coffee
> Sugar

Bring the water to just below the boiling point. Stir in the coffee, remove from the heat, and let stand for 2 minutes. Stir again and pour into the flannel funnel (see Note), which is set in your coffeepot. Serve immediately in demitasse cups, with sugar on the side.

NOTE Coffee filters are probably more readily available in the United States than the flannel funnels used in South America. You can use regular filters here without much loss of character in the final product.

VARIATION To make *café com leite* (coffee with milk), which is served at breakfast, mix equal amounts of brewed coffee and hot milk and serve in regular cups.

Bebidas con Harinas Tostadas
BEVERAGES PREPARED WITH
TOASTED FLOURS

SINCE PRE-HISPANIC TIMES, ANDEAN people have used toasted flours to make cold and hot beverages. Toasted flours still play an important role in the diets of the natives; they sustain millions of people. The flour was usually prepared at home, as it still is in some small towns. The Indians used mainly corn, fava beans, quinoa, and amaranth to make the flour. After the conquest, when the Spaniards introduced wheat, it became the grain of choice for making flour. It was easier to grind than dried corn, and not all varieties of corn were suitable for this purpose. When the Indians went on long journeys, they always carried a sack containing ground toasted corn to eat as is or to mix with water. After the conquest, another new ingredient, *panela* (unrefined brown sugar), was ground with the flour to make *pinol*, which is toasted corn flour ground three times with a piece of *panela*. This flour became the daily diet of the natives of the Altiplano, who took it not only on journeys but also to work and school. It can be eaten as is or mixed with water, milk, or aromatic teas.

In Bolivia, they have *pitu* or *pito*, a peasant food that has become very popular for its nutritional value. Bolivians have several varieties of *pitu* that go by the name of the cereal that is used. *Pitu de maíz* is toasted corn ground with dried apples, sweetened with sugar, and sometimes flavored with cinnamon. *Pitu de trigo* is toasted wheat ground with sugar. *Pitu de cebada* is toasted barley that is ground, sifted, and served mixed with a cup of milk or coffee. These cereals are often eaten as is or mixed with liquids. Not only grains are used to make *pitos*. Dried fava beans and peas also are used. In general, flours made of toasted grains and legumes were very important in the diets of all South American Indians.

In the *llanos* (open plains or grasslands) of Colombia, toasted corn flour is extremely important in the diet of the *llaneros* (cowhands), who use the flour to make drinks and *gofios* (sweet dried rolls). They toast the whole corn until golden, grind it into flour, and then toast it

again. To make *gofios*, the flour is mixed with *melado* (a liquid sweetener made of *panela* and honey) and formed into balls that are air-dried. The *llaneros* carry these balls on their long journeys across the *llanos*, hanging sacks filled with *gofios* and dried salt pork from their saddles—just as the Incas carried *tostado* (toasted dried corn) or flour, along with small dried fish, on their journeys. Venezuela, too, has *gofios*, but the Venezuelan version is made with cassava (yuca) and is eaten with a glass of water on the side.

Perhaps nowhere else in the Andes is toasted wheat flour more popular than in Chile. Here, where the Indians once used corn, wheat (which is more nutritious than corn) has become the grain of choice. The Mapuche Indians in south-central Chile, in particular, use flour in a variety of drinks, hot and cold. One of the most popular drinks is called *ulpo*, which is nothing more than water or milk mixed with flour and sugar and drunk cold. When *ulpo* is served hot, it is called *chercán*. It is a favorite drink to serve children for breakfast because it is highly nutritious. Unfortunately, these drinks are declining in popularity due to the advent of bottled drinks, which are generally less nutritious.

Bebidas Preparadas con Yuca Brava
BEVERAGES PREPARED WITH BITTER YUCA

IN THE AMAZON, THE MOST commonly used flour is made from *yuca brava* (bitter yuca) and is called *farina de mandioca* (manioc meal). This meal is made by grating the bitter yuca and squeezing out the juice. This juice is poisonous and must be boiled to remove the poison. It is then used as animal feed. The grated yuca is dried in the sun, then used to make bread or drinks. The drinks go by many different names; one is *chive*, which is usually made with manioc meal, water, and *melado*. (Here the *melado* is prepared by dissolving *panela* in a little hot water.) This *chive* mixture is kept in a covered container for two days, then strained and sweetened with honey.

The natives of Brazilian Amazonia make a drink called *mingau*, which is prepared with *caribé* paste. *Caribé* is made from cassava bread (sometimes called tapioca bread) that is soaked in water until it is reduced to a paste. More water is added to this paste to make a thin or thick drink, depending on the individual's taste. When it is served in the morning, lukewarm water is used; during the rest of the day, cold water is used.

Té TEA

TEA WAS FIRST GROWN IN CHINA about 5,000 years ago, but it did not arrive in the Western world until the beginning of the seventeenth century. In the eighteenth century, the English introduced tea to South America, where late-afternoon tea parties became fashionable. Tea gradually replaced hot chocolate as the favorite afternoon drink. The French, who also enjoyed afternoon tea, brought to the Americas the custom of serving tea with delicious pastries. In fact, tea was introduced in France in 1636, more than a decade before it appeared in England.

At the end of the nineteenth century, the English built tea plantations in South America. Throughout most of the continent, tea became an institution, whether it was *té completo*, tea and toast with butter and jam, or high tea, where an assortment of sandwiches and pastries was served.

After tea was introduced, many people, especially in the highlands, preferred to have only tea and a sandwich for supper. In Chile, they call this light meal *las once*, but it is not served at eleven (*once*) o'clock but at 4:00 or 5:00 P.M. The term *las once* originally referred only to the morning tea break. It was later applied to the afternoon break during *ley seca* (prohibition), when men who went out for a drink in the afternoon said they were going for *las once*, by which they meant *aguardiente*, which coincidentally has 11 letters.

Tea in Chile can be quite elaborate. When I was in Santiago in the late 1990s, Beatriz Toso, a very gracious hostess, invited a few of us to tea at the former palace of President Pinochet, which had been converted into an officers' club. Chileans love sweets, and this tea was sweet indeed. Called *las once completo*, it started with a large glass of fruit juice, followed by ice cream, a slice of a meringue *lucuma* torte, and finally sandwiches and tea.

Most South American countries favor finger sandwiches and *petits fours* or cakes as accompaniments to tea. Unless it is a casual invitation, which means toast and tea and maybe some cookies, you can be sure the best china, linens, and silver will be laid out to welcome you. The tea has to be perfectly brewed, whether it is plain or exotic. It is advisable to follow a few rules when brewing tea. Use 1 teaspoon of tea leaves for each cup of tea. Place the tea leaves in a teapot heated by rinsing it with boiling water. Bring freshly drawn cold water just to the boiling point—but do not let it boil—and immediately pour it over the tea leaves. Let the tea stand for three minutes for weak tea and five minutes for stronger tea. Serve immediately. Or make stronger tea and dilute it by adding a little boiling water to each cup. Tea can be served plain or with milk, which should be poured into the cup before the tea, or with lemon on the side.

Maté MATÉ

MATÉ, ALSO CALLED YERBA MATÉ or Paraguay tea, comes from the Quechua word *mati*, which is the name of the gourd from which it is drunk. It is made from the dried leaves of a shrub belonging to the holly family (*Ilex paraguariensis*) that grows wild along the upper reaches of the Paraguay River. There are two ways to brew *maté*. One is in a teapot, just like tea (see above). The other is to brew it in a gourd the size of an orange, called a *chimarrão* in Brazil. The gourd is filled about three-fifths full with leaves, then the *bombilla* (a straw-like wooden or metal stick with a flat, perforated end) is placed so that the perforated end touches the bottom of the gourd. Hot (*not* boiling) water is added until the gourd is full, and the leaves are steeped like tea. Sugar or milk also may be added. The *bombilla* is used to sip the tea. *El cebador* (a person who drinks *maté*) can add different ingredients to enrich its taste, such as orange or lemon zest, burnt sugar, even gin. As the level of the tea drops, more hot water is added. This can be repeated about four times, then the leaves are discarded.

Maté contains caffeine and is very popular in Paraguay, Argentina, Uruguay, and parts of Chile and southern Brazil. More than just a tea typical of these countries, *maté* is a bond that unites people. "When a hand extends a *maté* to another hand, it says *bienvenido* [welcome]," writes cookbook author Choly Berreteaga, "it is sharing confidences, intimacy and tranquility." *Maté* is popular with city dwellers, but even more popular in the countryside. The *gauchos* get up very early to go to work and would not think of leaving before sharing a *maté* and listening to ghost stories told by the oldest *gaucho*. In Uruguay, a common sight in cities, at resorts, and almost everywhere else is people walking along, sipping *maté* and carrying a thermos of hot water under one arm. They are called *sobaqueros*, which comes from the word *sobaco* (armpit).

Maté is available in Latin American and some Italian grocery stores, which is not surprising considering the number of Italians who immigrated to the southern countries of South America. Lately, *maté* has begun appearing in health food stores, because some studies have shown that it has more health benefits than green tea. *Maté* also comes in bags, which can be used like tea bags.

Aguitas Medicinales
HERBAL TEAS

IN PRE-HISPANIC TIMES, AMERICAN Indians were very advanced in the practice of pharmacology, with a vast knowledge of the curative (and lethal) powers of the plants around them. South American Indians discovered a wide range of cures for diseases such as scurvy, goiter, and malaria, using herbs, tree bark, and seaweed. Many of these cures have been incorporated into modern pharmacology. South Americans are very fond of herbal teas, which are taken at any time of the day but especially after meals. In fact, most restaurants offer a selection of native herbal teas, which are usually made with fresh herbs. Following are the most popular herbal teas, along with their traditional uses.

Boldo is an evergreen shrub (*Peumus boldus*) native to the Chilean Andes. It is used in the highlands as a tonic and activator of the liver and as an aid to digestion. It is especially good for promoting the excretion of the bile ducts. Infuse like tea; use ½ teaspoon crushed leaves per 1 cup water. Available in Latin American groceries.

Cachamai is a combination of herbs indigenous to Argentina, where it is popular as an aid to digestion. Infuse as you would tea. Available in tea bags in South American markets.

Cedrón (lemon verbena) is a fragrant shrub (*Lippia citriodora*) indigenous to Peru and Chile. It is used as a sedative, to reduce fevers, to aid in digestion, and to ease flatulence. It is also believed to relieve chronic inflammation of mucous membranes. Infuse like tea; use 2 teaspoons leaves per 1 cup water.

Hierbabuena (peppermint) and *menta verde* (spearmint) are very common throughout Latin America. They are used for stomach cramps and gas and to treat nervous or digestive problems. Steep fresh or dried leaves in boiling water.

Manzanilla (chamomile), though native to Europe, is one of the most popular teas in South America. Its properties are numerous. It acts as a calmative, tonic, and aromatic. It makes a wonderful wash for the eyes and skin and can be used in compresses for skin inflammation. It also reduces flatulence. Steep fresh or dried leaves in boiling water.

Toronjil (lemon balm) is a common perennial that grows throughout North and South America. It is perhaps the most used of the medicinal plants. It is very helpful in treating nervous problems and to relieve bronchial colds. Used in combination with valerian, it is especially good for insomnia. Steep fresh or dried leaves in boiling water.

Valeriana (valerian) is a perennial plant that grows in many parts of the Americas. It is used as a sedative for the heart and nervous system, without the side effects produced by narcotics. It is also used to treat migraines and insomnia. However, the use of large amounts of this herb, as well as prolonged use, can cause poisoning. Infuse 1 teaspoon of the root in 2 cups boiling water.

Bocaditos y Entradas

Hors d'Oeuvres and First Courses

Hors d'oeuvres served with drinks before dinner are not as popular in South America as in the United States. Nevertheless, small finger foods have a place in South American cuisine. Cold and hot hors d'oeuvres, cold and hot canapés, and finger sandwiches are served with drinks at bars, tea parties, cocktail parties, and all kinds of celebrations. Empanadas, a very popular first course, are now being made in small sizes to serve as hors d'oeuvres. Tamales and other savory pastries are also following suit.

Entradas, or first courses, are an essential component of any South American meal. No one would start a main meal without a first course. Often the first course includes one or more of the snack foods of which Latins are so fond. Snack foods permeate the Latin culture and show creole cuisine at its best. An endless variety of snack foods, such as empanadas, tamales, *cebiches* (marinated foods) *escabeches* (pickled foods), and fritters can be found throughout South America—at roadside stands along the highways, on city streets, in the marketplace, and in corner stalls, coffeehouses, tea rooms, and restaurants. The establishments that specialize in snack foods often have different names in different countries. In Argentina and Uruguay, one finds *confiterías*, in Brazil *confeitarias*, in Ecuador *cebicherías*, and in Venezuela *areperías*.

There is no question that the Spaniards left an indelible mark on the appetizers of the west coast of South America. Even typically Indian foods such as *arepas* (cornbread) and tamales went through a transformation after the Spaniards brought cattle, pigs, and chickens to the New World. Plain *arepas* are still prepared in the way the Indians made them 500 years ago. But the Spaniards introduced cheese and *chicharrón* (fried pork rind), which are now mixed with the dough in many areas of Colombia and Venezuela. In Venezuela, *areperías* offer *arepas* with a variety of fillings that can be traced to the arrival of the Spaniards, including chorizo, ground beef or pork, eggs, and goat cheese. For a selection of *arepa* recipes, see pages 348–349.

Tamales were originally an Indian food. The Indians ground corn, seasoned it with herbs and hot peppers, mixed in other vegetables, and wrapped the mixture in either corn-husks, plantain leaves, or *achira* (edible canna) leaves. Then they cooked the tamales on burning coals. With the arrival of the Spaniards, the *tamal* became the creole dish par excellence. The Spaniards added lard to the ground corn and also added meat, onions, eggs, olives, and raisins to the fillings. In his book *Geografía Gastronómica Venezolana*, Ramón David León talks about the *hallaca*, or *tamal*, being the national dish of Venezuela. When Venezuelans are abroad, he says, the *hallaca* makes them think of their country with longing and hope that by next Christmas, they will be able to enjoy this dish at home. If I had to pick two foods that define South American cooking, they would be empanadas and tamales. To me, they epitomize South American cuisine.

Most creole specialties are a mixture of Indian and Spanish or other European influence. Spanish *albóndigas* (meatballs) and croquettes, French vegetable puddings, Portuguese codfish balls, and Russian salad all reflect the blending of these cultures. Nowhere else in South America is this more visible than in Lima, Peru, which was the site of the most powerful Spanish viceroyalty. Historians talk about the great wealth of the Spanish aristocracy and the lavish parties they gave, with each host trying to surpass the other. From Spain they brought specialties such as *tapas*, which native cooks quickly adapted to local ingredients and techniques. The wide use of potatoes and hot peppers in appetizers reflects Inca cuisine. Spanish influence is seen in the use of cheese and nuts in the sauces and lard for frying. Peru's cuisine excels in the *tapas* that are served before a meal, including boiled potatoes topped with different sauces, tamales, empanadas, *torrejas* (thick vegetable pancakes), *cebiches*, and *escabeches*, all of which are a perfect blend of Inca and Spanish cuisine.

Cebiches
MARINATED FOODS

I T IS NOT QUITE CLEAR where *cebiches* originated. *Cebiche*, also spelled *ceviche* and *seviche*, is fish or seafood "cooked" by citrus juice. Traditionally, the citrus marinade was made with *naranja agria* (sour or bitter orange), but lemon, lime, and orange juices are used to prepare most *cebiches* today. More recently, the juices of other fruits, such as passion fruit and tamarillos, are used as the basis for the marinades. *Cebiches* are true creole dishes—the Spaniards brought the citrus fruits and paired them with the riches from South America's sea and land, creating this very original and wonderful specialty. It is not known whether the Indians used indigenous fruits, such as tamarillos, *naranjillas*, or passion fruit, to preserve some of their foods.

The most famous *cebiches* come from Ecuador and Peru, and Ecuadorian *cebiches* enjoy the reputation of being the best in South America. They are certainly the most unusual and varied. *Cebiches* fit beautifully into modern lifestyles, where people are searching for delicious and nutritious foods with few calories. Only a small amount of oil goes into the preparation of a *cebiche*, just enough to develop the flavors. Wonderfully refreshing, *cebiches* make terrific appetizers for any occasion and great picnic fare. In Peru and Ecuador, *cebiches* are popular snack foods, often served with a cold glass of beer. They can be found in *cebicherías*, restaurants that specialize in this type of food, which are favorite meeting places for friends and popular stops for late-night partygoers.

Cebiches can be made with just about any type of seafood—fish, shrimp, scallops, clams, mussels, squid, langostinos, or lobster. They also can be made with chicken, duck, mushrooms, hearts of palm, lupini beans, avocados, broccoli, and so on. The common denominator among the countries that prepare them is the lemon and lime juices used as the basis for the marinade. The fish is "cooked" by the acid in the marinade. Depending on the type of fish and the thickness of the pieces, this "cooking" takes anywhere from three to six hours, until the fish turns opaque. Shellfish is usually cooked or blanched first before adding it to the marinade. When I use green vegetables, I add them at the last minute; otherwise, the acidity of the marinade will turn the green color an unappetizing gray.

Peruvians serve their *cebiches* on lettuce leaves, without the marinade, garnished with pieces of corn on the cob, slices of hard-cooked eggs, sliced sweet potatoes, and cheese, and with a bowl of *cancha* (toasted dried corn) on the side. These make very nice luncheon dishes. Peruvians also like their *cebiches* spiced up with a generous amount of hot peppers, unlike their Ecuadorian neighbors, who use hot pepper sauce just to flavor the *cebiches* and serve a bowl of it on the side for their guests to determine the final level of heat. Peruvians use tuna, flounder, swordfish, and scallops, as well as a variety of shellfish, in their *cebiches*.

Ecuadorians serve their *cebiches* with the marinade and side dishes of *tostado* (toasted dried corn) or popcorn and French bread. *Cebiches* made with *corvina* (bass), shrimp, and *conchas prieta* (black clams) are the favorites of Ecuadorians. The flesh of the *concha prieta*, indigenous to the waters off Ecuador and Peru, is more tender than that of regular clams—similar to that of oysters—and is available canned or frozen in some Latin American groceries.

Colombian *cebiches* use citrus juices and tomato sauce for the marinade and are served on lettuce leaves, as in Peru. Colombians also have a unique *cebiche* made with coconut milk, an African contribution.

Chileans enjoy *cebiches* made from *corvina*, salmon, shrimp, and *cochayuyo* (seaweed). Chilean *cebiches* more nearly resemble the Peruvian types.

Cebiche Serrano

CEBICHE FROM THE HIGHLANDS

THIS *CEBICHE* IS A TREASURE of Ecuadorian cuisine. Typical of the Andean region of Ecuador, it has a sauce made with tomatoes and citrus juices, in contrast to *cebiches* from the coast, where only citrus juices are used. Both versions are excellent and worth trying. Once you have mastered the marinade, you can experiment with a variety of ingredients. The classic way of preparing this *cebiche* is with shrimp, langostinos (extra-large shrimp, also known as prawns), chicken, fish, or a variety of seafood. Hearts of palm or mushrooms, or a combination of both,

also make excellent *cebiches*. Or try the latest trend, a combination of broccoli (or any other suitable vegetable) and chicken or shellfish. *Naranja agria* (sour or bitter orange), available in Latin markets, used to be the most commonly used citrus fruit, but now it is being replaced with lemon, lime, and orange. I would advise you to use regular tomatoes (preferably beefsteak) in the summer and half pear-shaped tomatoes and half regular tomatoes in the winter; winter tomatoes make the sauce too thin and weak. Following are the master recipe for the sauce, some classic garnishes and side dishes, and the most popular *cebiche* combinations.

Classic Garnishes and Side Dishes for Cebiche Serrano

Cebiche Serrano is always served topped with 1 tablespoon of *cebollas encurtidas* and bowls of *tostado* and French bread. The *chifles* are optional. A sprig of parsley is the only garnish on top of the onions.

- ½ recipe *Cebollas Encurtidas* (marinated onions; page 340)
- *Tostado* (toasted dried corn; page 321), salted dry-roasted peanuts, or popcorn
- French bread
- *Chifles* (green plantain chips; page 120; optional)
- *Ají Criollo* (Creole hot pepper salsa; page 333)
- Fresh parsley sprigs or fresh basil leaves, cut into ribbons

Base de Tomate para Cebiches

TOMATO AND CITRUS MARINADE
Makes 2 1/2 to 3 cups

- 1 cup water
- About 1 pound medium-size ripe but firm tomatoes
- ¼ cup fresh lemon juice, or more to taste
- ¼ cup fresh lime juice
- ¾ cup fresh orange juice, or more to taste
- ¼ cup ketchup
- 1 teaspoon Worcestershire sauce
- 1 teaspoon Dijon mustard
- 1 tablespoon extra virgin olive oil
- ½ teaspoon salt
- ¼ teaspoon freshly ground black pepper
- Sugar (optional)
- 1 to 2 teaspoons fresh hot pepper puree, store-bought or homemade (page 332), or hot pepper sauce, to your taste

1. Bring the water and tomatoes to a boil in a large nonreactive saucepan. Reduce the heat to low, cover, and simmer for 5 minutes. Remove from the heat and let cool. With a slotted spoon, remove the tomatoes, let cool for a few minutes, and slip off the skins. Place the tomatoes in a blender or food processor and process until smooth. Then pass through a medium-mesh sieve to remove the seeds.

2. In a medium-size glass bowl, mix together the tomato puree, citrus juices, ketchup, Worcestershire, mustard, oil, salt, and black pepper. You may need to add a little more lemon juice or orange juice to balance the flavors; none of these flavors should be too pronounced. You also may add a little sugar if the taste is too acidic. Add the hot pepper puree and mix.

3. Cover and refrigerate for up to 1 day.

Cebiche de Camarones

SHRIMP CEBICHE *Serves 6*

This is the most popular *cebiche* in Quito. Many people prefer to use small shrimp because they are sweeter than the large ones. Others prefer langostinos, which should be cut into small pieces. All are delicious.

- 1 recipe *Base de Tomate para Cebiches* (this page)
- 1 recipe *Cebollas Encurtidas* (page 340)
- 4 cups water
- 2 scallions (white part and 1 inch of the green)
- 1½ pounds large shrimp, peeled and deveined
- ½ cup bottled lupini beans, peeled (page 307)
- 2 tablespoons finely chopped fresh cilantro or parsley leaves
- Salt and freshly ground black pepper
- Hot pepper sauce
- Sugar
- 6 sprigs fresh parsley or basil for garnish
- Classic Garnishes and Side Dishes for Cebiche Serrano (previous page)

1. Prepare the marinade. This can be done the day before.

2. About 4 hours before serving, prepare the *cebollas encurtidas*. Let stand at room temperature for about 3 hours, until the onions turn pink. Add half the recipe to the marinade and reserve the rest for garnish.

3. In a large saucepan, combine the water and scallions and bring to a boil. Reduce the heat to medium and simmer for a couple of minutes. Add the shrimp, remove from the heat, and let stand for a few seconds, until the shrimp turn pink. Drain, discard the scallions, and rinse the shrimp under cold running water (rinsing will prevent

the shrimp from becoming rubbery). Cut the shrimp in half crosswise, if desired. Add to the marinade along with the lupini beans and cilantro and stir to mix well. Cover with plastic wrap and refrigerate for 2 to 3 hours. The longer the shrimp stay in the marinade, the tougher they will get. This *cebiche* can be eaten the next day—the textures won't be as perfect, but it still will be perfectly delicious.

4. Before serving, season with salt and black pepper, hot pepper sauce, and sugar to taste. To serve, divide the shrimp among 6 small bowls and top each with 1 tablespoon of the *cebollas encurtidas* and a parsley sprig. Serve bowls of the garnishes on the side.

Cebiche de Hongos

MUSHROOM CEBICHE *Serves 6*

This is one of my family's favorite *cebiches*.

> 1 recipe *Base de Tomate para Cebiches* (page 63)
>
> 1 recipe *Cebollas Encurtidas* (page 340)
>
> 2 pounds fresh, firm, perfectly white mushrooms
>
> 1 scallion (white part and 1 inch of the green)
>
> 1 tablespoon fresh lemon juice
>
> 4 cups water
>
> ½ cup bottled lupini beans, peeled (page 307)
>
> 2 tablespoons finely chopped fresh cilantro or parsley leaves
>
> 1 ripe but firm Hass avocado
>
> Classic Garnishes and Side Dishes for Cebiche Serrano (page 62)

1. Prepare the marinade. This can be done the day before.

2. About 4 hours before serving, prepare the *cebollas encurtidas*. Let stand at room temperature for about 3 hours, until the onions turn pink. Add

half the recipe to the marinade and reserve the rest for garnish.

3. Wipe the mushrooms with a damp cloth or paper towel and cut into quarters or halves. Place the scallion, lemon juice, and water in a saucepan and bring to a boil. Reduce the heat and simmer for a couple of minutes. Add the mushrooms, boil for 30 seconds, drain, and discard the scallion.

4. Add the mushrooms to the marinade along with the lupini beans and cilantro and stir to mix well. Refrigerate for at least 2 hours.

5. Just before serving, peel and pit the avocado, then cut into ½-inch cubes. Serve with the rest of the garnishes.

Cebiche de Camarones con Hongos y Brocoli

SHRIMP CEBICHE WITH MUSHROOMS AND BROCCOLI *Serves 6 to 8*

This combination has proven to be a winner. When I entertain, I know my guests will be delighted to find this *cebiche* is a part of the menu. The broccoli is added at the last minute, because if it is left too long in the marinade, it will turn gray.

> 1 recipe *Base de Tomate para Cebiches* (page 63)
>
> 1 recipe *Cebollas Encurtidas* (page 340)
>
> 8 cups water
>
> 1 scallion (white part and 1 inch of the green)
>
> 1 pound medium-size shrimp, peeled and deveined
>
> 12 ounces fresh, firm, perfectly white mushrooms
>
> 1 tablespoon lemon juice
>
> 2 tablespoons finely chopped fresh cilantro leaves
>
> 2 cups small broccoli florets
>
> Classic Garnishes and Side Dishes for Cebiche Serrano (page 62)

1. Prepare the marinade. This can be done the day before.

2. About 4 hours before serving, prepare the *cebollas encurtidas*. Let stand at room temperature for about 3 hours, until the onions turn pink. Add half the recipe to the marinade and reserve the rest for garnish.

3. In a large saucepan, bring 4 cups of the water and the scallion to a boil. Reduce the heat to medium and simmer for a couple of minutes. Add the shrimp, remove from the heat, and let stand for a few seconds, until the shrimp turn pink. Drain, discard the scallion, and rinse the shrimp under cold running water (rinsing will prevent the shrimp from becoming rubbery).

4. Wipe the mushrooms with a damp cloth or paper towel and cut into quarters or halves to make uniform pieces. Place the remaining 4 cups water and lemon juice in a large saucepan and bring to a boil. Reduce the heat to medium and simmer for a couple of minutes. Add the mushrooms, boil for 30 seconds, and drain.

5. Mix the shrimp, mushrooms, and cilantro into the marinade. Cover with plastic wrap and refrigerate for at least 2 hours.

6. Meanwhile, steam the broccoli in a little salted water for 30 seconds. Drain, rinse with cold water, and refrigerate.

7. Just before serving, toss the broccoli in the marinade and serve with the garnishes and side dishes.

Cebiche Vegetariano de Palmitos, Hongos, y Brocoli

VEGETARIAN CEBICHE WITH HEARTS OF PALM, MUSHROOMS, AND BROCCOLI *Serves 6*

Because vegetables are so popular in the United States, I decided to create a vegetarian *cebiche* using the most loved vegetables. Needless to say, this *cebiche* is not only low in calories but also highly nutritious.

> 1 recipe *Base de Tomate para Cebiches* (page 63)
> 1 recipe *Cebollas Encurtidas* (page 340)
> One 14-ounce can hearts of palm
> 1 pound fresh, firm, perfectly white mushrooms
> 1 scallion (white part and 1 inch of the green)
> 1 tablespoon fresh lemon juice
> 4 cups water
> 1 cup broccoli or broccoflower florets, cut into ¾-inch pieces
> Classic Garnishes and Side Dishes for Cebiche Serrano (page 62)

1. Prepare the marinade. This can be done the day before.

2. About 4 hours before serving, prepare the *cebollas encurtidas*. Let stand at room temperature for a about 3 hours, until the onions turn pink. Add half the recipe to the marinade and reserve the rest for garnish.

3. Drain the hearts of palm and rinse thoroughly. Dry with paper towels and cut into ½-inch-thick rounds. Add to the marinade.

4. Wipe the mushrooms with a damp cloth or paper towel and cut into quarters or halves to make uniform pieces. Place the scallion, lemon juice, and water in a large saucepan and bring to a boil. Reduce the heat to medium and simmer for a couple of minutes. Add the mushrooms, boil for 30 seconds, drain, and remove the scallion. Stir into the marinade, cover with plastic wrap, and refrigerate for at least 4 hours.

5. Steam the broccoli in a little salted water for 30 seconds. (If using broccoflower, steam for 3 minutes.) Drain, rinse with cold water, and refrigerate.

6. Right before serving, add the broccoli or broccoflower to the marinade. Serve with the side dishes and garnishes.

Cebiche de Tomate de Arbol con Pollo y Alcachofas

TAMARILLO CEBICHE WITH
CHICKEN AND ARTICHOKE BOTTOMS *Serves 6*

This is not the classic *cebiche*, but rather a new way to play with various indigenous ingredients. The tamarillo (tree tomato) gives a more subtle taste to the marinade, which makes a wonderful foil for the combination of textures and flavors of the chicken, artichokes, and avocado.

- 3 large ripe but firm yellow or red tamarillos, pureed, or ¾ cup thawed frozen tamarillo puree
- 8 ounces ripe but firm tomatoes, cooked and pureed as instructed in step 1 for *Base de Tomate para Cebiches* (page 63)
- ½ cup fresh orange juice, or more to taste
- ¼ cup fresh lemon juice
- ½ cup chicken broth
- 2 tablespoons ketchup
- 1 teaspoon Worcestershire sauce
- 2 teaspoons Dijon mustard
- 2 tablespoons minced fresh cilantro leaves
- ½ teaspoon salt
- ¼ teaspoon freshly ground black pepper
- 1 tablespoon extra virgin olive oil
- 1 teaspoon fresh hot pepper puree, store-bought or homemade (page 332), or more to taste
- 1 whole bone-in chicken breast (about 1 pound), skin on, poached (page 407)
- 3 canned artichoke bottoms, cut into ½-inch cubes
- 1 ripe but firm Hass avocado
- 1 recipe *Cebollas Encurtidas* (page 340)
- 2 tablespoons minced fresh parsley leaves for garnish
- Classic Garnishes and Side Dishes for Cebiche Serrano (page 62)

1. In a large class bowl, mix together the tamarillo puree, tomato puree, orange juice, lemon juice, chicken broth, ketchup, Worcestershire, mustard, cilantro, salt, black pepper, and oil. Add the hot pepper puree, then taste and add more, if desired. Taste for salt and balance the flavors with a little more orange juice, if necessary.

2. Discard the bones and skin from the chicken and cut into strips ¼ inch wide and 1 inch long. Add to the tamarillo mixture along with the artichokes. Cover with plastic wrap and refrigerate for at least 2 hours.

Cebicherías RESTAURANTS

 Cebicherías are common in Peru and Ecuador. These restaurants specialize in *cebiches* (marinated foods), although sometimes they also serve other snack foods, such as small empanadas and fritters. In the past few years, many *cebicherías* have started offering seafood entrées and carryout service as well. They are favorite stops for people who want to have a snack or lunch, as well as for late-night partygoers. Along the coast, *cebicherías* are stands that sell *cebiches* made right there, with the catch of the day. *Cerveza* (beer) is a must with *cebiche*, but mineral water, soda, and fresh fruit juices are always available.

3. Just before serving, peel and pit the avocado, then cut into ½-inch cubes. Mix into the *cebiche*.

4. To serve, divide the *cebiche* among 6 small bowls or stemmed glasses. Top each with 1 tablespoon of the *cebollas encurtidas* and about 1 teaspoon parsley. Serve with the garnishes and side dishes.

Cebiche de Taxo (Curuba) con Langosta y Hongos

BANANA PASSION FRUIT CEBICHE
WITH LOBSTER AND MUSHROOMS *Serves 6*

As I mentioned in the introduction to this chapter, there is a possibility that the Indians used fruits of the passion fruit family to preserve fish and other foods. We know for sure that they used salt as a preservative and generous amounts of hot peppers to season their foods. This recipe spans more than 500 years of cooking, evolving as more and more European foodstuffs became available. Here another new ingredient is incorporated into the recipe—yellow tomatoes (although this is a case of what's old is new—yellow tomatoes were the first ones taken to Europe from South America). Yellow tomatoes have low acidity and make a good base for the more acidic banana passion fruit, which is related to the passion fruit. Indigenous to Colombia, Ecuador, and Bolivia, it is now available frozen (whole or pureed) in some South American groceries. The result is a light, wonderful marinade for lobster or shrimp, or a combination of both, with mushrooms, avocados, or hearts of palm.

1 pound ripe but firm yellow or orange tomatoes, cooked and pureed as instructed in step 1 for *Base de Tomate para Cebiches* (page 63)

¾ cup thawed frozen banana passion fruit pulp

⅓ cup fresh orange juice

¼ cup fresh lime juice

¼ cup ketchup

1 teaspoon Worcestershire sauce

1 teaspoon Dijon mustard

¾ teaspoon salt

⅛ teaspoon white pepper

1 tablespoon extra virgin olive oil

1 teaspoon fresh hot pepper puree, store-bought or homemade (page 332), or more to taste

8 ounces fresh, firm, perfectly white mushrooms

1 tablespoon lemon juice

4 cups water

1 pound cooked lobster meat, cut into ½-inch cubes (or use half lobster and half shrimp)

½ cup bottled lupini beans, peeled (page 307)

2 tablespoons minced fresh cilantro leaves

1 recipe *Cebollas Encurtidas* (page 340)

Chopped fresh parsley leaves for garnish

Classic Garnishes and Side Dishes for Cebiche Serrano (page 62)

1. Place the tomato puree, banana passion fruit pulp, orange juice, lime juice, ketchup, Worcestershire, mustard, salt, white pepper, oil, and hot pepper puree in a blender and pulse a few times until smooth. Transfer to a large glass bowl, cover with plastic wrap, and refrigerate. This can be done the day before.

2. Wipe the mushrooms with a damp cloth or paper towel and cut into quarters or halves to make uniform pieces. Bring the water and lemon juice to a boil in a large saucepan. Add the mushrooms, boil for 30 seconds, and drain.

3. About 2 to 3 hours before serving, add the lobster, mushrooms, lupini beans, cilantro, and half of the *cebollas encurtidas* to the marinade. Taste for salt and hot pepper puree. Cover with plastic wrap and refrigerate.

4. To serve, divide the *cebiche* among 6 small bowls or stemmed glasses. Top each with 1 tablespoon of the remaining *cebollas encurtidas* and garnish with the parsley. Serve with the side dishes and garnishes.

Cebiche al Estilo Montubio
CEBICHE FROM THE COAST OF ECUADOR

THIS IS THE CLASSIC *CEBICHE* from the coast of Ecuador and has become a favorite of the highlands as well. It can be made with fish (*cebiche de pescado*), just shrimp (*cebiche de camarones*), or any mixture of shellfish (*cebiche mixto*). It is wonderfully refreshing and light, ideal for the hot-weather months. This type of *cebiche* is served with a variety of side dishes, such as *tostado* (toasted dried corn), popcorn, *chifles* (green plantain chips), and sometimes French bread.

Cebiche Mixto
SHELLFISH CEBICHE *Serves 6*

Cebiche mixto usually includes shrimp, assorted shellfish, and sometimes fish. If you order *cebiche mixto* in a restaurant, expect to get squid and octopus in the dish.

> 4 cups water
>
> 1 scallion (white part and 1 inch of the green), sliced
>
> 1 pound medium-size shrimp, peeled and deveined
>
> ½ pound bay scallops, thoroughly rinsed
>
> ¼ cup dry white wine
>
> 1 pound mussels, scrubbed and debearded (page 408)
>
> 16 baby clams (optional)

MARINADE

> ⅓ cup fresh lemon juice
>
> ⅓ cup fresh lime juice
>
> ⅔ cup fresh orange juice
>
> ½ cup chicken broth
>
> 1 tablespoon extra virgin olive oil
>
> 1 teaspoon Dijon mustard
>
> 1 teaspoon Worcestershire sauce
>
> ½ teaspoon sugar
>
> ½ teaspoon salt
>
> ¼ teaspoon freshly ground black pepper
>
> Hot pepper sauce to taste

GARNISHES

> 1 medium-size ripe but firm tomato (5 to 6 ounces), peeled, seeded, and finely chopped
>
> 1 small green bell pepper, seeded and finely chopped
>
> 1 small onion, finely chopped (about ½ cup), rinsed with hot water, and drained
>
> 2 tablespoons minced fresh cilantro leaves
>
> 2 tablespoons minced fresh parsley leaves

SIDE DISHES

> Popcorn, *tostado* (page 321), *Chifles* (page 120), French bread, and *Ají Criollo* (page 333)

1. In a large saucepan, bring the water and scallion to a boil, reduce the heat to medium, and simmer for 5 minutes. Add the shrimp, remove from the heat, and let stand for a few seconds, until the shrimp turn pink. Remove with a slotted spoon (reserving the cooking liquid) and rinse under cold running water (rinsing will prevent the shrimp from becoming rubbery).

2. To the cooking liquid in the saucepan, add the scallops. Bring back to a boil, remove from the heat, cover, and let stand for 3 minutes, depending on the size of the scallops. Cut a scallop in half to see if it is cooked through (it should be milky white in the center). If so, drain and rinse under cold running water.

3.   Place the wine, mussels, and clams (if using) in a large skillet and bring to a boil over high heat. Cover and let continue to boil until the shells are open, 3 to 5 minutes. Discard any clams or mussels that do not open. Remove the clams and mussels from their shells and discard the shells.

4.   To make the marinade, combine all the ingredients in a large glass bowl. Stir in the shrimp, scallops, mussels, and clams. Mix well, cover with plastic wrap, and refrigerate for at least 2 hours.

5.   Right before serving, taste for salt, sugar, and hot pepper sauce. Serve in small bowls or stemmed glasses, each garnished in the center with 1 teaspoon each chopped tomato, bell pepper, onion, cilantro, and parsley. Serve with the side dishes.

Cebiche de Pescado

FISH CEBICHE *Serves 8*

This is one of the most popular *cebiches*. I make this only when I know the fish was flown in from the coast the same day. It is extremely important that the fish be absolutely fresh. Fish that has been frozen won't do. Make sure you check to see if the fish is "cooked" after three hours so that it will not get tough.

   Although the classic fish for this dish is *corvina* in Ecuador and tuna in Peru, you can use any white-fleshed fish, such as sea bass, flounder, red snapper, or sole (which I like because it "cooks" faster than other fish and is more delicate).

1½ pounds white-fleshed fish fillets (red snapper, *corvina*, sole, or any other firm, lean fish)

MARINADE
   ⅔ cup fresh lemon juice
   ⅓ cup fresh lime juice
   ⅔ cup fresh orange juice
   ½ cup chicken broth or clam juice
   1 tablespoon extra virgin olive oil
   1 teaspoon Dijon mustard
   1 teaspoon Worcestershire sauce
   ½ teaspoon sugar
   ½ teaspoon salt
   ¼ teaspoon freshly ground black pepper
   Hot pepper sauce to taste

GARNISHES
   1 medium-size ripe but firm tomato (5 to 6 ounces), peeled, seeded, and finely chopped
   1 small green bell pepper, seeded and finely chopped
   1 small onion, finely chopped (about ½ cup), rinsed with hot water, and drained
   2 tablespoons plus 2 teaspoons minced fresh cilantro leaves
   2 tablespoons plus 2 teaspoons minced fresh parsley leaves

SIDE DISHES
   Popcorn, *tostado* (page 321), *Chifles* (page 120), French bread, and *Ají Criollo* (page 333)

1.   Cut the fish fillets into strips about ¼ inch thick and 1 inch long.

2.   To make the marinade, combine the citrus juices in a large glass bowl. Add the fish, mix well, cover with plastic wrap, and let marinate in the refrigerator until it is "cooked" (it should be milky white throughout), 4 to 6 hours, but start checking at 3 hours.

3.   Add the remaining marinade ingredients and taste for sugar, salt, black pepper, and hot pepper sauce. Serve in small bowls or stemmed glasses,

each garnished in the center with 1 teaspoon each tomato, bell pepper, onion, cilantro, and parsley. Serve with the side dishes.

Cebiche Vuelve a la Vida

CEBICHE TO CURE HANGOVERS *Serves 6 to 8*

After a wild party, Quiteños (natives of Quito, Ecuador) stop at La Querencia Restaurant for a big bowl of *Cebiche Vuelve a la Vida* and, of course, a bottle of beer—guaranteed to restore you to health.

> 4 cups water
>
> 1 pound frozen large shrimp, thawed and peeled
>
> 1 pound shucked oysters, with their liquid
>
> 1 recipe marinade for *Cebiche Mixto* (page 68)
>
> Salt and hot pepper sauce

GARNISHES

> 1 medium-size ripe but firm tomato (5 to 6 ounces), peeled, seeded, and finely chopped
>
> 1 small green bell pepper, seeded and finely chopped
>
> 1 small onion, finely chopped (about ½ cup), rinsed with hot water, and drained
>
> 2 tablespoons plus 2 teaspoons minced fresh cilantro leaves
>
> 2 tablespoons plus 2 teaspoons minced fresh parsley leaves
>
> 1 ripe but firm Hass avocado, peeled, pitted, and diced (¼ inch) just before serving

SIDE DISHES

> Popcorn, *tostado* (page 321), *Chifles* (page 120), French bread, and *Ají Criollo* (page 333)

1. Bring the water to a boil in a large saucepan. Add the shrimp, remove from the heat, and let stand for a few seconds, until the shrimp turn pink. Drain, then rinse the shrimp under cold running water (rinsing will prevent the shrimp from becoming rubbery). Cut the shrimp in half, if desired.

2. In a large glass bowl, mix the shrimp and oysters with the marinade. Cover with plastic wrap and let marinate for at least 4 hours in the refrigerator.

3. Just before serving, season with salt and hot pepper sauce to taste. Divide the *cebiche* among 6 to 8 small bowls and garnish with the tomato, bell pepper, onion, cilantro, parsley, and avocado. Serve with the side dishes.

Cebiche de Concha Prieta

BLACK CLAM CEBICHE *Serves 4*

The *concha prieta* is a shellfish similar to the clam, only black in color, more assertive in taste, similar in texture to the oyster, and indigenous to the coast of Ecuador and Peru. This *cebiche* is one of the most popular Ecuadorian *cebiches*; in fact, it is the favorite of connoisseurs. *Concha prieta* is available in some Latin American markets, either canned or frozen.

> Two 5½-ounce cans *concha prieta en su jugo* (black clams in their own juice)
>
> 2 tablespoons fresh lemon juice
>
> 2 tablespoons fresh lime juice
>
> ½ cup ketchup
>
> 1 tablespoon extra virgin olive oil
>
> ¼ teaspoon freshly ground black pepper
>
> 1 teaspoon hot pepper sauce, or more to taste
>
> 2 tablespoons minced fresh cilantro or parsley leaves
>
> 1 recipe *Cebollas Encurtidas* (page 340)
>
> Sugar
>
> Salt
>
> 1 medium-size ripe but firm tomato (5 to 6 ounces), peeled, seeded, and diced (¼ inch)
>
> French bread, *tostado* (page 321), and *Ají Criollo* (page 333)

1. In a large glass bowl, mix together the clams and their juice, lemon juice, lime juice, ketchup, oil, black pepper, hot pepper sauce, cilantro, and half of the *cebollas encurtidas*. Cover with plastic wrap and let marinate in the refrigerator for at least 2 hours.

2. Right before serving, taste for sugar, salt, and hot pepper sauce. Serve the clams with the marinade in small bowls, each topped with some diced tomato and 1 tablespoon of the remaining *cebollas encurtidas*. Serve the French bread, *tostado*, and *ají* on the side.

Cebiche de Cochayuyo

CHILEAN SEAWEED CEBICHE *Serves 6*

Cochayuyo is a seaweed indigenous to the coast of Chile. Its texture lends itself to the preparation of any dish that uses meat or seafood. This highly nourishing food is the staff of life for the people on the coast. *Luche* (another type of seaweed) also can be used to make this *cebiche*. Although this version resembles Peruvian *cebiches*, it does not use hot peppers, only a very small amount of hot pepper sauce, and it is not served with corn or sweet potatoes, as Peruvian *cebiches* are.

2 cups cooked *cochayuyo* (page 421) cut into ½-inch pieces

1 cup fresh lemon juice

1 small red onion, halved, thinly sliced into half-moons, soaked in hot water for 5 minutes, and drained

2 cloves garlic, mashed into a paste with ½ teaspoon salt and ¼ teaspoon freshly ground black pepper

1 tablespoon extra virgin olive oil

2 tablespoons minced fresh cilantro leaves

½ teaspoon hot pepper sauce, or more to taste

Lettuce leaves

French bread

1. In a large glass bowl, mix together the lemon juice, onion, garlic paste, oil, cilantro, and hot pepper sauce. Taste for salt and hot pepper sauce. Add the *cochayuyo*, cover with plastic wrap, and marinate in the refrigerator for at least 2 hours.

2. Line 6 salad plates with the lettuce leaves. Drain the *cebiche* and serve on the lettuce, accompanied by the French bread.

Cebiche de Pescado con Leche de Coco

FISH CEBICHE IN COCONUT MILK *Serves 6*

In this specialty from the coast of Colombia, the fish is "cooked" in lemon juice, drained, and then marinated with the coconut milk and flavorings.

1 pound red snapper or *corvina* fillets

1 cup fresh lemon juice, or more if needed

2 cloves garlic, mashed into a paste with 1 teaspoon salt and ¼ teaspoon white pepper

1 small red onion, halved, thinly sliced into half-moons, soaked in hot water for 5 minutes, and drained

1 cup well-stirred canned unsweetened coconut milk

1 teaspoon fresh hot pepper puree, store-bought or homemade (page 332), or hot pepper sauce

2 tablespoons minced fresh cilantro leaves for garnish

Coconut flakes or shredded fresh coconut

1. Cut the fish fillets into strips ¼ inch thick and 1 inch long. Place in a large glass bowl with the lemon juice. (The juice should cover the fish; add more if needed.) Cover with plastic wrap and let marinate in the refrigerator until the fish is opaque through the center, 4 to 6 hours.

2. Drain the fish strips. Mix with the garlic paste, onion, coconut milk, and hot pepper puree.

Return to the refrigerator for about 2 hours to blend the flavors.

3. Divide the mixture among 6 small bowls or stemmed glasses and garnish with the cilantro and coconut.

Cebiche de Salmón Peruano

SALMON MARINATED IN CITRUS JUICES

Serves 6 to 8

Fish *cebiches* require perfectly fresh fish—it has to smell like the sea. On the coast of Peru, small stands sell *cebiche* made with just-caught fish without bothering to "cook" the fish in the marinade. It's more like Japanese *sashimi*, but in Peru they call it *cebiche*. A classic Peruvian appetizer, this recipe can be made with different kinds of fish, such as salmon, sole, flounder, tuna, or *corvina*, or with shellfish. For Peruvians, one of the essential ingredients is the hot pepper. Depending on your taste, the seasoning can be mildly hot or very hot. Many Peruvians add a jigger of *pisco* (Peruvian brandy) at the end. Peruvian *cebiches* are usually served as a first course or snack on a bed of lettuce, with slices of boiled sweet potatoes, slices of corn on the cob, Alfonso or Kalamata olives, and a bowl of *cancha* (toasted dried corn) on the side. Served this way, it makes a nice light luncheon dish. As an appetizer, serve it on lettuce and garnished with olives.

> 1½ pounds salmon fillets, skin and any
>   remaining pin bones removed
> 2 large cloves garlic, chopped
> 2 jalapeños, seeded and chopped
> 1 teaspoon granulated garlic
> 1 teaspoon salt
> ½ teaspoon freshly ground black pepper
> ½ cup fresh lime juice
> 1 cup fresh lemon juice, or more if needed
> 2 tablespoons minced fresh cilantro leaves
> 2 hot peppers (preferably 1 red and 1 green),
>   seeded and cut into very thin strips

> ½ small red onion, thinly sliced into
>   half-moons, soaked in hot water for
>   5 minutes, drained, and marinated in the
>   juice of 1 lemon and salt and white pepper
>   to taste for 2 hours
> Lettuce leaves
> Kalamata olives for garnish

1. Cut the salmon into strips ¼ inch thick and 1 inch long.

2. Place the chopped garlic, jalapeños, granulated garlic, salt, and black pepper, and a little of the lime juice in a blender and process until smooth. In a large glass bowl, mix the salmon with this paste until well combined. Pour the remaining lime juice and the lemon juice on top of the salmon. The juice should cover the fish completely; if it does not, add more lemon juice. Cover with plastic wrap and let marinate in the refrigerator until the fish is opaque through the center, 4 to 6 hours.

3. Drain away the marinade, season with salt and black pepper to taste, and toss with the cilantro, hot peppers, and marinated onion. Cover with plastic wrap and refrigerate until needed, up to 4 hours.

4. To serve, line 6 to 8 salad plates with the lettuce and divide the *cebiche* among the plates. Garnish with the olives and serve.

Cebiche de Champiñones

MUSHROOM CEBICHE *Serves 6 to 8*

Mushrooms have been popular in South America since pre-Hispanic times, when the indigenous peoples gathered them to supplement their diets. These wild mushrooms, called *callampas*, were found throughout South America, with different species growing in different areas. White mushrooms, called *champiñones*, were brought by the Spaniards and are definitely more appreciated than the wild ones because of their quality and looks.

This wonderfully refreshing *cebiche* from Peru is ideal to serve as an appetizer for a cocktail party. I don't use much hot pepper—just enough to give the *cebiche* a little heat.

1 pound fresh, firm, perfectly white mushrooms, wiped clean with a damp cloth or paper towel

½ cup thinly sliced celery

½ cup thinly sliced red onion cut into 1-inch pieces, soaked in hot water for 5 minutes and drained

4 cloves garlic, chopped

½ teaspoon salt

¼ teaspoon white pepper

½ teaspoon hot pepper sauce

½ teaspoon dried oregano

¾ cup fresh lime or lemon juice

1 tablespoon extra virgin olive oil

2 tablespoons thin red bell pepper strips

1 small jalapeño, seeded and minced

Alfonso or Kalamata olives for garnish

1.   Bring a large saucepan of water to a boil. Meanwhile, slice or quarter the mushrooms. Drop into the boiling water along with 1 tablespoon of the lime juice and cook for 30 seconds. Drain, mix with the celery and onion in a large glass bowl, and set aside.

2.   Place the garlic, salt, white pepper, hot pepper sauce, and oregano in a blender and process for a few seconds, until the garlic is minced. Add the remaining lime juice and oil and pulse until well blended. Toss with the mushroom mixture, then taste for salt and hot pepper sauce. Cover with plastic wrap and let marinate in the refrigerator for 2 to 3 hours.

3.   Drain, then mix with the red bell pepper and jalapeño. Cover with plastic wrap and refrigerate for up to 1 day.

4.   Serve in a bowl, garnished with the olives.

Cebiche de Sardinas

SARDINES WITH MARINATED VEGETABLES
Serves 4

Spaniards have a nice way of serving sardines, topped with either minced onions or garlic and chopped parsley. Peruvians added their own touch and came up with this recipe by adding the usual hot peppers and lemon juice. The tomatoes add a refreshing note. This is a truly lovely way to eat sardines.

Two 4½-ounce cans sardines (preferably packed in olive oil), drained

1 small onion, finely chopped (about ½ cup), rinsed with hot water, and drained

1 jalapeño, seeded and minced

2 tablespoons fresh lemon juice

¼ teaspoon salt

⅛ teaspoon ground cumin

¼ teaspoon freshly ground black pepper

Lettuce leaves

1 small ripe but firm tomato (about 3 ounces), peeled, seeded, and diced (¼ inch)

1.   Place the sardines in a glass pie plate and set aside.

2.   In a small glass bowl, combine the onion and jalapeño. In another small glass bowl, whisk together the lemon juice, salt, cumin, and black pepper, then toss with the onion mixture. Pour evenly over the sardines, cover with plastic wrap, and refrigerate until needed, at least 2 hours.

3.   To serve, line a plate with the lettuce leaves and transfer the sardines to the plate. Distribute the tomato around the edge and serve.

VARIATION   Substitute one 8-ounce can Atlantic salmon for the sardines, removing any skin and bones. Serve garnished with black olives, preferably Kalamata.

Escabeches
PICKLED FOODS

THE TECHNIQUE OF MAKING PICKLED foods, or *escabeches*, is of Arab origin and was introduced into Spanish cuisine during the centuries that the Moors occupied Spain. The Spaniards adopted pickling as a way of preserving foods such as fish, poultry, meat, and vegetables. *Escabeches* enjoy great popularity in South America, and little has changed in their preparation since colonial times. The basic ingredients are oil, vinegar, and sometimes wine, to which an assortment of herbs and vegetables can be added. Venezuelans love fish *escabeches* made with such local varieties as *carite*, *atún*, *sierra*, *mero*, and trout. Venezuelan *escabeches* are prepared with a sauce made of oil, vinegar, garlic, thyme, basil, bay leaves, and cloves that is used to marinate fish. Colombia, the only country in South America that enjoys two seacoasts, has a variety of fish *escabeches*. Like the Venezuelans, they use thyme, basil, and other herbs to flavor the sauce, but they also add capers, onions, red bell peppers, and olives. In Ecuador, fish and chicken are the favorite *escabeches* and are seasoned with various herbs and spices, such as oregano and cumin. Peruvians also season with oregano and cumin but add hot peppers and garnish their *escabeches* with sliced boiled sweet potatoes, chunks of corn on the cob, and Alfonso olives. Bolivians enjoy fish from the rivers and Lake Titicaca and prepare their *escabeches* with trout, catfish, *bogas* (small fish from Lake Titicaca), and *corvina*. Just like their Peruvian neighbors, Bolivians love to season their food with hot peppers. Chilean chicken *escabeche* is made with onions and carrots. Argentines and Uruguayans excel in the preparation *escabeches* made with fish, chicken, partridge, squab, quail, and other wild game. Landlocked Paraguay prepares *escabeche de muchacho* with beef, and *escabeches* also are popular in Brazil.

In general, *escabeches* are simple to prepare and, ideally, should be made the day before you intend to serve them, to allow the flavors to develop. They are usually served at room temperature but sometimes are served warm. Good-quality olive oil and vinegar are essential for a good *escabeche*. *Escabeches* are extremely versatile. They can be served as a snack, appetizer, lunch, or part of a buffet or picnic. They are especially good for summertime entertaining.

Alcauciles y Zanahorias en Escabeche

ARTICHOKES AND CARROTS IN ESCABECHE
Serves 8 to 12

This beautiful *escabeche*, an Argentine specialty, can be made a few days ahead of time and is perfect for large gatherings. Its piquant flavor goes well with savory tarts, quiches, roasted or grilled meats, fish, or fowl, or as part of an appetizer table. The cooked green beans should be added shortly before serving because the vinegar turns them brown if they are left in the marinade for a few hours. Always serve this salad at room temperature.

One 12-ounce package baby carrots, trimmed

1 medium-size red onion, sliced ⅛ inch thick

2 cloves garlic, minced

1 bay leaf

Two 14-ounce cans artichoke hearts, drained, rinsed, and quartered

Pinch of red pepper flakes, or more to taste

¾ cup extra virgin olive oil

½ cup white wine vinegar

¾ cup chicken broth

½ teaspoon salt

¼ teaspoon freshly ground black pepper

8 ounces fresh green beans (optional)

One 6-ounce can large black olives, drained and rinsed

1. Bring a large saucepan of salted water to a boil. Add the carrots and cook until crisp-tender, about 5 minutes. Drain.

2. Place the carrots, onion, garlic, bay leaf, artichokes, red pepper, oil, vinegar, chicken broth, salt, and black pepper in a large nonreactive saucepan. Cover, bring to a boil, reduce the heat to low, and simmer for 5 minutes. Remove from the heat, transfer to a glass bowl, and let cool completely. Cover with plastic wrap and refrigerate until needed, up to 5 days.

3. If using the green beans, trim and cut on the diagonal into 1-inch pieces. Bring a large saucepan of salted water to a boil. Add the beans and cook until crisp-tender, about 6 minutes. Drain and rinse under cold running water to stop the cooking. This can be done the day before. Just place the cooled beans in a zippered-top plastic bag and refrigerate until needed.

4. Remove the salad from the refrigerator 30 minutes before serving and discard the bay leaf. Toss with the green beans (if using) and olives, taste for salt and black pepper, and let sit at room temperature until ready to serve.

5. Just before serving, drain away the marinade. Serve the salad in a glass bowl.

Berenjena a la Vinagreta
EGGPLANT PICKLED IN VINAIGRETTE
Makes about 1 quart

This pickled eggplant is one of the most popular ways to prepare eggplant in Argentina. It is perfect as an appetizer and a favorite accompaniment to *asados* (grilled meats). It is so popular that many families preserve several quarts of it at a time. The unusual addition of anise seeds to the vinaigrette gives the eggplant a special flavor. Gloria de Russo, a businesswoman from Mar del Plata, graciously shared her very special recipe with me.

1½ pounds baby eggplants

Kosher salt

4 cups water

1¼ cups cider vinegar

¾ cup extra virgin olive oil, or more if needed

1 bay leaf

2 cloves garlic, minced

½ teaspoon salt

½ teaspoon dried oregano

¼ teaspoon dried thyme

Pinch of red pepper flakes

¼ teaspoon anise seeds

1. Peel the eggplant and cut into ¼-inch-thick rounds. Distribute in a glass baking dish and sprinkle generously with kosher salt. Let stand for at least 6 hours or overnight.

2. In a 4-quart stainless steel saucepan, bring the water and 1 cup of the vinegar to a boil. Rinse the eggplant and add to the boiling water. Cook, uncovered, over medium heat for 15 minutes, taking care not to overcook—the slices should hold their shape. Drain, carefully transfer to a clean kitchen towel, and let drain thoroughly.

3. Combine the remaining ¼ cup vinegar and all the remaining ingredients in a medium-size bowl and whisk until thickened. Pour a little of

the vinaigrette in the bottom of a wide-mouth 1-quart glass jar. Arrange the eggplant slices in layers, pouring some vinaigrette over each layer. The vinaigrette should cover the eggplant; add more oil, if needed. Cover tightly and refrigerate for at least 1 day to blend the flavors.

4. To serve, bring to room temperature and drain. Serve as an hors d'oeuvre with crackers or as a side dish for grilled meat or fish. This will keep for a couple of weeks in the refrigerator.

Berenjena Escabechada

PICKLED EGGPLANT *Serves 6 to 8*

The Lebanese settled in many South American countries and brought with them one of their favorite foods, eggplant. This dish, unlike *Berenjena a la Vinagreta* (page 75), is cooked in oil and vinegar. It is very popular in Argentina and Uruguay and makes an excellent accompaniment to grilled meat, fowl, or fish. It is also a nice addition to a buffet or served as a first course, with the bonus that it can be prepared a few days in advance.

- **4 to 5 baby eggplants or 1 medium-size eggplant (about 1 pound)**
- **Kosher salt**
- **2 medium-size carrots, sliced on the diagonal ¹⁄₁₆ inch thick**
- **1 medium-size onion, halved and thinly sliced into half-moons (about 1 cup)**
- **½ cup olive oil**
- **¼ cup white wine vinegar**
- **2 cups chicken broth or water**
- **Bouquet garni (2 bay leaves; 2 cloves garlic, crushed; and 10 black peppercorns, tied up in cheesecloth)**
- **1 teaspoon dried oregano or marjoram, crumbled**
- **Pinch of red pepper flakes**
- **½ teaspoon salt (omit if using chicken broth)**
- **¼ teaspoon sugar**
- **Freshly ground black pepper**

- **2 tablespoons minced fresh parsley leaves for garnish**
- **2 tablespoons chopped pimentos for garnish**

1. Peel the eggplants and cut into ¼-inch-thick rounds. Place in a large glass bowl, sprinkle with kosher salt, and let stand for about 4 hours at room temperature. The eggplant will release a brown, bitter liquid.

2. Rinse the eggplant well and place in a 10-inch stainless steel skillet. Add the carrots, onion, oil, vinegar, chicken broth, bouquet garni, oregano, red pepper, salt (if using), and sugar. Bring to a boil over medium-low heat and cook, stirring occasionally to make sure eggplant slices are cooking evenly, until there is only about ¾ cup liquid left in the pan, about 30 minutes. Add salt and black pepper to taste. Remove from the heat and let cool. Discard the bouquet garni and refrigerate the eggplant with its liquid in a covered glass container until needed. This will keep for up to 1 week in the refrigerator.

3. Serve at room temperature, garnished with the parsley and pimentos.

Faisán en Escabeche

PICKLED PHEASANT *Serves 4*

Argentina and Uruguay have an abundance of wild game, such as squab, partridge, and quail. A favorite way to prepare these birds is in *escabeche*, to serve the next day or preserve for the future. Pheasants are abundant in the United States; they have a very lean flesh that benefits from the *escabeche* sauce. This is a good formula for any wild bird, as well as for duck and goose. Of course, the cooking time will vary according to the bird used.

- **One 2½-pound pheasant**
- **¾ cup olive oil**
- **1 teaspoon sweet paprika**
- **4 cloves garlic, minced**

5 juniper berries

1 teaspoon rubbed sage

½ teaspoon salt

½ teaspoon black peppercorns

1 cup dry white wine

1 cup chicken broth

2 bay leaves

3 sprigs fresh parsley

1 small red onion, sliced into ¼-inch-thick rings

1 large carrot, cut into strips ¼ inch thick and 1 to 1½ inches long

½ cup sherry vinegar

1 cup small cauliflower or broccoflower florets

¼ cup dried cherries soaked in 2 tablespoons port or cream sherry for 1 hour

Freshly ground black pepper

French bread for serving

1. Cut the pheasant into serving-size pieces—legs, thighs, wings (remove the wing tips), and breasts. Wash thoroughly and dry with paper towels. In a 10-inch skillet, heat ¼ cup of the oil over medium heat. Add the pheasant pieces and lightly brown on both sides. Stir in the paprika, garlic, juniper berries, sage, salt, and peppercorns and cook for 1 minute. Add the wine, chicken broth, bay leaves, and parsley. Cover, bring to a boil, reduce the heat to low, and simmer until the pheasant is almost falling apart, about 1 hour, turning the pieces after 30 minutes.

2. Transfer the pheasant to a large glass bowl. Strain the broth through a fine-mesh strainer and set aside. The traditional way of serving these birds is to marinate the whole pieces with the skin and bones. I prefer at this point to remove the skin and bones and to shred the meat into bite-size pieces, then return the meat to the bowl.

3. In a heavy, 2-quart nonreactive saucepan, heat the remaining ½ cup oil over medium heat. Add the onion and carrot and cook for 1 minute. Add the vinegar, reserved pheasant broth, cauliflower, and cherries with the port and simmer until the cauliflower is just cooked, about 3 minutes; it should still be crisp. Add salt and black pepper to taste. Pour over the pheasant, let cool completely, cover with plastic wrap, and refrigerate overnight.

4. To serve, bring to room temperature and, with a slotted spoon, transfer to 4 salad plates. Serve French bread on the side.

Escabeche de Pollitos

PICKLED CORNISH HENS *Serves 8*

This type of *escabeche* is very popular in South America. Chicken or Cornish hens can be used, with the seasonings and vegetables varying according to the region. Some versions call for hot peppers, oregano, and cumin as the main flavorings; others for thyme, marjoram, and capers; and still others for just garlic, salt, and pepper. All make wonderful additions to the buffet table.

2 Cornish hens (about 1¼ pounds each)

3 cups chicken broth

1 cup dry white wine

½ teaspoon black peppercorns

2 bay leaves

4 ounces red or white pearl onions, peeled

4 ounces baby carrots, trimmed

1 cup small cauliflower florets

½ cup extra virgin olive oil

¼ teaspoon sweet paprika

4 large cloves garlic, thinly sliced

½ teaspoon dried marjoram

Pinch of red pepper flakes

¾ cup cider vinegar

Salt and freshly ground black pepper

12 black olives, pitted

¼ cup sweetened dried cranberries

1. Thoroughly wash the hens, then place in a 4-quart nonreactive saucepan. Add the chicken broth, ½ cup of the wine, the peppercorns, and bay leaves and bring to a boil over medium heat, skimming the froth as it rises to the top. Reduce the heat to low, cover, and simmer until the meat is pulling away from bones, about 1 hour. Transfer to a chopping board and let cool. Strain the broth through a fine-mesh strainer and set aside. Remove the skin from the hens and cut the birds into serving-size pieces, which is the traditional way of serving. I prefer to remove the bones and tear the meat into bite-size pieces; it is much easier to eat this way. Place the meat in a large glass bowl and set aside.

2. Bring the strained broth to a boil in a 2-quart saucepan. Add the onions, reduce the heat to medium-low, and simmer until tender but still slightly crisp, about 20 minutes. Remove with a slotted spoon and set aside. Bring the broth back to a boil, add the carrots, and cook until crisp-tender, about 10 minutes. Remove with a slotted spoon and add to the onions. Add the cauliflower to the broth and cook for 1 minute. Remove with a slotted spoon and add to the onions and carrots, reserving the broth.

3. Heat the oil in a large skillet over low heat. Stir in the paprika, garlic, marjoram, and red pepper flakes and cook for 30 seconds. Add the vinegar, remaining ½ cup wine, ½ cup of the reserved broth, and salt and black pepper to taste. Simmer for 5 minutes. Add the meat, onions, carrots, cauliflower, olives, and cranberries and simmer for 5 minutes more to blend the flavors. Taste for salt and black pepper. Let cool, transfer to a large glass bowl, cover with plastic wrap, and refrigerate overnight to develop the flavors.

4. To serve, bring to room temperature and, with a slotted spoon, transfer the *escabeche* to a serving platter. This dish can also be served warm.

Lengua a la Vinagreta

TONGUE MARINATED IN VINAIGRETTE *Serves 12*

When I was visiting my friend Yvonne Miles, we spent a few days on her farm in Paysandú, in northern Uruguay. All the farmers from the area do their banking and shopping in a very small town called Quebracho, which has a tavern, a restaurant, a bank, and a couple of grocery stores. It was in the tavern, which is a must stop for the farmers, that I learned that the alcohol of choice among the country people of Uruguay is *grapa*. The way to drink it is standing at the bar, from a large shot glass, accompanied by a beer chaser. I had not had lunch yet, and after three sips of *grapa*, I started to feel lightheaded. It was time for lunch.

I was pleasantly surprised to find a very continental menu at the restaurant. The *lengua a la vinagreta* was served with Russian salad as an appetizer. Both were delicious, as was the *Wienerschnitzel* that followed. Another surprise was the dessert I ordered. The flan came with a mound of *dulce de leche*, which I learned is a very popular way of serving it in Uruguay. The tavern and the restaurant reminded me of the *picanterías* of the Andean countries, where the gentlemen farmers and the farm hands congregate for their favorite drinks and foods. If tongue is not your favorite meat, this vinaigrette can be used with pork loin or roast beef.

> 1 beef tongue (about 3 pounds)
> ½ cup extra virgin olive oil
> ¼ cup sherry vinegar
> 1 tablespoon Dijon mustard
> ½ teaspoon salt
> ½ teaspoon freshly ground black pepper
> Pinch of sugar
> 2 hard-cooked eggs, peeled, whites chopped, and yolks pushed through a sieve

¼ cup seeded and minced red bell pepper

½ small onion, minced (about ¼ cup)

1 tablespoon capers, drained

2 tablespoon pitted and finely chopped Kalamata olives

½ teaspoon dried oregano, crumbled

1 tablespoon chopped fresh basil leaves

¼ cup minced fresh parsley leaves

French bread for serving

1. Rinse the tongue thoroughly. Place in a large casserole with salted water to cover by 1 inch. Bring to a boil over medium heat, skimming off the froth as it rises to the top. Reduce the heat to low, cover, and simmer until a fork inserted in the thickest part goes in without resistance, about 3 hours.

2. Transfer to a cutting board and let stand until cool enough to handle. The skin comes off easily when hot but not when cold, so remove all the skin as soon as possible and remove any small bones and gristle. Cut on the diagonal into ⅛-inch-thick slices, cutting toward the tip and the hump, almost parallel to the base. Arrange in overlapping layers in a large glass baking dish.

3. In a medium-size glass bowl, whisk together the oil, vinegar, mustard, salt, and black pepper until thickened. Add the sugar, egg whites, bell pepper, onion, capers, olives, oregano, basil, and parsley. Stir well to combine and pour evenly over the tongue. Cover with plastic wrap and let marinate in the refrigerator for at least 6 hours or overnight.

4. Arrange a few slices on salad plates and garnish with the egg yolks. Serve French bread on the side.

VARIATION A 3-pound pork loin or beef sirloin roast can be used instead of tongue. Rub the roast with salt and pepper to taste. Place in a shallow roasting pan with ½ cup dry white wine mixed with ½ cup beef broth and bake in a pre-heated 350°F oven for 2 hours. The juices should run clear when done. Slice ⅛ inch thick and continue with step 3 above.

Escabeche de Pescado Peruano

PERUVIAN-STYLE FISH ESCABECHE *Serves 8*

This *escabeche* is made with different spices than the *escabeches* from the southern countries of South America. As in most Peruvian specialties, hot peppers are a very important part of the seasoning. Tuna and *corvina* are the preferred fish for Peruvian and Venezuelan *escabeches*. Bolivians make a similar *escabeche* with *bogas*, small fish indigenous to Lake Titicaca, although fresh sardines also can be used. Peruvians serve their *escabeches* garnished with corn, olives, hard-cooked eggs, wedges of brick cheese, and sliced boiled sweet potatoes.

> 2 pounds tuna or *corvina* fillets
>
> Juice of 1 lemon
>
> 4 cloves garlic, mashed into a paste with 1 teaspoon salt and ¼ teaspoon freshly ground black pepper
>
> ½ cup extra virgin olive oil
>
> 8 ounces small onions, quartered
>
> 1 cup ¼-inch-wide red bell pepper strips
>
> 2 teaspoons fresh hot pepper puree, store-bought or homemade (page 332), or hot pepper sauce to taste
>
> ½ teaspoon ground cumin
>
> 1 teaspoon dried oregano, crumbled
>
> ¾ cup white wine vinegar
>
> ¾ cup chicken broth
>
> Lettuce leaves

GARNISHES

> 10 Alfonso or Kalamata olives
>
> 2 hard-cooked eggs, peeled and quartered
>
> 2 jalapeños, seeded and cut into very thin strips
>
> Small whole baby corn

1. Cut the fish fillets into 1 x 2-inch pieces. Rub with the lemon juice and garlic paste. Place in a large glass bowl, cover with plastic wrap, and let marinate in the refrigerator for 1 hour.

2. In a large skillet, heat the oil over medium heat. Add the onions, bell pepper strips, hot pepper puree, cumin, and oregano and cook, stirring, for 5 minutes. Add the fish with its marinade and cook for a couple of minutes, stirring. Add the vinegar and chicken broth, bring to a simmer, cover, and cook until the fish is opaque throughout, about 5 minutes. Season with salt and black pepper to taste. Transfer the fish to a glass dish, top with the sauce from the pan, and let cool. Cover with plastic wrap and refrigerate for at least a few hours or overnight to let the flavors develop. Let the fish come to room temperature before serving.

3. To serve, arrange the lettuce leaves on a serving tray. Remove the fish from the marinade using a slotted spoon, place on the lettuce, and top with the marinated onions and pepper strips and some of the marinade. Garnish with the olives, eggs, jalapeños, and baby corn.

Escabeche de Pescado

PICKLED FISH *Serves 8*

Fish *escabeches* are very popular in areas along the Pacific coast and regions where large rivers teem with a variety of fish. The most popular fish used for *escabeches* are tuna, *corvina*, *sierra*, red snapper, trout, and catfish, depending on the area. The fish fillets or steaks are usually first sautéed in olive oil, then the *escabeche* sauce is poured over them to marinate for a few hours or, better yet, overnight. This dish can be served warm or at room temperature. It is extremely easy because the fish is not sautéed first but cooked in the sauce.

2 pounds white-fleshed fish fillets (*corvina*, *sierra*, catfish, trout, or any other firm, lean fish)

2 tablespoons fresh lemon juice

1 teaspoon salt

½ teaspoon freshly ground black pepper

½ cup olive oil

1 cup thinly sliced red onion

½ cup seeded and thinly sliced red bell pepper

½ cup seeded and thinly sliced green bell pepper

4 cloves garlic, thinly sliced

2 tablespoons capers, drained

Bouquet garni (4 sprigs fresh thyme or 1 teaspoon dried, 2 sprigs fresh parsley, 2 bay leaves, and ½ teaspoon black peppercorns, tied up in cheesecloth)

½ cup dry white wine

½ cup sherry vinegar

½ cup fish stock (page 410) or chicken broth

Lettuce leaves

1. Rub the fish fillets with the lemon juice, ½ teaspoon of the salt, and the black pepper. Place in a glass baking dish and let marinate in the refrigerator for 1 hour. Cut into 1 x 2-inch pieces and set aside.

2. Heat the oil in a heavy casserole over medium heat. Add the onion and bell peppers and cook for 5 minutes, stirring a few times. Add the capers, remaining ½ teaspoon salt, black pepper to taste, the bouquet garni, wine, vinegar, and fish stock. Bring to a simmer, then reduce the heat to low. Add the fish, baste with the sauce, cover, and simmer until opaque through the center, 6 to 8 minutes. Discard the bouquet garni and taste for salt and black pepper.

3. Carefully transfer the fish to a glass baking dish, pour the sauce over the fish, and let cool. Cover with plastic wrap and refrigerate for a few

hours or overnight to let the flavors develop. Let the fish come to room temperature before serving.

4. To serve, arrange the lettuce leaves on 8 salad plates and divide the *escabeche* among them.

Tamales

I F I H A D T O C H O O S E one food that epitomizes the creole cuisine of South America, it would be the tamale. Felipe Rojas-Lombardi echoes my feelings in his book *The Art of South American Cooking*: "Whenever I get a longing for the foods of my childhood, visions of tamales fill my mind." Maybe it is the memories tamales bring back of holidays and family celebrations and the excitement found in the kitchen, where many loving hands labored together in the preparation of this beloved specialty. It is in this quintessential South American food that one can see most vividly the blend of European and Indian cuisines.

When the Spaniards came to the Americas, they discovered that the Indians made an unusual type of food wrapped in leaves. The Indians used ground fresh or dried corn and probably sweet potatoes and squash. They didn't have many spices or herbs, so their tamales were simply seasoned. After the conquest, the Spaniards introduced pigs, chickens, eggs, olives, and raisins, which helped embellish and enrich the tamales, taking them to culinary heights never dreamed of by the Indians.

The word *tamale* comes from *tamalli* in Nahuatl, the language of the Aztecs. Evidently, the Spaniards carried this term to South America. In Quechua, the language of the Incas, the word for corn tamale is *choclotanda*, which means "cornbread." In South America, tamales are found in Andean countries where there is a concentrated Indian population. The Amazonian Indians also make tamales with corn, yuca, or plantains. Each of the Andean countries has a variety of tamales, both savory and sweet. They go by different names depending not only on the country but also on the region. In Venezuela, they are called *ayacas* or *hallacas*, *bollos*, and *cachapas*; in Colombia *tamales*, *envueltos*, *hallacas*, and *bollos*; and in Ecuador *humitas*, *tamales*, *quimbolitos*, *hallacas*, and *chiguiles*. Peruvians have *tamales*, *humitas*, *juanes*, and *chapanas*; Bolivians *humintas* and *tamales*; Chileans and Argentines *humitas*; and Brazilians *pamonhas*.

Regardless of the name, preparing a good tamale is an art and requires *una buena mano* (a good hand) to feel if the dough is just right. Tamales have evolved from pre-Columbian times and now are made not only from corn and quinoa but also from potatoes, yuca, plantains, rice, squash, eggplants, sweet potatoes, and a variety of flours. The fillings usually include cheese, chicken, pork, beef, or fish. Raisins, prunes, hard-cooked eggs, hot peppers, almonds, and olives are the usual garnishes. The favorite wrappings are cornhusks, banana leaves, and *hojas de achira* (edible canna leaves). Once they are wrapped, they are either boiled or steamed in a special pot called a *tamalera*.

Preparation of Tamales

Follow these five simple steps when making tamales.

1. Prepare the filling the day before.

2. Prepare the leaves and cut strings for tying them a few hours ahead.

3. Make the dough. Get the garnishes ready.

4. Assemble and wrap the tamales.

5. Steam the tamales.

Fillings

Most fillings can be prepared the day before, with the exception of cheese. Although you cannot prepare the cheese filling early, you can grate the cheese ahead and keep it refrigerated in a zippered-top plastic bag. Leftover pork or poultry is ideal for making tamales. If they are going to be frozen, it is better not to use eggs in the filling, because the eggs will get rubbery when reheated.

Leaves to Wrap Tamales

The most popular leaves for wrapping tamales in South America are:

- Fresh cornhusks

- Banana leaves

- Edible canna leaves (not available in the United States)

In the United States, two kinds of cornhusks are available, fresh and dried.

Fresh Cornhusks Corn on the cob, with the husks on, is available most of the year, but it is most plentiful during the summer and early fall.

To remove the husks from the cob, use a sharp, heavy knife to cut through the corncob at the stem end, where the kernels start. Carefully remove the husks and select the largest for wrapping. Blanch them in boiling water for a minute to make them more pliable, dry with paper towels, and set aside. Save the rest of the husks for cutting strips to tie the tamales or for covering the tamales before steaming.

Dried Cornhusks These come mainly from Mexico, last indefinitely, and are available in most supermarkets and Mexican groceries. They come in packages and need to be reconstituted by soaking in hot water, without unfolding. Once they are softened, it is easy to remove the husks. Put them in a colander, rinse thoroughly, and dry with paper towels.

There are several ways to wrap tamales, depending on the region. The most popular method uses one large husk. Put the husk (or overlap two if small) on your worktable and place two heaping tablespoons of dough in the center, toward the lower half. Fold the left side of the husk over the dough, fold the pointed end over the center, and finally fold the right side over the center. Tie with kitchen twine or cornhusk strips. As you finish, place them in a baking pan with the open end up. I wrap *humitas* in only one or two leaves.

The other method uses three husks. Place two husks on the worktable, overlapping them by two inches on the lower, wide end. Place a third husk in the center. Add the dough, fold one side over the dough, fold the other side over the center, and then fold the pointed ends to form a rectangular package. Tie four ways with kitchen twine.

Banana Leaves In the United States, two kinds of banana leaves are available, fresh and frozen, although the fresh leaves are not available everywhere. The frozen leaves are available in large cities in Latin American and Mexican groceries. The frozen leaves come in one-pound packages and measure about 10 x 14 inches each. They have to be cut to the desired size. The problem I have found with frozen leaves is that they have been in the freezer too long or have been handled carelessly, resulting in brittle leaves that make it almost impossible to get a good-size leaf.

Because of this problem, I and other cooks have come up with the idea of cutting the leaves large enough to encase the tamale dough (about 7 x 8 inches) and then wrapping them in a 10 x 12-inch piece of aluminum foil. (If the leaves are bad, I cut smaller pieces and make smaller tamales.) Wrapped this way, the dough absorbs the flavor of the banana leaf and protects the tamale from the aluminum foil (many people are afraid of chemical reactions between aluminum foil and food). My friend Melissa Pearlman who was helping me test the tamale recipes for this book found aluminum foil sheets packed in large dispensers for food service use. They are made of lightweight aluminum foil, measure 10 x 12 inches, and are ideal for the second wrapping of tamales. For people who make 50 or more tamales at a time, especially during the Christmas season, this is a blessing, because you don't have to buy extra packages of banana leaves just in case they are not perfect, and you do not have to tie the tamales. Also, since I steam all types of tamales, the aluminum foil seals the tamales very well.

To work with frozen banana leaves, defrost them in the refrigerator overnight, cut to size, and rinse well. Dry with paper towels, always going with the grain; the leaves will shred if you go against the grain.

There are two ways of using banana leaves, either fresh or frozen: just as they are or passed through a flame or boiling water to soften them. Raw leaves have the tendency to break more easily, but it is up to the cook whether to soften them or not. If banana leaves in any form are not available, use parchment paper and tie the tamales with kitchen twine.

Wrapping Tamales with Banana Leaves

All the preparation for the banana leaves can be done ahead, even the day before. Once the leaves are cleaned, put them in plastic bags and refrigerate. Before you start assembling the tamales, make sure you have all the ingredients lined up on the counter—dough, filling, garnishes, leaves, and kitchen twine or aluminum foil. I always use aluminum foil instead of twine. Place one leaf on your work surface, with the grain going left to right. Place the required amount of dough in the center (many cooks divide the dough into 8 to 12 portions, depending on the size of tamales desired), spread it to form a rectangle measuring about 3 x 5 inches, make a slight indentation in the center, and top with the filling. Fold the leaves as an envelope: the left long side over the filling, then the long right side over, and finally the two ends under. Tie as a bundle or use the aluminum foil to make a second wrapping. To use the foil, bring the two long sides of the foil together, make a half-inch fold, make another half-inch fold, and then tuck the ends over or under.

Cooking Tamales

If you don't have a *tamalera* (I don't), use an 8-quart pot that has a steaming basket. Bring 2 to

4 cups of water (enough to come to the bottom of the basket when it's set in) to a boil. If you have pieces of broken husks or leaves, line the basket with them, then start placing the tamales on their sides in the basket. (*Humitas* are cooked standing up, with the open end on top.) Most cooks prefer to cook 4 or 5 tamales at a time, in one layer, so that they can rise freely; you can overlap them a little, if necessary. Another pot that is similar to a *tamalera* is an 8-quart steamer that comes with two baskets. With one of these, it is possible to cook 6 or 7 tamales at a time. Cover the tamales with leftover pieces of husks or leaves and a clean kitchen towel. Place the basket in the pot and cover. The specific cooking time will depend on the particular tamale, but they should be cooked until firm to the touch. A coin, such as a quarter, is usually put in the bottom of the pot. When it stops making noise, the water has evaporated, and you need to add more boiling water. Note that most tamales are eaten drizzled with a little hot pepper sauce.

Hallacas Venezolanas

VENEZUELAN TAMALES *Makes 24 hallacas*

Without a doubt, the *hallaca* (sometimes spelled *ayaca*) is the grand national dish of Venezuela. In *Geografía Gastronómica Venezolana*, Ramón David León describes the *hallaca* as being not only a culinary creation but also a spiritual one, which, more than any other tradition, binds Venezuelans together. A Christmas without *hallacas* would be unthinkable for a Venezuelan. The *hallaca* is a complex creation made of a variety of foods that can be traced back to colonial times. The dough is rather simple: the Indian *arepa* dough and *achiote* (annatto) are mixed with Spanish lard. The Spanish filling is quite elaborate, more so than for any other South American tamale. This recipe is one of the most complex *hallaca* recipes I have encountered in my research. My friend Helena Chapellín Wilson generously shared with me her family recipe and even came to my home to show me the preparation, especially the wrapping of the *hallaca*. Her aunt María Chapellín was a prominent Venezuelan cookbook author, and her *hallacas* are definitely the best I've ever had. They are lean and delicious and freeze extremely well for several months without losing their flavor. Prepare the filling in stages, invite a group of friends over for the assembly and cooking, and have a fun day making this wonderful specialty. Before starting to make *hallacas*, read all about the preparation of tamales on pages 82–84.

RELLENO (Filling)

- **4 whole bone-in chicken breasts (about 4 pounds), skin removed**
- **4 ounces salt pork**
- **2 medium-size onions, peeled**
- **1 leek (white part and 1 inch of the green), washed well**
- **2 scallions (white part and 1 inch of the green)**
- **2 celery stalks**
- **1 medium-size carrot, peeled**
- **3 sprigs fresh parsley**
- **3 sprigs fresh cilantro**
- **8 cups water**
- **1 pound ripe but firm tomatoes, peeled and seeded, or one 16-ounce can peeled whole tomatoes, drained and seeded**
- **1 small green bell pepper, seeded and cut into 1-inch pieces**
- **1 small red bell pepper, seeded and cut into 1-inch pieces**
- **1 large shallot, peeled**
- **One-half 16-ounce jar mild *jardinera* in oil, drained**

GUISO DE COCHINO (Braised Pork)

- **2 pounds pork tenderloin, trimmed of fat and silver skin and cut into ¾-inch cubes**
- **½ cup canola oil**

½ cup red or white wine vinegar

½ cup muscatel wine

1½ tablespoons capers, drained

Tabasco sauce

½ cup finely chopped *panela* or firmly packed dark brown sugar

2 teaspoons salt

½ teaspoon freshly ground black pepper

MASA (Dough)

One 2-pound bag *arepa* flour (page 417)

4½ cups reserved chicken broth, heated, or more if needed

2 tablespoons *Manteca de Color* (page 331), made with vegetable shortening, or more if needed

GARNISHES

Three 1-pound packages frozen banana leaves, prepared per instructions on page 83

One 5-ounce jar pimento-stuffed Spanish olives, drained

8 ounces blanched whole almonds

1 cup seedless black raisins

Parchment paper (optional), cut into twenty-four 10 x 12-inch rectangles

Kitchen twine, cut into twenty-four 30-inch lengths, or aluminum foil, cut into twenty-four 10 x 12-inch rectangles

1. To make the filling, place the chicken breasts, salt pork, one of the onions, the leek, scallions, celery, carrot, parsley, cilantro, and water in a large casserole or Dutch oven. Add more water, if needed, to cover the chicken by 1 inch. Bring to a boil over medium heat, skimming off the froth that comes to the surface. Reduce the heat to low, cover, and simmer for 1 hour. Remove the chicken and salt pork and let cool. Remove the chicken from the bones and cut into 2 x ½-inch strips. Cut the salt pork into ¼-inch dice. Cover with plastic wrap and refrigerate until needed.

Strain the broth, reserving the vegetables. Cool the broth and refrigerate. When the fat has hardened on top of the broth, discard it. Reserve the broth for the dough.

2. In a blender or food processor, finely chop the reserved vegetables along with the remaining onion, the tomatoes, bell peppers, shallot, and *jardinera*. This will be the basis for the braised pork. It can be made 2 days ahead and kept refrigerated.

3. To make the braised pork, place the pork tenderloin and the chopped vegetables in a 4-quart saucepan. Add the oil, vinegar, wine, capers, Tabasco to taste, and *panela*. Bring to a boil, reduce the heat to low, and simmer until the pork is tender, about 45 minutes, stirring occasionally until the *panela* has melted. Add the salt and black pepper. The braised pork can be made 2 days ahead and kept refrigerated.

4. The amount of dough needed varies with personal preference. Helena likes to spread a very thin layer of dough, while others prefer a thicker layer. A ⅛-inch-thick layer is perfect for my taste, because it gives a nice balance of filling and dough. The best way to start is to make the dough as described in the following paragraph. If more dough is needed as you assemble the tamales, make another cup—it takes only a few minutes. The proportion of flour to broth is 1 cup flour to 1½ cups broth. Add *manteca de color* and shortening as needed.

To make the dough, put 3 cups flour in a large bowl. Add the chicken broth and mix with a wooden spoon or your hands to make a soft dough. Work in the *manteca de color* and shortening and knead until smooth, about 5 minutes. The color should be light orange. If it's too light or you prefer a stronger annatto flavor, add more *manteca de color* as desired. Cover with a damp kitchen towel.

5. Assemble the *hallacas*. There are two ways of doing this. One is Helena's way, which is the better one but, because of the demands of modern life, not very practical. She uses 4 layers of banana leaves and boils her *hallacas*. The other way is to use 1 banana leaf square, placed on a work surface with the grain running left to right. Roll the dough into 2 logs, cut each into 12 rounds, and then cut each round into 2 pieces. Put 1 piece in the center of the banana leaf and, with your fingers, flatten it into a 3 x 5-inch rectangle, with the long side parallel to the grain of the leaf. The dough should be thin and it has a tendency to dry out, so keep on wetting your fingers to spread the dough on the banana leaf. Place 2 tablespoons of the braised pork along the center of the dough, parallel to the grain of the leaf. Arrange on top 1 piece of chicken, 1 piece of salt pork, 2 olives, 2 almonds, and 4 raisins. Take the other piece of dough, flatten it on top of another leaf into a larger rectangle, and place it on top of the filling, pressing down on all sides to contain the filling.

Fold the sides of the leaf along the grain over the *hallaca*, then bring the ends under. You should get a neat rectangle. To protect the filling, especially if there is a tear in the leaves, place the *hallaca* on a piece of parchment paper. Bring the long sides together, making a ½-inch fold, and fold again, then close the ends over the seam side. Tie four ways with a piece of twine, like a neat package. Or wrap in aluminum foil per the instructions on page 83.

6. Following the instructions on pages 83–84, steam the *hallacas* for 1 hour.

7. To freeze, place the steamed *hallacas* on baking sheets and place in the freezer. When frozen, pack them in zippered-top plastic bags and freeze for up to 6 months. To reheat, thaw and then steam for about 20 minutes, or steam for 30 minutes if not thawed. Or reheat one at a time on high in the microwave, starting with 1 minute cooking time.

NOTES **If there is any dough and filling left over, Helena puts both in the food processor and processes until pureed. She uses this dough to make small tamales (about 2 x 3 inches), and serves them for appetizers. This is also a good way to use smaller pieces of banana leaves. Steam these tamales until firm, about 30 minutes. They are delicious.**

Humitas/Choclotandas
FRESH CORN TAMALES

THE HISTORIAN FATHER JOSEPH DE Acosta called *humitas*, or tamales, the "bread of the Indians," and rightly so, because this was the only kind of food the Indians had that resembled bread in pre-Hispanic times. In fact, the Quechua word for these tamales is *choclotanda*, which means "cornbread." Before the conquest, the Indians made their *choclotandas* with ground fresh corn. Sometimes they filled them with meat or fish, if it was available. Simply seasoned with herbs, they were wrapped in cornhusks and cooked in clay pots set in hot coals. I'm sure the Quechuas were the first ones to use corncobs (placed in the bottom of the pot) to steam the tamales, a practice still popular among those who don't have steamer baskets or *tamaleras*.

After the Spaniards came, *humitas* evolved into a more sophisticated specialty with the addition of butter or lard, cheese, and eggs. Just about every country in South America has a version of fresh corn tamales, although the names vary. In Colombia, they are called *envueltos de mazorca*; in Venezuela *cachapas*; and in Ecuador, Chile, Paraguay, and Argentina *humitas* or *chumales*. In Peru, they go by either *humitas* or *tamalitos verdes*, and in Bolivia they are called *humintas*. In northern Brazil, the Amazonian version of the *humita* is the *pamonha*.

The classic Ecuadorian *humita* uses ground corn, cheese, scallions, eggs, and a mixture of half lard and half butter. The Colombian version is similar, except that *chicharrón* (fried pork rind) is ground with the corn. The Peruvian version mixes ground corn with lard, ground fresh cilantro leaves, garlic, and hot peppers. The Chilean version is similar to the Peruvian, except Chileans use basil instead of cilantro. Argentines and Paraguayans use onion and tomato to flavor their *humitas*, and Bolivians add onions, eggs, cheese, hot pepper sauce, and anise. All types are delicious. In Brazil, the Amazonian natives make their *pamonhas* with ground corn, coconut, and sugar. Sometimes they use a mixture of corn and yuca. The Andean towns bordering the Amazon also have special tamales, made with corn and yuca or plantains.

Humitas are usually savory and served as a first course. A sweet variety is served as a dessert with coffee. Leftover *humitas*, reheated in a frying pan or in the microwave, are wonderful with coffee in the morning.

The secret to a good *humita* is corn with a high starch content that has been picked when it is *cau* or *choclero* (very ripe but not dry). *Humitas* are always wrapped in fresh cornhusks, which give them a delicious, intense corn flavor. Unfortunately, the corn in the United States is not suitable for this dish because of its high water content. I have found a way to reproduce *humitas* in the States by adding cornmeal to the batter and buying extra ears of corn to get enough good husks to wrap them. Another possibility is to use Mexican dried cornhusks or parchment paper.

Recently, I found some frozen Peruvian corn, very *cau*, in a South American grocery. I discovered that when using this corn, you have to add water or milk because it is too dry. For my recipes, omit the cornmeal when using this type of corn. Many cooks combine the *cau* corn with fresh corn, which I think works better because you get a better texture and flavor.

Bolivians and Argentines also bake their *humintas* or *humitas* in the oven instead of steaming them. Baking works very well, especially if you line the baking dish with husks and add about ½ cup water to the pan. The cooking time is about the same.

Humitas Ecuatorianas

ECUADORIAN HUMITAS *Makes about 12* humitas, *depending on the size of the cornhusks*

A well-prepared *humita* is a gourmand's delight. These *humitas* are generally made plain, but some cooks prefer to fill them with a piece of cheese or chicken or some other tidbit.

> 6 to 8 ears corn (4 cups kernels)
> ¼ cup chopped scallions (white part only)
> ½ cup (1 stick) unsalted butter, melted
> 3 large eggs, separated
> ½ cup cornmeal, or more if needed
> 1 teaspoon baking powder
> 1 teaspoon salt
> 1 teaspoon sugar
> 6 ounces Chihuahua, mozzarella, or Muenster cheese, shredded
> 1 tablespoon brandy
> Kitchen twine, cut into twelve 15-inch lengths
> 2 cups water
> *Ají Criollo* (page 333)

1. Have a large pot of water boiling. To remove the husks from the corn, use a sharp, heavy knife to cut through the corncob at the stem end, where the kernels start. Carefully remove the husks. Select the largest for wrapping and blanch in the boiling water for a couple of minutes to make them more pliable. Remove from the water with tongs and set on paper towels to drain. Save the rest to cut into strips for tying or to cover the *humitas* before steaming.

2. With a brush, remove the silk from the corn and rinse. Use the knife to cut the kernels from the cobs (you need 4 cups). Place in a food processor or blender along with the scallions and process until finely ground. Add the butter, egg yolks, cornmeal, baking powder, salt, sugar, cheese, and brandy. Pulse until everything is well incorporated and smooth. Transfer to a large bowl; the mixture should be thick, not runny. Add more cornmeal if the batter is runny.

3. Whip the egg whites until soft peaks form. Carefully fold just enough into the corn mixture until it mounds.

4. To assemble the *humitas*, dry the cornhusks and place 2 on the worktable, overlapping them a little. Place a heaping ½ cup corn batter on the lower half of the husks, fold the left side over the center, fold the pointed end over, and finally fold the right side over toward the center. Tie around the middle with twine or cornhusk strips.

5. Place a quarter in the bottom of a steamer, add the water, and line the steamer basket with small cornhusks. Place a few *humitas* standing open end up in the steamer. Cover with leftover husks and a clean kitchen towel. Place the cover on the pot, bring to a boil, and steam until the *humitas* feel firm to the touch, about 30 minutes if small, 45 minutes if large. Add more boiling water if needed (the quarter will stop making noise when all the water has evaporated).

6. To serve, remove the twine and place on a plate with the husks opened to expose the *humita*. Serve with a dish of *aji* on the side.

NOTE **If using dried cornhusks, soak them in hot water for a few minutes, dry, and use as instructed.**

Humitas Verdes Peruanas

PERUVIAN GREEN TAMALES *Makes about 12 humitas, depending on the size of the cornhusks*

Seasoned with cilantro, onion, garlic, and hot pepper puree or sauce, these *humitas* don't have any eggs or cheese in the batter. They are close to the original Indian *humitas*. The same type of *humita* is made in Chile (see the next recipe), where basil is used instead of cilantro. In both cases, because of the difference between U.S. and South American corn, you have to use cornmeal to get the right texture. Adding a lightly beaten egg also will help. Sometimes Peruvians make *tamalitos verdes* with a pork filling.

6 to 8 ears corn (4 cups kernels)

R E L L E N O (Filling; optional)
> **12 ounces lean pork shoulder, trimmed of fat**
> **1 clove garlic, crushed**
> **4 cups water**
> **2 tablespoons canola oil**
> **1 medium-size onion, thinly sliced (about 1 cup)**
> **2 hot red or green peppers, seeded and cut into thin strips**
> **12 Alfonso or Kalamata olives, pitted**
> **2 hard-cooked eggs (optional), peeled and chopped**

> **6 tablespoons (¾ stick) unsalted butter or lard**
> **1 small onion, minced (about ½ cup)**
> **½ cup packed fresh cilantro leaves**
> **2 small cloves garlic, chopped**
> **1 teaspoon salt**
> **1 teaspoon sugar**
> **¼ teaspoon freshly ground black pepper**
> **2 teaspoons fresh hot pepper puree, store-bought or homemade (page 332), or hot pepper sauce to taste**

½ cup cornmeal

1 large egg (optional), lightly beaten

Kitchen twine, cut into twelve 15-inch lengths

2 cups water

Ají Criollo (page 333)

1. Have a large pot of water boiling. To remove the husks from the corn, use a sharp, heavy knife to cut through the corncob at the stem end, where the kernels start. Carefully remove the husks. Select the largest for wrapping and blanch in the boiling water for a couple of minutes to make them more pliable. Remove from the water with tongs and set on paper towels to drain. Save the rest to cut into strips for tying or to cover the *humitas* before steaming.

2. With a brush, remove the silk from the corn and rinse. Use the knife to cut the kernels from the cobs (you need 4 cups). Place in a blender or food processor and process until finely ground. Transfer to a large bowl and wash out the blender or processor.

3. If making the filling, place the pork, garlic, and water in a heavy casserole or Dutch oven. Bring to a boil, reduce the heat to medium-low, and let simmer until the pork is tender, about 45 minutes. The remaining filling ingredients will be added later.

4. Meanwhile, heat the butter in a large skillet over low heat. Add the onion and cook, stirring a few times, until transparent, about 3 minutes. Place the cilantro and garlic in a blender or food processor and process until smooth. Add to the skillet along with the salt, sugar, black pepper, and hot pepper puree. Cook for a few minutes, sprinkle the cornmeal on top, and cook, stirring constantly, until the mixture is thick, shiny, and separates from the bottom (it should be thick

enough to mound). Remove from the heat, let cool to lukewarm, and beat in the egg, if desired.

5. When the pork is tender, remove from the pan with a slotted spoon, let cool slightly, and cut into ½-inch pieces. Heat the oil in a large skillet over medium heat. Add the onion, hot peppers, and pork and cook, stirring a few times, for 5 minutes. Remove from the heat and stir in the olives and hard-cooked eggs (if using). The filling can be prepared the day before, cooled, covered, and refrigerated.

6. To assemble the *humitas*, dry the cornhusks and place 2 on the worktable, overlapping them a little. If not using the filling, place a heaping ½ cup corn batter on the lower half of the husks, fold the left side over the center, fold the pointed end over, and finally fold the right side over toward the center. Tie in the middle with twine or cornhusk strips. If using the filling, place a large spoonful of batter on the husks, spread out to a 3 x 4-inch rectangle, place 1 tablespoon of the filling in the center, and cover with another spoonful of batter. Fold up the same way.

7. Place a quarter in the bottom of a steamer, add the water, and line the steamer basket with small cornhusks. Place a few *humitas* standing open end up in the steamer. Cover with leftover husks and a clean kitchen towel. Place the cover on the pot, bring to a boil, and steam until the *humitas* feel firm to the touch, about 30 minutes if small, 45 minutes if large. Add more boiling water if needed (the quarter will stop making noise when all the water has evaporated).

8. To serve, remove the twine and place on a plate with the husks opened to expose the *humita*. Serve with a dish of *ají* on the side.

NOTE **If using dried cornhusks, soak them in hot water for a few minutes, dry, and use as instructed.**

Humitas Chilenas

CHILEAN HUMITAS *Makes about 12 humitas, depending on the size of the cornhusks*

These *humitas* resemble those made by the Indians—no eggs or cheese, just some fat, onion, and seasonings added. My addition of cornmeal and beaten egg is to make up for the lack of starch in the corn available in the United States.

> 6 to 8 ears corn (4 cups kernels)
> 6 fresh basil leaves, chopped
> 1 small jalapeño (optional), seeded and minced
> ¼ cup (½ stick) unsalted butter or lard
> 1 medium-size onion, finely chopped (about 1 cup)
> 1 teaspoon salt
> 1 teaspoon sugar
> ¼ teaspoon freshly ground black pepper
> ½ cup cornmeal
> 1 large egg (optional), lightly beaten
> Kitchen twine, cut into twelve 15-inch lengths
> 2 cups water
> *Ají Criollo* (page 333)

1. Have a large pot of water boiling. To remove the husks from the corn, use a sharp, heavy knife to cut through the corncob at the stem end, where the kernels start. Carefully remove the husks. Select the largest for wrapping and blanch in the boiling water for a couple of minutes to make them more pliable. Remove from the water with tongs and set on paper towels to drain. Save the rest to cut into strips for tying or to cover the *humitas* before steaming.

2. With a brush, remove the silk from the corn and rinse. Use the knife to cut the kernels from the cobs (you need 4 cups). Place in a blender or food processor along with the basil and jalapeño (if using) and process until finely ground.

3. Melt the butter in a large, heavy skillet over medium heat. Add the onion and cook, stirring a few times, until transparent, about 3 minutes.

4. Add the salt, sugar, black pepper, and cornmeal to the blender or food processor. Pulse until everything is well incorporated and smooth. The mixture should be thick, not runny. Add more cornmeal if the batter is runny. Add to the onion and cook, stirring constantly, until the mixture is thick, shiny, and separates from the bottom (it should be thick enough to mound). Remove from the heat, let cool to lukewarm, and beat in the egg, if using.

5. To assemble the *humitas*, dry the cornhusks and place 2 on the worktable, overlapping them a little. Place a heaping ½ cup corn batter on the lower half of the husks, fold the left side over the center, fold the pointed end over, and finally fold the right side over toward the center. Tie in the middle with twine or cornhusk strips.

6. Place a quarter in the bottom of a steamer, add the water, and line the steamer basket with small cornhusks. Place a few *humitas* standing open end up in the steamer. Cover with leftover husks and a clean kitchen towel. Place the cover on the pot, bring to a boil, and steam until the *humitas* feel firm to the touch, about 30 minutes if small, 45 minutes if large. Add more boiling water if needed (the quarter will stop making noise when all the water has evaporated).

7. To serve, remove the twine and place on a plate with the husks opened to expose the *humita*. Serve with a dish of *ají* on the side.

NOTE **If using dried cornhusks, soak them in hot water for a few minutes, dry, and use as instructed.**

Huminta en Fuente

BOLIVIAN HUMITA *Serves 8*

In Bolivia, this *huminta* is seasoned with a generous amount of hot pepper sauce. It can be assembled in cornhusks or baked in the oven in a casserole, as in this version. A puree of winter squash or carrots can be added to the corn instead of the cheese. There are many variations, depending on the region and the cook. This can be served as a first course, side dish, or dessert.

> 6 to 8 ears corn (4 cups kernels)
>
> ¾ cup cornmeal
>
> 4 ounces Chihuahua, mozzarella, or Muenster cheese, shredded
>
> ½ cup (1 stick) unsalted butter, melted
>
> 3 large eggs
>
> 1 teaspoon salt
>
> 1 teaspoon plus 2 tablespoons sugar
>
> 1 teaspoon baking powder
>
> Pinch of ground cinnamon, plus more for sprinkling
>
> ½ teaspoon anise seeds
>
> 2 tablespoons *pisco* (page 34)
>
> Hot pepper sauce to taste
>
> 1 large egg, lightly beaten

1.   Husk the corn. With a brush, remove the silk from the corn and rinse. With a sharp, heavy knife, remove the kernels from the cobs (you need 4 cups). Place in a blender or food processor, and process until finely ground. Add the cornmeal, cheese, melted butter, whole eggs, salt, 1 teaspoon of the sugar, the baking powder, cinnamon, anise, *pisco*, and hot pepper sauce. Pulse until well mixed. Taste for salt and sugar.

2.   Preheat the oven to 350°F.

3.   Spread the corn mixture evenly in a well-buttered 9-inch casserole, brush the top with the beaten egg, and sprinkle with the remaining 2 tablespoons sugar and a little cinnamon. Bake until a knife inserted in the center comes out clean, about 30 minutes. Let cool for 5 minutes, slice, and serve.

Humita en Cacerola

ARGENTINE HUMITA CASSEROLE *Serves 4 to 6*

Whether the *humitas* are made on top of the stove or baked in the oven, like this casserole, they are very tasty. This is a wonderful variation.

> 6 to 8 ears corn (4 cups kernels)
>
> ¼ cup (½ stick) unsalted butter
>
> 1 large onion, finely chopped (about 1½ cups)
>
> 1½ cups seeded and finely chopped green or red bell pepper
>
> 1 large ripe but firm tomato (about 8 ounces), peeled, seeded, and chopped
>
> ¾ cup cornmeal
>
> 1 teaspoon salt
>
> 1 teaspoon sugar
>
> ¼ teaspoon freshly grated nutmeg
>
> ¼ teaspoon freshly ground black pepper
>
> 8 fresh basil leaves, chopped
>
> 4 ounces Chihuahua, mozzarella or Muenster cheese, shredded
>
> 3 large eggs, lightly beaten
>
> ¼ cup freshly grated Parmesan cheese

1.   Husk the corn. With a brush, remove the silk from the corn and rinse. With a sharp, heavy knife, remove the kernels from the cobs (you need 4 cups). Place in a blender or food processor and process until finely ground.

2.   Melt the butter in a large, heavy skillet over medium heat. Add the onion and bell pepper and cook, stirring a few times, until softened, about 5 minutes. Add the tomato, reduce the heat to low, cover, and continue to cook until it forms a sauce, about 10 minutes. Stir in the ground corn, cornmeal, salt, sugar, nutmeg, pepper, and basil and

cook, stirring constantly, until thickened enough to form a soft dough, about 5 minutes. Remove from the heat and let cool to lukewarm. Mix in the Chihuahua cheese and eggs and taste for salt and sugar.

3.   Preheat the oven to 350°F.

4.   Transfer the corn mixture to a well-buttered 9-inch casserole (or to individual casseroles), sprinkle evenly with the Parmesan, and bake until lightly browned, about 45 minutes. Serve hot.

NOTE This *humita* can be wrapped in individual cornhusks to make *humitas en chala*, which may be baked or steamed.

Pamonhas de Milho Verde

SWEET CORN AND COCONUT HUMITAS
Makes about 8 pamonhas

Pamonhas de milho verde epitomize the blending of three different cultures from three different continents. The Indians ground their corn, wrapped it in cornhusks, and either steamed the packets or cooked them on hot coals. The Africans incorporated their own coconuts and the Portuguese sugar into the recipe and created one of the first and simplest Brazilian creole specialties.

This type of *humita* has the consistency of a pudding and is eaten with a spoon. It is very difficult to reproduce in the United States with local fresh corn, which does not have enough starch. If one is using coconut milk, a very starchy corn is needed to get a dough that can be wrapped in cornhusks. Fortunately, grated coconut is also used to make *pamonhas*, and I was able to find Brazilian corn in a can. The result is a *humita* with a firmer texture. Also, instead of using fresh cornhusks to make packets that look like little purses, as the Brazilians do, I use Mexican dried cornhusks, which I wrap as for *Humitas Ecuatorianas* (page 87).

8 to 16 dried cornhusks, depending on their size

Two 8-ounce cans Brazilian steamed corn kernels
¼ cup milk
1 cup sweetened shredded coconut
2 to 4 tablespoons sugar, to your taste
Kitchen twine, cut into eight 15-inch lengths
2 cups water

1.   Place the cornhusks in a large bowl and cover with very hot water. Let soak.

2.   Place 1 can of the corn, with the little liquid it has, in a blender and process, adding a little milk at a time, until ground. Add the other can of corn and process until as finely ground as possible. Transfer to a large bowl and add the coconut and 2 tablespoons of the sugar. Taste and add more sugar to get the sweetness desired. (Since the coconut is sweetened and the corn is sweet, the amount of sugar added depends on your taste.)

3.   To assemble the *pamonhas*, drain the cornhusks and dry with paper towels. Place 2 on the worktable, overlapping them a little. Place a heaping ½ cup corn batter on the lower half of the husks, fold the left side over the center, fold the pointed end over, and finally fold the right side over toward the center. Tie with twine or cornhusk strips.

4.   Place a quarter in the bottom of a steamer, add the water, and line the steamer basket with small cornhusks. Place a few *pamonhas* standing open end up in the steamer. Cover with leftover husks and a clean kitchen towel. Place the cover on the pot, bring to a boil, and steam until the *pamonhas* feel firm to the touch, about 30 minutes. Add more boiling water if needed (the quarter will stop making noise when all the water has evaporated).

5.   To serve, remove the twine and place on a plate with the husks opened to expose the *pamonhas*.

Tamales de Coliflor

CAULIFLOWER TAMALES *Makes 10 to 12 tamales*

I never cease to admire the creativity of Latin cooks, especially when it comes to making tamales. This delicious Ecuadorian tamale is not a common one. I ate it many years ago at a farm that had been converted into a restaurant. This tamale is one of those treasures that are becoming increasingly available as people open restaurants using old family recipes. The usual wrapping is *hojas de achira* (edible canna leaves), which are not available in the United States. Instead, use banana leaves or parchment paper.

> 1 medium-size head cauliflower (about 2½ pounds)
>
> 1 teaspoon fresh lemon juice
>
> 1 cup water
>
> 6 tablespoons (¾ stick) unsalted butter, melted
>
> 3 large eggs
>
> ¾ cup cornstarch mixed with 1 teaspoon baking powder, ½ teaspoon salt, and ¼ teaspoon white pepper
>
> 4 ounces fontina cheese, shredded

R E L L E N O (Filling)
> 2 tablespoons canola oil
>
> ½ teaspoon sweet paprika
>
> ⅓ cup chopped scallions (white part and 1 inch of the green)
>
> 1½ cups chopped or shredded cooked chicken breast or roasted pork
>
> ¼ teaspoon ground cumin
>
> ¼ teaspoon salt
>
> ¼ teaspoon freshly ground black pepper
>
> ¼ cup chicken broth, or more if needed

> One 1-pound package frozen banana leaves, prepared per instructions on pages 82–83, or parchment paper, cut into twelve 10 x 12-inch rectangles
>
> 20 to 24 pimento strips

> 10 to 12 black olives, pitted and halved
>
> Aluminum foil, cut into twelve 10 x 12-inch rectangles, or kitchen twine, cut into twelve 30-inch lengths

1.   Remove the florets from the cauliflower; you should have about 1½ pounds trimmed florets. Sprinkle with the lemon juice. Bring the water to a boil in a large saucepan. Add the florets and steam just until tender, about 10 minutes. Do not overcook. Drain well and let cool.

2.   Place the cauliflower in a food processor and coarsely chop. Add the melted butter and eggs and pulse until blended. The mixture should be coarse, not smooth. Add the cornstarch mixture and cheese and pulse just until well mixed. Transfer to a large bowl.

3.   To make the filling, heat the oil in a small skillet over low heat. Stir in the paprika and scallions and cook, stirring, for a couple of minutes. Add the chicken, cumin, salt, pepper, and chicken broth and cook for 5 minutes, adding a little more broth if the mixture is too dry (the filling should be moist). Taste for salt and pepper.

4.   To assemble the tamales, place a banana leaf square on the worktable with the grain running left to right. Place a heaping ½ cup of the cauliflower mixture in the center and flatten it a bit to make a rectangle about 3 to 5 inches long. Press 1 heaping tablespoon of the filling in the center and top with 2 pimento strips and 2 olive halves. Bring the long sides of the banana leaf over the filling. Fold the other ends under the tamale and place folded side down on a piece of aluminum foil, if desired. Fold up the aluminum foil as described on page 83. Or tie the tamale together with twine. (If using parchment paper, tie with twine.)

5.   Place 4 or 5 tamales in a steamer basket and cook for about 30 minutes, per the instructions on pages 83–84. Serve hot.

NOTE These tamales reheat well in the microwave.

Tamales de Mote

HOMINY TAMALES *Makes 10 to 12 tamales*

Tamales de mote are a specialty of the Andean countries. Like many other creole dishes, they vary not only from country to country but also from cook to cook. It is very difficult to give all the variations that I have found in the preparation of the dough and filling. I chose this very special recipe from Ecuador because it makes one of the best tamales I have ever eaten. It is the specialty of a famous caterer in Quito—even her cooks don't know the exact recipe. Aurora, a nurse who was taking care of my father, provided me with the list of ingredients she got from her neighbor, who worked for the caterer. Adding the *ají* and mustard to the dough really makes a difference in the taste—the flavor is subtle, and the texture is very light. In Ecuador, these tamales are wrapped in *achira* (edible canna leaves), but banana leaves are used in the other Andean countries. You also may use parchment paper. No matter how you wrap them, they will be wonderful.

Many people prefer to cook dried corn instead of using canned hominy. The problem with this is that the hilum has to be removed from each kernel of corn. (The hilum is the narrow tip of the corn kernel, where it was attached to the cob. It is called *hembrilla* in Spanish and *shungo* in Quechua.) This is the preferred method in South America, even though it is labor-intensive. Most of the canned hominy available in the United States already has the hilum removed.

RELLENO (Filling)

1 whole bone-in chicken breast (about 1 pound), skin on, poached (page 407)

2 tablespoons canola oil

½ teaspoon ground annatto or sweet paprika

¼ cup finely chopped scallions (white part and 1 inch of the green)

2 tablespoons natural peanut butter

½ cup milk

¼ teaspoon salt

½ teaspoon freshly ground black pepper

MASA (Dough)

Two 15-ounce cans white hominy (without the hilum), drained

4 ounces Chihuahua, mozzarella, or Muenster cheese, shredded

½ cup (1 stick) unsalted butter, softened

4 large eggs, separated (see Notes on page 95)

1 teaspoon fresh hot pepper puree, store-bought or homemade (page 332), or hot pepper sauce

1 teaspoon prepared mustard

1 teaspoon baking powder

½ teaspoon salt

One 1-pound package frozen banana leaves, prepared per instructions on pages 82–83, or parchment paper, cut into twelve 10 x 12-inch rectangles

GARNISHES

3 hard-cooked eggs (optional; see Notes), peeled and quartered

24 pimento-stuffed Spanish olives

½ cup seedless black raisins

4 hot red peppers, seeded, cut into thin strips, blanched in boiling water for 20 seconds, and drained, or 24 pimento strips

12 fresh parsley leaves

Aluminum foil, cut into twelve 10 x 12-inch rectangles, or kitchen twine, cut into twelve 30-inch lengths

1. To make the filling, remove the skin and bones from the chicken breast and discard. Cut the breast into strips about 2 inches long and ½ inch wide.

2. In a medium-size skillet, heat the oil over medium heat. Stir in the annatto and scallions and cook for a few seconds, stirring constantly.

Add the chicken, peanut butter, milk, salt, and black pepper. Stir until the peanut butter has melted, reduce the heat to low, and simmer, uncovered, until the chicken has absorbed most of the liquid, about 5 minutes. Set aside to cool.

3. To make the dough, grind the hominy in a food processor until smooth. Add the cheese and butter and pulse until blended. Add the egg yolks and pulse until well incorporated. Stop as necessary to push the mixture down from the sides. Add the hot pepper puree, mustard, baking powder, and salt. Process for a few seconds, until the mixture is light and fluffy, and transfer to a large bowl. In another large bowl, beat the egg whites with an electric mixer until they form glossy peaks. Fold one-third of the egg whites into the hominy mixture, then carefully fold in the rest.

4. To assemble the tamales, place a banana leaf square on the worktable with the grain running left to right. Place a heaping ½ cup of the hominy mixture in the center and flatten it a bit to make a rectangle measuring about 3 x 5 inches. Top with a wedge of hard-cooked egg, if using, in the center, 2 pieces of chicken on the sides, 2 olives and 2 raisins on each end, and 2 strips of hot pepper, crisscrossed. Place a parsley leaf on top. Bring the long sides of the banana leaf over the filling. Fold the other ends under the tamale and place folded side down on a piece of aluminum foil, if desired. Fold up the aluminum foil as described on page 83. Or tie the tamale together with twine. (If using parchment paper, tie with twine.)

5. Place 4 or 5 in a steamer basket and cook for about 30 minutes, per the instructions on pages 83–84. Serve hot.

NOTES If the tamales are going to be frozen, omit the hard-cooked eggs; they don't freeze well.

Many cooks add beaten whole eggs all at once, thus eliminating the step of beating the egg whites.

Tamales de Yuca

YUCA TAMALES *Makes 8 tamales*

Yuca is very important in the diets of the peoples of Brazil and the Andean countries, especially in the coastal and Amazonian towns. Yuca tamales are found wherever yuca grows, with variations depending on the cook and the region. In Amazonia, yuca is sometimes mixed with corn and coconut milk. Colombians also are fond of using coconut milk to flavor tamales.

RELLENO (Filling)

- 2 tablespoons canola oil
- ½ teaspoon ground annatto or sweet paprika
- 1 medium-size onion, thinly sliced (about 1 cup)
- 1 cup thin green bell pepper strips
- 1 cup thin yellow bell pepper strips
- 1 large ripe but firm tomato (about 8 ounces), peeled and chopped
- 1 clove garlic, mashed into a paste with ½ teaspoon salt and ¼ teaspoon freshly ground black pepper
- 1 teaspoon dried basil

MASA (Dough)

- 1 pound trimmed fresh yuca or frozen yuca, cooked (page 410)
- 6 tablespoons (¾ stick) unsalted butter
- 3 large eggs
- ½ cup freshly grated Parmesan cheese
- ⅓ cup cornstarch
- ½ teaspoon salt
- 1½ teaspoons sugar
- 1 teaspoon baking powder

One 1-pound package frozen banana leaves, prepared per instructions on pages 82–83, or parchment paper, cut into eight 10 x 12-inch rectangles

4 ounces pepperoni (1 to 1½ inches in diameter), sliced into 24 rounds

2 hard-cooked eggs, peeled and each cut into 4 wedges

8 black olives, halved and pitted

Aluminum foil, cut into eight 10 x 12-inch rectangles, or kitchen twine, cut into eight 30-inch lengths

1. To make the filling, heat the oil in a large skillet over medium heat. Add the annatto, onion, bell peppers, and tomato and cook, stirring occasionally, until the tomato has formed a thick sauce, about 10 minutes. Add the garlic paste and basil and cook for 1 minute. Remove from the heat and set aside.

2. To make the dough, mash the yuca with a potato masher. Do not use a food processor, because the yuca will get gummy. Add the butter and beat until smooth. Let cool, then add the eggs one at a time, beating well after each addition. Stir in the Parmesan. In a small bowl, mix together the cornstarch, salt, sugar, and baking powder and fold into the yuca mixture. Taste for salt and sugar.

3. To assemble the tamales, place a banana leaf square on the worktable with the grain running left to right. Put about one-eighth of the dough in the center of the leaf and flatten it a bit to make a rectangle measuring about 3 x 5 inches. Top with about one-eighth of the filling. Place 3 slices of the pepperoni on top of the filling, then 1 egg wedge and 2 olive halves. Bring the long sides of the leaf over the filling. Fold the other ends under the tamale and place folded side down on a piece of aluminum foil, if desired. Fold up the aluminum foil as described on page 83. Or tie the tamale together with twine. (If using parchment paper, tie with twine.)

4. Place 4 tamales in a steamer basket and cook for about 30 minutes, per the instructions on pages 83–84. Serve hot.

Tamales de Papa

POTATO TAMALES *Makes 12 tamales*

I have found this type of tamale only in the highlands of Ecuador. It is an old family recipe and was the specialty of my aunt Michita, who had *una buena mano* (a good hand) for tamales. She usually made these with a filling of chicken seasoned with peanut butter, but any kind of filling could be used, such as pork, tuna, sardines, or chorizo. I decided to innovate and use the Mexican chorizo, which is totally different from the Spanish chorizo used in Ecuador. Both are made with pork and garlic, but Mexican chorizo is seasoned with chili powder and is crumbled, whereas Spanish chorizo is spiced with paprika and is sliced. I think it is a great pairing of flavors and textures.

MASA (Dough)

2 pounds Idaho potatoes

1 clove garlic, peeled

Salt

½ cup (1 stick) unsalted butter, softened

4 ounces Chihuahua, mozzarella, or Muenster cheese, shredded

2 tablespoons all-purpose flour mixed with 2 teaspoons baking powder and ½ teaspoon salt

¼ teaspoon white pepper

4 large eggs, separated

RELLENO (Filling)

One 7½-ounce mild Mexican chorizo

1 medium-size onion, finely chopped (about 1 cup)

12 pimento-stuffed Spanish olives, sliced

¼ cup frozen peas

Two 1-pound packages frozen banana leaves, prepared per instructions on pages 82–83, or parchment paper, cut into twelve 10 x 12-inch rectangles

Aluminum foil, cut into twelve 10 x 12-inch rectangles, or kitchen twine, cut into twelve 30-inch lengths

1.   To make the dough, peel and slice the potatoes, place in a 4-quart saucepan, and add water to cover by 1 inch. Add the garlic and salt to taste and bring to a boil over medium heat. Reduce the heat to low and cook, covered, until tender, about 30 minutes.

2.   Meanwhile, make the filling. Remove the chorizo from its casing and crumble into a heavy 10-inch frying pan over medium heat. Break up the chorizo with a wooden spoon, stirring occasionally. When the chorizo starts to render its fat, about 3 to 4 minutes, stir in the onion. Reduce the heat to medium-low and continue to cook, stirring occasionally, until the onion is transparent. Add the olives and peas and mix well. Transfer to a large bowl and set aside to cool.

3.   Drain the potatoes well and mash with a potato masher. Add the butter, cheese, flour mixture, and pepper and mix until well blended. Season with salt to taste. In a large bowl with an electric mixer, beat the egg whites until they form soft peaks. While still beating, add the egg yolks, one at a time, beating well after each addition. Fold one-third of the eggs into the potato mixture, then carefully fold in the rest of the beaten eggs. Taste for salt.

4.   To assemble the tamales, place a banana leaf square on the worktable with the grain running left to right. Spread about 2 heaping tablespoons of the dough in the center of the leaf to make a rectangle measuring about 3 x 5 inches. Make a slight indentation in the center and put 2 table-spoons of the filling in it. Bring the long sides of the leaf over the filling. Fold the other ends under the tamale and place folded side down on a piece of aluminum foil, if desired. Fold up the aluminum foil as described on page 83. Or tie the tamale together with twine. (If using parchment paper, tie with twine.)

5.   Place 4 tamales in a steamer basket and cook for about 30 minutes, per the instructions on pages 83–84. Serve hot.

Tamales de Arroz

RICE TAMALES WITH CHICKEN FILLING
Makes 10 to 12 tamales

Rice tamales are very popular in Ecuador and Colombia. Each country has a special way of making them. In Colombia, the rice is usually cooked in coconut milk, and the filling is made with whole (bone-in) pieces of chicken and pork, diced cooked potatoes, and sometimes chickpeas. The version here comes from Ecuador and is suitable for any special occasion. The filling can be made with chicken or pork. The saffron lends an elegant touch, but it is not traditional.

R E L L E N O   (Filling)

   2 tablespoons canola oil

   1 teaspoon *Manteca de Color* (page 331) or sweet paprika

   1 medium-size onion, minced (about 1 cup)

   1 clove garlic, mashed into a paste with ½ teaspoon salt and ¼ teaspoon freshly ground black pepper

   ¼ teaspoon ground cumin

   1 medium-size ripe but firm tomato (5 to 6 ounces), peeled and chopped

   1½ cups shredded cooked chicken or turkey

   ½ cup frozen peas

   2 tablespoons chopped pimentos

MASA (Dough)

1 cup long-grain rice

3 cups water

¾ teaspoon salt

¼ teaspoon white pepper

¼ teaspoon saffron threads, crumbled

6 tablespoons (¾ stick) unsalted butter, softened

4 ounces Chihuahua, mozzarella, or Muenster cheese, shredded

2 tablespoons freshly grated Parmesan cheese

3 large eggs, separated

1 teaspoon baking powder

1 teaspoon sugar

Two 1-pound packages frozen banana leaves, prepared per instructions on pages 82–83, or parchment paper, cut into twelve 10 x 12-inch rectangles

GARNISHES

12 pimento-stuffed Spanish olives

24 seedless golden raisins

12 fresh parsley leaves

Aluminum foil, cut into twelve 10 x 12-inch rectangles, or kitchen twine, cut into twelve 30-inch lengths

1. To make the filling, heat the oil in a large, heavy skillet over medium heat. Add the *manteca de color* and onion and cook, stirring, for 5 minutes. Stir in the garlic paste and cumin, then add the tomato and chicken. Cover and cook over low heat, stirring occasionally, until most of the liquid has evaporated but the mixture is still moist, about 5 minutes. Mix in the peas and pimentos and season with salt and black pepper to taste. Transfer to a 9-inch plate and set aside.

2. To make the dough, place the rice and water in a 4-quart saucepan. Cook, uncovered, over medium-low heat until the water is absorbed, about 20 minutes. Remove from the heat, cover, and let sit for 5 minutes. Transfer to a food processor and let cool. Add the salt, white pepper, saffron, butter, Chihuahua cheese, Parmesan, egg yolks, baking powder, and sugar and process until smooth. In a medium-size bowl with an electric mixer, beat the egg whites until they form soft peaks, then fold them into the rice mixture. Transfer to a 9-inch pie plate.

3. To assemble the tamales, use a knife or spatula to cut the dough into 10 to 12 wedges. Do the same with the filling. Place a banana leaf square on the worktable with the grain running left to right. Place 1 wedge of dough in the center and spread into a 3 x 5-inch rectangle. Top with a wedge of the filling and garnish with 1 olive, 2 raisins, and 1 parsley leaf. Bring the long sides of the leaf over the filling. Fold the other ends under the tamale and place folded side down on a piece of aluminum foil, if desired. Fold up the aluminum foil as described on page 83. Or tie the tamale together with twine. (If using parchment paper, tie with twine.)

4. Place 4 tamales in a steamer basket and cook for about 30 minutes, per the instructions on pages 83–84. Serve hot.

Tamales de Verde

GREEN PLANTAIN AND SHRIMP TAMALES
Makes 10 to 12 tamales

This type of tamale is typical of the Pacific coast of Ecuador and Colombia, where plantains are the staff of life. There are many regional variations of this dish. In Colombia, the plantains are usually cooked in coconut milk, and the filling is made with potatoes and pieces of cooked ribs and chicken seasoned with *sofrito* (an onion-based flavoring). This Ecuadorian version is quite elegant and should be eaten within two days of being made.

1 pound medium-size shrimp, unpeeled

4 cups water

RELLENO (Filling)

2 tablespoons olive oil

1 teaspoon *Manteca de Color* (page 331) or sweet paprika

1 medium-size onion, finely chopped (about 1 cup)

½ cup seeded and chopped green bell pepper

½ cup seeded and chopped red bell pepper

2 large cloves garlic, mashed into a paste with ½ teaspoon salt and ½ teaspoon freshly ground black pepper

½ teaspoon ground cumin

1 large ripe but firm tomato (about 8 ounces), peeled and diced

2 tablespoons chopped fresh parsley leaves

2 tablespoons chopped fresh cilantro leaves

¼ cup pimento-stuffed Spanish olives, sliced

½ cup milk

2 tablespoons natural peanut butter

MASA (Dough)

2 large green plantains

1 cup milk

½ teaspoon salt

½ cup all-purpose flour

6 tablespoons (¾ stick) unsalted butter

3 large eggs

Two 1-pound packages frozen banana leaves, prepared per instructions on pages 82–83, or parchment paper, cut into twelve 10 x 12-inch rectangles

GARNISHES

2 hard-cooked eggs, peeled and sliced

12 hot red pepper strips, blanched in boiling water for 20 seconds and drained

Aluminum foil, cut into twelve 10 x 12-inch rectangles, or kitchen twine, cut into twelve 30-inch lengths

1. Peel and devein the shrimp, reserving the shells. Refrigerate the shrimp until needed. Place the shells and water in a 2-quart saucepan, bring to a boil, reduce the heat to medium, and cook, uncovered, for 15 minutes. Remove from the heat, let cool for 10 minutes, and transfer to a blender. Process for 5 seconds, strain through a fine-mesh strainer, and set aside.

2. To make the filling, heat the oil in a large, heavy skillet over medium heat. Add the *manteca de color*, onion, bell peppers, garlic paste, cumin, tomato, parsley, cilantro, and olives and cook, stirring occasionally, until thickened, about 10 minutes. Stir in the milk and peanut butter and cook, stirring constantly, until well blended and thickened, about 5 minutes. Season with salt and black pepper to taste. Stir in the shrimp and cook for 30 seconds. Remove from the heat and set aside.

3. To make the dough, peel the plantains, slice, and place in a food processor or blender. Process until pureed, then add 2 cups of the shrimp broth and process until smooth. If using a blender, do this in batches, adding some of the broth to each batch. Transfer to a heavy casserole and mix with the milk, salt, flour, and butter. Cook over medium heat, stirring until it thickens and forms a dough that pulls away from the side and bottom of the pan. Remove from the heat and let cool to lukewarm. Beat in the eggs one at a time.

4. To assemble the tamales, place a banana leaf square on the worktable with the grain running left to right. Spread about 3 heaping tablespoons of the dough in the center of the leaf about ½ inch thick. Top with about 2 tablespoons of the filling, 1 slice of egg, and 1 hot pepper strip. Bring the long sides of the leaf over the filling. Fold the other ends under the tamale and place folded side down on a piece of aluminum foil, if desired. Fold up the aluminum foil as described on page 83. Or tie the tamale together with twine. (If using parchment paper, tie with twine.)

5. Place 4 tamales in a steamer basket and cook for about 45 minutes, per the instructions on pages 83–84. Serve hot.

Tamales Colombianos de Calabaza

COLOMBIAN SQUASH TAMALES

Makes about 14 tamales

Colombians use corn in many different ways to make tamales. Some recipes start with dried corn—soaking, precooking, and even aging it. Other recipes, like this one, use *arepa* flour to make the dough, which is mixed with the filling. Squash is often mixed with the tamale dough in other Andean countries as well.

R E L L E N O (Filling)

2 tablespoons canola oil

12 ounces lean pork shoulder, trimmed of fat and cut into ½-inch cubes

2 medium-size onions, finely chopped (about 2 cups)

4 cloves garlic, mashed into a paste with 1 teaspoon salt and ¼ teaspoon freshly ground black pepper

2 large ripe but firm tomatoes (about 1 pound), peeled and chopped

1½ cups water

M A S A (Dough)

12 ounces calabaza or other winter squash, peeled, seeded, and cut into large chunks

1 cup peeled and diced (¼ inch) red potatoes

1 medium-size carrot, sliced ⅛ inch thick

1½ cups *arepa* flour (page 417), or more if needed

1½ cups hot water, or more if needed

Two 1-pound packages frozen banana leaves, prepared per instructions on pages 82–83, or parchment paper, cut into fourteen 10 x 12-inch rectangles

Aluminum foil, cut into fourteen 10 x 12-inch rectangles, or kitchen twine, cut into fourteen 30-inch lengths

1. To make the filling, heat the oil in a 4-quart saucepan over medium-low heat. Add the pork, onions, garlic paste, and tomatoes. Cover and cook for 20 minutes, stirring occasionally. Add the water, reduce the heat to low, and continue to cook until the pork is very tender, about 20 minutes more. If the mixture has too much liquid, cook, uncovered, until reduced to a thick sauce. Season generously with salt and pepper to taste.

2. Meanwhile, make the dough. Place the squash and salted water to cover in a medium-size saucepan, cover, and cook over medium heat until tender, about 20 minutes. Drain well and coarsely mash with a fork. In another medium-size saucepan, cook the potatoes and carrots in salted water to cover over medium heat until tender, about 15 minutes. Drain and set aside.

3. When the pork is done, mix the *arepa* flour and hot water together in a large bowl. Knead for a few minutes to make a soft dough. Add the squash and knead until smooth. Add the pork, potatoes, and carrots and mix well. The mixture should be moist and stiff enough to mound. If it is too dry, add a little more hot water. If it is too moist, add a little more *arepa* flour. Season with salt and pepper to taste, mixing thoroughly. It should taste a little overseasoned.

4. To assemble the tamales, place a banana leaf square on the worktable with the grain running left to right. Spread about ¾ cup of the pork mixture in the center of the leaf about ¾ inch thick.

Bring the long sides of the leaf over the filling. Fold the other ends under the tamale and place folded side down on a piece of aluminum foil, if desired. Fold up the aluminum foil as described on page 83. Or tie the tamale together with twine. (If using parchment paper, tie with twine.)

5.   Place 4 tamales in a steamer basket and cook for about 45 minutes, per the instructions on pages 83–84. Serve hot.

NOTE These tamales freeze well and reheat well in the microwave.

Quimbolitos

SWEET TAMALES *Makes 10 to 12 tamales*

Quimbolitos are the classic sweet tamales of Ecuador. They can also be found in Nariño, Colombia, which was part of what is now Ecuador during colonial times. *Quimbolitos* are served for dessert or as a snack with a cup of coffee. They also make a wonderful breakfast treat. The ingredients are fairly universal, except for the type of flour and fat. Many cooks prefer to make them with wheat flour only, while others prefer a combination of flour and cornstarch. In Colombia, these tamales are made with cornmeal. Most people still use a combination of lard and butter for fat. When I was visiting my father in Ecuador in the late 1990s, Maria, one of his nurses, made these *quimbolitos* for me because, she said, they were her specialty. Maria grew up in a small town, where cooking traditions are followed more than in the bigger cities and everyone has a specialty to show off. Maria used only wheat flour, but I prefer to combine wheat flour and cornmeal.

1 cup (2 sticks) unsalted butter, softened

¾ cup plus 2 tablespoons sugar

6 large eggs, separated

6 ounces Chihuahua, mozzarella, or Muenster cheese, shredded

½ cup cornmeal

1 cup all-purpose flour

1 teaspoon baking powder

1 tablespoon grated lemon zest

½ teaspoon anise seeds, crushed

2 tablespoons brandy or anise liqueur

Pinch of salt

One 1-pound package frozen banana leaves, prepared per instructions on pages 82–83, or parchment paper, cut into twelve 10 x 12-inch rectangles

GARNISH

Seedless black raisins

Aluminum foil, cut into twelve 10 x 12-inch rectangles, or kitchen twine, cut into twelve 30-inch lengths

1.   In a large bowl with an electric mixer, cream the butter and ¾ cup of the sugar together until light. Add the egg yolks one at a time and beat until light and fluffy. Stir in the cheese, cornmeal, flour, baking powder, zest, anise, and brandy. Wash and dry the beaters.

2.   In another large bowl, beat the egg whites and salt until they form soft peaks. Beat in the remaining 2 tablespoons sugar, 1 tablespoon at a time, and continue to beat until glossy peaks form. Fold one-third of the mixture into the batter, then gently fold in the rest.

3.   To assemble the *quimbolitos*, place a banana leaf square on the worktable with the grain running left to right. Spread about ¾ cup of the cheese mixture in the center of the leaf about ¾ inch thick. Place 3 or 4 raisins on top of the batter. Bring the long sides of the leaf together over the filling. Fold the other ends under the tamale and place folded side down on a piece of aluminum foil, if desired. Fold up the aluminum foil as described on page 83. Or tie the tamale together with twine. (If using parchment paper, tie with twine.)

4. Place 4 tamales in a steamer basket and cook for about 20 minutes, per the instructions on pages 83–84. Serve hot.

Huminta de Quinua al Horno

BAKED QUINOA TAMALE *Serves 8 to 9*

This Bolivian tamale can be made wrapped in cornhusks or, as in this version, baked in a casserole, which is a lot simpler than wrapping individual tamales. Peruvians and Ecuadorians also make quinoa tamales with different kinds of fillings, such as pork, chicken, or shrimp. The hot pepper puree is an important ingredient in the tamales of Peru and Bolivia; it gives the dish a special character. Serve this as an appetizer or as a side dish with grilled poultry or fish.

1 cup quinoa, cooked and steamed dry (page 327)

¼ cup (½ stick) unsalted butter

1 medium-size onion, minced (about 1 cup)

½ cup half-and-half

3 large eggs, lightly beaten

1 teaspoon salt

2 teaspoons sugar

½ teaspoon anise seeds, crushed

½ teaspoon ground cinnamon

1 tablespoon fresh hot pepper puree, store-bought or homemade (page 332), or hot pepper sauce to taste

4 ounces jalapeño or plain Chihuahua, mozzarella, or Muenster cheese, shredded

¼ cup freshly grated Parmesan cheese

1. Preheat the oven to 350°F.

2. Place the quinoa in a food processor and pulse for a few seconds, until coarsely ground. Melt the butter in a small skillet over low heat. Add the onion and cook, stirring, until transparent, about 3 minutes. Add to the quinoa along with the half-and-half, eggs, salt, sugar, anise, cinnamon, hot pepper puree, and Chihuahua cheese. Pulse until well mixed, then taste for salt.

3. Transfer the mixture to a well-buttered 9-inch square baking dish, sprinkle the Parmesan evenly over the top, and bake until golden brown, about 45 minutes. Let rest for 10 minutes before cutting into 9 squares.

Pastas de Sal

SAVORY PASTRIES

THERE IS A CONTROVERSY GOING on among some South American countries as to who created empanadas. Brazilians credit empanadas to the Portuguese, who first brought them to Brazil. In 1692, Rodrigues Domingo, the master cook for the king of Portugal, published a cookbook in Lisbon that had 88 recipes for empanadas and other savory pastries, such as tarts and pies. These pastries are a very important part of the famous Brazilian appetizers called *salgadinhos* (salty things).

Others believe that the Spaniards brought empanadas to South America. "La Molina," the maid of the Infanta María Teresa (a Spanish princess), is credited with inventing a special dough called *hojaldre* (puff pastry), with which she made *pastelitos* (pastries) filled with highly seasoned minced meat.

I am inclined to believe that both stories are correct. Puff pastry is widely used in South America, and pastry shops there carry a tremendous variety of sweet and savory pastries made with this dough. But this is just one of the types of dough used in making savory pastries. Every country has its specialty. Colombians and Venezuelans use cornmeal, yuca flour, and wheat flour in their dough. In Ecuador, empanadas can be made with dough fashioned from dried white corn, rice, or green plantains, and they are usually filled with cheese or seasoned ground beef or pork. Brazil also has many types of dough, and fillings range from cheese or hearts of palm to seafood, meat, or chicken. Argentina has a rich variety of savory pastries, each named after its town of origin, such as *empanadas de Tucumán* and *empanadas de Córdoba*. The dough is mostly made with wheat flour and either lard or butter, and the filling can be meat, fowl, shellfish, cheese, or vegetables.

Empanadas al Horno

BAKED TURNOVERS *Makes 12 main course empanadas*

While I was in Santiago, Chile, I was told that the celebration of Independence Day, September 18, is practically synonymous with empanadas and *chicha* (a fermented drink, made with grapes in this case). Luckily, this is not the only day when empanadas are enjoyed. Empanadas can be found in sit-down and carryout restaurants, as well as at home, any time of the day or year. I was also told that the poet Pablo Neruda loved empanadas so much that his major preoccupation five days before his death was with the empanadas he had ordered from his favorite restaurant. When they arrived, he ate them with gusto in the company of good friends.

On the way to the wineries outside Santiago, there are little huts where wonderful bread and empanadas are baked in beehive ovens. For a special treat, Chileans take a bottle of wine, a few empanadas, and a *tortilla de rescoldo* (a round, flat bread made with flour, lard, and fried pork rind) and have a picnic along the road.

This empanada is called *caldúa* (soupy) and is the most popular Chilean specialty. The name *caldúa* comes from the juicy, cumin-seasoned filling that is cooked with broth; the meat and onions absorb some of the liquid to keep the filling moist.

RELLENO (Filling)

2 tablespoons canola oil

3 medium-size onions, chopped (about 3 cups)

2 cloves garlic, minced

1 teaspoon salt

12 ounces lean ground beef

2 teaspoons sweet paprika

2 teaspoons ground cumin

½ teaspoon dried oregano, crumbled

½ teaspoon freshly ground black pepper

Hot pepper sauce of your choice

1 cup beef broth

1 tablespoon all-purpose flour

MASA (Dough)

4 cups all-purpose flour

1 tablespoon baking powder

1 teaspoon salt

1 cup vegetable shortening

1 cup warm milk

1 large egg white lightly beaten with 1 tablespoon water

12 pitted black olives, sliced

2 hard-cooked eggs, peeled and sliced

¼ cup seedless black raisins (optional)

1. To make the filling, heat the oil in a large skillet over medium heat. Add the onions and cook, stirring a few times, until transparent, about 5 minutes. Stir in the garlic and salt and cook for 30 seconds. Increase the heat to medium-high, add the beef, and cook, stirring constantly, until it loses its pink color. Stir in the paprika, cumin, oregano, black pepper, and hot pepper sauce to taste and cook for a couple of minutes. Add the beef broth and cook for a few minutes, until the meat absorbs some of the liquid. Sprinkle in the flour, stir, and cook until thickened. The mixture should be soupy. Let cool, cover with plastic wrap, and refrigerate overnight to let the flavors develop.

2. To make the dough, put the flour, baking powder, and salt in a food processor and process for 5 seconds. Add the shortening and process until the mixture looks like cornmeal. With the machine running, add the warm milk through the feed tube and process until the dough almost gathers into a ball. Transfer to a floured board and knead for a few seconds. Cover with plastic wrap and let rest for 30 minutes.

3. Form the dough into a log and cut into 12 portions. On a lightly floured board, roll each portion into a 6-inch circle. Lightly brush the edge of half of the circle with the egg white mixture. Place about 2 heaping tablespoons of the filling in the center, top with a few slices of olives, a slice of egg, and a few raisins (if using). Fold half of the circle over to form a half-moon and press the edges together firmly. Brush the top with the egg white mixture. Fold the rounded edge over ½ inch, making 3 separate folds—one on each side, then one on the bottom—to create a trapezoid shape. Brush the folds with the egg white mixture and place on a lightly greased baking sheet. Repeat with the remaining dough and filling.

4. Preheat the oven to 375°F.

5. Pierce the tops of the empanadas once with a fork and bake until lightly colored, about 20 minutes. Be careful not to overbake. Remove from the oven and let cool for 5 minutes before serving.

NOTE These empanadas freeze very well unbaked. When freezing, omit the hard-cooked eggs, because they will become rubbery. Freeze on baking sheets lined with waxed paper until hard, then store in covered containers. You can pop them into the oven frozen; just increase the baking time by 5 minutes.

VARIATION You can make hors d'oeuvre–size empanadas by dividing each piece of dough into 4 smaller pieces and rolling each into a 3-inch circle, then proceeding as directed above. Instead of adding sliced egg to the top of the filling, chop the egg and mix it into the filling. Reduce the baking time by about 5 minutes.

Empanadas de Hongos

MUSHROOM TURNOVERS
Makes 12 main course empanadas

This was one of my mother's favorite first courses for dinner parties. Of course, the puff pastry was always made at home. I remember my younger sister Ximena loved to make puff pastry; I think she was 10 years old when she learned how to make this dough. These empanadas were also a favorite of my cooking class students, and they are always a treat for family and friends. The bonus is that they freeze beautifully. To accommodate today's busy schedules, I often rely on ready-made puff pastry, as in this version of the dish.

RELLENO (Filling)

¼ cup (½ stick) unsalted butter

1 pound fresh, firm white mushrooms, wiped clean with a damp cloth or paper towel and finely chopped

¼ cup chopped scallions (white part and 1 inch of the green)

¼ cup whipping cream

½ teaspoon salt

¼ teaspoon freshly ground black pepper

Pinch of freshly grated nutmeg

2 tablespoons day-old bread crumbs (page 413)

2 tablespoons finely chopped fresh parsley leaves or dill

8 ounces cheddar cheese, shredded

2 packages Pepperidge Farm frozen puff pastry shells, thawed

1 large egg lightly beaten with 1 tablespoon water

1. To make the filling, melt the butter in a large skillet over medium heat. Add the mushrooms and scallions and cook, stirring, until all the liquid from the mushrooms has evaporated. Add the cream, and cook until reduced enough to just coat the mushrooms. Remove from the heat and add the salt, pepper, and nutmeg. Toss with the bread crumbs and parsley. Let cool, then stir in the cheese.

2. Remove 1 pastry shell and roll it out on a lightly floured work surface into a 5- to 6-inch circle. Place 2 heaping tablespoons of the filling in the center of the circle and lightly moisten the edge of half of the circle with the egg mixture. Fold the round in half and press firmly to seal the edges. Crimp the edge with a fork dipped in flour and pierce the top with a fork to allow steam to escape. Repeat with the remaining shells and filling, then refrigerate for 30 minutes before baking.

3. Preheat the oven to 375°F.

4. Brush the empanadas with the egg mixture and bake on the upper oven rack until golden brown, about 25 minutes. Let cool for a few minutes before serving.

NOTE These empanadas freeze very well unbaked. Freeze on baking sheets lined with waxed paper until hard, then store in covered containers. You can pop them into the oven frozen; just increase the baking time by 5 minutes.

Empanadas de Viento

WIND TURNOVERS

Makes 8 large or 24 small empanadas

These delicious empanadas from the highlands of Ecuador are very light, hence their name. They can be made in cocktail size or appetizer size. They are a must when preparing a meal around *fritada* (fried chunks of pork), or with *fanesca* (a vegetable stew with cod). Many restaurants in Quito serve these empanadas with *cebiches* for a midday snack or lunch. In Cuenca, a city in the southern part of Ecuador, a popular and unusual version of these empanadas is filled with white cheese, mashed ripe banana, and a little brown sugar. During religious holidays, country women fry these empanadas in front of the churches, and they are indeed puffy and light like the wind.

MASA (Dough)

2 cups all-purpose flour

1 teaspoon baking powder

1 teaspoon salt

¼ cup lard, vegetable shortening, or unsalted butter

¼ cup water mixed with 1 tablespoon fresh lemon juice

RELLENO (Filling)

4 ounces jalapeño or plain Chihuahua, mozzarella, or Muenster cheese, shredded

¼ cup minced scallions (white part and 1 inch of the green)

½ teaspoon ground annatto or sweet paprika

Peanut oil for frying

Sugar (optional) for sprinkling

1. To make the dough, sift together the flour, baking powder, and salt in a large bowl. Add the

lard and blend together with your fingers to make a coarse meal. Add the lemon water and mix well, adding a little more water if needed to make a soft dough. Knead until smooth and elastic. Cover with plastic wrap and let rest for 30 minutes.

To make the dough in a food processor, pulse the flour, baking powder, salt, and lard together to get a coarse meal. With the machine running, add the lemon water through the feed tube and process until the dough forms a ball. Knead just a couple of times.

2. To make the filling, combine all the ingredients in a medium-size bowl.

3. Divide the dough into 8 or 24 equal-size pieces. Roll the pieces into balls and cover with plastic wrap. On a lightly floured board, roll each ball into a thin round. Put 1 heaping tablespoon of the filling in the center for large empanadas and 1 teaspoon for small. Lightly moisten half of the edge with water. Fold in half, pressing firmly to seal the edges; crimp with a fork. Place the empanadas on a lightly floured tray and cover with a kitchen towel. These can be assembled a couple of hours before frying and left at room temperature.

4. In an electric skillet, heat ½ inch of the oil to 350°F. Fry a few empanadas at a time, carefully swishing the oil back and forth with a large spoon so that they puff up. Cook for a few minutes, until golden on both sides. Remove with a slotted spoon to a platter lined with paper towels. Serve immediately plain or, in the traditional manner, sprinkled with sugar.

Empadinhas de Siri

CRABMEAT TARTS *Makes 24 tarts*

Empadas (pies) and *pastéis* (turnovers) are among the famous Brazilian appetizers called *salgadinhos* (salty things). *Empadas* are made in different sizes, with the small ones called *empadinhas*. These very delicate tarts can be found throughout Brazil, with fillings such as shellfish, chicken, cheese, hearts of palm, and vegetables. They are delicious and freeze very well. Good-quality canned crabmeat works well for this recipe.

RELLENO (Filling)
 2 tablespoons olive oil
 ½ small onion, minced (about ¼ cup)
 3 cloves garlic, mashed into a paste with ½ teaspoon finely crumbled bay leaf and 1 teaspoon salt
 1 tablespoon seeded and minced green bell pepper
 1 tablespoon seeded and minced red bell pepper
 1 tablespoon minced fresh parsley leaves
 2 teaspoons grated lime zest
 8 ounces crabmeat, picked over for shells and cartilage
 ¼ teaspoon red pepper flakes
 2 tablespoons fresh lime juice
 1½ tablespoons all-purpose flour
 ½ cup milk

MASA (Dough)
 6 tablespoons (¾ stick) cold unsalted butter
 1½ cups all-purpose flour
 ½ teaspoon salt
 2 large egg yolks
 3 tablespoons cold water

 Freshly grated Parmesan cheese

1. To make the filling, heat the oil in a medium-size frying pan over low heat. Add the onion, garlic paste, bell peppers, parsley, and zest. Cook until the onion is transparent, about 4 minutes, stirring a few times with a wooden spoon. Add the crabmeat, red pepper flakes, and lime juice and cook until most of the liquid has evaporated. Sprinkle in the flour, mixing well. Add the milk

and cook, stirring, to obtain a creamy consistency. Remove from the heat and let cool.

2. To make the dough, cut the butter into small pieces, place in a medium-size bowl, and add the remaining ingredients. Mix with your hands, handling the dough just until it gathers into a ball. Add a few drops of water if it is too dry. Shape into 2 logs about 1 inch in diameter and cut each into 12 pieces. Using your fingers, fit each piece into a 1½-inch muffin cup or mold. Or using a small rolling pin on a lightly floured surface, roll each piece into a 3-inch round to fit into the cup or mold. With a knife, cut off the dough that extends beyond the edge of the cup. Fill the cups with the crabmeat mixture and sprinkle with the Parmesan. The filled tarts can be frozen for up to 2 months.

3. Preheat the oven to 375°F.

4. Bake the tarts on the lower oven rack until the crust is lightly golden, about 15 minutes. If frozen, increase the baking time by 5 minutes. Remove from the oven and let cool for a few minutes before removing the tarts from the cups with a small rubber spatula. Transfer to a platter and serve.

Pasteos de Aipim e Camarão

YUCA AND SHRIMP TURNOVERS

Makes about 24 turnovers

These turnovers are one of Brazil's favorite *salgadinhos* (salty things), common throughout the country, and they will become one of your favorites, too. The unusual dough is made with fresh yuca, the beloved tuber of Brazil. There *malagueta* peppers are used to spike the filling, but here we use the much milder jalapeño pepper instead. Make these turnovers ahead and keep them in the freezer for special occasions.

M A S A (Dough)

8 ounces trimmed fresh yuca or frozen yuca, cooked (page 410)

¾ cup (1½ sticks) unsalted butter, softened

1¾ cups all-purpose flour mixed with 2 teaspoons baking powder and 1 teaspoon salt

R E L L E N O (Filling)

1 pound small shrimp, peeled, deveined, and sliced ¼ inch thick

1 tablespoon fresh lime juice

1 tablespoon *dendê* (page 422)

2 tablespoons minced shallots

1 large clove garlic, minced

2 tablespoons all-purpose flour

½ cup well-stirred canned unsweetened coconut milk

1 jalapeño (optional), seeded and minced

1 teaspoon salt

3 tablespoons minced fresh cilantro leaves

1 large egg lightly beaten with 1 tablespoon water

1. To make the dough, remove the fibers from the cooked yuca and mash with a potato masher. (Don't use a food processor for this or the yuca will become gummy.) In a large bowl, mix the yuca puree with the butter and flour mixture, kneading gently to get a smooth dough and adding a little more flour if it is too sticky. Cover with plastic wrap and let rest for 30 minutes.

2. Meanwhile, make the filling. Place the shrimp in a large bowl and pour the lime juice over them. Let stand for 15 minutes. Heat the *dendê* in a 9-inch skillet over medium heat. Add the shallots and garlic and cook, stirring, for 2 to 3 minutes. Add the shrimp and cook over high heat until they begin to turn pink. Sprinkle in the flour and mix. Reduce the heat to low, and cook, stirring with a wooden spoon, for a couple of

minutes. Add the coconut milk and bring to a boil. Simmer until thickened, about 2 minutes; it will set when cooled. Stir in the jalapeño (if using), salt, and cilantro. Remove from the heat and let cool.

3. Preheat the oven to 400°F.

4. To assemble the turnovers, roll out the dough on a lightly floured surface to about ⅛ inch thick. Cut into 3-inch squares. Place 1 tablespoon of the filling in the center of each square, fold over in a triangular shape, and press the edges together with your fingers to seal. Brush with the egg mixture and bake in the upper third of the oven until golden, about 15 minutes. Serve hot.

NOTE **These turnovers freeze very well unbaked. Freeze on baking sheets lined with waxed paper until hard, then transfer to covered containers. You can pop them into the oven frozen; just increase the baking time by 5 minutes.**

Salteñas de Pollo

BOLIVIAN CHICKEN TURNOVERS *Makes 24 turnovers*

Salteñas are practically synonymous with Bolivia. These highly seasoned meat and vegetable turnovers are found throughout the country. They are usually served as a snack anytime during the day, though especially in the morning. There are many variations, depending on the region. The most popular versions are made with chicken or beef, or a combination of both. Turnovers made with cheese or vegetables also are wonderful. Whether they are served in restaurants or at home to welcome visitors, they are an exquisite way for Bolivians to show their hospitality. *Salteñas* have a definite bite, imparted by the *ají colorado* (hot red pepper) that Bolivians use in generous amounts. For the sake of expediency, I chose to use red pepper flakes instead.

The day before making the turnovers, make the filling. In Bolivia, the broth is usually made with beef bones or cow's feet to get the gelatin needed. I have found that chicken wings or, even better, chicken feet, work very well. You also can use commercial chicken broth to poach the chicken breast. If you do, after poaching soften one envelope of unflavored gelatin in two tablespoons cold water, then add to the hot broth.

RELLENO (Filling)

1 whole bone-in chicken breast (about 1 pound), skin on

6 chicken feet or wings

1 medium-size onion, peeled

1½ teaspoons salt

2 tablespoons canola oil

2 medium-size onions, minced (about 2 cups)

1 teaspoon ground annatto or sweet paprika

2 cloves garlic, minced

½ cup minced scallions (white part and 1 inch of the green)

¼ cup minced fresh parsley leaves

1 teaspoon ground cumin

½ teaspoon ground allspice

1 teaspoon dried oregano, crumbled

¼ teaspoon freshly ground black pepper

¾ teaspoon red pepper flakes, or more to taste

1 teaspoon sugar

¼ cup dry white wine or dry sherry

¾ cup peeled and diced (¼ inch) red potatoes, cooked in water to cover until tender and drained

½ cup frozen peas

½ cup finely chopped cooked carrots

MASA (Dough)

4½ cups all-purpose flour

1 teaspoon baking powder

1 tablespoon sugar

1 teaspoon salt

1 cup lard or vegetable shortening

1 large egg lightly beaten with 1 tablespoon milk or water

2 hard-cooked eggs (optional), peeled and sliced

24 pimento-stuffed Spanish olives, halved

¼ cup seedless golden raisins

2 large egg yolks lightly beaten with 2 tablespoons milk

1. To make the filling, place all the chicken and the whole onion in a 4-quart saucepan. Add water to cover and 1 teaspoon of the salt. Bring to a boil over medium heat, skimming off the froth as it rises to the top. Reduce the heat to low and simmer, partially covered, for 30 minutes. Remove the chicken breast and discard the feet and onion. When the breast is cool enough to handle, remove the skin and bones and discard. Chop the meat coarsely—you should have about 1½ cups—and set aside. Strain the chicken broth, degrease, and reduce over medium-high heat to about 2 cups.

2. Heat the oil in a large skillet over medium heat. Add the minced onions, and cook, stirring a few times, until transparent, about 5 minutes. Stir in the annatto, garlic, scallions, parsley, cumin, allspice, oregano, black pepper, red pepper, remaining ½ teaspoon salt, and sugar and cook for a couple of minutes. Add the chicken broth and wine and cook for 5 minutes. Remove from the heat and add the chicken, potatoes, peas, and carrots. Mix well and taste for salt and red pepper. The mixture should be very soupy; it will set when chilled. Let cool, cover with plastic wrap, and refrigerate overnight.

3. To make the dough, place the flour, baking powder, sugar, and salt in a large bowl or food processor. With a pastry blender or by pulsing, blend the ingredients together. Add the lard and

blend with your fingers or process until the mixture resembles coarse meal. Add the egg mixture and knead or process until smooth. Cover with plastic wrap and let rest for 30 minutes.

4. Preheat the oven to 375°F.

5. To assemble the turnovers, turn the dough out onto a lightly floured surface. Cut into 4 equal pieces and roll each piece into a log. Divide each log into 6 pieces. Roll each piece into an oval measuring about 4½ x 6 inches. Place 2 heaping tablespoons of the filling in the center and top with a slice of egg (if using), 2 olive halves, and a couple of raisins. Moisten the edge of half of the oval with the egg mixture, bring up both sides of the dough, press firmly to seal, then twist the corners and turn under to prevent the juices from running out. Make a scalloped edge with your fingers or crimp with a fork. Place the turnovers on a lightly greased baking sheet, making sure the crimped edge is on top, not on the side, as most turnovers are made. Pierce the top with a fork to allow steam to escape. Brush with the egg mixture and bake in the upper third of the oven until lightly colored, about 20 minutes. Let cool for 5 minutes and serve.

NOTE **These turnovers can be frozen before cooking. Place them on baking sheets lined with waxed paper and freeze until hard. Transfer to zippered-top plastic bags. You can bake them frozen, increasing the baking time by 5 minutes.**

Empanadas Antioqueñas
PORK TURNOVERS ANTIOQUIA STYLE
Makes about 24 empanadas

Like all South Americans, Colombians love empanadas and have a variety of regional doughs and fillings. The empanadas from Antioquia, in the northeast of Colombia, are very special, because the dough is made with the *arepa* and yuca flours, which gives them a chewy, delicious crust. The pork filling, which sometimes is made with half pork and half beef, is also full of flavor. These empanadas are always deep-fried and have to be eaten hot. The dough requires quick handling and has to be kept covered with a damp towel to prevent it from drying out. The finished empanadas also need to be covered with a damp towel so they don't crack. For people who dislike deep-frying, I have figured out a way to bake them instead, but I recommend very highly that you fry them. Colombians serve these with lemon wedges to squeeze over them or with a bowl of *Ají Pique* (page 333).

RELLENO (Filling)

    2 tablespoons canola oil

    12 ounces lean ground pork

    1 teaspoon ground annatto or sweet paprika

    1 small onion, finely chopped (about ½ cup)

    ¼ cup finely chopped scallions (white part and 1 inch of the green)

    1 large ripe but firm tomato (about 8 ounces), peeled and chopped

    2 tablespoons minced fresh cilantro leaves

    1 teaspoon ground cumin

    1 teaspoon salt

    ½ teaspoon freshly ground black pepper

    1 cup peeled and diced (¼ inch) all-purpose potatoes

    1 cup water

MASA (Dough)

    2 cups *arepa* flour (page 417)

    2 tablespoons firmly packed dark brown sugar

    ½ teaspoon salt

    3 cups hot water

    2 tablespoons unsalted butter, softened

    ½ cup yuca flour (page 434)

    Peanut oil for frying

1. To make the filling, heat the oil in a large frying pan over medium heat. Add the pork and cook, stirring, until it loses its pink color. Add the annatto, onion, scallions, tomato, cilantro, cumin, salt, and pepper. Cover and cook for 10 minutes, stirring occasionally. Add the potatoes and water, cover, and simmer until the potatoes are soft, about 20 minutes. Uncover and cook until the meat has absorbed most of the liquid; the mixture should be moist. Remove from the heat and set aside to cool. Or make ahead and refrigerate.

2. To make the dough, mix the *arepa* flour, brown sugar, and salt together in a medium-size bowl. Add the hot water and mix with a wooden spoon until the dough forms a ball. With your hands, work in the butter until well incorporated. Transfer to a floured board, add the yuca flour little by little, and knead well until the dough is smooth and pliable. If too dry, add water a little at a time. Or do as Colombians do: rinse your hands with cold water and keep on kneading until the dough is soft enough to roll easily. Shape into a log about 2 inches in diameter, then cut into rounds about ¼ inch thick (but keep the rounds together until needed). Cover with a damp towel and work with one round at a time.

3. Place the dough round between 2 pieces of plastic wrap and roll it into a circle about ³⁄₁₆ inch thick. Peel off the top piece of plastic wrap and put 1 tablespoon of the filling in the center. Lifting the edge of the bottom piece of plastic wrap, fold half of the round over the filling. Remove the plastic wrap and press the edges to seal. Pinch between your thumb and forefinger to form an edge that looks like a rope, or just press firmly on both sides with the tines of a fork. Repeat with the remaining dough and rounds. Keep the finished empanadas covered with a damp cloth, as they dry out very fast. It is better

to make them only a couple of hours ahead. Refrigerate until needed.

4. In an electric skillet, heat ½ inch of the oil to 350°F. Fry a few empanadas at a time until lightly colored on both sides, about 4 minutes. Remove from the oil with a slotted spoon, drain on paper towels, and serve hot.

For people who don't like to fry, brush both sides of the empanadas with canola oil and bake in a preheated 400°F oven until lightly colored, about 30 minutes. The texture will be a little chewy.

NOTES **I find it easier to make the dough one half at a time. It is not only easier to knead but also easier to roll out the fresher it is.**

To freeze uncooked empanadas, place on baking sheets lined with aluminum foil and cover with plastic wrap. (This dough has a tendency to crack if left uncovered.) When hard, pack into containers. To fry frozen empanadas, place on baking sheets lined with aluminum foil, cover with plastic wrap, thaw at room temperature for 30 minutes, and then fry as directed above.

Empanadas Venezolanas

VENEZUELAN TURNOVERS *Makes 48 empanadas*

This is a classic Venezuelan empanada made with either wheat flour or *arepa* flour, depending on the cook's preference. To serve these turnovers for a cocktail party, make them ahead and freeze. Your guests will really appreciate them.

- **2 tablespoons canola oil**
- **12 ounces lean ground pork or beef, or a combination**
- **½ teaspoon dried oregano**
- **½ teaspoon ground cumin**
- **1 teaspoon salt**
- **¼ teaspoon freshly ground black pepper**
- **1 medium-size onion, chopped (1 cup)**
- **2 medium-size ripe but firm tomatoes (10 to 12 ounces), peeled, seeded, and quartered**
- **1 small red bell pepper, seeded and cut into pieces**
- **1 clove garlic, chopped**
- **1 teaspoon capers, drained**
- **¼ cup muscatel wine or cream sherry**
- **6 small black olives, pitted and finely chopped**
- **2 tablespoons dried currants**
- **1 recipe *Masa para Empanadas al Horno* (page 112)**
- **1 large egg lightly beaten with 1 tablespoon water**

1. In a large frying pan, heat the oil over medium heat. Add the pork, oregano, cumin, salt, and black pepper and cook, breaking up the meat, until the pink color disappears.

2. Place the onion, tomatoes, bell pepper, garlic, and capers in a blender or food processor and process until smooth. Add the puree to the meat along with the muscatel, olives, and currants and cook until most of the liquid has evaporated but the mixture is still moist. Taste for salt. Remove from the heat, let cool, cover with plastic wrap, and refrigerate for a couple of hours or overnight to let the flavors develop.

3. On a lightly floured surface, roll the dough into 4 logs and cut each into 12 pieces. Roll each piece into a 3-inch circle. Place 1 teaspoon of the filling in the center, lightly brush half of the edge with the egg mixture, fold in half to form a half-moon, and press the edges together firmly.

4. Preheat the oven to 375°F.

5. Just before baking, brush the empanadas with the egg mixture and bake on the upper oven rack until lightly colored, about 20 minutes. Be careful: overcooking will dry out the filling. Serve warm.

NOTE These empanadas freeze very well unbaked. Freeze on baking sheets lined with waxed paper until hard, then transfer to covered containers. You can pop them in the oven frozen; just increase the baking time by 5 minutes.

Masa para Empanadas al Horno
DOUGH FOR BAKED TURNOVERS

Makes enough dough for 16 large or 48 small empanadas

This is the classic, basic dough used for making baked turnovers throughout South America. The variations are endless, depending on the cook. Sometimes a teaspoon of baking powder is added to the flour, milk is used instead of water, or eggs are used. Prepared dough rounds can be found frozen in most supermarkets throughout South America and in some Latin American supermarkets in the Unites States. If pressed for time, you can use frozen puff pastry for making most empanadas. A range of fillings for these pastries can be found in this chapter.

> 3 cups all-purpose flour
>
> 1 teaspoon salt
>
> 1 teaspoon baking powder (optional)
>
> ½ cup lard or unsalted butter, cut into 8 pieces
>
> ¼ cup vegetable shortening
>
> ½ cup warm water

1. *Hand method:* In a large bowl, mix together the flour, salt, and baking powder (if using). Add the lard and shortening and blend together with your fingers to make a coarse meal. Add the water and mix well, adding more flour or water if needed to make a soft dough. Knead in the bowl until smooth and elastic. Cover with plastic wrap and let rest for 30 minutes.

Food processor method: Put the flour, salt, and baking powder (if using), in a food processor fitted with the steel blade and pulse for 5 seconds. Add the lard and shortening and process until the mixture looks like coarse meal, about 15 seconds. With the machine running, pour the water through the feed tube in a steady stream and process until the dough almost comes together into a ball. Remove from the bowl, knead a few times, and let rest for 30 minutes.

2. Place the dough on a lightly floured work surface, cut into 2 pieces, and roll each piece into a log. Cut each log into 8 rounds for large turnovers; you will have 16 rounds. With a lightly floured rolling pin, roll one round at a time into a circle about 5 inches in diameter. For smaller turnovers, cut the dough into 4 pieces and roll each into a log. Cut each log into 12 rounds; you will have 48 rounds. Roll one round at a time into a thin 3-inch circle.

For the larger turnovers, place 2 heaping tablespoons of filling in the center of each circle, lightly moisten the edge of half the circle, fold it in half, and press firmly to seal the edges. Trim and crimp the edge with a fork dipped in flour, then pierce the top once with the fork to allow steam to escape during baking. For the smaller turnovers, use 1 heaping teaspoon of filling and proceed as for the larger turnovers. Refrigerate for 30 minutes. The turnovers can be frozen at this point. Place on baking sheets lined with waxed paper and freeze, uncovered, for 1 hour. Store in tightly covered containers, separating the layers with waxed paper.

Empanadas de Avestruz
OSTRICH TURNOVERS *Makes 18 empanadas*

The ostrich, native to Africa, is a relative of the *ñandú* (rhea), which roams the *pampas* of Argentina, Uruguay, and southern Brazil. The rhea is a little smaller than the ostrich, and in the southern countries of South America, its meat is used to make stews, meatballs, sausage, empanadas, and *charqui* (dried meat, or jerky). *Charqui* is sold as a snack food or to use in stews and soups. Ostriches and rheas are raised in the United States, and their meat, packaged as frozen fillets or patties, is available in some supermarkets. Ostrich and rhea meat is becoming more popular because it is leaner than, but similar to, beef. This recipe was adapted from the Argentine cookbook *La Cocina de Nuestra Tierra* by Choly Berreteaga. You can use either ostrich or rhea meat here.

2 large onions, cut into 1-inch pieces

Two 8-ounce packages frozen ostrich patties, thawed and broken up

1 teaspoon salt

½ teaspoon freshly ground black pepper

1 teaspoon sweet paprika

1 teaspoon ground cumin

¼ teaspoon red pepper flakes

½ teaspoon sugar

2 tablespoons olive oil

2 tablespoons unsalted butter

½ cup chicken broth

¼ cup chopped pimentos

⅓ cup sweetened dried cranberries or seedless black raisins, soaked in 3 tablespoons port or cream sherry for 1 hour

⅓ cup pimento-stuffed Spanish olives, sliced

2 packages Pepperidge Farm frozen puff pastry shells, thawed

1 large egg lightly beaten with 1 tablespoon water

1.   Place the onions in a food processor and process for a few seconds until finely chopped. Add the ostrich, salt, black pepper, paprika, cumin, red pepper, and sugar and process for about 5 seconds, until mixed. Transfer to a covered container and refrigerate overnight for the flavors to develop.

2.   In a large skillet, heat the oil and butter together over medium-high heat until the butter has melted. Add the meat mixture and cook, breaking up the meat with a wooden spoon, until it is cooked through, about 5 minutes. Stir in the chicken broth, pimentos, cranberries with port, and olives. Cook until the liquid is reduced but the mixture is still moist. Remove from the heat and set aside to cool; better yet, refrigerate for a couple of hours.

3.   Remove 1 pastry shell and roll it out on a lightly floured work surface to a 5-inch circle. Place 2 heaping tablespoons of the filling in the center of the circle and lightly moisten the edge of half of the circle with the egg mixture. Fold in half and press firmly to seal the edges. Crimp the edge with a fork dipped in flour and pierce the top with the fork to allow steam to escape. Repeat with the remaining shells and filling and refrigerate for 30 minutes.

4.   Preheat the oven to 375°F.

5.   Brush the turnovers with the egg mixture and bake on the upper oven rack until golden, about 20 minutes. Eat hot or warm.

NOTE These turnovers freeze very well unbaked. Freeze on baking sheets lined with waxed paper until hard, then transfer to covered containers. You can pop them into the oven frozen; just increase the baking time by 5 minutes.

Empanadas de Jamón y Queso

HAM AND CHEESE TURNOVERS *Makes 16 empanadas*

The combination of ham and cheese for empanadas is very popular in South America, especially in Argentina and Uruguay, where empanadas come in a huge range of sizes, shapes, and fillings. This recipe is a winner. Not only does it taste delicious, but it is also easy to prepare. There is not much cooking involved, especially if you happen to have some ready-made pastry rounds in your freezer. Ready-to-fill frozen pastry rounds from Argentina are available in some Latin American markets and come in two sizes. They are a good alternative to the puff pastry shells.

2 tablespoons olive oil

1 large onion, finely chopped (about 1½ cups)

1 cup day-old bread crumbs (page 413), soaked in ½ cup milk for 30 minutes

8 ounces imported boiled ham, chopped

8 ounces Edam cheese, shredded

½ teaspoon freshly ground black pepper

1 large egg, lightly beaten

2 packages Pepperidge Farm frozen puff pastry shells, thawed

1 large egg lightly beaten with 1 tablespoon water

1. In a small frying pan, heat the oil over medium heat. Add the onion and cook, stirring a few times, until transparent, about 3 minutes. Remove from the heat and let cool. Squeeze the bread crumbs and place in a medium-size bowl. Add the onion, ham, cheese, black pepper, and egg and mix well.

2. Remove 1 pastry shell and roll it out on a lightly floured work surface to a 5- to 6-inch circle. Place 2 heaping tablespoons of the filling in the center of the round and lightly moisten the edge of half of the circle with the egg mixture. Fold in half and press firmly to seal the edges. Crimp the edge with a fork dipped in flour and pierce the top with the fork to allow steam to escape. Repeat with the remaining shells and filling and refrigerate for 30 minutes.

3. Preheat the oven to 375°F.

4. Brush the turnovers with the egg mixture

and bake on the upper oven rack until golden, about 25 minutes. Let cool for a few minutes and serve.

NOTE These turnovers freeze very well unbaked. Freeze on baking sheets lined with waxed paper until hard, then transfer to covered containers. You can pop them into the oven frozen; just increase the baking time by 5 minutes.

Tequeños

CHEESE PASTRIES *Makes about 40 pastries*

This classic Venezuelan hors d'oeuvre can be made with different types of cheese, as long as it is a firm, good melting cheese. They also freeze well and can go directly from the freezer into the hot oil.

2 cups all-purpose flour

¼ cup (½ stick) unsalted butter, softened

1 large egg yolk

1 teaspoon sugar

1 teaspoon salt

½ cup water

8 ounces Chihuahua, mozzarella, or Muenster cheese, cut into 2 x ½-inch sticks

Peanut oil for frying

1. In a large bowl, combine the flour, butter, egg yolk, sugar, salt, and water. Knead until very smooth, adding a little more water if too dry, about 10 minutes. Set aside to rest for 30 minutes.

2. On a lightly floured work surface, roll out the dough until very thin. Cut into strips 6 inches long and 2 inches wide. Take 1 stick of cheese and wrap it diagonally, overlapping the dough. Pinch

together the ends. Repeat with the remaining cheese and dough.

3. In an electric skillet, heat 1 inch of the oil to 350°F. Drop in a few *tequeños* at a time and fry until golden brown on both sides, 1 to 2 minutes. Remove using a slotted spoon, drain on paper towels, and let stand for 5 minutes before serving.

NOTE Uncooked *tequeños* may be frozen for up to 6 months. Fry them right out of the freezer; do not thaw.

Biscoitinhos de Castanha com Pimenta

CASHEW AND THREE-PEPPERCORN SABLÉS
Makes about 48 sablés

Brazilians adapted many French specialties to the local cuisine. These *sablés* are a good example of the creativity of native cooks, combining French techniques with local ingredients, such as the cashews and pink peppercorns indigenous to Brazil (as well as to many other countries in South America, including Peru and Ecuador). Enjoy them with cocktails.

- 7 tablespoons unsalted butter
- ⅓ cup freshly grated Parmesan cheese
- 2 ounces raw cashews, ground
- ½ teaspoon salt
- ½ teaspoon white peppercorns, crushed in a mortar
- ¼ teaspoon black peppercorns, crushed in a mortar
- ¾ teaspoon pink peppercorns, crushed in a mortar
- 1 large egg yolk
- ½ large egg white
- 1 cup plus 2 tablespoons all-purpose flour

1. In a large bowl with an electric mixer, cream the butter until light. Add the Parmesan, ground cashews, salt, white pepper, black pepper, and pink pepper, egg yolk, and egg white and beat until well blended. Quickly stir in the flour just until the dough gathers into a ball. Cover with plastic wrap and refrigerate for at least 3 hours or overnight.

2. Preheat the oven to 425°F.

3. Roll out the dough on a lightly floured surface to ³⁄₁₆ inch thick. With a biscuit cutter, cut into 2½-inch rounds and place on baking sheets lined with parchment paper. Bake until lightly colored, about 8 minutes. Let cool and store in a cookie tin.

Torta Pascualina de Verduras

VEGETABLE PIE *Makes one 9-inch pie; 8 to 12 servings*

I call this the queen of the *tortas* because it is not only beautiful to look at but delicious as well. Whenever I prepare this *torta* for a special occasion, it never fails to impress my guests.

The classic *torta Pascualina*, whose roots go back to Italy, is made with spinach or Swiss chard, or a combination of both. It is one of the most beloved and popular foods in Argentina, Chile, and Uruguay. I prefer this version because, visually and nutritionally, it offers more variety. It is very versatile and can be served as a first course, snack food, or side dish. It makes a wonderful meatless meal and is simple enough for a picnic yet elegant enough for a buffet.

One 10-ounce package frozen chopped spinach

1 pound carrots, sliced

¼ cup dried porcini mushrooms (optional)

1 cup fresh or frozen peas, cooked in water to cover until tender and drained

1 pound Swiss chard, cooked (page 411)

¼ cup olive oil

¼ cup finely chopped scallions (white part and 1 inch of the green)

¼ cup finely chopped fresh parsley leaves

1 teaspoon salt

¼ teaspoon freshly ground black pepper

⅛ teaspoon freshly grated nutmeg

3 large eggs, lightly beaten

4 ounces Swiss cheese, shredded

1 package Pepperidge Farm frozen puff pastry sheets, thawed

1 large egg lightly beaten with 1 tablespoon water

5 large eggs

1. Cook the spinach according to the package directions. Drain, rinse under cold running water, and squeeze dry.

2. Cook the carrots in boiling salted water until very tender, about 15 minutes. Drain and mash with a fork; the texture should be very coarse.

3. If using, soak the mushrooms in hot water to cover for 30 minutes. Drain, rinse thoroughly, and chop.

4. Combine the peas, Swiss chard, spinach, carrots, and mushrooms (if using) in a large bowl.

5. In a large, heavy skillet, heat the oil over medium heat. Add the scallions and cook, stirring, for 2 to 3 minutes. Stir in the cooked vegetables, salt, pepper, and nutmeg. Cook, stirring constantly, for a couple of minutes, then remove from the heat and let cool. Stir in the beaten eggs and cheese.

6. On a lightly floured board, roll out 1 puff pastry sheet into a 14-inch circle. Butter a 9-inch cake pan with removable sides and line with the pastry, fitting it into the bottom. Pierce the bottom with a fork and brush with the egg mixture. Spread the filling evenly on top and, with the bottom of a soup spoon, make 5 indentations. Break 1 egg into each indentation and season with salt and pepper to taste. Roll the second puff pastry sheet into a 9-inch circle and fit it on top of the filling, pressing the top and bottom edges together to seal. Trim away the excess pastry with a knife. With the tines of a fork, press all around the edge of the *torta*. Cut a vent in the center and decorate the top with cutouts made with the leftover pastry. Brush with the egg mixture and refrigerate for 15 minutes.

7. Preheat the oven to 375°F.

8. Bake on the center oven rack for 1 hour. If the pastry is browning too fast, cover loosely with aluminum foil. Remove from the oven and let cool for 20 minutes before removing the side of the pan. Slice and serve warm or at room temperature.

NOTE **The *torta* can be made a day ahead. After baking, cooling, and removing the outer ring of the pan, let cool completely, then refrigerate, loosely covered with aluminum foil. It is easier to handle if the bottom of the cake pan is left under the *torta*. To reheat, place the *torta* on a baking sheet and bake in a preheated 300°F oven for 20 minutes.**

Torta Pascualina de Chancho y Alcachofas

PORK AND ARTICHOKE PIE

Makes one 9-inch pie; 8 to 12 servings

Pork is the meat of choice in the Andean countries, and when combined with artichokes, it makes a pie that is hard to resist.

2 tablespoons olive oil

1 medium-size onion, minced (about 1 cup)

½ cup minced scallions (white part and 1 inch of the green)

1 pound lean ground pork

1 teaspoon salt

½ teaspoon freshly ground black pepper

¼ teaspoon freshly grated nutmeg

2 tablespoons unsalted butter

4 ounces fresh, firm white mushrooms, finely chopped

One 9-ounce package frozen artichoke hearts, cooked and coarsely chopped, or one 14-ounce can artichoke hearts, drained, rinsed, and coarsely chopped

3 large eggs, lightly beaten

4 ounces Chihuahua, mozzarella, or Muenster cheese, shredded

¼ cup freshly grated Parmesan cheese

1 package Pepperidge Farm frozen puff pastry sheets, thawed

1 large egg lightly beaten with 1 tablespoon water

5 large eggs

1. In a large, heavy skillet, heat the oil over medium heat. Add the onion, scallions, and pork and cook, stirring and breaking up the meat, until the pork is lightly browned. Add the salt, pepper, and nutmeg and stir to combine.

2. In a medium-size skillet, melt the butter over medium heat. Add the mushrooms and cook, stirring constantly, until dry. Add the artichokes and cook for a couple of minutes. Add to the pork mixture and cook for 2 to 3 minutes to blend the flavors. Taste for salt and pepper (it should taste highly seasoned). Set aside to cool. Mix with the 3 beaten eggs, Chihuahua cheese, and Parmesan.

3. On a lightly floured surface, roll out 1 puff pastry sheet into a 14-inch circle. Butter a 9-inch cake pan with removable sides and line with the pastry, fitting it into the bottom. Pierce the bottom with a fork and brush with the egg mixture. Spread the filling evenly on top and, with the bottom of a soup spoon, make 5 indentations. Break 1 egg into each indentation and season with salt and pepper to taste. Roll the second pastry sheet into a 9-inch circle and fit it on top of the filling, pressing the top and bottom edges together to seal. Trim away the excess pastry with a knife. With the tines of a fork, press all around the edge of the *torta*. Cut a vent in the center and decorate the top with cutouts made with the leftover pastry. Brush with the egg mixture and refrigerate for 15 minutes.

4. Preheat the oven to 375°F.

5. Bake on the center oven rack for 1 hour. If the pastry is browning too fast, cover loosely with aluminum foil. Remove from the oven and let cool for 20 minutes before removing the side of the pan. Slice and serve warm or at room temperature.

NOTE The *torta* can be made a day ahead. After baking, cooling, and removing the outer ring of the pan, let cool completely, then refrigerate, loosely covered with aluminum foil. It is easier to handle if the bottom of the cake pan is left under the *torta*. To reheat, place the *torta* on a baking sheet and bake in a preheated 300°F oven for 20 minutes.

Tarta de Palmitos

HEARTS OF PALM TART

Makes one 9-inch pie; 8 servings

This exquisite tart from Argentina is bound to become a favorite for a luncheon or as a first course. The native hearts of palm blend beautifully with the European ingredients. A Vidalia or white Spanish onion is perfect for this delicate tart.

    2 tablespoons unsalted butter
    1 cup thinly sliced leeks (white part only),
        washed well
    1½ cups thinly sliced Vidalia or white
        Spanish onion
    ½ teaspoon sweet paprika
    ¼ teaspoon salt
    ¼ teaspoon white pepper
    Pinch of sugar
    2 tablespoons cornstarch
    1 cup whipping cream or half-and-half
    2 hard-cooked eggs, peeled and chopped
    One 14-ounce can hearts of palm
    One 9-inch pie pan lined with *Masa Corta*
        (recipe follows), partially baked
    1 large egg white, lightly beaten
    2 tablespoons freshly grated Parmesan cheese

1. Melt the butter in a large, heavy skillet over low heat. Add the leeks and onion, cover, and cook for 15 minutes, stirring a few times. Do not let the onion brown. Stir in the paprika, salt, pepper, and sugar and cook for a few seconds. Add the cornstarch, whipping cream, and chopped eggs and cook, stirring constantly, until it comes to a boil. Reduce the heat to low and simmer until thickened. Remove from the heat and set aside to cool.

2. Drain and rinse the hearts of palm. Pat dry with paper towels. Cut each heart crosswise into 8 rounds.

3. To assemble the tart, brush the bottom of the prebaked tart shell with the egg white. Spread half

the leek sauce over the bottom of the tart. Arrange the hearts of palm over it, cover with the remaining sauce, and sprinkle evenly with the Parmesan. If desired, cover with plastic wrap and refrigerate for up to 4 hours.

4. Preheat the oven to 375°F.

5. Bake the tart on the center oven rack of the oven until the top is lightly browned, about 20 minutes. Let cool for 5 minutes, then cut into 8 wedges and serve as an appetizer. I often serve this tart as an entrée for a luncheon, with a salad on the side and preceded by a soup.

Masa Corta PÂTE BRISÉE

Makes one 9-, 10-, or 11-inch crust

This dough comes from France—the classic *pâte brisée* (short pastry) that is used to make most pies and tarts, both sweet and savory. I must confess that my hands are rather heavy when it comes to making fine dough, so I consider the food processor heaven-sent, because it allows me to turn out consistently good pastries with the process I give here. Often cooks use half lard and half butter.

    1½ cups all-purpose flour
    ½ teaspoon salt
    Pinch of sugar
    ½ cup (1 stick) cold unsalted butter
    2 to 3 tablespoons ice water, as needed

Hand method: Place the flour, salt, sugar, and butter in a large bowl. Rub together quickly with the tips of your fingers until the dough looks like corn flakes. Add 2 tablespoons of the water and blend quickly with a wooden spoon, adding a little more water if the dough is too dry. Gather the dough and shape it into a ball. Place on a lightly floured work surface and knead with the heel of your hand 2 or 3 times to blend well.

Form into a ball, wrap in waxed paper, and refrigerate for 1 hour.

Food processor method: Place the flour, salt, sugar, and butter in a food processor fitted with the steel blade and process until the mixture looks like coarse meal, about 10 seconds. With the machine running, pour 2 tablespoons of the water through the feed tube in a steady stream and process until the dough almost comes together into a ball. If the dough is too dry, add 1 more tablespoon water. The dough should hold together without crumbling, but too much water will toughen it. Remove from the food processor and knead on a lightly floured work surface 2 or 3 times with the heel of your hand. Form into a ball, wrap in waxed paper, and refrigerate for 1 hour.

Partially baked tart shell: On a floured work surface, roll the dough into a 15-inch round. Lift over the rolling pin and place in a 9-, 10-, or 11-inch tart pan with fluted sides and a removable bottom set on a baking sheet. Press the dough firmly into the pan and trim it so that it overlaps the rim of the pan by ½ inch. Turn the excess under and, with your thumbs, push it down to about ⅛ inch above the edge of the pan. With a fork, prick the bottom of the dough at ¼-inch intervals to prevent it from puffing. Cover with plastic wrap and refrigerate for 30 minutes.

To bake, line the shell with waxed paper, cover with aluminum foil, and fill with pie weights or dried beans. Bake in a preheated 425°F oven on the lower rack until set, about 10 minutes. Carefully remove the foil (with beans) and waxed paper. Prick the crust again with a fork. Bake until lightly colored, about 5 minutes more. Let cool completely and fill as instructed in specific recipes.

Tarta de Choclo y Porcini

CORN AND PORCINI MUSHROOM QUICHE *Makes one 11-inch quiche; 8 to 12 servings*

This *tarta* is very popular throughout South America. It is truly a wonderful quiche that travels well, can be made ahead, and excels as a first course for a dinner party or as a main course for a luncheon. It also makes a great side dish to accompany grilled fish, fowl, or meat.

> **3 cups thawed frozen corn kernels**
>
> **3 tablespoons unsalted butter**
>
> **1 medium-size onion, finely chopped (about 1 cup)**
>
> **¼ cup dried porcini mushrooms, soaked in hot water for 30 minutes**
>
> **1 cup whipping cream or milk**
>
> **4 ounces white cheddar cheese, shredded**
>
> **4 large eggs, lightly beaten**
>
> **½ teaspoon salt**
>
> **¼ teaspoon sugar**
>
> **¼ teaspoon white pepper**
>
> **One 11-inch quiche pan lined with *Masa Corta* (previous page)**
>
> **2 tablespoons freshly grated Parmesan cheese**

1. Place the corn in a food processor or blender and process until smooth. Transfer the puree to a large bowl.

2. Melt 2 tablespoons of the butter in a small skillet over medium-low heat. Add the onion, cover, and cook, stirring occasionally, until soft, about 10 minutes. Do not let it brown.

3. Drain and thoroughly rinse the mushrooms, chop finely, and add to the onion. Cook, stirring, for a couple of minutes, then add to the corn. Stir in the cream, cheddar cheese, eggs, salt, sugar, and pepper. Transfer the mixture to the shell, sprinkle the top evenly with the Parmesan, and dot with the remaining 1 tablespoon butter.

4. Preheat the oven to 350°F.

5. Place the quiche on a baking sheet and bake on the lower oven rack until golden brown, about

1 hour. Let cool for 10 minutes before cutting into wedges. Serve warm.

Varios Bocaditos y Entradas
MISCELLANEOUS APPETIZERS

MANY OF THESE APPETIZERS, ESPECIALLY the ones made with potatoes, show their Indian roots, which were embellished by Hispanic ingredients. The technique of deep-frying was brought by the conquistadors, along with the pigs. *Bolinhos de bacalhau* (codfish balls) and fritters made with quinoa and yuca are some of the great creations of the South American kitchen.

Patacones

FRIED GREEN PLANTAINS *Serves 8 to 10*

Also known as *tostones*, fried green plantains are quite popular in the Andean countries of South America, especially in coastal areas, where the daily diet consists of rice, beans or lentils, and plantains prepared in this way or roasted. They are equally good as appetizers with drinks or to accompany meat, poultry, or fish dishes. They must be eaten hot, because they harden as they cool. *Patacones* are fried first at a low temperature to allow the plantains to cook through, then fried a second time at a high temperature to brown and crisp them.

> 4 green plantains
> Peanut oil for frying
> Salt

1. Peel the plantains by trimming both ends with a sharp knife, cutting incisions along the natural ridges, and then pulling away the skin. Slice into 1- to 1½-inch-thick rounds.

2. In an electric skillet, heat ½ inch of the oil to 325°F. Fry the rounds in batches, being careful not to crowd them, until golden. Using a slotted spoon, transfer to paper towels to drain.

3. Place the fried slices between waxed paper or brown paper bags and flatten with a mallet or the flat side of a cleaver to about ⅓ inch thick.

4. Once all the slices have been fried and flattened, increase the temperature of the oil to 375°F and fry the rounds in batches again until brown. Drain on paper towels, season with salt to taste, and serve immediately.

Chifles

GREEN PLANTAIN CHIPS *Serves 4 to 6*

When plantains are thinly sliced and fried, they are called *chifles*. In South America, they are sold in plastic bags, like potato chips. They are a very popular snack food and also are good with *cebiches* and drinks.

> 2 green plantains
> Peanut oil for frying
> Salt

1. Peel the plantains by trimming both ends with a sharp knife, cutting incisions along the natural ridges, and then pulling away the skin. Cut into very thin slices and place in ice-cold water for 15 minutes (this helps keep them crisp). Drain well and dry on paper towels.

2. In an electric skillet, heat 1 inch of the oil to 375°F. Fry the rounds in batches, being careful not to crowd them, until golden, about 2 minutes. Using a slotted spoon, transfer to paper towels to drain. Sprinkle with salt to taste and serve when cool.

Emborrajados de Patas

PIG'S FEET FRITTERS *Serves 8*

I still remember how much we looked forward to lunch whenever we heard *emborrajados* were the appetizer of the day. Depending on the occasion, we had two or three kinds of these delicious fritters, an Ecuadorian treat. One popular version was made by putting a slice of cheese on top of a slice of raw ripe plantain, which was then dipped into the batter and dropped into the hot fat. Another variety was made with a slice of cooked potato topped with a slice of cheese, fried the same way. Cooked pieces of pig's feet were put in the batter with the bones in. Now things have changed, and only the meat from the pig's feet is used, which simplifies eating the fritters—you don't have to worry about removing the bones. My family's recipe is a little different from the standard in that it uses some cornmeal to make the fritters crispier. This batter can also be used to make *torrejas* (thick vegetable pancakes), which are especially popular in Peru and are nothing more than cooked vegetables mixed with the batter and dropped by the tablespoonful into hot oil.

2 pounds pig's feet
1 medium-size onion, peeled
½ small green bell pepper, seeded
2 large cloves garlic, peeled
1 teaspoon dried oregano
1 teaspoon salt
10 black peppercorns

BATTER

¾ cup all-purpose flour
¼ cup cornmeal
1 teaspoon salt
1 teaspoon baking powder
3 large eggs, lightly beaten
½ cup milk

Peanut oil for frying
Ají Criollo (page 333)

1. Place the pig's feet in a 4-quart saucepan with water to cover by 2 inches. Add the onion, bell pepper, garlic, oregano, salt, and peppercorns and bring to a boil over medium heat. Cover and simmer until the meat is falling apart, about 2 hours. Transfer the feet to a platter and let cool. Discard the bones and cut the meat into bite-size pieces. Cover and set aside.

2. To make the batter, combine all the ingredients in a large bowl and stir with a wooden spoon until smooth, or process in a blender. The batter should be thick enough to coat the food that is going to be fried. Add more flour, if needed. Mix in the cooked meat.

3. In an electric skillet or a wok, heat 1 inch of the oil to 350°F. Drop large spoonfuls of well-coated meat into the hot oil. Fry 2 to 4 fritters at a time, depending on the size of the pan. Be careful not to let the oil cool down by cooking too many at once. When golden brown on one side, turn over and cook until golden brown. Using a slotted spoon, transfer to a tray lined with paper towels to drain. Keep warm in a low oven while frying the rest.

4. Serve hot, with a bowl of *ají* on the side.

Bocados de Quinua

QUINOA FRITTERS *Makes about 36 fritters*

Bolivia is one of the main producers of quinoa and has a variety of specialties made with this nutritious grain. These delicious fritters are also popular in the other quinoa-producing countries, such as Peru and Ecuador.

- 1 tablespoon canola oil
- ½ teaspoon sweet paprika
- ¼ cup minced scallions (white part and 1 inch of the green)
- 1 tablespoon minced fresh parsley leaves
- 1 tablespoon minced fresh cilantro leaves
- 1 cup cooked quinoa (page 327)
- ¼ cup all-purpose flour
- ½ teaspoon salt
- ¼ teaspoon white pepper
- Pinch of cayenne pepper
- ¼ cup freshly grated Parmesan cheese
- 2 large eggs, lightly beaten
- Peanut oil for frying
- *Ají Criollo* (page 333)

1. In a small skillet, heat the canola oil over medium heat. Add the paprika and scallions and cook for a couple of minutes, stirring. Remove from the heat, add the parsley and cilantro, and mix in the quinoa. Transfer to a bowl and add the flour, salt, white pepper, cayenne, Parmesan, and eggs and mix well.

2. In an electric skillet, heat 1 inch of the peanut oil to 350°F. Drop heaping teaspoonfuls of the quinoa mixture into the hot oil, being careful not to crowd the fritters, and fry on both sides until golden. Using a slotted spoon, transfer to paper towels to drain. Keep warm in a low oven while frying the rest.

3. Serve hot, with a bowl of *ají* on the side.

Bolitas de Mandioca

YUCA COCKTAIL BALLS *Makes about 30 balls*

Also known as *frituras de yuca*, this specialty from Paraguay is also found in countries where *mandioca* (yuca) is abundant. The balls are very light and delicious and are usually served plain, but if a dip is desired, try them with *Chimichurri* (page 337).

- 8 ounces trimmed fresh yuca or frozen yuca
- ¼ cup freshly grated Parmesan cheese
- ¼ cup all-purpose flour mixed with ½ teaspoon salt and 1 teaspoon baking powder
- 2 tablespoons unsalted butter, softened
- 1 large egg, lightly beaten
- Peanut oil for frying

1. In a medium-size saucepan, cook the yuca in salted water to cover until tender, about 20 minutes. Drain, remove the fibers, and mash with a potato masher (don't use a food processor, or the yuca will become gummy). Combine thoroughly with the Parmesan, flour mixture, butter, and egg.

2. To form the balls, drop about 1 teaspoon dough onto a lightly floured surface and roll to coat with flour. Set on a baking sheet lined with waxed paper. The balls should be about 1 inch in diameter. They can be made a few hours ahead, loosely covered with waxed paper, and refrigerated until serving time.

3. When ready to serve, heat 1 inch of the oil to 350°F in an electric skillet. Drop a few of the balls at a time into the hot oil, being careful not to crowd them, and fry until golden brown. Swish the oil over the balls while frying, turning them as they brown. Remove with a slotted spoon, drain on paper towels, and serve immediately.

Picante con Ají a la Santandereano

TOMATO AND AVOCADO SALSA SANTANDER STYLE *Serves 6 to 8*

This salsa is similar to the Venezuelan *guasacaca* sauce, which is made with fresh tomatoes instead of canned. What intrigued me about this recipe was the use of canned tomatoes, which are beginning to infiltrate the cooking of South American countries. Also, I had never seen any recipe using only the seeds of hot peppers. In Venezuela, this is the usual accompaniment for *parrilladas* (barbecues), fish, or *marrano horneado con guasacaca* (pig baked with this sauce). It is truly a national dish, with the only difference between regions being in the amount of *ají* (hot pepper) used. In the *llanos*, a lot of *ají* is used. This recipe was given to me by María Borrero, a nurse from Bogotá, who served it with fried yuca wedges and claimed it was a favorite of the American doctors who worked at the hospital. You can also use this as a sauce for chicken or as a dip for tortilla chips.

Seeds of 1 hot pepper (preferably a *pequín*; see Note)

¼ teaspoon salt

One 16-ounce can peeled whole tomatoes, with juices

2 hard-cooked eggs, peeled and finely chopped

2 tablespoons finely chopped fresh cilantro leaves

1 small onion, finely chopped (about ½ cup)

1 to 2 ripe but firm Hass avocados, peeled, pitted, and finely chopped

¼ cup seeded and finely chopped red bell pepper

¼ cup seeded and finely chopped green bell pepper

2 to 3 tablespoons white wine vinegar, to your taste

Canola oil

1. In a mortar, pound the hot pepper seeds with the salt until pulverized, then pass through a fine-mesh sieve.

2. Finely chop the tomatoes and transfer with their juices to a medium-size bowl. Add the crushed hot pepper seeds, eggs, cilantro, onion, avocados, bell peppers, and vinegar and mix well. Add a small amount of the oil to distribute the flavors. Taste for salt. Serve at room temperature.

NOTE Instead of the hot pepper seeds, you can use ¼ teaspoon or more red pepper flakes.

Bolinhos de Bacalhau

CODFISH BALLS *Makes about 30 balls*

These delicious codfish balls, of Portuguese origin, are probably the most popular *salgadinhos* (salty things) in Brazil, as they are in Portugal. I remember the first time I ordered *bolinhos* in a restaurant in Rio, they brought me a deep dish with enough *bolinhos* to feed a family. They were oval-shaped, but balls are just as popular. Some cooks scoop out some of the dough with a tablespoon and with another spoon shape the oval and drop it into the hot oil. I prefer my method because it allows me to prepare them ahead and keep them refrigerated, ready to fry just before serving. These balls are usually served plain, but if you want to serve them with a dip, try *Molho de Pimenta e Limão* (page 335). Salt cod was brought to South America by the Portuguese and Spaniards. It was used more often in the past, when Catholics had to fast on Fridays. Salt cod specialties are much more popular in Brazil than in the Andean countries.

8 ounces boneless salt cod

3 tablespoons olive oil

1 medium-size onion, minced (about 1 cup)

1 clove garlic, minced

3 tablespoons minced fresh parsley leaves

10 to 12 ounces all-purpose potatoes

3 large eggs

¼ teaspoon salt

Freshly ground black pepper

Peanut oil for frying

All-purpose flour for dusting

1. Soak the salt cod in cold water to cover for at least 4 hours or overnight, changing the water twice. Drain and remove the skin and bones, if not using boneless.

2. In a large skillet, heat the olive oil over medium heat. Add the onion, garlic, parsley, and salt cod and cook for about 20 minutes, stirring with a wooden spoon and trying to shred the cod a bit. Transfer to a food processor and process until smooth.

3. Place the potatoes in a large saucepan with salted water to cover. Bring to a boil, reduce the heat to medium, and let simmer until tender, about 30 minutes. Drain and, when cool enough to handle, peel. Return to the pan and mash with a potato masher. Add the cod mixture and cook over medium heat for about 5 minutes, beating all the time with a wooden spoon. It is very important to beat the mixture well in order to have good-quality fritters. Remove from the heat and beat in the eggs one at a time. Add the salt and season with pepper to taste. Shape the mixture into 1-inch balls.

4. When ready to serve, heat 1 inch of the peanut oil to 360°F in an electric skillet. When the oil is hot, dip the codfish balls in flour to dust lightly and fry a few at a time until golden brown on both sides. Using a slotted spoon, transfer to paper towels to drain. Keep warm in a low oven for up to 1 hour if not serving immediately.

Salsa de Berenjenas con Chichocas

EGGPLANT RELISH WITH SUN-DRIED TOMATOES
Makes about 2 cups

The Zona Cuyana of Argentina, bordered by the Andes, has the perfect climate to grow grapes, wheat, and vegetables. Spanish and Italian immigrants settled here in the nineteenth century and planted grapes. These grapes are rated the best in the country, as are the wines made from them. The Italians also cultivated vegetables such as tomatoes and eggplants. They dried pear-shaped tomatoes, which they called *chichocas de tomate*. These tomatoes are ideal to add to sauces, and in some areas cooks prefer to use them in the *sofritos* for *locros* (hominy-based soups). The immigrants also brought this eggplant relish from Italy. The sun-dried tomatoes add a new dimension to this wonderful condiment, which is usually served with grilled meats. Sometimes I serve it as an hors d'oeuvre, with crackers or pita bread crisps.

1 medium-size eggplant (about 1 pound)

1 small onion, minced (about ½ cup)

¼ cup minced oil-packed or reconstituted sun-dried tomatoes

1 large ripe but firm pear-shaped tomato, peeled, seeded, finely chopped, and well drained

½ small Granny Smith apple, peeled, cored, grated, and tossed with 1 tablespoon fresh lemon juice

2 cloves garlic, mashed into a paste with ½ teaspoon salt and ¼ teaspoon freshly ground black pepper

1 tablespoon sherry vinegar

2 tablespoons extra virgin olive oil

¼ cup finely chopped fresh basil leaves

1. Place the eggplant on a baking sheet, pierce in a couple of places with a knife, and bake in a preheated 400°F oven until soft, about 45 minutes. Remove from the oven and let cool. Peel the eggplant and discard the parts that have too many seeds. Finely chop the pulp—it should be like a coarse puree. Place in a nonreactive strainer and let drain for a couple of hours.

2. In a glass bowl, mix together the eggplant, onion, sun-dried tomatoes, fresh tomato, and apple. In a small bowl, beat the garlic paste with the vinegar and oil until creamy. Toss with the eggplant mixture and 2 tablespoons of the basil. Taste for salt and pepper. Cover with plastic wrap and refrigerate for a few hours or overnight to allow the flavors to develop.

3. Strain, then serve in a glass bowl, garnished with the remaining 2 tablespoons basil.

Chorros a la Criolla

CREOLE MUSSELS *Serves 4*

This is a classic Peruvian *tapa*, always found on the menu in restaurants in Peru, as well as in Peruvian restaurants in the United States.

30 large mussels, scrubbed and debearded (page 408)

¼ cup water

1 medium-size onion, finely chopped (about 1 cup)

Juice of 2 limes

1 to 2 jalapeños, to your taste, seeded and minced

Pinch of red pepper flakes

1 teaspoon olive oil

Salt and freshly ground black pepper

1 cup cooked corn kernels, drained

1 large ripe but firm tomato (about 8 ounces), peeled, seeded, and finely chopped

2 tablespoons minced fresh cilantro leaves

Lettuce leaves, shredded

1. Put the mussels and water in a large saucepan, bring to a boil, cover, and cook until they open, about 5 minutes. Discard any mussels that don't open. Remove the meat and save 20 clean shell halves.

2. Soak the onion in cold water for 10 minutes, then drain and rinse well. In a medium-size bowl, combine the onion, lime juice, jalapeño(s), red pepper, oil, and salt and black pepper to taste. Let sit for 30 minutes to blend the flavors. Stir in the corn, tomato, and cilantro.

3. To serve, place one mussel in each shell and top with some of the corn mixture. Arrange the lettuce on 4 individual plates and top with 5 mussels each.

NOTE **An alternative way of serving this specialty for a buffet is to omit the shells and just serve the mussels mixed with the corn mixture in a bowl.**

Anticuchos

SKEWERED BEEF HEART *Serves 8*

This ancient dish preceded the Spanish conquest of Peru. Before the arrival of Europeans, who introduced cattle to South America, the Incas used the heart of the llama to prepare this specialty. *Anticucho* in Quechua means "food from the Andes cooked on skewers." It is a very popular appetizer, and it must be served with beer or *chicha* to quench the heat. The classic *anticuchos* are still made with beef heart and can be found in the streets of Lima, where vendors grill the skewers on portable charcoal grills. *Anticuchos* also are made with other meats, such as beef or chicken breast, or with fish or shrimp. In Bolivia, *anticuchos* are so popular that there are special establishments called *anticucheras*, which specialize in the preparation of these delicacies for evening snacks. Bolivians alternate meat and small potatoes on the skewers and serve them with a peanut sauce—a hearty snack indeed. For the Peruvian version, omit the oregano in the marinade and serve the *anticuchos* without the peanut sauce.

1 beef heart (about 4 pounds) or 3 pounds sirloin steak or boneless, skinless chicken breasts

MARINADE

½ cup red wine vinegar

4 cloves garlic, chopped

3 fresh hot yellow or red peppers, seeded

1 teaspoon ground cumin

1 teaspoon dried oregano, crumbled (for the Bolivian version)

1 teaspoon salt

½ teaspoon freshly ground black pepper

Pinch of sugar

BASTING SAUCE

3 dried *panca* peppers

¼ cup canola oil mixed with 2 tablespoons *Manteca de Color* (page 331)

16 small red potatoes (for the Bolivian version), cooked in water to cover until tender and drained

SALSA DE MANI
(Peanut sauce; for the Bolivian version)

2 tablespoons canola oil

Leftover basting sauce

¼ cup unsalted dry-roasted peanuts, ground, or natural peanut butter

1½ cups water

Salt

1.   Remove the fat and nerves from the heart and cut into 1-inch cubes. Put the cubes in a large glass bowl.

2.   To make the marinade, combine all the ingredients in a blender, puree and pour over the heart, tossing to coat. Cover with plastic wrap and let marinate in the refrigerator for at least 6 hours or overnight, turning the cubes occasionally.

3.   Soak 8 wooden or bamboo skewers in cold water at the same time the meat is put in the refrigerator.

4.   To make the basting sauce, break the dried peppers in half and discard the seeds. Crumble the peppers and soak in hot water to cover for 30 minutes. Using a slotted spoon, transfer the peppers to a blender or food processor. Add ½ cup of the soaking liquid and the oil mixture and process until smooth. Set aside.

5.   To make the peanut sauce, if using, heat the oil in a medium-size saucepan over medium heat. Add the leftover basting sauce and cook, stirring, until hot. Add the ground peanuts and water and simmer until the sauce is creamy, about 5 minutes. Season with salt to taste and keep warm.

6.   Remove the meat cubes from the marinade. For the Peruvian version, thread 4 or 5 cubes onto each skewer, keeping them apart, and brush on all sides with the basting sauce. Cook the skewers over a medium-hot charcoal fire or under the preheated broiler for about 4 minutes, turning frequently and basting with the basting sauce. Serve hot (see To Serve).

For the Bolivian version, alternate the meat cubes with 2 potatoes on each skewer and brush with the basting sauce. Cook as described above. Serve with the peanut sauce.

TO SERVE **Some people serve the Peruvian version with *Salsa Criolla Peruana* (page 334).**

Papas Huancaínas

POTATOES WITH SPICY CHEESE SAUCE
Serves 6 to 12

One of the best-known Peruvian appetizers, this dish originated in the Andean region of Huancayo. Potatoes with cheese sauce are also very popular in Bolivia. *Palillo*, an indigenous herb, gives the sauce a bright yellow color. This herb is sometimes available in Latin American markets, but it can easily be replaced with turmeric. *Papas huancaínas* are not only easy to prepare and lovely to look at, but they are also versatile. They make a dramatic addition to a buffet table and are ideal to serve as an hors d'oeuvre for a cocktail party. If serving this as an hors d'oeuvre, consider using small blue potatoes, if available. Medium-size potatoes can be cut into ½-inch-thick rounds and served with small plates and forks.

> 6 medium-size red or Yukon gold potatoes
> 1½ teaspoons salt
> 8 ounces imported feta cheese, crumbled
> One 3-ounce package cream cheese
> 1 tablespoon fresh lemon juice
> 1 large clove garlic, minced
> One 3-inch hot yellow pepper, seeded and minced
> ½ teaspoon *palillo* (page 427) or turmeric
> ¼ teaspoon freshly ground black pepper
> ½ cup whipping cream, or more if needed
> ¼ cup olive oil
> Boston or red leaf lettuce, shredded
> Black olives, halved and pitted, for garnish
> *Salsa Criolla Peruana* (page 334) for serving

1. Place the potatoes in a large saucepan with water to cover by at least 1 inch. Add 1 teaspoon of the salt, bring to a boil, and cook over medium heat until the potatoes are tender, about 30 minutes. Do not overcook. Drain, peel when cool enough to handle, cover, and set aside.

2. In a blender or food processor, place the feta, cream cheese, lemon juice, garlic, hot pepper, *palillo*, remaining ½ teaspoon salt, black pepper, whipping cream, and oil and process until smooth. Transfer to a small saucepan and cook over low heat, stirring constantly, until smooth, about 3 minutes. If the sauce is lumpy, return to the blender and process for a few seconds. If the sauce is too thick, stir in a little extra cream. Taste for salt and black pepper. The sauce can be made ahead, covered, and refrigerated until needed. Reheat until smooth enough to pour over the potatoes. It should be thick but runny enough to cover the potatoes smoothly.

3. To serve, line a plate or serving tray with lettuce, cut the potatoes in half lengthwise, and arrange on top of the lettuce. Pour the sauce over the potatoes and garnish each potato with an olive half. Scatter the *salsa criolla* around the potatoes.

Causa Rellena de Pollo

POTATO CAKE FILLED WITH CHICKEN SALAD *Makes one 9-inch cake; 8 to 12 servings*

Causa is a very old Peruvian specialty that, in its most primitive form, goes back to the Andean highlands of Peru. After the conquest, the Spaniards introduced the use of different fillings and garnishes to make this cake a feast for the eyes as well as the palate. The potatoes used in Peru are the *papa amarilla* (yellow potato) and *papa morada* (blue or purple potato). In the United States, Yukon gold potatoes work very well for this dish. Occasionally, blue potatoes are available in some U.S. supermarkets and are my favorite for making *causas*; the blue color is intensified by refrigeration and lends itself to a very dramatic presentation. *Causas* are usually served cut into wedges as an appetizer, but they also make a very nice main course for lunch or supper. Choose any of the garnishes listed here for a colorful platter.

2 hot green peppers

2 hot red peppers

3 pounds Yukon gold potatoes, scrubbed

6 tablespoons olive oil, or more to taste

1 tablespoon fresh lemon or lime juice, or
more to taste

1 tablespoon fresh hot yellow pepper puree,
store-bought or homemade (page 332)

1 teaspoon salt

¼ teaspoon white pepper

RELLENO (Filling)

2 cups finely chopped cooked chicken breast

½ cup finely chopped cooked carrots

1 small onion, minced (about ½ cup)

2 tablespoons minced fresh parsley leaves

1 tablespoon minced fresh basil or cilantro
leaves

½ cup mayonnaise, store-bought or homemade (page 341)

1 teaspoon Dijon mustard

¼ teaspoon salt

¼ teaspoon freshly ground black pepper

GARNISHES

Salad greens

3 hard-cooked eggs, peeled and quartered

8 ounces *queso panela* or feta cheese
(optional), cut into 8 wedges

1 ripe but firm Hass avocado, peeled, pitted,
and cut into 8 wedges

6 black olives, pitted

1.   Seed the hot peppers and cut into ⅛-inch-
wide strips. Blanch 3 times in boiling water for 20
seconds each time. Drain and set aside for garnish.

2.   Place the potatoes in a large saucepan with
cold salted water to cover and bring to a boil.
Reduce the heat to medium and let simmer until
tender, about 30 minutes. Drain and, when cool
enough to handle, peel and pass through a potato
ricer or mash with a potato masher until smooth.
In a small bowl, mix together the oil, lemon juice,

hot pepper puree, salt, and white pepper. Pour
over the potatoes and mix thoroughly. Season
carefully, adding more oil, lemon juice, hot peppers, or salt as needed to make a smooth, spicy
dough. Cover with plastic wrap and set aside.

3.   To make the filling, in a medium-size bowl,
mix together the chicken, carrots, onion, parsley,
and basil. In a small bowl, mix together the mayonnaise, mustard, salt, and black pepper. Toss the
mayonnaise mixture with the chicken mixture,
then taste for salt and black pepper.

4.   To assemble the cake, place a lightly oiled
ring from a 9-inch springform pan on a serving
platter. Transfer half of the potato mixture to the
ring, spreading it evenly. Top with the chicken
salad and spread the remaining potato mixture on
top. Cover with plastic wrap and refrigerate for at
least 2 hours or overnight.

5.   To serve, carefully remove the springform
ring, surround the *causa* with greens, and decorate
the top with the garnishes of your choice.

Ocopa Arequipeña

POTATOES WITH CHEESE,
WALNUTS, AND HOT PEPPER SAUCE   *Serves 8*

This is another example of the wonderful way
Peruvians use potatoes. Like *Papas Huancaínas*
(page 127), *ocopas* can be served at room temperature, making it a very special buffet or picnic dish,
although it is also a traditional first course. Typical
of Arequipa, this dish has spread not only to other
parts of Peru but abroad as well. Sometimes the
potatoes are mashed, mixed with the sauce ingredients, and served spread on a tray, garnished with
shrimp, pieces of sautéed fish, and turnip greens.
The classic *ocopa Arequipeña* is made with dried
mirasol (hot yellow) peppers, roasted onion and
garlic, nuts, cheese, and oil and is flavored with the
indigenous Peruvian herb *huacatay*, which has a
very distinctive flavor that is not very appealing to

many people. (There is no substitute for this. You can find *huacatay* in South American markets.) Another popular *ocopa* is *ocopa de camarones*, which uses shrimp and *huacatay*. One constant is the generous amount of hot peppers that Peruvians use, although this can be adjusted to the individual's taste. I usually puree three *mirasol* peppers, then add one tablespoon of the puree at a time to get the degree of heat I want. People who like hot food would use six peppers.

> 3 to 6 dried *mirasol* (hot yellow) peppers, to your taste
>
> 1 cup warm water
>
> 2 tablespoons plus 1/3 cup canola oil, or more if needed
>
> 1 small onion, minced (about 1/2 cup)
>
> 2 cloves garlic, minced
>
> 1/2 cup chopped walnuts
>
> 4 ounces fresh goat cheese or imported feta cheese, crumbled
>
> 1/2 cup milk, or more if needed
>
> 1 tablespoon fresh lemon juice
>
> 1/4 teaspoon salt
>
> 1/8 teaspoon white pepper
>
> 2 tablespoons *huacatay* puree, or to taste
>
> Lettuce leaves
>
> 8 small Yukon gold or red potatoes, peeled, cooked in water to cover until tender, drained, and halved
>
> 4 hard-cooked eggs, peeled and halved
>
> 1 recipe *Salsa Criolla Peruana* (page 334)
>
> 8 black olives, halved and pitted

1. Remove the seeds from the dried hot peppers and soak in the warm water for 1 hour. Puree the peppers in a blender with a little of the soaking liquid. If using bottled peppers, just seed and puree in a blender.

2. In a small skillet, heat 2 tablespoons of the oil over medium heat. Add the onion, garlic, and 1 tablespoon of the hot pepper puree and cook,

stirring, until the onion is transparent, about 3 minutes. Transfer to a blender or food processor. Add the walnuts, cheese, milk, lemon juice, salt, white pepper, and *huacatay* and process until smooth. With the machine running, add the remaining 1/3 cup oil through the feed tube in a thin stream and process until the sauce has the consistency of very thin mayonnaise. (It should cover the potatoes when poured.) Add a little more milk or oil if too thick. Season with salt and hot pepper puree to taste.

3. Line a serving platter with lettuce leaves. Arrange the potatoes cut side down on the lettuce. Distribute the eggs between the potatoes, then mound the *salsa criolla* in the center of the platter. Spoon the sauce over the potatoes and decorate each potato with an olive half.

Arrollado Fiambre

COLD SAVORY ROULADE *Makes about 24 rounds*

Cold savory *roulades* are very popular in Argentina and Uruguay. They come in main course and hors d'oeuvre sizes. I still remember with awe a very small *roulade* I had in a tea salon in Montevideo. It was about one inch in diameter, beautiful, and delicious—a perfect savory *petit four*. My Argentine friends make them for luncheons or buffets, decorated with mayonnaise and whatever ingredient goes with the filling. I love making them for tea parties in small sizes, with a variety of fillings.

PIONONO (Roulade)

> 4 large eggs
>
> Pinch of salt
>
> 2 tablespoons sugar
>
> 2 tablespoons all-purpose flour

RELLENO (Filling)

> 1/2 cup mayonnaise, store-bought or home-made (page 341), plus more for spreading

1 teaspoon Dijon mustard

1 teaspoon fresh lemon juice

Salt

¼ teaspoon white pepper

6 ounces imported boiled ham, finely chopped

2 hard-cooked eggs, peeled and finely chopped

2 tablespoons finely chopped fresh parsley leaves

1 teaspoon drained and chopped capers

1. Butter a 10 x 15-inch jellyroll pan, line it with aluminum foil or parchment paper, butter it again, and dust it with flour, knocking out the excess. Preheat the oven to 375°F.

2. To make the *roulade*, in a large bowl with an electric mixer, beat the eggs and salt until thick, about 10 minutes. While beating, add the sugar 1 tablespoon at a time. Sift the flour over the mixture and fold in carefully. Spread the batter evenly on the prepared pan. Bake in the upper third of the oven until golden, 8 to 10 minutes. Let rest for 5 minutes, then turn onto a clean kitchen towel, roll up with the long end facing you, and let cool.

3. To make the filling, in a medium-size bowl, mix together the mayonnaise, mustard, lemon juice, salt, and pepper. Add the ham, eggs, parsley, and capers. Mix well, then taste for salt and pepper.

4. Unroll the *roulade* and spread evenly with a thin layer of mayonnaise, leaving a ½-inch border around the edges. Spread the filling evenly on top. Roll up tightly, then wrap in aluminum foil and refrigerate for up to 6 hours.

5. To serve, cut into ½-inch-thick rounds and arrange on a serving platter.

Sopas

SOUPS

SOUPS PLAY A PARAMOUNT ROLE in South American cuisine. They are an indispensable part of the main meal and frequently appear alone, as meals in themselves. The type of soup varies, depending on the occasion, time of the day, geography, and season. From the wonderful *consommés*, which are a must for dinner parties, to the hearty, *pot-au-feu*–type soups, the varieties are almost endless and include *pucheros*, *locros*, *cocidos*, *sancochos*, and many others.

Although most South American soups originated in European kitchens, a few date back to pre-Hispanic times. In the Andean countries, there are the *mazamorras* or *coladas*, cream-like soups made with ground dried corn, ground dried beans, quinoa, amaranth, or squash. Potatoes and sometimes greens might be added. Variations of this type of soup, called *sangos*, are probably the oldest Indian food. In fact, *el sanco* was the sacred dish of the Incas, who used it not only as an energy food but also as an offering to the gods, asking for good health. These porridge-like soups have been described by the Ecuadorian food writer Luis Cordero as *polenta espesa* (thick polenta). Their preparation is similar to that of the *mazamorras* or *coladas*, and they are then flavored with ground peanuts and annatto. The Inca version originally called for fat, cornmeal, and fresh blood from a just-killed animal. After the arrival of Spanish settlers, onions, garlic, and milk were incorporated. In the coastal areas, the plantain became the basis for the *sango*, which in these areas goes by the name *cocuma* or *colada*. These soups have survived over the centuries and are still part of the daily diet of the poor.

The Spaniards introduced *potajes* (hearty soups), *pucheros* (*pot-au-feu*–type soups), and *cocidos* (meat and vegetable soups), which were quickly adapted to include local ingredients, such as corn, beans, potatoes, tomatoes, peppers, squash, and yuca. African slaves created unusual soups made with plantains, yuca, coconut milk, and peanuts. The Portuguese brought chicken and rice soup, which became one of the two most popular soups in Brazil, along with black bean soup.

Chile, Argentina, Uruguay, Bolivia, and Paraguay have *locros*, thick soups made with hominy, beans, squash, and sweet potatoes. They may be prepared with or without meat, depending on a family's economic means. These *locros* resemble the Andean *locros* in name only, as Andean *locros* are cream-type soups made with a base of potatoes or squash and milk, cheese, and eggs.

Chupés are stew-like soups prepared with fish, chicken, or meat, along with potatoes, cheese, vegetables, and sometimes eggs. They are very popular in Bolivia, Chile, Peru, and Ecuador. When these countries went to war to gain their independence, Venezuelan and Colombian soldiers joined in the battles. While in the southern countries, the soldiers fell in love with these soups and brought the recipes home, where they also became favorites. The Colombian *ajiaco* is a type of *chupé* made with chicken and three kinds of potatoes. The Bolivian *chupés* are typical lunches of the Altiplano and valleys and are made with meat, potatoes, and vegetables, especially squash. No milk, cheese, or eggs are used in this region's *chupés*. Sometimes dried sheep meat, called *chalona*, is used instead of fresh meat.

Sancochos are nothing more than boiled dinners or *pot-au-feu* and appear throughout the Andean countries. They can be as simple as the type of *sancochos* eaten in Ecuador, which feature meat or fish, yuca, and plantains, or as elaborate as some found in Colombia and Venezuela, which use a variety of meats and vegetables, such as yuca, *arracacha*, *ñame* (yam), squash, potatoes, plantains, corn, and sweet potatoes. They are meals in themselves.

The term *mazamorra* is of Indian origin. It means different things in different countries. Plain *mazamorra* (hominy) was the basis for the Argentine *locro* that was prepared in colonial times in big pots to feed the slaves and field workers. In Ecuador, *mazamorra*, also called *colada*, means any type of cream soup made with different types of dried bean flours. There are also sweet types of *mazamorra*, such as *mazamorra morada*, which is made with blue corn and berries and served as a dessert or snack.

Pucheros and *cazuelas* are especially popular in the southern countries of South America, where leftovers from the noon meal are converted into different soups for the evening meal. The favorite soups among Latins are *sopas claras*. These include light vegetable soups made with homemade chicken or beef broth, a few diced or julienned vegetables, and a little rice, as well as similar soups made with small meatballs or cornmeal dumplings.

MEATLESS SOUPS ARE OFTEN FOUND in the South American kitchen, using tubers, vegetables, legumes, and sometimes fruit. The most popular soups among the working classes are those made with diverse ground dried beans or with noodles or rice.

Sopa de Manga a la Margarida

MARGARIDA'S MANGO SOUP *Serves 6*

This soup was created by my talented Brazilian friend and colleague Margarida Nogueira. It is very light and refreshing and is ideal for summer, when mangoes are in season. It takes only a few minutes to prepare and can be made a day ahead. The taste of curry is so faint that it shouldn't bother those who aren't fond of this spice. The cilantro is indispensable because it rounds out the taste of the soup.

> Three 10-ounce or two 1-pound ripe but firm mangoes (see Notes)
> 1 tablespoon unsalted butter
> 1 tablespoon canola oil
> 2 tablespoons minced shallots
> 1 teaspoon curry powder
> 2 cups water
> 1 teaspoon beef bouillon granules
> 1 teaspoon fresh lime juice
> Cayenne pepper
> $\frac{1}{2}$ teaspoon salt
> Minced fresh cilantro leaves

1. Peel the mangoes, cut the flesh from the seeds, and then cut it into small dice (you should get about 3 cups). Place in a food processor or blender and process until smooth.

2. In a large nonreactive saucepan, heat the butter and oil together over medium heat until the butter has melted. Add the shallots and curry powder and cook, stirring constantly, for a couple of minutes, until the curry is fragrant. Add the mango puree, water, beef bouillon, lime juice, and cayenne to taste. Bring to a boil over medium heat, reduce the heat to low, and simmer for 5 minutes. The texture of the soup should be like that of heavy cream. If it is too thick, add a little more water. Stir in the salt.

3. Pour the soup through a medium-mesh sieve, let cool, and then chill completely. Serve cold, sprinkled with the cilantro.

NOTES If the mangoes are too soft, it will be difficult to remove the flesh from the seeds and skin, and the soup will taste very sweet.

This amount of soup will serve 6 if using very small bowls, such as 6-ounce tulip-shaped bowls. Half-cup servings are sufficient when served as part of a meal.

This soup freezes well for up to 2 months. When you're ready to use it, thaw in the refrigerator overnight and, even if partially frozen, whirl in the blender for a few seconds before serving.

Locro Ecuatoriano

POTATO SOUP WITH AVOCADO AND CORN
Serves 4

Potatoes were a staple food of the Incas, and today they are still the staff of life for the Andean peoples. Each country has a variety of soups and dishes that are centered on this noble root. *Locro* is a wonderful, hearty soup from Ecuador. Standard fare on the Ecuadorian table, it is bound to become a favorite, even for people who don't generally care much for potatoes. It can be served in small portions as a first course or in larger portions to make a very satisfying meal. A dish of *aji* on the side is a must.

2 tablespoons unsalted butter

½ teaspoon ground annatto or sweet paprika

¾ cup finely chopped scallions (white part and 1 inch of the green)

2 teaspoons salt

¼ teaspoon freshly ground black pepper

1½ pounds Idaho, Yukon gold, or other all-purpose potatoes, peeled and sliced crosswise 1½ inches thick

3 cups hot water, or more if needed

1 cup milk, or more if needed

4 sprigs fresh cilantro

1 large egg white

2 ounces Chihuahua, mozzarella, or Muenster cheese, shredded, or imported feta cheese, crumbled

1 large egg yolk lightly beaten with ½ cup whipping cream

GARNISHES

1 tablespoon extra virgin olive oil

1 teaspoon fresh lemon juice

Pinch of salt

4 romaine lettuce leaves, shredded

1 large ripe but firm Hass avocado, peeled, pitted, and cut into ½-inch cubes

1 cup cooked corn kernels, drained

2 hard-cooked eggs, peeled and coarsely chopped

Ají Criollo (page 333)

1. In a heavy 4-quart saucepan, heat the butter over medium-low heat until melted. Stir in the annatto, scallions, salt, and pepper and cook, stirring occasionally, until the scallions are softened, about 3 minutes. Add the potatoes and cook, stir-ring often, for about 3 minutes, without browning. Add the water and bring to a boil. Reduce the heat to low and simmer until the potatoes begin to fall apart, about 30 minutes. With a wooden spoon, stir the potatoes so that some do fall apart and press a few against the side of the saucepan, mashing them a little. This will thicken the soup. Add the milk and cilantro and bring the soup back to a boil. Reduce the heat to medium-low, add the egg white, and simmer for 5 minutes without stirring. Add the cheese and stir until melted. If the soup is too thick, add more milk or water to achieve the desired consistency. Discard the cilantro. Just before serving, stir in the egg yolk mixture and heat thoroughly.

2. For the garnishes, whisk the oil, lemon juice, and salt together in a small bowl. Combine the lettuce and avocado in a medium-size bowl and toss with the dressing until lightly coated. Ladle the soup into bowls, adding to each bowl ¼ cup of the corn. Mound about ¼ cup of the salad in the center of the soup and top with some of the chopped eggs. Serve with a bowl of *aji* on the side.

Chupé de Quinua

QUINOA CHOWDER *Serves 4*

Chowders are everyday items on the tables of the Andean peoples. These chowders can be as simple as a combination of squash, wheat, or quinoa with potatoes, or they may also include meat or fish. In Bolivia, beef or lamb is used, as well as the dried potatoes called *chuño* or *tunta*. The basic seasoning is fairly standard in all the Andean countries, except that in Peru and Bolivia ground hot peppers are added to the *sofrito*. (*Sofrito* is the universal South American seasoning. Its base is always onion, but it can include, as it does here, garlic, hot peppers, and other flavor elements.) This is a great soup for vegetarians.

2 tablespoons butter or olive oil

1 medium-size onion, finely chopped (about 1 cup)

2 cloves garlic, mashed into a paste with 1 teaspoon salt and ½ teaspoon freshly ground black pepper

½ teaspoon ground cumin

½ teaspoon sweet paprika

¼ teaspoon red pepper flakes (optional)

4 cups boiling water or chicken or vegetable broth

2 cups cooked quinoa (page 327)

1 pound boiling potatoes, peeled and cut into 1-inch cubes

1 cup milk

1 cup fresh or frozen corn kernels

½ cup fresh or frozen peas, or shelled fava beans, blanched and peeled (page 308)

4 ounces cheddar cheese, shredded

2 large eggs, lightly beaten

Minced fresh mint and cilantro leaves for garnish

1 ripe but firm Hass avocado (optional), peeled, pitted, and diced (¼ inch), for garnish

1. In a heavy 4-quart saucepan, melt the butter over low heat. Add the onion and cook, stirring occasionally, for 10 minutes, without letting it color. Stir in the garlic paste, cumin, paprika, and red pepper (if using) and cook for 1 minute. Add the water, quinoa, and potatoes and simmer, partially covered, until the potatoes are tender, about 15 minutes. Add the milk, corn, and peas and simmer for 5 minutes. Add the cheese and eggs and cook, stirring constantly, until the cheese is melted and the eggs have set.

2. Serve hot, garnished with the mint and cilantro leaves and the avocado, if using.

Repe (Sopa de Guineo Verde)

CREAM OF GREEN BANANA SOUP *Serves 8*

This is a delicious soup and can be a conversation starter if you make your guests guess what the main ingredient is. *Repe* originated in one of the southern provinces of Ecuador, where it is sometimes made like a thick puree to be served as a vegetable with rice. This soup has a subtle taste, reminiscent to some of asparagus soup and to others of potato and cheese soup. Regardless of the difficulty in defining the taste, it is always a hit.

When working with bananas, keep in mind that you should not use aluminum utensils, because they will discolor the soup. Use green, hard bananas. If the bananas are beginning to yellow, the soup will have a slightly sweet taste.

4 medium-size very green and hard bananas (about 1½ pounds)

4 cups water

2 cups milk

½ cup whipping cream

3 ounces white cheddar cheese, shredded

½ teaspoon salt

¼ teaspoon white pepper

Pinch of sugar (optional)

Minced fresh cilantro leaves or sweet paprika for garnish

Pesto de Cilantro (page 339; optional) for garnish

1. To peel the bananas, cut incisions along the ridges, then pull away the skin. Put them in a bowl of cold water to prevent discoloration.

2. In a 4-quart nonreactive saucepan, bring the water to a boil. Add the bananas (the water should cover them), cover, and cook over low heat until the bananas are soft, about 15 minutes. Drain, reserving the cooking liquid. Wash out the saucepan. With a fork, cut each banana into 6

pieces. Remove any black spots that may be found in the center. Place in a food processor or blender in batches along with 2 cups of the reserved cooking liquid and process until smooth.

3. Transfer to the clean saucepan. Add the milk and cream and bring to a boil. The soup should have the consistency of heavy cream. If it is too thick, thin it with a little water or milk. Add the cheese and stir until melted. Remove from the heat and stir in the salt and pepper. If the bananas are very green, a pinch of sugar will enhance the flavor.

4. Serve hot in soup bowls, garnished with cilantro or paprika, or with a swirl of the pesto, if desired.

NOTE **This soup can be made ahead and reheated, or it can be frozen for up to 2 months.**

Crema Anaranjada
WINTER SQUASH SOUP *Serves 8*

Some version of squash soup shows up in every South American country. In Venezuela, it is often made with a base of meat stock and flavored with mint and cilantro. In Uruguay, it is prepared with onions and tomatoes and, in the French style, enriched with cream and garnished with croutons. This particular recipe was inspired by one given to me by the chef/owner of one of the best restaurants in Montevideo, Lo de la Carlota. He called it *Crema Anaranjada* because of its beautiful orange color. I sometimes use (as Brazilians do) unsweetened coconut milk instead of cream, but I like to flavor it as Venezuelans do, with mint and cilantro. The result is a truly South American soup.

2 tablespoons unsalted butter

2 pounds calabaza or butternut squash, peeled, seeded, and cubed

2 medium-size onions, thinly sliced (about 2 cups)

2 large ripe but firm tomatoes (about 1 pound), quartered

1 teaspoon salt

¼ teaspoon freshly grated black pepper

Pinch of cayenne pepper

4 cups hot water or chicken broth

½ cup whipping cream or well-stirred canned unsweetened coconut milk

Croutons (page 412), minced fresh mint and cilantro leaves, or a few cooked corn kernels for garnish

1. In a heavy 6-quart casserole, melt the butter over medium heat. Add the squash and onions, cover, and cook, stirring occasionally, for 5 minutes. Add the tomatoes, salt, black pepper, cayenne, and water and bring to a boil. Cover, reduce the heat to medium-low, and simmer until the vegetables are soft, about 30 minutes. Remove from the heat and let cool for 30 minutes.

2. Transfer to a blender or food processor and process in batches until smooth. Push through a coarse-mesh sieve, return to the casserole, and add the cream. Taste for salt and heat through over low heat. If too thick, add a little water to obtain the desired consistency. It should be a little thicker than whipping cream.

3. Serve hot, garnished with croutons, mint and cilantro, or corn kernels.

NOTE **This soup is also excellent prepared without the cream or coconut milk.**

Crema de Aguacate
CREAM OF AVOCADO SOUP *Serves 8*

This exquisite soup from my childhood is a favorite throughout South America. Each country has its own version: some cooks use béchamel sauce as a base, others use potatoes, and the Brazilians use chicken stock, avocados, and a pinch of curry. I like my mother's recipe, which is delicious, fast, and easy to make. Keep in mind that avocados cannot be cooked, because they curdle and become bitter.

4 cups chicken broth

1 cup half-and-half

1 tablespoon grated onion

½ teaspoon salt

¼ teaspoon white pepper

¼ teaspoon hot pepper sauce, or to taste

2 large ripe but firm Hass avocados

1 tablespoon fresh lemon juice

1 cup croutons (page 412) for serving

1. In a heavy 4-quart saucepan or large bowl, mix together the chicken broth, half-and-half, onion, salt, white pepper, and hot pepper sauce. This can be done hours ahead and kept refrigerated until ready to serve.

2. A couple of hours before serving, peel the avocados, then pit and cut into 1-inch pieces. Place in a medium-size nonreactive bowl, sprinkle with the lemon juice, cover with Saran wrap, and refrigerate until ready to use.

3. Just before serving, put ½ cup of the chicken broth mixture in a blender. Bring the rest to a boil in a heavy 4-quart saucepan, then reduce the heat to low. Add the avocado to the blender and process until smooth. Pass this mixture through a coarse-mesh sieve, then add to the simmering broth and heat, but do not let it come to a boil. Taste for salt.

4. Serve immediately, with croutons on the side. This soup can also be served chilled. Make it only a couple of hours ahead, cover with Saran wrap, let cool, and then chill completely.

Gazpacho

COLD VEGETABLE SOUP   *Serves 8*

This world-famous cold soup originated in Spain after the discovery of the New World. When the Spaniards brought back to their homeland tomatoes and peppers, cooks paired them with onions, garlic, and bread to create this fabulous soup. Like many other Old World specialties, gazpacho traveled back to South America to become a popular specialty there, too. This particular recipe is one of the best I know; it has been refined over the years. Like the ladies of colonial times, I learned this recipe in Madrid. The chef of the restaurant O'Xeito taught me his secret for the best gazpacho I had ever eaten—the beautiful taste and salmon color come from the addition of a roasted red pepper. When I brought this secret back home, my mother tried it first and then told the cook how to prepare it.

2 cups cubed day-old bread (preferably French or Italian; see Note), crusts removed

3 large ripe but firm tomatoes (about 1½ pounds), peeled, seeded, and chopped

1 medium-size cucumber, peeled, seeded, and chopped

1 medium-size green bell pepper, seeded and chopped

1 roasted red pepper (page 411)

2 cloves garlic, minced

3 tablespoons olive oil

3 tablespoons red wine vinegar

2 cups water

2 teaspoons salt

½ teaspoon ground cumin

¼ teaspoon cayenne pepper

¼ teaspoon freshly ground black pepper

2 tablespoons tomato paste, if using winter tomatoes

> 1 large ripe but firm tomato (about 8 ounces), peeled, seeded, and finely chopped
>
> 1 medium-size cucumber, peeled, seeded, and finely chopped
>
> 1 small green bell pepper, seeded and finely chopped
>
> 1 medium-size onion, finely chopped (about 1 cup)
>
> Croutons (page 412)

1. Mix all the soup ingredients together in a large bowl, cover with plastic wrap, and refrigerate for 1 day.

2. Transfer the mixture in batches to a blender or food processor and process until smooth. Taste for salt and black pepper. Return to the bowl, cover with plastic wrap, and refrigerate for at least 4 hours. Add a little water if the mixture is too thick.

3. When ready to serve, stir the soup and ladle it into chilled bowls. Garnish with 1 teaspoon of each of the garnishes, or put the garnishes in separate bowls for your guests to add to their own taste.

NOTE Do not use commercial sliced bread that comes packaged in plastic bags; it will form lumps instead of thickening the soup.

Sopa de Zanahoria

PARAGUAYAN CARROT AND CHEESE SOUP *Serves 8*

In the course of my research, I have found many soups that are so simple and plain, such as the *mazamorras*, that they can only be classified as comfort foods. This is one such soup. I think the key to this recipe is to have fresh carrots and a flavorful cheese. Cheddar or Gouda not only gives the soup a good flavor and texture but also intensifies the beautiful orange color of the carrots. Many vegetable-based soups from Paraguay use cheese to give the soup taste and texture. This soup can also be made with winter squash instead of carrots.

> ¼ cup (½ stick) unsalted butter
>
> 1 pound carrots, sliced about ½ inch thick
>
> 1 teaspoon salt
>
> 1 teaspoon sugar
>
> 4 cups hot water
>
> 4 ounces cheddar or Gouda cheese, shredded
>
> Croutons (page 412) for serving

1. Melt the butter in a heavy 4-quart saucepan over medium heat. Add the carrots and cook, stirring, until they are covered with the butter. Add the salt, sugar, and water. Bring to a boil, cover, reduce the heat to low, and cook until soft, about 20 minutes.

2. Drain, reserving the cooking liquid. Transfer the carrots to a blender and process until smooth, adding a little of the cooking liquid. Return to the saucepan with the remaining liquid and bring to a boil. Reduce the heat to low, stir in the cheese, and simmer until it melts. The texture should be like that of heavy cream. Taste for salt and sugar.

3. Serve in soup bowls, with croutons on the side.

Sopa de Palmito

HEARTS OF PALM SOUP *Serves 4*

Hearts of palm are an old-time favorite vegetable for South Americans. They are not only delicious but also very versatile, and you can find them incorporated into sauces, salads, *cebiches*, tamales, empanadas, soups, and more. Hearts of palm are easy to find in all supermarkets and come packed in cans or glass jars. In the United States, fresh hearts of palm are available only in Miami, as far as I know, but the ones in jars and cans are still delicious and work well in all my recipes.

2 tablespoons unsalted butter

1 cup thinly sliced leeks (white part and 1 inch of the green), washed well

1 tablespoon all-purpose flour

1 tablespoon cornstarch

¼ teaspoon white pepper

One 14-ounce can hearts of palm, drained, rinsed, and cut into 1-inch pieces

2 cups chicken broth

1 cup milk

Sweet paprika or cayenne pepper for garnish

1. In a heavy 4-quart saucepan, melt the butter over low heat. Add the leeks and cook, stirring occasionally, for 3 minutes, without letting them color. Sprinkle in the flour, cornstarch, and pepper and toss to coat the leeks. Add the hearts of palm and chicken broth and cook, stirring, until well mixed.

2. Transfer to a blender, in batches if necessary, and process until smooth. Pass through a medium-mesh sieve and return to a clean pan. Add the milk and bring to a boil. Reduce the heat to low and simmer for a couple of minutes. Taste for salt and pepper.

3. Serve hot in soup bowls, garnished with paprika.

Sopas con Pollo o Carne
SOUPS WITH CHICKEN OR MEAT

SOUPS WITH CHICKEN OR MEAT have always been the most popular in South America. When we had chicken (more likely hen) as a main course, it needed long cooking. For instance, before being fried, it had to be boiled. So we could always count on a follow-up meal of chicken soup made from the broth, the chopped gizzards, carrots, peas, and rice.

Soups made with beef are also loved, and the array is endless. Although beef soups usually have vegetables, cooks often make do with whatever is available in the kitchen.

Locro Argentino
ARGENTINE HOMINY AND BEAN SOUP
Serves 10 to 12

The Argentine *locros* have nothing to do with the Ecuadorian or Peruvian *locros*, which have potatoes and milk as a base. The Argentine *locros* are mildly flavored, thick soups that are made by cooking the cracked dried kernels of hulled white corn

(hominy) for a couple of hours, until tender. In Argentina, there are basically three kinds of *locros*. One is made with a base of hominy and beans, another with fresh corn, and the third with wheat berries. Beef, sausage, or dried meat is added, depending on the circumstances. And when there is no meat, it is called *locro guascho*. Vegetables such as squash and sweet potatoes are included. Some people add cabbage, which makes the soup even more nutritious, although leafy greens, according to purists, should never be added. The variations are endless, depending on the season, the vegetables available, and the cook's preferences. At the end of the cooking time, a "fried sauce," or *sofrito*, is stirred into the soup.

Locros are very popular in the central zone of Argentina, as well as in Bolivia and Paraguay, with regional differences. Paraguayans have a simple *locro* made only with hominy and seasoned with onions and lots of cheese. They also have *locros* made with either fresh or dried meat and various vegetables, such as *mandioca* (yuca), instead of potatoes. *Iopará* is a type of *locro* that contains hominy and dried beans and is standard fare for soldiers. Bolivian *locros* are made with the whole hominy (not cracked) and *charqui* (dried meat) on the bone. It is seasoned with a *sofrito* made with onions, peppers, tomatoes, and garlic and is served with yuca or plantain and a Bolivian salsa.

For this recipe, I use canned hominy for convenience. Cracked dried corn is available at South American grocery stores. If you are using cracked corn instead of canned, soak one cup of the corn in water, just as you do the beans, then cook the corn and beans together. This is a truly wonderful soup to have on a wintry night. The recipe makes enough to keep a few quarts in the freezer for future enjoyment.

8 cups water

1 cup dried Great Northern or other white beans, picked over, rinsed, and soaked in water to cover for at least 4 hours

1 medium-size onion, chopped (about 1 cup)

1 small green bell pepper, seeded and chopped

1 pound beef brisket

Two 15-ounce cans hominy, undrained and coarsely chopped

2 cups coarsely chopped cabbage

1 pound calabaza or other winter squash, peeled, seeded, and cut into 1-inch cubes

2 medium-size sweet potatoes (about 12 ounces), peeled and cut into 1-inch cubes

2 teaspoons salt

½ teaspoon freshly ground black pepper

8 ounces Polish or Hungarian sausage (optional)

SOFRITO

2 tablespoons canola oil

1 tablespoon sweet paprika

½ teaspoon red pepper flakes

1 cup minced scallions (white part and 1 inch of the green)

1 teaspoon dried oregano, crumbled

1 teaspoon ground cumin

1 teaspoon salt

¼ teaspoon freshly ground black pepper

2 tablespoons minced fresh cilantro leaves

2 tablespoons minced fresh parsley leaves

1. Place the water, beans, onion, green pepper, and beef in a large soup kettle. Bring to a boil over medium heat, skimming off the froth as it rises to the top. Reduce the heat to low, cover, and simmer until the brisket is tender, about 1½ hours.

2. Remove the meat, cut into ½-inch pieces, and return to the pot. Add the hominy, cabbage, squash, sweet potatoes, salt, black pepper, and sausage (if using) and simmer for 30 minutes. By this time, the squash should start falling apart. Remove the sausage, cut into ¼-inch-thick rounds, and return to the pot.

3. Meanwhile, make the *sofrito*. In a medium-size skillet, heat the oil over medium heat. Add the paprika and stir in quickly. Add the remaining ingredients and cook, stirring, until softened, about 3 minutes. Stir the *sofrito* into the soup, taste for salt and pepper, and simmer for 5 minutes. The soup should have a thick broth. If it is too thick, add a little boiling water. If it is too thin, simmer for a few minutes, until thickened. Serve hot.

Caldo de Patas (Mondongo)

COW'S FEET SOUP *Serves 6 to 8*

This is a classic creole soup from the highlands of Ecuador, with a reputation for being an excellent remedy for *chuchaquis* (hangovers). In Quito, there are all-night restaurants that specialize in this soup and cater to partygoers until daybreak. On Sundays and holidays, huge kettles of it are common sights in the plazas of small towns and resorts around Quito. Typically made with cow's feet (available in ethnic groceries), it is equally good with pig's feet, which are easier to obtain in U.S. supermarkets.

> 1 cow's foot (about 2 pounds) or 2 pounds pig's feet, cut into 2-inch pieces (ask your butcher to do this)
>
> 2 leeks (white and green parts), ends trimmed and washed well
>
> 1 medium-size onion, quartered
>
> 4 cloves garlic, peeled
>
> 4 sprigs fresh parsley
>
> 8 cups water
>
> 2 teaspoons salt
>
> 1 tablespoon canola oil
>
> 1 teaspoon ground annatto or sweet paprika
>
> ½ teaspoon freshly ground black pepper
>
> 1 teaspoon dried oregano
>
> ½ teaspoon ground cumin
>
> Two 15-ounce cans hominy, undrained
>
> 1 cup milk, or more if needed
>
> ¼ cup natural peanut butter
>
> ½ cup whipping cream (optional)

GARNISHES

> ½ cup minced scallions (white part and 1 inch of the green)
>
> 1 jalapeño, seeded and cut into slivers
>
> ¼ cup chopped fresh cilantro leaves
>
> ¼ cup minced fresh parsley leaves

1. Put the cow's foot, leeks, onion, garlic, parsley, water, and salt in a large soup kettle. Bring to a boil, skimming off the froth that rises to the top. When the froth stops rising, reduce the heat to medium-low, cover, and simmer until the meat is tender, about 3 hours. Remove the meat and strain the broth through a sieve, pressing down on the vegetables to extract as much liquid and flavor from them as possible. Discard what is left of the vegetables. Degrease the broth. Remove the meat from the bones, discard the bones, and cut the meat into bite-size pieces.

2. In a 4-quart saucepan, heat the oil over low heat. Stir in the annatto, then add the black pepper, oregano, and cumin and cook, stirring, for a few seconds. Add the broth and bring to a boil. Add the meat and hominy and simmer for 10 minutes. Add the milk and peanut butter and simmer for another 10 minutes, stirring until the peanut butter has melted. Taste for salt and pepper.

3. Just before serving, stir in the whipping cream, if using. Do not let it boil. There should be plenty of broth, but add more milk, if needed.

4. Serve in soup plates, sprinkled with the garnishes.

Ch'airo

ANDEAN MEAT AND VEGETABLE SOUP WITH CHUÑO NEGRO *Serves 6*

This Bolivian soup is one of those traditional foods associated with a festival. According to the cookbook *Cocina Tradicional Boliviana* by Emilia de Velasco and Carola de Muzevich, *ch'airo* is always served for the Alasitas Festival (a festival of the indigenous Aymara people), which takes place in La Paz and around Lake Titicaca on January 24. This festival was originally celebrated in September, to pray for a good harvest, which takes place in the Bolivian spring (our fall). When the Spaniards came, they moved the festival to January.

The Alasitas Festival centers on Ekeko, the Aymara god of fertility, happiness, and prosperity.

Ekeko is also considered the god of the household and possessions, which is the reason he is portrayed loaded with tiny reproductions of things that are considered indispensable for the family. *Alasitas* means "buy me" in the Aymara language, and each year the streets are full of stalls selling figurines that represent Ekeko. Artisans also make tiny gifts that people buy to offer to Ekeko.

This festival is celebrated throughout Bolivia, though not always on the same day, in the same way, or with the same version of *ch'airo*. In the capital, La Paz, people celebrate Alasitas with *ch'airo paceño*, made with two kinds of meat—fresh lamb or beef and dried sheep (*chalona*). In the valley, they celebrate with the *ch'airo cochabambino*, made with fresh meat only. A constant ingredient is the two types of potatoes—fresh and dried black (*chuño negro*). *Chuño* is such an intrinsic part of this soup that there is a saying: "A *ch'airo* without *chuño* is like life without love." (You can find *chuño negro* in South American markets.) In La Paz, *ch'airo* is always served with *plato paceño*, a main course typical of Bolivia that is served during the corn harvest. It consists of large platters of corn on the cob cooked with anise seeds, fresh fava beans (cooked with a sprig of mint), boiled potatoes, and fresh cheese.

Ch'airo is not unique to Bolivia. It is also popular in the southern part of Peru. The Indians of the Altiplano always make their *ch'airo* with *chalona*, although the amount of meat used depends on the economic means of the family. Following is a simplified version of *ch'airo paceño*, similar to the *ch'airo con chuño negro* of the highlands of Peru.

½ cup *chuño negro*

10 cups water

2 pounds lean beef chuck, trimmed of fat and cut into 6 pieces

1 medium-size onion, chopped (about 1 cup)

1 large carrot, cut like thick French fries

1 medium-size turnip, peeled and cut into 6 wedges

2 large jalapeños, seeded and sliced

Red pepper flakes to taste

1 tablespoon salt

1 cup cooked wheat berries (page 412) or barley (see Note)

One 15-ounce can hominy, undrained

½ cup frozen peas

1 cup shelled fava beans, blanched and peeled (page 308)

1 pound all-purpose potatoes, peeled and cut like thick French fries

1 teaspoon dried oregano

Freshly ground black pepper to taste

GARNISHES

¼ cup thinly sliced scallions (white part and 1 inch of the green)

Minced fresh parsley leaves

Minced fresh mint leaves

1. Place the *chuño* in a bowl with lukewarm water to cover and let soak for at least 2 days, changing the water often. Rinse thoroughly, peel if needed, and squeeze dry. With a meat mallet, pound to break into small pieces. Set aside.

2. Place the water and beef in a large casserole and bring to a boil over medium heat, skimming off the froth as it rises to the top. Reduce the heat to low, cover, and simmer until the meat is tender, about 1 hour. Add the remaining ingredients, except the garnishes, including the *chuño*, and cook until the vegetables are tender, about 20 minutes. Taste for salt.

3. Serve hot in soup plates, adding 1 piece of beef to each plate. Sprinkle with the scallions and parsley. Serve the mint on the side so that people can add it to taste.

NOTE To cook barley, bring 1 cup salted water to a boil in a 2-quart saucepan. Stir in ¼ cup barley, reduce the heat, cover, and simmer for about 35 minutes, until tender.

Picanterías Creole Restaurants

The real flavor of the Andes is found in the *picanterías*, small restaurants where spicy dishes (very hot in Peru and Bolivia) are prepared and served, always complemented with *chicha de jora* (a fermented corn drink). These *restaurantes criollos*, as they are called in some countries, originated in the countryside and eventually moved to the outskirts of the big cities. Partygoers go there in the early hours of the morning to eat special foods that they believe will help them sober up before going home. The restaurants' specialties vary from country to country, but one thing they have in common is the atmosphere and the way their creole specialties, especially roasted or fried pig, attract people from the big cities and nearby areas, especially on weekends.

The name *picantería* comes from the generous use of *ajíes* (hot peppers), which makes the food *picante* (hot). These restaurants have been an institution in the countryside for hundreds of years, and there one can find the true flavor of the peasant's life. The *picanterías* found in the cities lack this quality.

Of special interest are the *picanterías* in Arequipa, a colonial city in southern Peru. The *picanterías* there are a novelty because they have retained the country look, the atmosphere, the service, and the flavor of the food. In Arequipa, the *picanterías* have a special emblem: a small red flag placed on the roof of a modest building. Each is furnished with rustic tables and benches. The food is prepared in enormous cauldrons, with lavish amounts of *rocotos* (a type of very hot pepper), which characterizes the cooking of this area. The menu changes every day: *ocopas* (potatoes with nut sauce), *cha'iro* (beef and hominy soup), stuffed *rocotos*, and stewed rabbit are just a few of the specialties, all made very hot and spicy, so that customers drink a lot of *chicha* to wash them down.

The use of hot peppers is also prevalent in Bolivia, but the food in the *picanterías* of the other Andean countries is not hot. Instead, it is served with a bowl of hot pepper sauce on the side. Dogs, flies, chickens, and ducks are part of the scene in most *picanterías*, as are decks of cards and a game called *sapo* (toad). The music played in Andean *picanterías* is sad, typical of the Andes. When people go to the *picanterías* in the countryside, it is with the intention of spending a whole afternoon. People from all walks of life—rich country gentlemen to peasant families (including babies) gather there.

Sapo is often played in *picanterías* in small-town taverns, and on farms. Whenever my family was invited to the farms of friends or relatives, we could count on finding a *sapo* game to keep us occupied for a while. *Sapo* consists of a simple console with an open-mouthed toad on top. There are some holes around the toad. People stand at a predetermined distance and throw heavy copper disks at the console, aiming for the toad's mouth. Getting a disk in the mouth earns the most points, while hitting the surrounding holes earns fewer points. The winner is the one who accumulates the most points.

Sopa de Quinua con Chancho

QUINOA SOUP WITH PORK *Serves 8 to 10*

This is one of the oldest soups made in South America, dating back to the time of the Inca Empire. After the conquest, pork and seasonings were added to it. This is a superb soup, full of taste and nutrition. I get numerous requests for this recipe from people who have moved to the United States from Ecuador and are delighted to find that quinoa is becoming more readily available in this country.

> 2 tablespoons olive oil
>
> 1 teaspoon ground annatto or sweet paprika
>
> ½ cup chopped scallions (white part and 1 inch of the green)
>
> 1 cup finely chopped leeks (white part and 1 inch of the green), washed well
>
> 1 medium-size ripe but firm tomato (5 to 6 ounces), peeled and chopped
>
> 4 cloves garlic, mashed into a paste with 1 teaspoon salt and ½ teaspoon freshly ground black pepper
>
> ½ teaspoon ground cumin
>
> ¾ pound lean pork from the leg or shoulder, trimmed of fat and cut into ½-inch cubes
>
> 6 cups hot water
>
> 1 pound boiling potatoes, peeled and cut into 1-inch cubes
>
> ¾ cup cooked quinoa (page 327)
>
> ¼ cup unsalted dry-roasted peanuts or natural peanut butter pureed with 1 cup milk
>
> 1 cup frozen peas
>
> 8 large fresh basil leaves, chopped
>
> Pinch of cayenne pepper
>
> Minced fresh parsley leaves for garnish

1. Heat the oil in a heavy 4-quart saucepan over low heat. Stir in the annatto, then add the scallions, leeks, tomato, garlic paste, and cumin and cook, stirring occasionally, for 5 minutes. Increase the heat to medium, add the pork cubes, and cook for a couple of minutes, tossing so they are well coated with the vegetable mixture. Add the water and bring to a boil. Cover, reduce the heat to low, and simmer for 45 minutes.

2. Add the potatoes, quinoa, and peanut puree. Partially cover and continue to cook until the potatoes are tender, about 20 minutes. Add the peas, basil, and cayenne and cook for a couple of minutes to heat the peas through. Taste for salt and black pepper.

3. Serve hot, garnished with the parsley.

Caldo Verde

GREEN BROTH (POTATO AND KALE SOUP) *Serves 6*

This Portuguese soup, named for its color, is the favorite soup of Portugal. It is believed to have originated in the north, after the Portuguese brought the potato home from the New World. When driving in the Minho province of Portugal, one can see Portuguese kale growing alongside grapevines—just about every house in the country has a patch of kale. This soup also has become a favorite in Brazil, especially in the southwest, because it is cheap, nourishing, and *saborosa* (tasty).

> 6 cups water
>
> 1 pound Yukon gold or other all-purpose potatoes, peeled and quartered
>
> 1 medium-size onion, coarsely chopped (about 1 cup)
>
> 2 teaspoons salt
>
> ¼ teaspoon freshly ground black pepper
>
> 1 bunch (about 12 ounces) kale or collard greens (see Notes), washed well, stems removed, and leaves cut lengthwise into ⅛-inch-wide strips, then cut crosswise into shorter strips
>
> 3 tablespoons extra virgin olive oil, plus more for serving
>
> 5 ounces chorizo or Polish sausage, sliced ¼ inch thick

1. In a 4-quart saucepan, bring the water, potatoes, and onion to a boil over medium heat. Add the salt and pepper, cover, reduce the heat to low, and cook until the potatoes are very tender, about 20 minutes. Drain, reserving the cooking liquid.

2. Mash or puree the potatoes, then return them and the reserved liquid to the saucepan and bring back to a boil. Add the kale and oil and cook until the kale is bright green and barely cooked, about 3 minutes. Taste for salt and pepper. The soup will thicken as it cools; add more boiling water if a thinner soup is desired.

3. In a medium-size skillet, lightly brown both sides of the sausage over medium heat. Add the sausage to the soup and serve immediately, with extra oil on the side so that people can add it to their taste.

NOTES For people who use a lot of greens, there is a special machine that slices and cuts them into thin slivers, so they are easier to eat. This machine, called a kale cutter, can be found in markets that carry Portuguese products.

The amount of greens used here will vary according to your taste.

Ajiaco de Pollo Bogotano

CREAMY POTATO SOUP WITH CHICKEN *Serves 8*

This famous soup from Bogotá, Colombia, makes an ideal main course for a lunch or light supper. The classic *ajiaco* is made with white, yellow (*papas criollas*), and purple potatoes. The different textures of these potatoes contribute to the flavor and texture of the soup. *Papas criollas* are available canned in Latin American markets; a good substitute is Yukon gold potatoes, which are sold in many supermarkets. They give flavor and color to the soup. Purple potatoes are occasionally available in some supermarkets and farmers' markets. Because they can be difficult to find, you may substitute new red potatoes in this recipe. Like the purple potatoes, they retain their shape when cooked. Idaho potatoes are used to give texture to the soup. They fall apart when cooked and, when mashed, provide the soup's creamy base. The chicken can be served in whole pieces or cut into bite-size slices, as in this recipe. Some versions also use a piece of beef along with or instead of the chicken. A Colombian herb, *guasca*, is sometimes added five minutes before the soup is finished cooking. There is no substitute for this herb.

The classic way to serve *ajiaco* is in soup plates, with bowls of capers, heavy cream, slices of corn on the cob (with corn holders), and either avocado slices or *ají de aguacate* (a guacamole-type specialty), so that each guest can garnish and flavor the soup to taste.

1 large whole bone-in chicken breast (about 1½ pounds), skin on

5 cups chicken broth

1 onion, peeled

2 carrots, peeled

2 scallions (white part and 1 inch of the green)

1 clove garlic, peeled

1 bay leaf

½ teaspoon dried thyme

¼ teaspoon ground cumin

4 sprigs fresh cilantro

10 black peppercorns

12 ounces small Yukon gold potatoes, peeled

12 ounces new red or purple potatoes, peeled and halved

1 tablespoon tomato paste (optional)

1 pound Idaho potatoes, peeled and sliced ¼ inch thick

4 cups water

2 teaspoons beef bouillon granules

1 cup frozen peas

4 ears corn, each cut into 4 pieces and cooked, or 2 cups cooked corn kernels, drained

½ cup whipping cream mixed with ½ cup crème fraîche or sour cream

One 3-ounce jar capers, drained

2 ripe but firm Hass avocados, peeled, pitted, and each cut right before serving into 8 slices or diced (¼ inch)

½ cup finely chopped fresh cilantro leaves

1. In a large casserole or saucepan, combine the chicken, chicken broth, onion, carrots, scallions, garlic, bay leaf, thyme, cumin, cilantro, and peppercorns and bring to a boil, skimming off the froth as it rises to the top. When the froth stops forming, reduce the heat to low, cover, and cook until the chicken is cooked through, about 20 minutes. Remove the chicken and carrots and set aside. Strain the broth through a fine-mesh sieve, return to the casserole, and bring to a boil over medium heat. Add the yellow and red potatoes and the tomato paste, if using. Cover and cook until the potatoes are soft, about 20 minutes.

2. While the red and yellow potatoes are cooking, place the Idaho potatoes in another saucepan with the water and beef bouillon. Bring to a boil, reduce the heat to medium, and cook until they begin to fall apart, about 30 minutes. Drain. Remove about a fourth of the slices and set aside; mash the rest. Add the mashed potatoes and reserved slices to the soup.

3. Remove the skin and bones from the chicken and discard. Cut the meat into strips about ¼ inch wide and 1 inch long. Add to the soup together with the peas and simmer for 5 minutes. Slice the carrots into rounds and add to the soup. Taste for salt. If the soup is too thick, add boiling water, a little at a time; the consistency should be like that of heavy cream. Keep in mind that as the soup stands, it will thicken.

4. Serve hot in soup plates, with bowls of the garnishes on the side.

Caldo de Albondiguillas de Pollo

CHICKEN SOUP WITH
CHICKEN MEATBALLS *Serves 6 to 8*

This unusual soup comes from Uruguay, brought by the Italian and Spanish immigrants who settled there. Instead of the croutons, many cooks use some kind of small pasta or rice.

1 boneless, skinless chicken breast half (about 6 ounces)

2 slices pancetta or strips bacon

¼ cup day-old bread crumbs (page 413)

¼ cup pine nuts

¼ teaspoon white pepper

1 large egg, lightly beaten

All-purpose flour

5 cups chicken broth

1 small carrot, cut into matchsticks

½ cup thinly sliced celery

½ cup peeled red potato cut into matchsticks

½ cup thinly sliced leeks (white part and 1 inch of the green), washed well

6 to 8 thin slices French bread, toasted

Freshly grated Parmesan cheese

Minced fresh parsley leaves for garnish

1. Place the chicken breast, pancetta, bread crumbs, pine nuts, and pepper in a food processor or meat grinder and grind together. Add the egg little by little, until the mixture is bound together enough to form balls. On a floured work surface, roll the mixture into small balls the size of grapes.

2. In a 4-quart saucepan, bring the chicken broth, carrot, celery, potato, and leeks to a boil over medium heat. Drop the meatballs into the broth a few at a time, until they are all added. Reduce the heat to low, cover, and simmer until the meat and vegetables are cooked, about 15 minutes.

3. To serve, place one piece of toast in each soup plate, top with a spoonful of Parmesan, pour some of the soup over, and garnish with the parsley. Serve immediately.

Canja

BRAZILIAN CHICKEN SOUP WITH RICE *Serves 6*

Chicken soups with rice are extremely popular in South America. Whether they are made with whole chickens or just the giblets, they are found in every country. *Canja* comes from Brazil, where it and black bean soup are the two most beloved soups. This soup is spiced up with hot pepper sauce, which is always present on the table.

> 2 tablespoons canola oil
>
> One 3- to 4-pound chicken, cut up, rinsed, and patted dry
>
> 1 medium-size onion, chopped (about 1 cup)
>
> 1 teaspoon minced garlic
>
> 8 cups water
>
> 1 large ripe but firm tomato (about 8 ounces), peeled, seeded, and coarsely chopped
>
> 2 medium-size carrots, sliced
>
> 1 leek (white part and 1 inch of the green), washed well and thinly sliced
>
> 2 teaspoons salt
>
> Freshly ground black pepper
>
> ½ cup long-grain rice
>
> 2 tablespoons minced fresh parsley leaves

1. In a soup pot, heat the oil over medium-high heat. Add the chicken a few pieces at a time and brown on all sides. Add the onion and garlic and cook, stirring, for a couple of minutes. Add the water, tomato, carrots, leek, salt, and pepper to taste. Bring to a boil and skim off the froth that rises to the top. When there's no more froth, reduce the heat to low, partially cover, and simmer for 1 hour.

2. Using a slotted spoon, transfer the chicken to a bowl. Remove the meat and discard the skin and bones. Strain the broth into another soup pot, reserving the vegetables. Bring the broth to a boil and skim off the froth. Add the rice, reduce the heat to medium-low, and simmer until tender, about 15 minutes. Add the chicken meat, reserved vegetables, and parsley and simmer for 5 minutes. Taste for salt and pepper. Serve hot in soup plates.

Sancocho de Gallina

BOILED CHICKEN WITH ROOT VEGETABLES
Serves 6

This famous soup from the northern Andes (Venezuela, Colombia, and Ecuador) dates back to colonial times. The Spanish brought their *cocidos* and *pucheros* with them, and the native cooks adapted them using local ingredients. *Sancocho* is the generic name for a broth-based soup made with meat, chicken, or fish and various root vegetables. There are many variations, depending on the country, region, and cook. *Sancocho* can be a simple soup made with yuca, plantains, and corn on the cob, or a veritable feast for a special occasion. In Venezuela, *sancocho* is considered the creole dish par excellence, chosen for picnics in the countryside and family celebrations. It is the dish that unifies all races and classes. Ramón David León, in his *Geografía Gastronómica Venezolana* (1984), wrote that the colonial rule of thumb for figuring out how many chickens were needed for *sancocho de gallina* was one-half chicken per person, and this rule is still used today. The most popular root vegetables for *sancocho* are *ñame* (yam), yuca, *ocumo*, *apio*, *ahuyama*, *batatas* (sweet potatoes), potatoes, and corn on the cob.

Colombians also enjoy this elaborate *sancocho*. In Santander, several kinds of meat are used—chicken, chorizo, beef, and pork ribs—and all of the above-mentioned root vegetables, plus cabbage, plantains (green and ripe), and chickpeas. This abundance in the Colombian *sancocho* actually resembles more nearly the Spanish *cocido*. Sometimes rice also is added. *Sancocho* from the Atlantic coast uses dried meat, which imparts a special flavor that does not appeal to everyone's taste. But this region also has *sancocho de pescado*, which is a simple *sancocho* made with coconut milk, fish, yuca, and plantains. In Ecuador, the most popular *sancochos* are the simple ones, whether made with beef or fish. Whichever *sancocho* you are making, make sure you have a side dish of *Ají Pique* (page 333).

8 ounces frozen *arracacha* (page 296)

8 ounces fresh yuca

8 ounces *ñame* (page 300)

8 ounces red potatoes

1 medium-size sweet potato (about 6 ounces)

12 ounces calabaza or other winter squash

10 cups water

One 3- to 4-pound chicken, cut up, rinsed, and patted dry

2 small onions, quartered

1 large leek (white part only), washed well and cut into 1-inch pieces

2 medium-size carrots, cut into 1-inch pieces

1 green plantain (optional), peeled and sliced ¼ inch thick

2 ears corn (optional), cut into 2-inch pieces

Bouquet garni (1 bay leaf, 3 sprigs fresh parsley, and 2 sprigs fresh thyme or ½ teaspoon dried, tied up in cheesecloth)

2 teaspoons salt

½ teaspoon freshly ground black pepper

Minced fresh cilantro or mint leaves, or a combination, for garnish

1. Peel the *arracacha*, yuca, *ñame*, red potatoes, sweet potato, and calabaza. Seed the calabaza and cut everything into 2-inch cubes.

2. Place the water and chicken pieces in a large soup kettle and bring to a boil. Skim off the froth that rises to the top. Add the cut-up root vegetables and the remaining ingredients, except the cilantro. Bring back to a boil, reduce the heat to medium-low, partially cover, and simmer until the chicken is cooked through and the vegetables are tender, about 1 hour. Discard the bouquet garni and taste for salt and pepper.

3. Serve in soup plates, making sure each plate has plenty of broth, a piece of each vegetable, and a piece of chicken. Garnish with the cilantro. Sometimes the soup is strained and the broth is served separately with cooked pasta. The vegetables and meat are then served on separate platters.

Sopa Juliana

CHICKEN SOUP WITH JULIENNED VEGETABLES

Serves 8

This type of soup is hard to find in the United States. In South America, variations of it are very popular. The soup is flavorful yet light and is a perfect start to a meal, especially if the rest of the meal is heavy. It is popular throughout South America, and each cook makes it with whatever she has in her kitchen.

- 2 tablespoons olive oil
- 2 medium-size carrots, cut into matchsticks
- 1 small turnip, peeled and cut into matchsticks
- 1 celery stalk, cut into matchsticks
- 1 small onion, thinly sliced (about ½ cup)
- 2 leeks (white part only), washed well and thinly sliced
- 1 boneless, skinless chicken breast half (about 6 ounces), cut into ⅓-inch cubes
- 6 cups chicken broth
- ¼ cup long-grain rice
- ¼ cup frozen peas
- 2 tablespoons dry sherry (optional)
- 2 tablespoons minced fresh parsley leaves for garnish
- Freshly grated Parmesan cheese for garnish

1. In a 4-quart saucepan, heat the oil over medium heat. Add the carrots, turnip, celery, onion, and leeks and cook, stirring occasionally, until soft, about 10 minutes. Add the chicken and cook, stirring constantly, for a couple of minutes. Add the chicken broth and rice and cook over low heat, uncovered, until the rice is tender, about 15 minutes. Add the peas and sherry (if using) and cook for 5 minutes.

2. Serve hot in soup cups, sprinkled with the parsley and Parmesan.

Sopas de Frutos del Mar

SEAFOOD SOUPS

THE SEAFOOD SOUPS IN SOUTH America trace their origins back to the Iberian Peninsula. The Spaniards and Portuguese had a rich tradition of soups based on the bounty of the sea. The Indians, on the other hand, did not make fish soups (at least no research indicates that they did). To the classic soups brought by the colonists, native cooks added flavorful New World ingredients. Tomatoes and peppers (sweet and hot) gave a new dimension to the soups. In the Andean regions, potatoes, yuca, and plantains were added, while in the coastal towns, plantains and yuca were used as a basis for seafood soups that were seasoned with coconut milk and ground toasted peanuts. In Colombia and Venezuela, hearty fish soups were created by the addition of a variety of indigenous root vegetables. In the southern countries of South America, the Spanish influence is more visible, especially in the thin broth-based soups, flavored with onions, garlic, tomatoes, and peppers, and sometimes with saffron and wine or port. A variety of the most representative of these creole soups follows.

Biche de Pescado

FISH SOUP WITH PLANTAINS AND VEGETABLES
Serves 8

This classic soup from Manabí, a province on the coast of Ecuador, is almost a stew. It is usually served as a main course, always preceded by *cebiche montubio*, which contains fish or shrimp (or both), or green plantain empanadas. This soup epitomizes the blend of the three cultures that have influenced the cooking of the coast. The Spanish *sofrito* blends beautifully with the African slaves' love of peanuts and plantains and the Indians' squash, yuca, corn, beans, and sweet potatoes. This is one of those dishes that varies from family to family, as every cook has her own version. Many cooks add green plantain balls instead of pieces of plantain, as in this recipe. The classic way to serve this soup is with pieces of corn on the cob, but because it is a little messy to eat, I substitute corn kernels. I also prefer to use only the ripe plantain and omit the green, although the green is a must among the Costeños (people from the coast).

- 1 medium-size red onion, chopped
- 1 cup chopped leeks (white part and 1 inch of the green), washed well
- 1 small green bell pepper, seeded and chopped
- 6 large cloves garlic, peeled
- 1 tablespoon peeled and minced fresh ginger
- 2 tablespoons minced fresh parsley leaves
- 2 tablespoons minced fresh cilantro leaves
- 2 tablespoons *Manteca de Color* (page 331)
- ½ teaspoon ground cumin
- 1 teaspoon dried oregano
- 1 teaspoon salt
- ½ teaspoon freshly ground black pepper
- 12 cups water
- 1 cup unsalted dry-roasted peanuts pureed with ½ cup milk
- 1 pound trimmed fresh yuca or frozen yuca, sliced 1 inch thick
- 8 ounces winter squash, peeled, seeded, and cut into 1-inch cubes
- 2 small sweet potatoes (about 8 ounces), peeled and quartered
- 2 small ripe (yellow) plantains, peeled and sliced 1 inch thick
- 1 cup cooked corn kernels, drained
- ½ cup bottled lupini beans, peeled (page 307), or cooked lima beans, drained
- 1½ pounds tuna, marlin, halibut, or *corvina* fillets, cut into 8 pieces and marinated in the juice of 1 lemon and salt and freshly ground black pepper to taste for 1 hour

Minced fresh cilantro leaves for garnish

1. Place the onion, leeks, bell pepper, garlic, ginger, parsley, and cilantro in a blender or food processor and process until smooth. Heat the *manteca de color* in a Dutch oven over medium heat. Add the onion puree, cumin, oregano, salt, and black pepper and cook, stirring frequently, for 10 minutes. Add the water and peanut puree and simmer for 20 minutes. Add the yuca, squash, sweet potatoes, and plantains and cook for 20 minutes. Add the corn, lupini beans, and marinated fish. Bring to a boil, reduce the heat to low, and cook for 10 minutes. Taste for salt and black pepper. The soup should have the consistency of heavy cream; if it is too thick, add more milk.

2. Serve in soup plates. Add about 1 tablespoon corn and a few lupini beans to each plate first, making sure there is a piece of everything else in the plate. Add the broth, sprinkle with the cilantro, and serve hot.

Caldillo de Congrio a la Neruda

NERUDA'S FISH SOUP *Serves 6 to 8*

This famous Chilean soup was immortalized by the Chilean poet Pablo Neruda, well known for his love of good food and a "happy table." In his poem "Oda al Caldillo de Congrio" (Ode to Congrio Soup), he sings the praises of this delicious soup. This is the dish, he writes, where the essences of Chile come together. In the soup, the just-married flavors of the sea and earth come to the table so that some lucky people can be introduced to heaven. *Congrio* is a delicious fish indigenous to the coast of Chile. Considered to be the king of the fish found in Chilean waters, it has a firm, delicate, white flesh. Unfortunately, it is not available in the United States, but Chilean sea bass, red snapper, and halibut are good substitutes. Depending on the cook, *caldillo de congrio* can be a light fish broth made with fish or shellfish or a substantial fish soup, made even richer if cream and shrimp are added, as in Neruda's version.

2 pounds Chilean *congrio* fillets (1½ to 2 inches thick) or other firm, white-fleshed fish (such as Chilean sea bass, red snapper, or halibut)

Juice of 1 lemon

Salt and freshly ground black pepper

2 tablespoons olive oil

2 medium-size onions, thinly sliced (about 2 cups)

1 teaspoon sweet paprika

3 cloves garlic, mashed into a paste with ½ teaspoon salt and ½ teaspoon freshly ground black pepper

2 small carrots, thinly sliced on the diagonal

One 4-ounce jar pimento strips, drained

1 tablespoon chicken bouillon granules

1 bay leaf

Pinch of sugar

1 teaspoon dried marjoram

¼ teaspoon hot pepper sauce or cayenne pepper

One 16-ounce can pear-shaped tomatoes, drained and chopped

1 cup dry white wine or dry sherry

3 cups water

1 cup milk

6 medium-size all-purpose potatoes, peeled, quartered, cooked in water to cover until tender, and drained

1 pound large shrimp, peeled and deveined

½ cup whipping cream (optional)

¼ cup minced fresh parsley leaves for garnish

¼ cup finely chopped scallions (white part and 1 inch of the green) for garnish

1. Cut the fish fillets into 2- to 3-inch pieces. Sprinkle with the lemon juice and salt and black pepper to taste, cover with plastic wrap, and refrigerate until needed.

2. Heat the olive oil in a Dutch oven or large casserole over low heat. Add the onions and paprika, cover, and cook, stirring occasionally, until soft, about 10 minutes. Do not let brown. Stir in the garlic paste, carrots, pimentos, bouillon, bay leaf, sugar, marjoram, and hot pepper sauce and cook, stirring constantly, for a couple of minutes. Add the tomatoes, wine, and water and bring to a boil. Reduce the heat to low, cover, and simmer for 30 minutes. Discard the bay leaf. The soup base can be made ahead up to this point. Let cool, cover, and refrigerate until needed.

3. To finish, bring the soup to a boil over medium heat and add the milk, fish, and potatoes. Cover and simmer until the fish is cooked through, about 8 minutes. Just before serving, add the shrimp and cook until they turn pink and begin to curl, about 1 minute. Add the cream, if using, and heat through. Taste for salt, black pepper, and sugar.

4. Serve in soup plates, sprinkled with the parsley and scallions.

Chupé de Pescado con Habas Verdes

FISH CHOWDER WITH FRESH FAVA BEANS *Serves 6*

There is nothing better than a bowl of *chupé* on a cold winter night. I especially like this variation from Peru because it is flavored with hot peppers and, instead of peas, it uses fava beans. This chowder can be made with either fish or shrimp, or a mixture of both. Peruvians always add eggs before serving. They either stir in the lightly beaten eggs or put one poached egg in each soup plate and pour the soup on top. This is a hearty soup that can be used as a main course for a light supper.

2 tablespoons olive oil

1 teaspoon ground annatto or sweet paprika

1 medium-size onion, minced (about 1 cup)

3 cloves garlic, mashed into a paste with ½ teaspoon salt and ½ teaspoon white pepper

2 medium-size ripe but firm tomatoes (about 10 ounces), peeled, seeded, and chopped

1 tablespoon tomato paste

1 tablespoon fresh *mirasol* pepper puree, store-bought or homemade (page 332)

2 tablespoons plus ¼ cup minced fresh cilantro leaves

½ teaspoon dried oregano, crumbled

½ teaspoon ground cumin

¼ teaspoon sugar

3 cups fish stock (page 410) or chicken broth

¼ cup long-grain rice

4 medium-size all-purpose potatoes, peeled and sliced 1 inch thick

1½ pounds firm white-fleshed fish fillets (such as sea bass, monkfish, catfish, or halibut), cut into 6 pieces

¾ cup shelled fava beans, blanched and peeled (page 308), or fresh peas

2 ears corn, each cut into 3 pieces, or 1 cup fresh corn kernels

5 ounces fresh goat cheese

1 cup milk, or more if needed

1 large egg (optional), lightly beaten

8 ounces large shrimp, peeled and deveined

1. In a large, heavy saucepan, heat the oil over medium heat. Stir in the annatto, onion, garlic paste, tomatoes, tomato paste, pepper puree, 2 tablespoons of the cilantro, oregano, cumin, and sugar. Cover and cook, stirring occasionally, until the tomatoes have softened and the mixture is like a thick sauce, about 20 minutes. (Add a little water while the tomatoes are cooking if the mixture begins to get dry.) Add the fish stock and simmer for 15 minutes. The soup can be prepared ahead up to this point. Let cool, cover, and refrigerate up to overnight.

2. To finish, bring the soup back to a boil, add the rice and potatoes, and cook for 15 minutes. Add the fish, fava beans, and corn and simmer for 8 minutes. Add the cheese and milk and cook, stirring constantly, until the cheese has melted and the milk is heated through. The soup should have the consistency of heavy cream; add more milk or water if it is too thick. (Keep in mind that potato-based soups thicken as they stand.) Taste for salt and white pepper. If using the egg, add in a stream and stir until it forms strands. Just before serving, stir in the shrimp and cook for a couple of minutes, until they turn pink and begin to curl.

3. To serve, in each soup plate place 1 piece of fish, a couple of shrimp, 3 or 4 potato slices, and 1 piece of corn (if using ears of corn). Ladle the chowder over these, sprinkle each plate with some of the remaining ¼ cup cilantro, and serve immediately.

Crema de Espárragos con Chorros

CREAM OF ASPARAGUS SOUP WITH MUSSELS
Serves 6

I had this soup in the Carrera Hotel in Santiago, Chile, and fell in love with it. The soup's beautiful deep green color provides a lovely contrast to the salmon color of the mussels. To achieve a bright green color, it is essential to cook the asparagus just until done and no longer. The time required for that will depend on the freshness of the asparagus; new asparagus takes only about 3 minutes. If mussels are not your favorite food, omit them and add the sherry at the end of the cooking time.

2½ pounds asparagus

4 cups chicken broth, or more if needed

2 tablespoons unsalted butter

1 small onion, chopped (about ½ cup)

1 large clove garlic, chopped

2 tablespoons all-purpose flour

⅛ teaspoon white pepper

30 mussels, scrubbed and debearded (page 408)

¼ cup dry sherry or dry white wine

Salt

Cayenne pepper (optional)

1. Wash the asparagus thoroughly, then cut off the bottoms and discard. You should have at least 1½ pounds after trimming. Cut the spears into 1-inch pieces.

2. In a large saucepan, bring the chicken broth to a boil over medium heat. Add the asparagus, bring back to a boil, and cook, uncovered, until the asparagus is just getting tender but is still crunchy, about 3 minutes. Drain, reserving the cooking liquid.

3. In a 4-quart saucepan, melt the butter over low heat. Add the onion and garlic and cook, stir-ring occasionally, until the onion is softened, about 5 minutes. Add the flour and cook, stirring constantly, until bubbling, about 1 minute. Remove from the heat and whisk in the white pepper and reserved cooking liquid. Bring back to a boil, stirring constantly, then simmer for 5 minutes. Remove from the heat and let cool for 30 minutes.

4. Place the asparagus in a blender or food processor and process until smooth, adding some of the thickened cooking liquid as needed. If using a blender, puree the asparagus in batches, with some of the liquid, and strain through a medium-mesh sieve. If the puree is too thick, add a little more chicken broth before passing it through the sieve. Return to a clean saucepan.

5. Place the mussels and sherry in a large saucepan, cover, bring to a boil over medium heat, and cook until the shells open, about 5 minutes. With a slotted spoon, transfer the opened mussels to a bowl and let cool. Discard any unopened mussels. Pull the meat from the shells and rinse thoroughly under cold water to remove any leftover sand. Strain the mussel broth through a sieve lined with cheesecloth.

6. Bring the soup back to a simmer and add the mussel broth. Season with salt and cayenne (if using) to taste.

7. Serve hot in soup plates or bowls, each garnished with at least 3 mussels.

NOTE **This soup freezes very well. Whisk while reheating to get a smooth cream, or puree in a blender before reheating.**

Sancocho de Pescado Ecuatoriano

**ECUADORIAN FISH SOUP WITH
GREEN PLANTAINS AND YUCA** *Serves 6*

Simple *sancochos*, whether made with meat or fish, are everyday soups in the homes of Venezuelans, Colombians, Ecuadorians, and Peruvians. All *sancochos* have as a basis a well-flavored broth made with meat or fish, to which yuca and plantains are added. In Venezuela and Colombia, other root vegetables may be added, and Colombians sometimes flavor their *sancochos* with coconut milk. Peruvians substitute potatoes for plantains in *sancochado a lo pobre* (*sancocho* of the poor). Of course, there are many variations, depending on the cook and the fish of choice in the country. Mackerel is often used in Venezuela, where it goes by the name *carite*. Shad, *corvina*, grouper, and cod also are good choices.

Four 6-ounce firm, white-fleshed
    fish fillets (about 1 inch thick),
    each cut into 2 pieces

Juice of 1 lemon

Salt and freshly ground black pepper

8 cups water

2 heads of white fish

2 green plantains, peeled, cut into 2-inch
    chunks, and halved lengthwise

1 pound fresh yuca, peeled and cut into
    2-inch chunks

2 tablespoons olive oil

1 teaspoon *Manteca de Color* (page 331)

1 large onion, minced (about 1½ cups)

1 cup seeded and finely chopped green bell
    pepper

¼ teaspoon red pepper flakes

1 large ripe but firm tomato (about 8
    ounces), peeled, seeded, and chopped

4 cloves garlic, mashed into a paste with 1
    teaspoon salt and ½ teaspoon freshly
    ground black pepper

½ teaspoon dried thyme

1 small leek (white part and 4 inches of the
    green), end trimmed and washed well

2 ears corn, cut into 2-inch pieces

1. In a glass baking dish in the refrigerator, marinate the fish fillets in the lemon juice and salt and black pepper to taste.

2. In a large saucepan, bring the water and fish heads to a boil, reduce the heat to medium-low, and simmer for 20 minutes. Drain, discard the heads, and return the broth to the pan over medium-low heat. Add the plantains and cook for 15 minutes. Add the yuca and cook for 20 minutes more.

3. While the vegetables are cooking, heat the oil in a medium-size skillet over medium heat. Add the *manteca de color*, onion, bell pepper, red pepper, tomatoes, garlic paste, thyme, and leek and cook, stirring occasionally, for 10 minutes. Stir in the fish pieces, making sure they are well coated with the sauce. Remove from the heat, discard the leek, and set aside.

4. When the yuca is almost done, add the fish mixture and corn and cook, without stirring, until the fish is opaque throughout, 8 to 10 minutes. Taste for salt and black pepper and serve hot in soup plates.

Crema de Coco con Camarones

CREAM OF COCONUT SOUP WITH SHRIMP *Serves 4*

There are many versions of shrimp soup throughout South America. Where there was a large concentration of Africans, such as on the coast of Venezuela, Colombia, Ecuador, Peru, and northern Brazil, this soup was made with coconut milk, as in this version.

    1 small onion, chopped (about ½ cup)

    2 large cloves garlic, chopped

    1 medium-size ripe but firm tomato
        (5 to 6 ounces), chopped

    3 cups chicken broth

    8 ounces medium-size shrimp, peeled,
        deveined, and halved

    1 teaspoon Worcestershire sauce

    1 teaspoon dry mustard

    Pinch of cayenne pepper

    1 cup well-stirred canned unsweetened
        coconut milk

    2 tablespoons cornstarch or potato starch
        mixed with ¼ cup cold water

    Salt and freshly ground black pepper

    4 thin lemon slices for garnish

    Minced fresh mint and cilantro leaves for
        garnish

1.   Place the onion, garlic, and tomato in a blender or food processor and process until smooth, adding a little of the chicken broth at a time until the mixture is ground. Add the rest of the chicken broth and process for a few seconds, until the mixture is smooth. Pass the puree through a medium-mesh sieve. Put half of the shrimp in the blender or food processor and process until smooth, adding a little of the chicken broth puree as necessary.

2.   In a 4-quart saucepan, combine the remaining chicken broth puree and the shrimp puree and mix well. Bring to a boil over medium heat, reduce the heat to low, and simmer for 5 minutes. Add the Worcestershire, mustard, cayenne, and coconut milk and bring back to a boil. Stir in the cornstarch mixture and simmer until thickened, stirring constantly. Add the rest of the shrimp and cook until the shrimp turn pink and begin to curl, about 1 minute. Add salt and black pepper to taste.

3.   Serve in soup bowls, garnished with a lemon slice and the mint and cilantro.

Crema de Cangrejo

CRABMEAT SOUP *Serves 6*

In South America, there are a variety of cream soups that don't necessarily have cream—they owe their creaminess to being pureed. This crabmeat soup is perfect without cream, but for cream lovers like me, adding a bit of whipping cream just makes the soup taste better. Sometimes I serve the cream in a separate bowl, so that guests can add a tablespoon to the soup, if they so desire. Though expensive, crab is found in abundance along the Pacific coast of South America, including Ecuador, where this recipe comes from.

    1 tablespoon olive oil

    1 small onion, chopped (about ½ cup)

    2 cloves garlic, minced

    ½ cup chopped carrots

    ½ cup peeled and diced (¼ inch) all-purpose
        potatoes

    1 celery stalk, chopped

    1 tablespoon minced fresh cilantro leaves

    1 tablespoon minced fresh parsley leaves

    1 teaspoon dry mustard

¼ teaspoon white pepper

½ teaspoon salt

2 teaspoons chicken bouillon granules

4 cups hot water

6 ounces fresh or canned good-quality crabmeat, undrained but picked over for shells and cartilage

1 tablespoon fresh lemon juice

½ cup whipping cream (optional)

Cayenne pepper or sweet paprika for garnish

1. Heat the oil in a 4-quart saucepan over low heat. Add the onion and cook, stirring, until softened, about 3 minutes. Add the garlic, carrots, potatoes, celery, cilantro, and parsley and cook, stirring, for a couple of minutes. Add the mustard, white pepper, salt, bouillon, and water. Bring to a boil, reduce the heat to low, and simmer for 15 minutes. Add the crabmeat and cook for 5 minutes.

2. Remove from the heat, let cool for a few minutes, transfer to a blender, and process until smooth. Return to the saucepan, bring back to a boil, and taste for salt and white pepper. Stir in the lemon juice and cream (if using), keeping the soup on the burner just long enough to heat through.

3. Serve in soup cups, sprinkled with cayenne.

Ensaladas

SALADS

SALADS OF MANY KINDS ARE found in South America, although in general they are somewhat different from the salads to which we are accustomed in the United States. The most popular salads served with a main course are cooked-vegetable salads. Ecuador is rich in this type of salad, with endless variations of the combination of vegetables (always artfully arranged), depending on the season and what is available at the market. Salads made with fresh beans are always welcome throughout South America. A common characteristic of South American salads is the sparse use of dressing, because, like the French, we don't want the dressing to mask the flavor of the vegetables, just enhance them.

One exception to the cooked-vegetable salad is the tossed salad (*ensalada mixta*), which is common to many countries. In South America, it is always made with lettuce and tomatoes, to which thinly sliced onions, shredded carrots, and radishes or watercress are added. This combination is, like other salads in the region, dressed sparingly, usually simply tossed with a little oil and vinegar.

Main course salads are made with a variety of meat, poultry, and seafood. Beef, chicken, tongue, ham, shrimp, tuna, and salmon are favorite choices. They are typically served surrounded by cooked and fresh vegetables and seasoned with a vinaigrette or some kind of mayonnaise. These types of salads are very popular in the southern countries, especially during the hot summer months. Potato and rice salads, which are common, may be simple or complex. Black rice salad, made with squid ink, is very popular. Squid ink is not easy to find in the United States, although the squid itself is widely available.

Of course, now, with the revolution of food that is going on in South America, new American-style salads are appearing. Olive oil, once a costly commodity in South America, is now available at lower prices, and a variety of vinegars, such as balsamic, can be found at local supermarkets. For the salads in this book, I have used extra virgin olive oil and canola oil, instead of the more traditional corn oil, because of their appeal to North American palates and their considerable health benefits.

Ensalada de Langosta y Papa

LOBSTER AND POTATO SALAD *Serves 8*

This salad is a specialty from the coast of Ecuador. It is on the menu of every restaurant in the coastal towns. In Ecuador, everything *except* the tail of the lobster is used to make the salad. In the United States, I use only the tails for the sake of convenience. When I want to make a very elegant buffet dish, I mound the salad on a large platter lined with watercress and surround the salad with hard-cooked quail eggs, halved and topped with a little black caviar—truly dramatic. The use of saffron is optional, as is the amount of lobster, depending on the size of your wallet. In some specialty shops, I have found canned frozen lobster meat that is quite reasonable and could be substituted for the tails; it comes cut into small pieces.

> Two to three 8-ounce frozen lobster tails, thawed
>
> 1 clove garlic, lightly crushed
>
> 3 pounds new red or white boiling potatoes
>
> ¼ teaspoon saffron threads, crumbled and softened in ⅓ cup chicken broth (optional)
>
> 1 small red onion, thinly sliced and cut into 1-inch pieces
>
> 2 tablespoons minced shallots
>
> 2 hard-cooked eggs, peeled and chopped
>
> 2 tablespoons minced fresh parsley leaves
>
> 2 tablespoons minced fresh cilantro leaves
>
> ⅔ cup mayonnaise, store-bought or homemade (page 341)
>
> ½ cup whipping cream, or more if needed
>
> 1 tablespoon Dijon mustard
>
> 1 tablespoon fresh lemon juice
>
> 1 teaspoon salt
>
> ¼ teaspoon white pepper
>
> Freshly ground black pepper
>
> GARNISHES
>
> Watercress
>
> 8 to 12 hard-cooked quail eggs (page 412), peeled and halved lengthwise
>
> One 2-ounce jar black caviar

1. Place the lobster tails and garlic in salted boiling water to cover. Bring back to a boil, reduce the heat to medium, cover, and simmer for 3 minutes. Remove the tails, rinse with cold water, and remove the meat from the shells. Cut into ½-inch cubes and set aside.

2. Place the potatoes in a 6-quart casserole. Add salted cold water to cover by 2 inches and cook over medium-low heat until tender, about 20 minutes. Drain and, when cool enough to handle, peel. Cut into ½-inch cubes. Toss with the saffron mixture, if using.

3. Rinse the onion and shallots in hot water to mellow their flavor a bit. Drain well and add to the potatoes along with the lobster, eggs, parsley, and cilantro.

4. In a small mixing bowl, combine the mayonnaise, cream, mustard, lemon juice, salt, and white pepper until well mixed. Toss with the potato-lobster mixture, adding more cream, if needed. Taste for salt and season with black pepper to taste.

5. To serve, line a platter with the watercress. Mound or spread the salad on the watercress. Surround with the quail egg halves, cut side up. Put ¼ teaspoon caviar on each egg half and serve immediately.

Ensalada de Arroz con Jamón y Alcachofas

RICE SALAD WITH HAM AND ARTICHOKES
Serves 8 to 10

Rice salads are very popular in most South American countries. Sometimes they are very simply made; other times they are more elaborate. They can be meatless or include meat, chicken, or seafood. Vinaigrette or mayonnaise is used to bind the salad. This is a great salad that comes from my Argentine friend Doris Rucci. It is ideal to take on a picnic or to serve as part of a buffet.

SALAD

2 cups converted rice, cooked with 1 clove garlic (page 322)

One 14-ounce can artichoke hearts, drained, rinsed, and cut into bite-size pieces

2 cups cooked corn kernels, drained

One 2-ounce jar pimento strips, drained

1 slice (⅛ inch thick) imported boiled ham, cut into in ½-inch-wide matchsticks

¼ cup minced fresh cilantro or basil leaves

CREAMY MUSTARD DRESSING

½ cup extra virgin olive oil

3 tablespoons aged white wine vinegar

1 teaspoon Dijon mustard

2 tablespoons whipping cream

½ teaspoon salt

½ teaspoon freshly ground black pepper

Pinch of sugar

GARNISHES

Black olives

Cooked asparagus spears

1. To make the salad, in a large salad bowl, mix together all the ingredients.

2. To make the dressing, in a small mixing bowl, beat all the ingredients together until the mixture thickens.

3. Toss the salad with dressing to taste. The recipe can be made up to this point the day before. Just cover and refrigerate until needed.

4. To serve, remove from the refrigerator 30 minutes before needed. Season with salt and pepper to taste, transfer to a serving platter, and garnish with the olives and asparagus.

Ensalada de las Américas

THE ALL-AMERICAN SALAD *Serves 8*

North American wild rice pairs with several South American classics—Andean quinoa and Indian corn and peppers—to produce this very special and delicious salad that celebrates the riches of the Pan-American larder. The combination of flavors and textures, as well as the eye appeal, will make this refreshing salad a favorite for the buffet table.

SALAD

1 cup wild rice

1 bay leaf

10 cups water

Salt

¾ cup quinoa

1 pound good-quality cooked salad shrimp

2 cloves garlic, mashed into a paste with ½ teaspoon salt and ¼ teaspoon freshly ground black pepper

2 teaspoons fresh lemon juice

¾ cup seeded and diced (¼ inch) green bell pepper

¾ cup seeded and diced (¼ inch) red bell pepper

1 cup diced (¼ inch) red onion, soaked in hot water for 5 minutes and drained

¼ cup finely chopped fresh parsley leaves

¼ cup finely chopped fresh cilantro leaves

1 cup cooked corn kernels, drained

½ cup pine nuts, lightly toasted (page 413)

    ¼ cup extra virgin olive oil

    ½ cup canola oil

    3 tablespoons sherry vinegar

    1 tablespoon Dijon mustard

    1 teaspoon salt

    ½ teaspoon freshly ground black pepper

    Pinch of sugar

    ¼ cup minced fresh herbs (such as chives, basil, thyme, or mint)

GARNISH

    2 medium-size ripe but firm tomatoes, each cut into 8 wedges

1. To make the salad, place the wild rice in a fine-mesh strainer and rinse thoroughly. Transfer to a 4-quart saucepan, add the bay leaf and 6 cups of the water, and bring to a boil. Season with salt to taste, reduce the heat to medium-low, and simmer, uncovered, until the rice is tender, about 45 minutes. Drain, discard the bay leaf, and set aside to cool.

2. Place the quinoa in a fine-mesh strainer and rinse thoroughly under cold running water until the water runs clear. In a medium-size saucepan, bring the remaining 4 cups water to a boil, add the quinoa, and cook until the grains are transparent throughout, about 12 minutes. Drain, rinse, and return to the saucepan. Cover and dry the quinoa over low heat for 5 minutes. Toss with a wooden spoon and transfer to a mixing bowl to cool.

3. While the quinoa is cooking, rub the shrimp with the garlic paste and lemon juice. Cover with plastic wrap and refrigerate until needed.

4. In a large mixing bowl, combine the rice, quinoa, shrimp, and remaining salad ingredients.

5. To make the dressing, in a small mixing bowl, beat all the ingredients together with a fork until the mixture thickens.

6. Toss the salad with dressing to taste. Taste for salt and pepper. Cover with plastic wrap and refrigerate until needed.

7. Serve chilled, garnished with the tomato wedges.

Ensalada de Quinua con Frejoles Negros y Choclo

QUINOA SALAD WITH BLACK BEANS AND CORN
Serves 8 to 10

This salad, which comes from my booklet *The Art of Cooking with Quinoa*, is my favorite dish to take whenever I'm asked to bring something to a party. It never fails to elicit words of praise, even from people who may be doubtful about quinoa. This bright, colorful salad, appealing to the eye as well as the appetite, is substantial enough to stand alone as a main course. It can be served with or without meat.

SALAD

    1 cup quinoa

    6 cups water

    One 15-ounce can black beans, drained and rinsed

    1 cup cooked corn kernels, drained

    ½ cup seeded and diced (¼ inch) red bell pepper

    ½ cup seeded and diced (¼ inch) green bell pepper

    ½ cup chopped red onion, soaked in hot water for 5 minutes and drained

    ¼ cup thinly sliced scallions (white part and 1 inch of the green)

    8 ounces good-quality salad shrimp, cut into ½-inch pieces, or 2 cups cooked chicken, smoked turkey, or imported boiled ham cut into ½-inch cubes (optional)

    ¼ cup minced fresh cilantro leaves

⅓ cup extra virgin olive oil

3 tablespoons sherry vinegar

1 tablespoon Dijon mustard

½ teaspoon salt

½ teaspoon freshly ground black pepper

Pinch of sugar

GARNISH

8 cherry tomatoes, halved, or tomato wedges (optional)

Salad greens (optional)

1. To make the salad, place the quinoa in a fine-mesh strainer and rinse under cold running water until the water runs clear. Bring the water to a boil in a medium-size saucepan, add the quinoa, and cook until the grains are transparent throughout, about 12 minutes. Drain, rinse, and return to the saucepan. Cover and dry the quinoa over low heat for 5 minutes. Toss with a wooden spoon and transfer to a large mixing bowl to cool.

2. Add the beans, corn, bell peppers, onion, scallions, and shrimp (if using) and toss to combine well.

3. To make the vinaigrette, in a jar with a screw-type cover, combine all the ingredients and shake for a few seconds, until the mixture thickens.

4. Toss the salad with the vinaigrette (use a little less for the vegetarian version). Taste for salt. Cover and refrigerate until needed.

5. Just before serving, toss the salad with the cilantro. Garnish with the tomatoes, or serve on a bed of greens.

Aguacates Rellenos con Pollo o Jamón

AVOCADOS FILLED WITH CHICKEN OR HAM
Serves 6

This is a great way to use up leftover chicken or ham. Finely diced cooked carrots or beets, peas, and potatoes or rice are favorite choices for stuffing avocados.

1 cup finely chopped cooked chicken or imported boiled ham

¼ cup finely chopped red onion, soaked in hot water for 5 minutes and drained

¼ cup coarsely chopped walnuts

½ cup peeled and finely chopped cooked all-purpose potatoes

1 tablespoon minced fresh chives

½ cup mayonnaise, store-bought or homemade (page 341)

2 tablespoons whipping cream

1 teaspoon fresh lemon juice

1 teaspoon sherry vinegar

½ teaspoon curry powder (optional)

¼ teaspoon salt

White pepper

3 large ripe but firm Hass avocados

Salad greens, cut into thin strips

Pimento strips for garnish

1. In a medium-size mixing bowl, combine the chicken, onion, walnuts, potatoes, and chives.

2. In a small mixing bowl, combine the mayonnaise, cream, lemon juice, vinegar, curry powder (if using), salt, and pepper to taste, beating until creamy. Toss with the chicken mixture and taste for salt and pepper.

3. Prepare the avocados as instructed on page 166. Fill the avocado hollows with the salad. Arrange the greens on 6 salad plates, place the

avocados on the greens, decorate with the pimento strips, and serve right away.

VARIATION The chicken salad can be served without the avocado, on a bed of greens and garnished with thinly sliced avocado and tomato.

Paltas con Cangrejo

AVOCADOS FILLED WITH CRABMEAT *Serves 4*

Avocados filled with crabmeat are a very special first course in South America, and for some Chilean families, they are a traditional appetizer for Christmas Eve dinner.

> **One 6-ounce can good-quality crabmeat**
> **¼ cup minced celery**
> **2 tablespoons minced shallots**
> **2 tablespoons seeded and finely chopped green or red bell pepper**
> **¼ cup mayonnaise, store-bought or homemade (page 341)**
> **1 tablespoon ketchup**
> **1 teaspoon fresh lemon juice**
> **¼ teaspoon salt**
> **Freshly ground black pepper**
> **Cayenne pepper**
> **2 large ripe but firm Hass avocados**
> **Salad greens**
> **Black olives, halved and pitted, for garnish**

1. Place the crabmeat in a strainer and let stand until thoroughly drained. Pick out any shells or cartilage. In a medium-size mixing bowl, combine the crabmeat, celery, shallots, and bell pepper.

2. In a small mixing bowl, beat together the mayonnaise, ketchup, lemon juice, salt, and black pepper to taste until smooth. Toss with the crabmeat mixture, taste for salt, and add cayenne to taste.

3. Prepare the avocados as instructed on page 166. Fill the avocado hollows with the salad, mounding the mixture. Serve on a bed of greens, garnished with the olives.

Ensalada de Calamares

SQUID SALAD *Serves 2*

In South America, squid often appears in seafood soups, stews, rice dishes, and salads. In the United States, it is especially easy to prepare squid dishes because you can buy it already cleaned and ready to stuff or cut into rings. Squid rings also are available frozen. One thing to keep in mind is that squid should be cooked quickly; otherwise, it becomes tough and requires longer cooking to soften it again.

> **8 ounces cleaned squid**
> **2 tablespoons extra virgin olive oil**
> **1 roasted red pepper (page 411), cut into 1-inch pieces**
> **2 Belgian endives, cored and sliced crosswise 1 inch thick**
> **1 cup frisée**
> **One 2-ounce can flat anchovies, drained and rinsed**
> **1 recipe *Vinagrete Tricolor* (page 166)**
> **French bread for serving**

1. Rinse the squid and dry with paper towels. Cut the tentacles in half and slice the tubes (the squids' bodies) into ½-inch-thick rings. Heat the oil in a large skillet over medium-high heat, add the squid, and cook, stirring, until it begins to shrink and turns milky white. This takes only a few seconds. Transfer to a plate lined with paper towels and let cool.

2. In a medium-size salad bowl, combine the squid, roasted pepper, endives, frisée, and as many anchovy fillets as desired. Toss with vinaigrette to taste and serve with French bread.

Vinagrete Tricolor
TRICOLOR VINAIGRETTE

Makes about 1 cup

1 recipe *Vinagrete Clásico* (page 168)
2 tablespoons chopped fresh parsley leaves
2 tablespoons chopped fresh cilantro leaves
2 tablespoons minced red onion
2 tablespoons minced black olives

Combine all the ingredients in a glass jar with a screw-type cover. Shake well.

VARIATION Sometimes chopped hard-cooked eggs are added to this dressing.

Aguacates (Paltas) y Tomates Rellenos
STUFFED AVOCADOS AND TOMATOES

One of the most popular ways of serving avocados is stuffed. A tremendous variety of fillings may be used, including seafood, chicken, ham, grains, or vegetables. The fillings are generally simply dressed with mayonnaise or vinaigrette. Stuffed avocados make a wonderful luncheon dish when served on a bed of greens and garnished with hard-cooked eggs, asparagus, tomatoes, or other vegetables. They are also the most popular first course in many regions.

There are two ways to serve avocado halves—peeled or unpeeled. To peel an avocado, cut it in half lengthwise, moving your knife around the pit in the center. Remove and discard the pit. Carefully peel the halves by pulling strips off with a paring knife. Place the halves in a glass pie plate and cover tightly with Saran wrap (this will prevent them from discoloring). If using unpeeled avocados, simply cut them in half, removing and discarding the pit.

To serve, place avocado halves on a plate lined with greens, sprinkle with salt and pepper to taste, and fill the hollows left by the pit, mounding the filling appetizingly. Garnish and serve. The recipes on pages 164 and 165 can be garnished with quartered hard-cooked eggs, cooked asparagus, black olives, artichokes, and/or tomatoes, just to mention the most commonly used garnishes. Two very popular fillings are *Ensalada Rusa* (page 169) and shrimp or crabmeat tossed with *Salsa Golf* (page 341).

Large ripe but firm tomatoes also can be stuffed and served in this way. Just peel the tomatoes (page 411), cut a slice off the top where the stem is, and, with a spoon, remove the heart with the seeds. Turn the tomatoes upside down to drain. Sprinkle salt and pepper to taste inside, and they are ready to stuff. Serve like the avocados.

Atún en Ají

TUNA WITH ONION AND HOT PEPPER SALSA

Serves 4 to 6

This Bolivian specialty is an easy-to-prepare salad
for a hot summer day or picnic. Use canned white
tuna, good-quality canned salmon, or any leftover
fish. Bolivians season this salad with an onion
sauce spiced with lots of hot pepper. I wouldn't be
surprised if it were the result of a wealthy Bolivian
lady coming back from Europe and telling her cook
about the wonderful niçoise salad she had in the
south of France. This is, I think, the clever cook's
interpretation of what the lady described.

SALAD
- Two 8-ounce cans white tuna (albacore),
  drained
- 1 pound small boiling potatoes, cooked in
  salted water to cover until tender, drained,
  halved, and sliced ¼ inch thick
- 1 cup green beans (trimmed and cut
  diagonally into 1-inch pieces), cooked in
  water to cover until crisp-tender and
  drained, or ½ cup fresh or frozen peas,
  cooked in water to cover until tender and
  drained
- 2 hard-cooked eggs, peeled and chopped
- 2 tablespoons minced fresh parsley leaves

ONION AND HOT PEPPER SALSA
- 2 tablespoons olive oil
- 1 medium-size onion, halved and thinly
  sliced into half-moons (about 1 cup)
- ½ teaspoon salt
- 1 clove garlic, minced
- ½ teaspoon dried oregano, crumbled
- 1 tablespoon fresh hot yellow pepper puree,
  store-bought or homemade (page 332), or
  ½ teaspoon red pepper flakes
- 1 cup chicken broth, or more if needed

GARNISH
- Black olives

1. To make the salad, place the tuna in the center of a large platter. Arrange the potatoes around it, then scatter the green beans, eggs, and parsley over all. Cover with plastic wrap and set aside.

2. To make the salsa, heat the oil in a medium-size skillet over medium heat. Add the onion and salt and cook, stirring a few times, until transparent, about 3 minutes. Stir in the garlic, oregano, and hot pepper puree and cook over low heat for 2 minutes, stirring so it doesn't burn. Add the chicken broth and simmer for 5 minutes. Add more chicken broth, if necessary; there should be enough salsa to drizzle over the tuna and potatoes. After drizzling, the salad can be covered with plastic wrap and refrigerated for up to a few hours.

3. To serve, bring the salad to room temperature, carefully toss it, and garnish with the olives. Provide a slotted spoon for serving.

Salpicón de Carne

SALAD GREENS WITH MEAT *Serves 4*

This salad is particularly popular in Argentina. I
think it was probably invented as a way to use up
leftover meat, chicken, or fish. I usually make this
when I have leftover roast beef or steak that was
cooked on the grill. The base for this salad is always
julienned lettuce, to which onions, tomatoes, bell
peppers, celery, and hard-cooked eggs can be
added. A simple vinaigrette is sufficient to dress the
salad. With garlic bread on the side, it makes a
wonderful luncheon dish.

1 small red onion, sliced into rings, soaked in hot water for 5 minutes, and drained

Juice of 1 lime

Salt and freshly ground black pepper

6 cups mesclun salad mix, rinsed well and dried

1 pound grilled steak, sliced ⅛ inch thick

2 medium-size red potatoes, cooked in water to cover until tender, drained, sliced ¼ inch thick, and cut into bite-size pieces

1 recipe *Vinagrete Clásico* (recipe follows)

1. In a small mixing bowl, mix together the onion, lime juice, and salt and pepper to taste. Let stand at room temperature for 1 hour.

2. In a large salad bowl, toss together the mesclun, marinated onion, steak, and potatoes. Shake the vinaigrette well and toss some of it with the salad—just enough to coat the ingredients without drowning them. Serve immediately.

Vinagrete Clásico
CLASSIC VINAIGRETTE DRESSING

Makes a generous ½ cup

¼ cup extra virgin olive oil

¼ cup canola oil

2 tablespoons aged white wine vinegar or fresh lemon juice

1 teaspoon Dijon mustard

½ teaspoon salt

½ teaspoon freshly ground black pepper

Pinch of sugar

Combine all the ingredients in a glass jar with a screw-type cover. Shake well.

NOTES Vinaigrettes can be made with just canola oil, but extra virgin olive oil boosts the flavor.

I don't care for acidic salad dressings, so I use an aged vinegar. You can substitute any other vinegar.

Side Salads

Ensalada de Tía María

AUNT MARIA'S POTATO SALAD *Serves 8*

This recipe really intrigued me. I would never have tried it if not for Helena Chapellín Wilson, a lady with a wonderful palate. This salad was the creation of her aunt María Chapellín, a well-known Venezuelan cookbook author. The way Helena gave me the recipe is typical of how most South American cooks prepare dishes: by eye and feel. She said just cook a few potatoes, cut them up, and add some creamed corn, relish, mayonnaise, and so on. Quantities? Just enough. Here is my version.

3 pounds small Yukon gold or red potatoes

One 8-ounce can creamed corn

One 14-ounce can corn kernels, drained

½ cup hot dog relish, or more to taste

½ cup mayonnaise, store-bought or homemade (page 341)

½ teaspoon salt

¼ teaspoon freshly ground black pepper

1. Place the potatoes in a large saucepan with water to cover by 1 inch. Bring to a boil, reduce the heat to medium, and cook until tender, about 20 minutes. Drain, let cool for a few minutes,

peel, cut in half, and cut into ½-inch-thick half-moons.

2.   In a large serving bowl, toss the potatoes with the remaining ingredients until well combined. Taste for salt, pepper, and relish. Cover with plastic wrap and refrigerate until serving time.

Ensalada Rusa

RUSSIAN SALAD *Serves 8 to 10*

Russian salad is one of the oldest and most beloved salads of South America. Perhaps the secret of its appeal rests on the fact that it is not only very tasty (we always made it with homemade mayonnaise) but also can be arranged beautifully, depending on the occasion. I remember a spectacular first course I had in a restaurant in Lima, Peru. The salad was piled in the shape of a dome on top of a large artichoke bottom. It was decorated with chicken strips, pimentos, and asparagus tips and surrounded with a julienne of lettuce, tomatoes, and pickles. My mother was fond of Russian salad made with shrimp or with ham and chicken. It is safe to say that there is not one single recipe for Russian salad, but there are a few traditional ingredients that always show up, such as those in this recipe. Some cooks prefer to use green beans instead of peas, as well as apples or nuts. The ingredients can vary as much as the imagination of the cook.

> About 1 pound red potatoes, peeled, cooked in water until tender, drained, and diced (¼ inch)
>
> 1 cup diced (¼ inch) cooked carrots
>
> 1 cup diced (¼ inch) cooked beets
>
> ½ cup fresh or frozen peas, cooked in water to cover until tender and drained
>
> ⅓ cup minced onion, rinsed with hot water and drained
>
> ¼ cup hot chicken broth
>
> ⅔ cup mayonnaise, store-bought or homemade (page 341)
>
> 2 teaspoons Dijon mustard

> 1 tablespoon fresh lemon juice
>
> ¼ cup whipping cream
>
> ¼ teaspoon salt
>
> ¼ teaspoon white pepper
>
> 2 hard-cooked eggs, peeled and finely chopped
>
> Finely chopped fresh parsley leaves for garnish
>
> Black olives for garnish

1.   In a large glass bowl, toss together the potatoes, carrots, beets, peas, onion, and chicken broth.

2.   In a small mixing bowl, combine the mayonnaise, mustard, lemon juice, cream, salt, pepper, and chopped eggs until well mixed. Toss the dressing with the potato mixture until well coated, then taste for salt and pepper. The salad can be made up to a day ahead, covered with plastic wrap, and refrigerated until needed.

3.   To serve, mound the salad in the center of a platter, sprinkle with the parsley, and arrange the olives around the mound. Or put the salad in individual molds, then unmold on a platter around meat, chicken, or shrimp and garnish with the parsley and olives.

Ensalada de Berros, Chochos, y Aguacate

WATERCRESS, LUPINI BEAN, AND AVOCADO SALAD *Serves 6*

This luscious salad from Ecuador has been brought up to date by leaving the avocado in chunks rather than mashing it in the traditional style. The softness of the avocado and tomato mixed with the crispness of the watercress and romaine provides a stimulating contrast of textures and flavors. This vibrant salad makes a beautiful first course served on individual plates.

3 cups packed watercress, tough stems
removed and torn into bite-size pieces

3 cups packed shredded romaine lettuce

1 medium-size onion, diced (¼ inch; about
1 cup)

1 cup bottled lupini beans, peeled (page 307)

2 large ripe but firm tomatoes (about
1 pound), peeled, seeded, and diced
(¼ inch)

3 tablespoons minced fresh cilantro leaves

1 ripe but firm Hass avocado

¼ cup extra virgin olive oil

2 tablespoons aged white wine vinegar

¼ teaspoon salt

¼ teaspoon freshly ground black pepper

1. Put the watercress and romaine lettuce in a bowl lined with paper towels, cover with plastic wrap, and refrigerate until needed.

2. In a small bowl, soak the onion in hot water for 2 minutes to remove the sharpness. Drain and place in a large serving bowl with the lupini beans, tomatoes, and cilantro. Cover with plastic wrap and refrigerate until needed.

3. Just before serving, peel and pit the avocado and cut into ¼-inch dice. Toss with the onion mixture.

4. In a small mixing bowl, beat together the oil, vinegar, salt, and pepper until the mixture thickens. Remove the paper towels from the watercress and romaine. Toss with half of the dressing. Toss the onion mixture with the remaining dressing.

5. To serve, divide the greens among 6 salad plates. Mound the onion mixture on top of the greens and serve immediately.

Ensalada de Apio y Palta

CELERY AND AVOCADO SALAD *Serves 6*

This unusual and lovely salad is typical of Chilean cooking. It is a required side dish for turkey at Christmas, whether it is made with walnuts or pomegranate seeds. The version made with walnuts is more popular. I prefer the color and texture of the pomegranate seeds, but the salad is excellent either way. The celery and dressing can be prepared ahead of time. Cut the avocados a couple of hours before serving, cover with Saran wrap, and refrigerate until needed.

SALAD

3 ripe but firm Hass avocados, peeled, pitted,
and cut into ½-inch cubes or balls

3 cups diced (¼ inch) celery

DRESSING

2 tablespoons extra virgin olive oil

2 tablespoons fresh lemon juice

1 teaspoon Dijon mustard

½ teaspoon salt

¼ teaspoon freshly ground black pepper

Pinch of sugar

GARNISH

¼ cup pomegranate seeds or coarsely
chopped walnuts

1. To make the salad, in a medium-size mixing bowl, mix together the avocado and celery.

2. To make the dressing, in a small mixing bowl, beat together all the ingredients until the mixture thickens.

3. Toss the dressing with the avocado mixture until evenly coated. Transfer to a glass bowl, garnish with the pomegranate seeds, and serve immediately.

Ensalada de Verdolaga

PURSLANE SALAD *Serves 4 to 6*

This very special salad from Bolivia is usually made with purslane or watercress. Purslane is available in the spring and fall in Latin American and ethnic groceries. To take advantage of the wonderful selection of salad greens now available in supermarkets, try a mesclun salad mix, tender baby spinach leaves with frisée, or any other variety of greens. *Quilquiña* is an herb indigenous to Bolivia and is available dried in South American groceries.

4 cups packed purslane, watercress leaves and tender stems, or mesclun salad mix

SARZA DE CEBOLLA (Onion salsa)

2 tablespoons extra virgin olive oil

1 tablespoon aged white wine vinegar

¼ teaspoon salt

¼ teaspoon freshly ground black pepper

1 medium-size onion, diced (¼ inch; about 1 cup), rinsed with hot water, and drained

1 large ripe but firm tomato (about 8 ounces), seeded and diced (¼ inch)

2 jalapeños, seeded and minced

2 tablespoons minced fresh parsley leaves

1 teaspoon dried *quilquiña* (optional)

2 ounces feta cheese, crumbled

1. Thoroughly wash the purslane and dry with paper towels. Refrigerate until needed.

2. To make the salsa, in a small mixing bowl, beat together the oil, vinegar, salt, and black pepper. In a medium-size mixing bowl, mix together the onion, tomato, jalapeños, parsley, and *quilquiña* (if using). Toss with the dressing until well combined.

3. Divide the greens among 4 to 6 salad plates, top each with some of the onion salsa, and sprinkle the cheese on top.

Ensalada de Endivias, Palmitos, y Paltas

BELGIAN ENDIVE, HEARTS OF PALM, AND AVOCADO SALAD *Serves 8*

South Americans love hearts of palm, avocados, and olives. To ensure complete rapture, I have combined all of them with Belgian endives and a wonderful vinaigrette to make a very light and refreshing salad. Samples of this salad were always so well received while I was promoting my book *Cooking with a Latin Beat* that I thought it deserved to be repeated here. Served in your prettiest glass bowl, it is ideal for a buffet, picnic, or any other get-together.

One 14-ounce can hearts of palm

1 cup pitted black olives

4 Belgian endives

2 tablespoons minced fresh parsley leaves

2 ripe but firm Hass avocados

1 recipe *Vinagrete Clásico* (page 168)

1. Drain the hearts of palm and rinse thoroughly. Cut into ¼-inch-thick rounds. Drain and rinse the olives. Core the endives and cut into ½-inch-thick slices. This can all be done ahead of time; keep each ingredient in a separate covered container in the refrigerator.

2. About 2 hours before serving, peel and pit the avocados, then cut into ½-inch cubes. Cover with Saran wrap and refrigerate until needed.

3. When ready to serve, place all the ingredients in a medium-size mixing bowl, toss with the vinaigrette (shaking it well before adding), and divide among 8 salad plates.

Ensalada de Tomate y Cebolla

TOMATO AND ONION SALAD *Serves 4*

This salad is a "bread and butter" type of salad for Chileans—very simple but wonderfully refreshing. It is a very useful salad, especially enjoyable when summer tomatoes are at their peak. One time, when I was shopping at a supermarket, I saw an Italian woman buying a big bag of jalapeño peppers. I got curious and asked her what was she going to do with them. She said that she just adds sliced jalapeños to a wonderful Italian tomato and onion salad that her family loves. It was interesting to find the roots of this Chilean salad in a Chicago supermarket. Many Chileans use finely chopped hot peppers, but others prefer just minced parsley, cilantro, or basil.

> 4 medium-size ripe but firm tomatoes (1¼ to 1½ pounds)
>
> 1 medium-size Vidalia onion
>
> 1 large jalapeño, seeded and chopped
>
> 2 tablespoons extra virgin olive oil
>
> 1 tablespoon sherry vinegar or fresh lemon juice
>
> ¼ teaspoon salt
>
> ¼ teaspoon freshly ground black pepper
>
> 2 tablespoons minced fresh cilantro, basil, or parsley leaves

1. Core the tomatoes and cut into bite-size pieces. Cut the onion into ¼-inch dice and rinse well with hot water. Drain and mix with the tomatoes and jalapeño in a medium-size mixing bowl.

2. In a jar with a screw-type cover, combine the oil, vinegar, salt, and black pepper and shake until the mixture thickens. Pour over the tomato mixture, sprinkle with the cilantro, and toss to combine well. Cover with plastic wrap and refrigerate until needed, 2 to 4 hours.

Salada de Chuchu

CHAYOTE SALAD *Serves 6*

Chayote is as not as popular in all South American countries as it is in Brazil. This is a very refreshing and light salad. Be careful not to overcook the *chayote*; it should retain a crunchy texture.

> 3 large *chayotes* (about 1½ pounds)
>
> 1 small onion, sliced into rings (about ½ cup), rinsed with hot water, and drained
>
> 1 cup seeded red bell pepper, cut into ¾-inch pieces
>
> 1 large jalapeño (optional), sliced into rings and seeded
>
> ⅓ cup canola oil
>
> 1 tablespoon white wine vinegar
>
> 1 tablespoon fresh lime juice
>
> 2 cloves garlic, mashed into a paste with ¼ teaspoon salt and ¼ teaspoon freshly ground black pepper
>
> ¼ cup thinly sliced scallions (white part and 1 inch of the green) for garnish

1. Peel the *chayotes* with a vegetable peeler. Cut in half and cook in boiling salted water to cover until tender but still firm, about 10 minutes. The best way to test it is to take one half out and cut a thin slice; it should be slightly crunchy when done. Drain, let cool, and remove the seed, which can be eaten. Cut into ¾-inch cubes.

2. In a medium-size mixing bowl, combine the *chayotes*, onion, bell pepper, and jalapeño. The salad can be prepared ahead up to this point. Cover and refrigerate until needed, 2 to 4 hours.

3. In a small mixing bowl, beat the oil, vinegar, lime juice, and garlic paste together until the mixture thickens. Toss with the salad until evenly coated and season with salt and pepper to taste. Serve garnished with the scallions.

Ensalada de Frutas Tropicales

TROPICAL FRUIT SALAD *Serves 8 to 10*

This is a beautiful, sweet, refreshing salad that celebrates the glorious fruits and vegetables (papayas, tomatoes, avocados, and hearts of palm) that the Americas have contributed to the world. The colors, textures, and flavors of the ingredients are enhanced by the fragrant aroma of the passion fruit in the dressing, and all combines to create a truly ambrosial salad.

PASSION FRUIT VINAIGRETTE

½ cup canola oil

¼ cup honey

¼ cup thawed frozen passion fruit pulp

¼ cup fresh orange juice

¼ cup red wine vinegar

2 teaspoons dry mustard

½ teaspoon salt

Freshly ground pepper mélange (mixture of 3 kinds or colors of peppercorns)

SALAD

1 ripe but firm papaya (about 1 pound; see Notes)

4 pink grapefruits

One 14-ounce can hearts of palm

1 cup cherry or grape tomatoes

1 medium-size red onion, halved and thinly sliced into half-moons

Juice of 1 lime

Salt and freshly ground black pepper

2 ripe but firm Hass avocados (see Notes)

Baby spinach, rinsed well and dried

1. To make the vinaigrette, combine all the ingredients in a jar with a screw-type cover and shake until the mixture thickens. Set aside.

2. To make the salad, cut the papaya lengthwise into quarters and remove the seeds with a tea-spoon. Peel and cut crosswise into ¼-inch-thick slices. Put in a plastic container, cover, and refrigerate until needed.

3. With a sharp knife, remove a slice from the ends of the grapefruits. With a grapefruit knife, remove the peel and membrane. Take the sections out with the knife, carefully arrange them in a plastic container, and refrigerate until needed.

4. Rinse the hearts of palm and drain well. Cut into ½-inch-thick rounds, cover, and refrigerate until needed.

5. Rinse the tomatoes thoroughly and cut in half.

6. Soak the onions in hot water for 5 minutes and drain. Place in a glass bowl and toss with the lime juice. Season with salt and pepper to taste. The salad can be prepared to this point up to 4 hours ahead.

7. Up to 2 hours before serving, peel and pit the avocados, then cut crosswise into ¼-inch-thick slices. Cover tightly with Saran wrap and refrigerate.

8. To assemble the salad, place the spinach on a large platter and arrange the papaya, grapefruit sections, hearts of palm, tomatoes, and avocados on top. Scatter the onions over all. Shake the vinaigrette and drizzle over the salad. Serve immediately.

NOTES Small papayas are not always available. If necessary, buy a larger one and save what's left over—papaya is especially nice for breakfast.

The papaya and avocados should be purchased a couple of days before needed, because they should be perfectly ripe and firm for this recipe. They are not always easy to find at that stage and usually need a couple of days of ripening at room temperature.

Ensalada de Vigilia

EASTER SALAD *Serves 6 to 8*

Most South Americans are Catholic, and many of their food specialties are associated with the celebration of Catholic holidays. This salad is usually served on Good Friday, when the faithful fast. It combines ingredients that were basic to the diet of the Andean Indians with an essentially southern European dressing. Some versions use *queso fresco* as a garnish, and sometimes the salad is served with a dressing made with cheese. Prepared this way, it is a meal in itself. In the southern countries, various versions use lettuce, beans, apples, and celery as the main ingredients, depending on what is easily available. The recipe here calls for new red or Yukon gold potatoes, but I have also made this salad using purple potatoes, which provide a nice contrast of colors. If you decide to use purple potatoes, remember that they cook much faster than red or yellow ones.

SHALLOT VINAIGRETTE

¼ cup extra virgin olive oil

¼ cup canola oil

3 tablespoons sherry vinegar

1 tablespoon Dijon mustard

¾ teaspoon salt

½ teaspoon freshly ground black pepper

Pinch of sugar

2 tablespoons minced shallots

SALAD

1½ pounds new red or Yukon Gold potatoes

Salt

1 cup shelled fava beans, blanched and peeled (page 308)

1 cup cooked corn kernels (preferably white), drained

½ cup lupini beans, peeled (page 307)

½ cup fresh or frozen peas, cooked in water to cover until tender and drained

Freshly ground black pepper

GARNISHES

1 medium-size Vidalia onion, halved, thinly sliced into half-moons, rinsed in hot water, drained, and mixed with the juice of 1 lime

12 grape or cherry tomatoes, halved

1 ripe but firm Hass avocado, peeled, pitted, and cut into 8 wedges

1. To make the vinaigrette, combine all the ingredients in a jar with a screw-type cover and shake until the mixture thickens. Set aside.

2. To make the salad, place the potatoes and water to cover by 1 inch in a large saucepan. Bring to a boil, add salt to taste, reduce the heat to medium, and cook until just tender, about 20 minutes. Drain and, when cool enough to handle, peel and cut into ½-inch-thick rounds. Cut the rounds into halves or quarters, depending on the size.

3. In a large glass bowl, mix together the potatoes, fava beans, corn, lupini beans, and peas. Shake the dressing again, pour over the salad, and toss to coat evenly. Season with salt and pepper to taste. Cover with plastic wrap and refrigerate until needed, up to 6 hours.

4. To serve, bring the salad to room temperature. Transfer to a serving platter or bowl and garnish with the onion, tomatoes, and avocado.

Ensalada de Espárragos Blancos

WHITE ASPARAGUS SALAD *Serves 4*

For many years, the only way to get white asparagus was in jars, which were usually imported from Spain. If white asparagus is not available, hearts of palm or avocados are wonderful substitutes. This is a very easy and elegant salad that can be served as a first course or as a side salad. Any kind of greens can be used. If a lighter dressing is desired, use *Vinagrete Tricolor* (page 166).

SALAD

1 pound bottled white asparagus

Bibb lettuce

One 4-ounce jar pimento strips, drained

PINK VINAIGRETTE DRESSING

¼ cup canola oil

½ cup whipping cream

2 tablespoons ketchup

1 teaspoon Dijon mustard

½ teaspoon Worcestershire sauce

¼ teaspoon salt

¼ teaspoon white pepper

1. To make the salad, drain and rinse the asparagus and dry with paper towels. Line 4 salad plates with the lettuce, divide the asparagus among the plates, and place pimento strips across the asparagus.

2. To make the vinaigrette, whisk all the ingredients together in a small bowl until creamy. Spoon over the asparagus and serve immediately.

Ensalada de Vegetales con Vinagreta

VEGETABLE SALAD WITH VINAIGRETTE DRESSING *Serves 8 to 10*

This salad is the most popular type in South America. The vegetables change according to the weather and individual needs, but basically the salad is served with meat, fish, or poultry, always nicely arranged on a platter and with just a little dressing, so as not to mask the flavors of the wonderfully fresh vegetables. It is one of my favorite salads to serve for buffets and picnics. The vegetables can be sliced, diced, or julienned and cooked ahead, so that the salad can be quickly assembled before serving. Now that there are so many baby vegetables available, it is a pleasure to prepare a salad like this. Tiny squash, zucchini, eggplants, French beans, fava beans, red cabbage, and different-colored beets are wonderful choices. If you can find purple potatoes, by all means use them, too.

1 pound green beans or asparagus

1 pound baby carrots, trimmed, cooked in water to cover 5 minutes, and drained

1 medium-size head cauliflower or broccoflower (about 2½ pounds), cut into florets

1 pound beets

2 tablespoon minced fresh herbs (such as chives, parsley leaves, or cilantro leaves)

1 recipe *Vinagrete Clásico* (page 168)

1. Wash the green beans and snap off the ends, pulling down the strings. Cut into 1-inch pieces, drop into salted boiling water, and cook, uncovered, for about 4 minutes, until crisp-tender. Drain, rinse under cold running water, dry, and refrigerate. If using asparagus, remove the tough bottoms, cut on the diagonal into 1-inch pieces, and steam for a couple of minutes, until crisp-tender.

2. Cook the cauliflower the same as for the green beans; it will take about 3 minutes. Drain and rinse under cold running water.

3. To prepare the beets, cut off the tops, and cook in boiling water until tender, 30 minutes to 1 hour, depending on the size. Drain and, when cool enough to handle, slip off the skins and slice or cut into matchsticks.

4. To serve, toss each vegetable with a little of the vinaigrette and arrange decoratively on a serving platter. Sprinkle the cauliflower with the herbs.

Aves y Animales de Caza

POULTRY AND GAME

CHICKEN IS AMONG THE MOST appreciated contributions of the conquistadors to the Americas, for chicken has become the favorite bird to serve for special occasions. It is only in recent years that, thanks to mass production, chicken has become an inexpensive bird, affordable for more people and not just for holidays. However, the mass-produced birds are not the most desirable ones. These cheaper chickens are fattened on fishmeal, and when they started appearing in the supermarkets, the ladies of the house complained about their strong fish flavor. Cooks would first blanch the birds in boiling water a couple of times to remove the flavor. Unfortunately, there was nothing they could do about the texture. Free-range chickens provide a firmer meat than chickens raised in confined spaces. Hence, although fish-fed birds are more affordable, free-range chickens remain more popular among those who can afford them. (Luckily, some specialty shops and finer groceries in the United States also offer free-range chickens.)

A once familiar sight in the residential neighborhoods of Quito were country women loaded with baskets of live chickens, going from door to door, offering for sale their firmer and more flavorful country-raised birds. In most of South America, it is more common to see these women in the streets, bus stations, and open markets. Also common are the maids accompanying the ladies of the houses to "market," checking the chickens, pressing the feathers to feel what is beneath them, making sure they pick a plump, meaty bird. These birds are kept in the buyers' backyards until needed and fed with corn to improve their taste and texture. Then it is up to the cook to plan the bird's demise and prepare it for cooking—

quite a laborious task. In the big cities, this task is often bypassed, and chickens are bought from the grocer. But in the countryside, this process still goes on.

South American cooks have a variety of ways to prepare chicken. However, one commonality is to marinate it in lemon juice, along with a bit of salt and pepper. This, many cooks claim, tenderizes and whitens the meat. Then they rub the bird with the seasonings for the specific dish. Because the meat from free-range chickens is tougher than that of birds raised in small spaces, the former are poached before they are sautéed or cooked in a sauce.

Hens are used to make soups, and most of the meat from them is then used to make fillings for tamales, casseroles, salads, or empanadas. Not too surprisingly, given its presence in so much of South American cooking, *sofrito*, an onion-based flavoring seasoned with herbs and spices, is the base for many sauces used to prepare chicken. Traditionally, the whole chicken was used to make the various chicken specialties, but today homemakers and chefs in South America more often use chicken breasts, thighs, legs, and wings, which are now available in supermarkets.

The turkey, indigenous to Mexico, is mostly served for Christmas dinner. In the past, it, too, was purchased live, usually a few weeks before the holidays, in order to fatten it and improve its flavor with a diet of corn. The problem was that turkeys were favorite targets of thieves and were often stolen just before Christmas, no matter how many precautions were taken to protect the bird. Even so, this has not lessened the turkey's popularity.

Duck, called *xuta* in Quechua, was one of the domesticated birds the Spanish found in Ecuador (on the coast and in the Andes) and Peru. The historian Eduardo Estrella has found that ducks are often depicted in ceramics made between A.D. 500 and 1500, which has led him to believe that the natives had a special love for this bird. Pedro Cieza de León, in his book *La Crónica del Perú*, describes *xutas* as big ducks, which the Indians raised in their homes and were good to eat. It seems that ducks were especially popular in the Andean region, and when the conquistador Sebastián de Benalcázar was making his way to conquer Quito, the Cañaris made him a peace offering of *charqui* (dried meat), fish, pigeons, and ducks.

Game birds and animals are also common in South America. In Argentina and Uruguay, an abundance of large, flightless rheas roam the *pampas*. In Argentina, rhea is made mainly into jerky. Throughout South America, there is also an abundance of partridge, quail, and squab, which are prepared in many imaginative and tasty ways.

In Peru, early peoples hunted the *vizcacha*, an animal about the size of a hare, and in Ecuador, there was such an abundance of rabbits that natives could catch them with clubs. Originally, these animals were dried and used for barter or in the preparation of stews. (Rabbits are still used, but today they are prepared fresh.) Indigenous peoples also relied on the *cuy* (guinea pig), a domesticated animal raised by Andean Indians living from Ecuador south through northern Chile. Because the indigenous peoples also used this animal for divination and sacrifices, which the Catholic Spaniards viewed as pagan, at one time an effort was made to eradicate *cuy*, though without success, because every household raised them. As with other meat and poultry, *cuy* was, and still is, prepared mainly for special occasions.

Xinxim de Galinha

CHICKEN WITH CASHEW AND COCONUT SAUCE
Serves 4

This Bahian specialty clearly shows the African influence in the cooking of Brazil. The use of *dendê*, nuts, and coconut milk in the sauce is typical of Bahian cooking and gives the dish a very special color and taste. The use of dried shrimp dates back to the Indians, who used to preserve fish and shellfish by drying them. Some people don't care for the flavor of dried shrimp and make *xinxim* without it. Either way, this is a delicious way to prepare chicken. Brazilians serve it with rice and, of course, *Farofa de Ouro* (page 304).

1 large onion, chopped (about 1½ cups)

½ cup chopped scallions (white part and 1 inch of the green)

¼ cup chopped fresh cilantro leaves

2 tablespoons finely chopped fresh parsley leaves, plus more for garnish

3 large cloves garlic, mashed into a paste with 1 teaspoon salt

1 tablespoon peeled and minced fresh ginger

Juice of 1 lemon

4 small bone-in chicken breast halves, skin removed and halved crosswise

4 bone-in chicken thighs or legs, skin removed

2 tablespoons olive oil

2 tablespoons *dendê* (page 422)

½ cup peeled dried shrimp (page 433; optional), ground

⅓ cup ground unsalted dry-roasted cashews

½ cup well-stirred canned unsweetened coconut milk

Malagueta pepper sauce or Tabasco sauce

¼ cup unsalted dry-roasted whole cashews

1. Place the onion, scallions, cilantro, 2 tablespoons parsley, garlic paste, ginger, and lemon juice in a blender and process until smooth. Place the chicken in a zippered-top plastic bag, add the onion puree, and toss to coat well. Seal and let marinate in the refrigerator for 1 hour.

2. In a large casserole, heat the olive oil and *dendê* together over medium heat. Drain the chicken pieces, reserving the marinade, and pat dry with paper towels. Lightly brown on both sides without crowding them. Do it in batches, if necessary. Remove the pieces as they are done and set aside. When all the pieces are browned, return to the skillet together with the marinade. Add the dried shrimp (if using), ground cashews, coconut milk, and hot pepper sauce to taste. Cover, reduce the heat to low, and simmer until the chicken is tender, about 30 minutes, turning the pieces after 15 minutes. Season with salt and hot pepper sauce.

3. Transfer the chicken to a heated serving platter, scatter the whole cashews on top, and pour the sauce over. Sprinkle with parsley and serve.

Picante de Pollo (Sajta)

CHICKEN WITH SPICY HOT SAUCE *Serves 4 to 6*

Picante de pollo, also called *sajta*, is part of a famous Bolivian specialty called *picante mixto*, a very elaborate feast that is usually served for special occasions and festivities. *Picante mixto* consists of *picante de pollo*, *picante de lengua* (spicy tongue), *chuño phuti de huevo* (egg and dried potato omelet), *papa rellena* (stuffed potato), *pastel de macarón al horno* (pasta torte), and, of course, a good *llajwa* (salsa). When prepared as a single entrée, *picante de pollo* is usually served with two kinds of potatoes, fresh and dried (*chuño*).

In Bolivia, *picante* means "very hot," but the amount of hot peppers used can be adjusted to your taste. The best thing to do is add one tablespoon of the puree at a time, tasting and adding more until the desired level of heat is achieved.

2 tablespoons canola oil

2 medium-size onions, finely chopped (about 2 cups)

1 teaspoon salt

¼ cup finely chopped scallions (white part and 1 inch of the green)

2 cloves garlic, minced

1 large ripe but firm tomato (about 8 ounces), peeled, seeded, and chopped

½ cup seeded and finely chopped green bell pepper

¼ cup finely chopped fresh parsley leaves

1 teaspoon dried oregano

1 teaspoon ground cumin

½ teaspoon freshly ground black pepper

3 dried hot red peppers, seeded, soaked in hot water for 30 minutes, drained, and pureed in the blender with a little of the soaking liquid

One 3- to 4-pound chicken, cut up, rinsed, patted dry, and skin removed (if desired)

1 cup chicken broth

1 cup frozen peas, or shelled fava beans, blanched and peeled (page 308)

½ cup dry bread crumbs

Minced fresh parsley leaves for garnish

1. In a large frying pan, heat the oil over medium heat. Add the onions and salt and cook for 10 minutes, stirring occasionally. Add the scallions, garlic, tomato, bell pepper, chopped parsley, oregano, cumin, black pepper, and hot pepper puree. Cover and cook, stirring occasionally, for 10 minutes. Add the chicken and chicken broth and bring to a boil. Cover, reduce the heat to low, and simmer until the chicken is cooked all the way through, about 40 minutes. Add the peas and bread crumbs and cook for 5 minutes more. Season with salt and black pepper to taste.

2. Transfer the chicken to a heated serving platter, and sprinkle with the minced parsley.

TO SERVE Serve with boiled potatoes or rice.

Tallarín de Pollo con Salsa de Espinaca

SPAGHETTI WITH CHICKEN AND SPINACH SAUCE

Serves 4

Combinations such as this are very popular, especially in the southern countries of South America. I have some young friends who have made this dish a staple. It is an excellent way to use leftover chicken, turkey, or fish. The sauce can be served as a topping or tossed with the pasta.

¼ cup olive oil

½ cup finely chopped scallions (white part and 1 inch of the green)

8 ounces fresh, firm white mushrooms, sliced

2 tablespoons chopped fresh parsley leaves

8 fresh basil leaves, cut into ribbons, or 1 teaspoon dried basil

½ teaspoon salt

¼ teaspoon freshly ground black pepper

One 10-ounce package frozen chopped spinach, cooked according to package directions, drained, and squeezed dry

2 cups cooked chicken cut into ½-inch cubes

2 tablespoons tomato paste

1 cup whipping cream or half-and-half

One 10-ounce package fresh spaghetti or fettuccine

¼ cup freshly grated Parmesan cheese, plus more for serving

1. Heat the oil in a large, heavy skillet over medium heat. Add the scallions and cook, stirring, for 1 minute. Add the mushrooms and cook, stirring, until tender, about 5 minutes. Stir in the parsley, basil, salt, and pepper. Add the spinach, chicken, tomato paste, and cream and bring to a boil. Immediately reduce the heat to medium-low and simmer for a couple of minutes. Taste for salt and pepper. The sauce can be prepared ahead up

to this point, cooled, covered, and refrigerated. Reheat before serving.

2. Bring a large pot of salted water to a boil. Add the spaghetti, stir, and cook until *al dente*. Drain thoroughly and transfer to a heated serving bowl or platter. Top with the sauce, sprinkle with the Parmesan, and serve immediately, with additional Parmesan on the side.

Pollo a la Mariana

MARIANA'S CHICKEN *Serves 4*

Mariana was our family cook for 50 years. She was like a member of the family and stayed with us long past retirement. I have such fond memories of her. I include this recipe not only because it is simple and good but also to honor Mariana's love and dedication to us. She cooked the way my mother taught her, although sometimes she would come up with her own adaptations of traditional recipes. This was one of her improvisations, and, I must say, everybody enjoyed chicken prepared her way.

One 3-pound chicken, rinsed and patted dry

A D O B O (Marinade)
> **1 small onion, chopped (about ½ cup)**
> **½ cup fresh orange juice**
> **1 tablespoon fresh lemon juice**
> **½ teaspoon salt**
> **½ teaspoon sweet paprika**
> **½ teaspoon freshly ground black pepper**
> **½ teaspoon granulated garlic**
> **Pinch of freshly grated nutmeg**
> **½ teaspoon Worcestershire sauce**

1. Remove all the extra fat from the chicken.

2. To make the marinade, place all the ingredients in a blender and process until smooth. Rub the chicken inside and out with the marinade.

Cover with plastic wrap and refrigerate for a few hours or overnight.

3. Preheat the oven to 425°F.

4. Place the chicken on a rack in a shallow baking pan. Bake for 30 minutes, then reduce the oven temperature to 350°F and bake until the juices run clear when the thigh is pierced with a knife, about 30 minutes. Baste with the juices every 20 minutes throughout the cooking time.

5. Remove from the oven and let cool for 10 minutes. Cut into serving-size pieces and serve.

TO SERVE **Serve with rice and peas or beans.**

Vatapá de Galinha

CHICKEN IN NUT AND DRIED SHRIMP SAUCE
Serves 4 to 6

This classic dish from Bahia has been hailed as the glory of the Afro-Brazilian kitchen. Some researchers believe that this specialty came from the Iberian Peninsula and was modified by African slaves, who added their own ingredients, such as *dendê* (palm oil) and coconut milk. Many cooks thicken the *vatapá* with bread, which is the Portuguese way of thickening their stews, while others use either rice flour or manioc meal. Ground nuts are an essential ingredient, and cooks use either peanuts, almonds, or cashews. The dried shrimp is also essential to the dish, as is the *dendê*, which gives the *vatapá* its characteristic taste and color. When *dendê* is not available, some cooks replace it with annatto oil. *Vatapá* can be made with fish, shrimp, dried cod, or chicken. Serve with *Pirão de Arroz* (page 326).

1 medium-size onion, chopped (about 1 cup)

½ cup chopped scallions (white part and 1 inch of the green)

2 cloves garlic, chopped

1 tablespoon peeled and chopped fresh ginger

1 tablespoon seeded and chopped serrano or *manzano* pepper, or more to taste

2 medium-size ripe but firm tomatoes (10 to 12 ounces), peeled, seeded, and chopped

1 small green bell pepper, seeded and cut into pieces

½ cup fresh cilantro sprigs, chopped

3 tablespoons *dendê* (page 422), or 2 tablespoons olive oil mixed with 1 tablespoon *Manteca de Color* (page 331)

One 3-pound chicken, cut up, rinsed, patted dry, and skin removed

1 teaspoon salt

¼ teaspoon freshly ground black pepper

½ cup cubed day-old bread, soaked in ½ cup water for 30 minutes and pureed

¼ cup peeled dried shrimp (page 433), ground

½ cup ground lightly toasted peanuts, almonds, or cashews (page 413)

1 tablespoon fresh lime juice

One 14-ounce can unsweetened coconut milk, well stirred

1. Place the onion, scallions, garlic, ginger, hot pepper, tomatoes, bell pepper, and cilantro in a blender or food processor and process until smooth.

2. In a large skillet or heavy casserole, heat the *dendê* over medium heat. Add the onion puree and cook, stirring occasionally, until it loses its raw taste, about 10 minutes.

3. Season the chicken with the salt and black pepper and add to the sauce, tossing to coat. Cover and cook until the chicken is cooked all the way through, about 25 minutes.

4. Transfer the chicken to a chopping board and let cool for a few minutes. Remove the bones and cut the meat into pieces about ½ inch wide and 1½ inches long. Return the chicken to the sauce. Add the bread, shrimp, nuts, lime juice, and coconut milk and simmer until the sauce thickens. Taste for salt and black pepper and serve.

Crepas de Pollo

CHICKEN CREPES *Makes 12 to 14 crepes; 4 to 5 servings*

For an elegant luncheon, these very special Uruguayan crepes are sure to be a hit. The whipping cream is a touch that some good Latin cooks add to the assembled crepes, but they seldom bother to tell you this if you ask for their secret. Like seasoning with salt, you ought to know it without being told. I believe it is a secret that was inherited from some Italian cooks. (Many years ago, I heard of an Italian lady who made the best and lightest lasagna. She would not reveal her secret, until one day someone saw her pouring cream around the edges of the pan.) This recipe can be doubled or tripled.

RELLENO (Filling)

1 whole bone-in chicken breast (about 1 pound), skin on, poached (page 407)

½ cup dried porcini mushrooms, soaked in hot water for 30 minutes

1 tablespoon unsalted butter

2 tablespoons minced shallots

1 tablespoon all-purpose flour

¾ cup half-and-half

2 tablespoons dry sherry

¼ teaspoon salt

Pinch of white pepper

⅓ cup sliced almonds

2 tablespoons minced fresh parsley leaves

3 ounces soft fontina cheese, shredded

1 recipe *Crepas* (plain or basil; page 405)

1 recipe *Salsa Blanca* (page 405), heated

¼ cup freshly grated Parmesan cheese

¼ cup sliced almonds

½ cup whipping cream

1. To make the filling, let the poached chicken breast cool, then remove the skin and bones and cut the meat into ¼-inch dice.

2. Drain the mushrooms, rinse to remove any sand, and chop.

3. Melt the butter in a medium-size skillet over medium heat. Add the shallots and mushrooms and cook, stirring constantly, for a couple of minutes. Stir in the flour and cook for 1 minute. Add the half-and-half, sherry, salt, and pepper and cook, stirring constantly, until thickened. Remove from the heat and let cool. Stir in the almonds, parsley, and fontina. This can be done the day before, covered, and refrigerated. Gently reheat before proceeding.

4. To assemble the crepes, place 2 heaping tablespoons of the filling in the center of each crepe and roll up tightly into a cylinder. Arrange the filled crepes in a single layer in 2 buttered shallow baking dishes, making sure they are not crowded. The dish can be made a day ahead up to this point, covered, and refrigerated. Bring the crepes to room temperature before proceeding.

5. Preheat the oven to 375°F.

6. Cover the crepes with the *salsa blanca*, sprinkle with the Parmesan and almonds, and drizzle the cream around edges. Bake in the upper third of the oven for 20 minutes. Serve hot.

TO SERVE **Serve with steamed baby squash flavored with a little butter or with a good salad.**

Arroz con Pollo

CHICKEN WITH RICE *Serves 4 to 6*

Another all-time favorite from South America, this flavorful and easy-to-prepare dish is a staple throughout the continent. In some countries, it was reserved for special occasions, due to the high cost of chicken prior to the introduction of mass production. Each country has its own version, but the basic ingredients are always the same. In some countries, red kidney beans or chickpeas are sometimes used instead of peas. (Use one can of beans, drained and thoroughly rinsed.) Artichoke hearts also can be added to dress up the dish.

3 tablespoons olive oil

One 3-pound chicken, cut up, rinsed, patted dry, and skin removed

½ teaspoon salt

½ teaspoon freshly ground black pepper

1 medium-size onion, minced (about 1 cup)

1 cup thin green bell pepper strips

2 cloves garlic, minced

2 medium-size ripe but firm tomatoes (10 to 12 ounces), peeled, seeded, and chopped

1 teaspoon sweet paprika

1½ cups converted rice

3 cups chicken broth

½ teaspoon saffron threads, crumbled and softened in ¼ cup chicken broth or water (optional)

¼ cup pimento-stuffed Spanish olives, sliced

1 tablespoon capers, drained

1 cup frozen peas

Pimento strips for garnish

1. Heat the oil in a large, heavy skillet over medium heat. Cook the chicken pieces on both sides, without crowding, until they turn white. Do not brown. Sprinkle with the salt and pepper and transfer to another dish.

2. Add the onion and bell pepper to the skillet and cook, stirring a few times, until softened, about 5 minutes. Add the garlic, tomatoes, and paprika and cook for a couple of minutes. Add the rice and cook, stirring constantly, for a couple of minutes. Add the 3 cups chicken broth, saffron and broth (if using), olives, and capers. Bring to a boil, season with salt and pepper, and cook, uncovered, for 5 minutes. Transfer to a shallow baking dish and cover loosely with aluminum foil.

3. Preheat the oven to 350°F.

4. Bake the casserole until the rice has absorbed all the liquid and the chicken is almost cooked all the way through, about 30 minutes. Stir in the peas and bake for 5 minutes more. Serve decorated with the pimento strips.

TO SERVE **Serve with a green salad dressed with a simple vinaigrette.**

Picante de Pollo Ecuatoriano

MARINATED CHICKEN WITH PEPPERS AND POTATOES ECUADORIAN STYLE *Serves 6*

This is a prized recipe that comes from the house-keeper of a bishop friend of my parents. This housekeeper was a gifted cook who was very secretive about her techniques. As was typical of the culture long ago, she did not believe in sharing her recipes. Luckily for me, she had a fondness for my mother and was somehow convinced to share the magic formula for *picante de pollo*. This recipe is similar to the *escabeches* in the hors d'oeuvres chapter, except that in this case the ingredients are not "cooked" in the vinaigrette, so the vegetables retain their freshness. Blanching them in flavored chicken broth removes the raw taste of the onions and peppers. The entire dish can be prepared the day before. It can be served as is or topped with chopped fresh herbs, such as parsley, cilantro, chives, basil, or tarragon. It is truly a wonderful summertime meal, great for picnics and outdoor entertaining. Traditionally, it was prepared with the whole chicken, but I prefer to use chicken breasts. I like to mix different colors of peppers for visual appeal as well as taste.

> 2 whole bone-in chicken breasts (about 2 pounds), skin on, poached (page 407), poaching liquid reserved
>
> 1 pound small new red or Yukon gold potatoes, cooked in water to cover until tender, drained, and peeled
>
> 2 small red onions, sliced ⅛ inch thick
>
> 1 cup thin red bell pepper strips
>
> 1 cup thin green bell pepper strips
>
> 1 cup thin yellow bell pepper strips
>
> 2 to 4 large jalapeños (see Note), to your taste, seeded and thinly sliced
>
> 1 tablespoon pickling spices
>
> ½ cup olive oil
>
> ¼ cup sherry vinegar
>
> 1 teaspoon salt
>
> ¼ teaspoon freshly ground black pepper
>
> Finely chopped fresh parsley leaves, cilantro leaves, and chives

1. Strain the poaching liquid from the chicken breasts and reserve 2 cups. While the chicken is still warm, remove the skin and bones. Pull the meat into strips about ½ inch wide and 2 inches long. Place in a large glass bowl, add the potatoes, and set aside.

2. In a medium-size glass bowl, combine the onions, bell peppers, and jalapeños. Set aside.

3. In a small saucepan, bring the reserved poaching liquid and pickling spices to a boil, reduce the heat to medium-low, and simmer for 5 minutes. Strain over the onions and peppers and let stand until lukewarm. Add the oil, vinegar, salt, and black pepper and mix well. Add to the chicken mixture, stirring carefully until everything is coated with the liquid. Adjust the seasonings, cover with plastic wrap, and refrigerate for at least 6 hours or overnight, stirring occasionally.

4. Bring to room temperature and drain. Serve sprinkled with the chopped herbs. This dish can also be reheated and served warm.

NOTE **This dish should be a little piquant. Jalapeños are sometimes hot, sometimes quite mild. The only way to know whether they are hot or mild is to sample a piece of each. If this dish is made for hot-pepper lovers, add a pinch of red pepper flakes to the poaching liquid when simmering.**

Calalú Matutero

CHICKEN WITH OKRA AND CABBAGE *Serves 4*

This specialty from the Paria coast of Venezuela, was brought from Trinidad in colonial times and became very popular among both rich and poor. The people from the coast eat *calalú* at least once a week. Originally, it was made with goat, but now it is prepared with either goat or chicken. Some cooks add coconut milk to the sauce.

2 tablespoons olive oil

1 pound boneless, skinless chicken breasts

1 large onion, finely chopped (about 1½ cups)

2 large cloves garlic, mashed into a paste with 1 teaspoon salt and ½ teaspoon freshly ground black pepper

½ cup seeded and diced green bell pepper

½ cup seeded and diced red bell pepper

4 large ripe but firm pear-shaped tomatoes, peeled and finely chopped

1 bay leaf

1 cup chicken broth or water

8 ounces frozen sliced okra

2 cups shredded cabbage (preferably Savoy)

1. In a large, heavy skillet with a cover, heat the oil over medium-high heat. Dry the chicken breasts with paper towels and cook on both sides until lightly golden. Transfer to a plate and set aside. Reduce the heat to low, add the onion to the skillet, and cook, stirring a few times, until softened, about 5 minutes. Stir in the garlic paste and cook for 1 minute. Add the bell peppers, tomatoes, and bay leaf. Cover and cook, stirring occasionally, until the tomatoes have formed a sauce, about 15 minutes. Add a little water if the mixture becomes too dry.

2. Return the chicken to the skillet and add the chicken broth. Cover and simmer until the chicken is cooked all the way through, 15 minutes or more, depending on the size of the breasts.

3. While the chicken is cooking, prepare the vegetables. Bring a 4-quart saucepan of salted water to a boil, add the okra and cabbage, bring back to a boil, and cook for 10 minutes.

4. Transfer the chicken to a cutting board, cool for a few minutes, and slice or tear into pieces about ½ inch wide and 1½ inches long. Discard the bay leaf. Drain the vegetables and add to the skillet along with the chicken. Make sure there is enough sauce to cover the meat and vegetables; if not, add more water. Simmer for 5 minutes to blend the flavors. Season with salt and black pepper and serve.

TO SERVE **Serve with rice.**

Pechugas de Pollo al Cilantro

CHICKEN BREASTS WITH CILANTRO SAUCE
Serves 4 to 6

If you like cilantro, you will enjoy this vivid, full-flavored recipe from Chile. It is a quick and healthy way to prepare chicken breasts.

- 6 boneless, skinless chicken breast halves (about 6 ounces each)
- Juice of 1 lemon
- Salt and freshly ground black pepper
- 2 tablespoons canola oil
- 1 small onion, chopped (about ½ cup)
- 2 scallions (white part and 1 inch of the green), chopped
- 2 large cloves garlic, chopped
- 1 teaspoon dried oregano, crumbled
- ½ teaspoon ground cumin
- 1 bunch fresh cilantro, tops only, coarsely chopped
- 1 cup chicken broth
- Pinch of cayenne pepper
- 1 teaspoon cornstarch mixed with 2 tablespoons cold water (optional)

1. Place the chicken between 2 pieces of plastic wrap and pound on both sides with a meat mallet to get a fairly even thickness. Sprinkle with the lemon juice and salt and pepper to taste. Cover with plastic wrap and let marinate in the refrigerator for 1 hour.

2. In a large skillet, heat the oil over medium heat. Dry the breasts with paper towels and cook on both sides until lightly colored, about 3 minutes per side. Transfer the breasts to a platter and set aside.

3. Add the onion, scallions, garlic, oregano, and cumin to the skillet. Reduce the heat to low and cook, stirring a few times, for 5 minutes. Transfer to a blender, add the cilantro and chicken broth, and process until smooth. Return to the skillet and add the chicken and cayenne. Simmer until cooked all the way through, about 10 minutes, turning the chicken once after 5 minutes. Season with salt and black pepper to taste. If the sauce is too thin, thicken with the cornstarch slurry. Serve hot.

TO SERVE **Serve with white rice and sliced zucchini sautéed with corn.**

Pechugas de Pollo con Salsa de Quinua a la Huancaína

CHICKEN BREASTS WITH QUINOA, CASHEW, AND GOAT CHEESE SAUCE *Serves 6*

This sauce is rich and flavorful and is especially good when served on top of grilled chicken breasts. In Peru and Bolivia, this sauce is a variation of one used for the Peruvian specialty *Papas Huancaínas* (page 127). Three hot peppers will give just enough heat, although Peruvians and Bolivians use many more than three, as they like their sauces very hot. Bolivians make this sauce with peanuts.

- 6 small boneless, skinless chicken breast halves
- Juice of 2 limes
- Salt and freshly ground black pepper
- 5 tablespoons olive oil
- 3 *mirasol* (hot yellow) peppers
- 1 small onion, chopped (about ½ cup)
- 1 clove garlic, minced
- 1 cup milk, or more if needed
- ½ cup cooked quinoa (page 327)
- ¼ cup unsalted dry-roasted cashews or peanuts
- 2 ounces fresh goat cheese or imported feta cheese, crumbled
- *Salsa Criolla Peruana* (page 334)

Comidas MEALS

Most urban families eat three meals a day. *Desayuno* (breakfast) is taken early in the morning and consists of a glass of fresh fruit juice and a roll or toast with *café en leche* (coffee and milk). The next meal is *almuerzo* (lunch), which is the big meal of the day. Lunch is eaten anytime between noon and 2:00 P.M., depending on the country. It starts most often with soup, but a first course is sometimes served instead, such as stuffed avocados, *cebiche*, empanadas, or fritters of some kind, depending on the country and people's means. The main course is meat, chicken, or seafood, accompanied by rice or potatoes and some kind of cooked vegetable or salad. A light dessert follows; it may be stewed fruits or custard, or simply fresh fruit, which is served on a plate with a small fork and knife to peel the fruit. In some countries, such as Brazil, rice and beans are served every day at lunch. In some of the Andean countries, rice and beans are the daily diet of the masses. In the southern countries, the diet is more European, with pasta being more predominant.

Until a few years ago, businesses used to close at noon for two to three hours, and families had time to have a leisurely lunch, since this was the biggest and most important meal of the day. Now businesses are becoming Americanized, and people are working what is called *jornada única* (an eight-hour day, with 30 minutes for lunch), with no time for a *siesta* (nap). Most corporations serve lunch in their cafeterias.

Teatime is still popular among urban South Americans. The traditions and recipes associated with this are covered in greater depth on pages 54–55.

Many people are trying to cut down on the evening meal, making a more substantial afternoon tea, with soup and sandwiches, the last meal of the day. Nevertheless, the custom of going out for a late dinner or party (after 9:00 P.M.), brought by the Spaniards and Portuguese, still exists today.

1. Place the chicken breasts between 2 pieces of plastic wrap and lightly pound on both sides with a meat mallet to get a fairly even thickness. Sprinkle with the lime juice, season with salt and black pepper to taste, and drizzle with 1 tablespoon of the oil. Cover and let marinate in the refrigerator for a couple of hours.

2. Seed the hot peppers, crumble, and soak in hot water to cover for 1 hour. Puree in a blender with a little of the soaking liquid.

3. To make the sauce, heat the remaining 4 tablespoons oil in a small skillet over medium heat. Add the onion, garlic, and pepper puree and cook, stirring a few times, until soft, about 5 minutes.

4. Place the milk, quinoa, cashews, and onion mixture in a blender or food processor and process until smooth. Add the cheese, pulse for a few seconds to blend, and return to the skillet. Cook over low heat, stirring constantly, until

creamy. The sauce should be thick enough to cover the chicken without being runny. If the sauce is too thick, thin it with milk. Season with ½ teaspoon salt and black pepper to taste. The sauce can be made a day ahead, covered, and refrigerated until needed. Reheat before proceeding.

5. Preheat the broiler.

6. Place the chicken on a broiler pan and broil until cooked through, 2 to 3 minutes per side. Serve each breast topped with about ¼ cup of the sauce and some *salsa criolla*.

Pechugas de Pollo con Salsa de Almendras y Jerez

CHICKEN BREASTS WITH ALMOND AND SHERRY SAUCE *Serves 4*

Peruvians excel in the preparation of wonderful chicken dishes made with nut sauces, which have Indian and Spanish roots. The Incas probably used the native peanuts and squash seeds to make sauces to flavor their foods. Perhaps sometimes they even used the nuts called Chachapoyas almonds (*Caryocar amygdaliferum*), which are grown in Chachapoyas, in northern Peru. They are three times the size of true almonds and have a very delicate flesh. Chachapoyas almonds have always been coveted and considered a luxury item, even before the Spaniards arrived. The Spaniards, for their part, learned from the Moors how to use nuts (almonds and pine nuts) in sauces and brought this knowledge (and true almonds) to South America. This sauce also can be made with peanuts or walnuts, and it is excellent on fish, lobster, or langostinos (extra-large shrimp). The dish makes an elegant entrée for a special dinner party.

> **4 boneless, skinless chicken breast halves (about 6 ounces each)**
> **Juice of 1 lemon**
> **Salt and freshly ground black pepper**
> **¼ cup olive oil**
> **All-purpose flour for dredging**
> **1 medium-size onion, sliced (about 1 cup)**
> **1 large ripe but firm tomato (about 8 ounces), chopped**
> **¼ teaspoon dried thyme**
> **½ cup chicken broth, or more if needed**
> **½ cup blanched whole or sliced almonds**
> **½ cup milk**
> **2 tablespoons dry sherry**
> **Snipped fresh chives for garnish**

1. Cut each breast half in half again crosswise. Place between 2 pieces of plastic wrap and lightly pound the thicker parts with a meat mallet to flatten a bit. Sprinkle with the lemon juice and season with salt and pepper to taste. Cover and refrigerate for at least 30 minutes.

2. In a large, heavy skillet, heat the oil over medium heat. Dry the chicken pieces with paper towels and dredge in the flour, tapping off any excess. Quickly pan-fry, without crowding, until lightly colored on both sides. Transfer to a platter. Once all the chicken has been browned, add the onion, tomato, thyme, and ¼ teaspoon each salt and pepper to the skillet. Reduce the heat to low, cover, and cook, stirring occasionally, until softened, about 8 minutes. Add the chicken broth and cook for 5 minutes more.

3. Transfer to a blender and process until smooth. Strain through a coarse-mesh sieve and return to the skillet. Add the chicken, cover, and simmer for 6 minutes, turning the chicken after 3 minutes.

4. Place the almonds and milk in the blender and process until smooth. (Some cooks prefer a coarse sauce, with little pieces of almond left in. Do whichever appeals to you.) Stir into the chicken mixture, add the sherry, and simmer for 5 minutes to blend the flavors. Season with salt

and pepper to taste. The sauce should be thicker than heavy cream. If it is too thick, add a little more chicken broth or water.

The entire dish can be made a few hours ahead. Store in a covered plastic or glass container and keep refrigerated until needed. Before serving, bring to room temperature and heat, covered, over low heat.

5. To serve, sprinkle with the chives.

TO SERVE **Serve with rice and steamed vegetables dressed with a little butter.**

Pechugas de Pollo en Salsa de Maracuyá

CHICKEN BREASTS WITH PASSION FRUIT SAUCE *Serves 4*

Chicken with fruit sauce was not part of the traditional creole cuisine. Instead, it is a rather new addition to the South American table. Passion fruit is an incredibly fragrant and delicious fruit, which is usually made into drinks, mousses, and desserts. Now it is beginning to show up in exotic sauces for game and chicken. This velvety sauce is not only easy to make but also provides a touch of elegance to the chicken breasts.

    4 boneless, skinless chicken breast halves
        (about 6 ounces each)
    Juice of 1 lime
    Salt and white pepper
    2 tablespoons unsalted butter
    1 tablespoon canola oil
    ¼ cup brandy or rum
    ¼ cup thawed frozen passion fruit pulp
    ½ cup orange juice
    2 teaspoons sugar
    ¼ cup whipping cream

1. Place the chicken breasts between 2 pieces of plastic wrap and lightly pound on both sides with a meat mallet to get a fairly even thickness. Sprinkle with the lime juice and season with salt and pepper to taste. Cover and let marinate in the refrigerator for about 1 hour.

2. In a large skillet, heat the butter and oil together over medium heat until the butter melts. Dry the chicken breasts with paper towels and pan-fry for a couple of minutes on each side without letting them brown. Transfer to a plate and set aside.

3. Drain the fat from the pan, add the brandy, and scrape any browned bits from the bottom of the pan. Add the passion fruit pulp, orange juice, and sugar and cook until the sauce is reduced to about ½ cup. Add the cream, return the chicken to the pan, cover, and simmer until the juices from the chicken run clear when pierced with a knife, about 3 minutes per side. Taste for salt, sugar, and pepper. Serve hot, with some of the sauce on top.

Pastel de Choclo con Pollo Boliviano

CORN TORTE WITH CHICKEN FILLING BOLIVIAN STYLE *Serves 6 to 8*

Corn tortes are very popular in all South American countries. They are made with a base of ground fresh corn kernels mixed with butter, eggs, cheese, onions, or tomatoes, depending on the country. This base can be wrapped in cornhusks and steamed; these packets are called *humintas* in Bolivia and *humitas* in Argentina, Peru, and Ecuador. Or it can be baked in a shallow baking dish (*huminta al horno*). Sometimes it is layered with cheese or with a savory mixture of ground beef or chicken.

There is a considerable difference between South American and North American corn varieties. Because South American corn is drier and starchier, it is important for U.S. cooks to look for mature corn, and it is necessary to add cornmeal to get the right consistency for the *huminta* mixture. This particular corn torte hails from Bolivia, where it is usually cut into slices and served with a cup of coffee.

RELLENO DE POLLO (Chicken filling)

2 tablespoons canola oil

1 medium-size onion, halved and thinly sliced into half-moons (about 1 cup)

2 medium-size ripe but firm tomatoes (10 to 12 ounces), peeled, seeded, and finely chopped

1 teaspoon dried oregano

1 bay leaf

1 teaspoon salt

Pinch of sugar

1 tablespoon dried hot red pepper puree, store-bought or homemade (page 332), or ¼ teaspoon red pepper flakes

½ cup dry white wine

½ cup chicken broth

2 cups shredded cooked chicken

¼ cup seedless black raisins (optional)

HUMINTA (Corn batter)

2 pounds frozen corn kernels, thawed

½ cup cornmeal

2 teaspoons baking powder

2 teaspoons salt

1 teaspoon sugar

5 large eggs

1 large egg white

1 tablespoon *pisco* (page 34)

½ cup (1 stick) unsalted butter, melted

4 ounces Swiss, Emmental, or other good melting cheese, shredded

1 large egg white, lightly beaten

1. To make the filling, heat the oil in a large skillet over medium heat. Add the onion and cook until transparent, about 5 minutes. Add the tomatoes, oregano, bay leaf, salt, sugar, and hot pepper puree. Cover and cook over low heat for 10 minutes. Add the wine and chicken broth and cook, uncovered, until thickened. Stir in the chicken and raisins (if using) and continue to cook for a few minutes, until the sauce has thickened a little more. Discard the bay leaf and taste for salt and sugar. Let cool, then refrigerate for a few hours or overnight.

2. To make the *huminta*, place the corn in a food processor and process until smooth. Mix the cornmeal, baking powder, salt, and sugar together in a small bowl and add to the food processor. Add the eggs, egg white, and *pisco*. Process until smooth. Add the butter and cheese and pulse until well mixed. Transfer the mixture to a large mixing bowl.

3. Preheat the oven to 350°F. Generously butter a shallow 6-cup baking dish.

4. To assemble the torte, spread half of the *huminta* in the prepared dish. Spread the chicken mixture on top and cover with the rest of the *huminta*. Brush with the beaten egg white and bake on the middle oven rack until golden and a knife inserted in the center comes out clean, about 1 hour. It can be made ahead, cooled, and refrigerated. To serve, bring to room temperature and bake in a preheated 350°F oven until heated through, about 20 minutes.

Arroz con Pato a la Chiclayana

DUCK WITH RICE CHICLAYAN STYLE *Serves 4 to 6*

This specialty comes from Chiclayo, a city in north-western Peru. It is traditionally made with *chicha de jora* (a fermented corn drink) or dark beer. This is an ideal dish for a dinner party: not only is it an all-in-one meal, but it can be completely prepared ahead of time. The wonderful combination of spices makes this dish very special. If you like the flavor of cilantro, use more; Peruvians add up to two cups. This dish can also be made with chicken.

One 4- to 5-pound duckling

¼ cup fresh lemon juice

1 teaspoon salt

½ teaspoon freshly ground black pepper

¼ cup olive oil

2 medium-size onions, finely chopped (about 2 cups)

6 large cloves garlic, minced

2 tablespoons seeded and minced jalapeños or serranos

1 teaspoon ground cumin

½ teaspoon dried oregano, crumbled

One 12-ounce can or bottle beer (preferably dark)

2 cups chicken broth

1 cup packed fresh cilantro leaves

2 tablespoons *pisco* (page 34)

2 cups converted rice

1 cup frozen peas

Hot green and red peppers, cut into thin strips, or 1 large ripe but firm tomato (about 8 ounces), seeded and diced (¼ inch), for garnish

1. Cut the duck into serving-size pieces: cut each breast half in half crosswise, separate the legs and thighs, and remove the tips from the wings. Remove all the fat and skin from these pieces and discard. Put the pieces in a non-aluminum bowl. Rub with the lemon juice, salt, and black pepper. Cover with plastic wrap and refrigerate for a couple of hours.

2. In a large, heavy casserole, heat the oil over low heat. Add the onions and cook, stirring occasionally, until softened, about 5 minutes. Add the garlic, jalapeños, cumin, oregano, and salt to taste and cook for 1 minute. Add the duck pieces, toss

with the onions, and cook on both sides only until they turn white. Add the beer and chicken broth, cover, and simmer until the duck is just cooked through, about 45 minutes. Sometimes, if the duck is old, it will take more than an hour to cook. Season with salt and black pepper to taste.

3. Place the cilantro and *pisco* in a blender and pulse until the cilantro is minced. Add to the casserole along with the rice. Cover, bring to a boil, reduce the heat to medium-low, and simmer until the rice has absorbed most of the liquid, about 20 minutes. By this time, the rice should be cooked. Stir in the peas and cook for 5 minutes. Remove from the heat, fluff the rice, cover, and let stand for 5 minutes.

4. Transfer the rice mixture to an ovenproof serving dish, arrange the duck pieces on top, cover, and keep warm in a low oven until ready to serve. This can be made ahead and reheated, covered, in a preheated 350°F oven until heated through, about 20 minutes. Garnish with the hot pepper strips or diced tomatoes and serve immediately.

TO SERVE Serve with a tossed salad.

Canelones de Acelgas, Espinaca, y Palmitos

SWISS CHARD, SPINACH, AND HEARTS OF PALM CREPES *Makes 12 to 14 crepes; 4 to 5 servings*

In Paraguay, crepes are called cannelloni, perhaps because the pasta for *canelones* is not readily available, as it is in neighboring Argentina and Uruguay. Paraguayans trim the edges of the crepe to look like cannelloni. The filling in this recipe could be used with either pasta squares or crepes. This type of filling is very popular throughout the southern countries of South America, where Swiss chard and spinach are widely used to fill turnovers and tortes. It is a delicious and winning combination.

2 tablespoons olive oil

2 tablespoons minced shallots

2 cloves garlic, minced

8 ounces Swiss chard (leaves and stems), cooked (page 411), drained, and squeezed dry

One 10-ounce package frozen chopped spinach, cooked according to package directions, drained, and squeezed dry

½ teaspoon salt

¼ teaspoon freshly ground black pepper

Pinch of freshly grated nutmeg

2 tablespoons finely chopped fresh parsley leaves

1 cup canned hearts of palm, rinsed well and cut into ⅓-inch cubes

One 4-ounce can *pâté de foie gras*

1 large egg, lightly beaten

1 cup day-old bread crumbs (page 413)

1 recipe *Crepas con Albahaca* (page 405)

1 recipe *Salsa Blanca* (page 405), heated

½ cup freshly grated Parmesan cheese

½ cup whipping cream

1. In a large, heavy skillet, heat the oil over medium heat. Add the shallots and garlic and cook, stirring, for 1 minute. Add the Swiss chard, spinach, salt, pepper, nutmeg, and parsley and cook, stirring, until well blended, about 1 minute. Carefully fold in the hearts of palm. Remove from the heat and let cool to lukewarm. Mix in the *pâté*, egg, and bread crumbs. Season with salt and pepper to taste.

2. To assemble, place 2 heaping tablespoons of the filling in the center of each crepe and roll up tightly into a cylinder, tucking the ends under. Arrange the crepes in a single layer in 2 buttered shallow baking dishes, making sure they are not too crowded. These can be made the day before, covered, and refrigerated. Bring to room temperature before baking.

3. Preheat the oven to 375°F.

4. Pour the *salsa blanca* evenly over the crepes. Sprinkle with the Parmesan and drizzle with the cream. Bake until bubbling, about 20 minutes. Serve hot.

TO SERVE **Serve with a tomato and onion salad.**

Perdices Encocadas

PARTRIDGE IN COCONUT SAUCE *Serves 4 to 6*

Partridge abound in most of South America and are prepared in a variety of ways. In the southern countries, they are very popular in *escabeches*; in the northern countries, they are seasoned in delightful ways and braised. This is a wonderful combination of tropical flavors, made even tastier by the addition of the very popular portobello mushrooms. You may use dried mushrooms instead, if you wish. This is also a good way to prepare pheasants, squab, or any other wild birds.

4 partridge, trussed

Juice of 1 lemon

½ cup dry white wine

½ teaspoon salt

½ teaspoon freshly ground black pepper

2 strips bacon

1 tablespoon olive oil

½ teaspoon ground annatto or sweet paprika

1 medium-size onion, finely chopped (about 1 cup)

1 medium-size carrot, finely chopped

4 cloves garlic, minced

1 teaspoon dried thyme

1 bay leaf

½ cup pineapple juice

1 cup beef broth

¾ cup well-stirred canned unsweetened coconut milk

½ cup water

4 medium-size portobello mushrooms, stems discarded, caps sliced and cut into 1-inch pieces

2 tablespoons minced fresh parsley leaves for garnish

Small pineapple wedges for garnish

1. Place the partridge in a glass bowl and sprinkle with the lemon juice, wine, salt, and pepper. Cover with plastic wrap and let marinate in the refrigerator for at least 2 hours or overnight.

2. Heat a 12-inch casserole over medium heat, then fry the bacon until crisp. Drain on paper towels and set aside.

3. Add the oil to the bacon grease in the casserole and heat. Lightly brown the partridge on both sides. Transfer to a platter and set aside. Add the annatto, onion, carrot, garlic, thyme, and bay leaf to the casserole. Cover and cook over low heat for 5 minutes, stirring a few times. Return the partridge to the casserole and add the pineapple juice and beef broth. Cover and simmer for 1 hour, turning the birds after 30 minutes. If the liquid evaporates too fast, add a little water; always maintain some sauce.

4. Stir in the coconut milk, water, and mushrooms. Cover and cook until the meat is tender, about 20 minutes. Discard the bay leaf and season with salt and pepper to taste.

5. To serve, transfer the birds to a cutting board, remove the trussing strings, and cut each in half. Arrange on a heated serving platter, spooning some of the sauce on top. Crumble the bacon and sprinkle on the partridge along with the parsley. Garnish with the pineapple wedges and serve immediately.

Codorniz Rellena con Higaditos de Pollo

QUAIL STUFFED WITH CHICKEN LIVERS *Serves 2*

Quail is abundant in South America. My Venezuelan friend Helena Chapellín Wilson prepares quail seasoned and stuffed with pieces of chicken livers. It is so simple that she doesn't use a recipe. This is my version of her dish.

4 quail, washed well

Juice of 1 lime

4 whole chicken livers, trimmed of membranes

2 tablespoons olive oil

2 tablespoons minced shallots

½ teaspoon salt

¼ teaspoon freshly ground black pepper

1 tablespoon minced fresh parsley leaves

4 strips bacon

1. Dry the quail with paper towels, then rub inside and out with the lime juice.

2. Rinse the livers, trim off any fat, and separate into halves. In a small frying pan, heat the oil over low heat. Add the shallots and cook, stirring, for 1 minute. Increase the heat to medium and cook the chicken livers quickly on both sides, just to sear them. Add the salt, pepper, and parsley and toss together quickly. Remove from the heat.

3. Preheat the oven to 425°F.

4. When the mixture is cool enough to handle, stuff the quail loosely with it, then wrap each quail with 1 strip of bacon. Secure the bacon with a toothpick. Set the quail in a shallow baking pan and bake until the bacon is crispy, about 40 minutes. Remove from the oven and serve.

TO SERVE **Serve with *Acelga con Almendras* (page 293).**

Christmas Traditions

More than any other holiday, Christmas brings families together in a celebration of deep-seated traditions. For South Americans, this is a religious holiday—a time of rejoicing at the triumph of light over darkness, a promise of hope and peace on earth. It is a time of giving. It is also a time of sharing in the special foods and customs of the season. South American Yuletide traditions reflect the native heritage as well as the mingling of Spanish, Portuguese, German, and Italian cultures. Each country has its own celebrations—especially in rural areas—that embody the folklore of the country, such as the pageants, tableaus, and dances in Brazil and the processions and *villancicos* or *aguinaldos* (Christmas songs) in the Andean countries. And to complete celebrations, traditional foods are served: tamales, *buñuelos* and *pristiños* (fritters), *pan de Pascua* (Christmas bread), and a wide variety of drinks, such as hot chocolate and fruit punches.

Christmas also evokes childhood memories, locked in our hearts, of family and friends sharing in these special foods and traditions. I fondly remember the hustle and bustle prior to Christmas in my native Ecuador. The men helped set up the manger and the tree, while the women concocted delicious cookies and sweets to be shared not only with family and friends but also with the needy. Several days before Christmas, my mother would start sewing colorful bags out of crepe paper, which would be filled with cookies and candy to be distributed on Christmas Eve.

One Christmas tradition common to all South American countries is midnight Mass, attended by the whole family to celebrate the birth of Jesus Christ. After Mass, the family returns home to partake in the *cena de Navidad* (Christmas dinner). Some families prefer to have the *cena* before going to Mass.

In southern South America, it is quite warm during the Christmas season, because it is summer. But that does not deter the people from celebrating the season with Santa Claus and with traditional foods after midnight Mass. The meats used vary depending on the country—turkey, roast beef, lamb, duck, and chicken are all quite popular. From Spain we also inherited the suckling pig, which is served in the Andean countries, sometimes alone and sometimes with turkey, depending on the number of people. In Bolivia, *picana de Navidad* (meat and chicken stew) is eaten after midnight Mass or for lunch on Christmas Day, depending on each family's customs. This stew is made with big chunks of meat and chicken, plus a variety of vegetables, pieces of corn on the cob, and potatoes, all seasoned with spices, beer, and wine. The cooks also add raisins—tied up in cheesecloth bags to prevent them from getting lost in the pot. Each person is served the contents of a bag in a small bowl.

Pavo Relleno de Navidad

**STUFFED TURKEY FOR THE
CHRISTMAS CELEBRATION** *Serves 12*

The turkey is the star of the Christmas *cena* in most South American countries. Cooks have created many excellent ways to prepare this bird. If it is served roasted without stuffing, it has to be marinated for two to three days in fruit juices, wine or beer, and seasonings, then slowly roasted. It also may be stuffed (with or without the bones) with different combinations of ground meats, fresh and dried fruits, nuts, olives, and capers, in the European tradition.

> One 12- to 14-pound turkey
> ½ cup cognac or brandy
> Salt and freshly ground black pepper

R E L L E N O (Stuffing)

> 2 tablespoons unsalted butter
> 1 medium-size onion, minced (about 1 cup)
> 8 ounces lean ground pork
> 8 ounces ground veal
> 8 ounces imported boiled ham, cut into ¼-inch dice
> One 4-ounce can *pâté de foie gras*
> 2 cups day-old bread crumbs (page 413)
> 1 teaspoon salt
> ½ teaspoon freshly ground black pepper
> ½ teaspoon ground allspice
> ½ teaspoon ground cinnamon
> 1 cup coarsely chopped pitted prunes
> 1 cup chopped dried apricots
> ½ cup sliced blanched almonds
> 4 large eggs, lightly beaten
> ½ cup dry sherry
> ½ cup (1 stick) unsalted butter, melted

S A L S A (Gravy)

> Neck and giblets from turkey
> 4 cups chicken broth, plus more as needed
> ½ cup dry sherry
> 3 tablespoons all-purpose flour
> 3 tablespoons quince or apple jelly
> 1 tablespoon cognac or brandy
> Salt and freshly ground black pepper

1. A day or two before roasting, wash the turkey thoroughly inside and out, then dry with paper towels. Rub inside and out with the cognac and salt and pepper to taste. Cover with plastic wrap and refrigerate.

2. The stuffing can be prepared a day ahead. Melt the butter in a large skillet over medium heat. Add the onion and cook, stirring occasionally, until softened, about 5 minutes. Add the ground pork, ground veal, and ham and cook, stirring occasionally, until the ground meat loses its pink color.

3. Remove from the heat and add the *pâté*, mashing it with a fork to blend with the other meat. Let cool. Add the bread crumbs, pepper, allspice, cinnamon, prunes, apricots, almonds, eggs, and sherry and mix until well blended. Cover with plastic wrap and refrigerate until needed.

4. Preheat the oven to 325°F.

5. Stuff the turkey loosely just before roasting. Don't pack the stuffing in. Truss the bird, if desired, and brush with some of the melted butter. (Any leftover stuffing can be cooked separately in a buttered baking dish. Bake for about 45 minutes with the turkey.) Place in a buttered roasting pan and roast until an instant-read thermometer inserted in the thigh registers 180° to 185°F, about 4 hours. Baste with the melted butter or pan drippings every 30 minutes.

6. While the turkey is roasting, begin to make the gravy. Place the neck and giblets and the chicken broth in a medium-size saucepan and simmer for 1 hour. Strain through a fine-mesh sieve and set aside. This is the turkey stock.

7. When the turkey is done, transfer to a heated serving platter. Remove the trussing strings and skewers (if using) and cover loosely with aluminum foil to keep warm while you finish the gravy.

8. Skim the fat off the juices in the roasting pan and reserve 3 tablespoons of the fat. Add the sherry to the pan juices and warm the pan over medium heat, scraping up the browned bits that cling to the bottom. Strain and set aside.

9. In a 2-quart saucepan, combine the reserved fat and the flour and cook over medium heat for a couple of minutes, stirring constantly. Add the turkey stock and strained pan juices and bring to a boil, stirring constantly with a wire whisk. Reduce the heat to low and simmer for 5 minutes, adding more chicken broth as needed to make a thin sauce. Stir in the jelly and cognac, then season with salt and pepper to taste. Cover and keep warm over low heat.

10. Remove the stuffing from the bird and transfer to a serving bowl. Carve the turkey and serve with the gravy and stuffing on the side.

Conejo en Salsa de Chocolate

RABBIT IN CHOCOLATE SAUCE *Serves 4*

In the course of my research, I found a few recipes that use chocolate to flavor savory sauces, but this is not a common way of preparing South American specialties. I firmly believe that those recipes are offshoots of the Mexican *mole*, a rich, dark sauce made with chocolate. Perhaps a few wealthy ladies traveled to Mexico and were exposed to *mole*. When they returned home, they had their cooks experiment with adding a small piece of chocolate and sometimes some ground nuts to their sauces. I found rabbit with chocolate sauce in Brazil, Argentina, Ecuador, and Peru, as well as chocolate sauce in a version of the Bolivian *ají de pollo* (spicy chicken) and *ají de conejo* (spicy rabbit). Chileans use their version of chocolate sauce with langostinos.

> One 2½-pound rabbit
> 2 tablespoons olive oil
> 1 medium-size onion, finely chopped (about 1 cup)
> 4 cloves garlic, chopped
> 1 teaspoon salt
> ¼ teaspoon freshly ground black pepper
> ½ teaspoon dried rosemary
> ½ teaspoon dried thyme
> ¼ teaspoon red pepper flakes
> 2 large ripe but firm tomatoes (about 1 pound), peeled, seeded, and chopped
> 1 bay leaf
> 1 cup dry red or white wine
> 1 cup water or chicken broth
> 1 ounce unsweetened chocolate, grated
> ¼ cup unsalted dry-roasted peanuts, coarsely ground

1. Rinse the rabbit, dry with paper towels, and cut into 5 pieces—the loin, front legs, and hind legs. Separate each of the legs into 2 pieces.

2. In a large, heavy casserole, heat the oil over medium heat. Add the rabbit pieces and cook on both sides until golden. Add the onion and cook, stirring a few times, until softened, about 5 minutes.

3. In a mortar, mash the garlic with the salt, pepper, rosemary, thyme, and red pepper. Add to the rabbit, stirring to coat. Add the tomatoes, bay leaf, wine, and water and mix well. Reduce the heat to low, cover, and simmer until the meat is very tender, about 1½ hours.

4. Stir in the chocolate and peanuts. If the sauce is too dry, add more water; there should be

enough sauce to coat all the pieces. Discard the bay leaf and season with salt and pepper to taste. Serve immediately.

TO SERVE **Serve with buttered pasta and green beans and carrots.**

Cuy Asado

ROASTED GUINEA PIG *Serves 1 to 2*

Guinea pigs are widely used for food, especially in Ecuador and Peru, where locals prepare a variety of specialties that date back to precolonial times. *Cuy* shows up stuffed, in *picantes*, braised with peanut sauce, and in soups. The Peruvian *cuy chactado* (*cuy* fried very crisp) and the Ecuadorian *cuy asado* are some of the most popular ways of preparing *cuy*. Restaurants specializing in local cuisine serve a whole *cuy* per person; it is baked just like *lechón asado* (roasted young pig), with a crunchy skin. *Cuy* and rabbit are often prepared the same way.

The Andean Indians use *chicha de jora* (a fermented corn drink) to marinate the meat, but because *chicha* is not widely available in the United States, I use beer here. *Cuy* and Peruvian *chicha* can be purchased in some Andean and Latin American markets.

1 frozen *cuy*, thawed and washed
One 12-ounce can or bottle beer
½ small onion, chopped (about ¼ cup)
4 cloves garlic, chopped
1 teaspoon salt
1 teaspoon ground cumin
1 teaspoon freshly ground black pepper
¼ cup canola oil
1 tablespoon *Manteca de Color* (page 331)

1. The *cuy* can be prepared whole or cut into serving-size pieces. I prefer to cut it into pieces.

2. Put the beer, onion, garlic, salt, cumin, and pepper in a blender and process until smooth. Place the *cuy* and beer mixture in a zippered-top plastic bag, seal, and turn to coat the meat. Let marinate in the refrigerator for at least 4 hours or overnight.

3. Preheat the oven to 350°F. Coat a shallow baking pan with oil.

4. Place the *cuy* and marinade in the prepared pan, cover with aluminum foil, and bake for 1 hour. Uncover, brush with the *manteca de color*, and bake until cooked through, about 30 minutes more, brushing with the oil every 15 minutes. The skin should be crisp.

TO SERVE **Serve with rice and fried potato wedges, and perhaps a peanut sauce.**

Carnes

MEATS

BEFORE THE CONQUEST, SOUTH AMERICAN Indians had very few animals that were used for meat. The Incas had two species of domesticated animals—the llama and alpaca. There were also two related wild species available—the vicuña and guanaco. All these animals supplied milk, meat, and wool. Llamas also were used as pack animals. When the Incas killed a llama, the meatier parts were made into *charqui* (dried meat), which was tightly controlled by the state and given to the people only for holidays. Most Indians had to rely on the *cuy* (guinea pig) for meat, and that, too, was only for special occasions. These animals were grown at home and had a great capacity for reproducing quickly. *Cuyes* were prepared in many ways, roasting over an open fire or boiling being the most common. To this day, *cuyes* are very popular with the Andean people and are prepared roasted, grilled, and stewed. In Peru and Ecuador, they are a regular feature in restaurants that specialize in creole cuisine.

Pedro Cieza de León, in his book *La Crónica del Perú*, reported in the sixteenth century that there was an abundance of deer in Peru and Ecuador, as well as rabbits, Muscovy ducks, partridge, doves, pigeons, and other wild game. This was true for most of South America. When Columbus first landed in what is now Venezuela, he thought he had discovered the Garden of Eden, so incredible was the lush vegetation and the abundance of fresh water. The horses, cattle, sheep, goats, pigs, and chickens he brought multiplied so quickly that the Spaniards could count on a good supply of meat throughout the conquest. The introduction of these animals dramatically increased the number of food animals available to the indigenous peoples as well.

Carne de Res y Carne de Ternera
BEEF AND VEAL

WHEN THE CONQUISTADORS ARRIVED IN South America, they found areas that were particularly suited to raising cattle. The *llanos* of Venezuela and Colombia and the *pampas* of southern Chile, Argentina, Uruguay, Paraguay, and southern Brazil offered endless prairies of tall grasses, where large herds of cattle could graze and multiply at a rate almost beyond belief. This abundance of meat not only affected the eating habits of the people but also spawned an entire culture of South American "cowboys"—*llaneros*, *huasos*, and *gauchos*. In Venezuela alone, five million cattle roam the *llanos* under the watchful eyes of the *llaneros*, who will occasionally kill a cow for their own meals, preparing their meat *"llano* style"—roasting it over great open fires, seasoning it with garlic and salt, and serving it with boiled cassava (yuca), *guasacaca* (tomato and avocado) sauce, and cassava bread. And with the barbecue come the singing of ballads and the dancing of the *joropo*. During the revolution of emancipation, this *llano*-style open barbecue was the soldiers' favorite way of preparing meat.

Argentina's cattle industry grew so large that it is now South America's largest exporter of meat and leather goods. Argentine beef is famous throughout the world and Argentines have the reputation of consuming more beef per capita than people in any other South American country. Charles Darwin wrote that when he visited Argentina in 1832, he was startled by the eating habits not only of the *gauchos* but also of the well-to-do people, who ate mostly large amounts of meat and sometimes a piece of squash on the side. It is the *gauchos* of Argentina and Uruguay who started the tradition of the *asado* (barbecue), which in the old days consisted of impaling large cuts of meat on long skewers with a crosspiece to keep the meat flat. The skewers were thrust into the ground at an angle toward a wood fire. Now reserved only for rare and special occasions, this original method of cooking has long been replaced by backyard barbecue grills.

The Porteños (people from the port, meaning those who live in Buenos Aires) indulge in *parrilladas*, huge barbecues widely available in the restaurants of Buenos Aires. The *parrillada mixta* (mixed grill) that normally feeds two Argentines would be more than enough for four outsiders. A very popular side dish is boiled squash, Swiss chard, and carrots, which is doused with olive oil to taste. *Parrilladas* have become an institution in Argentina. If Argentina's favorite dance, the tango, is the first thing that comes to most people's minds when thinking of this country, the *asado a la parrilla*, or *parrillada*, is probably the second, at least among locals. In the past few years, however, the eating habits of the Porteños have changed, and the consumption of meat has decreased due to dietary concerns and the cost of living.

In Uruguay, as in Argentina, meat is the staff of life, and *parrilladas* are found everywhere. Beef and veal are the most popular meats in the cities, and lamb is the most popular in the countryside. On the *estancias* (ranches) and farms, lamb is the daily diet of the farm hands. It is also the diet of outdoor workmen, such as construction workers, road builders, and field workers, who can easily improvise a grill on the ground to roast a leg of lamb for lunch.

On the *llanos* in the Orinoco basin of Colombia, raising livestock—mainly cattle, horses, pigs, sheep, and chickens—is the most important industry. Colombians eat a lot of beef and pork, as do Ecuadorians and Peruvians. Lamb is also very popular in these countries.

The fertile soil along Chile's border with Argentina is ideal for pastures. This "frontier" is home to the *huasos*, this region's version of the *gauchos*. Beef is very popular in Chile, and Chileans love to have *parrilladas* on Sundays. In Santiago, some restaurants specialize in barbecues and serve a mixed grill that consists of different cuts of beef and an assortment of sausages. Just as in Argentina, the portions are so generous that they could serve twice as many people as are dining.

In the past, *charqui* (dried meat) was very important to the *gauchos* and *huasos*, because they could chew it for hours as they herded their cattle. They also carried *charqui* that had been pounded in a mortar and broken into small pieces to make "instant" soups. Today *charqui* is also an essential ingredient in *guisos* (stews).

The Mapuche Indians live along the Chile-Argentine frontier on *reducciones* (reservations). They make a livelihood through pastoral activities and agriculture. In this area, the lamb is known for its high quality, and the inhabitants still prepare *asados* like the original Argentine *gauchos* did. Chileans have a repertoire of recipes using every part of the animal. The *asado al palo* (lamb barbecue) has even inspired poets to write odes to it. In the interior, the Aymara Indians have the *guatia*, which is the Altiplano version of the *curanto* (a clambake-like feast). They roast llama and sheep meat and serve it with cheese. All is accompanied by *pusitunka* (a fermented drink), which flows like water during such events.

Cattle ranching on large *estancias* is prevalent in the Chaco, the plains of Paraguay, where there are several German-speaking colonies of Mennonites, who first came to Paraguay in 1920. Cattle are also raised in the southern departments of Misiones and Ñeembucú. Meat, dairy products, and hides are used for local consumption and for export. Paraguayans eat a lot of meat, especially beef, and *parrilladas* are quite popular, served with *maté* tea. A favorite food for lunch is a stew made with beef, beans, corn, and manioc (yuca). Also popular are *pucheros*, *locros*, and *caldos*—soups made with meat, sausage, rice, and vegetables.

Brazil is one of the world's largest producers of meat. The southern part of Brazil, especially around Rio Grande do Sul, is a tall-grass prairie, where large herds of cattle and sheep graze the *pampas*. This is Brazil's main cattle-raising area. Southeastern Brazil has the country's finest cattle ranches and the most fertile farms. It is also the most industrialized area, known as the economic heartland. Rio Grande do Sul is the center of the meatpacking industry. This is also the land of the Brazilian *gauchos*, who are of Spanish and Indian ancestry. They are renowned for opulent barbecues described as "everything-on-the-spit barbecues," as well as for *maté* tea, which is drunk from a *chimarrão* (gourd). Brazil's *gaucho* eats his meat with manioc meal and also enjoys *charqui*, which is used to make rice casseroles, barbecued *charqui*, and bean dishes.

In Brazil, the European influence on the preparation of meat can be seen in the clay pot stews and savory calf's foot jellies. Restaurants offer *gaucho*-style barbecues, which have become quite popular in Rio and São Paulo. The *churrascarias* in Rio offer barbecues *rodisio* style: a parade of waiters, carrying a variety of meats impaled on sword-like skewers, slice the meats to order at your table. A fabulous salad bar offers not only a variety of salads but also side dishes such as the Brazilian staples of rice, beans, manioc, and enormous hearts of palm. *Rodisio*-style restaurants have gone international and can now be found in some big cities outside South America.

Northeastern Brazil has large areas of fertile, rolling hills where raising cattle and goats has become a very important industry. This is the land of *carne seca* (beef jerky) and meat specialties that show Portuguese and African influence, such as *paçoca de carne* (beef with manioc meal). Jerky is eaten more often than fresh meat here, and throughout Brazil it is the staple food of the masses, along with beans, rice, and manioc. *Carne seca*, one of the ingredients in *feijoada*, is dried in chunks, different from *charqui*, which is cut into thin strips and dried.

The new meat dishes that have evolved in the local cuisines of South America are variations of Spanish or Portuguese specialties. Many of the beef specialties have an Arab influence, a vestige of the Moorish occupation of Spain and Portugal. Dishes cooked with almonds, raisins, cinnamon, and cloves, as well as with either fresh or dried fruit, trace their origins to that period. A good example is *carbonada*, a classic meat stew of Argentina and Uruguay that is prepared with pears and peaches.

Estofado

BRAISED BEEF *Serves 6*

Estofados (braised meats) are very important in the South American diet. This dish can be made with a whole piece of beef or with two-inch cubes, as for beef stew. It is a delicious and practical choice for entertaining, because it can be made ahead of time and reheated just before serving. Braising meat is an old European tradition, found in just about every country in Europe. Braising in wine was practiced by the Spaniards, Portuguese, and French, and when they came to South America, they incorporated tomatoes, bell peppers, and potatoes into the mix. For cuts of meat such as eye of the round or bottom round of beef, it is necessary to lard them with larding pork or bacon.

¼ cup dried porcini mushrooms, soaked in 1 cup hot water for 30 minutes

One 3-pound beef sirloin roast, whole or cut into 2-inch cubes

1 teaspoon salt

½ teaspoon sugar

½ teaspoon freshly ground black pepper

3 tablespoons olive oil

1 medium-size onion, finely chopped (about 1 cup)

1 small green bell pepper, seeded and finely chopped

1 medium-size carrot, shredded

4 cloves garlic, minced

2 large ripe but firm tomatoes (about 1 pound), peeled, seeded, and chopped

2 tablespoons tomato paste

¾ cup dry white or red wine

Bouquet garni (3 sprigs fresh parsley, 1 bay leaf, and 2 sprigs fresh thyme or ½ teaspoon dried, tied up in cheesecloth)

1 to 2 cups beef broth, as needed

1½ teaspoons unsalted butter, softened, then kneaded together with 1½ teaspoons all-purpose flour to make a *beurre manié* (page 414; optional)

4 medium-size all-purpose potatoes, peeled, cooked in water to cover until tender, drained, quartered, buttered, and kept warm

Minced fresh parsley leaves for garnish

1. Drain the mushrooms, reserving the liquid. Rinse thoroughly under cold running water to remove any sand. Chop and set aside.

2. Trim any excess fat from the roast, then rub with the salt, sugar, and black pepper. In a heavy casserole or Dutch oven, heat the oil over medium heat and brown the roast on all sides. Transfer to a platter. Add the onion to the casserole and cook over medium heat, stirring occasionally, until transparent and softened, about 8 minutes. Add the bell pepper, carrot, garlic, tomatoes, and tomato paste. Cover, reduce the heat to medium-low, and cook until the tomatoes have formed a sauce, about 15 minutes. Return the roast to the casserole, add the wine, and cook, uncovered, for 15 minutes. Turn the roast over and add the chopped mushrooms, ¼ cup of the soaking liquid, the bouquet garni, and 1 cup of the beef broth. Cover and simmer until a fork goes through the meat easily, about 2 hours. Turn the roast after 1 hour. If the sauce reduces too much, add more broth. When the meat is done, the sauce should be thick enough to coat the back of a spoon. If it is too thin, either boil it down or thicken with the *beurre manié*; it should be the consistency of whipping cream. The amount of sauce will depend on the type of casserole used.

3. Discard the bouquet garni. Season with salt and black pepper to taste. Remove the roast, cut into ¼-inch-thick slices, and place on a platter. Arrange the potatoes around the meat. Sprinkle the potatoes with the parsley and serve.

Carbonada Uruguaya
URUGUAYAN BEEF STEW WITH
VEGETABLES AND FRUIT   Serves 6

"*Carbonadas* are for Uruguayans what paellas are for Spaniards," says cookbook author Maria Rosa García de Hérmala. This Uruguayan specialty was probably created by the Basques, who had a penchant for using fruit in savory dishes, a tradition left in Spain by the Arab occupation. It is usually cooked in a *cazuela de barro* (earthenware crock) and served in the shell of a calabaza (winter squash). Uruguayans use a mature veal that looks more like beef. This specialty is also popular in Argentina, with slight variations.

2 tablespoons canola oil

2 medium-size onions, chopped (about 2 cups)

1 medium-size green bell pepper, seeded and chopped

4 cloves garlic, minced

2 pounds boneless beef sirloin or veal cut from the leg, trimmed of fat and cut into 1½-inch cubes

1 bay leaf

1 teaspoon dried oregano, crumbled

½ teaspoon dried thyme

½ teaspoon freshly ground black pepper

1 teaspoon salt

One 16-ounce can pear-shaped tomatoes, with juices

2 cups beef broth, or more if needed

2 ears corn, cut into 1-inch-thick rounds

8 ounces winter squash, peeled, seeded, and cut into 1-inch cubes

8 ounces boiling potatoes, peeled and cut into 1-inch cubes

1 large sweet potato (about 8 ounces), peeled and cut into 1-inch cubes

2 large ripe but firm Anjou or Bartlett pears, peeled, cored, and cut into 1-inch cubes

2 large ripe but firm peaches, peeled, pitted, and cut into 1-inch cubes

¼ cup freshly grated Parmesan cheese

1. In a heavy 6-quart casserole or Dutch oven, heat the oil over medium heat. Add the onions, green pepper, and garlic and cook, stirring a few times, until the onions are transparent, about 5 minutes. Add the meat, bay leaf, oregano, thyme, black pepper, and salt and cook, stirring a few

times, for about 5 minutes. Put the tomatoes and their juices in a blender and process until coarsely chopped. Add to the casserole along with the beef broth. Bring to a boil, reduce the heat to low, cover, and simmer until the meat is tender, about 1 hour.

2. Remove the bay leaf. Add the corn, squash, potatoes, and sweet potato and simmer until the potatoes are tender, about 20 minutes. Add the pears and peaches. If the juices in the pan have dried up, add more beef broth; there should be plenty of sauce to cover the meat and vegetables. Heat the fruit through and taste for salt and black pepper. Serve hot, sprinkled with the Parmesan.

TO SERVE **Uruguayans serve *carbonadas* with rice.**

Matambre

ROLLED FLANK STEAK *Serves 8 to 10*

Matambre is one of the best-known Argentine specialties, but it is also popular in Uruguay and Chile. I can't think of a more colorful way to serve meat. This version deviates a little from the classic in that I don't use sliced hard-cooked eggs in the filling. Instead, I prefer fresh asparagus. The cut of meat for *matambre* in Argentina is from mature veal and similar to flank steak. You can find *matambre* in Argentine markets. Otherwise, substitute two flank steaks and have the butcher butterfly them for you. Although *matambre* can be served warm, the most popular way to present it is cold, thinly sliced, as an appetizer, with *Ensalada Rusa* (page 169) and *Chimichurri* (page 337) on the side. I especially like *matambre* for large parties, arranged on a big platter with a mound of the salad in the center.

> **One 3- to 4-pound Argentine matambre, or two 1½- to 2-pound flank steaks, butterflied**
>
> **¼ cup red wine vinegar**

2 tablespoons canola oil

1 teaspoon dried oregano

3 cloves garlic, minced

1 teaspoon salt

¼ teaspoon freshly ground black pepper

¼ cup finely chopped fresh parsley leaves

½ teaspoon red pepper flakes

½ cup freshly grated Parmesan cheese

Spinach or Swiss chard leaves, washed well and stems removed

1 large carrot, cut into matchsticks

4 to 6 asparagus spears, bottoms trimmed

1 roasted red pepper (page 411), cut into ¼-inch-wide strips

2 large eggs, lightly beaten

4 cups beef broth

4 cups water, or as needed

1. Remove any excess fat from the steak (the Argentine cut has more fat than the flank) but leave some of the fat. Rub with the vinegar and oil. Sprinkle with the oregano, garlic, salt, and black pepper. Place in a nonreactive dish, cover with plastic wrap, and refrigerate for at least 4 hours or overnight.

2. To assemble the *matambre*, place the steak fat side down on a cutting board. (If using flank steaks, lay the steaks cut side up, overlapping the two ends by about 2 inches. Pound the overlapping ends a little with a meat mallet to join them together more firmly.) Sprinkle with the parsley, red pepper, and ¼ cup of the Parmesan, then cover with the spinach leaves. Arrange the carrots, asparagus, and roasted pepper across the grain in rows about 2 inches apart. Pour the beaten eggs on top, then sprinkle with the remaining ¼ cup Parmesan.

3. Carefully roll up the meat, going with the grain. Tie with kitchen twine at about 1-inch intervals. Wrap in cheesecloth or a kitchen towel,

tying the ends with twine. (This step is not required. Many cooks cook the roll without wrapping it.)

4. To cook the roll, you will need an oval casserole. Alternatively, a fish poacher (which is what I use) also works well. Place the *matambre* in the casserole and add the beef broth. Add enough water to reach two-thirds of the way up the side of the roll. Bring to a boil over medium heat and skim off the froth as it rises to the top. Reduce the heat to low, cover, and simmer for 2 hours, turning the meat after 1 hour.

5. If serving hot, transfer to a board and let rest for 10 minutes. Remove the cheesecloth and twine, if necessary, and cut into ½-inch-thick slices with a sharp knife. Arrange the slices on a heated serving platter and pour a few spoonfuls of stock over them.

If serving cold, allow the meat to cool in the stock for 30 minutes. Transfer to a shallow baking pan and press the meat by placing a board with cans on top. Refrigerate for a few hours or overnight. Slice and serve.

El Pabellón Criollo

VENEZUELAN SHREDDED BEEF WITH RICE AND BEANS *Serves 6*

Few specialties capture the essence of Venezuelan cuisine as well as this dish. Even the name has a patriotic and ethnic connotation. *Pabellón* means "flag," and *pabellón criollo* is a creole dish in which shredded beef (*carne mechada*, a version of the Spanish *ropa vieja*, literally "old clothes"), rice, and black beans are arranged in a way to resemble the tricolor flag of Venezuela. These three colors of the flag represent the three primary peoples of this country: native Indians, Europeans, and Africans. Sometimes this dish is served surrounded with slices of fried *maduro* (ripe plantain), in which case it is called *pabellón con barandas*. It is a hearty dish, loved by all Venezuelans, rich and poor. *Pabellón*, along with the *hallaca* (tamale), *sancocho* (soup), and *arepa* (cornbread), epitomizes the colors, textures, and flavors of Venezuelan cuisine.

> One 1½-pound flank steak, trimmed of fat and cut into 4 pieces
>
> 1 medium-size onion, halved and sliced into half-moons (about 1 cup)
>
> Beef broth as needed
>
> 6 tablespoons canola oil
>
> 1 teaspoon ground annatto or sweet paprika
>
> 2 medium-size onions, finely chopped (about 2 cups)
>
> 3 cloves garlic, minced
>
> 1 small red bell pepper, seeded and chopped
>
> 2 large ripe but firm tomatoes (about 1 pound), peeled, seeded, and chopped
>
> 1 teaspoon salt
>
> ½ teaspoon freshly ground black pepper
>
> 1 ripe (yellow) plantain
>
> 1 recipe *Arroz Blanco Venezolano* (page 323)
>
> 1 recipe *Caraotas Negras* (page 308)

1. Place the meat and sliced onion in a 4-quart saucepan and add beef broth to cover. Bring to a boil over medium heat, reduce the heat to low, cover, and simmer until the meat is tender enough to pull apart with a fork, about 1½ hours. Let cool in the stock. Remove from the stock and shred (¼ inch thick) with your fingers. Strain the stock and set aside.

2. In a 12-inch skillet, heat 4 tablespoons of the oil over medium-high heat, add the shredded meat, and brown, stirring occasionally. Reduce the heat to medium and stir in the annatto, chopped onions, garlic, bell pepper, tomatoes, salt, and black pepper. Cook, uncovered and stirring occasionally, until the tomatoes have formed a sauce, about 20 minutes. If the mixture gets too dry, add some of the reserved stock a little at a time; the meat should be juicy. Taste for salt and black pepper.

3. Just before serving, peel the plantain, cut into 3 chunks, and halve each chunk lengthwise. Heat the remaining 2 tablespoons oil in a medium-size skillet over low heat. Add the plantain and cook on both sides until golden, about 3 minutes per side.

4. To assemble the *pabellón*, arrange the beef in the center of a heated platter and place a mound of rice on one side and a mound of beans on the other side. Arrange the plantain slices all around. Serve at once.

Rabada com Lingüiça

BRAISED OXTAILS WITH SAUSAGE *Serves 4 to 6*

Although braised oxtails are prepared in different ways in different parts of Brazil, they are popular throughout the country. In the northeast, they are prepared very much like the Portuguese *rabada* (stew), using a simple *sofrito* of onion and garlic, along with linguiça (sausage). African slaves quickly adopted this dish, adding their own spices, and made it a specialty to be used as an offering to the goddess *Xangô* in the *Candomblé* religion. In southern Brazil, where the Spanish influence is more prevalent, a *sofrito* is made with tomatoes, onions, garlic, and wine. In Rio and São Paulo, watercress is added just before serving. I'm including two versions here (see the next recipe) not only because they are equally delicious but also because they clearly show how the foreign dishes evolved in different environments.

> **4 pounds oxtails, cut into 2-inch pieces**
> **Juice of 1 lemon**
> 2 tablespoons *Manteca de Color* (page 331), or 2 tablespoons canola oil mixed with 1 teaspoon sweet paprika
> 2 medium-size onions, finely chopped (about 2 cups)
> ¼ cup finely chopped scallions or leeks (white part and 1 inch of the green)
> 2 tablespoons chopped fresh cilantro leaves
> 2 tablespoons chopped fresh parsley leaves
> 4 cloves garlic, mashed into a paste with 1 teaspoon salt and ½ teaspoon freshly ground black pepper
> 1 teaspoon ground cumin
> 2 bay leaves
> 2 cups hot water
> ¼ cup red wine vinegar
> 1 pound linguiça, chorizo, or Polish sausage, cut into 1-inch pieces

1. Wash the oxtails, dry, and rub with the lemon juice. Let stand for 30 minutes at room temperature while you prepare the *sofrito*.

2. In a large casserole, heat the *manteca de color* over medium heat. (If using oil and paprika, heat the oil, then stir in the paprika.) Add the onions, scallions, cilantro, parsley, garlic paste, cumin, and bay leaves and cook, stirring a few times, until the onions are softened, about 5 minutes. Add the oxtails, water, and vinegar. Cover and simmer over low heat for about 3 hours, turning the meat after 1 hour. The secret of delicious oxtails is the slow cooking. Add the sausage and cook for 30 minutes. The meat should be very, very tender. If the liquid dries up, add more water as needed. There should always be enough liquid to provide a sauce that will coat the meat; however, this is not a soupy stew. *Rabada* can be prepared the day before; bring to room temperature before reheating. Serve hot.

TO SERVE **Serve with white rice.**

Rabada com Agrião

OXTAIL STEW WITH WATERCRESS *Serves 4*

Here is Margarida Nogueira's version of Brazilian oxtails that is popular in Rio and São Paulo.

- **4 pounds oxtails, cut into 2-inch pieces**
- **1 tablespoon white wine vinegar**
- **2 large cloves garlic, mashed into a paste with 1 teaspoon salt and ½ teaspoon freshly ground black pepper**
- **2 tablespoons fresh lime juice**
- **1 cup dry red wine**
- **¼ cup olive oil**
- **1 large onion, chopped (about 1½ cups)**
- **1 large ripe but firm tomato (about 8 ounces), peeled and chopped, or 1 cup canned peeled tomatoes, with juices, chopped**
- **1 bay leaf**
- **2 tablespoons chopped fresh parsley leaves**
- **2 cups beef broth, or more if needed**
- **1 bunch watercress**

1. Wash the oxtails, remove any excess fat, and put in a large casserole with water to cover. Add the vinegar, bring to a rapid boil, and continue to boil for 10 minutes.

2. Meanwhile, in a glass baking dish, combine the garlic paste, lime juice, and wine. Remove the oxtails from the water, add to the marinade, and coat well with the mixture. Cover with plastic wrap and let marinate in the refrigerator for at least 4 hours or overnight, occasionally turning the pieces.

3. Remove the oxtails from the marinade, reserving the marinade, and dry with paper towels. Heat the oil in a clean casserole over medium heat. Add the oxtails and brown on all sides, working in batches, if necessary, and transferring the pieces to a plate as they are browned. When all the pieces are browned, add the onion to the casserole and cook, stirring occasionally, until golden brown, about 5 minutes. Add the tomato, bay leaf, and parsley, and cook for about 10 minutes. Return the oxtails to the casserole, cook for 5 minutes, turn over, and cook for 5 minutes more, so that both sides absorb the flavors. Add the beef broth and reserved marinade, reduce the heat to low, cover, and cook until the meat is very soft, about 3 hours, turning the meat after 2 hours. If the sauce reduces too much, add more beef broth or water. Once the meat is done, discard the bay leaf and season with salt and pepper to taste. This dish can be prepared up to this point the day before; bring to room temperature before reheating.

4. Wash the watercress thoroughly, remove the tough stems, and dry. Just before serving, add to the *rabada*, waiting for just a few seconds until the watercress wilts. Serve immediately.

TO SERVE **Serve with boiled potatoes or creamy polenta.**

Pastel de Choclo Chileno

CHILEAN CORN TORTE *Serves 6*

This is a national dish of Chile, the glory of its gastronomy. The corn topping is basically the dough for *humitas*, an Indian specialty, and the filling, called *pino*, is very Spanish—the perfect union of two cuisines. Because the corn has to be mature, called *choclero* in Chile, it is a little difficult to reproduce the topping in the United States. Look for large corn kernels, avoiding what is called young corn, and cook the puree until it is very thick. Some cooks in the United States add a little cornstarch or cornmeal to thicken the puree. The traditional way to serve this *pastel* is in a large clay casserole or in individual casseroles. Another popular way to prepare this specialty, not only in Chile but also in the rest of South America, is with a potato topping similar to mashed potatoes with eggs and cheese mixed in. In Paraguay, it is usually made with yuca. Chileans also make this *pastel* with a combination of meat and chicken.

RELLENO (Filling)

    1 whole bone-in chicken breast (about
        1 pound; optional), skin on, poached
        (page 407)
    2 hard-cooked eggs, peeled
    Filling for *Empanadas al Horno* (page 103)

CORN TOPPING

    2 pounds frozen corn kernels, thawed
    Milk as needed
    2 tablespoons unsalted butter
    ½ teaspoon salt

    ¼ cup sugar, or more to taste

1. To make the filling, if using the poached chicken breast, let cool, then remove the skin and bones and cut into bite-size piece. Slice the eggs into rounds. Cover both and set aside. Have the filling for the empanadas handy.

2. To make the corn topping, place the corn in a food processor or blender and process, adding a little milk at a time, until finely ground.

3. In a large, heavy skillet, melt the butter over medium heat. Add the corn puree and salt and cook, stirring constantly, until it forms a thick puree, about 10 minutes. Taste for salt.

4. Preheat the oven to 375°F. Butter a shallow, 8-cup ovenproof casserole.

5. Distribute the empanada filling evenly over the bottom of the casserole. Top with the chicken, if using, and then with the sliced eggs. Spread the corn topping on top and bake for 30 minutes. Sprinkle with the sugar (some Chileans add more) and broil briefly, until the sugar caramelizes to a dark brown.

6. Remove from the oven and let cool for a few minutes. Divide into 6 portions and dish out with a metal spatula and a large spoon.

VARIATION Some cooks omit the granulated sugar and just dust the *pastel* with confectioners' sugar before baking.

Pastelón de Mandioca (Pastelón Mandi'ó)

YUCA PIE WITH BEEF FILLING *Serves 8*

Paraguay is the only country in South America where there are two official languages, Guarani (an indigenous language) and Spanish. Guarani is spoken by 90 percent of the people, and 50 percent are bilingual. The Guarani name for yuca is *mandi'ó*. Paraguayans sometimes name their specialties using both Spanish and Guarani terms, such as *pastelón mandi'ó*. Yuca is one of the staple foods of Paraguayans, who use this root in many ways. It is a wonderful alternative to potatoes. This hearty pie reminds me of the potato-topped English shepherd's pie. The meat filling is the typical *pino* (seasoned ground meat), similar to the one used in the previous recipe.

RELLENO (Filling)

    2 tablespoons canola oil
    1 pound lean ground beef
    2 medium-size onions, finely chopped (about
        2 cups)
    2 medium-size ripe but firm tomatoes (10 to
        12 ounces), peeled and chopped
    1 small green bell pepper, seeded and
        chopped
    4 cloves garlic, minced
    1 teaspoon ground cumin
    1 teaspoon salt
    ¼ teaspoon freshly ground black pepper
    ¼ teaspoon red pepper flakes

MASA (Dough)

3 pounds fresh or frozen yuca

⅓ cup milk

8 ounces Chihuahua, mozzarella, or
Muenster cheese, shredded

2 tablespoons unsalted butter or canola oil

1 teaspoon salt

3 large eggs, lightly beaten

1. To make the filling, heat the oil in a large skillet over medium heat. Add the ground beef and cook, stirring occasionally and breaking up any clumps, until all the pink is gone. Add the remaining filling ingredients, mix well, cover, reduce the heat to low, and cook until the vegetables are soft, about 20 minutes. The mixture should be juicy; if it's too dry, add a little water. Remove from the heat and let cool.

2. To make the dough, peel the yuca, if using fresh. If using frozen, do not thaw. Whether fresh or frozen, cook in boiling salted water until tender, about 20 minutes. Do not let it get too soft, or it will absorb too much water. Drain well, mash, and let cool for 5 minutes. Add the milk, cheese, butter, salt, and eggs and knead well for a few minutes.

3. Preheat the oven to 350°F. Butter and flour a 7 x 12-inch ovenproof dish.

4. Spread half of the dough evenly over the bottom of the dish. Spread the filling on top and cover with the rest of the dough, spreading it with a rubber spatula until smooth. Bake until golden, about 1 hour.

5. Remove from the oven, let rest for a few minutes, and cut into squares. Serve hot.

TO SERVE **Serve with cooked peas and carrots.**

Paçoca de Carne com Banana-da-Terra

**BEEF WITH MANIOC MEAL
AND RIPE PLANTAINS** *Serves 4*

Paçoca is a Brazilian specialty that shows the blending of Portuguese, African, and Indian influences at its best. It is usually made with *carne seca* (beef jerky) and either manioc meal or cornmeal. The dried meat has to be pounded in a mortar until practically ground. Thanks to the advent of the food processor, this can be done by machine, but in the remote villages of Brazil, it is still done by hand. Plantains are used often throughout Brazil. They are a staple among the working classes and are particularly popular in the northeast.

In the month of June, which is the month of São João (Saint John), the Indians of Brazil celebrate the Harvest of the Corn, very much like the Peruvians and Bolivians celebrate the Inti Raymi, or Festival of the Sun.

At the end of the seventeenth century and into the eighteenth, an increasing number of settlers ventured into the interior of southeastern Brazil. The most famous group was the *bandeirantes*. These nomads from São Paulo were the descendants of Portuguese settlers and Indian women. Their main purposes in going to the interior were to capture Indians to be sold as slaves and, later on, to search for gold, silver, diamonds, and other hidden wealth. Because the *carne seca* and manioc meal kept for several days without spoiling, the *bandeirantes* carried *paçoca* on their forays. It is for this reason that this specialty is also called *comida de guerra* (food of war).

In Rio Grande do Sul, the Spanish settlers had an interesting variation of *paçoca*, using rice instead of manioc meal or cornmeal. The *carreteiros* (drivers of mule wagons) carried *carne seca* that had been previously crushed in a mortar to eat on the trails, and when the wagon train stopped, the people would congregate to make *arroz de carreteiro* (mule driver's rice), which is rice cooked with seasoned jerky. (Rice was plentiful in this area.) To this day, *arroz de carreteiro* is considered a great dish to serve to a group of friends.

Paçoca de carne can also be made with fresh meat, and this is the version I give here. This savory dish has an interesting texture—sort of chewy and crunchy—and a delightfully full flavor. It is surprisingly addictive.

1 pound lean beef chuck

1½ teaspoons salt

5 tablespoons canola oil

1 medium-size onion, chopped (about 1 cup)

1 tablespoon red wine vinegar

1 teaspoon hot pepper sauce

2 tablespoons butter

2 cups manioc meal or coarse-ground cornmeal

2 ripe (yellow) plantains

1. Put the meat and 1 teaspoon of the salt in a medium-size saucepan and add water to cover. Bring to a boil, reduce the heat to low, and simmer until fork tender, about 1 hour. Remove from the water, cut into 4 pieces, and shred.

2. Heat 3 tablespoons of the oil in a medium-size skillet over low heat. Add the onion and cook, stirring a few times, until softened, about 5 minutes. Add the shredded meat, remaining ½ teaspoon salt, the vinegar, and hot sauce. Cook, stirring occasionally, for 10 minutes. Transfer to a food processor and process until coarsely ground.

3. In a large skillet, melt the butter over medium heat. Add the manioc meal and cook, stirring constantly, until it begins to turn golden, about 5 minutes. Remove from the heat and stir in the reheated meat.

4. Peel the plantains and cut diagonally into ¼-inch-thick slices. In another large skillet, heat the remaining 2 tablespoons oil over medium heat and cook the plantains, a few slices at a time, on both sides until golden brown. Transfer to a plate lined with paper towels.

5. Place the shredded meat on a serving platter, decorate with the plantain slices, and serve right away.

Chatasca (Charqui con Arroz)

DRIED BEEF WITH RICE *Serves 4*

I was so happy to find this recipe in a very old Argentine book, *El Libro de Doña Petrona*, which was virtually a cooking bible for my mother, as well as for other housewives throughout Spanish South America. The dog-eared appearance of my mother's book attests to how much it was used. Women who had this cookbook considered themselves privileged because, years ago, it was terribly expensive and difficult to find. It features not only Argentine cooking but also European cuisine, especially French and Italian. Unfortunately, it doesn't include any information about the history of the recipes. This one reminded me of the Brazilian *arroz de carreteiro* (mule driver's rice), and I believe its roots had to be similar. When rice became available in the New World, onions and garlic were already growing there, so it was easy to take these foods, along with *charqui* (dried meat) on long trips. And that is what the mule drivers of the Argentine plains did. They took *charqui* to chew on the road, and when mealtime came, they would toast the *charqui* on a grill, pound it into small pieces, and add it to a pot of boiling water to make a soup or stew. (Actually, it is likely that the *charqui* that was taken on long journeys was already pounded into small pieces.) This recipe has survived over the years, although other ingredients, such as tomatoes and herbs, have been added. Years ago, this specialty was usually cooked with cow's fat, but it is rarely used today.

Bolivians also make a specialty with *charqui* called *charquicán*, which is just like the Argentine *chatasca*. Bolivians fry the *charqui* first to get it crisp. The Mapuche Indians of Chile had a specialty also called *charquicán*, made with *charqui de guanaco* (dried guanaco meat), which supposedly has a strong, very unappealing taste. After the Spaniards brought cattle to South America, *charquicán* began to be made with fresh beef instead.

This is a modernized version of *chatasca*. As far as I know, South American *charqui* is not available in the United States, but the Mexican *cecina or cecina seca* is a good substitute and can be found in some large Mexican supermarkets. The meat is very thin and comes in large, uneven sheets that are difficult to chop unless they are soaked first. During one of my shopping trips to buy *cecina*, a Mexican lady who was also buying the dried meat told me she quickly fries the *cecina* in oil, then breaks it into small pieces to put into the pot. Because the dried meat is salted, there is no need to add salt to the dish.

> 2 sheets *cecina* (Mexican dried meat) or *charqui* (about 3 ounces)
>
> ¼ cup canola oil
>
> 1 large onion, finely chopped (about 1½ cups)
>
> 2 medium-size ripe but firm tomatoes (10 to 12 ounces; optional), peeled and chopped
>
> 1½ cups long-grain rice
>
> 3 cups water or beef broth
>
> Freshly ground black pepper

1. Wash the *cecina* thoroughly and dry with paper towels. Heat 2 tablespoons of the oil in a large skillet over medium heat. Fry the *cecina* for a few seconds on each side, until lightly colored. Dip the meat in a bowl of cold water for a few seconds to crisp it. Pound the meat to break it into small pieces, or break into 1-inch pieces and coarsely chop in a food processor.

2. Heat the remaining 2 tablespoons oil in a casserole over medium heat. Add the onion and cook, stirring, until softened, about 5 minutes. Add the tomatoes, if using, and cook for 5 minutes. Add the rice, meat pieces, water, and pepper to taste. Cover and cook over low heat until the rice is tender and still has a little liquid left. Fluff and serve immediately.

Saice

SEASONED GROUND BEEF WITH POTATOES AND ONION SAUCE *Serves 4*

This specialty comes from Bolivia and is nothing more than the popular *picadillo* (seasoned chopped beef) served on top of boiled potatoes. It reveals the Bolivian penchant for onion sauces.

> 2 tablespoons canola oil
>
> 1 medium-size onion, finely chopped (about 1 cup)
>
> 2 cloves garlic, minced
>
> 1 pound lean ground beef
>
> 2 large ripe but firm tomatoes (about 1 pound), peeled and coarsely chopped
>
> 1 teaspoon salt
>
> ½ teaspoon freshly ground black pepper
>
> ½ teaspoon ground cumin
>
> 1 teaspoon dried oregano
>
> 1 to 2 tablespoons dried hot red pepper puree, store-bought or homemade (page 332), to your taste, or ½ teaspoon red pepper flakes
>
> Pinch of sugar
>
> 1 cup beef broth
>
> 1 cup frozen peas

2 small onions, thinly sliced into rings (about 1 cup), rinsed with hot water, and drained

2 to 4 jalapeños, to your taste, seeded and minced

2 tablespoons canola oil

1 tablespoon white wine vinegar

¼ teaspoon salt

¼ teaspoon freshly ground black pepper

1 pound boiling potatoes, peeled, cooked in water to cover until tender, drained, and kept warm

Minced fresh parsley leaves for garnish

1. Heat the oil in a large, heavy skillet over medium heat. Add the onion and cook, stirring occasionally, until golden, about 4 minutes. Add the garlic and ground beef and cook, breaking up the meat with a wooden spoon, until the beef looses its pink color. Add the tomatoes and cook until they form a sauce, about 10 minutes. Stir in the salt, black pepper, cumin, oregano, hot pepper puree, and sugar. Add the beef broth and peas and cook until the peas are tender, about 5 minutes. The mixture should be saucy. Taste for salt.

2. Meanwhile, make the onion sauce. Mix the onions and jalapeños together in a small mixing bowl. In another small bowl, beat the oil, vinegar, salt, and black pepper together with a fork. Pour over the onion mixture and toss. Set aside.

3. Slice the potatoes into ¼-inch-thick rounds and arrange on a serving platter. Top with the meat mixture and then the onion sauce. Serve immediately, sprinkled with the parsley.

TO SERVE **Serve with rice or** *Chuño Phuti de Huevo* **(page 303).**

Inti Raymi FESTIVAL OF THE SUN

The Inca solstice celebration, Inti Raymi, occurred each year on June 24, which is the shortest day of the year in the Southern Hemisphere. On June 23, fires were left burning all night to welcome the return of the sun. The celebration featured grandiose pageants and llamas being sacrificed to the sun.

When the Spanish and Portuguese laid claim to large parts of the Americas, they often did so in partnership with the Roman Catholic Church. As the church worked to spread Catholicism, it adapted many of the "pagan" celebrations to its religious holidays. In this way, Inti-Raymi, which coincides with the feast of Saint John the Baptist, was converted into a Christian holiday.

Because June also marks the end of the harvest, it is a time for giving thanks. The foods associated with Inti Raymi, such as corn, now also are part of the St. John's Day celebrations. In Brazil, the Indians dedicate the whole month of June to the celebration of the corn harvest and prepare a variety of dishes based on corn. These specialties range from the humble *paçoca de carne*, made with cornmeal and dried meat, to fancy corncakes and drinks. In Paraguay, St. John's Day begins with a special Mass, which is followed by many festivities.

Lampreado

YUCA AND BEEF PATTIES

Make 8 patties; 4 to 8 servings

In Paraguay, yuca is a mainstay that appears on the table, in one form or another, almost every day. *Lampreado* is one of the many tasty, wholesome recipes that use this versatile root vegetable. It is of Spanish origin, although in a way it also resembles the *kibbeh*, or *kibbi*, of the Arabs, which is made with ground meat and bulgur (thanks, no doubt, to centuries of Moorish occupation of Spain). In this dish, a crunchy exterior gives way to a soft, savory interior. It is both fun and comfortingly familiar. *Lampreado* may also be made with finely chopped boiled beef or *carne seca* (beef jerky), if you wish to try different variations.

> 1 pound fresh or frozen yuca
>
> 2 tablespoons canola oil, plus more for frying
>
> 1 medium-size onion, minced (about 1 cup)
>
> 1 clove garlic, minced
>
> 8 ounces lean ground beef
>
> ½ teaspoon salt
>
> ¼ teaspoon freshly ground black pepper
>
> Fresh or dry bread crumbs

1. If using fresh yuca, peel it. If using frozen yuca, do not thaw it. Cook the yuca in boiling salted water until tender. Do not let it get too soft, or it will become watery. Drain and mash.

2. While the yuca is cooking, heat the oil in a large skillet over medium heat. Add the onion and garlic and cook, stirring a few times, until the onion is softened, about 5 minutes. Stir in the ground beef, salt, and pepper and cook, breaking up the meat with a wooden spoon or fork, until the beef loses its pink color.

3. Mix the beef with the yuca until well blended and shape into 8 patties, just like hamburgers. Dredge in the bread crumbs until evenly and

completely covered. This recipe can be prepared to this point up to a day ahead. Just cover loosely with waxed paper and refrigerate until needed.

4. To serve, heat a large skillet over medium heat. Add enough oil to coat the bottom of the skillet and, when it is sizzling hot, add the patties 4 at a time. Fry on both sides until golden brown, about 4 minutes per side. Serve hot.

TO SERVE **Serve with a tossed salad.**

Milanesas

BREADED CUTLETS *Serves 4*

Milanesas occupy a very important place in the cuisine of South America, especially in the southern countries, such as Argentina and Uruguay. This hearty dish consists of thin cutlets pounded to an even thickness, well seasoned, and dipped in egg and bread crumbs, then fried until golden brown. Garlic and parsley are two of the essential seasonings. Just about any kind of meat can be used, veal or young beef being the most popular. Pork, chicken breast, fish, sweetbreads, brains, sweet potatoes, eggplant, and zucchini also are alternatives. *Milanesas* are so popular in Uruguay that they had to be made portable; they are incorporated into very large sandwiches and sold everywhere, especially in train stations.

The art of making *milanesas* was brought to South America by Italian immigrants, and Argentines and Uruguayans have embraced it wholeheartedly. The Germans also brought their *Wienerschnitzel*, which is the same as *milanesas*. Breading meats, chicken, fish, and vegetables is popular throughout South American. Paraguayans make all kinds of *milanesas*, especially with beef, fish, and even tripe.

> **4 thinly sliced veal cutlets (about 4 ounces each)**

1 teaspoon salt

¼ teaspoon freshly ground black pepper

2 tablespoons minced fresh parsley leaves or dried parsley

2 large eggs lightly beaten with 1 tablespoon water

1 cup dry bread crumbs

Canola oil for frying

2 cloves garlic (see Note), peeled

4 lemon wedges for garnish

1. Rub the cutlets on both sides with the salt and pepper. Place between 2 pieces of plastic wrap and pound with a meat mallet to an even thickness. Pat both sides with the parsley. Dip in the egg mixture, then in the bread crumbs, being careful to coat evenly, and set on a wire rack to dry a little. You can do this ahead and refrigerate on the rack for up to 6 hours.

2. There are two methods of cooking *milanesas*: pan-frying and oven-frying. I find oven-frying is practical when cooking 8 or more. To pan-fry, heat ¼ inch of the oil in a large skillet over medium heat until hot. Add the garlic and cook until golden. Discard the garlic and add a drop of water to the oil; if it sizzles, the oil is hot enough (but don't let it get so hot that it starts to smoke—smoking oil will burn the batter). Cook the cutlets for a minute or so on each side, until golden brown. Drain on paper towels.

To oven-fry, preheat the oven to 400°F. Put ¼ cup canola oil in a large baking pan, place in the oven, and heat until very hot but not smoking, about 5 minutes. Place a few of the breaded cutlets in the pan, without overlapping them, and bake until golden brown, about 5 minutes per side. Drain on paper towels. Oven-frying can be done in 2 batches, but add more oil after the first batch and reheat before adding the remaining cutlets.

3. Serve immediately, garnished with the lemon wedges.

NOTE If you wish to use granulated garlic instead of fresh garlic, mix ¼ teaspoon granulated garlic with the salt.

Ragout de Ternera

VEAL RAGOUT *Serves 4*

Ragouts of different types can be found throughout South America. Veal is the meat of choice in the southern countries, while pork is often used in the Andes. In Brazil, ragouts are mostly made with beef and are usually served with *Farofa de Ouro* (page 304). This version is very much appreciated by those seeking a more substantial meal. In the other South American countries, ragouts are served with potatoes or pasta.

2 tablespoons canola oil

2 pounds veal stew meat, trimmed of fat

1 slice (¼ inch thick) imported boiled ham (about 2 ounces)

1 tablespoon all-purpose flour

½ teaspoon salt

¼ teaspoon freshly ground black pepper

½ teaspoon dried oregano

¼ cup tomato paste

1 bay leaf

1 cup dry white wine

1 cup water or chicken broth

Pinch of sugar

One 4-ounce can mushrooms, drained

1. Heat the oil in a 4-quart casserole over medium heat. Dry the meat cubes with paper towels, add to the hot oil, and brown on all sides. Add the ham and cook, stirring, for 1 minute. Sprinkle the flour, salt, pepper, and oregano over the meat, stirring to mix well.

Add the tomato paste, bay leaf, wine, water, and sugar. Stir to combine well and bring to a boil. Reduce the heat to low, cover, and simmer until the meat is tender, about 1 hour.

2. Add a little more water if the sauce has reduced too much. Add the mushrooms and simmer for 5 minutes to blend the flavors. Taste for salt and pepper, discard the bay leaf, and serve.

TO SERVE **Serve with pasta and a green salad.**

Chuletas de Ternera a la Criolla

VEAL SHOULDER STEAK CREOLE STYLE
Serves 4 to 6

Veal shoulder steak is an inexpensive, flavorful cut, ideal for braising. In South America, the liquid used for braising might be *chicha de jora* (a fermented corn drink), beer, or wine, depending on the country. In the Andean countries, *chicha* is often used, while in the southern countries, wine is preferred. The spices also vary. This type of braising is typical of Peru and Ecuador. The shoulder cut is available in some U.S. supermarkets and in ethnic markets.

> 2 shoulder veal steaks (about 1½ pounds each) or 4 to 6 veal chops
>
> Juice of 1 lemon
>
> 1 teaspoon salt
>
> ¼ teaspoon freshly ground black pepper
>
> 2 tablespoons canola oil

> ½ teaspoon granulated garlic
>
> 1 teaspoon dried marjoram
>
> 1 bay leaf
>
> 1 cup light beer
>
> 1 tablespoon tomato paste
>
> 1 tablespoon firmly packed dark brown sugar
>
> 2 tablespoons minced fresh cilantro leaves for garnish

1. Wash and dry the steaks. Trim off all the fat and gristle. (By trimming, the steaks can be separated into smaller steaks, or chops.) Leave the bones in because they give the sauce more flavor. Squeeze the lemon juice over the chops and sprinkle both sides with the salt and pepper. Place in a glass baking dish and refrigerate for a couple of hours.

2. Heat the oil in a large casserole over medium heat. Dry the chops with paper towels and add to the casserole without crowding. Brown on both sides. Sprinkle the garlic and marjoram over the chops and add the bay leaf, beer, tomato paste, and brown sugar. Bring to a boil, then reduce the heat to a low simmer, cover, and cook until the meat is very tender, about 2 hours, turning the chops after 1 hour.

3. Remove the bay leaf. Taste for salt and pepper, then serve sprinkled with the cilantro.

TO SERVE **Serve with pasta or potatoes and green beans.**

Cerdo, Jamón, y Chorizo
PORK, HAM, AND SAUSAGE

ALTHOUGH BEEF IS THE FAVORITE meat of most South Americans, pork is king among those who live in the Andes. When the Spaniards introduced the pig to the highlands, the Indians quickly took to it and incorporated it into their small repertoire of meats. The variety of dishes prepared from the pig ranges from simple pork chops baked with a marinade of orange and lemon juices and spices to stews made with beer or, preferably, *chicha de jora*, the Indians' beloved fermented corn drink. Soups that feature different parts of the pig are made with hominy and seasoned with toasted ground peanuts and cumin. Fresh leg of pork, called *pernil* in most countries, is very popular throughout most of South America. The leg is also stuffed with a variety of dried fruits, then braised in beer or *chicha*.

Brazilians are big consumers of pork, both fresh and cured. *Feijoada* (bean stew), for example, uses several kinds of cured meats and sausages. In the Southeast, in particular, one finds many specialties made with pork, including *tutu á Mineira* (black beans Minas style) and *feijao tropiero* (beans cattle herder style), which consists of fried eggs served with kale, sausage, beans, and *farofa* (page 304), along with rice and bacon rind. The Germans, who settled in Rio Grande do Sul and Santa Catarina, developed the industries that produce pork, cattle, sheep, and rice. (This area also produces ham, salami, and cheese.) The Portuguese, too, brought many specialties centered on pork. In São Paulo, one can find dishes such as *lombo de porco com ameixas* (roasted loin of pork with prunes), *leitão recheado* (stuffed roasted pig), and *lombo de porco ao leite* (roasted loin of pork with milk).

The Andean countries have a unique way of preparing a country-style fiesta that centers on the pig. In the past in Ecuador, the *matanza del cerdo* (killing of the pig) was the ideal way to celebrate any festive occasion. People who owned farms usually gave this type of party, and invitations were most coveted. Unfortunately, this custom is disappearing, and with it the wonderful specialties made with every part of the pig.

The killing of the pig is a complex undertaking, with lots of hands and expertise needed to prepare the dishes that go with this ritual. It is an all-day affair that starts with the *cuchicara* (cracklings), seasoned with salt and *ají* (hot pepper salsa) and accompanied by a shot of *aguardiente* (sugar cane liquor) to prevent stomach problems. In the afternoon, it is time for the *fritada* (fried chunks of pork), *empanadas de viento* (cheese turnovers), *mote* (hominy), *tostado* (toasted dried corn), and *chicha de jora*. Then there is a much-needed break to take a *siesta* (nap). Last but not least, in the evening, everyone enjoys the wonderful black and white *morcillas* (pork sausages) and soup made with the innards of the pig.

In Chile, the *fiesta del chancho* is very similar to the *matanza del cerdo*. However, the specialties are a little different from those in Ecuador. In general, depending on the region and country, the dishes prepared from the pig are so varied that it is not within the scope of this book to cover them all. In Colombia, for example, they stuff the pig with a filling of rice. In Venezuela, the young pig is seasoned with onions, orange juice, and spices and then roasted. Most South Americans roast the whole pig, and the crunchy skin is one of the delicacies everyone covets. Nothing goes to waste.

Ham and sausages were brought to South America by the Spaniards, Portuguese, and Germans. These meats have always been available in delicatessens, along with salami and *mortadela* (a smoked Italian sausage), and have been widely used in creole cuisine. The Spanish Serrano and the Italian Parma are cured hams that are very thinly sliced and served as an appetizer. They are also used for flavoring foods. Chorizo and *longaniza* are the favorite sausages on the Spanish side of South America, while the Portuguese have their own *chouriço* and linguiça. All these sausages are made from finely chopped pork seasoned with paprika, garlic, salt, pepper, and herbs. Chorizo is heavily seasoned with paprika and has an orange color. The Portuguese marinate the meat mixture for linguiça in wine before stuffing it into the casings. Both types are air-dried for several days. Polish sausage is a good substitute for *longaniza* and linguiça. Blood sausage is another favorite. This and other sausages are available in the United States in South American, Argentine, and Portuguese groceries. I have also found blood sausage in German delicatessens.

Carapulcra

PORK AND DRIED POTATO STEW *Serves 4*

This classic specialty from the highlands of Peru is a mainstay of the region's people. It is usually made with pork, although it is also sometimes prepared with pork and chicken. Most Peruvian cooks serve *carapulcra* with rice or small boiled potatoes on the side. You also may serve it with cooked yuca. It is generously seasoned with *mirasol* peppers, which give the dish a very special taste. If you can't find dried potatoes, use all-purpose potatoes. (And note that if you do find dried potatoes, you have to start preparing them two to three days in advance.) This is a hearty, tasty dish, which was prepared in a simpler form in pre-Hispanic times, using llama meat instead of pork.

1 cup *papa seca* (dried potatoes; see pages 298–299)

2 tablespoons canola oil

1 pound boneless lean pork, trimmed of fat and cut into ¾-inch cubes

1 medium-size onion, finely chopped (about 1 cup)

2 large cloves garlic, minced

1 teaspoon ground cumin

1 teaspoon ground annatto or sweet paprika

¼ teaspoon ground cloves

1 teaspoon salt

½ teaspoon freshly ground black pepper

1 tablespoon dried *mirasol* or *panca* pepper puree, store-bought or homemade (page 332), or more to taste

4 cups beef broth or water

½ cup unsalted dry-roasted peanuts, ground, or natural peanut butter

¼ cup cream sherry or sweet wine

12 black olives, pitted, for garnish

2 hard-cooked eggs, peeled and sliced, for garnish

1. Preheat the oven to 400°F.

2. Place the *papa seca* on a jellyroll pan and roast for 7 minutes, stirring once. Transfer to a strainer and shake to remove any excess starch. Place in a large mixing bowl, cover with plenty of water, and let stand until soft, about 1 day, changing the water two or three times during the day. Drain well and set aside.

3. Heat the oil in a large, heavy casserole over medium heat. Add the pork and lightly brown on all sides. Transfer to a platter. Add the onion, garlic, cumin, annatto, cloves, salt, black pepper, and pepper puree to the casserole and cook, stirring constantly, for about 5 minutes. Return the pork to the casserole, add the beef broth, and bring to a boil. Reduce the heat to medium-low, cover, and simmer for 30 minutes. Add the potatoes and stir to combine. Cook for 30 minutes, stirring occasionally so the potatoes don't stick to the bottom of the casserole. Add the ground peanuts and stir to combine. Continue to cook, stirring occasionally, until the meat is tender, 20 to 30 minutes. Add more water if the stew becomes too dry; there should be enough sauce to cover the meat and potatoes. Stir in the sherry and taste for salt and black pepper.

4. Remove from the heat and serve hot, garnished with the olives and eggs.

Fricasé

FRICASSEE *Serves 6*

This is a very old and delicious specialty from Bolivia. It is most commonly sold in the morning, as an invigorating energy booster to help people start the day. A specialty of creole cooking, *fricasé* is always found in the markets, small restaurants, and other places that cater to locals. It is also the favorite food of people who have been partying all night and want to restore their strength before they go home or face the day.

Fricasé is a highly spiced pork stew, always served with hominy and potatoes. In the Altiplano, *chuño* (dried potatoes) is the potato of choice and the hot peppers are yellow. The meat is always cut into big chunks, but I prefer to cut it into smaller pieces. Because this dish is considered a restorative, the primary identifying characteristic is that it is very spicy and hot, although the amount of dried

peppers (red or yellow) used varies. I have seen recipes that use as many as 20 or more peppers for this amount of meat. The quantity I've specified here may be more than you will be comfortable with, but you can adjust it to your taste.

> **6 dried hot yellow or red peppers, or to taste, seeded, soaked in hot water for 30 minutes, and drained, soaking liquid reserved**
>
> **2 medium-size onions, chopped (2 cups)**
>
> **4 large cloves garlic, chopped**
>
> **¼ cup packed fresh parsley leaves**
>
> **1 teaspoon salt**
>
> **1 teaspoon freshly ground black pepper**
>
> **1 teaspoon dried oregano**
>
> **1 teaspoon ground cumin**
>
> **2 pounds lean pork shoulder, trimmed of fat and cut into 1½-inch cubes**
>
> **6 cups water**
>
> **2 tablespoons dry bread crumbs**
>
> **Two 15-ounce cans white hominy, heated and drained just before serving**
>
> **6 medium-size boiling potatoes, peeled, cooked in water to cover until tender, drained, and kept warm**

1. Place the hot peppers, onions, garlic, parsley, salt, black pepper, oregano, and cumin in a blender or food processor. Add a little of the peppers' soaking liquid and process until smooth.

2. Transfer to a casserole, add the pork, and coat with the puree. Add the water and bring to a boil over medium heat. Reduce the heat to low, cover, and simmer for 2 hours. The meat should be very tender. Taste for salt, add the bread crumbs, and simmer for 5 minutes. The sauce should be the consistency of heavy cream, and the stew should be soupy.

3. Place ½ cup of the hominy in each of 6 soup plates. Add 1 potato and some of the pork stew. Serve immediately.

Costelinha com Canjiquinha

PORK RIBS WITH HOMINY *Serves 4*

The settlers who came to Brazil's inland state of Minas Gerais during the gold rush quickly adopted corn because it took less time to grow than *mandioca* (yuca). It could be used fresh or dried, and could be prepared in innumerable ways. It appeared in *pamonhas* (tamales), *angús* (molded porridges), and *canjica*, a dessert made with *canjiquinha* (cracked dried white corn). To the Indians' corn, African slaves added greens, and these, together with beans and pork, characterize the cooking of Minas Gerais.

When my friend Margarida Nogueira sent me this recipe, it reminded me of the Ecuadorian *morocho de sal*, one of the oldest specialties that falls in the category of *mazamorras* (hominy stews; page 282). African slaves made the old *mazamorras* more nutritious by adding collard greens, which they probably grew in their backyards. The onions and pork, Portugal's contributions to the cultural and culinary mélange, makes this specialty a true creole dish.

> 2 tablespoons canola oil
>
> 1 medium-size onion, finely chopped (about 1 cup)
>
> 1 cup cracked dried white corn (*maíz pisado* or *maíz quebrado*; available in South American groceries), rinsed and soaked in water to cover overnight
>
> 6 cups hot water or beef broth
>
> 4 country-style pork ribs
>
> 3 tablespoons fresh lemon juice
>
> 1 teaspoon salt
>
> ¼ teaspoon freshly ground black pepper
>
> 1 cup water
>
> 6 collard green leaves, washed well, stems removed, and torn into small pieces

1. In a heavy saucepan or casserole, heat the oil over low heat. Add the onion and cook, stirring a few times, until softened, about 5 minutes. Drain and rinse the soaked corn and add to the onion. Cook for about 1 minute, stirring so the grains absorb the flavor. Add the hot water, cover, and cook until tender, about 1 hour, stirring occasionally. The mixture should be soupy.

2. While the corn is cooking, remove the excess fat from the ribs, rub with the lemon juice, and sprinkle with the salt and pepper. Let stand at room temperature for 30 minutes.

3. Place the ribs in a 4-quart saucepan, add the water, cover, and cook over low heat for about 1 hour. Uncover and continue to cook until all the water has evaporated and the meat has started to brown in its own fat. Brown on all sides. Drain on paper towels and keep warm.

4. When the corn is cooked, add the collard greens to the pan and cook until softened, about 20 minutes. Season with salt and pepper to taste.

5. To serve, divide the corn mixture among 4 plates and place 1 rib on each plate.

Fritada/Chicharrón

PORK ANDEAN STYLE *Serves 8*

Fritada, also called *chicharrón* in the Andes, is one of the classic creole dishes from this region and dates back to the time of the conquest. Very little about this dish has changed over the centuries, although there are some regional differences (including different names). What is the same is the irresistible aroma of the frying pork, which conjures up images of the wonderful feast ahead.

Throughout the Andean countries, along the highways close to the big cities, rows of small open storefronts are a typical sight. Each one displays a large *paila* (cauldron), where the meat is cooked. People from the city go for weekend rides into the surrounding areas to enjoy the scenery and to search out this specialty and its trimmings. The cosas finas (fine things—that is, suitable accompaniments for the pork) vary from country to country. In Ecuador, cosas finas include potatoes and ripe plantains sautéed in the fat rendered by the pork, hominy, chochos (lupini beans), tostado (page 321), Cebollas Encurtidas (page 340), and Ají Criollo (page 333). One can also find fritada on the streets of Quito, where vendors set up small braziers to keep the fritada warm in copper pailas. The venta de fritada (seller of fritada), who caters to workers in the nearby areas, also sells sacks of hominy and lupini beans.

In the streets of Lima, Peru, one can smell the wonderful aroma of chicharrones, which are served with boiled or fried sweet potatoes, bread, and salsa criolla. In Bolivia, after the chicharrón is cooked, it is tossed with a puree of ají amarillo (hot yellow pepper) and cooked for 5 minutes more to blend the flavors. Sometimes chicharrón includes pieces of pig skin that have been cooked for 30 minutes to render the fat. (In other regions, this fried pork rind itself is called chicharrón.) Bolivians serve chicharrón with pataska (hominy) or tunta (dried white potatoes). During harvest season, corn on the cob is commonly served and always with a good llajwa (salsa). In Colombia, chicharrón is usually part of a specialty called fritanga, which also includes heart, liver, feet, and sausages all fried together. Papas Chorreadas (page 301), corn on the cob, and fried plantains are the usual accompaniments. In Venezuela, chicharrón is accompanied by the ubiquitous aged rum or black coffee. This dish used to be available only on weekends, and thus arose the ominous saying, "To every fat pig comes its Saturday," a warning usually applied to Venezuelan politicians.

When we visit Ecuador, our relatives or friends always invite us for a big creole party, which takes place at one of their weekend homes in the countryside. The menu varies very little. We start with cocktails and empanaditas de queso (small cheese turnovers). The first course is always some kind of cebiche, followed by fritada or hornado (roasted leg of pork), Llapingachos (page 300) or sautéed potatoes and plantains, mote (hominy), corn on the cob, a lettuce and avocado salad, and ají. Pilsner beer is a must with the cebiche, as is wine with the main course. A refreshing homemade fruit ice cream or sherbet is the best ending to this hearty meal.

The best fritada is made with a mixture of meat from the ribs and shoulder; very lean pork won't work for this dish. Only excess fat is removed; the rest of the fat melts during cooking and keeps the meat from drying out. Whatever fat is left after cooking can be removed from the ribs before eating.

One 2-pound pork shoulder roast

2 pounds country-style pork ribs, halved crosswise

8 large cloves garlic, peeled

1 tablespoon salt

½ teaspoon ground cumin (optional)

1 cup water or beer

1 bunch scallions (white part and 1 inch of the green), cut into 2-inch pieces

1. Remove some of the large pieces of fat from the pork roast and discard. Cut the remaining large pieces of fat into small pieces. Cut the meat into 2-inch chunks. Put the cut-up fat in a large heavy skillet or Dutch oven along with the pork chunks, ribs, garlic, salt, cumin (if using), and water. Bring to a boil over medium-high heat and cook, turning the pork occasionally, until all the water has been absorbed, about 45 minutes. Some of the fat will have been released by this time and will start browning the meat. Reduce the heat to low.

2. As the meat browns, stir with a wooden spoon so that it browns evenly. (Remove small pieces of pork when they are browned and crispy and drain on paper towels. These pieces can be mixed with the tostado or used as a garnish for the hominy—delicious.) When the meat is almost done, stir in the scallions and cook for about 10

minutes, stirring occasionally so that the meat absorbs their flavor. The *fritada* is done when it is dark brown, crispy on the outside, and moist on the inside. Using a slotted spoon, transfer to a platter lined with paper towels.

3. Use the leftover fat, called *mapahuira*, to fry any of the side dishes mentioned in the headnote, such as potatoes, sweet potatoes, yuca, plantains, or *tostado*, and to season the hominy. Serve as indicated in the headnote.

Hornado

ROASTED LEG OF PORK ANDEAN STYLE *Serves 20*

This has to be one of the best ways to eat roasted pig. It is popular in all the Andean countries, with the seasoning varying from country to country. The whole pig, prepared this way, is made in the countryside. It is baked in brick ovens overnight, at a low temperature, so that when it is done, the meat is moist and delicious and the skin is crunchy. This is another weekend specialty in many countries, available in towns near the cities or on the way to the resorts. It is possible to buy any part of the pig by the pound, or even a whole leg, from vendors who have prepared it. This is the ideal way to entertain when there is no time to prepare the leg at home.

Thanks to an increasing number of ethnic markets in the United States, it is possible to find fresh leg of pork easily. This is a family recipe that we have made many times, and with the leftovers we make delicious sandwiches the next day. For sandwiches, we use kaiser rolls spread with mayonnaise, then add a slice of meat, some lettuce, a slice of tomato, and *Cebollas Encurtidas* (page 340).

One 8- to 10-pound fresh leg of pork, skin on, if desired

Juice of 1 to 2 large lemons, as needed

1 tablespoon ground annatto or sweet paprika

¼ cup salt

2 teaspoons ground cumin

2 teaspoons freshly ground black pepper

1 head garlic, peeled

1 small onion, cut into small pieces

1 cup water or beer

1 recipe *Agrio* (recipe follows)

1. Remove the excess fat from the pork. With a sharp paring knife, deeply pierce every inch of the leg. Rub the lemon juice into the holes and all over the leg.

2. Place the remaining ingredients, except the *agrio*, in a blender and process until smooth. With your finger, push this mixture into the holes. Wrap the leg well in plastic or place in a large glass container or plastic bag. Refrigerate overnight, turning it every few hours, rubbing it with the marinade, and pushing the marinade into the holes with the back of a wooden spoon. Some people prefer to let it marinate for 2 to 3 days.

3. Preheat the oven to 450°F.

4. Remove the pork from the marinade and place in a large roasting pan. Roast for 45 minutes. Reduce the oven temperature to 300°F and roast until very well done, about 4 hours. Baste every hour with the fat released from the leg. If at the end of the cooking time, the skin is not crunchy, increase the oven temperature to 400°F and roast until crunchy.

5. Break the skin into roughly 2-inch pieces, then slice the meat about ½ inch thick on the diagonal. (The meat may break into chunks.) Drizzle a little of the *agrio* over the meat and serve the rest on the side.

Agrio Creole Vinaigrette

Makes about 2 1/4 cups

Agrio is a type of vinaigrette that, I believe, was created to cut down on the richness of the pork. It is usually drizzled on top of the meat before serving.

- 2 cups water
- 2 tablespoons white wine vinegar
- 1 teaspoon olive oil
- 1 teaspoon salt
- 1 tablespoon firmly packed dark brown sugar
- 1 small jalapeño, seeded and minced
- 2 scallions (white part only), thinly sliced
- 1 tablespoon minced fresh parsley leaves
- 1 tablespoon minced carrot

Mix all the ingredients together in a large measuring cup. Add more salt or brown sugar to achieve a mild sweet-sour taste.

Pernil

FRESH LEG OF PORK CREOLE STYLE
Serves 16

Pernil is very similar to *hornado*, the difference being that for *pernil*, the skin is always removed and the *aliño* (rub) is made not only with the standard cumin, garlic, and annatto, but also with sweet spices such as cloves, allspice, and cinnamon. In Ecuador, *pernil* is the standard meat used to make sandwiches sold in small delicatessens that specialize in creole food. Many cooks press the meat after it is cooked so that it can be cut into thin slices, but I don't think this is necessary.

- One 8- to 10-pound fresh leg of pork, skin removed
- 1 recipe *Aliño para Carne de Cerdo* (page 339)

1. Remove the excess fat from the pork. With a sharp paring knife, pierce every inch of the leg and, with your finger, push the *aliño* into the holes. Spread the *aliño* all over the leg. Wrap in plastic or place in a large glass container or plastic bag. Refrigerate overnight, turning it every few hours, rubbing it with the *aliño*, and pushing the *aliño* into the holes with the back of a wooden spoon. Some cooks prefer to let it marinate for 2 to 3 days.

2. Preheat the oven to 325°F.

3. Place the meat in a roasting pan lined with a sheet of aluminum foil large enough to fold over the leg. Roast for 3 hours, uncover, and continue to roast until very well done, about 2 hours more. You should be able to pull the meat apart with a fork. (Cook the meat to an internal temperature of 180°F, which is more than the recommended temperature on the meat thermometer.)

4. Serve warm or at room temperature, cut into 1/8-inch-thick slices, as part of a buffet. Or use it to make sandwiches (see Note).

NOTE To make sandwiches, spread kaiser rolls with mayonnaise or butter. Add some lettuce, a thin slice of tomato, and a few slices of *pernil*. Top with *Ají Criollo* (page 333) and *Cebollas Encurtidas* (page 340).

Lomo de Cerdo Relleno con Frutas

PORK LOIN STUFFED WITH PRUNES AND APPLES *Serves 6 to 8*

My cousin Gladys Almeida de Franco loves to entertain, and she does it with flair and elegance. This type of pork is a favorite of South American hostesses when they want to prepare something special. They may use prunes, raisins, or other dried fruit for the stuffing, with beer and/or cola frequently used for marinating and basting. These ingredients emphasize the natural sweetness of the pork. In South America, the whole leg of pork is usually boned and stuffed, but I find that boneless pork loin is more readily available in U.S. meat markets and can easily be stuffed. If using a leg of pork, remove the skin and excess fat. Whichever cut you use, this dish is excellent.

One 3- to 4-pound boneless pork loin

12 to 16 bite-size pitted prunes

1 small Granny Smith apple, peeled, cored, and chopped

¾ cup dark beer

¾ cup cola (*not* diet)

¾ cup barbecue sauce

2 teaspoons beef bouillon granules

6 cloves garlic, mashed into a paste with 2 teaspoons salt and ½ teaspoon freshly ground black pepper

1 teaspoon ground cumin

1 bay leaf

1 teaspoon dried rosemary, crumbled

¼ cup firmly packed dark brown sugar

Maraschino cherries for garnish

Canned pineapple rings for garnish

1. With a sharp knife, carefully cut through the middle of the pork loin lengthwise, but do not cut all the way through; stop about ½ inch from the bottom, as if you were butterflying the loin. Place the prunes and apple along the center and either sew or tie the loin together with kitchen twine at 1-inch intervals, making sure it is completely closed.

2. In a medium-size mixing bowl, combine the beer, cola, barbecue sauce, bouillon, garlic paste, cumin, bay leaf, and rosemary and pour over the loin. Cover with plastic wrap and let marinate in the refrigerator all day or overnight.

3. Preheat the oven to 350°F.

4. Place the pork in a shallow baking pan and pour half of the marinade over the top. Roast until the pork is very well done, 2½ to 3 hours,

basting with the remaining marinade every 20 to 30 minutes. You should be able to pull it apart with a fork.

5. Remove from the oven and let rest for 10 minutes. Remove the twine and cut into ½-inch-thick slices. Arrange on a heated platter, drizzle some of the sauce on top, and garnish with the cherries and pineapple rings. Serve any extra sauce in a gravy boat.

TO SERVE **Serve with tiny new potatoes sautéed in olive oil and buttered peas.**

Chuletas Ahumadas con Col

SMOKED PORK CHOPS WITH CABBAGE *Serves 4*

Many years ago, my sister Ximena had a lady friend from Germany who made this dish. Her friend said that since she could not get sauerkraut in Ecuador, she had figured out a way of preparing something that resembles the famous German specialty *kasseler Rippenspeer*. I'm happy she shared this recipe with my sister, because it has become a favorite of my family and friends.

2 tablespoons unsalted butter

1 tablespoon canola oil

4 smoked pork chops

1 medium-size onion, halved and thinly sliced into half-moons (about 1 cup)

1 small head cabbage (about 1½ pounds), cored and shredded

¼ teaspoon salt

¼ teaspoon freshly ground black pepper

½ cup dry white wine or dry vermouth

Sweet paprika for garnish

4 medium-size boiling potatoes, peeled, cooked in water to cover until tender, and drained

In a large, heavy casserole, heat the butter and oil together over medium heat until the butter melts.

Brown the pork chops on both sides. Add the onion and cook, stirring a few times, until softened, about 5 minutes. Add the cabbage, salt, pepper, and wine. Reduce the heat to low, cover, and simmer, stirring occasionally, to blend the flavors, about 20 minutes. The cabbage should be soft but not mushy. Check the seasonings, sprinkle with the paprika, and serve with the boiled potatoes.

Arroz con Chorizo y Pasas

RICE WITH CHORIZO AND RAISINS *Serves 3 to 4*

Rice with ground beef or chorizo is a staple for millions of Latins. The chorizo we use in South America, however, is the Spanish type, which is more like a sausage, as opposed to the Mexican chorizo, which is a crumbly meat seasoned with hot peppers. I decided to try this recipe with Mexican chorizo, which is more readily available in U.S. markets. It turned out to be excellent. As a bonus, it can be prepared ahead and easily reheated in a frying pan or the oven.

> One 7½-ounce mild Mexican chorizo
> 1 medium-size onion, finely chopped (about 1 cup)
> 1 to 2 tablespoons canola oil, as needed
> 1½ cups converted rice
> ⅓ cup seedless golden raisins
> 3 cups hot water
> 1 teaspoon salt
> ¼ teaspoon freshly ground black pepper
> 1 cup frozen peas
> 2 tablespoons chopped fresh cilantro leaves
> 1 large ripe (yellow) plantain
> 2 hard-cooked eggs, peeled and cut into wedges, for garnish
> Pimento strips for garnish

1. Remove the chorizo from its casing and place in a heavy 10-inch skillet with a cover. Cook over medium heat, stirring occasionally and breaking up the chorizo with a wooden spoon. When the chorizo starts rendering its fat, 3 to 4 minutes, stir in the onion. Reduce the heat to low and cook, stirring a few times, until the onion is transparent, about 5 minutes. If there is not enough fat and the onion starts sticking, add up to 1 tablespoon of the oil to finish cooking the onion. Add the rice and cook, stirring constantly, for 1 minute to coat the grains with the fat. Add the raisins, water, salt, and pepper and bring to a boil. Cover and cook over the lowest possible heat for 15 minutes. Scatter the peas and cilantro on top, cover, and finish cooking until all the water has been absorbed and the peas are heated through, about 5 minutes. Fluff the rice with a fork, cover, and set aside to dry for 5 minutes.

2. While the rice is cooking, peel the plantain and cut into thirds, then cut each third lengthwise into three slices. Heat 1 tablespoon of the oil over low heat in a medium-size nonstick skillet. Add the plantain, cover, and cook until golden on both sides, about 5 minutes per side. Drain on paper towels and keep warm.

3. Transfer the rice mixture to a serving platter and arrange the plantain slices, egg wedges, and pimento strips on top.

TO SERVE **Serve with a tossed salad.**

Cazuela de Garbanzos y Espinaca con Jamón

CHICKPEA AND SPINACH STEW WITH HAM
Serves 4

This type of dish is very popular in the southern countries of South America. *Cazuelas* (stews cooked in earthenware crocks) were brought by the Spaniards and underwent the usual changes, including the addition of local ingredients. This is a versatile type of stew, because it can be made with or without meat. In the past, whenever meat was available, people would use ham, salt pork, or chorizo in small quantities, just to flavor the stew. Another flavoring was salt cod. During Lent, the dish was made without meat, with cooks either using the salt cod or simply relying on the flavors of the vegetables. Sometimes Swiss chard was used instead of spinach, and sweet potatoes instead of regular potatoes.

2 tablespoons canola oil

1 medium-size onion, minced (about 1 cup)

½ cup seeded and chopped green bell pepper

4 cloves garlic, minced

2 large ripe but firm tomatoes (about 1 pound), peeled and chopped

2 tablespoons tomato paste, if using winter tomatoes

1 bay leaf

1 teaspoon salt

½ teaspoon freshly ground black pepper

Two 15-ounce cans chickpeas, undrained

2 cups water

2 medium-size all-purpose potatoes, peeled and cut into 1-inch cubes

8 ounces calabaza or other winter squash, peeled, seeded, and cut into 1-inch cubes

8 ounces spinach leaves, washed well, stems removed, and coarsely chopped

4 ounces imported boiled ham, cut into ½-inch cubes, or Polish sausage, thinly sliced

2 tablespoons minced fresh parsley leaves for garnish

In a large, heavy casserole, heat the oil over medium heat. Add the onion, bell pepper, and garlic and cook, stirring a few times, until the onion is softened, about 5 minutes. Add the tomatoes, tomato paste (if using), bay leaf, salt, and pepper. Cover and simmer until the tomatoes have formed a sauce, about 10 minutes. Add the

chickpeas and water and bring to a boil. Reduce the heat to low, add the potatoes, cover, and cook for 10 minutes. Add the calabaza and cook until fork tender, about 10 minutes. Add the spinach and ham, mix well, and simmer for 5 minutes to blend the flavors. Add more water if the stew is too thick; it should have some sauce but not be too soupy. Discard the bay leaf and taste for salt and pepper. Serve hot, sprinkled with the parsley.

Porotos con Longaniza y Calabaza

LIMA BEANS WITH SAUSAGE AND SQUASH *Serves 3 to 4*

When a Chilean friend gave me this recipe, I was pleasantly surprised to discover its Yugoslavian roots. It is almost identical to the recipe my Yugoslavian sister-in-law gave me years ago. The only difference is that the Chilean version calls for calabaza, which Chileans add to many of their bean stews. The Yugoslavs immigrated to Chile in the 1850s and 1860s, and they obviously incorporated New World foods into their specialties. In this case, more nutrition and flavor were added to the dish in the form of the squash.

2 tablespoons canola oil

1 large onion, finely chopped (about 1½ cups)

1 teaspoon sweet paprika

6 ounces Polish or Hungarian sausage, sliced ¼ inch thick

12 ounces calabaza or other winter squash, peeled, seeded, and cut into 1-inch cubes

1 cup water

Two 15-ounce cans lima beans, undrained

Salt and freshly ground black pepper

Heat the oil in a large skillet over low heat. Add the onion and paprika and cook, stirring occasionally, until golden, about 7 minutes. Add the sausage and cook on both sides until golden brown. Add the calabaza and water, cover, and cook until the squash is fork tender, about 10 minutes. Add the beans with their liquid and bring to a boil over medium heat. Cover, reduce the heat to low, and simmer until all the flavors are blended, about 10 minutes. By this time, some of the squash will have fallen apart and thickened the sauce. Chileans usually remove 1 cup beans, mash them, and add them back to the dish to thicken the sauce even more. Season with salt and pepper to taste. Serve hot.

TO SERVE **Serve with a green salad.**

Polenta Rellena con Jamón y Queso

**POLENTA WITH HAM AND
CHEESE FILLING** *Serves 4 to 6*

In the Río de la Plata region of Argentina and Uruguay, one of the most important river systems in South America, cornmeal, mozzarella cheese, tomatoes, onions, and garlic, some brought by the Italians, are staples. This recipe comes from Estela de Costa, a businesswoman from Punta del Este, an exclusive resort in Uruguay. For unexpected guests (of which there are many), Estela is always ready with *copetines* (cocktails) and a quick meal, which she calls *saca de apuros* (saves the day). The polenta can be made with water, and the recipe can easily be doubled and baked in a 10 x 13-inch baking dish. The leftovers reheat well in the microwave. This is a very simple dish, yet it is tremendously appealing.

SOFRITO
> 2 tablespoons canola oil
> 1 medium-size onion, finely chopped (about 1 cup)
> 2 cloves garlic, minced

> 2 medium-size ripe but firm tomatoes, peeled, seeded, and chopped
> ¼ teaspoon salt
> ¼ teaspoon freshly ground black pepper
> Pinch of sugar

POLENTA
> 1½ cups milk or water
> 1½ cups water
> 1 teaspoon salt
> ½ teaspoon white pepper
> 1 cup cornmeal

> 6 ounces thinly sliced imported boiled ham
> 6 ounces mozzarella cheese, thinly sliced
> ¼ cup freshly grated Parmesan cheese
> ½ cup whipping cream

1. To make the *sofrito*, heat the oil in a medium-size skillet over low heat. Add the onion and cook, stirring a few times, until softened, about 5 minutes. Add the garlic and tomatoes, cover, and cook until the tomatoes have formed a sauce, about 10 minutes. If the tomatoes dry out too quickly, add a little water to obtain the consistency of a thick sauce. Add the salt, black pepper, and sugar. Set aside.

2. To make the polenta, bring the milk, water, salt, and white pepper to a boil in a heavy 4-quart saucepan over medium heat. Reduce the heat to low and add the cornmeal in a slow, thin stream, stirring constantly with a wire whisk. Cook, stirring frequently with a wooden spoon, until thick and smooth, about 7 minutes. When done, the polenta should pull away from the side of the pan as you stir. Spread half the polenta in a buttered, shallow 9-inch square baking dish. Top with half of the *sofrito* and arrange half of the ham slices on top, followed by half of the mozzarella. Pour the remaining polenta on top and spread it out evenly. Repeat the layers of *sofrito*, ham, and mozzarella. Sprinkle the Parmesan evenly on top and drizzle with the cream, especially around the edges. The dish can be prepared to this point up to a day ahead; simply cover and refrigerate until needed.

3. Preheat the oven to 375°F.

4. Bake the polenta on the upper oven rack until golden, about 20 minutes. Remove from the oven and let rest for 10 minutes. Cut into squares and serve warm.

TO SERVE **Serve with a fresh spinach salad.**

Crepas de Choclo y Jamón a la Blanca

BLANCA'S CREPES FILLED WITH CORN AND HAM *Makes about 16 crepes; 6 to 8 servings*

Crepes have always occupied a place of honor on the South American table. Their roots go back to France and Italy. Along the way, native cooks began using indigenous ingredients, creating delicious new fillings. These corn crepes are just one example of the ingenuity of the Latin cook. No two cooks prepare them the same way. Some prefer to grind the corn, and others use it whole. Some use ham in the filling, and others prefer porcini mushrooms. Uruguayans and Argentines, in particular, excel in the preparation of crepes, and *crepas de choclo* is a specialty of Uruguay. While I was in Montevideo visiting my friend Yvonne Miles, her cook, Blanca, prepared these crepes for me, and they have become a favorite of family and friends. Because crepes can be assembled the day before, they are ideal for entertaining. The *salsa blanca* also can be made the day before and reheated before finishing the dish.

2 tablespoons canola oil

1 medium-size onion, minced (1 cup)

½ cup seeded and finely chopped green or red bell pepper

4 ounces thickly sliced imported boiled ham, minced

4 ounces Emmental cheese, shredded

½ teaspoon salt

¼ teaspoon freshly ground black pepper

2 hard-cooked eggs, peeled and chopped

2 cups cooked corn kernels, drained

1 recipe *Crepas con Albahaca* (page 405)

2 cups *Salsa Blanca* (page 405)

1 cup whipping cream, or more if needed

½ cup freshly grated Parmesan cheese

1. Heat the oil in a large skillet over medium heat. Add the onion and bell pepper and cook, stirring a few times, until softened, about 5 minutes. Remove from the heat and let cool to lukewarm. Stir in the ham, cheese, salt, pepper, eggs, and corn.

2. Place 2 heaping tablespoons of the filling in the center of each crepe and roll tightly into a cylinder. Arrange the crepes in a single layer in 2 buttered shallow baking dishes, making sure they are not crowded. The crepes can be made the day before up to this point, then covered and refrigerated.

3. Preheat the oven to 375°F.

4. Bring the crepes to room temperature, if refrigerated. In a medium-size saucepan, reheat the *salsa blanca* over medium-low heat. If it is too thick, add a little of the cream to thin it to the consistency of a medium-light sauce. Pour evenly over the crepes. Drizzle ½ cup of the cream around the edges of each pan, sprinkle the Parmesan evenly over the top, and bake until bubbling, about 20 minutes. Serve immediately.

TO SERVE **Serve with a vegetable salad.**

Capeletis a la Yvonne

YVONNE'S CAPPELLETTI *Serves 6 to 8*

In Argentina and Uruguay, some type of pasta is always served on Sunday, a custom brought by Italian immigrants. At the home of my friend Yvonne Miles in Uruguay, the pasta is cappelletti, which the whole family looks forward to, and with good reason. Yvonne prepares this with a wonderful white sauce, made lighter by the addition of cream.

2 tablespoons unsalted butter

2 tablespoons all-purpose flour

1 cup hot milk

1 tablespoon beef bouillon granules

1 cup whipping cream

2 tablespoons dry sherry

2 tablespoons freshly grated Parmesan cheese

Salt and white pepper

1 slice (¼ inch thick) imported boiled ham, cut into matchsticks

One 4-ounce can mushrooms, drained

Two 9- to 12-ounce packages frozen cheese-filled cappelletti (see Note)

1. In a small, heavy saucepan, melt the butter over medium heat. Add the flour and cook, stirring, for a couple of minutes, until bubbling. Do not let it color. Off the heat, whisk in the milk until smooth and return to the heat. Add the bouillon and cream and cook, stirring, until it comes to a boil. Reduce the heat to medium-low and simmer for a couple of minutes. Stir in the sherry, Parmesan, and salt and pepper to taste. Stir in the ham and mushrooms, cover, and set aside.

2. In a large pot, cook the cappelletti in salted boiling water until done. Drain thoroughly, return to the pot, and toss with the sauce to coat well. Serve immediately.

TO SERVE **Serve with a refreshing green salad dressed with a light vinaigrette.**

NOTE **Cappelletti comes in packages that weigh anywhere from 9 to 12 ounces. Anything in this weight range will work. This type of pasta is usually sold under the name *tortelloni* for the medium size that I use for this recipe. It is shaped in the form of hats, which is where it gets its name: "little hats." Cappelletti comes with different fillings, so choose what you like.**

Cordero y Chivo
LAMB AND GOAT

ALONG WITH BEEF AND PORK, lamb (called both *cordero* and *borrego*, depending on where you are) is widely used in most South American countries. Goat (*chivo* if grown, *cabrito* when a kid) is popular in some countries, and sometimes recipes that call for goat can also be made with lamb. In Ecuador, there is an old specialty called *seco de chivo*, which is always made with lamb, perhaps because goat is not readily available. Lamb is prepared in many ways, depending on the country and the cook. It is barbecued over an open pit; legs are roasted in the oven; chops are prepared in sauces or in fancy French dishes. But the most popular way is stewed with a variety of seasonings and ingredients. Peruvians and Bolivians have similar specialties, always highly seasoned with hot peppers. Chileans raise excellent-quality lamb in the southern part of their country.

There they specialize in grilling the whole lamb over charcoal, in the *gaucho* fashion. In fact, from there all the way to the Strait of Magellan, the favorite way to prepare lamb (and also kid) is grilling it in that fashion. But lamb is prepared in many other ways as well, using every part of the animal. Famous is *guiso de sangre de cordero* (blood, potato, and cabbage stew), along with *chanfaina* (a sauté made with the innards of the lamb, potatoes, carrots, and peas). In Brazil, lamb is not as popular as in the rest of South America, but it is raised in the southeast, where the specialties include roasted leg of lamb, rack of lamb, and lamb casseroles.

Goat meat, fresh or salted, is widely consumed in Venezuela, as is the butter and cheese made from goat's milk. Some of the specialties date from colonial times. Grilling baby lamb and kid is a very popular way of preparing these young animals. In some areas of Venezuela, the *cabrito* has to be male and not more than 10 months old. The grilling takes place in the countryside, with plenty of guests, food, drink, and music. Such meals are usually reserved for birthdays, engagement parties, holidays, and so on. Trade with the island of Trinidad, just off the northeast coast of Venezuela, influenced the popularity of goat, and some dishes can be traced back to that island. Good examples are *talkari de chivo* (goat stew) and *quimbombó porteño* (salted goat, fish, and okra soup). Another dish prepared with salted goat is *chivo con fríjoles* (goat with beans), which is also one of the oldest specialties in Sucre, a state in northern Venezuela.

Carne de Borrego en Coco

LAMB BRAISED IN COCONUT MILK *Serves 4*

Coconut milk, which appears in many dishes from Brazil and the Andean countries, especially those from coastal towns, is an important contribution of African slaves to creole cuisine. This recipe hails from the Pacific coast of Colombia, where coconut milk is used to flavor meat, poultry, fish, and rice. Extracting milk from coconuts is a labor-intensive task. Fortunately, unsweetened coconut milk is available frozen or canned in Latin American and Oriental supermarkets, as well as in the ethnic food aisles of many larger supermarkets.

2 tablespoons unsalted butter

1 tablespoon canola oil

2 pounds boneless leg of lamb, trimmed of fat and gristle and cut into 1-inch pieces

1 medium-size onion, minced (about 1 cup)

½ cup seeded and chopped green bell pepper

½ cup seeded and chopped red bell pepper

½ cup finely chopped celery

6 large cloves garlic, mashed into a paste with 1 teaspoon salt and ½ teaspoon freshly ground black pepper

2 tablespoons minced fresh parsley leaves

2 tablespoons minced fresh cilantro leaves

Pinch of cayenne pepper

Pinch of ground allspice

1 tablespoon firmly packed dark brown sugar

2 cups hot water

1 cup well-stirred canned unsweetened coconut milk

Salt and freshly ground black pepper

1. In a heavy 6-quart casserole, heat the butter and oil together over medium heat until the butter melts. Add the lamb and brown on all sides. Add the onion, bell peppers, celery, garlic paste, parsley, cilantro, cayenne, allspice, and brown sugar and cook, stirring a few times, until the onion is softened, about 5 minutes. Add the water and bring to a boil. Reduce the heat to low, cover,

and simmer, stirring occasionally, until the meat is tender, about 1½ hours. If the mixture gets too dry, add more hot water.

2. Stir in the coconut milk, season with salt and black pepper to taste, and cook for 5 minutes. Serve hot.

TO SERVE Serve with rice and green beans.

Pierna de Cordero Doña "O"

MRS. O'S LEG OF LAMB *Serves 8*

When I was visiting friends in the fashionable resort of Punta del Este in Uruguay, a well-known painter, Cristina Lorenzo y Lozada de Infantozzi, prepared this leg of lamb. She said that the reason some people don't care for lamb is because a gland called the *catinga* is not removed from the inside of the leg, and that is what gives it a bad taste. *Catinga* in Guarani means "that which smells bad." This gland is also called *catinga* in Brazil, where recipes for leg of lamb specify that the gland be removed before cooking. In the United States, this gland is usually removed before the meat is packaged for sale.

Cristina does not subscribe to the idea of using many condiments to foil the taste of lamb. On the contrary, she tries to preserve the delicate taste of this meat. She could not tell me the origin of this dish, only that it has been in her family for generations. I believe that the ideas, if not the actual recipe, were probably brought to South America from Italy, because the recipe uses two types of sauce that are commonly used in northern Italian cooking. No matter what its pedigree, Cristina's leg of lamb is superb.

Two 2-pound boneless legs of baby lamb (see Note)

3 tablespoons olive oil

2 medium-size onions, finely chopped (about 2 cups)

4 cloves garlic, minced

1 teaspoon dried oregano

One 16-ounce can pear-shaped tomatoes, with juices

1 teaspoon salt

1 tablespoon sugar

½ teaspoon freshly ground black pepper

1 teaspoon Worcestershire sauce

¾ cup dry white wine

1 recipe *Salsa Blanca* (page 405), heated

1. Remove all the fat and tendons from the lamb. Tie the legs closed with kitchen twine. In a large Dutch oven, heat the oil over medium heat. Add the lamb and brown on all sides until golden. Add the onions and cook, stirring a few times, until softened, about 5 minutes. Add the garlic and oregano and cook, stirring constantly, for 1 minute.

2. Drain the tomatoes, reserving the juices. Chop the tomatoes and add to the pan. Stir in the tomato juices, salt, sugar, pepper, and Worcestershire. Reduce the heat to low, cover, and cook for about 30 minutes. Add the wine and continue to cook until the meat is tender, about 1 hour, turning it after 30 minutes. Taste for salt and pepper. The dish can be made to this point up to a day ahead. Simply cool, cover, and refrigerate. Before serving, bring to room temperature and bake, covered, in a preheated 350°F oven until heated through, about 20 minutes.

3. To serve, cut into ¼-inch-thick slices and arrange on a heated serving platter. Top with the tomato sauce and drizzle with a little of the *salsa blanca*. Serve the remaining *salsa blanca* in a sauceboat.

TO SERVE Serve with sautéed potato wedges.

NOTE A 4-pound leg of lamb can be used instead of 2 legs of baby lamb. It will take about 30 minutes longer to cook.

Costillitas de Cordero al Horno

BAKED BABY LAMB CHOPS *Serves 4*

Lamb is very popular in Argentina and Uruguay. This is a great Argentine party dish, which can be prepared ahead and baked just before serving. It really is a wonderful, easy way to serve baby lamb chops.

- 5 tablespoons olive oil
- ¼ cup minced shallots
- 4 cloves garlic, minced
- 4 ounces fresh, firm white mushrooms, finely chopped
- 1 cup dry white wine
- 1 tablespoon tomato paste
- 1 bay leaf
- 1 tablespoon fresh rosemary leaves, finely chopped, or 1 teaspoon dried, crumbled
- ½ teaspoon salt
- ½ teaspoon freshly ground black pepper
- 2 tablespoons day-old bread crumbs (page 413)
- 2 tablespoons minced fresh parsley leaves
- 8 baby lamb chops (1 to 1½ inches thick)

1. In a heavy skillet, heat 4 tablespoons of the oil over medium heat. Add the shallots and garlic and cook, stirring constantly, for 1 minute. Add the mushrooms and cook, stirring a few times, until lightly colored. Stir in ½ cup of the wine, the tomato paste, bay leaf, rosemary, salt, and pepper and cook until most of the liquid has evaporated and the mixture is thick, about 5 minutes. Remove from the heat, discard the bay leaf, and stir in the bread crumbs and parsley. Set aside to cool. This can be done the day before, covered, and refrigerated.

2. Trim the fat from around the chops, if desired, and season with salt and pepper to taste. Heat the remaining 1 tablespoon oil in a large skillet over medium-high heat. Add the chops, without crowding them, and quickly brown on both sides. Remove from the pan and set aside. Drain the fat from the skillet, pour in the remaining ½ cup wine, and deglaze the pan over low heat, scraping up any browned bits from the bottom.

3. Preheat the oven to 375°F.

4. Spread the mushroom mixture in a shallow ovenproof dish large enough to hold the chops in a single layer. Lay the chops on top of the mushrooms. Drizzle the juices from deglazing the pan over the chops, cover with aluminum foil, and bake until done, about 20 minutes, depending on the thickness. They should be pink in the center, unless you or your guests want them well done. If well-done chops are desired, increase the baking time by 5 minutes.

5. To serve, place 2 lamb chops on each dinner plate. Stir the mushroom mixture well and top each chop with about 1 tablespoon if it.

TO SERVE **Serve with parsleyed potatoes and** *Zapallitos Rellenos con Choclo* (page 293).

Talkari de Chivo

GOAT STEW *Serves 6 to 8*

Talkari is a stew of Indian origin that came to Venezuela via the island of Trinidad, undergoing some changes along the way. It is very popular on the Paria coast. In some coastal towns, it would be unthinkable to throw a party without having a big pot of *talkari* simmering while the music is playing and guests are dancing and drinking. It is believed to cure depression and restore vitality. Its particulars change from town to town, depending on what is available. Sometimes the stew is made with chicken stock instead of wine. Some people use potatoes in the stew (as here), while others serve it with rice. Eggplant may or may not be used. The meat of choice is goat, but chicken or lamb may be substituted. If goat is available, it is deliciously savory in this stew.

- **6 pounds leg of baby goat, bone in, cut into 2-inch pieces (ask your butcher to do this)**
- **Juice of 2 lemons**
- **1 head garlic, peeled**
- **1 teaspoon dried oregano**
- **1 teaspoon ground cumin**
- **1 tablespoon curry powder**
- **½ teaspoon ground cloves**
- **2 teaspoons plus 1 tablespoon salt**
- **½ teaspoon freshly ground black pepper**
- **½ teaspoon cayenne pepper**
- **¼ cup olive oil**
- **3 medium-size onions, finely chopped (about 3 cups)**
- **One 28-ounce can peeled whole tomatoes, with juices**
- **Bouquet garni (6 sprigs fresh thyme or 1 teaspoon dried, 2 sprigs fresh rosemary or 1 teaspoon dried, 6 sprigs fresh parsley, and 2 bay leaves, tied up in cheesecloth)**
- **2 cups dry red wine**
- **1 medium-size eggplant (about 1 pound)**
- **1½ pounds boiling potatoes**

1. Trim the fat and membranes from the goat. Thoroughly rub with the lemon juice to remove any gamy taste. Rinse well, drain, and dry with paper towels.

2. Put the garlic, oregano, cumin, curry powder, cloves, 2 teaspoons of the salt, the black pepper, and cayenne in a blender and process until smooth. Rub the goat with this paste, cover with plastic wrap, and let marinate in the refrigerator for a few hours or overnight.

3. Heat the oil in a large Dutch oven over medium heat. Add the onions and cook, stirring a few times, until softened, about 5 minutes. Add the meat and cook, stirring occasionally, for 30 minutes. Chop the tomatoes with their juices in a blender. Add to the pan along with the bouquet garni, reduce the heat to low, cover, and simmer for 2 hours. Add the wine and continue to cook until the meat is tender, about 1 hour.

4. While the meat is cooking, prepare the eggplant. Peel and cut into 1-inch cubes. Place in a large bowl of cold water mixed with the remaining 1 tablespoon salt to remove the bitterness. After 30 minutes, drain well. Add to the stew when the meat is tender. Cook until the eggplant is very soft, about 20 minutes.

5. Also while the meat is cooking, peel the potatoes, cut into 1-inch-thick rounds, and then cut into quarters. Cook in salted boiling water until tender. Add to the finished stew and simmer for 5 minutes to allow the potatoes to absorb some of the flavor. Taste for salt and black pepper and serve.

TO SERVE **Serve with rice and *Patacones* (page 120).**

Seco de Cabrito a la Chiclayana

BRAISED BABY GOAT STEW CHICLAYO STYLE *Serves 4 to 6*

Seco means dry, and in the case of these stews, it denotes that the sauce is not soupy but rather thick. Chiclayo, a city located on the northwest coast of Peru, is famous not only for *arroz con pato* (rice with duck) and many Peruvian sweets but also for its *secos*. Peruvians enjoy their *secos* very *picante* (spicy). *Secos* also are quite popular in Ecuador and are made with a variety of meats, chicken, and fish. In Ecuador, *seco de chivo* is now made only with lamb, but somehow it has kept the name from a time when goat (*chivo*) was more readily available. It has a tomato-based sauce. Like its Peruvian counterpart, it can be made with either *chicha de* jora or beer. In Ecuador, it is often made with the juice of the *naranjilla,* a fruit indigenous only to Ecuador and Colombia, but this is not necessary to have an authentic (and delicious) *seco.* You can find *chicha* in some South American markets.

6 pounds leg of baby goat, bone in, cut into 2-inch pieces (ask your butcher to do this)

Juice of 2 lemons

1 to 3 tablespoons dried pepper puree, store-bought or homemade (page 332), or ½ to 1 teaspoon red pepper flakes, to your taste

2 cups packed fresh cilantro tops

1 teaspoon salt

½ teaspoon freshly ground black pepper

1 teaspoon ground cumin

6 cloves garlic, chopped

3 tablespoons canola oil

2 medium-size onions, finely chopped (about 2 cups)

1 cup light beer or *chicha de jora*

Beef broth, if needed

Boiled potatoes or yuca (page 410), cut into wedges and fried

Cooked white rice (page 322)

1. Trim the fat and membranes from the goat. Thoroughly rub with the lemon juice to remove any gamy taste. Rinse well, drain, and dry with paper towels.

2. In a blender or food processor, process the hot pepper puree, cilantro, salt, black pepper, cumin, and garlic until smooth. Blend with the beer. Rub the meat with the puree, cover with plastic wrap, and refrigerate for a couple of hours.

3. Heat the oil in a large, heavy casserole over medium heat. Add the onions and cook, stirring occasionally, until golden, about 7 minutes. Add the meat with its marinade and cook, stirring constantly, until all the pieces are coated with the onions and the flavors of the spices have developed, 2 to 3 minutes. Cover and simmer, stirring occasionally, for 3 to 4 hours. If it gets too dry, add beef broth as needed. The meat should be very soft, and the sauce should cover the meat.

4. Serve with potatoes or yuca and white rice.

TO SERVE **Sometimes peas or beans are also served with the rice.**

Varias Carnes
VARIETY MEATS

SOUTH AMERICANS ENJOY A WIDE range of what are commonly called variety meats. Most variety meats are classified under the headings *interiores* and *exteriores* (interior and exterior organs). Interior organs are those found inside the animals, such as intestines, tripe (stomach lining), liver, kidneys, heart, sweetbreads (thymus gland and pancreas), and brains. Exterior organs are those that can be see on the outside of the animals, such as tongue, udder, testicles, and feet. The numerous ways these meats are prepared attest to their popularity. Most of these organs have strong flavors and textures that do not always appeal to everyone. Because animals were not a very important part of the Indians' diets, most of these foods can be traced back to Europe. The Indians did have llamas, however, and were fond of cooking the llama hearts on skewers. (This favored treat has its modern counterpart in *Anticuchos,* page 125, a popular appetizer and street food. The one change over the centuries is that today the heart being skewered is beef heart.)

Reuniones Festivas Festive Gatherings

As in most of the rest of the world, festivals in South America involve family, friends, and food. However, when speaking of festival foods in South America, it is nearly impossible to categorize them precisely by ingredients, largely because people in a family, neighborhood, or village contribute everything they have to the party preparations. Peru's *pachamanca* (cookout) can involve pork, goat, chicken, duck, corn, potatoes, and much more. The classic *feijoada* (bean stew) of Brazil combines beef, pork, sausages, tongue, and beans. The great *asados* and *parrilladas* (barbecues) of the continent's southern countries can include just about any part of the animal, including the innards, as well as a variety of sausages. It is because these feasts are so varied—and because they often feature those items classified as variety meats—that they are included in this section.

In Peru, the *pachamanca* is a traditional feast. It usually takes place once a year, on May 3, during the feast of Santa Cruz. It is an elaborate affair that requires the cooperation of family and friends, as it must be organized according to rules that have been observed throughout the centuries. Men and women each have a task to perform. It is up to the men to find a place in the countryside where there is an abundance of stones, large and small, preferably close to a river. They dig a hole about 10 inches deep by 30 inches in diameter. Then they build what they call a *pirca* (pyramid), with the larger stones at the base and a door. The pyramid should not be taller than 25 inches. Inside, they build a fire with logs to heat the stones until they are almost red. The logs are then removed, and foods prepared by the women are put inside. The most common meat used for a *pachamanca* is a young pig or baby goat, sometimes stuffed like a turkey. Chickens, *cuyes* (guinea pigs), ducks, *humitas* (tamales), sweet potatoes, fava beans, corn on the cob, cheese, and even whole cabbages, all well seasoned, are brought to the stone oven. The meats are wired so that they can be removed easily. Heated stones are placed between the foods, everything is covered with greens or banana leaves and then with large sacks, and the pyramid is covered with sand, forming a small "mountain." A cross with flowers is placed on top. It is the Santa Cruz (Holy Cross), which will bless all the food, so that it comes out perfect. The food is served with freshly made *ají* (hot pepper salsa) and generous amounts of *chicha de jora*, called *champagne Peruano*. The musicians arrive early to get the people in the spirit of the feast that is to come.

Chanfaina

SAUTÉED KIDNEYS WITH POTATOES *Serves 4*

Chanfaina can be made with just kidneys, as in this recipe, or with the kidneys, liver, and heart of a lamb, baby cow, or pig. This type of specialty, prepared in different ways, is found everywhere in South America. When buying the kidneys, make sure they smell fresh, with only a faint ammonia odor.

- 1 pound veal or lamb kidneys
- Juice of 1 lemon and milk, as needed, or 1 tablespoon vinegar and water as needed
- 2 medium-size all-purpose potatoes, cooked in water to cover until tender, drained, peeled, and cut into ½-inch cubes
- 1 large egg, lightly beaten
- ½ teaspoon salt
- ¼ teaspoon freshly ground black pepper
- ½ teaspoon dried oregano, crumbled
- 2 tablespoons unsalted butter
- 1 tablespoon canola oil
- ½ teaspoon sweet paprika
- 2 tablespoons finely chopped fresh parsley leaves for garnish

1. Remove the thin filament surrounding the kidneys, as well as the button fat on the underside. Cut into ¼-inch-thick slices, place in a medium-size glass bowl, and add the lemon juice and milk to cover. Cover and refrigerate for about 2 hours. Drain well, rinse with hot water, and dry with paper towels. Return to the bowl and refrigerate until ready to use.

2. Add the potatoes, egg, salt, pepper, and oregano to the kidneys and mix. Heat the butter and oil in a large skillet over medium heat. When very hot, stir in the paprika and immediately add the kidney mixture. Cook, without stirring, for a few seconds, until the kidneys begin to set, then start stirring as for scrambled eggs. When the kidneys have stiffened but not hardened, they are done. Serve immediately, sprinkled with the parsley.

TO SERVE **Serve with white rice.**

Cau-Cau

TRIPE LIMA STYLE *Serves 4 to 6*

Tripe is considered a delicacy throughout South America, as it is in many other parts of the world, and every country has many delicious ways of preparing it. Whether it is called *mondongo, callos, guatita,* or *librillo,* tripe is always seasoned with a *sofrito* that starts with garlic and onions and includes bell peppers, tomatoes, and the cook's favorite herbs. This version comes from Lima, Peru, and is flavored with dried *mirasol* peppers and *palillo,* a native herb that turns food yellow. (You can substitute turmeric if *palillo* is unavailable.) With rice on the side, this makes a very satisfying meal.

- 1½ pounds tripe
- Juice of 1 lemon
- 1 clove garlic, peeled
- 1 bay leaf
- 2 sprigs fresh mint

SOFRITO
- ¼ cup olive oil
- 2 medium-size onions, minced (about 2 cups)
- 1 to 2 tablespoons *mirasol* pepper puree, store-bought or homemade (page 332), to your taste; or ½ teaspoon red pepper flakes
- 2 large cloves garlic, mashed into a paste with 1 teaspoon salt and ¼ teaspoon freshly ground black pepper
- ½ teaspoon ground cumin
- ½ teaspoon ground *palillo* (page 427) or turmeric
- 1 sprig fresh mint
- 1½ pounds boiling potatoes, peeled, cooked in water to cover until tender, drained, and cut into ½-inch cubes

2 tablespoons fresh lemon juice

2 tablespoons minced fresh cilantro leaves

1 cup fresh or frozen peas, cooked in water to cover until tender, drained, and kept warm

1 medium-size firm ripe but firm tomato, cut into thin wedges

1. Rub the tripe with the lemon juice, then rinse with water. Place the tripe, garlic, bay leaf, and mint in a 4-quart saucepan and add water to cover by 1 inch. Bring to a boil over medium heat, skimming off the froth as it rises to the top. Reduce the heat to low, cover, and simmer until the tripe is fork tender, about 1 hour. Transfer to a cutting board and let cool. Reserve 1 cup of the broth. Cut the tripe into strips about 1 inch long and ¼ inch wide and set aside.

2. While the tripe is cooking, make the *sofrito*. Heat the oil in a large skillet or casserole over low heat. Add the onions and *mirasol* pepper puree, cover, and cook, stirring occasionally, until the onions are very soft, about 10 minutes. Do not let brown. Stir in the garlic paste, cumin, *palillo*, and mint and cook, stirring frequently, for a couple of minutes. Add the tripe and potatoes, mix well, and cook, uncovered, until most of the liquid has disappeared, about 5 minutes. The characteristic of this dish is that it does not have a sauce; it is just moist. Remove the mint. Toss the tripe with the lemon juice and cilantro and season with salt and black pepper to taste.

3. To serve, transfer to a heated serving platter, scatter the peas on top or around the edges, and decorate with the tomato wedges.

Librillo en Salsa de Maní

TRIPE IN PEANUT SAUCE *Serves 4 to 6*

Dishes with peanut sauce are specialties of the highlands of some of the Andean countries. This is a very tasty way to prepare tripe. Try to get the honeycomb type, which is the best, but the plain is also good.

1½ pounds tripe

2 tablespoons canola oil

1 teaspoon ground annatto or sweet paprika

2 medium-size onions, finely chopped (about 2 cups)

4 cloves garlic, minced

1 cup seeded and chopped green bell pepper

1 medium-size ripe but firm tomato (5 to 6 ounces), peeled and chopped

½ teaspoon ground cumin

1 teaspoon salt

½ teaspoon freshly ground black pepper

2 tablespoons finely chopped fresh parsley leaves, plus more for garnish

2 tablespoons finely chopped fresh cilantro leaves

½ cup fresh or frozen peas, cooked in water to cover until tender and drained

1 large carrot, diced (¼ inch), cooked in water to cover until tender, and drained

3 tablespoons natural peanut butter or unsalted dry-roasted peanuts pureed with ½ cup milk

2 hard-cooked eggs, peeled and each cut into 8 wedges, for garnish

1. Wash the tripe thoroughly. Place in a 4-quart saucepan and add water to cover by 1 inch. Bring to a boil over medium heat, skimming off the froth as it rises to the top. Reduce the heat to low, cover, and simmer until the tripe is fork tender, about 1 hour. Drain, rinse, and cut into strips about 1 inch long and ½ inch wide. Set aside.

2. Heat the oil in a large casserole over medium heat. Stir in the annatto and onions and cook, stirring occasionally, until softened, about 5 minutes. Add the garlic, bell pepper, tomato, cumin, salt, and pepper, cover, and cook over low heat until the tomato has formed a sauce, about 10

minutes. Add the tripe, parsley, cilantro, peas, carrot, and peanut butter mixture and cook, stirring, until smooth. Simmer for 5 minutes to blend the flavors.

3. Serve hot, garnished with the eggs and parsley.

Lengua de Ternera con Porotitos y Espinaca

VEAL TONGUE WITH BEANS AND SPINACH *Serves 3 to 4*

Tongue has to be one of the most popular specialties throughout South America. It is prepared with many different sauces, all of which are delicious. It can be simply braised in a tomato-onion, peanut, olive, or wine sauce, to mention just a few. This version reminds me of the Italian heritage of South America. I have had a similar sauce in Italian restaurants in the United States, served with fish such as salmon or tuna.

- 1 veal tongue (1½ to 2 pounds), cooked (page 407), 1 cup broth reserved
- 2 tablespoons olive oil
- 2 cloves garlic, crushed
- 1 large ripe but firm tomato (about 8 ounces), peeled, seeded, and chopped
- Pinch of red pepper flakes
- One 15-ounce can Great Northern beans, undrained
- Pinch of nutmeg
- Pinch of sugar
- Salt and freshly ground black pepper
- 2 cups packed well-washed and coarsely chopped spinach leaves

1. Peel and trim the tongue as instructed on page 407. Cut into ¼-inch-thick slices and set aside.

2. Heat the oil in a large, heavy skillet over low heat. Add the garlic and cook for a few seconds, until golden, then discard. Add the tomato and red pepper, cover, and simmer until softened,

about 5 minutes. Stir in the beans and their liquid and ½ cup of the reserved tongue broth. Bring to a boil, reduce the heat to medium, and simmer for 5 minutes. Add the nutmeg, sugar, and salt and black pepper to taste. The recipe can be prepared ahead up to this point. Let cool, cover, and refrigerate. Tongue can refrigerated in its cooking broth for up to 1 day.

3. To serve, reheat the tomato sauce. Add the spinach, cover, and steam for 3 minutes. Do not overcook, or the spinach will lose its bright green color. Reheat the tongue. Divide among 4 heated dinner plates and spoon some of the sauce on top.

TO SERVE **Serve with rice, if desired.**

Lingua com Passas

BEEF TONGUE WITH RAISIN SAUCE *Serves 6*

Tongue with raisin or prune sauce is a popular specialty in South America. I like this Brazilian version because of its simplicity and good taste. Many people are afraid of making caramel, but Latin cooks do it all the time without any problem. They usually caramelize the sugar in a large spoon directly over the flame on the stove (hold it with an oven mitt). An easier way is to caramelize the sugar in the microwave. This sauce is also great on roasted pork tenderloin or chicken breast; just use chicken broth instead of the tongue broth.

- 1 beef tongue (about 3 pounds), cooked (page 407), broth reserved
- 2 tablespoons sugar
- 2 teaspoons water
- 1 tablespoon red wine vinegar
- 1 teaspoon soy sauce or Brown Coloring (page 414)
- 3 tablespoons finely chopped onion
- ½ cup seedless black raisins
- 8 black olives for garnish

1. Cut the cooked tongue diagonally into ¼-inch-thick slices and return to the broth to keep warm.

2. Put the sugar and water in a 2-cup Pyrex measuring cup, microwave on high for 1 minute, stir, and microwave for 1 minute more. When it is ready, it should smell like caramel and be dark brown. (To make the caramel on the stovetop, place the sugar and water in a small skillet and bring a boil, stirring. Cook over low heat until it turns dark brown.) Pour into a 2-quart saucepan and let cool for a couple of minutes. Add the vinegar, soy sauce, onion, raisins, and 1 cup of the tongue broth. Bring to a boil, stirring, and cook until the caramel melts. Simmer for 5 minutes, then remove from the heat and let cool for a few minutes. Transfer to a blender and process until the sauce is still a bit coarse. Return to the saucepan and hold over low heat.

3. To serve, drain the tongue slices well and arrange on a heated serving platter. Drizzle with the hot sauce and garnish with the olives.

TO SERVE **Serve with rice and buttered baby carrots.**

Estofado de Hígado

BRAISED CALF'S LIVER WITH POTATOES *Serves 4*

Estofados (braised meats), made with chicken, fish, and just about any kind of meat, are popular throughout South America. This is a nice way of preparing liver. All that is needed is rice on the side to satisfy South Americans' love for the combination of rice and potatoes.

> **3 tablespoons olive oil**
> **1 pound calf's liver fillets, filaments removed and fillets cut crosswise into 1½-inch pieces**
> **Salt and freshly ground black pepper**
> **All-purpose flour for dredging**

> **1 medium-size onion, halved and thickly sliced into half-moons (about 1 cup)**
> **1 clove garlic, thinly sliced**
> **½ teaspoon dried oregano, crumbled**
> **2 medium-size ripe but firm tomatoes (10 to 12 ounces), peeled and chopped**
> **3 medium-size red potatoes, peeled and cut into wedges**
> **1 cup beef broth, or more if needed**
> **Finely chopped fresh parsley leaves for garnish**

1. Heat the oil in a large skillet over medium heat. Season the fillets with salt and pepper to taste and dredge in the flour, shaking off any excess. Quickly pan-fry, a few at a time, until golden on both sides. Transfer to a tray lined with paper towels.

2. Add the onion and garlic to the skillet and cook, stirring a few times, until softened, about 5 minutes. Add the oregano, tomatoes, potatoes, and beef broth. Cover and cook until the potatoes are tender, about 20 minutes. Add more broth if the mixture is too dry. Add the liver and cook, uncovered, for about 3 minutes. The liver should still be pink in the center, and there should be enough sauce to cover it and the potatoes. Season with salt and pepper to taste and serve sprinkled with the parsley.

Crepas de Sesos y Hongos

CREPES FILLED WITH CALF'S BRAINS AND MUSHROOMS *Makes about 12 crepes; 6 servings*

Calf's brains, like sweetbreads, have a very delicate texture and need special handling to remove the filament that covers them. Brains are especially perishable; they should be cooked within 24 hours of purchase, or at least soaked and blanched within that time period. The most popular way of preparing brains in South America is breaded, as for *milanesas* (breaded cutlets), but a variety of interesting dishes use this elegant ingredient.

In the United States, it is not always easy to find a butcher who carries calf's brains. Some Mexican meat markets have them occasionally. Your best bet may be a Middle Eastern meat market, many of which sell them frozen. Or you can check with your butcher to see if he can order them. In this recipe, I like portobello mushrooms, but you can use any kind.

- 1 pound frozen veal or calf's brains, thawed overnight in the refrigerator
- 1 tablespoon red or white wine vinegar
- 2 tablespoons butter
- 1 tablespoon canola oil
- 4 ounces portobello mushrooms, caps wiped clean with a damp cloth or paper towel and stems coarsely chopped
- ½ cup finely chopped scallions (white part and 1 inch of the green)
- 2 tablespoons finely chopped fresh parsley leaves
- 10 fresh basil leaves, cut into ribbons
- ½ teaspoon salt
- ¼ teaspoon white pepper
- ¾ cup whipping cream
- ¼ cup day-old bread crumbs (page 413)
- 1 recipe *Crepas* (plain or basil; page 405)
- 1 recipe *Salsa Blanca* (page 405), heated
- ½ cup freshly grated Parmesan cheese

1.   Rinse the brains and place in a bowl with water to cover. Add the vinegar. After 1 hour, it should be easy to pull the filaments away from the brains. I have found that frozen brains often require less work than fresh, and some have hardly had any filaments to pull. Blanch the brains in boiling salted water for 10 minutes. Let cool in the liquid, then drain well. Cut into ½-inch-thick slices, then dice.

2.   In a large skillet, heat the butter and oil together over medium heat. Add the mushrooms

and cook, stirring, until tender. Stir in the scallions, parsley, basil, salt, and pepper. Add ¼ cup of the whipping cream and cook until reduced to a creamy sauce. Stir in the brains and bread crumbs and taste for salt and pepper. Remove from the heat and set aside.

3.   To assemble, place 2 heaping tablespoons of the filling in the center of each crepe and roll tightly into a cylinder, tucking the ends under, if desired. Arrange in a single layer in 1 or 2 buttered shallow baking dishes, making sure they are not crowded. The crepes can be made a few hours ahead up to this point, then covered and refrigerated.

4.   Preheat the oven to 375°F.

5.   Bring the crepes to room temperature, if necessary. Cover with the *salsa blanca*, sprinkle with the Parmesan, and drizzle the remaining ½ cup cream on top of the crepes and around the sides of the pan. Bake until bubbling, about 20 minutes. Serve hot.

Asado de Achuras
GRILLED INNARDS

THE INDISPENSABLE PART OF A *parrillada*, besides the steaks, is the *achuras*. *Achura* comes from the Araucanian word *achuraj*, meaning "throw away," because the *gauchos* and Indians used to discard all the innards and use only the meat. Generally, the *achuras* include the sweetbreads, udder, kidneys, heart, and intestines.

Asado de Mollejas
GRILLED SWEETBREADS

Sweetbreads are the star of a *parrillada* in any Latin American country. People are always waiting by the grill to snatch them up as soon as they are ready; you can never have enough of them. Argentines usually grill the whole sweetbreads, without any precooking and without removing the outer membrane. Argentine sweetbreads are larger and thicker than the American variety, so after grilling, the whole sweetbreads are cut into ½-inch-thick slices and thrown back on the grill for a few minutes to finish cooking.

Sweetbreads are highly perishable and should be cooked the same day they are bought. To prepare them, wash thoroughly and place in a bowl of cold water. Soak for a couple of hours in the refrigerator, changing the water at least twice. Carefully pull off as much filament as can be easily removed, being careful to leave the sweetbreads whole. Soak again in the refrigerator for 1 hour in water mixed with 1 tablespoon vinegar. Drain and soak in plain water for 1 hour more. Drain and pull off any remaining filament that can be removed easily. Now they are ready to cook.

For grilling, just put sweetbreads on the grill where the fire is not too hot. Grill both sides until golden brown, basting with *Adobo de Salmuera* (page 243), or just season with salt and pepper to taste after removing them from the grill.

Asado de Ubre
GRILLED UDDER

This is considered a delicacy throughout South America, especially if it comes from a young animal, because it is more tender. To grill, cut into small steaks measuring about 2 by 4 inches. Grill over a hot fire without any seasonings, turning frequently to avoid browning. After each side has see the fire once, begin basting with *Adobo de Salmuera* (page 243). When done, the udder be lightly colored, feel firm to the touch, and be juicy and tender when cut. If overdone, it will be dry

and tough. (It takes only a few seconds to overcook udder.) Season with salt and pepper to taste before serving.

Asado de Riñones
GRILLED VEAL KIDNEYS

Peel off the fat and filaments, trying to keep the kidneys in one piece. Cut into ½-inch-thick slices. Although washing or marinating is not generally recommended for kidneys, because they absorb too much water, Argentines marinate the slices in red wine or red or white wine vinegar, with a little salt added, for 15 minutes before cooking. Drain, place over a hot fire, and turn often, so they don't get too hard. When done, they should be browned on the outside and juicy on the inside. Season with salt and pepper and serve with *Chimichurri* (page 337) or a mustard sauce.

Asado de Chorizos y Morcillas
GRILLED CHORIZOS AND BLOOD SAUSAGES

All *asados* begin with *chorizos* and *morcillas*. An Argentine secret to prevent bursting of the casing is to soak the sausages in water for a couple of hours, then pierce the casing with a fork before putting the sausages on the grill. Cook over a medium fire, turning them as they brown.

Tripa Mishqui (Chinchulín)
GRILLED SMALL INTESTINE Serves 3 to 4

The small intestine of pork, lamb, and veal is much appreciated throughout South America and is an indispensable part of a *parrillada*. In Ecuador, this dish is called *tripa mishqui*, which is part Spanish and part Quechua. The Spanish *tripa* in Quechua is

Asados o Parrilladas BARBECUES

Asados and parrilladas are extremely popular in the southern countries of South America, especially in Chile, Argentina, Uruguay, and southern Brazil. *Asados* date back to a time when cattle roamed the *pampas* freely and the nomadic herdsmen, called *gauchos*, prepared their meat out in the open. Large cuts of beef were impaled on long iron skewers with crosspieces to keep the meat flat. These skewers were thrust firmly into the ground, angled toward a wood fire. The only seasoning was from brining beforehand. Sometimes, especially in the countryside, the meat was cooked with the skin still on, and it was usually served cold. Prepared this way, the meat lasted longer than when it was cooked without the skin. This original method of cooking is now reserved for special occasions and has been replaced by backyard barbecue grills, or *parrillas*.

The classic Argentine and Uruguayan *parrillada* was carefully planned to provide maximum enjoyment for the participants, and the process developed in these countries became the unofficial protocol for most of South America. (Of course, because of the pressures of modern life, *parrilladas* are not often as elaborate as they used to be.) The classic *parrillada* begins with empanadas and grilled chorizos and *morcillas* (blood sausages), accompanied by a glass of wine. The idea is to whet the appetite for things to come. *Achuras* (innards) are a popular second course and usually include sweetbreads, kidneys, udder, heart, and lower intestines (*chinchulines*). Meats are the main course, and a generous one pound of meat per person is normally allotted. Short ribs, rump or chuck steak, and flank steak are popular choices. The classic way to prepare *bifes* and *churrascos* (steaks) is to grill them without seasoning, although not everybody adheres to this practice. Salt and pepper, or other desired seasonings, are added once the meat is cooked and removed from the grill, because this keeps the meat juicy. To keep the steaks even moister, they can be basted with brine on the side that has already been cooked. Tougher cuts of meat, such as chuck, are usually marinated overnight to tenderize them.

chunchulli and *mishqui* is the Quechua word for sweet, meaning the flavor of the small intestine is delicate and sweet. Colombians, Argentines, and Uruguayans call it *chinchuli*, Venezuelans *chinculla*, and Chileans *chinchule*. Ecuadorians use mostly the small intestine from either pigs or lambs, whereas Argentines, Chileans, and Colombians more often use the small intestine from calves. The part most appreciated is the thinner part of the beginning of the intestine. *Tripa* is highly perishable and should be prepared the day it is bought.

In Ecuador, *tripa mishqui* is considered a great remedy for stomach problems, thanks to an enzyme found inside the small intestine. After cooking, this enzyme becomes a tasty, creamy substance. *Tripa mishqui* is the specialty of some street vendors, who grill it on small braziers. Most restaurants in Buenos Aires, Argentina, offer it as part of their regular menus. Colombians prepare *chinchulín* as an appetizer. First, it is seasoned and boiled for 30 minutes. Then it is cut into bite-size pieces, fried until golden, and served with plantain chips or *humitas*. Chileans

Plenty of salads and bread are a must, as are *salsa criolla* and *chimichurri*. Wine, beer, or *maté*—or all three—is always on hand to help everyone get into the spirit of the festivities. The finale normally consists of fresh fruit, fruit salads, or fruit compotes. As much a part of the festivities as the food are the music and dancing—things that no true Latin could do without.

The Brazilian cookout is called *churrasco à gaúcha*, and there are two ways of preparing it, depending on the region. The *churrasco à Rio Grande* (from Rio Grande do Sul) is similar to the Argentine *asado*. After the meat starts to cook, it is basted with a brine made with hot water and salt, and sometimes crushed garlic. It is served with *farofa* (page 304) and *Molho de Pimenta e Limão* (page 335). The custom is to dip the meat into a bowl of *farofa*, then sprinkle it with the *molho*.

The *churrasco Paulista* (from São Paulo) is marinated overnight in a mixture of lemon juice, salt, and pepper. It is served with a sauce made with lemon juice, hot peppers, minced onion, and parsley. Banana *farofa* is the usual accompaniment.

Adobo de Salmuera BRINE MARINADE *Makes about 2 cups*

2 cups lukewarm water
2 tablespoons kosher salt
½ teaspoon freshly ground black pepper
Juice of 1 lemon

Mix all the ingredients together in a medium-size bowl. Marinate tough cuts of meat in the brine overnight, or use to baste less tough cuts as they are grilled.

---

serve *chinchule* grilled or pan-fried, with boiled potatoes and *Pebre de Cilantro* (page 336) on the side.

1 pound *tripa* (small intestine)
4 cloves garlic, peeled
1 teaspoon ground cumin
1 cup packed fresh cilantro leaves
1 tablespoon *Manteca de Color* (page 331)
1 teaspoon salt
½ teaspoon freshly ground black pepper
¼ cup water

1. Remove the membranes from the outside of the intestine. The easiest way to clean the inside is to attach the intestine to a faucet and run water through for a few minutes until the water runs clear. Cut the intestine into 4-inch pieces and place in a glass bowl.

2. Place all the remaining ingredients in a food processor and process until smooth. Mix with the intestine pieces until well coated, cover with

plastic wrap, and let marinate in the refrigerator for a few hours.

3. Preheat the oven to 400°F.

4. Using a slotted spoon, transfer the intestine to a baking dish. Reserve the marinade. Bake until cooked through, about 30 minutes. The intestine will shrink a lot by the time it is done.

5. Remove from the oven and grill over a hot fire, basting with the marinade, until golden brown on all sides. Serve immediately; intestines get tough as they cool.

Especialidades con Varias Carnes
SPECIALTIES WITH VARIOUS MEATS

 SOME SOUTH AMERICAN SPECIALTIES COMBINE a variety of meats. Following are just a few of the most popular.

Feijoada Completa

BLACK BEANS WITH SMOKED AND FRESH MEATS *Serves 10 to 12*

When talking about Brazilian food, the first specialty that comes to mind is *feijoada completa*, hailed as the national dish of Brazil. Its origin is obscure. Some believe it was created in Rio de Janeiro, then spread to the rest of the country. Others believe it was created by the slaves who worked in the Big Houses of the plantations; they prepared a bean stew seasoned with the odds and ends of meat given to them by their masters, such as the ears, tails, and feet of pigs. Or it could be of Portuguese origin. When I was in Portugal, I had the opportunity to taste the Portuguese *feijoada*, which has been made there for hundreds of years and uses all the parts of a pig, plus blood sausage. The Portuguese *feijoada* has white beans and never includes beef jerky, which is essential to the Brazilian *feijoada*.

In the major cities of Brazil, *feijoada* has become a specialty to be enjoyed on Saturday. The reason for this is that *feijoada* is such a heavy dish, it should be eaten for lunch, after which people can go to the beach to sleep it off. *Feijoada* is considered a ceremonial dish, requiring long and careful preparation of the beans and meat, and a certain protocol has to be observed in its presentation. The smoked meats are usually cooked separately in Brazil, but in the United States, the meats come precooked, and all they need is 30 minutes cooking with the beans to blend the flavors. *Feijoada* can be served simply but is traditionally assembled on platters and in bowls, for an impressive presentation at the table or on a buffet or sideboard. This is a party dish that serves anywhere from 10 to 12 people. It is even more festive (and more authentic) when accompanied by *cachaça*-based drinks, such as *caipirinhas* or *batidas*, Brazilian beer, and wonderful music.

There are many variations of *feijoada* in Brazil, depending on the region and the cook. The following recipe comes from the files of Luisa Nogueira, whose family came from Ceará, in northeastern Brazil. Like most South American ladies, she loved to have a houseful of family and friends; her reward was seeing how much her guests enjoyed her food. Saturday *feijoadas* at her home in Rio were always very joyful.

2 pounds dried black beans

1 pound Brazilian dried beef (jerky), wax removed

1 pound beef sirloin roast

1 pound smoked pork loin (preferably boneless)

1 pound lean slab bacon, fresh or smoked

1 pound smoked pork ribs

1 pound linguiça, chorizo, or other smoked sausage

1 pound fresh linguiça

1 small smoked beef tongue (about 1 pound)

2 tablespoons canola oil

2 medium-size onions, finely chopped (about 2 cups)

4 cloves garlic, minced

¼ cup minced fresh parsley leaves

¼ cup minced fresh cilantro leaves

1 bay leaf

Salt

1 teaspoon freshly ground black pepper

1 teaspoon ground cumin

½ teaspoon red pepper flakes

Molho de Pimenta e Limão (page 335) or other hot pepper sauce

SIDE DISHES

Couve à Mineira (page 292)

4 seedless oranges, peeled and sliced ¼ inch thick

Arroz Brazileiro (page 323)

Farofa de Ouro (page 304)

1.   Pick over and rinse the beans well. Place in a large mixing bowl and soak in water to cover by 4 inches overnight. In another large bowl, soak the dried beef in water to cover overnight in the refrigerator, changing the water 2 or 3 times. (After soaking, I usually blanch the meat in boiling water for a few seconds, just to make sure all the wax is removed.)

2.   Drain the beans and place in an 8-quart soup pot. Add cold water to cover by 2 inches and bring slowly to a boil over medium heat. Drain the dried beef and add it to the beans along with the sirloin. Partially cover and cook over low heat, skimming off the froth that rises to the surface. Simmer until the beans are cooked but still firm, about 2 hours, depending on the age of the beans.

3.   Transfer half of the beans and cooking liquid to another large pot. Divide the rest of the meats between the 2 pots and simmer for 30 minutes, making sure there is enough liquid to cover the beans by 2 inches. When adding water to the beans, use only boiling water; cold water will discolor them.

4.   Meanwhile, heat the oil in a large skillet over medium heat. Add the onions, garlic, parsley, cilantro, and bay leaf and cook, stirring a few times, until the onions are softened, about 5 minutes. Season with salt to taste, the black pepper, cumin, and red pepper flakes. Add 2 ladles of the cooked beans and mash with a wooden spoon. Remove ½ cup of this mixture and return everything else to the bean pot. Cook, stirring occasionally, for 30 minutes.

Feijoada can be prepared up to this point the day before; refrigerate the beans and meats separately. To serve, bring the beans to room temperature and reheat over low heat. Place the meats in a large baking pan, cover with aluminum foil, and reheat in a preheated 350°F for 20 minutes.

5.   To make a sauce, add enough bean liquid to the ½ cup reserved bean mixture so that it has the consistency of whipping cream. Add the *molho* to taste.

6.   To serve, remove the meats from the bean pot (or baking pan) and slice ⅛ inch thick. Arrange on a heated platter, with the tongue in the center, the smoked meats at one end, and the fresh meats at the other end. Moisten with a little of the bean liquid. Place in the center of the table or serving area. On another platter, arrange the *couve* (kale) in the center and surround with the orange slices. Serve the beans, which should be very soupy, in a soup tureen. Put the *arroz* (rice)

in a large serving bowl and the *farofa* in a medium-size serving bowl. Serve the sauce in a sauceboat or small bowl.

Pastel de Fideos con Carne y Jamón

PASTA TORTE WITH BEEF AND HAM *Serves 4 to 6*

This type of dish is particularly popular in the southern countries of South America, where many Spanish and Italian immigrants settled. The combination of beef and ham also appears in the fillings of many other specialties; it is delightfully tasty.

2 tablespoons olive oil

1 medium-size onion, finely chopped (about 1 cup)

½ cup seeded and finely chopped red bell pepper

8 ounces lean ground beef

4 ounces thickly sliced imported boiled ham, minced

½ teaspoon salt

¼ teaspoon freshly ground black pepper

2 cups small broccoli florets, blanched in boiling water for 30 seconds and drained

One 9-ounce package linguine

1 recipe *Salsa Blanca* (page 405)

½ cup milk

½ cup freshly grated Parmesan cheese

¾ cup whipping cream

1. Heat the oil in a large skillet over medium heat. Add the onion and bell pepper and cook, stirring a few times, until softened, about 5 minutes. Add the ground beef and ham and cook, stirring frequently, until the beef loses its pink color. Add the salt, black pepper, and broccoli and mix well.

2. Cook the linguine in a large pot of boiling salted water. Check the timing, because you will want it to be *al dente*. Drain, rinse under cold running water, and mix with the meat mixture.

3. Preheat the oven to 350°F. Generously butter a shallow 2-quart baking dish.

4. Heat the *salsa blanca* over low heat. Add the milk and ¼ cup of the Parmesan and stir until the cheese melts. Pour over the pasta and meat mixture and combine well. Transfer to the prepared dish and drizzle with the cream, especially around the edges. Sprinkle the remaining ¼ cup Parmesan evenly over the top. Bake until heated through, about 20 minutes. Serve at once.

TO SERVE **Serve with garlic bread and a green salad.**

Achogchas/Caiguas Rellenas con Carne y Jamón

ACHOGCHAS/CAIGUAS STUFFED WITH BEEF AND HAM *Serves 3 to 4*

Achogcha, also spelled *achoccha* in Ecuador, goes by the name *caigua* in Peru and *achojcha* in Bolivia. This member of the squash family is widely used in these three Andean countries. It looks like a poblano pepper, has a mild flavor, and is available frozen in some South American groceries. A variety of dishes are made with this vegetable, but the most popular is stuffed with different kinds of meat, rice, and vegetables. In Ecuador, the favorite way to serve it is as a first course, filled with a mixture of meat, rice, and peas and topped with white sauce. *Achogchas* also are used in soups and stews. There is no substitute, but because the fillings are very tasty and the *achogchas* (sold frozen as *caiguas*) are not always available, I decided to find a suitable substitute. Cubanelle peppers seem to be the ideal choice for this type of dish because they are sweet and mild and their shape is similar to that of the *achogcha*. Look for the widest peppers, so it is easier to remove the seeds and to stuff them.

1 package frozen *caiguas*, thawed, or 6
  Cubanelle peppers

1 tablespoon canola oil

1 medium-size onion, finely chopped (about
  1 cup)

1 large ripe but firm tomato (about 8
  ounces), peeled and chopped

1 clove garlic, minced

½ teaspoon dried oregano

½ teaspoon ground cumin

½ teaspoon salt

½ teaspoon freshly ground black pepper

4 ounces lean ground beef

4 ounces imported boiled ham, ground into
  a paste in a food processor

½ cup frozen peas

½ cup day-old bread crumbs (page 413)
  soaked in ½ cup water for 30 minutes

1 large egg, lightly beaten

2 tablespoons seedless black raisins
  (optional)

1 cup beef broth

Cornstarch mixed with cold water
  (optional), for thickening

1. Wash the *caiguas* well and cut a slice off the stem end. Using a teaspoon, carefully remove the heart with the seeds. Cook in a large pot of boiling salted water until softened, about 15 minutes. (If using peppers, cook for about 5 minutes.) Drain, rinse under cold running water, and set aside.

2. Heat the oil in a medium-size skillet over medium heat. Add the onion and cook, stirring a few times, until softened, about 5 minutes. Add the tomato, garlic, oregano, cumin, salt, and black pepper and cook until the tomato has formed a sauce, about 10 minutes. Stir in the ground beef, ham, and peas and continue to cook until the mixture has absorbed all the juices, about 5 minutes. Taste for salt and black pepper, remove from the heat, and let cool.

3. Squeeze the bread crumbs and add to the meat mixture along with the egg and raisins (if using); mix well. Stuff the *caiguas* with this mixture and place in a single layer in a greased baking pan.

4. To the remaining meat mixture, add the beef broth and bring to a boil. If desired, thicken the sauce with the cornstarch mixture to taste. Pour the sauce over the *caiguas* and cover the pan with aluminum foil. The dish can be made up to this point, allowed to cool, and then refrigerated for up to 1 day. Bring to room temperature before baking.

5. Preheat the oven to 350°F.

6. Bake the *caiguas* until heated through, about 20 minutes. Serve hot.

TO SERVE **The usual way to serve this dish is with white rice. I prefer to serve it with mashed potatoes.**

Pescados y Mariscos

FISH AND SHELLFISH

S OUTH AMERICA HAS BEEN BLESSED with many waters. It is flanked by two oceans, the Atlantic and Pacific, and is crossed, almost from coast to coast, by the mighty Amazon River. In addition, there are several other river systems and many small lakes. All of this water provides a tremendous variety of fish. The Amazon River alone, with approximately 1,000 tributaries (17 of which are about 1,000 miles long), is believed to be home to 1,800 species of fish. The Atlantic Ocean offers a variety of fish and shellfish, some of which are unusual species indigenous only to this part of the world. There is an abundance of sea bass, flounder, grouper, snapper, swordfish, croakers, sardinellas, lobsters, crabs, shark, swordfish, marlin, and shrimp, just to name a few of the more common, and more familiar, varieties.

Thanks to the cold Humboldt Current, the Pacific coast of South America is the world's richest fishing ground for tuna, *corvina*, shark, swordfish, anchovies, cod, sea bass, grouper, *robalo* (snook), salmon, and gray mullet, as well as some unusual species, such as the Chilean *congrio*, giant abalones called *locos*, sea urchins called *erizos*, and more. Fishermen from the seaport of Iquique, Chile, boast of having caught the largest albacore tuna ever—a monster weighing about 1,180 pounds. In the Región de los Lagos (Lake District) of Chile, the fishing industry is very important. There are many factories that process and can a variety of fish and shellfish, including tuna, *congrio*, mackerel, lobsters, clams, mussels, and eels. Chile also has La Playa de las Machas (the beach of the mussels) in Arica, where thousands of tourists come every year to eat steamed mussels by the bucketful. The demand for fish and shellfish has escalated to the point where it is increasingly raised commercially in special ponds. This commercial aquaculture is now producing shrimp in Ecuador and salmon in Chile, both of which are largely exported to the United States.

Ecuador and Peru enjoy the riches of the Pacific Ocean and many rivers, which provide an abundance of *truchas* (trout) and other species of fish. Ecuador is one of the main harvesters of shrimp, tuna, and *corvina*. I especially like the freshwater fish (by which I mean saltwater fish that are actually born in the rivers and caught when young), such as snook, tilapia, catfish, and mullet, some of which are unfortunately disappearing in this area. Peru's coast is rich in sea lions, abalone, shark, mullet, and all kinds of mollusks. The Atlantic coast of Venezuela is teeming with *pargo* (red snapper), *sábalo* (shad), snook, and more. Historically, anchovies have been the major catch in this region. Now shellfish, marlin, and tuna also are plentiful. Alligators and turtles are common in the many streams. The fish are prepared in many interesting ways that reflect the strong Spanish and African influences in the coastal cuisine.

The coast of Argentina and the Río de la Plata are rich with barracuda, *dorado* (dolphin), and *palometa*. In Tierra del Fuego, there is plenty of Atlantic salmon, and the rivers are teeming with trout. This area is also home to giant crabs, which unfortunately are becoming rare.

The fishing grounds off the coast of Uruguay are said to be the richest in the world and haven't yet been exploited. *Corvina*, skate, and shark are some of the fish caught here. The Uruguay River also provides a variety of fish, such as dolphin and catfish.

The east coast of Brazil is bounded by the Atlantic Ocean and offers croakers, shrimp, lobsters, sardinellas, cod, red snapper, and many other types of fish. Northern Brazil is the site of the justly famous Amazon rain forest and Amazon River. It encompasses the largest river basin in the world. The basin's rivers are rich in fish such as piranha, dolphin, *surubí* or *surubim* (a large catfish abundant in big rivers throughout Brazil, Paraguay, and Bolivia), *tucurané*, *pintado*, and electric eel. Some of the species of fish have yet to be identified. The preparation of fish in this area reflects Indian, Portuguese, and African influences. Fish and shellfish are also dried and used along with fresh fish. Seafood is seasoned with *refogado* (an onion sauce also called *sofrito*), peanuts, coconut milk, *dendê*, and *malagueta* peppers. In southern Brazil, wine and *refogado* made with olive oil prevail as flavorings for fish.

Venezuela has the Orinoco River, which, along with its tributaries, drains most of the country. The Orinoco system contains a great variety of fish, including dolphin and catfish (which can reach up to 300 pounds), as well as crocodiles and manatees.

Colombia is the only country in South America that has access to both the Pacific and Atlantic Oceans, which are rich in such locally popular fish as red snapper, snook, trout, and shad. In the rivers, there is an abundance of iguanas and turtles, which are prepared in many ways. The iguana is used mainly in *guisos* (stews) made with generous amounts of *sofrito* and potatoes. With turtles, Colombians make *pinchos* (small shish kebabs), *picadillo* (seasoned minced turtle), and the classic *sarapaté de charapa* (innards of turtle with plantain). Sweets are made with turtle eggs and *panela*. In addition, *cachama* (a river fish) is popular. Anaconda (a river snake) is much appreciated, especially the tenderloin, and is usually smoked and prepared in many different dishes in the *llanos* of Venezuela and Colombia.

Every country in South America enjoys an abundance of freshwater fish, especially trout. Even landlocked countries such as Bolivia and Paraguay have a variety of fish because of the many streams that flow into the Amazon River, as well as other river systems and the lakes, all of which offer a wealth of fish, large and small.

In pre-Hispanic times, fish was a major source of protein for the natives, who called it "meat of the water." The Indians were adept at preserving fish and shellfish by salting or sun-drying them. In fact, dried fish was a mainstay of the Inca army.

The Indians cooked fresh fish on an open fire or wrapped it in leaves and roasted it over hot coals. The Mapuches prepared the *curanto* (a clambake-like feast), which is a Mapuche word meaning "stony ground." The most primitive way of preparing a *curanto* consisted of digging a pit in the ground, which was then lined with hot rocks and layered with the fruits of the sea and a few potatoes. *Nalca* or *panqué* leaves (similar to banana leaves) were put on top, then covered with dirt. After the Spaniards came, new foods, such as sausages, chicken, and pork were added. Modern *curantos* are usually quite elaborate and include layers of lobsters, crabs, mussels, clams, *cholgas* (large mussels), *picorocos* (large, rough-shelled barnacles), sausages, and *milcaos* or *chapaleles* (potato patties), which are covered with leaves and then with cloth and dirt. The classic postcolonial *curanto* also calls for a whole suckling pig. The modern *curanto*, called *pulmay*, is prepared in big pots or steamers. Layers of shellfish, *chapeleles*, and meats are placed on a bed of *sofrito* and steamed until done. These foods are then served on separate platters, and the resulting broth, which connoisseurs think is the best part, is served in cups.

The Aymara Indians, who live around Lake Titicaca, sit around bonfires, as their ancestors did hundreds of years ago, and cook freshly caught *bogas* (small fish) with fresh and dried potatoes, serving it all topped with lots of *ají* (hot pepper salsa). They also dry these small fish and mix them with toasted dried corn to make *charqui de bogas*, which they take with them on long journeys.

Most South American fish dishes are of Spanish or Portuguese origin. Adapted also to use the continent's bounty, such as tomatoes, peppers, potatoes, and yuca, they constitute a unique creole fish cuisine.

Pescado a la Chorrillana al Estilo Chino

FILLETS OF FISH CHINESE STYLE *Serves 4*

In 1850, Chinese workers started arriving in Peru. Within 30 years, more than 100,000 Chinese were brought over to work mainly on the plantations. Some were put to work on the railroads and in the guano pits, which were excavated to provide fertilizer. Eventually, the Chinese workers achieved economic independence and many opened restaurants. The style of cooking that developed, called *cocina Chifa* (Chinese cuisine), became an integral part of South American cuisine. *Cocina Chifa* is very much like the Chinese cuisine in the regions from which the workers came, with variations due to differences in ingredients. Today, in many South American cities, some restaurants, called simply Chifa, specialize in this South American–Chinese cuisine.

This recipe is a very interesting rendition of the classic *Chorrillana* sauce, which originated in the coastal village of Chorrillos, a suburb of Lima, Peru. Usually served on top of sautéed fillets of beef, *Chorrillana* is normally made with onions, peppers (sweet and hot), tomatoes, and *salsa de tamarindo*—a mixture of soy sauce, vinegar, and sugar (it has nothing to do with the fruit called tamarind). This salsa is an indication of Asia's contribution to a very traditional South American dish.

¼ cup canola oil

Four 6-ounce firm, white-fleshed fish fillets (such as cod)

Salt and freshly ground black pepper

All-purpose flour for dredging

1 medium-size onion, halved and sliced into half-moons (about 1 cup)

1 small green bell pepper, seeded and thinly sliced

1 to 2 jalapeños, to your taste, halved lengthwise, seeded, and thinly sliced crosswise

2 cloves garlic, mashed

1 teaspoon peeled and minced fresh ginger

2 medium-size ripe but firm tomatoes (10 to 12 ounces), peeled and chopped

2 tablespoons ketchup

2 tablespoons white wine vinegar

1 tablespoon soy sauce

1 teaspoon sugar

3 scallions (white part and 1 inch of the green), cut into 1-inch pieces

1 teaspoon cornstarch mixed with 2 tablespoons cold water

2 tablespoons minced fresh cilantro leaves for garnish

1. In a wok or large skillet, heat the oil over medium heat. Season the fillets with salt and black pepper to taste and dredge in the flour to coat, shaking off the excess. Pan-fry the fish until firm to the touch, 2 to 4 minutes per side. Transfer to a heated serving platter and keep in a low oven while you prepare the sauce.

2. Increase the heat under the pan to high. When hot, add the onion, bell pepper, jalapeños, garlic, and ginger and stir-fry for 30 seconds. Add the tomatoes, ketchup, vinegar, soy sauce, and sugar and stir-fry for 30 seconds. Add the scallions and season with salt and black pepper to taste. Stir in the cornstarch mixture and simmer for a few seconds, until the sauce thickens.

3. Pour the sauce over the fish, sprinkle with the cilantro, and serve immediately.

TO SERVE Serve with white rice.

Salmón con Salsa de Palmitos

SALMON WITH HEARTS OF PALM SAUCE *Serves 4*

If you want to treat your friends to something special, this recipe from Chile, where salmon are now being farmed, is the way to go. It is not only delicious but also easy to prepare. White sauces are very popular in South America, especially in the southern countries, and there are many variations. Both hearts of palm and avocado are luxurious ingredients that add flavor and depth to the dish. However, if avocado is not your favorite fruit, you can omit it.

SAUCE

- 2 tablespoons unsalted butter
- 2 tablespoons minced shallots
- 1 tablespoon all-purpose flour
- ¼ teaspoon salt
- ¼ teaspoon white pepper
- 1 teaspoon dry mustard
- Pinch of sugar
- 1 cup hot milk
- ½ cup whipping cream
- 2 tablespoons dry sherry
- 2 tablespoons freshly grated Parmesan cheese
- 1 cup canned hearts of palm, rinsed well and diced (¼ inch)

Four 6-ounce salmon fillets

Juice of 1 lemon

Olive oil

Salt and freshly ground black pepper

½ ripe but firm Hass avocado (optional), peeled, pitted, and diced (¼ inch), for garnish

Cayenne pepper or sweet paprika for garnish

1.   To make the sauce, melt the butter in a small saucepan over medium-low heat. Add the shallots and cook for 1 minute. Add the flour and cook, stirring constantly, until bubbling, about 1 minute. Stir in the salt, white pepper, mustard, and sugar. Remove from the heat, whisk in the milk, return to the heat, and bring to a boil. Reduce the heat to medium-low and simmer for 2 minutes. Add the cream, sherry, and Parmesan and cook until the cheese has melted. The sauce can be prepared to this point up to 2 days in advance. Place a piece of waxed paper on top, let cool, and refrigerate until needed.

2.   Preheat the oven to 425°F.

3.   Rinse the salmon fillets and pat dry. Rub with the lemon juice and oil and season with salt and black pepper to taste. Place on a baking sheet lined with aluminum foil and roast until firm to the touch and opaque throughout, 8 minutes for 1-inch-thick fillets, slightly longer for thicker fillets.

4.   While the salmon is cooking, reheat the sauce, if necessary, stirring until smooth and adding a little milk if it is too thick. Add the hearts of palm and simmer for a couple of minutes. Remove from the heat.

5.   To serve, place a salmon fillet on each serving plate and pour one-quarter of the sauce on top. Decorate with a few pieces of the avocado, if using, and the cayenne. Serve immediately.

TO SERVE Serve with buttered steamed broccoli and parsleyed potatoes.

Truchas a la Parrilla

GRILLED TROUT *Serves 2*

Trout is found in all South American countries, and it is the most popular fish in inland areas, simply because the rivers and streams teem with them. Patagonia, in southern Argentina, is a trout fisherman's paradise. Trout is usually pan-fried or grilled, but there are many other ways to prepare it. In Bolivia and Peru, it often comes boned and baked with sliced onion, pepper, and tomato. Sometimes it is stuffed with fillings such as bread and mushrooms. I'm particularly fond of this grilled trout, which is easy to prepare and delicious.

2 trout, dressed

Juice of 2 lemons or limes

1 teaspoon salt

½ teaspoon freshly ground black pepper

½ teaspoon ground cumin

½ teaspoon granulated garlic

½ cup (1 stick) unsalted butter, melted

1. Make 3 deep incisions in both sides of each trout. In a small bowl, mix together the lemon juice, salt, pepper, cumin, and garlic and coat the trout with it, making sure it gets into the incisions. Cover with plastic wrap and refrigerate for at least 1 hour.

2. When ready to serve, place the trout on a well-oiled perforated grill rack. Grill over a low fire, basting frequently with the melted butter, until just cooked through, about 5 minutes per side. Serve right away. Be careful to remove the bones when eating.   .

TO SERVE **Serve with rice or potatoes and a salad.**

El Corbullón Mantuano

FISH CATALÁN STYLE *Serves 4*

This is one of Venezuela's most famous dishes. The ideas behind the recipe were brought to South America during colonial times by the Catalans, who dominated commerce on the eastern coast of Venezuela, especially in Cumaná. Local ingredients were incorporated, then the dish spread rapidly to other areas of Venezuela, to become a national dish. In the beginning, it was part of the daily diet of many people. Gradually, it became a favorite of gourmets, undergoing some changes along the way.

A variety of fish can be used, such as *mero* (sea bass or grouper), *pargo* (red snapper), or *cherna* (stone bass or grouper). The classic way of serving this dish is with cornmeal dumplings and boiled potatoes. I prefer to serve it on a bed of steamed spinach, surrounded with the sauce and dumplings.

Four 6-ounce fish fillets

Juice of ½ lemon

Salt and freshly ground black pepper

¼ cup olive oil

1 medium-size onion, halved and thinly sliced into half-moons (about 1 cup)

1 cup thinly sliced leeks (white part only), washed well

1 small green bell pepper, seeded and cut into thin strips

1 small red bell pepper, seeded and cut into thin strips

1 cup dry white wine

1 tablespoon capers, drained

10 pimento-stuffed Spanish olives, sliced

Sugar

CORNMEAL DUMPLINGS

1 cup *Masa de Arepa* (page 348)

1 tablespoon unsalted butter

1 pound spinach leaves, washed well, stems removed and chopped, or one 10-ounce package frozen chopped spinach

1. Rub the fish fillets with the lemon juice, season with salt and black pepper to taste, and set aside in the refrigerator.

2. In a large skillet with a lid, heat the oil over low heat. Add the onion, leeks, and bell peppers. Cover and cook, stirring a few times, for 5 minutes. Add the wine and cook, uncovered, for 5 minutes. Add the fish fillets, baste with the sauce, cover, and simmer for 8 minutes for 1-inch-thick fillets, slightly longer for thicker fillets. Remove the fish from the sauce and set aside.

3. Let the sauce cool for about 5 minutes. Transfer to a blender and process until smooth. Return to the skillet and bring back to a simmer. If the sauce is too thick, add a little water. Stir in the capers and olives and season with salt and sugar to taste. The dish can be prepared a few

hours ahead up to this point. Transfer the sauce (reserve 1 tablespoon for the dumplings) and fish to a nonmetallic container, let cool, and refrigerate until needed.

4. Meanwhile, make the dumplings. Combine the *masa*, butter, and 1 tablespoon of the sauce in a small bowl. Make small dough balls about ½ inch in diameter. Place on a plate in a single layer, cover with plastic wrap, and refrigerate until needed. Just before serving, cook in boiling salted water for 5 minutes.

5. If using fresh spinach, steam over boiling water, then drain. If using frozen, cook according to the package directions, then drain. Keep warm.

6. To reheat the fish and sauce, bring to room temperature, place in a skillet, cover, and bring to a boil. Reduce the heat and simmer for a couple of minutes.

7. To serve, place one-quarter of the warm spinach on each heated serving plate, top with 1 fillet, drizzle with sauce, and arrange corn dumplings around the edge.

Filetes de Sábalo en Leche de Coco

FILLETS OF SHAD IN COCONUT MILK *Serves 4*

This specialty is popular along the coast of Colombia. Coconut milk imparts a delicate taste to the fish. I remember the first time I had this dish in Cartagena, I was presented with a fish that covered the whole oval platter, which was full of a delicious broth. The dish was very light indeed—if you didn't eat the whole fish. Just remember, shad has a lot of bones, and many stay behind even after filleting.

> **Four 6-ounce shad or haddock fillets**
> **2 tablespoons fresh lemon juice**
> **½ teaspoon salt**

> **¼ teaspoon freshly ground black pepper**
> **2 tablespoons olive oil, plus more for frying (optional)**
> **1 medium-size onion, minced (about 1 cup)**
> **1 tablespoon all-purpose flour**
> **3 cloves garlic, peeled**
> **1 small green or red bell pepper, seeded and diced**
> **1 tablespoon minced fresh cilantro leaves**
> **¼ teaspoon dried thyme**
> **¼ teaspoon saffron threads, crumbled**
> **2 tablespoons tomato paste**
> **½ cup well-stirred canned unsweetened coconut milk**

1. Rub the fish fillets with the lemon juice, salt, and black pepper. Cover with plastic wrap and refrigerate for at least 2 hours.

2. Heat the oil in a large skillet over medium heat. Add the onion and cook, stirring a few times, until softened, about 5 minutes. Sprinkle in the flour and cook, stirring constantly, for 1 minute.

3. In a blender or food processor, process the garlic, bell pepper, cilantro, thyme, saffron, and tomato paste until smooth. Add to the onion and cook over low heat for 10 minutes, stirring occasionally. Add the coconut milk, bring to a boil, reduce the heat to medium-low, and simmer for 5 minutes. The sauce can be made ahead up to this point, cooled, and refrigerated until needed. Reheat before proceeding.

4. The fillets can be pan-fried in hot olive oil over medium-high heat or baked in a preheated 400°F oven until milky white throughout, about 10 minutes.

5. Transfer to 4 heated plates and top with the sauce.

TO SERVE Serve with *Arroz Negro con Tocineta y Plátano* (page 322).

Surubí con Fariña

**CATFISH FILLETS BREADED
WITH MANIOC MEAL** *Serves 4*

A very popular way to prepare fish fillets in all South American countries is breading and frying them. The breading can be done with flour or cornmeal, or with egg and bread crumbs. Catfish are found everywhere, especially in the Amazon, and they can get big. In Paraguay and Amazonia, catfish fillets are breaded with manioc meal just before frying—very simple and very delicious. Any kind of fish fillet can be prepared this way. Manioc meal is available in some Latin American markets.

> Four 6-ounce catfish fillets (about 1 inch thick)
>
> Juice of 1 lemon
>
> Salt and freshly ground black pepper
>
> ½ cup manioc meal
>
> Canola oil for frying
>
> Lemon wedges

1. Rub the fillets with the lemon juice and season with salt and pepper to taste. Cover with plastic wrap and refrigerate for 1 hour.

2. Dredge the fillets on both sides in the manioc meal, shaking off any excess.

3. In a large skillet, heat about ¼ inch of the oil over medium heat. The oil is ready when a few drops of water sprinkled in the pan sizzle. Add the fillets and cook until golden, about 1 minute per side. Serve immediately with the lemon wedges.

TO SERVE **Serve with mashed or boiled potatoes and a lettuce and tomato salad.**

Picante de Cojinova

**AMBERJACK WITH POTATOES
AND PEANUT SAUCE** *Serves 4 to 6*

Cojinova, or amberjack, is a fish indigenous to the waters off Peru. Pompano or any semifat fish can be used instead. This is a wonderful dish, whether it is prepared for the family or for company. The sauce can be made ahead and kept refrigerated. This dish is usually made *muy picante* (very spicy) in Peru, but it is just as good with only a hint of heat. The potatoes can be cooked a couple of hours ahead and kept at room temperature. Just before serving, assemble the whole thing and cook until the fish just flakes. Yuca can be used instead of potatoes.

> 1½ pounds amberjack fillets, cut into 1½-inch pieces
>
> Juice of 1 lemon
>
> 4 cloves garlic, mashed into a paste with 1 teaspoon salt and ¼ teaspoon freshly ground black pepper
>
> 2 tablespoons fresh hot yellow or red pepper puree, store-bought or homemade (page 332), or 1 teaspoon red pepper flakes
>
> ¼ cup olive oil
>
> 1 large onion, chopped (about 1½ cups)
>
> 2 large ripe but firm tomatoes (about 1 pound), peeled and finely chopped
>
> ½ cup unsalted dry-roasted peanuts pureed with ¼ cup water
>
> 1 pound boiling potatoes, cooked in water to cover until fork tender, drained, peeled, and cut into 1-inch cubes

1. In a glass bowl, mix the fish with the lemon juice, garlic paste, and hot pepper puree. Rub the fish pieces with this mixture and set aside while you prepare the sauce.

2. Heat the oil in a large, heavy skillet over medium heat. Add the onion and cook, stirring a few times, until softened, about 5 minutes. Add

the tomatoes, cover, and cook over low heat, stirring occasionally, until the onion and tomatoes have softened and formed a sauce, about 15 minutes. Stir in the peanut puree and cook, stirring, until thickened, about 5 minutes. Mix in the fish and potatoes, cover, and cook, stirring occasionally, until the fish flakes, about 7 minutes. Season with salt and black pepper to taste and serve.

TO SERVE **Serve with rice.**

Guiso de Pescado Seco

DRIED FISH STEW *Serves 4*

Dried codfish is one of the Portuguese and Spanish legacies that were quickly adopted by cooks along the Atlantic and Pacific coasts of South America. It is interesting to notice the different ways of preparing codfish in the different regions. The coastal towns favor the use of coconut milk, while the Andean regions follow more closely the ways of the Iberian Peninsula, using chickpeas and potatoes, which makes for a more rounded meal.

On the island of Chiloé, in southern Chile, there is such abundance of fish that what is not consumed locally is salted and sun-dried in the summer and smoked in the winter. Red *congrio* and hake are the fish destined to be dried. They have very few bones, which can easily be removed after soaking. This type of dried fish is not available in U.S. markets, but you can use salt cod or dried *abadejo* (pollock) instead. Both are available year-round in Latin American markets. This is my adaptation of a recipe from *Chilenos Cocinando a lo Chileno* by Roberto Marín Vivado.

> **1 pound boneless salt cod or dried pollock**
> **¼ cup olive oil**
> **3 cloves garlic, finely chopped**
> **1 teaspoon sweet paprika**
> **½ teaspoon ground cumin**
> **1 teaspoon dried oregano**

¼ teaspoon freshly ground black pepper
⅛ teaspoon cayenne pepper
4 medium-size all-purpose potatoes, peeled and quartered
3 cups coarsely chopped cabbage
2 cups water
1 cup frozen peas
1 medium-size ripe but firm tomato (5 to 6 ounces), peeled, seeded, and diced, for garnish

1. Soak the salt cod in water to cover overnight, changing the water once or twice. Drain and cut into small pieces.

2. Heat the oil in a large skillet over low heat. Add the garlic and cook, stirring, for 15 seconds. Add the cod and cook, stirring a few times, for 5 minutes. Stir in the paprika, cumin, oregano, black pepper, cayenne, and potatoes and cook for a couple of minutes, stirring until the spices are evenly distributed. Add the cabbage and water, cover, and cook until the potatoes are tender, about 20 minutes. Add the peas and cook for 3 minutes. The stew should have enough liquid to cover the vegetables and cod. Add more water, if needed, and simmer for a couple of minutes.

3. Serve hot in soup plates, garnished with the tomato.

Fanesca

ECUADORIAN EASTER SALT COD AND VEGETABLE STEW *Serves 10 to 12*

Fanesca is one of the traditional dishes of the Ecuadorian highlands, faithfully preserved for generations. It is a unique dish, served only once a year on Holy Thursday, to tide people over during the fast of Good Friday. Perhaps this is the reason *fanesca* is sometimes called *la comida del hambre* (food for the hungry). In all my research on Latin

American foods, I have been unable to find another country in the Americas that prepares this specialty.

Very little is known about the origin of this dish, other than that its roots go back to Europe. According to some researchers, *fanesca* represents a Christian ritual that was practiced in the catacombs in Rome during the persecution of the Christians. During Holy Week, the Christians would sneak into the catacombs carrying food, mainly grains and legumes, which were put into one big pot to be distributed among all. That is why, even to this day, it is the custom to give *fanesca* to relatives, friends, neighbors, and the needy.

The origins of the name are not clear either. Some historians believe that *fanesca* came to America via Galicia, in Spain. Others think that the name could have come from the old Spanish name for a soup called *juanesca* or *fuanesca*. Still others believe that it could have come from *faneca*, the Portuguese name of a fish in the cod family. Whatever the origin, *fanesca* is a complex, milk-based vegetable stew that has been prepared for hundreds of years. It consists of an assortment of grains, legumes, vegetables, and salt cod. As the story goes, there should have been 12 different grains and legumes in the dish to signify the 12 Apostles. Because the faithful could come up with only 8, other vegetables had to be added over time. The grains and legumes most commonly used in Ecuador are corn, rice, peas, fresh beans (common beans or lima beans), peanuts, lupini beans, fava beans, lentils, chickpeas, and hominy. The other ingredients are squash, cabbage, *ullucos*, and *zambo* (a kind of squash occasionally available in some ethnic groceries in the United States under the name winter melon; zucchini is a good substitute). Cooks have total freedom to use or not to use some of these ingredients.

Preparing *fanesca* is labor-intensive and requires a lot of hands. Preparation usually starts two to three days ahead. Common beans, fava beans, lupini beans, and corn have to be peeled or husked; vegetables have to be cleaned and chopped. It becomes a communal ritual in which most members of the household take part. Neighbors also drop by to help. All the ingredients have to be cooked separately. There is never a consensus as to whether one should use cabbage (because it is hard to digest) or *ullucos* (because of their mucilaginous texture). Chickpeas are a must for some families. Lentils are not commonly used because they are too hard to digest. Salt cod is the essential ingredient, not only because it symbolizes Jesus Christ (because he fed fish to the masses) and the cross, but also because some people feel that it gives the *fanesca* its characteristic flavor. The seasoning is also controversial. Some people like a very spicy sauce, while others prefer a more subtle seasoning, so that each ingredient can be tasted. Purists use only milk and cream for the sauce; others also use some of the liquid in which the vegetables were cooked.

The recipe here is my mother's basic *fanesca*. She always added the cod to the *fanesca*, but my cousin Lucy de Almeida, who is a well-known caterer in Quito, prefers to cook it separately, to please those who don't care for the cod flavor. She also adds pureed lupini beans to give another dimension to the dish. And, as French chefs do, she adds a big chunk of butter to the finished dish. Her *fanesca* is really luxurious.

Galo Plaza, former president of Ecuador, often served this specialty to company while he was an ambassador in Washington. His chef recommended some ingredient substitutions, such as replacing *zambo* with zucchini, and Muenster cheese with cream cheese, which gives the sauce an even creamier texture.

Fanesca is a great dish. When prepared in stages, it is not such a chore. The garnishes are important, especially the little fritters and *empanaditas* that are served on the side. Preparation through the cooking of the rice can be done the day before.

Molo (page 302) is the classic side dish, along with pickled vegetables. For dessert, serve rice pudding or figs stewed in brown sugar, along with sliced brick cheese.

1 pound boneless salt cod (preferably white)

2 cups shelled fava beans, blanched and peeled (page 308)

2 cups cooked corn kernels, drained

One 15-ounce can Great Northern beans, drained and rinsed, or 1½ cups frozen baby lima beans, cooked and drained

1 cup fresh or frozen peas, cooked in water to cover until tender and drained

1½ cups bottled lupini beans, peeled (page 307)

1 head garlic, unpeeled

2 cups shredded zucchini or *zambo* (winter melon)

2 cups peeled, seeded, and cubed (1 inch) calabaza or other winter squash

2 cups shredded cabbage

½ cup long-grain rice

1½ cups water

2 tablespoons canola oil

2 tablespoons unsalted butter

½ teaspoon ground annatto or sweet paprika

1 cup finely chopped scallions (white part only)

2 cups finely chopped leeks (white part only), washed well

½ teaspoon ground cumin

½ teaspoon dried oregano

2 teaspoons salt

1 teaspoon white pepper

½ cup unsalted dry-roasted peanuts

5 cups milk, or more if needed

4 ounces cream cheese

1 cup whipping cream

¼ cup (½ stick) unsalted butter (optional), softened

GARNISHES

2 hard-cooked eggs, peeled and sliced

1 ripe (yellow) plantain, peeled, sliced ¼ inch thick, and fried in hot canola oil until golden on both sides

1 small red bell pepper, seeded and cut into strips, or 4 hot red peppers, seeded, cut into thin strips, blanched in boiling water for 20 seconds, and drained

1 recipe small *Empanadas de Viento* (*empanaditas*; page 105)

Ball-shaped fritters made from the dough left over from making the *empanaditas*

Fresh parsley sprigs

1. Soak the salt cod in water to cover overnight, changing the water a couple of times. Drain, cut into bite-size pieces, and set aside.

2. Prepare the fava beans, corn, Great Northern beans, peas, and 1 cup of the lupini beans. Place in a large mixing bowl, cover with plastic wrap, and refrigerate until ready to use.

3. Preheat the oven to 400°F.

4. Roast the garlic in a baking dish until the cloves are soft, about 20 minutes. Remove from the oven, let cool, and squeeze out the garlic; it should be like a paste. Cover with plastic wrap and refrigerate.

5. Steam the zucchini until tender, about 5 minutes. Steam the calabaza until soft, about 20 minutes. Steam the cabbage until tender, about 20 minutes. Place the zucchini, squash, and cabbage in a food processor and process until smooth. Transfer to a large bowl, cover with plastic wrap, and refrigerate.

6. In a small saucepan, combine the rice and water and cook over low heat until most of the water has been absorbed, 25 to 30 minutes. Mash with a fork, transfer to a bowl, cover, and refrigerate.

7. In a large, heavy casserole, heat the oil, butter, and annatto together over medium heat until the butter has melted. Add the cod and cook, stirring, for a couple of minutes. Remove with a slotted spoon and set aside. Add the scallions, leeks, roasted garlic, cumin, oregano, salt, and white pepper to the casserole and cook, stirring constantly, for 5 minutes. Do not let brown. Transfer to a blender and add the remaining ½ cup lupini beans, the peanuts, and a little of the milk. Process until smooth. Return to the casserole, add the cod and remaining milk, and bring to a boil. Reduce the heat and simmer for 5 minutes. Add the squash and cabbage, rice, and bean mixture and simmer for 15 minutes, stirring frequently so it doesn't stick to the bottom of the casserole. Cut the cream cheese into small cubes and add, stirring until it melts. Add the cream and heat through. *Fanesca* should have the consistency of a thick soup; if it is too thick, add a little more milk. Taste for salt and stir in the butter, if using.

8. Serve hot in soup plates, garnished with the eggs, plantain, bell pepper, *empanaditas*, fritters, and parsley.

NOTES You may serve the cod separately, as a side dish. Place the cod pieces in boiling water, cover, reduce the heat to low, and simmer for 15 minutes. Drain and set aside until ready to serve.

You can prepare everything through step 6, as well as chop the leeks and scallions, the day before. If done this way, *fanesca* need not be a chore.

Water is never used in the classic *fanesca*, just milk.

Pescado Relleno

BAKED WHOLE STUFFED FISH *Serves 4 to 6*

In pre-Hispanic times, South America's Indians wrapped fish in different types of leaves, such as *achira* (canna lily), and cooked it over hot coals. Later, after the conquistadors planted banana trees, the trees provided not only bananas but also leaves used to wrap fish (and, even more important, tamales). The stuffing here is post-Hispanic, with some native seasonings. A wide range of items can be used to make the stuffing. Mushrooms, vegetables, shellfish, and, in the coastal regions of the Andean countries, green plantains are all popular.

One 3- to 4-pound whole fish (such as red snapper, *corvina*, or striped or black sea bass), with head and tail, dressed

3 cloves garlic, mashed with 1 teaspoon salt, ¼ teaspoon freshly ground black pepper, ½ teaspoon ground cumin, and ½ teaspoon dried oregano

1 tablespoon fresh lemon or lime juice

1 tablespoon *Manteca de Color* (page 331), or 1 tablespoon canola oil mixed with ½ teaspoon sweet paprika

1 medium-size onion, minced (about 1 cup)

¼ cup seeded and minced green bell pepper

1 medium-size ripe but firm tomato (5 to 6 ounces), peeled, seeded, and finely chopped

One 6-ounce can good-quality crabmeat, drained well and picked over for shells and cartilage

½ cup day-old bread crumbs (page 413)

Olive oil for rubbing

All-purpose flour for dusting

1. Rinse the fish and dry thoroughly with paper towels. In a small bowl. combine the garlic paste and lemon juice. With a sharp knife, make 3 deep incisions on both sides of the fish and rub this paste inside the incisions. Set aside.

2. In a medium-size skillet, heat the *manteca de color* over low heat. Add the onion, bell pepper, and tomato and cook, stirring a few times, for about 5 minutes. Season with a pinch each of salt, black pepper, and cumin. Mix in the crabmeat and bread crumbs until well incorporated. Stuff the fish with this mixture, then secure it closed with skewers. If there is any stuffing left over, bake it in a separate oiled baking dish with a cover.

3. Preheat the oven to 400°F. Cover a broiler pan with heavy-duty aluminum foil and punch

holes in the foil to match the holes in the broiler pan. Butter or oil the foil.

4.   Rub the fish with the oil and dust lightly on both sides with the flour. Place on the prepared pan. Cover the tail and fins with foil to keep them from burning. Bake until the juices run clear, 30 to 40 minutes.

5.   When done, transfer the fish and foil to a hot platter and remove the foil, carefully pulling it from under the fish. Remove the skewers, being careful not to damage the fish. To serve, cut along the fish's back and remove the fins and skin. With a metal spatula, carefully remove the fillets from the backbone. Serve right away, with dressing from the cavity.

TO SERVE **Serve with rice, thick French fries, and a few leaves of lettuce topped with sliced tomato.**

Encocados de Langostinos

LANGOSTINOS IN COCONUT MILK SAUCE *Serves 6*

Langostinos are oversize shrimp, which are used often in Ecuador. *Encocados* is a type of specialty popular on the coasts of Ecuador and Colombia, as well as on the Galápagos Islands, with regional differences. The name means "in coconut sauce," and the dish can be made with shellfish and/or white fish, such as *corvina*. The preparation starts with a very well seasoned *refrito* (onion-based sauce) to which coconut milk and any kind of seafood is added. The *refrito* can be made ahead, and the dish finished just before serving. The classic way to serve *encocados* is with white rice and any kind of plantain—fried ripe plantain, roasted green plantain, or *patacones* (fried green plantain). Sometimes fried yuca is served as well.

Juice of 1 lemon

4 large cloves garlic, mashed into a paste with ½ teaspoon salt and ½ teaspoon freshly ground black pepper

3 pounds langostinos (extra-large shrimp), peeled and deveined

2 tablespoons olive oil

1 teaspoon ground annatto or sweet paprika

1 medium-size onion, minced (about 1 cup)

½ cup minced scallions (white part and 1 inch of the green)

½ cup seeded and minced red bell pepper

½ cup seeded and minced green bell pepper

2 medium-size ripe but firm tomatoes (10 to 12 ounces), peeled, seeded, and chopped

1 tablespoon tomato paste, optional

¼ cup minced fresh parsley leaves

¼ cup minced fresh cilantro leaves

½ teaspoon ground cumin

1 cup well-stirred canned unsweetened coconut milk, or more if needed

1.   Combine the lemon juice and garlic paste in a small bowl, then rub into the langostinos. Cover with plastic wrap and refrigerate until needed.

2.   In a large casserole or skillet, heat the oil over low heat. Stir in the annatto, then add the onion, scallions, bell peppers, tomatoes, and tomato paste (if using). Cover and cook, stirring occasionally, until soft, about 20 minutes. If the mixture starts to dry out, add a little water. Stir in the parsley, cilantro, and cumin. Cover and cook for 5 minutes. The recipe can be prepared ahead up to this point; let cool and refrigerate.

3.   To finish the dish, bring the sauce to a boil, add the langostinos, and mix well. Cook, stirring a few times, until the langostinos begin to curl and turn pink, 3 to 5 minutes. Add the coconut milk, reduce the heat to medium-low, and stir until heated through. Add more coconut milk if the sauce is too thick; it should have a creamy consistency. Season with salt and black pepper to taste and serve immediately.

TO SERVE **Serve with white rice, fried ripe plantain, and buttered asparagus.**

Carurú de Camarão

SHRIMP WITH OKRA AND NUT SAUCE *Serves 4 to 6*

Carurú is a traditional dish of Bahia, usually served in honor of the "twin saints," Cosme and Damian. Families with twins invite friends and neighbors to celebrate the feast of the twin saints, which takes place in September. This custom, called "*carurú* of the two-two," features a large platter of *carurú*. The dish itself is of Sudanese origin, and as with many specialties of this type, every cook has her own rendition. The sauce clearly shows its African roots, with the use of *dendê* (palm oil), okra, and coconut milk. The Indians' contribution is the dried shrimp, tomatoes, and bell pepper. Some cooks use peanuts and cashews to thicken and season the sauce, while others prefer to use manioc meal. Bahians use generous amounts of hot peppers to season *carurú*, but the most common way to serve it is with a bowl of *Molho de Pimenta e Limão* (page 335) on the side, so that each person can add the hot sauce to his or her taste.

- 1½ pounds large shrimp, peeled and deveined
- Juice of 1 lime
- 2 tablespoons *dendê* (page 422) or canola oil
- 1 medium-size onion, minced (about 1 cup)
- 4 large cloves garlic, mashed into a paste with 1½ teaspoons salt and ¼ teaspoon freshly ground black pepper
- ¼ cup seeded and minced green bell pepper
- 2 medium-size ripe but firm tomatoes (10 to 12 ounces), peeled and chopped
- ¼ cup minced scallions (white part and 1 inch of the green)
- 2 tablespoons finely chopped fresh cilantro leaves
- 1 tablespoon peeled and minced fresh ginger
- ¼ teaspoon red pepper flakes
- 3 cups sliced okra, fresh or frozen
- ½ cup water
- ¼ cup peeled dried shrimp (page 433), ground
- ¼ cup unsalted dry-roasted peanuts, ground, or 4 tablespoons natural peanut butter
- ¼ cup unsalted dry-roasted cashews, finely chopped
- 1½ cups well-stirred canned unsweetened coconut milk
- 2 tablespoons minced fresh parsley leaves for garnish

1. Place the large shrimp in a large mixing bowl, pour the lime juice over the top, and toss to coat the shrimp with the juice. Cover with plastic wrap and let marinate in the refrigerator for 1 hour.

2. Heat the *dendê* in a large, heavy skillet over medium heat. Add the onion, garlic paste, bell pepper, tomatoes, scallions, cilantro, ginger, and red pepper and cook, stirring a few times, for 5 minutes. Add the okra and water, cover, reduce the heat to low, and cook until the okra is almost tender, about 10 minutes for fresh and according to the package directions for frozen. Stir in the dried shrimp, peanuts, cashews, and coconut milk. Cover and simmer until the okra is completely tender, another few minutes. Add the marinated shrimp and cook, stirring, until they turn pink and curl, 3 to 5 minutes. If the sauce is too thick, add a little water; it should have the consistency of heavy cream. Season with salt to taste.

3. Transfer to a heated serving platter, sprinkle with the parsley, and serve immediately.

TO SERVE **Serve with white rice and hot pepper sauce.**

Crepas con Camarones y Cangrejo

CREPES FILLED WITH SHRIMP AND CRABMEAT

Makes 16 crepes; 5 to 6 servings

When the South American hostess needs an elegant first course, this is the specialty of choice. The filling can be made with a mixture of seafood, or with shrimp or crabmeat alone. These crepes are also great for a luncheon or light supper.

> 1 pound medium-size shrimp, peeled,
>   deveined, cooked in boiling water just
>   until pink, and drained
> 8 ounces crabmeat (see Note)
> 1 recipe *Salsa Blanca* (page 405)
> 6 tablespoons tomato sauce
> 1 tablespoon cognac or brandy
> Salt and white pepper
> Tabasco sauce or cayenne pepper
> 1 recipe *Crepas* (plain or basil; page 405)
> 1 cup whipping cream
> ½ cup freshly grated Asiago cheese

1.   Cut half of the shrimp into thirds. Place the other half in a food processor and pulse until coarsely ground. In a non-aluminum bowl, mix all the shrimp with the crabmeat and set aside.

2.   Heat the *salsa blanca* in a medium-size saucepan. Stir in the tomato sauce and cognac and season with salt, white pepper, and Tabasco. The sauce should be thick. Mix 1 cup of this sauce with the shrimp.

3.   Place 2 heaping tablespoons of the shrimp filling in the center of each crepe and roll up tightly into a cylinder. Arrange in a single layer in 2 buttered shallow baking dishes, making sure they are not crowded. At this point, the crepes can be covered and refrigerated for a few hours.

4.   Preheat the oven to 375°F.

5.   Reheat the remaining sauce, adding just enough of the cream to make a light sauce. Pour over the crepes, sprinkle on the cheese, and drizzle the rest of the cream around the edges of the pan. Bake until bubbling, about 20 minutes. Serve hot.

TO SERVE **Serve with asparagus spears tossed with a little butter and lemon juice.**

NOTES **The best way to get good-quality crabmeat is to buy the legs. You'll want to buy about 12 ounces of crab still in the shells to end up with 8 ounces picked over. Have the fishmonger cut the legs into 2-inch pieces so that you can remove the meat easily. Cut into bite-size pieces.**

You may use a 6-ounce can of good-quality crabmeat instead. Just pick over for shells and cartilage.

Ají de Camarones

SHRIMP IN HOT PEPPER AND WALNUT SAUCE *Serves 4 to 6*

Peruvians excel in the preparation of *ajíes*, dishes using their beloved *mirasol* (hot yellow) peppers. The most famous is *ají de gallina* (chicken in hot pepper sauce). But *ajíes* also are made with shrimp, langostinos, corn, potatoes, squash, eggs, and *cuy* (guinea pig). Everything can be made a few hours ahead, then assembled and cooked just before serving. The indigenous peoples used walnuts and peanuts to make sauces, and when the Spaniards came, they brought almonds and pine nuts to make other, thinner sauces, which they learned from the Moors.

2 pounds extra-large shrimp or langostinos, unpeeled

4 cups water

1 small onion, halved

1 clove garlic, peeled

Juice of 1 lemon

Salt and freshly ground black pepper

3 dried *mirasol* (hot yellow) peppers, seeded, or red pepper flakes to taste

¼ cup olive oil

½ teaspoon ground annatto or sweet paprika

1 medium-size onion, finely chopped (about 1 cup)

2 large cloves garlic, minced

½ teaspoon dried oregano, crumbled

½ teaspoon ground cumin

½ cup milk

½ cup ground walnuts

2 tablespoons freshly grated Parmesan cheese

GARNISHES

6 small all-purpose potatoes, cooked in water to cover until tender, drained, and halved

2 hard-cooked eggs, peeled and quartered

12 Kalamata olives

1. Peel the shrimp and place the shells, water, onion halves, and garlic clove in a 3-quart saucepan. Bring to a boil, reduce the heat to medium-low, and simmer for 20 minutes. Strain and discard the shells, onion, and garlic. Set the broth aside.

2. Place the shrimp in a large glass bowl. Add the lemon juice and salt and black pepper to taste and toss to coat. Cover with plastic wrap and let marinate in the refrigerator.

3. Break the dried peppers into small pieces and soak in warm water for 30 minutes. Drain, transfer to a blender, and process until smooth. Set aside. (If using red pepper flakes, add in place of the puree in the next step.)

4. In a heavy 12-inch skillet, heat the oil over medium heat. Stir in the annatto, add the shrimp, and cook, stirring constantly, until they turn pink, about 1 minute. With a slotted spoon, transfer to a clean bowl. Add the chopped onion to the skillet and cook, stirring a few times, until softened, about 5 minutes. Add the minced garlic, hot pepper puree, oregano, cumin, and ½ teaspoon salt and cook for 1 minute. Add the milk, walnuts, and 2 cups of the reserved shrimp broth. Cook, stirring constantly, until the sauce thickens; it should be a little thicker than whipping cream. At this point, the shrimp and sauce can be cooled and refrigerated in covered containers until needed.

5. To finish, bring the shrimp and sauce to room temperature, if necessary. Transfer the sauce to a large skillet and bring to a simmer over medium heat. Stir in the Parmesan and shrimp and simmer until the shrimp are heated through. Season with salt and black pepper to taste. Serve garnished with the potatoes, eggs, and olives.

Frigideira de Camarão
PUFFED EGGS WITH SHRIMP AND VEGETABLES *Serves 4*

Some people believe that this Brazilian specialty comes from the Portuguese *frittata* (omelet). As with many European dishes, it went through a transformation with the addition of *dendê* (palm oil) and coconut milk, both characteristic of African cooking. In Bahia, where the African influence is strong, *frigideira* generally means a baked dish that has eggs on top. The main ingredient can be sausage, fish, shrimp, crabmeat, hearts of palm, or dried cod. It is a lovely dish to serve for brunch.

2 tablespoons olive oil

1 tablespoon *dendê* (page 422)

1 large onion, halved and thinly sliced into half-moons (about 1½ cups)

2 cloves garlic, mashed into a paste with ½ teaspoon salt and ¼ teaspoon freshly ground black pepper

2 tablespoons finely chopped fresh cilantro leaves

2 tablespoons finely chopped fresh parsley leaves

Juice of 1 lime

1 pound large shrimp, peeled and deveined

½ cup well-stirred canned unsweetened coconut milk

4 large eggs

1 medium-size ripe but firm tomato, peeled, seeded, and thinly sliced

1.   In a medium-size skillet, heat the olive oil and *dendê* together over medium-low heat. Add the onion, garlic paste, cilantro, and parsley and cook, stirring, until the onion is softened, about 5 minutes. Add the lime juice and shrimp and cook for 30 seconds. Add the coconut milk and cook until it comes to a boil. Remove from the heat.

2.   Preheat the oven to 350°F. Butter a shallow 4-cup baking dish.

3.   In a large mixing bowl with an electric mixer, beat the eggs until they are foamy and have increased in volume. Mix the eggs with the shrimp. Pour the mixture into the prepared dish and decorate the top with the tomato. Bake until spongy but not dry (it should look moist), 12 to 15 minutes. Serve immediately.

TO SERVE **Serve with white rice.**

Langostinos a la Normandy

PRAWNS NORMANDY STYLE *Serves 4 to 6*

Many years ago in Quito, Ecuador, before eating out became so popular, there were only a few restaurants, where we went for special occasions. The French restaurant Normandy was one of them. Its specialty was prawns covered with a mixture of herbs, garlic, and lots of olive oil and butter, then quickly baked—absolutely sinful. Years later, when I went back to Quito with my husband, we went to the Normandy, and Peter fell in love with this dish. When we got back to the States, we reproduced it, and I have made it many times since. Unfortunately, the owners of the restaurant retired and closed the doors a few years later.

2 pounds prawns (12 to 14 per pound), unpeeled

Salt and freshly ground black pepper

1 small onion, minced (about ½ cup)

2 medium-size shallots, minced (about ¼ cup)

6 cloves garlic, minced

¼ cup minced fresh parsley leaves

¼ cup minced fresh cilantro leaves

¼ cup (½ stick) unsalted butter, melted

½ cup olive oil

1.   With kitchen scissors or a sharp paring knife, cut along the backs of the prawns about ⅛ inch deep and remove the dark vein. Rinse thoroughly, pat dry with paper towels, and place on a jellyroll pan, pressing down a little to flatten. Season with salt and pepper to taste.

2.   Preheat the oven to 425°F.

3.   In a small mixing bowl, mix together the onion, shallots, garlic, parsley, and cilantro and distribute the mixture over the top of the prawns, loosening their shells a bit so that the mixture

gets under and inside. Drizzle the melted butter and oil on top and bake for 5 minutes. Toss the prawns to coat with the butter mixture and bake for about 5 minutes more, until the prawns curl like half-moons. Toss well to make sure they are covered with the butter mixture and serve.

TO SERVE **Serve with white rice and your favorite salad.**

Quinua Atamalada con Camarones

QUINOA STEW WITH SHRIMP *Serves 4*

Atamalados are very thick stews made with quinoa, barley, wheat, or rice, along with pork, dried shrimp, fresh shrimp, or mussels. It is said that the test of a good *atamalado* is that when it cools, it should harden like a tamale. This is a specialty of Peru.

> **2 large cloves garlic, mashed into a paste with 1 hot pepper, seeded and chopped, and ½ teaspoon salt**
>
> **½ teaspoon dried oregano**
>
> **½ teaspoon ground cumin**
>
> **¼ teaspoon freshly ground black pepper**
>
> **8 ounces medium-size shrimp, peeled and deveined**
>
> **2 tablespoons canola oil**
>
> **1 medium-size onion, finely chopped (about 1 cup)**
>
> **½ cup chicken broth made with 1 teaspoon chicken bouillon granules**
>
> **1 cup quinoa, cooked (page 327)**
>
> **2 ounces Chihuahua, mozzarella, or Muenster cheese, shredded**

GARNISHES

> **2 hard-cooked eggs, peeled and each cut into 4 wedges**
>
> **8 black olives**
>
> **Minced fresh cilantro or parsley leaves**

1. In a small mixing bowl, combine the garlic paste, oregano, cumin, and black pepper. Rub the shrimp with this paste, cover, and refrigerate for at least 30 minutes.

2. Heat the oil in a large skillet over medium heat. Add the shrimp and cook, stirring steadily, for 10 to 15 seconds, just until the shrimp begin to change color—they should not be fully cooked. Remove with a slotted spoon and set aside. Add the onion to the skillet and cook, stirring a few times, until softened, about 5 minutes. Add the chicken broth, quinoa, and cheese. Mix well, season with salt and black pepper to taste, and simmer for a couple of minutes. Stir in the shrimp and cook until they begin to curl.

3. To serve, transfer to a heated serving platter and decorate with the eggs, olives, and cilantro.

Arroz con Mejillones a la Walter

WALTER'S RICE WITH MUSSELS *Serves 4 to 6*

When I was a guest of the Costas, friends and long-time residents of Punta del Este, Uruguay, Walter Costa prepared this specialty using local white mussels. He went in the morning to buy a few pounds of the shucked mussels, just taken from the sea. These mussels are so fresh that they smell like the ocean and taste like heaven. Walter said that he likes these mussels so much, he sometimes uses more mussels than rice in the recipe. Even though we don't have the pleasure of getting that particular type of mussel in the United States, this dish is still a treat for mussel lovers. I use New Zealand mussels because they are readily available here.

> **One 2-pound package frozen New Zealand mussels in the half shell**
>
> **3 tablespoons olive oil**

1 large onion, chopped (about 1½ cups)

½ cup seeded and diced (¼ inch) green bell pepper

½ cup seeded and diced (¼ inch) red bell pepper

3 large cloves garlic, minced

2 teaspoons sweet paprika

3 cups boiling water

½ teaspoon saffron threads, crumbled

1½ cups converted rice

1 teaspoon salt

½ teaspoon freshly ground black pepper

1 cup dry white wine

Tabasco sauce

2 tablespoons minced fresh parsley leaves for garnish

1. Thaw the mussels in the refrigerator a few hours before starting the dish. Remove from the shells and rinse thoroughly to remove any sand. Cut in half crosswise and set aside.

2. In a heavy 10-inch skillet with a tight cover or a large, heavy casserole, heat the oil over medium heat. Add the onion and cook, stirring frequently, until softened, about 5 minutes. Add the bell peppers and garlic and cook for a couple of minutes, stirring a few times. Mix the paprika with 1 cup of the boiling water and add to the skillet. Stir the saffron into 1 cup of the boiling water and let it soften for a couple of minutes. Add to the skillet along with the rice, mussels, salt, black pepper, and remaining 1 cup boiling water. Stir, reduce the heat to medium-low, cover, and cook for 10 minutes. Add the wine, season with Tabasco and salt to taste, and continue to cook until the rice has absorbed all the liquid, about 20 minutes.

3. Remove from the heat, stir, cover, and let stand for 5 minutes. Serve sprinkled with the parsley.

Arroz con Cangrejo y Coco

RICE WITH CRABMEAT AND COCONUT MILK *Serves 4 to 6*

There is nothing more typical of the Pacific and Atlantic coasts of South America than rice cooked with some type of seafood. Brazil, Venezuela, Colombia, Ecuador, and Peru all excel in the preparation of this dish, which may be made with shrimp, crabmeat, lobster, fish, mollusks, or a combination and flavored with coconut milk.

2 tablespoons olive oil

½ teaspoon ground annatto or sweet paprika

1 medium-size red onion, finely chopped

1 cup finely chopped leek (white part and 1 inch of the green), washed well

½ cup minced celery

½ cup seeded and diced (¼ inch) red bell pepper

½ cup seeded and diced (¼ inch) green bell pepper

2 cloves garlic, mashed into a paste with 1 teaspoon salt and ¼ teaspoon freshly ground black pepper

2 tablespoons minced fresh parsley leaves

2 tablespoons minced fresh cilantro leaves

¾ cup well-stirred canned unsweetened coconut milk

Two 6-ounce cans good-quality crabmeat, drained well and picked over for shells and cartilage

1½ cups cooked converted rice (page 322), kept warm

Heat the oil in a large, preferably nonstick skillet over medium heat. Add the annatto, onion, leek, celery, bell peppers, parsley, and cilantro and cook, stirring a few times, until the onion is wilted, about 5 minutes. Add the coconut milk and crabmeat. Reduce the heat to low and cook for 5 minutes, carefully stirring occasionally so that it doesn't stick to the pan. Toss with the rice and serve.

TO SERVE Serve with *Ensalada de Endivias, Palmitos, y Paltas* (page 172).

Sinfonía del Mar

A SEAFOOD SYMPHONY *Serves 8*

This splendid stew reflects not only its Spanish heritage but also the bounty from Chile's long seacoast, which has been blessed with some of the richest and finest seafood in the world. It takes some time to prepare, but most of the work can be done ahead. This is a real treat for seafood lovers.

Four 4-ounce lobster tails

16 langostinos (extra-large shrimp)

2 pounds sea bass or other firm, white-fleshed fish fillets

1 tablespoon fresh lemon juice

Salt and freshly ground black pepper

1 pound mussels

10 to 12 clams

1 tablespoon all-purpose flour or cornmeal

¼ cup olive oil

2 medium-size onions, minced (about 2 cups)

1 tablespoon minced garlic

One 16-ounce can crushed tomatoes

½ cup ground blanched almonds

2 bay leaves

1 teaspoon sweet paprika

¼ to ½ teaspoon saffron threads, to your taste, crumbled

¼ teaspoon red pepper flakes

2 cups chicken broth or water

½ cup dry sherry

1. Cut each lobster tail into 4 slices. With a small knife, loosen the flesh a bit so it is easier to remove from the shell when eating. Peel the lan-gostinos, leaving the tails on. Remove the black vein. Cut the fish fillets into 8 roughly equal-size pieces. Rub with the lemon juice and salt and black pepper to taste. Set all aside.

2. Wash the mussels and clams thoroughly. Pull the beards off the mussels, if necessary. Mix the flour into a large pot of cold water, then add the clams and mussels, making sure they are covered by the water. (The flour makes the shellfish open and release the sand.) Rinse after 30 minutes and drain. Set aside.

3. Heat the oil in a large, heavy casserole over medium heat. Add the onions and cook, stirring occasionally, until very soft, about 10 minutes. Add the garlic and cook for a few seconds. Stir in the tomatoes and almonds, cover, and cook for 20 minutes. Add the bay leaves, paprika, saffron, 1 teaspoon salt, ½ teaspoon black pepper, and the red pepper and cook for 1 minute. Add 1 cup of the chicken broth, cover, and bring to a boil. Reduce the heat to medium-low and simmer for 20 minutes. Discard the bay leaves. The sauce can be prepared up to this point the day before. Let cool, cover, and refrigerate. Reheat before proceeding.

4. To cook the shellfish, bring the remaining 1 cup broth to a boil. Add the lobster, cover, and simmer for 3 minutes. Remove with a slotted spoon and set aside. Add the mussels and clams, cover, and cook until the shells open, about 5 minutes. Remove with a slotted spoon, discarding any that don't open. Strain the broth through a sieve lined with cheesecloth.

5. Add the strained broth and sherry to the sauce and season with salt and black pepper to taste. Add the fish pieces, cover, and simmer for 8 minutes. Add the lobster and langostinos and cook just until the langostinos turn pink and curl, 3 to 5 minutes.

6. Serve immediately in soup plates. In each plate, put 1 piece of fish, 2 pieces of lobster, 2 langostinos, 2 mussels, and 1 clam. Pour some of the sauce over all.

Moqueca do Frutos del Mar

BRAZILIAN SEAFOOD STEW *Serves 8*

The natives of Brazil had a way of preparing fish called *pokeka*, which was nothing more than pieces of fish wrapped in leaves and roasted over hot coals. The Africans who worked in the kitchens of the Big Houses of the plantations baked the fish in banana leaves and eventually modified the technique, calling it *moqueca*, which became a famous Brazilian fish stew. There are many interpretations of this stew. It can be made with shrimp, fish, or a mixture of fish and shellfish. It might have only a small amount of broth, like one I had in Rio, or a lot of liquid, like the *moqueca* I enjoyed on the coast, in a restaurant in Florianópolis. The locals thicken the broth with *farofa* (page 304), the toasted manioc that is always present on the table, and if they like it spicy, they add more of the equally ubiquitous *Molho de Pimenta e Limão* (page 335).

Four 4-ounce lobster tails

1 cup water

3 tablespoons *dendê* (page 422)

2 medium-size onions, finely chopped (about 2 cups)

1 small green bell pepper, seeded and finely chopped

1 small red bell pepper, seeded and finely chopped

2 cloves garlic, minced

2 large ripe but firm tomatoes (about 1 pound), peeled, seeded, and finely chopped

¼ cup minced fresh cilantro or parsley leaves

1 cup well-stirred canned unsweetened coconut milk

Malagueta pepper sauce or Tabasco sauce

Salt

¼ teaspoon freshly ground black pepper

3 tablespoons olive oil

16 large shrimp, peeled and deveined

1½ pounds firm, white-fleshed fish fillets (such as cod, halibut, or catfish), cut into 1- to 1½-inch pieces

All-purpose flour for dredging

12 ounces lump crabmeat, picked over for shells and cartilage

1 pound cleaned squid, sliced ½ inch thick, or frozen squid rings, thawed and blanched in boiling water for a few seconds, until milky white

1 pound mussels, scrubbed and debearded, then steamed (page 408), broth strained and reserved

½ cup chopped scallions (white part and 1 inch of the green) for garnish

1. Cut each lobster tail into 4 slices. With a small knife, loosen the flesh a bit so it is easier to remove from the shell when eating. In a small saucepan, bring the water to a boil, add the lobster, and cook for 3 minutes. Drain the lobster, reserving the broth, and set aside. Strain the broth and set aside.

2. Heat the *dendê* in a large skillet over medium heat. Add the onions, bell peppers, and garlic and cook, stirring a few times, for 5 minutes. Add the tomatoes, cilantro, coconut milk, and hot pepper sauce to taste, then cover and simmer for 15 minutes. Season with salt to taste and stir in the black pepper. Set aside. The sauce can be prepared the day before, cooled, and refrigerated.

3. In another large skillet, heat the oil over medium heat. Add the shrimp and cook, stirring, for a few seconds, until the shrimp just turn pink. Remove with a slotted spoon and set aside. Lightly dredge the fish in the flour, tapping off any excess, and cook on both sides for a couple of minutes, until lightly colored. Add the sauce, bring to a boil, reduce the heat to medium-low, and simmer for 5 minutes. Add the lobster, shrimp, crabmeat, squid, and mussels and cook only until heated through. It is better to remove the mussels from the shells, leaving only 8 in the shells for garnish. If the sauce is too thick, add some of the broth from cooking the mussels or lobster. There should be enough sauce just to coat the seafood; this is not a soupy stew. Taste for salt and hot pepper sauce.

4. Serve in heated bowls or soup plates, each garnished with 1 mussel in the shell and some of the scallions.

TO SERVE Serve with white rice.

Bobó de Camarão

SHRIMP WITH YUCA SAUCE *Serves 4 to 6*

Bobó is one of the great African-Brazilian specialties from northern Brazil—an ingenious blend of African cooking and native ingredients, namely tomatoes, yuca, and hot pepper. The yuca puree is combined with coconut milk to make a creamy sauce. I have heard that a famous cook in northern Brazil has brought this recipe up to date by adding whipping cream to make a thinner sauce. With or without cream, it is an unusual and delicious dish.

1½ pounds large shrimp, unpeeled

Juice of 1 lime

4 cups water

1 pound peeled fresh yuca or frozen yuca

1 tablespoon olive oil

2 tablespoons *dendê* (page 422)

1 medium-size onion, minced (about 1 cup)

3 cloves garlic, minced

½ cup seeded and finely chopped green bell pepper

2 large ripe but firm tomatoes (about 1 pound), peeled, seeded, and chopped

2 tablespoons minced scallions (white part and 1 inch of the green)

2 tablespoons minced fresh parsley leaves

2 tablespoons minced fresh cilantro leaves

½ teaspoon salt

¼ teaspoon white pepper

Red pepper flakes

1 cup well-stirred canned unsweetened coconut milk

Whipping cream, if needed

1. Peel the shrimp, reserving the shells, and devein. Rinse the shrimp well and dry with paper towels. Place in a large glass bowl and toss with the lime juice. Cover and refrigerate until needed.

2. Place the shrimp shells in a medium-size saucepan, add the water, and bring to a boil. Reduce the heat to low and simmer for 10 minutes. Strain the broth and discard the shells.

3. In a 4-quart saucepan, bring the shrimp broth to a boil. Add the yuca and, if necessary, enough boiling water to cover. Cook over low heat until the yuca is tender, about 20 minutes. Drain, reserving the cooking liquid. Mash the yuca with a potato masher, adding enough cooking liquid to get a coarse puree. (Some cooks prefer to leave small pieces of yuca unmashed for texture.)

4. While the yuca is cooking, heat the oil and *dendê* together in a large skillet over medium heat. Add the onion and cook, stirring a few times, until softened, about 5 minutes. Stir in the garlic, bell pepper, tomatoes, scallions, parsley, cilantro, salt, white pepper, and red pepper. Cover and cook until the tomatoes have formed a sauce, about 10 minutes. Stir in the coconut milk and cook for 5 minutes.

5. To finish the dish, bring the tomato mixture to a boil. Stir in the shrimp and simmer until the shrimp begin to curl, about 1 minute. Stir in the yuca puree (reserve a few spoonfuls if making the hot pepper sauce; see To Serve) and season with salt and white pepper to taste. If the mixture is too thick, add enough whipping cream to get the desired consistency, which should be like that of heavy cream. (I have never needed to thin this sauce.) Serve hot.

TO SERVE **Serve with rice and homemade hot pepper sauce. To make the sauce, remove a few spoonfuls of the yuca puree, thin with a little water, and mix with prepared hot pepper sauce to taste.**

Platos Vegetarianos

MEATLESS MAIN DISHES

MOST OF SOUTH AMERICA'S INDIGENOUS peoples ate to nourish their bodies and souls. Their diets were essentially vegetarian. The Indians of the Altiplano depended on quinoa, amaranth, corn, beans, squash, and potatoes and other tubers. In the coastal and Amazonian regions, yuca was the basic food, eaten three times a day. The Indians used only a few herbs to flavor their foods, and these herbs were not always available. Salt was rare and costly, so their main flavoring agent was, and still is, hot pepper sauce. In fact, many of the dishes that South Americans still enjoy today taste bland to foreigners, who are not accustomed to flavoring their foods with anything but hot pepper sauce.

The earliest bean and vegetable stews were very simply prepared and flavored mainly with sun-ripened produce. The Europeans brought onions, garlic, and various herbs and spices, such as oregano, basil, cumin, and black pepper, which all became essential ingredients in creole cuisine. But what really revolutionized local cooking was the introduction of dairy products. Simple specialties such as *humitas* (ground corn wrapped in cornhusks) were transformed into gourmet delights by the addition of cheese, butter, and eggs. Cheese became part of the daily diet throughout South America, whether it was used on its own or as part of more complicated dishes. With the introduction of wheat, meatless pasta dishes became regular fare, especially in the southern countries and Brazil. And let us not forget the indigenous potato, which was transformed by the addition of cheese, butter, and eggs into wonderful specialties that delight the palate.

Unfortunately, the basic daily diet of the Indians has changed since the conquest, as they have had to do without quinoa and amaranth, which contain almost twice as much protein as other grains and all the amino acids that are absent from most plant proteins. Today people are rediscovering the value of these grains, and perhaps they will regain their rightful place on the South American table. In the tropics, the Indians' diet is still based on yuca and, since the conquest, also on plantains.

Pastel de Quinua

QUINOA TORTE *Serves 8*

Some of the best quinoa comes from Bolivia, and Bolivians excel in the preparation of many dishes using this nourishing grain. Tortes such as this one are also called baked soups, because the mixture looks soupy before going into the oven. This dish can be made with pasta, chickpeas, bread, or other grains as the starch element. It makes a wonderful luncheon dish, accompanied by a salad. Make sure there is enough for seconds.

> 6 cups water
>
> 1½ cups quinoa, rinsed (page 327)
>
> 2 tablespoons canola oil
>
> 1 medium-size onion, finely chopped (about 1 cup)
>
> 2 medium-size ripe but firm tomatoes (10 to 12 ounces), peeled and finely chopped
>
> 2 tablespoons minced fresh parsley leaves
>
> 1 teaspoon dried oregano
>
> ½ teaspoon sugar
>
> 1 teaspoon salt
>
> ½ teaspoon ground allspice
>
> ½ teaspoon freshly ground black pepper
>
> 1 tablespoon fresh hot red or yellow pepper puree, store-bought or homemade (page 332), or hot pepper sauce to taste
>
> 1 cup chicken broth
>
> ½ cup all-purpose flour
>
> 3 large eggs, lightly beaten
>
> ¾ cup milk
>
> 8 ounces white cheddar, Chihuahua, mozzarella, or Muenster cheese, shredded
>
> 2 hard-cooked eggs, peeled and sliced
>
> ½ cup freshly grated Parmesan cheese

1. Preheat the oven to 375°F. Butter and flour a shallow 8-cup baking dish.

2. Bring the water to a boil in a large saucepan. Add the quinoa, reduce the heat to medium-low, and cook until tender, about 12 minutes. Drain and set aside.

3. Heat the oil in a medium-size, heavy skillet over low heat. Add the onion and tomatoes and cook, stirring occasionally, until the tomatoes have formed a sauce, about 10 minutes. Add a little water if it gets too dry. Add the parsley, oregano, sugar, salt, allspice, black pepper, hot pepper puree, and chicken broth and simmer for 10 minutes.

4. Toss the quinoa with the flour. Add half of the tomato mixture, the beaten eggs, milk, and half of the cheddar cheese and mix well. Spread half of the quinoa mixture in the prepared dish. Top with the sliced eggs, the remaining tomato mixture, and the remaining cheddar. Cover with the remaining quinoa mixture. Sprinkle the Parmesan evenly over the top and bake until the top is browned and crispy, about 40 minutes.

5. Remove from the oven and let rest for 5 minutes, then slice and serve.

TO SERVE **Serve with a green salad.**

NOTE **This torte reheats very well. Cover loosely with aluminum foil and place in a preheated 350°F oven until heated through, about 20 minutes.**

Souflé de Kiwicha/Amaranto

AMARANTH SOUFFLÉ *Serves 4*

Amaranto, better known in the Andes as *kiwicha*, was another sacred grain of the Indians that almost disappeared after the arrival of the Spaniards. Fortunately, these grains are coming back, thanks to the efforts of the scientific community, and are spreading worldwide because of an impressive nutritional profile. This soufflé is absolutely delicious, the best way to prepare amaranth. It is also good with quinoa, and either way it makes a great luncheon dish served with buttered asparagus or broccoli.

Dry bread crumbs

2 tablespoons unsalted butter

2 tablespoons all-purpose flour

½ teaspoon salt

¼ teaspoon white pepper

Pinch of freshly grated nutmeg

1 cup hot milk

4 large eggs, separated

4 ounces Gouda or other good melting cheese, shredded

1 cup cooked amaranth (page 328)

1.   Preheat the oven to 400°F. Prepare a 6- to 8-cup soufflé mold (or any similar size mold) by buttering it thoroughly, especially the sides, and sprinkling it evenly with the bread crumbs. Shake out any excess crumbs.

2.   To make the sauce, heat the butter over medium heat in a small saucepan. Add the flour, salt, pepper, and nutmeg and cook, stirring with a wooden spoon, until foamy, about 2 minutes. Do not let brown. Remove from the heat and, with a wire whisk, beat in the milk, stirring until smooth. Return to the heat and bring to a boil. Cook, stirring with a wooden spoon, for 1 minute. Remove from the heat and beat in the egg yolks one at a time. Add the cheese and stir until melted. Mix in the amaranth.

3.   In a large mixing bowl with an electric mixer, beat the egg whites with a pinch of salt until they hold firm peaks. Fold a third of the whites into the amaranth mixture to lighten it, then fold in the rest.

4.   Transfer the mixture to the prepared mold. Place in the middle of the oven, reduce the oven temperature to 375°F, and bake until golden brown and puffed, 30 to 35 minutes. Turn off the

oven and leave the soufflé inside for another 5 minutes, if necessary.

5.   Serve hot, dipping a serving spoon in the center and dishing the soufflé out with the help of a serving fork.

NOTES If using quinoa instead of amaranth, you will need 2 cups cooked quinoa.

Leftovers reheat very well in a preheated 300°F oven. Of course, they won't puff.

You can cut the recipe in half and bake in a 1-quart dish to serve 2.

Ahogado de Berenjenas

EGGPLANT LAYERED WITH
TOMATOES AND CORN   Serves 8

In this delicious casserole of Italian origin, Old World eggplant pairs with Indian corn and tomatoes to give us a most unusual treat. It is like a New World lasagna, a specialty of my friend Kika Keefe, who lives in Santiago, Chile.

3 medium-size eggplants (about 1 pound each)

Olive oil or olive oil cooking spray

Salt and freshly ground black pepper

2 pounds ripe but firm pear-shaped tomatoes

2 cups thawed frozen corn kernels

¼ cup milk

¼ teaspoon white pepper

Pinch of freshly grated nutmeg

2 tablespoons unsalted butter

8 ounces Chihuahua, mozzarella, or Muenster cheese, shredded

½ cup whipping cream

¼ cup freshly grated Parmesan cheese

1.   Preheat the oven to 425°F.

2.   Peel the eggplant and cut lengthwise into ¼-inch-thick slices. With a pastry brush, coat the

slices with oil on both sides, or use olive oil spray. Brush or spray a jellyroll pan with oil, arrange the eggplant in a single layer in the pan, and season with salt and black pepper to taste. Bake until lightly colored, about 20 minutes. Remove from the oven and set aside.

3.   Reduce the oven temperature to 350°F. Lightly oil a 9 x 13-inch baking dish.

4.   Blanch the tomatoes in a large pot of boiling water for 30 seconds. Peel and cut into ⅛-inch-thick rounds. Lay on paper towels to drain.

5.   Process the corn in a blender or food processor until smooth, adding the milk, ½ teaspoon salt, the white pepper, and nutmeg. Heat the butter in a large skillet over medium heat. Add the corn mixture and cook, stirring, until thickened, about 5 minutes.

6.   To assemble, place a layer of eggplant in the prepared baking dish, cover evenly with half of the tomato slices, season with salt and black pepper to taste, cover evenly with half of the corn mixture, and top with half of the mozzarella. Repeat the layers, ending with a layer of eggplant. Drizzle the cream over the top, then sprinkle evenly with the Parmesan. Bake in the middle of the oven until lightly browned, about 45 minutes.

7.   Remove from the oven, let rest for 10 minutes, and serve, using a metal spatula and a large spoon to dish it out.

Ajiaco de Ollucos

ULLUCO STEW   *Serves 2 as a main course, 4 as a side dish*

This tuber, along with the potato, was a staple of the Incas. It is still a major source of carbohydrates in many of the Andean countries. It has a somewhat earthy taste and, like okra, a slightly mucilaginous texture that turns some people off. It grows at altitudes between 6,000 and 12,000 feet, and some scientists hope that it will travel around the world just as the potato did, to provide a nutritious crop in areas not suitable for growing other foods. *Ullucos* are available frozen or canned in some Latin American groceries.

> **1 pound frozen or canned *ullucos***
>
> **2 tablespoons canola oil**
>
> **1 medium-size onion, minced (about 1 cup)**
>
> **4 cloves garlic, crushed**
>
> **½ teaspoon *palillo* (page 427) or turmeric**
>
> **1 teaspoon salt**
>
> **1 pound all-purpose potatoes, peeled, cooked in water to cover until tender, drained, and cut into ¾-inch cubes**
>
> **2 cups chicken broth, or more if needed**
>
> **Freshly ground black pepper**
>
> **Fresh hot pepper puree, store-bought or homemade (page 332), or red pepper flakes**
>
> **4 ounces imported feta cheese, cubed**
>
> **2 hard-cooked eggs, peeled and each cut into 8 wedges, for garnish**
>
> **2 tablespoons minced fresh parsley leaves for garnish**

1.   If using frozen *ullucos*, cook in boiling salted water, covered, for 10 minutes. Drain, let cool, and cut into ¾-inch-thick rounds. If using canned *ullucos*, drain, rinse, and slice.

2.   Heat the oil in a large saucepan over low heat. Add the onion and garlic and cook until the onion is soft, about 10 minutes. Stir in the *palillo*, salt, potatoes, *ullucos*, and chicken broth. Season with black pepper and hot pepper puree to taste. Bring to a boil, reduce the heat to medium-low, and simmer until thickened, about 5 minutes. There should be enough sauce to cover the vegetables; add more chicken broth if it's too dry.

3.   Just before serving, stir in the cheese. Serve in soup plates garnished with the eggs and parsley.

Rotolo di Pasta de Brocoli

BROCCOLI PASTA ROLL

Makes 16 rotolo or 24 cannelloni; 8 to 12 servings

I had this marvelous pasta dish in Montevideo, Uruguay, in the restaurant of my friend Felipe Miles. This gifted young chef served slices of the pasta roll on a bed of fresh tomato sauce. Although this presentation is beautiful, I think that the average cook would find it difficult to deal with the process of handling the pasta sheets, assembling, slicing, warming up, and serving. A much easier way for home use is to make cannelloni, which are assembled and placed in an ovenproof pan, ready to go into the oven when needed. When I make them this way, I serve two or three on a plate, with the sauce running over the middle and the basil scattered on top, which I think is just as beautiful as the more complex presentation. I include both options here, so that you can choose the one you prefer.

When I prepare this dish, I usually serve *Ensalada de Berros, Chochos, y Aguacate* (page 170) as a first course and a flan, surrounded with fresh fruit, as dessert. This luncheon has a definite Italian accent, which is fitting, considering the fact that many Italian immigrants came to Uruguay. These cannelloni can be made up to two days ahead and kept in the refrigerator, or they can be frozen up to three months.

RELLENO (Filling)

¼ cup olive oil

6 anchovy fillets

4 large cloves garlic, mashed into a paste with 1½ teaspoons salt and ½ teaspoon freshly ground black pepper

2 pounds fresh or frozen broccoli florets

1¼ cups seedless golden raisins

12 ounces ricotta cheese

1 cup freshly grated Parmesan cheese

1 tablespoon salt

1 tablespoon olive oil

3 fresh pasta sheets, about 12 inches square, if making *rotolo*, 4 sheets if making cannelloni

¼ cup (½ stick) unsalted butter, melted, if making cannelloni

2 recipes *Salsa de Tomate* (page 406)

8 fresh basil leaves, cut into ribbons, for garnish

1.   To make the filling, heat the oil in a heavy 12-inch skillet over medium heat. Add the anchovies and garlic paste and stir until the anchovies melt into the oil. Add the broccoli, cover, reduce the heat to low, and steam the broccoli, stirring occasionally, until fork tender, 5 to 7 minutes. Do not overcook. Uncover and let cool, then drain thoroughly.

2.   Place the broccoli mixture and ½ cup of the raisins in a food processor and process until coarsely pureed. Add the ricotta and Parmesan and process for a few seconds, until well blended. Transfer to a large bowl.

3.   *To make* rotolo: Bring a large pot of boiling water to a boil. Add the salt and oil and cook the pasta 1 sheet at a time until *al dente*, about 5 minutes each. Place a colander in the pot to make removing the pasta easier, or use slotted spoons to transfer the pasta to a bowl of ice water to cool. Carefully remove 1 pasta sheet from the bowl, place on a dry kitchen towel, and dry with another towel. Spread one-third of the filling evenly on the pasta, leaving a ½-inch margin all around. Scatter ¼ cup of the raisins evenly over the filling. With the help of the towel, roll up tightly, like a jellyroll. Cut the roll in half (it is easier to handle) and wrap each half tightly in plastic wrap. Repeat with the remaining ingredients. Cut each roll into ¾-inch-thick slices and place cut side down in a buttered shallow baking

dish. Cover with aluminum foil and refrigerate or freeze, if desired.

To make cannelloni: Cut the 4 pasta sheets in half lengthwise and then into thirds crosswise, to get 6 rectangles from each sheet. Cook the pasta as for the *rotolo*, 4 rectangles at a time. When cooked, remove with a large slotted spoon, drain well, place on a dry kitchen towel, and cover with another kitchen towel. Repeat until all the rectangles are cooked. To assemble, spread about 2 heaping tablespoons of the filling on each rectangle, leaving a ¼-inch margin all around. Scatter 3 or 4 raisins on top, roll up tightly starting from the long end, and place seam side up in a buttered shallow baking dish, making sure you don't crowd them. Brush with the melted butter. Cover with aluminum foil and refrigerate or freeze, if desired.

4. Preheat the oven to 350°F. Bring the pasta to room temperature, if necessary. Bake, covered, until just heated through, about 15 minutes for the *rotolo* or 20 minutes for the cannelloni.

5. Just before serving, heat the *salsa de tomate* over low heat. For the *rotolo*, pour ¼ cup of the *salsa* on each heated plate. Arrange 3 to 5 slices of pasta on top and garnish with the basil. For the cannelloni, place 3 on each plate, pour the sauce along the middle of each, and scatter the basil on top. Serve either as a first course or as a main course for dinner.

Noquis de Espinaca

SPINACH GNOCCHI *Serves 3 to 4*

In Uruguay and Argentina, *ñoquis* are traditionally served on the 29th of each month. The idea is that one's pockets are almost empty at the end of the month, and potatoes and flour are about the only ingredients left in the pantry. In Argentina, neigh-borhood restaurants follow this tradition, serving *ñoquis* as a special on the 29th. Uruguayans place money under their plates of *ñoquis* to ensure prosperity. This version is similar to the Italian *gnocchi alla Romana*, which are made with semolina and are usually cut into medallions. When I make these for dinner, I precede them with a vegetable soup.

> 2 cups water
> ½ teaspoon salt
> 1 teaspoon dry mustard
> ¼ teaspoon white pepper
> Pinch of freshly grated nutmeg
> ⅔ cup instant polenta flour or cornmeal
> 1 large egg, lightly beaten
> ½ cup plus 2 tablespoons freshly grated Parmesan cheese
> 2 cups well washed packed spinach leaves, cooked in a little water until completely wilted, drained, squeezed dry, and minced (about ⅓ cup)
> ¼ cup (½ stick) unsalted butter, melted

1. Place the water, salt, mustard, white pepper, and nutmeg in a medium-size saucepan and bring to a boil. Sprinkle the polenta flour over the boiling water and stir with a wire whisk until well blended. Cook, stirring constantly with a wooden spoon, until the dough pulls away from the side and bottom of the pan, 5 to 7 minutes. The dough should be quite stiff but still workable. Remove from the heat and beat in the egg, ½ cup of the Parmesan, and the spinach. Pour into a greased shallow baking pan and spread to a thickness of about ½ inch. Let cool, cover, and refrigerate for at least 2 hours.

2. Preheat the oven to 375°F. Butter a baking sheet.

3. When the dough is firm, cut into 2-inch squares. Place on the prepared sheet, brush with the melted butter, and sprinkle with the remaining 2 tablespoons Parmesan. Bake until golden on top, about 15 minutes. Let rest for a few minutes and serve.

TO SERVE **Serve with a tomato and onion salad.**

Porotos Granados

CRANBERRY BEAN, CORN, AND SQUASH STEW *Serves 4*

This popular Chilean dish traces its origin to the time before the arrival of the Spaniards. The Mapuche Indians probably made a simple stew with the summer bounty of beans, calabaza, corn, tomatoes, and peppers. In Chile, as in the rest of the Andean countries, cooks use fresh beans for most of their specialties. The beans, though, are mature, sold in the shell, and take about 45 minutes to cook. It is difficult to find fresh cranberry beans in the United States, so you can use dried cranberry beans or other types of fresh beans, such as navy beans or black-eyed peas.

A variation of this dish uses fresh baby lima beans. The corn is sometimes pureed and passed through a sieve, as is the squash. Some cooks prefer to use the vegetables as they are, letting the squash cook until it falls apart and forms a sauce. Calabaza is becoming more popular in the United States and is available in some supermarkets here. Any winter squash can be used instead. Some people enrich the stew with a little whipping cream.

> 2 tablespoons canola oil
>
> ½ teaspoon sweet paprika
>
> 1 medium-size onion, minced (about 1 cup)
>
> 1 small green bell pepper, seeded and finely chopped
>
> 2 cloves garlic, mashed into a paste with 1 teaspoon salt and ½ teaspoon freshly ground black pepper
>
> ¼ teaspoon ground cumin
>
> 1 large ripe but firm tomato (about 8 ounces), peeled and chopped

> 8 fresh basil leaves, chopped, or 1 teaspoon dried basil
>
> 2 cups cooked cranberry beans or one 15-ounce can black-eyed peas, drained and rinsed
>
> 1 pound winter squash, peeled, seeded, and cut into 1-inch cubes
>
> 1 cup fresh or frozen corn kernels
>
> 2 tablespoons freshly grated Parmesan cheese
>
> Fresh basil leaves, cut into ribbons
>
> *Color Chileno* (page 331), *Pebre de Cilantro* (page 336), or cayenne pepper

1. Heat the canola oil in a 4-quart saucepan over medium heat. Stir in the paprika, onion, and bell pepper and cook, stirring a few times, for about 5 minutes. Add the garlic paste, cumin, tomato, and chopped basil and cook over low heat until the tomato has formed a sauce, about 10 minutes. Add the beans, squash, and enough water just to cover them. Bring to a boil, reduce the heat to medium-low, cover and simmer until the squash begins to fall apart, about 20 minutes. Add more water if the stew dries out too much; it should have enough sauce to cover the vegetables. Add the corn and cook for 5 minutes.

2. Serve in soup bowls, sprinkled with the Parmesan and basil ribbons and drizzled with the *color Chileno.*

Frijol Boludo/ Frisoles Colombianos

COLOMBIAN-STYLE BEANS
Makes about 8 cups; 4 to 6 servings

Frisoles or *frijoles* (beans) are a staple in Colombia, a comfort food for all classes. There are many ways of preparing beans, and methods vary from region to region. I like this rendition because of its simplicity. Served with rice and a green salad, it makes a perfect vegetarian meal. My Colombian neighbor, Sol Name, used to make these beans often, and I always appreciated it when she brought some to me.

> 2 cups *frijol boludo* or *bala* (see Notes), picked over and rinsed
>
> 1 small carrot, thinly sliced
>
> 1 small all-purpose potato, peeled and thinly sliced into rounds
>
> 2 cloves garlic, chopped
>
> ½ cup vegetable broth, or more if needed
>
> 4 scallions (white part and 1 inch of the green)
>
> 1 green plantain, peeled and cut into ½-inch cubes
>
> 2 teaspoons salt
>
> ½ teaspoon freshly ground black pepper

1. Soak the beans overnight per the instructions on page 412. Drain and place in a heavy casserole with fresh water to cover by 2 inches. Bring to a boil over medium heat, reduce the heat to low, and simmer for 1 hour.

2. While the beans are cooking, place the carrot, potato, garlic, and vegetable broth in a food processor and process until smooth. Add to the hot beans along with the scallions and plantain. Cover and simmer until the beans are soft, about 30 minutes. Discard the scallions and add the salt and pepper. Simmer for a few more minutes, adding boiling water or broth if too dry; the beans should be soupy. Serve hot.

TO SERVE Colombians serve these beans with rice on the side, which they add to the beans to taste.

NOTES The large, dark red beans called *frijol boludo* or *bala* are available in Latin American markets. Red kidney beans may be substituted.

Some versions of this recipe call for diced bacon or salt pork to be added along with the puree. Others use *sofrito* (an onion-based flavoring) as the main seasoning.

Porotos Guisados

BEAN AND VEGETABLE STEW *Serves 4*

In Uruguay and Argentina, hearty casseroles made with or without meat are quite popular—a tradition inherited from the Spaniards. White beans or chickpeas, root vegetables, and sometimes cabbage go into the pot. These casseroles always start with a good *sofrito* made with onions, garlic, peppers, and tomatoes.

SOFRITO
> 2 tablespoons olive oil
>
> 1 large onion, chopped (about 1½ cups)
>
> ½ teaspoon sweet paprika
>
> 1 small green bell pepper, seeded and chopped
>
> 2 medium-size ripe but firm tomatoes (10 to 12 ounces), peeled and chopped
>
> 4 cloves garlic, mashed into a paste with 1 teaspoon salt and ¼ teaspoon freshly ground black pepper
>
> 1 teaspoon dried oregano, crumbled
>
> Pinch of freshly grated nutmeg
>
> 2 tablespoons chopped fresh parsley leaves
>
> ¼ teaspoon red pepper flakes

> 4 cups vegetable or chicken broth
>
> ½ pound boiling potatoes, peeled and cut into 1-inch cubes
>
> 2 small sweet potatoes (about 8 ounces), peeled, sliced 1 inch thick, and quartered
>
> 8 ounces winter squash, peeled, seeded, and cut into 1-inch cubes
>
> One 15-ounce can Great Northern beans or chickpeas, undrained
>
> 1 cup chopped cabbage
>
> ½ cup frozen peas
>
> Finely chopped fresh parsley leaves for garnish

1. To make the *sofrito*, heat the oil in a heavy 4-quart saucepan over low heat. Add the onion and paprika and cook, stirring occasionally, until very soft, about 8 minutes. Add the bell pepper, tomatoes, garlic paste, oregano, nutmeg, parsley, and red pepper. Cover and cook, stirring occasionally, until the tomatoes have formed a sauce, about 10 minutes. If the sauce is too dry, add a little water.

2. Add the vegetable broth to the *sofrito* and bring to a boil. Add the potatoes, sweet potatoes, squash, beans with their liquid, and cabbage. Cover and simmer until the vegetables are soft, about 20 minutes. There should be plenty of liquid to cover the vegetables; add more water, if needed. Add the peas and simmer for 5 minutes.

3. Serve in soup bowls, sprinkled with the parsley.

Mazamorra

DRIED CORN STEW *Serves 4*

Mazamorra is one of the oldest and simplest Indian foods and has survived virtually unchanged throughout the continent's human history. It is a simple stew made with water and cracked dried corn, except in some countries, such as Venezuela and Brazil, where fresh corn is used as well. In pre-Hispanic times, it was probably served seasoned with herbs or honey. After the conquest, milk and sugar, *panela* (molded brown sugar), or *arope* (brown sugar syrup) were served with this simple stew.

Mazamorra is a dish that sustains the masses, a cure-all specialty, and a beloved comfort food. Depending on the region, it is prepared with either yellow or white corn and made into a savory or sweet dish. The whole kernels of dried corn have to be pounded to break them into smaller pieces, called *maíz quebrado*, literally "broken corn." The stew can then be thickened with the starch left after pounding. The broken corn has to be soaked overnight and cooked the next day in the same water with a little lye or a teaspoon of baking soda to soften the corn. (Lye was made by mixing fine

ashes with hot water and straining it through a fine-mesh sieve.) This stew had to be stirred often during the last hour of cooking to thicken it.

In Ecuador, this cooked corn is made into *morocho de sal o de dulce* (savory or sweet *mazamorra*). In the coastal region of Colombia, there is a savory version called *peto*. In Paraguay, the corn stew is served with milk and sugar or sugar cane syrup. This cooked corn is the basis for the famous *locros* (hominy-based soups) of Argentina, Paraguay, and Uruguay. In Bolivia, it is called *pataska* and is the basis for *tojorí* (a breakfast pudding that also can be served cold as a dessert), which is a specialty of Cochabamba and eastern Bolivia, where it goes by the name of *tujuré*. When prepared as a dessert, it is cooled in a shallow pan and cut into slices to serve with sugar cane syrup. Brazilians call cracked dried white corn *canjiquinha* and use it, among other things, to make *mungunzá*, a *mazamorra* made with milk or coconut milk, depending on the region.

> 1 cup cracked dried white corn (*maíz pisado* or *maíz quebrado*; see Note)
>
> 6 cups water
>
> 1 tablespoon ground white corn (see Note) dissolved in ¼ cup water
>
> Pinch of baking soda
>
> Milk (optional) for serving
>
> Grated *panela* or dark brown sugar for serving

1. Thoroughly wash the cracked corn and soak overnight in plenty of cold water to cover. Alternatively, put it in a heavy casserole with water to cover and bring to a boil. Turn off the heat, cover, and let it stand for 1 hour.

2. Drain the corn and place in a heavy casserole. Add the water, bring to a boil, reduce the heat to medium-low, and simmer until soft, about 1 hour. Stir in the white corn paste and baking soda and continue to cook, uncovered and stirring often, until thickened, about 30 minutes. Serve with milk, if desired, and *panela* on the side.

NOTE Cracked dried white corn is available in some Hispanic markets in 1-pound boxes under the name of *mazamorra Colombiana*. It comes with a pouch of ground white corn to thicken it. It is also available in 1-pound bags under the name *canjiquinha*. This does not have the ground corn, which is not necessary for some recipes.

Mazamorra Campesina

SWEET CORN STEW *Serves 4*

This *mazamorra* is typical of the diet of the Venezuelan countryside. Just as many people view chicken soup as a cure-all, so do the *campesinos* (country people) attribute healing powers to this stew. It is considered especially good for children, the elderly, and women who have given birth.

6 to 8 ears corn (4 cups kernels)

2 cups water

2 cups milk

½ teaspoon anise seeds, crushed

Pinch of salt

Granulated or dark brown sugar for serving

In a food processor or blender, puree the corn with a little of the water until smooth. Transfer to a large saucepan and add the rest of the water, the milk, anise, and salt. Bring to a boil over medium heat, reduce the heat to low, and simmer, stirring constantly, until thickened, about 10 minutes. Serve warm, with the sugar on the side.

Chipá Guasú

PARAGUAYAN CORN TORTE *Serves 6*

This torte is one of the classic examples of what can be done with corn. I especially like this dish because of its versatility: it can be used as a main course for a meatless meal, as part of a buffet, or as a side dish for any fish or meat. Whichever way I serve it, it is always a hit. The classic cheese used for this torte is Chihuahua, but you can experiment with different cheeses, such as fontina, which works very well here.

1 cup water

1 medium-size onion, halved and thinly sliced into half-moons (about 1 cup)

1 cup thinly sliced leeks (white part and 1 inch of the green), washed well

1 teaspoon salt

6 to 8 ears corn (4 cups kernels), or one 20-ounce package frozen corn, thawed

½ cup (1 stick) unsalted butter, melted

3 large eggs, separated

½ cup cornmeal mixed with 2 teaspoons baking powder and 1 teaspoon sugar

½ cup milk

8 ounces fontina cheese, shredded

2 tablespoons freshly grated Parmesan cheese

1. Preheat the oven to 375°F. Butter a 7 x 11-inch baking dish.

2. In a small saucepan, bring the water to a boil. Add the onion, leeks, and salt. Cover, reduce the heat to medium-low, and simmer for 10 minutes. Remove from the heat and let cool.

3. In a food processor, process the corn until smooth. Add the butter, egg yolks, cornmeal mixture, and milk and process until well mixed. Add the fontina and pulse until the ingredients are well blended. Transfer to a large mixing bowl, add the onion mixture, and mix well.

4. In a medium-size mixing bowl, beat the egg whites with an electric mixer until stiff (but not dry) peaks form. Carefully fold into the corn mixture. Turn into the prepared baking dish, sprinkle evenly with the Parmesan, and bake in

the middle of the oven until golden brown, about 45 minutes.

5. Remove from the oven and let rest for 5 minutes before cutting into serving-size portions.

Charquicán de Cochayuyo

COCHAYUYO (SEAWEED) BRAISED WITH VEGETABLES *Serves 4 to 6*

This chapter would not be complete without at least one dish made with *cochayuyo*. Open any Chilean cookbook, and you will find a variety of recipes using this outstanding, wholesome seaweed. There it is usually sold dried in one-pound packages of four bundles. It has a firm texture that makes it a good substitute for meat. This seaweed—along with *luche* (a dried algae) and *hulte* (the trunk of the seaweed and always sold cooked)—is a very important part of the coastal people's diet. This recipe was given to me by my travel guide because, she said, it is typical of what Chileans eat. It is not only loaded with nutritive value, but it is also delicious and a good way to get acquainted with this very special seaweed. I hope that we can soon find it in North American markets.

12 ounces calabaza or other winter squash

1 cup water

1½ pounds all-purpose potatoes, peeled

2 tablespoons unsalted butter

½ cup hot milk

Salt

2 tablespoons canola oil

1 small onion, finely chopped (about ½ cup)

½ cup seeded and chopped green bell pepper

1 teaspoon sweet paprika

2 cups finely chopped cooked *cochayuyo* (page 421)

1 cup fresh or frozen corn kernels

½ cup water

¼ teaspoon freshly ground black pepper

8 ounces green beans, ends trimmed and cut on the diagonal into ½-inch pieces

Pinch of baking soda

Color Chileno (page 331) or cayenne pepper

4 to 6 large eggs (optional), fried sunny-side up

1. Peel the calabaza, remove the seeds, and cut the flesh into chunks. Bring a medium-size saucepan of salted water to a boil. Add the calabaza, reduce the heat to medium-low, cover, and cook until tender, about 15 minutes. Drain and mash.

2. Meanwhile, place the potatoes in a large pot of salted water. Bring to a boil and continue to boil until tender. Drain and mash, adding the butter and milk to make a smooth puree. Mix the potatoes with the squash and season with salt to taste. Spread in a buttered, shallow ovenproof serving dish. Cover and keep warm.

3. In a large skillet, heat the canola oil over medium heat. Add the onion and bell pepper and cook, stirring occasionally, until soft, about 5 minutes. Stir in the paprika and *cochayuyo* and cook for 5 minutes. Add the corn, water, ½ teaspoon salt, and the black pepper. Cover and cook until all the water has evaporated, about 10 minutes. Taste for salt and black pepper.

4. Meanwhile, bring a medium-size saucepan of salted water to a boil. Add the baking soda (to preserve the bright green color of the beans) and green beans and cook until crisp-tender, about 5 minutes. Drain and add to the *cochayuyo* mixture. Spread over the potato-squash mixture. Drizzle with the *color Chileno*.

5. Serve warm, topped with 1 fried egg per person, if desired.

Vegetales y Legumbres

VEGETABLE AND BEAN SIDE DISHES

VEGETABLES AND LEGUMES ARE AN integral part of the creole cuisine of South America. In fact, beans, squash, and corn make up the so-called "Indian triad" that sustained the indigenous peoples for centuries. The arrival of the Spaniards and, later, the Portuguese enriched the diets of peoples on both sides of South America with onions, garlic, and numerous other vegetables. Creole cooks found new uses for these vegetables, usually in combination with the American tomato and pepper. The now ubiquitous *sofrito* (an onion-based flavoring or sauce) was the most important creation and plays a paramount role in South American cuisine.

Many of the vegetables in South America are served as a sauce. Vegetables served as side dishes vary by region and season. Although the use of vegetables differs from country to country, a variety of cooked vegetables, prepared in different ways, are an important part of South American meals.

Greens

South America's original inhabitants enjoyed a wide variety of greens, though not ones with which we are familiar. They ate the green leaves from plants such as quinoa, amaranth, Andean lupine, and cassava (yuca), as well as whatever they could gather in the fields. Garcilaso de la Vega, the first Inca historian, writes in his book *Comentarios Reales* (1609) about the abundance of greens called *ch'iwa*, how small some of them were, and how highly the Indians thought of them, to the point of preserving them by drying them in the sun. Seaweed on the coast, such as the Chilean *cochayuyo* (page 421), was eaten fresh or dried. In the interior, algae from the rivers or lakes, called *yuyo* or *llullucha*, was consumed fresh. So-called Indian cress (actually the flowering plant we call nasturtium, unrelated to true cress), *verdolaga*, and other wild greens, such as sorrel, wild lettuce, ferns, chicory, and herbs, were eaten fresh and added to soups and stews.

In Brazil, in areas where there was a concentration of slaves, the Africans brought with them their love for greens. West Africans have a tremendous variety of greens, wild and cultivated. Ghana alone claims to have more than 40 edible green vegetables. And a friend of mine from Sierra Leone said that they have more than 100 varieties of greens. The women collect them in season and dry them for later use. African slaves brought this tradition—and also, inadvertently, the seeds—to the Americas. African women had the custom of braiding their hair and carrying seeds on their heads (because they didn't have pockets) when they went to other towns. When these women were captured by slave traders and sent to the Americas as slaves, the experience was so traumatic that they didn't undo their hair until they got to their new home. Then out came the seeds of okra and greens. The Africans also quickly adopted the greens of the new land, which they used fresh or dried, just as they did back home.

The Europeans brought kale, collard greens, Swiss chard, cabbage, garlic, and lettuce, to name a few. They used these vegetables to make soups, stews, and side dishes that were highly seasoned with the indigenous hot peppers.

Kale or Collard Greens?

 Ana Patuleia Ortins, in her cookbook *Portuguese Homestyle Cooking*, addresses this question, which all cooks have when a recipe calls for *couve*. Some cooks believe that this is kale, others that it is collard greens. Patuleia describes two kinds of *couve*—the broad, flat-leaved *couve*, which is more common on the Portuguese mainland and resembles collard greens in flavor and color, and the curly-leaved *couve*, which comes from the Azores (islands belonging to Portugal) and is similar to the kale grown in the United States. She says that Portuguese immigrants brought the flat-leaved type of *couve* to Brazil. Thus, it is likely that the word *couve* refers to what we know as collard greens rather than to our kale.

Swiss Chard

 This plant brought by the Spaniards is very popular in the southern countries of South America. It has large leaves and fleshy stalks, with a taste that is slightly bitter. The green leaves have a texture similar to that of spinach. There is also a ruby-colored variety, as well as a rainbow type that displays an array of colors—yellow, orange, red, and green. When fresh, the leaves should be bright and crisp. Most supermarkets carry Swiss chard all year round.

Tomatoes

The word *tomato* derives from the Aztec word *tomatl*. Tomatoes first made their appearance as wild cherry tomatoes in Peru, Ecuador, and northern Chile. No evidence has ever been found of tomatoes being cultivated in South America prior to the conquest. By the time the Spaniards arrived, tomatoes were being cultivated in Mexico, although no one knows for sure how they got there. Over the years, tomatoes became increasingly important in the preparation of Mexican foods. The Incas apparently did not use tomatoes widely, although they may have used tomatoes in stews and salads. Now tomatoes appear on the South American table in a variety of ways. According to historians, the first tomato introduced in Europe was the yellow variety, which is probably why Europeans knew the tomato initially as *pomodoro*, "golden apple."

Peppers

Peppers, both sweet and hot, are another of America's great contributions to the world. Sweet peppers, or bell peppers, are widely used in South American countries and come in different colors: green, red, yellow, orange, and purple. They are especially used as part of *sofrito*. Hot peppers also are used extensively, especially in hot pepper salsas, which, in their varied forms, are common table condiments.

When Columbus first encountered the hot pepper (*Capsicum* species), which was different from the black pepper (*Piper nigrum*) for which he was looking, he called it *pimienta de las Indias* (pepper of the Indies). *Ajíes* (hot peppers) were an integral part of the Indian diet. They were used to season foods that were otherwise tasteless and were consumed as vegetables and as medicine. Hot peppers also had a ritual value, and the Incas required them as a tribute. According to the Indian chronicler Guaman Poma de Ayala, the Inca warehouses always had a generous supply of hot peppers, which were considered a very important commodity. Historian Bernabé Cobo believes that hot peppers were second in importance only to corn.

Squash

Sophie D. Coe, in her book *America's First Cuisines*, lists three genera in the squash family having culinary significance in the New World: *Cyclanthera*, *Sechium*, and *Cucurbita*.

Achogcha, *caigua*, or *cyua* (*Cyclanthera pedata*) is native to Peru, Ecuador, and Bolivia. The fruit of this climbing plant looks like a hot green pepper and is often stuffed with meat, rice, or vegetables, as in the Mexican dish *chiles rellenos*. Used in soups, main courses, or salads, the *achogcha/caigua* has a thin green skin that is sometimes smooth and sometimes wrinkled, depending on the species, and flat black seeds. It has just become available frozen in the United States in some South American groceries. There is no substitute.

Chayote (*Sechium edule*), from Mexico, Central America, and the Caribbean, goes by a number of names, including mango squash, vegetable pear, and vegetable squash. The word *chayote* comes from the Aztec word *chayotl*. This squash is used widely in Guatemala and other countries in Central America, as well as in Brazil and a few other South American countries. It is about four inches long and pear-shaped, with a very light green, smooth skin and cream-colored flesh. It is firmer in texture than other squash and should be purchased free of blemishes. When very young, it can be eaten raw, but it must be peeled, either before or after cooking. Its single pit is edible after cooking. *Chayote* may be baked, fried, boiled, or stuffed. A versatile vegetable, it is used not only for soups, stews, and savory dishes but also for desserts. *Chayote* is available throughout the year in most supermarkets.

The third genus mentioned by Coe, *Cucurbita*, encompasses squash, pumpkins, and gourds. There is evidence that by the year 6000 B.C., indigenous peoples in South America were cultivating some species of *Cucurbita*. These species can be eaten in different stages of maturation. For instance, immature fruits can be eaten as green vegetables, such as *zambo*, *zapallitos* (small squash), or *calabacín*.

Zambo, *vitoria*, and *lacayote* are different names for *Cucurbita ficifolia* or *C. pepo*, called winter melon in the United States. It traveled from Mexico centuries ago to become the most popular *Cucurbita* species throughout South America, except in Brazil, where people evidently didn't take to it. Therefore, I was surprised to find in the pastry shops of Portugal a variety of pastries made with this squash.

Zambo is cultivated in colder climates, in poor soils. It doesn't need special care and has excellent keeping qualities. In a cool, dry storage area, it can last up to two years. It looks like a watermelon, weighing up to 25 pounds, and can be white, green, or white with green stripes. The flesh is white with black seeds, known as *pepitas* When young, *zambo* tastes like zucchini and can be used in the same ways. When mature, it tastes like an overgrown zucchini and is used to make soups, stews, and compotes. When "aged," its flesh resembles that of the spaghetti squash and is used to make preserves. The seeds can be toasted and eaten like peanuts or made into a sauce. The liquid that exudes from the skin of the *zambo* when pierced was once used to remove hair. There is not much information about the uses of this squash in colonial times because all squash were referred to as *calabazas*.

The winter squash *Cucurbita maxima* is called *zapallo* in the Andes and *calabaza* elsewhere on the continent. Its origin seems to have been in northern Argentina, Bolivia, northern Chile, and southern Peru, from where it spread slowly to other areas. Recent excavations in northern Argentina show that the *zapallo* was cultivated by at least around 500 B.C. After the conquest, it spread throughout the world. This species includes what we call the pumpkin, as well as other varieties of winter squash, such as acorn, buttercup, and hubbard. These fruits grow to enormous sizes, which amazed the conquistadors. It is not unusual to find *zapallos* that weigh 60 pounds or more.

Crookneck winter squash (*Cucurbita moschata*), similar to *C. maxima*, is also called *zapallo*. Excavations made in Peru and Ecuador indicate that it was being cultivated around 4000 B.C. The Spaniards called it *melón de la tierra* and sometimes *calabaza*. It also is large, commonly weighing around 50 pounds. The indigenous peoples used it in soups and sweets. The seeds were dried in the sun and eaten toasted or in sauces. This squash also was used as a medicine and to remove hair. It is still widely used today, especially by the country people. In the United States, this is the main canning pumpkin. Other varieties include butternut and cushaw.

Eggplant

Although eggplant is not native to the Americas, it has become a favorite vegetable, especially among people of Mediterranean and Lebanese descent. Thanks to the influx of Japanese and Middle Eastern immigrants to the United States, we now enjoy a variety of eggplants that range in color from white to purple, and even green and orange. The sizes also vary, from tiny finger eggplants to the more traditional large ones. The smaller varieties can be round, in the shape of an egg, or long and thin like the Asian varieties. These are firmer than the larger ones and are ideal for slicing. When choosing an eggplant, make sure the skin is firm, taut, and shiny. It should feel heavy for its size, and the stem should look fresh. Supposedly, the male eggplant has fewer seeds than the female. To tell which is male, look at the round end of the eggplant—it will have an oval-shaped indentation,

whereas the female will have a round indentation. As for salting the sliced eggplant to remove bitterness, it is not necessary for most dishes. I have found only a few instances where the eggplant was so bitter that even salting didn't help. I believe it was picked when not fully ripe.

Okra

Okra (*Hibiscus esculentus*) is widely used in the Caribbean islands, Central America, and Brazil. This long, tapered, dark green pod originated in Africa and was imported to South America with the slave trade. Called gumbo by West African slaves, it quickly lent its name to the creole stews in which it was most widely used. Okra exudes a gummy substance that naturally thickens stews, broths, and sauces.

Plantain

Plantains, or cooking bananas, were first introduced to the Americas in 1516 by Tomás de Berlanga, discoverer of the Galápagos Islands and later bishop of Panama. He brought bananas from West Africa, where they had been cultivated for centuries. Plantains are always eaten cooked. They are bigger, heavier, and starchier than regular bananas. When unripe, their skin is dark green; when ripe, they turn yellow; when very ripe, they are black. There are specific uses for each stage of ripening. Plantains become sweeter as they ripen.

Green and yellow plantains are used very much like root vegetables in soups and stews. Black plantains are used in many specialties, such as drinks, scrambled eggs, and *Boronia* (next page). Cooked plantains are mashed to make empanadas, tamales, and casseroles. The plantain is one of the most versatile fruits, especially loved in the tropics, where it always appears alongside rice and beans or as fried rounds called *tostones* or *Patacones* (page 120). Thinly sliced and deep-fried plantains are called *Chifles* (page 120), which resemble potato chips. Plantains can be stored at room temperature or refrigerated to stop ripening.

To peel green and yellow plantains, trim off the ends with a sharp knife, then make incisions along the natural edges and pull away the skin. To prevent green plantains from turning brown, rub the flesh with half a lemon, let stand for 5 minutes, and rinse with cold water. This removes the substance that makes soups turn gray. After cooking, green plantains turn very hard when cold, so it is advisable to keep them in hot liquid until ready to eat. Plantains are available all year round in most supermarkets.

Boronia

EGGPLANT AND PLANTAIN CASSEROLE
Serves 4 as a main course, 8 as a side dish

This excellent dish from Cartagena, Colombia, can be made ahead, frozen if desired, and reheated in the oven. It doubles as a side dish or a meatless main course. Another version from the Pacific side of Colombia uses grated white cheese, such as Muenster, instead of tomato sauce. This is good served with charcoal-broiled meat and white rice.

> 2 medium-size eggplants (about 2 pounds)
> 2 very ripe (black) plantains
> 3 cups cold water
> 2 tablespoons canola oil
> 2 cloves garlic, peeled
> 1 tablespoon *Manteca de Color* (page 331) or 1 teaspoon sweet paprika
> 1 medium-size onion, finely chopped (about 1 cup)

> 2 pounds ripe but firm tomatoes, peeled, seeded, and chopped, or 3 cups canned pear-shaped tomatoes, with juices
> ½ teaspoon salt
> ¼ teaspoon freshly ground black pepper
> Sugar

1. Peel the eggplants and cut into 1-inch cubes. Put in a large bowl of salted water and let stand for 30 minutes.

2. Peel the plantains and thinly slice. Put in a 4-quart nonreactive saucepan along with the water and bring to a boil over medium heat. Drain the eggplant, add to the plantains, cover, reduce the heat to low, and simmer until the vegetables are soft, about 20 minutes. Drain thoroughly, mash the vegetables until smooth, and set aside.

3. While the vegetables are cooking, heat the oil in a heavy skillet over low heat. Add the garlic cloves and cook for a couple of minutes until golden brown. Discard the garlic, add the *manteca de color* and onion, and cook for 5 minutes, stirring occasionally. Add the tomatoes, salt, and pepper and simmer until thick, about 20 minutes. Mix ½ cup of this sauce with the vegetable puree. Season with salt, pepper, and sugar to taste.

4. Preheat the oven to 300°F.

5. Transfer the puree to a shallow baking pan, cover, and bake until heated through, about 20 minutes. Meanwhile, reheat the sauce. To serve, remove the puree from the oven and top with the sauce.

Budín de Coliflor con Salsa de Choclo

CAULIFLOWER PÂTÉ WITH CORN SAUCE *Serves 8*

Budines, whether prepared in individual molds for dinner parties or in large molds for buffets, are an elegant way to serve vegetables in South America. During colonial times, wealthy ladies traveled abroad and brought back descriptions of the marvelous creations they had seen overseas. It was then up to the house cook to try to re-create these delicacies. French cuisine—the cuisine of choice for entertaining—inspired *budines*, which are nothing more than what we now call vegetable *pâtés*. Virtually any kind of vegetable can be used to prepare *budines*, which are served with a variety of sauces.

- 1 medium-size head cauliflower or broccoflower (about 2½ pounds), cut into florets
- ¼ cup (½ stick) unsalted butter
- ¼ cup all-purpose flour
- 1 cup milk
- ½ teaspoon salt
- ¼ teaspoon white pepper
- Pinch of freshly grated nutmeg
- Pinch of cayenne pepper
- 4 large eggs, lightly beaten
- ¼ cup day-old white bread crumbs (page 413)
- 1 recipe *Salsa de Choclo* (page 406), heated

1. Bring a large saucepan of salted water to a boil. Add the cauliflower and cook until just tender, about 5 minutes. Drain and mash with a fork; the mixture should be coarse.

2. Melt the butter in a medium-size, heavy saucepan over medium heat. Blend in the flour and cook, stirring constantly, for a couple of minutes until bubbling, making sure it doesn't color. Remove from the heat and, with a wire whisk, blend in the milk. When smooth, return to the heat and add the salt, white pepper, nutmeg, and cayenne. Cook, stirring constantly, until it comes to a boil. Remove from the heat, beat in the eggs, and mix with the cauliflower. Taste for salt and white pepper. This may be prepared ahead up to this point, covered, and refrigerated for a few hours or overnight.

3. Preheat the oven to 350°F. Oil eight 6-ounce timbale molds. Sprinkle the bread crumbs in the molds to cover the bottom and sides. Knock out any excess crumbs.

4. Divide the cauliflower mixture evenly among the molds, then set the molds in a baking pan containing 1 inch of boiling water. Bake in the lower third of the oven until a knife inserted in the center comes out clean, 30 to 35 minutes.

5. Remove the molds from the water and let sit for 5 minutes. Run a thin knife around the edge of each mold and invert onto a warm plate. Top with a couple of tablespoons of the *salsa de choclo* and serve immediately as a first course or side dish.

NOTE **This pudding can be baked in a 6-cup soufflé mold. Increase the baking time to 45 minutes. If not served immediately, leave it in the pan of hot water for up to a couple of hours, reheating the water as needed. Unmold when ready to serve.**

Couve à Mineira

BRAISED COLLARD GREENS (OR KALE)
MINAS GERAIS STYLE *Serves 6 to 8*

A common sight in the open markets of Rio de Janeiro is enormous bowls filled with finely shredded collard greens. Braised collard greens are the indispensable side dish of *feijoada*, the black bean and meat stew that is virtually Brazil's national dish and a very popular dish in Minas Gerais. The classic way of braising collard greens is with lard or bacon fat, but vegetable shortening or oil can be used instead. Sometimes a little minced onion or garlic is added. Although there is some dispute among cooks as to whether *couve* means collard greens or kale (page 287), both are used, and either works in this recipe, so use whichever you prefer.

2 pounds collard greens or kale

¼ cup bacon fat or olive oil

2 cloves garlic, mashed into a paste with ½ teaspoon salt and ¼ teaspoon freshly ground black pepper

1.   Wash the collard greens or kale well and remove the stems. Gather a few leaves at a time, roll into a tight cylinder, and slice crosswise as finely as possible to create thin ribbons.

2.   Heat the bacon fat in a large skillet over medium heat. Add the garlic paste and stir quickly. Add the greens and cook for a few minutes, stirring. Reduce the heat to low, cover, and simmer, stirring occasionally, until the greens are tender, 5 to 10 minutes. Do not overcook; they should be a little crisp. Taste for salt and pepper and serve immediately.

Acelga con Almendras

SWISS CHARD WITH ALMONDS *Serves 4*

Argentine and Uruguayan cuisines are heavily influenced by Italian and Spanish cooking. Swiss chard shows up in a variety of dishes. It can be prepared by simply steaming the chard, both the leaves and stems, and serving it drizzled with olive oil. This is a popular side dish for grilled meat, poultry, or fish. Chard is often used to make fillings for empanadas and tortes, as well as in soups and casseroles. This dish is a nice mixture of flavors and textures. The sweetness of the roasted pepper mellows the strong taste of the chard.

1 pound Swiss chard

½ roasted red pepper (page 411)

1 medium-size all-purpose potato, cooked in water to cover until tender and drained

2 tablespoons olive oil

½ cup chicken broth mixed with 1 teaspoon all-purpose flour

Salt and freshly ground black pepper

¼ cup sliced almonds, lightly toasted (page 413), for garnish

1.   Wash the Swiss chard thoroughly and remove any bruised spots. With a small knife, remove the middle rib and cut into ½-inch pieces. Set aside. Shred the leaves into ½-inch-wide strips. Bring a large saucepan of salted water to a boil. Add the diced ribs, cover, and cook for 3 minutes. Add the leaves, cover, and cook for 3 minutes. Drain, rinse with cold water, and squeeze the liquid out of the leaves. Set aside.

2.   Cut the roasted pepper and potato into bite-size pieces and set aside.

3.   Heat the oil in a large skillet over medium heat. Add the Swiss chard, roasted pepper, and potatoes and cook for a couple of minutes, until all the flavors have blended. Add the broth mixture and cook, stirring, until thickened. Season with salt and pepper to taste. Serve hot, topped with the almonds.

Zapallitos Rellenos con Choclo

ZUCCHINI STUFFED WITH CORN *Serves 4*

Italian immigrants quickly adopted native ingredients, such as the zucchini, and created wonderful specialties like this. Stuffed vegetables are very popular in the southern countries of South America, where many Spanish and Italian immigrants settled. These immigrants brought with them a tradition for such preparations. The zucchini used for stuffing in South America is the round variety, which may be hard to find in the United States. Here I use the Mexican variety, which is shaped like a pear and is available in Mexican markets.

2 Mexican zucchini

2 tablespoons olive oil

2 tablespoons chopped shallots

¼ cup seeded and chopped green bell pepper

2 tablespoons chopped oil-packed sun-dried tomatoes

½ cup cubed day-old bread, soaked in ¼ cup milk for 30 minutes

1 cup fresh or frozen corn kernels

2 tablespoons minced fresh basil leaves or 1 teaspoon dried

½ teaspoon salt

¼ teaspoon freshly ground black pepper

¼ cup freshly grated Parmesan cheese

½ cup water

1. Preheat the oven to 375°F.

2. Wash the zucchini thoroughly, remove the stems, and split in half lengthwise. With a small spoon or melon baller, scoop out the flesh from the center, leaving a ¼-inch-thick wall. Set the flesh aside. Place the zucchini halves in a shallow baking pan and bake for 10 minutes.

3. While the zucchini halves are baking, heat the oil in a medium-size, heavy skillet over medium heat. Add the shallots and cook for 1 minute. Add the zucchini flesh, bell pepper, tomatoes, bread, corn, basil, salt, and black pepper. Cook, stirring constantly, until all the liquid disappears, about 5 minutes. Taste for salt and black pepper and stir in 2 tablespoons of the Parmesan. Divide the filling among the zucchini halves and sprinkle with the remaining 2 table-

spoons Parmesan. The recipe can be made to this point up to a few hours ahead, covered, and refrigerated.

4. Preheat the oven to 400°F.

5. Place the zucchini halves in a shallow baking pan, pour the water into the pan, and bake until lightly colored, about 20 minutes. Serve immediately.

Kiveve

WINTER SQUASH WITH CORNMEAL *Serves 4*

This very typical Paraguayan specialty is made with *andaí* (winter squash) and is a wonderful side dish for *asados* (grilled meats). It can also be served, topped with a chunky tomato sauce, as a main course for a vegetarian meal. Like polenta, the consistency can be changed to accommodate your taste. Adjust the amount of water or milk for a softer or firmer texture.

1 pound winter squash

1 cup water

½ teaspoon salt

2 teaspoons sugar

2 tablespoons unsalted butter

1 cup milk

½ cup cornmeal

2½ ounces Mexican *queso fresco*, crumbled

1. Peel the squash, seed, and cut into chunks. Place in a large saucepan with ½ cup of the water, the salt, and sugar. Cover and cook over low heat until tender, about 15 minutes.

2. Using a potato masher, mash the squash with the cooking liquid. Add the butter and milk and bring to a boil. Reduce the heat to low and start sprinkling in the cornmeal, beating all the time with a wire whisk until smooth. Continue to cook over low heat, stirring with a wooden spoon, until

thickened, about 10 minutes. Cover and cook, stirring occasionally, until the cornmeal is cooked and the consistency is thick, at least 5 minutes. Serve immediately, sprinkled with the cheese.

Alcauciles y Champiñones a la Crema

ARTICHOKES AND MUSHROOMS WITH CREAM *Serves 4*

The southern countries of South America have a variety of dishes that feature the beloved artichoke, an Old World import. This is a delicious and versatile recipe. It can be used as a side dish with broiled fish or chicken, but also makes a lovely first course served in hollowed puff pastry rounds. This was adapted from a recipe by Choly Berreteaga in the book *Berreteaga Express*.

2 tablespoons unsalted butter

1 teaspoon canola oil

2 cloves garlic, lightly crushed

1 tablespoon minced shallots

8 ounces fresh, firm white mushrooms, sliced

One 9-ounce package frozen artichoke hearts (see Notes), cooked and cut into eighths, or one 14-ounce can artichoke hearts, drained, rinsed, and cut into eighths

1 slice (⅛ inch thick) imported boiled ham or 4 thin slices prosciutto, finely chopped

¼ teaspoon salt

⅛ teaspoon white pepper

½ cup whipping cream

Fresh basil leaves, cut into ribbons, or snipped fresh chives for garnish

Melt the butter with the oil in a heavy casserole over medium heat. Add the garlic and cook, stirring, until golden on all sides. Discard the garlic. Add the shallots and cook for 1 minute, stirring.

Increase the heat to medium-high, add the mushrooms, and cook, stirring, for 3 minutes. Stir in the artichokes, ham, salt, and pepper and cook for a couple of minutes. Add the cream and cook until thickened, 2 to 3 minutes. Taste for salt and pepper and serve hot, garnished with the basil.

NOTES **When working with artichokes, whether frozen or canned, remove the dark green outer leaves; they are tough and inedible.**

Fast cooking of the mushrooms is essential. Low heat causes the mushrooms to release a grayish liquid that will give the dish an unappealing color. The fresher the mushrooms, the nicer the dish will look.

Plátanos Verdes Asados

BAKED GREEN PLANTAINS *Serves 4*

Plantains prepared this way sustain millions of people in the tropics. It is the usual side dish for rice and stewed beans, lentils, or chickpeas.

4 green plantains

1. Preheat the oven to 400°F.

2. Trim the ends of the plantains, place in a shallow baking pan, and bake until soft to the touch, about 45 minutes. Peel and serve.

Plátanos Maduros Asados

BAKED RIPE PLANTAINS *Serves 4*

This plantain dish is from Venezuela and Colombia.

4 very ripe (black) plantains

4 ounces Chihuahua, mozzarella, or Muenster cheese, shredded

4 slices guava paste, cut into small pieces

1. Preheat the oven to 400°F.

2. Trim the ends of the plantains, place in a shallow baking pan, and bake for 15 minutes.

3. Remove the pan from the oven. Holding a plantain with a folded kitchen towel and using a sharp knife, make a lengthwise slit in the skin. Peel the plantain and split lengthwise to the heart. Remove the black center strip and fill the space with the cheese and guava paste. Return to the oven for a few minutes until the cheese begins to melt. Serve hot.

Root Vegetables

ROOT VEGETABLES PLAY AN ENORMOUS role in the everyday lives of South Americans, especially those in the Andean countries. Perhaps because tubers are protected by the soil against weather conditions, people have always depended on them to prevent starvation. Some of them, such as potatoes and cassava (yuca), are the staff of life for millions. In Venezuela, Colombia, and Ecuador, the *arracacha*, also called *zanahoria blanca* (white carrot), is a very important root vegetable that is used in side dishes, soups, and stews. Many tubers, such as the *ulluco*, *mashua*, and *oca*, are important to the daily diet of many people of the Andean Altiplano.

Arracacha/Zanahoria Blanca

Arracacha (*Arracacha xanthorriza*, *A. esculenta*) is a root vegetable indigenous to the subtropics of the Andean part of South America, although now it is also grown in southern Brazil. Some researchers believe that this relative of the carrot and celery is the oldest cultivated plant in South America. In fact, it has been domesticated for so long that its wild ancestor is unknown. It seems likely that it originated in Ecuador and adjacent areas of Colombia and Peru, where it is still most commonly used, and spread to other areas. The Spanish chronicler Fernández de Oviedo described the *arracacha* as a very nutritious plant that was important to the indigenous peoples. It looks like a large white carrot, only fatter. The fresh root should be peeled with a potato peeler. The flesh can be white or yellow, with a texture similar to that of the potato, and is slightly sweet, with a faint taste of celery. It is used as a vegetable, either boiled, fried, or roasted; in soups and stews; and in tamales, empanadas, and many other dishes. The aboveground stems can be boiled or eaten raw like celery. It is also made into a starch that is used for thickening soups. This vegetable is called *arracacha* in Colombia, *zanahoria blanca* in Ecuador, and *apio* in Venezuela. It is available in the United States frozen, and sometimes fresh, in Latin American markets.

Yuca

Yuca, also known as cassava and manioc, is consumed mainly in the tropics of the Andean countries, Paraguay, and Brazil. It was used by the Indians centuries before the Spaniards and Portuguese arrived. Archaeological evidence indicates that bitter yuca (*Manihot utilissima*) was probably being cultivated in the lowlands of Venezuela and Colombia by about 3,000 years ago, and sweet yuca (*Manihot dulcis pax*) was cultivated in Peru by about 2,000 years ago.

Some researchers believe that yuca was first used in Brazil around 3,500 years ago. Amazingly, the Indians figured out how to process bitter yuca, whose roots are highly poisonous, for consumption. Edible derivatives of bitter yuca are made into many products, the most important being *farinha de mandioca* (manioc meal), which is consumed daily in Brazil, throughout the Amazon, and in the tropical areas and *llanos* of Venezuela and Colombia. In fact, Ramón David León, author of *Geografía Gastronómica Venezolana*, believes that in these areas of Venezuela, cassava bread is consumed in greater quantities than wheat bread and *arepas* (cornbread). Cassava bread was, and is, the bread of the Indians. In the Amazon, indigenous peoples eat it with all their meals.

Slightly toasted manioc meal, called *farofa*, is placed in a special shaker called a *farinheira* and included among the condiments that appear on every Brazilian table. *Farofa* is sprinkled on all kinds of food and is used to thicken soups, stews, and beans. It is also the basis of *angús* and *pirãos* (starchy mixtures). The unprocessed root is not available in North America, but processed manioc meal is available in some Latin American groceries. Another byproduct of bitter yuca is a very delicate flour that is deposited after yuca is grated, pressed, and washed. It is called *harina de yuca* (yuca flour) in the Andean countries and *polvilho* in Brazil. This flour is used to make breads and cakes.

Sweet yuca has a rough, dark brown skin and a shelf life of only a few days. When selecting sweet yuca, make sure it is free of blemishes, mold, soft spots, and cracks. The flesh should be completely white and hard, and it should smell clean. Discard it if it has a sour or ammonia-like smell. When cooked, sweet yuca has a dry, mealy texture and a slightly sweet taste. It is quite popular in tropical and semitropical areas of South America, where it appears in soups, stews, side dishes, and even desserts. Sweet yuca is a good substitute for potatoes and is available fresh in many supermarkets and Latin American groceries in the United States. It is also available frozen.

Jícama

Jícama (*Pachyrhizus erosus*), the tuber of a leguminous plant, is sometimes called Mexican potato. It is native to Mexico but can be found in some South American countries and is widely available in the United States. It has a white, slightly sweet flesh with a crunchy texture, similar to that of a water chestnut. It comes in a variety of sizes, ranging from one-half to five pounds. It is usually eaten raw but can be cooked, and it is used in appetizers or salads. The beige-brown skin can be more easily removed if you cut off the ends, cut the *jícama* into wedges, and then pull off the skin with a paring knife. Whole *jícama* can be stored unwrapped in the refrigerator for a couple of weeks. Once it is cut, it should be wrapped in plastic and used within two to three days.

Potato

The potato is one of the Americas' most important contributions to the world larder, rivaled only by corn. Potatoes probably originated and were domesticated in the Altiplano of Bolivia, close to Lake Titicaca, about 8,000 years ago. From there they spread north to Ecuador and southern Colombia and south into Chile. The Incas of Peru cultivated potatoes at high altitudes, between 3,000 and 3,500 feet. They developed a tremendous variety of potatoes, many of which have disappeared over time. It has been estimated that at one time, more than 200 varieties of potatoes existed, of different colors, shapes, and sizes. *Papas criollas* (yellow potatoes) and *papas moradas* (blue or purple potatoes) are two of the unique species still found in Peru, Colombia, and Ecuador. Fortunately, some of these species are increasingly available in U.S. markets, especially from specialty growers. The yellow potatoes are small and do not fall apart when cooked, which makes them ideal for stews and similar dishes. The blue potatoes come in small and medium sizes. Their beautiful blue color is intensified when they are refrigerated after cooking.

Potatoes are used throughout South America, but they are most important in the areas that were once under Inca control and among the Mapuche Indians of Chile. The potato reigns supreme in the Altiplano of Bolivia, Peru, Ecuador, and Colombia, where it is consumed daily. Sometimes potatoes, seasoned only with hot pepper sauce, are the only food available to the Indians and poor people of the high Andes. There is evidence that although the potato was important to early indigenous peoples, it was looked down on by the Incas, who later conquered these peoples. The Incas thought that corn was superior to the potato, and they destroyed many potato fields. During the early colonial period, some Spaniards considered the potato an appealing delicacy, but others adopted the Inca attitude, viewing it as the food of lesser races. Another reason for the potato's lack of cultural prestige may be that religious ceremonies related to the potato were not as common as ceremonies pertaining to corn. New findings indicate, however, that early potato growers performed some ceremonies. Eduardo Estrella, in his book *El Pan de América*, describes how the planting season was celebrated in some areas of the Andes before the conquest. It was an occasion for big gatherings, where family members and neighbors got together for the planting. It started with a prayer or invocation to the appropriate spirits, and then everybody would proceed with the planting. After they were finished, a ritual meal was served—a soup made with fava bean flour and *cuy* (guinea pig), along with boiled potatoes served with hot peppers, *cuy*, and *mote* (hominy). Lots of *chicha de jora* (a fermented corn drink) was consumed, and when the meal was finished, there was music, dancing, and more *chicha*.

The men of the Altiplano are in charge of harvesting the potatoes, but the women are the keepers of the seed potatoes. When the potatoes are brought in, the mother, grandmother, and children sort them, separating them into three groups: The best-looking medium-size potatoes (without blemishes) are saved as seed for the coming year. The large ones without blemishes or worms are reserved for eating. And the small ones that are not so perfect are used for *papa seca* or *chuño* (dried potatoes).

The importance of the potato in the diet of the people of the Altiplano is exemplified by the variety of dishes that are prepared using potatoes. Investigators have found that in some areas, about 35 potato specialties are consistently prepared with one, two, or three varieties of potatoes. For instance, the Colombian *ajiaco* uses three kinds of potatoes. In Bolivia, most of the stews and soups have two kinds of potatoes, dried and fresh. In Chile, the Mapuche Indians, and Chileans in general, make good use of potatoes. The Mapuches are the only ones in South America who cook potatoes on wooden skewers over hot coals.

In the highlands of Peru and Bolivia, the Indians have a way of preserving potatoes by freeze-drying them at high altitudes. When the temperature drops below freezing, the potatoes are left on the ground to freeze overnight, then thawed in the sun during the day. The moisture is then squeezed out, and the potatoes are frozen again. This process of freezing, thawing, squeezing, and refreezing is repeated for a few weeks, until the potatoes are completely dehydrated. At that point, they become white and very light. Called *chuño*, these dehydrated potatoes can last indefinitely. To use *chuño*, you have to soak it in lukewarm water for two to three days (depending on how old it is), changing the water every day, until the peel is easy to remove. The best way to determine whether the *chuño* is completely rehydrated is to cut a potato in half; if it is not chalky in the center, it is ready. Cut it up, removing the skin as it comes off, and cook in salted boiling water for 5 to 10 minutes. Cooking any longer than that will harden it, and you will have to cook it for a much longer time to soften it again. Fortunately, *chuño* is now available canned and already cooked.

The Quechuas of Peru also had a process of freeze-drying potatoes, which produced what is called *papa seca*. For this, the potatoes were cooked first, left to freeze overnight, thawed in the sun during the day, and squeezed dry. This process was repeated until the potatoes were completely dried. During the process, the potatoes were broken into small pieces. The Aymaras of southern Peru and Bolivia had a process of aging potatoes in water, and they also dried potatoes using two methods. The results were *chuño* and *tunta*. *Chuño* is also the name given to a potato starch made from dehydrated potatoes. It looks like cornstarch and it is used to thicken sauces or to make drinks for sick people or children.

Sweet Potato

It is not entirely clear where the sweet potato, called *batata*, *boniato*, or *camote* in South America,

originated. Almost all evidence indicates that it is indigenous to tropical America, where it dates back several millennia. However, early European explorers reported something similar to the sweet potato growing on some Pacific islands. This may have been a yam, which is different from the sweet potato, although it is possible that voyagers in canoes reached the islands from South America. It seems unlikely that the sweet potato was introduced to the Americas from the islands, but this is not impossible.

In Peru, dried sweet potatoes have been found in pre-Columbian tombs, and fossilized sweet potatoes dating to about 10,000 years ago have been discovered in Chilca. However, these fossils are the remains of wild sweet potatoes, gathered rather than cultivated ones. It is not known precisely when the sweet potato made the leap from wild to domesticated, but it was widely cultivated in South America, especially in Peru, by 750 B.C. It then spread across South America and the Caribbean. According to some researchers, the Incas used sweet potatoes as food and ceremonial objects.

When the Spaniards arrived in the Americas, they quickly took to the sweet potato because, in the words of Fernández de Oviedo, "a *batata* well cured and well prepared is like marzipan." This tuber, unlike the potato, grows well in the warm Andean valleys and in tropical regions.

Sweet potatoes in the United States are sweeter and moister than those grown in South America. The colors of sweet potatoes range from white to yellow to purple. Unfortunately, in the past few years, the production of sweet potatoes in Ecuador has decreased due to a lack of interest among consumers. In Peru, however, the sweet potato is still very much a part of *cebiches* and other specialties. In most countries, they are used to make soups, stews, French fries, and desserts.

Ulluco

The *ulluco* (*Ullucus tuberosus*) is another tuber from the highlands of Colombia, Ecuador, Peru, and Bolivia, where it is the staple food of many people and is known as the poor man's potato. In Bolivia, the *ulluco* is called *papalisa*, and it seems that *papalisa* is the name most commonly used to market the tuber in the supermarkets of the Andean countries. It comes in different shapes and brilliant and striking colors—yellow, pink, red, orange, brown, and purple. The skin is thin and soft, and it does not need to be removed before eating. The flesh is white or pale yellow. It has a mucilaginous texture but retains its crispness after cooking. The flavor is earthy. The leaves are similar in taste and texture to spinach and are rich in nutrients. In Peru, the Incas freeze-dried *ullucos* and ate them with dried meat.

This is a versatile vegetable that lends itself to a wide variety of culinary uses and is especially good added to soups and stews. It also can be cooked and used in salads. Like okra, it is either loved or reviled. Unfortunately, it remained only a local crop until recently. Studies have shown that *ullucos* are a wonderful crop for high altitudes and may have potential for introduction in areas that have trouble growing other food crops. In the United States, *ullucos* are available frozen and canned in some Latin American supermarkets, and sometimes the yellow and purple varieties can be found frozen.

Yacon

Yacon (*Polymnia sonchifolia*) is a root that can be eaten raw. Because of its sweet taste and crunchy texture, it has been called the apple of the earth. The main stem of the plant also is edible and can be cooked as a vegetable. *Yacon* grows from Venezuela to Argentina at high altitudes. In Ecuador, it is called *jícama*, which causes confusion with the real *jícama* (page 297). In Latacunga, an Andean city in Ecuador, it is associated with the Day of the Dead (November 2, when people pay their respects to deceased relatives) and is sold in great quantities for offerings to the dead.

Yam

The yam (*Dioscorea alata*), called *ñame* in South America, is native to Africa but now grows in many tropical regions of the world. Yams are usually the size of large potatoes, but some may weigh up to 100 pounds. They have a tough, thick, brown skin and white, yellow, or even reddish flesh with a starchy texture. Yams should not be confused with sweet potatoes, which are occasionally called yams in the United States. The two are unrelated. Yams are available fresh in some supermarkets and fresh and frozen in Hispanic markets year-round.

Llapingachos
POTATO AND CHEESE PATTIES
Makes about 20 patties

This dish is a true treasure of Ecuadorian creole cuisine. On weekends, when people go to resorts around Quito, the roads are full of local Indians cooking these patties over hot coals in portable braziers. People often make special trips to resorts where there are small eateries specializing in *llapingachos* and roasted pig. They can be served as a first course, side dish, or main course. They are often presented on a bed of shredded lettuce and carrots and decorated with strips of avocado and tomato, with, of course, a dish of *aji* (hot pepper salsa) on the side. For a main course, *llapingachos* are generally served with a fried egg on top and are sometimes accompanied by fried bananas. On the coast of Ecuador, they are often served with *Salsa de Maní* (page 343).

2 pounds Idaho potatoes, peeled and quartered

1 teaspoon salt

¼ cup *Manteca de Color* (page 331) or ¼ cup canola oil mixed with 1 teaspoon sweet paprika, plus more for brushing

½ cup minced scallions (white part only)

8 ounces Chihuahua, mozzarella, or Muenster cheese, shredded

4 cups mixed shredded lettuce and carrots

2 tablespoons canola oil

Juice of 1 lemon or lime

2 medium-size ripe but firm tomatoes (10 to 12 ounces), sliced

2 ripe but firm Hass avocados, peeled, pitted, and sliced

1. Bring a large pot of water to boil. Add the salt and potatoes and cook until soft, about 30 minutes. Drain thoroughly and mash with a potato masher.

2. In a small skillet, heat the *manteca de color* over low heat, add the scallions, and cook, stirring, for a couple of minutes. Add to the mashed potatoes, combining well. Let the mixture cool, then stir in the cheese. Shape into patties about 3 inches in diameter and 1 inch thick. Cover with plastic wrap and refrigerate until needed.

3. The best way to cook these patties is on a nonstick griddle, as for pancakes. Heat the griddle over medium heat, brush with *manteca de color* (see Note), add the patties, and cook until browned and crispy on the bottom, about 5 minutes. Brush the tops with *manteca de color*, turn over, and

brown the other side. When properly done, the patties will have a beautiful brown crust and should be tender inside. Too much fat in the pan will make the patties fall apart; that is why a nonstick pan works best.

4. Place the lettuce and carrots in a large bowl. Add the oil and lemon juice and toss. Line a serving platter with the salad and top with the *llapingachos*. Decorate with the tomatoes and avocados and serve.

NOTE Many cooks make a "paintbrush" out of a large scallion, slicing the end to make the "bristles," then use it to brush on the *manteca de color*.

Papas Chorreadas

POTATOES WITH TOMATO AND CHEESE SAUCE *Serves 6*

For this dish, a tomato sauce, well seasoned with herbs and spices and enriched with cheese and cream, is poured over boiled potatoes. It is traditionally served with *sobrebarriga*, oven-braised rolled flank steak. This is a famous specialty from Bogotá and one of Colombia's most beloved dishes. It can also be served with grilled meat, chicken, or sausage, or as a first course.

6 medium-size all-purpose potatoes, peeled

2 tablespoons unsalted butter or olive oil

1 small onion, minced (about ½ cup)

½ cup thinly sliced scallions (white part only)

2 large ripe but firm tomatoes (about 1 pound), peeled, seeded, and chopped

2 tablespoons minced fresh cilantro leaves

¼ teaspoon dried oregano, crumbled

¼ teaspoon ground cumin

¼ teaspoon salt

¼ teaspoon freshly ground black pepper

½ cup whipping cream

2 ounces Chihuahua, mozzarella, or Muenster cheese, shredded

1. Place the potatoes in a large saucepan with salted water to cover by an inch. Bring to a boil, partially cover, and cook over low heat until the potatoes are tender, about 20 minutes.

2. Meanwhile, melt the butter in a medium-size, heavy skillet over medium heat. Add the onion and scallions and cook, stirring a few times, until transparent, about 5 minutes. Add the tomatoes, cilantro, oregano, cumin, salt, and pepper and cook, stirring a few times, for 5 minutes. Add a little water if the sauce dries out. The tomatoes should form a sauce when done. Add the cream and cheese and cook, stirring constantly, until the cheese melts. Taste for salt and pepper. Cover and keep warm over very low heat.

3. Drain the potatoes thoroughly. With a paring knife, make a cross in each potato so that it opens a bit. Arrange the potatoes on a serving platter, pour the sauce over them, and serve immediately.

Papas Doradas

BROWNED POTATOES *Serves 4 to 6*

These potatoes, popular throughout South America, are simply wonderful to serve with braised meat, fish, or poultry. Whenever I serve them to my family or guests, there are never any left. If you can find small new potatoes, scrub them well and cook them with their skins on. Absolutely delicious.

> 6 medium-size all-purpose potatoes
> 2 tablespoons unsalted butter
> 2 tablespoons canola oil
> Salt and freshly ground black pepper
> Minced fresh parsley leaves for garnish

1. Peel and quarter the potatoes, or use with a melon baller to scoop them into balls.

2. In a large, heavy skillet, heat the butter and oil together over medium heat until the butter melts. Add the potatoes and cook, tossing frequently, until lightly browned on all sides. Season with salt and pepper to taste. Reduce the heat to low, cover, and cook, stirring occasionally, until soft, about 10 minutes.

3. Drain the potatoes on paper towels. Transfer to a serving platter, sprinkle with the parsley, and serve hot.

Molo

MASHED POTATOES WITH PEANUT BUTTER *Serve 8 to 10*

In Ecuador, this is the traditional accompaniment for *Fanesca* (page 257), and even though it sounds totally out of place in a menu with such a heavy main course, it works. It is served after the *fanesca*, on a bed of lettuce, dressed up with parsley, cheese, and hard-cooked eggs.

> 2 pounds Idaho potatoes, peeled
> 1 cup milk, heated with ¼ cup whipping cream (do not boil)
> 4 ounces Chihuahua, mozzarella, or Muenster cheese, shredded
> Salt and white pepper
> ¼ cup (½ stick) unsalted butter
> ½ cup finely chopped scallions (white part only)
> Pinch of ground cumin
> 1 tablespoon natural peanut butter pureed with ¼ cup milk

GARNISHES
> Lettuce leaves
> Scallions, cut into 2-inch pieces, sliced lengthwise to within 1 inch of one end, and placed in ice water until the ends open like a broom
> Brick cheese, cut into wedges
> Hard-cooked eggs, peeled and cut into wedges
> Minced fresh parsley leaves

1. Place the potatoes in a large saucepan with salted water to cover by 2 inches. Bring to a boil, reduce the heat to medium, and cook until tender, about 30 minutes. Drain and mash with a potato masher. Stir in the hot milk mixture and shredded cheese. Season with salt and pepper to taste.

2. Meanwhile, melt the butter in a small skillet over medium heat. Add the chopped scallions and cook, stirring, for a couple of minutes. Add the cumin and salt and pepper to taste. Stir in the peanut butter puree and set aside. When the potatoes are ready, reheat and mix with the potatoes.

3. Arrange the lettuce on a platter and top with the potatoes. Garnish with the scallion "brooms," cheese wedges, eggs, and parsley and serve immediately.

Chuño Phuti de Huevo

EGG AND DRIED POTATO OMELET *Serves 4*

A classic dish from the Bolivian highlands, this recipe can be made with *chuño negro* (dried black potatoes) or *chuño blanco* or *tunta* (dried white potatoes). It is a very important side dish, served with many specialties, especially *Picante de Pollo* (page 179).

> One 10-ounce can cooked *chuño blanco* (see Note)
>
> 2 tablespoons canola oil
>
> 1 medium-size onion, finely chopped (about 1 cup)
>
> 1 cup seeded and chopped green bell pepper
>
> 1 large ripe but firm tomato (about 8 ounces), seeded and chopped
>
> 4 large eggs
>
> 5 ounces Mexican *queso fresco*, crumbled

1. Drain the *chuño* and rinse thoroughly. Cut into small (about ¼ inch) pieces and place in a small saucepan. Add a little water and warm over low heat. Do not boil. Drain, cover, and keep warm.

2. Heat the oil in a large frying pan over medium heat. Add the onion, bell pepper, and tomato and cook, stirring, for about 5 minutes. Add the eggs one at a time, cracking them right over the pan, and cook, stirring occasionally, until they are almost set. Carefully distribute the *chuño* on top of the eggs, being careful not to disturb them. Sprinkle the cheese on top, but do not stir—the cheese should not melt. Serve as soon as the eggs are fully cooked.

NOTE **If using uncooked *chuño*, see the directions on page 299 for rehydrating it.**

Yuca Sancochada y Frita

BOILED AND FRIED YUCA *Serves 4*

This is a very popular way to serve yuca and is especially good as a side dish. These wedges also can be served with *guasacaca* (tomato and avocado sauce) as an hors d'oeuvre.

> 1 pound trimmed fresh yuca, cooked (page 410), or frozen yuca, cooked (see Notes)
>
> ¼ cup canola oil
>
> Salt

1. Cut the yuca into 2 or 3 wedges each.

2. Heat the oil in a large skillet over medium-high heat. Add the yuca and fry until golden on both sides, about 3 minutes per side. Drain on paper towels, sprinkle with salt, and serve.

NOTES **Most cooks prefer frozen yuca because the "fresh" yuca found in some supermarkets is not always truly fresh.**

Some people prefer to freeze the yuca after it has been cooked and then fry it frozen. This method produces a very light yuca, but the fat splatters quite a bit when adding the frozen wedges to the hot oil.

Enyucado

YUCA AND COCONUT TORTE *Makes 16 squares*

This is a specialty from the Atlantic coast of Colombia, where it is not unusual to mix savory dishes with sweet ones. *Enyucado* is served as a side dish with meat or as a snack with coffee in the afternoon. Some versions use coconut milk, others just grated coconut, and some cooks prefer to mix both. Most classic versions do not use eggs, as this recipe does. This version comes from a friend, Sol Name, who prefers the lighter texture the eggs create.

> 1 pound fresh yuca, trimmed
>
> ½ cup sugar
>
> 4 ounces brick cheese, shredded, or 5 ounces Mexican *queso fresco*, crumbled
>
> ¾ cup grated fresh or frozen unsweetened coconut
>
> ½ cup whipping cream
>
> ¼ cup (½ stick) unsalted butter, melted
>
> ½ teaspoon anise seeds, crushed, or ½ teaspoon pure vanilla extract
>
> 2 large eggs, lightly beaten

1. Cut the yuca crosswise into 2- to 3-inch pieces. With a sharp knife, make a cut lengthwise through the bark and pink skin of each piece. Place the knife under the skin to loosen it and pull the skin and bark away. Rinse each piece as you peel it and keep submerged in cold water until you finish all the pieces. Cut the peeled yuca into 1-inch pieces, place in a food processor fitted with the steel blade, and process until grated. Transfer to a large bowl, add all the remaining ingredients, and mix well.

2. Preheat the oven to 350°F. Butter a 9-inch square baking pan.

3. Transfer the mixture to the prepared pan. Bake on the upper oven rack until golden, about 45 minutes. Let cool to lukewarm, cut into squares, and serve warm or at room temperature.

Farofa de Ouro

GOLDEN MANIOC MEAL *Serves 6*

Brazilians love *farinha de mandioca* (manioc meal), especially prepared in the form of *farofa*, which is nothing more than the meal toasted to a pale golden color, either in a skillet on top of the stove or in the oven. This is put in a *farinheira*, a shaker that appears on every Brazilian table, and is sprinkled on all kinds of savory foods. The recipe here is for the basic *farofa*. There are other, more elaborate ones, such as *farofa de dendê*, which is fried in *dendê* (palm oil) after being toasted, and *farofa de ameixas*, which is made with prunes. Cooks, depending on the menu, may add onions, crispy bacon, passion fruit pulp, or shredded kale, to name just a few favorite ingredients.

> 2 cups manioc meal or fine dry bread crumbs
>
> ¼ cup (½ stick) unsalted butter
>
> 4 hard-cooked eggs
>
> Salt
>
> 8 black olives for garnish

1. In a large, heavy skillet, toast the manioc meal over low heat, stirring constantly, until it begins to turn a pale beige. Remove from the heat.

2. In a medium-size saucepan, melt the butter over medium heat. Add the toasted manioc meal slowly, stirring so that it doesn't burn, and cook until all of the butter is absorbed and there are no clumps. Remove from the heat.

3. Peel the eggs, cut in half lengthwise, and remove the yolks. Chop the whites and set aside. Finely chop the yolks and add to the *farofa*. Season with salt to taste. Transfer to a serving bowl and decorate with the egg whites and olives.

TO SERVE **Serve with *feijoada*, fowl, fish, or barbecued meat.**

Puré de Camote y Nueces

MASHED SWEET POTATOES WITH WALNUTS

Serves 6

The combination of sweet potatoes and walnuts shows up in Argentina, Peru, and Ecuador. The South American sweet potatoes, or *camotes*, are different from the ones grown in the United States. They are white or purple and dry and mealy, so you need to increase the amount of cream and butter. I'm sure this recipe was inspired by the American sweet potato casserole topped with marshmallows. Many years ago in South America, marshmallows had to be made at home because they were not available in local markets. Because of that, this was considered a very special dish, fit for special receptions. A popular way to prepare *camotes* in Bolivia is to mash them with cream and bake them topped with grated *chancaca* or *panela* (molded brown sugar) or caramel.

> **2 pounds sweet potatoes**
> **¼ cup (½ stick) unsalted butter**
> **½ cup whipping cream, or more if needed**
> **½ cup ground walnuts**
> **Marshmallows for topping**

1. Place the sweet potatoes in a large pot with cold water to cover by 1 inch. Bring to a boil, reduce the heat to medium, and cook until soft, about 20 minutes. Drain, let cool a bit, and peel. Mash with a potato masher in a medium-size bowl. Add the butter and mix well. Add the cream little by little, beating it into the mashed sweet potatoes with a wooden spoon. Add the walnuts, continuing to beat. If the puree is too dry, add more cream.

2. Preheat the oven to 375°F. Butter a gratin dish.

3. Transfer the puree to the prepared dish, top with the marshmallows, and bake until the marshmallows are browned, about 20 minutes. Serve hot.

Arracacha/Zanahoria Blanca con Salsa de Queso

ARRACACHA WITH CHEESE SAUCE *Serves 4*

This tuber, which resembles a fat carrot, is very popular in Colombia and Ecuador, as well as in Venezuela, where it is called *apio*. A versatile tuber, it can be boiled, fried, made into *pastelitos* (patties), or used in soups and many other dishes. It is available frozen in some Latin American supermarkets.

> **1 pound frozen *arracacha* (page 296)**
> **2 tablespoons canola oil**
> **1 teaspoon *Manteca de Color* (page 331)**
> **¼ cup minced scallions (white part and 1 inch of the green)**
> **2 tablespoons minced fresh cilantro leaves**
> **¼ teaspoon ground cumin**
> **4 ounces cream cheese, cubed**
> **¼ cup milk**
> **Salt and freshly ground black pepper**

1. Bring a large saucepan of salted water to a boil. Add the *arracacha* and continue to boil for 10 minutes. At this time, smaller pieces are usually tender. Remove them with a slotted spoon. Larger pieces may take up to 10 minutes more. Drain, cover, and set aside.

2. In a small skillet, heat the canola oil and *manteca de color* together over medium-low heat. Add the scallions, cilantro, and cumin and cook for 1 minute. Add the cream cheese and milk and cook, stirring, until the cheese melts. Season with salt and pepper to taste.

3. Cut the *arracacha* in half lengthwise, place in a heated serving dish, and pour the sauce over. Serve hot.

VARIATION Another way of serving *arracacha* is with *Salsa de Pepas de Zambo* (page 343) instead of this cream cheese sauce.

Picante de Ollucos

ULLUCOS IN HOT SAUCE *Serves 4*

Peruvians and Bolivians like their food *muy picante* (very spicy). Picantes are very popular in these countries, and so is this tuber, which goes by the name *olluco* in Peru and *papalisa* in Bolivia. *Picante* denotes a dish that has generous amount of hot peppers. I put in just enough to give a tinge of heat; you can ratchet it up or down from there.

One 20-ounce can *ullucos* packed in brine

2 tablespoons canola oil

1 teaspoon *Manteca de Color* (page 331) or ½ teaspoon sweet paprika

1 small onion, finely chopped (about ½ cup)

1 tablespoon dried *mirasol* pepper puree, store-bought or homemade (page 332), or ½ teaspoon red pepper flakes

⅓ teaspoon ground cumin

¼ teaspoon salt

¼ teaspoon freshly ground black pepper

1 tablespoon natural peanut butter pureed with ½ cup milk

2 hard-cooked eggs, peeled and quartered, for garnish

1. Drain the *ullucos* and rinse well. Cut into ³⁄₁₆-inch-thick rounds and set aside.

2. In a 4-quart saucepan, heat the oil and *manteca de color* together over medium heat. Add the onion and hot pepper puree and cook, stirring a few times, until soft, about 5 minutes. Add the cumin, salt, and black pepper and cook for a couple of minutes. Add the *ullucos* and peanut butter puree and cook, uncovered, over low heat until most of the liquid has evaporated, about 5 minutes.

3. Serve hot, garnished with the eggs.

Legumes

BEANS ARE BELIEVED TO BE one of the first foods that were domesticated in the New World, at the beginning of the development of agriculture, becoming an important part of the Indians' diet. They are now cultivated in all parts of the world, in all types of climates. Beans are leguminous plants (plants with seeds in pods) and have been used in many parts of the world since ancient times. The beans indigenous to the Americas include kidney beans, black turtle beans, string beans, snap beans, and lima beans. The pod is eaten in some varieties (string beans), but most beans are used minus the pod, either fresh or dried. Contrary to some beliefs, dried beans don't have an unlimited shelf live, as they continue to dry and harden with time and become progressively more difficult to cook properly.

The common, kidney, turtle, string, or snap bean (*Phaseolus vulgaris*) was domesticated in the New World thousands of years ago. This appears to have occurred simultaneously in different parts of the Americas. In archaeological excavations made in Mexico and Peru, for instance, there is evidence that it was being cultivated 4,000 years ago. These beans are called *frijoles* in Spanish.

The conquistadors found lima beans (*Phaseolus lunatus*) in the vicinity of what is now Lima, Peru, which gave the bean its name. It is believed that this bean was developed in the highlands of Peru because the common bean doesn't do well at high altitudes. From there it spread to other South

American countries. Lima beans have been found in excavations that date back to 6000 B.C. A smaller lima bean, called *sieva*, has been found in Central America. After the conquest, lima beans began to be cultivated throughout the world in climates that range from temperate to subtropical. Called *tortas* in Spanish and *pallares* in Quechua, they are widely used, both fresh and dried.

Lupini beans (*Lupinus mutabilis*) are the seeds of the leguminous lupine, a member of the pea family, which has long flower spikes. There is evidence that the beans of this beautiful flowering plant were cultivated 1,500 years ago in southern Peru and Bolivia. The Andean lupini bean is about the size of a Great Northern bean, only rounder and flatter, with an ivory color. Currently, lupini beans are used primarily in Bolivia, Peru, and Ecuador, where they are a very important part of the Indians' diet, along with corn, quinoa, and potatoes. A common sight at the markets there, and sometimes on the streets, is Indians selling hominy and lupini beans from baskets or sacks. The two combined make for an almost ideal diet nutrition-wise. In South America, lupini beans are variously called *tarwis*, *chochos*, or *tremoços*.

Lupini beans are high in protein (more than 40 percent) but are naturally bitter and toxic, so they must be treated to remove the alkaloids. The beans are soaked for 24 hours, boiled for 5 minutes, and then soaked again in plenty of water for a few days. The water must be changed three times a day. A sweet variety of the bean, without the alkaloid, has been developed. A newcomer to the market is the dehydrated lupini bean from Ecuador, which needs only to be soaked in lukewarm water overnight and is ready to eat. Ecuadorian lupini beans also come packed in brine and are available in the United States in Ecuadorian groceries and some Latin American markets. These beans can be eaten without peeling. There is also a Middle Eastern or Italian variety, which is larger and darker in color than the Ecuadorian variety. It comes packed in brine and is available in the Italian section of most supermarkets and in Middle Eastern or Italian groceries. This is a good substitute for the Andean variety, although the skin has to be removed before eating. To do this, tear a little opening in the skin with your fingers and squeeze the bean until it pops.

The peanut (*Arachis hypogaea*) is a member of the legume family, like beans, and was domesticated in the foothills of the Andes between Bolivia and Argentina about 4,000 years ago. From there it spread to Peru, Brazil, and the Caribbean. The Spanish first found this plant in the sixteenth century in Haiti, where the Taino people called it *maní*. This is now the Spanish name for peanut, except in Mexico, where the Aztec name, *cacahuate*, was adopted. The peanut is not a nut, as the pea-like seeds develop in pods. The plant produces a white flower at the end of a stalk. After the flower is fertilized, the stalk bends down and grows about two inches into the ground, where the seedpods develop. Green peanuts can be eaten whole and in the southern United States go by the name goobers. When ripe, peanuts are toasted to remove the bitter flavor. Ground peanuts are used in many specialties in northern Brazil, Bolivia, Peru, and Ecuador, as well as in some of the other Andean countries. Sweet confections containing peanuts are found everywhere in South America. Peanuts are also made into oil, margarine, and flour and have become a very important ingredient in African and Asian cuisines.

Basul is not a well-known bean, even in the Andean countries, but it looks promising for agroforestry. Scientists believe that this tree bean can make a difference between malnutrition and good health for the inhabitants of these regions. *Basul* in combination with cereals or root vegetables makes for a balanced diet.

Nuñas, or popping beans, are another member of the vast bean family indigenous to the Americas. They are grown in Peru and Ecuador, mainly for family consumption, at altitudes above 8,000 feet. They are sun-dried right after being harvested. *Nuñas* are popped in a little hot oil, much like popcorn, and served as a side dish or snack. This cooking method is ideal for high altitudes, because popping requires less fuel than does the long boiling required for other beans.

From the Old World came fava beans, lentils, and chickpeas, which the Indians adopted whole-heartedly. In time, especially in some of the Andean countries, fava beans became so popular that they were thought to be indigenous to the Americas. And lentils are the daily diet of the masses in some Andean countries. Chickpeas, also called garbanzo beans, also became very popular, especially in the southern countries of South America.

Fava beans (*Vicia faba*), also known as broad beans, originated in the Mediterranean region and were cultivated thousands of years ago in Egypt, Greece, and Rome. They are very popular in the Andean countries, especially when fresh. Fava bean pods vary in size, depending on the degree of ripeness. Look for pods that are firm, not spongy. The beans have to be removed from the pods, then either blanched in salted boiling water for one minute to remove the outer skin so they can be used in recipes for further cooking, or cooked for about five minutes or more, depending on the degree of ripeness, to be eaten plain. The outer skin is usually removed before eating, although some people eat the skin, especially if the beans are very young. One pound of fava beans will render one cup of shelled beans.

A very popular way of serving fresh fava beans in Andean countries is on big platters with corn on the cob and brick cheese. Some people are sensitive to an illness called favism, which is a potentially lethal allergic reaction triggered by eating fava beans or by inhaling the scent of beans grown in marshy ground. This predisposition is found only in some people of Mediterranean descent. Fresh fava beans can be found in Italian and ethnic grocery stores and in some supermarkets in the spring, summer, and early fall. They also are available frozen.

Caraotas Negras

BLACK BEANS *Serves 8*

Black beans and rice are the staff of life for Venezuelans and Brazilians. Black beans are eaten as a side dish, as a main dish with rice and plantains, or with meat and fish. This particular version is an indispensable part of the famous dish from Caracas called *El Pabellón Criollo* (page 206).

2 cups dried black beans
10 cups water

2 tablespoons olive oil

1 medium-size onion, finely chopped (about 1 cup)

1 medium-size red bell pepper, seeded and finely chopped

6 cloves garlic, mashed into a paste with 1 teaspoon salt and ½ teaspoon freshly ground black pepper

½ teaspoon ground cumin

1 teaspoon dark brown sugar

1 tablespoon red or white wine vinegar or dry sherry

1. Thoroughly wash and pick over the beans. Place in a large saucepan with the water and let soak for at least 3 hours. (Alternatively, you could bring the beans to a full boil, turn off the heat, cover, and let stand for 1½ hours.) Bring the beans and their soaking water to a boil, reduce the heat to low, cover, and let simmer until soft, about 1 hour.

2. While the beans are cooking, heat the oil in a large skillet over medium-low heat. Add the onion, bell pepper, garlic paste, cumin, and brown sugar and cook, stirring occasionally, until soft, about 10 minutes. Add 1 cup of the cooked beans and mash with a fork. Add to the bean pot, stir, and simmer over low heat for 30 minutes. Taste for salt and black pepper, stir in the vinegar, and serve.

TO SERVE **Serve over white rice.**

Puré Picante de Garbanzos

SPICY MASHED CHICKPEAS *Serves 4*

This is a very popular side dish in Chile, usually served with roasted pork or beef. The flavoring varies; some cooks use garlic, others onions or bacon. This is an Old World specialty creolized by the addition of the Indians' favorite condiment, hot peppers, from which the dish gets its name.

2 tablespoons olive oil

2 cloves garlic, minced

One 15-ounce can chickpeas, drained and rinsed

½ cup chicken broth

1 teaspoon fresh hot pepper puree, store-bought or homemade (page 332)

¼ cup whipping cream

Salt and white pepper

1. Heat the oil in a medium-size, heavy saucepan over low heat. Add the garlic and cook, stirring, for a few seconds. Add the chickpeas, chicken broth, hot pepper puree, and cream and cook, stirring, for 5 minutes.

2. Transfer to a blender or food processor and process until smooth. Return the puree to the saucepan, season with salt and white pepper to taste, and simmer over medium-low for a few minutes, adding a little water if the puree becomes too dry. Serve hot.

Frijoles en Nueces y Ají

BEANS WITH WALNUTS AND HOT PEPPERS *Serves 6*

This Peruvian specialty is a very interesting and delicious way to prepare beans. It could be that the Incas used one of South America's indigenous nuts to flavor the beans, or perhaps the Spanish, who have a tradition of using almonds in stews, introduced the use of nuts along with the bacon. This dish can be made with black beans, but it is also good made with *frijoles mayocoba* (Peruvian white beans), which are similar to Great Northern beans. For many people, this is a meal in itself, eaten with lots of rice.

1 pound dried black or white beans, or three 15-ounce cans, undrained

4 ounces lean slab bacon, sliced ¼ inch thick and cut into ¼-inch cubes

1 medium-size onion, finely chopped (about 1 cup)

4 dried *mirasol* (hot yellow) peppers, seeded, soaked in hot water for 30 minutes, drained, and pureed

2 large cloves garlic, mashed into a paste with 1 teaspoon salt and ½ teaspoon freshly ground black pepper

½ cup ground walnuts

1. If using dried beans, thoroughly wash and pick over. Place in a large saucepan with the water and let soak for at least 3 hours. (Alternatively, you could bring the beans to a full boil, turn off the heat, cover, and let stand for 1½ hours.) Bring the beans and their soaking water to a boil, reduce the heat to low, cover, and let simmer until soft, about 1 hour. If using canned beans, place with their juice in a large saucepan.

2. Place 1 cup of the beans in a blender and process until smooth. Return to the saucepan.

3. Heat a large skillet over medium heat. Add the bacon and fry until browned. With a slotted spoon, transfer the bacon to paper towels to drain. Remove all but 1 tablespoon of the bacon fat from the skillet. Reduce the heat to low, add the onion, and cook, stirring occasionally, until softened, about 5 minutes. Stir in the *mirasol* pepper puree and garlic paste and cook, stirring constantly, for 3 minutes.

4. Add the onion mixture, bacon, and walnuts to the beans. Simmer over medium-low heat, stirring occasionally, for 20 minutes to blend the flavors. If the mixture gets too thick, add a little boiling water; the beans should have some sauce. Taste for salt and black pepper and serve hot.

TO SERVE **Serve over rice, if desired.**

Menestra de Lentejas

STEWED LENTILS *Serves 16*

Menestras, whether made with lentils, dried beans, or chickpeas, are the staple of millions of people in South America. This version is typical of the Pacific coast of the Andean countries and it is usually served with white rice, fish or beef grilled on skewers, and fried plantains. Without meat, it makes for a wonderful vegetarian meal. It freezes very well and is handy to have on hand for a nour-ishing side dish that goes well with rice topped with a fried egg. If frozen, thaw in the microwave or overnight in the refrigerator, then reheat in the microwave or on top of the stove. If it's too dry, add a little water and simmer for a minute.

1 pound dried brown lentils

1 small green bell pepper, seeded but left whole

1 small onion, peeled

6 cups cold water

2 medium-size onions, coarsely chopped (about 2 cups)

1 large green bell pepper, seeded and chopped

4 cloves garlic, chopped

½ cup packed fresh parsley leaves

½ cup packed fresh cilantro leaves

½ cup water

¼ cup tomato paste

2 teaspoons beef bouillon granules

1 teaspoon ground cumin

1 teaspoon salt

½ teaspoon freshly ground black pepper

2 tablespoons canola or olive oil

1 teaspoon ground annatto or sweet paprika

1. Pick over the lentils and rinse thoroughly. Place in a 4-quart saucepan and add the whole bell pepper, whole onion, and water. Bring to a boil over medium heat, then reduce the heat to low, cover, and simmer until the lentils are soft, about 30 minutes. Transfer 1 cup of the lentils, the bell pepper, and onion to a blender and process until smooth. Return the puree to the pan.

2. Place all the remaining ingredients, except the canola oil and annatto, in a blender or food processor and process until smooth.

3. Heat the canola oil in a Dutch oven (preferably nonstick) over medium-low heat. Stir in the annatto and vegetable puree, partially cover, and

cook, stirring occasionally, until the vegetables lose their raw taste, about 15 minutes. If the puree dries out, add a little water. Add the lentils and simmer for 15 minutes to blend the flavors, adding more water if it gets too thick. The lentils should be soupy, because they will thicken as they stand. Taste for salt and black pepper and serve. (A standard serving is about ½ cup.)

TO SERVE **Serve with grilled whole green plantains or *Patacones* (page 120).**

VARIATIONS On the Andean coast of Colombia and Ecuador, some cooks add ½ green plantain pureed with ½ cup water to the vegetable puree. Others add ½ boiled green plantain, cut into ½-inch cubes, when adding the lentils to the vegetable puree.

Granos

GRAIN DISHES

GRAINS HAVE ALWAYS OCCUPIED A place of importance in South Americans' diets. Thousands of years before Columbus landed in the Americas, the Indians cultivated grains, which played a central role in their lives. The most important and versatile grain was maize, or corn, which is easily cultivated and grows at low altitudes. The other significant grains were quinoa, amaranth, and kaniwa, which grow at higher altitudes. After the conquest, the Spaniards introduced wheat, rice, barley, and oats, which the Indians quickly embraced. These Old World cereals were nutritionally superior to corn but, unfortunately, possessed less nutritional value than quinoa, amaranth, and kaniwa, although they were easier to use.

The introduced grains dramatically increased the options available to South American cooks, and today both Old World grains and New are part of the continent's culinary landscape.

Maíz
MAIZE, CORN

THE SINGLE MOST IMPORTANT GIFT of the Americas to the world was maize, or what we now call corn. The word *corn* originally referred to the most important grain in a particular region, and this is still true in many parts of the world. Today in the Americas, however, the word *corn* is used almost exclusively to mean maize, although the earlier name is still reflected in the Spanish word for the grain, *maíz*.

Corn was the most important foodstuff of the Indians, many of whom considered it sacred. The Inca emperor himself planted the first corn seeds each year, and ceremonies were performed throughout the year to attract rain, give thanks for water, and to celebrate a successful harvest. Scholars believe that corn was domesticated in Central America (Honduras, Guatemala, and southern Mexico), then traveled throughout the Americas. Recent archaeological excavations seem to indicate that by 5,000 years ago, corn was being widely cultivated in South America.

When the Spaniards arrived there, they found corn growing in virtually all geographical regions of the land. It used to feed the body and soul—as food, medicine, and a part of ceremonies honoring the gods. The Guarani Indians of Brazil celebrated a good corn crop as Colheita Sagrada, or Sacred Harvest. The Indians had a special respect for corn, and when they planted the seeds, they prayed to Mother Earth, acknowledging their reliance on nature.

There are many types of corn, which are used in different ways. Some varieties are good for toasting, others for boiling or roasting, and still others for popping. The starchy types have been used for centuries for *arepas* (cornbread), *humitas* (tamales), and *pasteles* (casseroles made with ground corn, eggs, and cheese). Many of these ancient specialties, such as *arepas*, have survived intact. Others, such as *humitas*, have undergone changes.

The importance of corn in the Andean countries is typified by the diet of the people of Ecuador. In Cuenca, a city in southern Ecuador that boasts the first university in Ecuador and is the birthplace of a number or eminent writers, 30 corn-based specialties are prepared to celebrate the anniversary of the founding of the city. No wonder so many writers have written poems praising this sacred grain! In other areas of the Ecuadorian Andes, investigators have found more than 45 corn-based specialties, from appetizers to desserts. This reliance on corn is also true in the other Andean countries.

Corn was, and is, consumed at three stages of maturation: young or fresh, called *choclo* or *maíz tierno*; semimature, called *choclero* or *maíz cau*; and dried, called simply *maíz*.

Choclo or Maíz Tierno

YOUNG OR FRESH CORN

THE QUALITY OF SOUTH AMERICAN corn is quite different from the sweet corn we have in the United States. Because of its high starch content, South American corn has to be cooked much longer, and it has a chewy consistency. Young corn is mainly boiled or cooked over a fire with the husks left on. It is often sold on the streets or in little storefront restaurants that also feature some kind of pork specialty. Sometimes the kernels are removed and fried in butter. Young corn is also used to make soups.

The favorite way of serving fresh corn in season is boiled. The ears are brought to the table on large trays, where bowls of butter and hot pepper sauce are waiting to season them. In Ecuador, trays of fresh fava beans boiled with the skins on are served with the corn, along with platters of brick cheese. In Bolivia, corn on the cob is boiled with anise and sugar and served with fava beans cooked with a sprig of mint. Boiled potatoes and slices of brick cheese that have been quickly fried in a little oil are also part of this feast, called *plato paceño*, which is found throughout Bolivia during corn season. In Peru, the most delicious way to serve ears of corn is with *huancaína*, a cheese sauce flavored with hot peppers. Some of the most popular dishes made with fresh corn kernels are *choclo frito* (fried corn), *pailita de choclo y crema* (corn casserole with butter and cream), *Mazamorra Campesina* (page 283), soups, pancakes, cakes, and flans.

Choclero or Maíz Cau

SEMIMATURE CORN

MAÍZ CAU IS IN BETWEEN young and fully mature, or dried, corn. The corn "milk" starts thickening at this stage, as the starch content increases. This is the corn that is used to make the famous *humitas*, *pasteles*, and *picantes de choclo*. It is also added to soups such as *locros*, and it is used in a variety of stews. It can be eaten boiled, but it takes a lot longer to cook than young corn.

Maíz DRIED CORN

WHEN THE EARS OF CORN have dried out, the milk is converted completely into starch. To make sure they are completely dried, they can be spread out on blankets and dried in the sun. Traditionally, the kernels of dried corn were used to prepare several foodstuffs that were basic to the Indians' diet. Today dried corn is still used in many ways. *Tostado* (toasted dried corn) is eaten as an accompaniment to some foods or as a snack. *Mote* or *muti* (hominy) is dried corn that has been soaked, peeled, and boiled. It is eaten plain or used in a variety of specialties. Dried corn also may be ground to make a whole spectrum of dishes, from appetizers to desserts.

Arroz
RICE

LONG-GRAIN RICE, BROUGHT OVER by the Spaniards and Portuguese, has become a staple grain in South America, where many people survive on a diet of rice and beans. In some countries, such as Brazil, everyone, both rich and poor, has rice and beans every day as part of the main meal. The coastal people of countries in the tropics, such as Colombia and Ecuador, serve a bowl of rice on the side to eat with beans or soups. In some countries, people eat leftover rice for breakfast. Whatever form it takes, rice is a common and well-established part of South American cuisine.

Quinua
QUINOA

PRONOUNCED "KEEN-WA," QUINOA IS A grain native to the western slopes of the Andes. It is very resistant to the hardships of high altitudes, where cold and wind often defeat less hardy plants. It can grow at altitudes above 9,800 feet and is often planted around fields of potatoes and corn to protect these more sensitive plants from the elements.

Quinoa was first domesticated somewhere in northern Chile or in Peru. Seeds have been found in excavations in northern Argentina and Peru at sites that date back 2,000 years. Long before the Spaniards arrived, the Incas had spread the methods of cultivating and using quinoa throughout the area of their conquests.

By the time the Spaniards arrived, quinoa's range extended from the Colombian *sabanas* (prairies) in the north to Argentina, Chile, and Bolivia in the south. The Chibcha people of Colombia called it *suba* or *supha*, while the Araucanians of Chile called it *dahue*. Quinoa was sacred to the Incas, who revered it for its nutritional value. According to legend, quinoa was the remains of a heavenly banquet, so each planting season began with the Inca ruler reverently planting the first row with a golden spade. The time of planting was also an occasion for ceremonial offerings to Mother Earth. Guinea pigs, some kind of fat, coca leaves, *chicha de jora* (a fermented corn drink), and other foods were offered, while celebrants indulged in drinking and dancing. The Incas also had objects of worship called *quinuamamas*, which were dolls fashioned from flour ground from the grain.

After the harvest came the tedious task of removing the saponin, a naturally occurring insecticide produced by the plant, from the quinoa grains. The grains were rinsed by hand until the bitterness disappeared. Then the quinoa was used to make soups, *mazamorras* (hominy stews), and a type of bread shaped like a cigar. The cooked quinoa was also mixed with *mishque*, the sweet liquid obtained from a cactus plant, to make tamales or *arroz de mishque*, which basically is a type of *mazamorra*. In the Altiplano of Bolivia, quinoa is mixed with amaranth and cooked in water to make *macuna*, a porridge that could sustain people at work or on long journeys. Most of these foods are still prepared in some villages. Every part of the quinoa plant had some kind of use. The leaves of the plant were much appreciated by the Indians and Spaniards for making soup. The bitter water from washing the quinoa was used to make soap and cure fevers. The ashes left from burning the stalks after the harvest were used to make little buns that were chewed with coca leaves.

According to the author Eduardo Estrella, the decline of quinoa began in the nineteenth century. He believes that the Spaniards rejected the grain as "Indian food" and over the years other people followed suit. To make matters worse, the peasants developed a superstition about quinoa. They believed that pigs that ate quinoa developed *mal de la quinua* (quinoa sickness) and died. Because quinoa looks like the cysts that develop in the muscles of pigs with cysticercoids (tapeworms), they thought that there must be a connection between the grain and the disease. So the peasants stopped planting quinoa, to the point where it nearly disappeared.

Quinoa is now being revived, thanks to the growing interest in health and nutrition. It is now not only imported to the United States, but it is cultivated in Colorado, New Mexico, northern California, Washington, and Oregon, as well as in other parts of the world. There are about 2,000 varieties of quinoa, which range in size from as small as a grain of sand to the size of a sesame seed, and in color from ivory to yellow, brown, and black. It has an amazing nutrient profile, characterized by an outstanding balance of protein, minerals, and amino acids. It is one of only a few high-protein grains in the world. Some advocates claim medicinal and stamina-giving qualities for the grain. From a cook's point of view, quinoa is an extremely versatile grain, suitable for almost any kind of dish. It is a good substitute for rice and bulgur, and it can be used in salads, soups and stews, croquettes, and casseroles, as well as to stuff vegetables.

Kiwicha
AMARANTH

UNLIKE QUINOA, WHICH GREW ONLY in South America, amaranth spread throughout the Americas, almost as widely as corn. It was the sacred grain of the Aztecs but was almost wiped out by the Spaniards, who identified it solely with the human-blood rituals in which the Aztecs frequently used it. Amaranth was also one of the staple grains of the Incas and other pre-Columbian Indians.

The most important type of amaranth in the Andes is called *kiwicha* in Quechua. The Quechuas used it for ceremonial dishes, such as *colada morada* (a purple corn and fruit soup), prepared for the Day of the Dead. Other common names for amaranth are *quihuicha*, *ataco*, and *sangurachi*. This beautiful, colorful plant grows in the highlands of Ecuador, Peru, Bolivia, and parts of Chile, where most conventional grain crops cannot grow. It is drought, heat, and pest tolerant, and the stems, leaves, and flowers come in beautiful colors—purple, red, and gold. From the red variety, a nontoxic coloring called *betalaina* is extracted. The tiny amaranth seeds are smaller than those of quinoa—about the size of poppy seeds. Each plant produces more than 400,000 seeds, which have a nutritional profile similar to that of quinoa. They can be popped like popcorn, ground into flour, and made into porridge. After the grain is threshed, the leavings are used for animal fodder. Like the leaves of the quinoa plant, amaranth leaves can be used in soups or simply cooked like spinach or Swiss chard.

Cañihua

KANIWA

LIKE QUINOA AND AMARANTH, KANIWA (*Chenopodium palladicaule*) is a nutritious grain that grows at high altitudes, thriving in places where even quinoa cannot survive. The staff of life for the Indians of the Bolivian and Peruvian Altiplano, it is grown for its seeds, which are smaller than those of quinoa and amaranth, and for its leaves, which are used as greens. The seeds are toasted and ground into a flour that is used to make soups or beverages. A hot beverage made with kaniwa is sold in the streets of Cuzco, Peru. Kaniwa is not available in the United States.

Mote de Trigo

WHEAT BERRIES

DRIED COOKED CEREALS SUCH AS wheat berries, barley, and corn come under the generic name of *mote* in some South American countries. *Mote de trigo* (wheat berries) is very popular in the South American kitchen. An import from Europe, the berries (which are simply whole, unground wheat grains) are used to make stews, soups, and even desserts. In some countries, there are two varieties—dried and precooked. The precooked variety is not available in the United States. To cook dried wheat berries, see the instructions on page 412.

Cachapitas de Jojoto

CORN PANCAKES *Makes 24 small pancakes; 4 servings*

Like *arepas* (cornbread) these delicious pancakes are a very popular snack food in Venezuela and are sold in *areperías* (snack shops) garnished with cheese or chorizo. They make a nice hors d'oeuvre or side dish, with or without the cheese or chorizo.

> 2 cups fresh corn kernels
> ½ cup whipping cream
> 2 large eggs
> ¼ cup all-purpose flour
> ½ teaspoon salt
> ¼ teaspoon sugar
> 1 tablespoon unsalted butter, melted, plus more for brushing
> Sliced chorizo (optional)
> Sliced Chihuahua, mozzarella, Muenster, or imported feta cheese (optional)

1. Place the corn, cream, eggs, flour, salt, sugar, and melted butter in a blender or food processor and process until smooth. The mixture should have the consistency of heavy cream. If it's too thick, add a little more cream.

2. Heat a griddle (preferably nonstick) over medium heat. Brush with melted butter, then drop 1 tablespoon of the mixture at a time onto the griddle and cook on both sides until golden brown.

3. Serve hot, with a slice of chorizo or cheese on top, if desired.

Flan de Choclo

CORN CUSTARD *Serves 6*

I had this heavenly corn custard in the Carrera Hotel in Santiago. It had been prepared in small, individual molds and was so delicate that it melted in my mouth.

2 tablespoons unsalted butter

1 small onion, chopped (about ½ cup)

2 cups fresh corn kernels

2 cups milk

½ teaspoon salt

½ teaspoon sugar

3 large eggs, lightly beaten (see Note)

Dry bread crumbs

1. Melt the butter in a large, heavy skillet over medium heat. Add the onion and cook, stirring occasionally, until softened, about 5 minutes. Add the corn and cook, stirring, for a couple of minutes. Add the milk, salt, and sugar and simmer, stirring a few times, for 5 minutes. Do not let boil.

2. Remove from the heat and let cool for a few minutes. Transfer to a blender or food processor and process until smooth. Pass the puree through a medium-mesh sieve. You should have about 3 cups corn puree. Place in a medium-size mixing bowl and, using a wire whisk, beat in the eggs just enough to blend them with the puree.

3. Preheat the oven to 325°F. Butter six 6-ounce ovenproof molds, then coat the insides evenly on the sides and bottoms with the bread crumbs. Knock out any excess crumbs.

4. Fill the prepared molds evenly with the custard to ¼ inch below the top. Place in a baking pan half-filled with hot water and lay a sheet of aluminum foil over the molds. Bake on the lower oven rack until a knife inserted in the center comes out clean, about 45 minutes.

5. Remove from the oven and let cool for a few minutes. Run a small paring knife around the inside of each mold to release the custard, then unmold onto a heated serving plate and serve.

NOTE For a firmer custard, you can add 1 egg yolk or 1 whole egg.

Mote con Picadillo

HOMINY WITH SCALLIONS AND CILANTRO
Serves 6 to 8

This specialty is always present when serving pork in Ecuador, whether the pork is in the form of *hornado* (roasted leg of pork) or *fritada* (fried pork chunks). *Mote* (hominy) is especially good when tossed with the fat left over from cooking either version of pork. This type of hominy is sold in the open markets, and sometimes on the street, to workers who need a quick snack. For many people, hominy with *ají* (hot pepper salsa) and *tostado* (toasted dried corn) is a meal.

> Two 15-ounce cans white or yellow hominy, drained and rinsed
>
> ½ cup canned black-eyed peas or pinto beans, drained and rinsed
>
> 3 tablespoons fat rendered from cooking pork, or unsalted butter

GARNISHES

> ¼ cup finely chopped scallions (white part and 1 inch of the green)
>
> 2 tablespoons finely chopped fresh cilantro leaves
>
> 1 small ripe but firm tomato (about 3 ounces), seeded and finely chopped

1. Place the hominy and beans in a 4-quart saucepan with water to cover. Bring to a boil, reduce the heat to medium, and simmer for 5 minutes. Drain thoroughly and toss with the fat.

2. Transfer to a heated serving bowl. Top with the scallions, cilantro, and tomato and serve.

Mote Pillo Cuencano

HOMINY CUENCA STYLE *Serves 4*

There are some regions in Ecuador that are well known for their passion for *mote* (hominy). Ecuadorian hominy is much larger than the variety found in the United States and is the comfort food of many, rich and poor. Cuenca is a colonial city located in southern Ecuador, where it is possible to find a great variety of specialties that center on hominy. This dish is usually served with pork or chorizo.

2 tablespoons unsalted butter

1 teaspoon *Manteca de Color* (page 331) or sweet paprika

½ cup finely chopped scallions (white part and 1 inch of the green)

1 small clove garlic, mashed into a paste with ¼ teaspoon salt and ¼ teaspoon freshly ground black pepper

Two 15-ounce cans white or yellow hominy, heated and drained

½ cup milk

4 large eggs, lightly beaten

2 tablespoons finely chopped fresh parsley leaves

1. In a large skillet (preferably nonstick), heat the butter and *manteca de color* together over medium heat. When the butter has melted, add ¼ cup of the scallions and the garlic paste. Cook, stirring constantly, for 1 minute. Stir in the hominy and cook for a few seconds, then add the milk. Simmer until all the milk is absorbed, about 5 minutes. Add the eggs and continue to cook, stirring frequently, until the eggs are just set. Do not let them dry out.

2. In a small bowl, combine the remaining ¼ cup scallions and the parsley. Transfer the hominy mixture to a heated serving bowl and sprinkle with the scallions and parsley.

Corpus Christi

 Corpus Christi is a holiday celebrated by most Catholics around the world 60 days after Easter. It honors Jesus Christ and the sacrament of Holy Communion. In South America, the most famous celebration is found in Cuzco, Peru, which was the stronghold of the Incas. After the conquest, the Spaniards started the tradition of dressing statues of the saints in elaborate, brightly colored costumes to attract the indigenous people. This succeeded to such an extent that now people come from far away to attend the celebration. They bring their best costumes to take part in processions and compete with other villages to see which group is wearing the most elaborate and colorful costumes. The streets are lined with stalls selling dishes made with corn, *cuy* (guinea pig), and other foods, and there is lots of drinking and dancing.

To a lesser extent, other countries celebrate Corpus Christi with special foods and festivities. In Ecuador, for example, *champuz* and *rosero* (fruit and hominy drinks) are the traditional desserts served on Corpus Christi. Going to church and receiving Communion on this day is a must.

Maíz Tostado

TOASTED DRIED CORN *Makes about 3 cups*

The Spanish chronicler Father Joseph de Acosta called *maíz tostado* the bread of the Indians. It was indeed a staple of the Incas, especially useful for long journeys. As settlers arrived from Spain and Portugal, it became a popular snack food. Children in the countryside still carry some *tostado* in their pockets to eat during recess at school. Toasted dried corn is a truly democratic food, enjoyed by rich and poor alike. It is the indispensable ingredient in *cebiches*, especially in Ecuador, where it goes by the name *tostado*, and in Peru, where it is called *cancha*. In Bolivia, it is called *tostado de maíz* to differentiate it from *tostado de trigo* (toasted wheat berries). *Tostado* is also an integral part of the Ecuadorian *hornado* (roasted leg of pork) and *fritada* (fried pork chunks). In Bolivia, it is sometimes mixed with dried *bogas* (small fish from Lake Titicaca) to take on journeys. It is also mixed with *charqui seco* (dried meat), *chicharrón* (fried pork rind), or a piece of *chancaca* (molded brown sugar). In the olden days, Bolivians thought so highly of *tostado* that they served it to guests accompanied with slices of cheese, still a favorite way to eat *tostado*. *Tostado* also can be found in Paraguay, where the Guarani name for it is *abatí pororó* and the Spanish name is *maíz saltado*.

The corn used to make *tostado* is a special, medium-size, yellow kernel that in Ecuador goes by the Quechua name *mishka*. There is also another type of corn that is used for toasting, called *chuspillo* or *chulpi* in Ecuador and *maíz cancha chulpi* in Peru. It has a small kernel and is very sweet. In the United States, you can find *maíz* for *tostado* in South American groceries. In precolonial times, the corn was toasted in clay pots set into a fire, without any fat. After the Spaniards introduced the pig, the corn was toasted in lard, and this is the most popular way of preparing it now. The best *tostado* is made with leftover lard from frying pork.

2 cups dried corn
1 cup lard or canola oil
1 large clove garlic, peeled
Salt

1.   In a medium-size bowl, soak the corn in water to cover for 1 hour, then drain.

2.   Heat the lard and garlic in a 4-quart aluminum saucepan over low heat. When the garlic is lightly browned, discard and add the corn all at once and start stirring with a wooden spoon. Have a cover ready, and when the corn starts "jumping" or popping, partially cover the saucepan but continue to stir occasionally to achieve even browning. It should take about 10 minutes for the corn to be fully cooked and golden brown. When done, some of the kernels will have popped open.

3.   With a slotted spoon, transfer the corn to a bowl lined with paper towels and add salt to taste. Let cool before serving. The leftover fat can be reused.

Mbaipy/Polenta

PARAGUAYAN POLENTA *Serves 4*

Polenta is very popular in South American countries wherever large numbers of Italian immigrants settled. Venezuelans use *arepa* flour (precooked corn flour) to make their polenta, which is often prepared with some meat filling. In Argentina, it is made with cream and cheese and topped with tomato sauce or stuffed with meat. This Paraguayan version is interesting because it uses onion, cheese, and sour cream and is finished in the oven. It is very tasty and takes only a few minutes to prepare. It's a great do-ahead dish that can be reheated in the oven or microwave.

2 tablespoons canola oil

1 small onion, minced (about ½ cup)

2 cups water

1½ cups milk

1 teaspoon salt

1 cup cornmeal

1 cup sour cream

2 ounces Chihuahua, mozzarella, or Muenster cheese, shredded

2 tablespoons freshly grated Parmesan cheese

1. Heat the oil in a heavy 4-quart saucepan over medium heat. Add the onion and cook, stirring occasionally, until softened, about 5 minutes. Add the water, milk, and salt and bring to a boil. Sprinkle the cornmeal over the boiling liquid, stirring constantly, until all is added. Add the sour cream and cook, stirring frequently (almost constantly), until thickened and pulling away from the side of the pan, about 15 minutes. Mix in the Chihuahua cheese.

2. Preheat the oven to 350°F. Butter a shallow 1-quart baking dish.

3. Transfer the cornmeal mixture to the prepared dish. Sprinkle the top evenly with the Parmesan and bake until golden, about 30 minutes. Let cool for 5 minutes, then cut into 4 portions and serve.

TO SERVE **Serve topped with tomato sauce or any kind of stew.**

Arroz Blanco Graneado

WHITE RICE *Serves 6*

Rice, especially plain white rice, is one of the staples of South America and is part of most meals in the Andean countries and Brazil. Latin cooks know how to prepare it to perfection. It is very

important to have a heavy, wide saucepan with a tight cover. To obtain a very tender rice, with the grains separated, cover the rice after it has finished cooking and let it stand off the heat for five minutes. If the rice dries out before it is cooked, sprinkle a couple of tablespoons of hot water over it, cover, and finish cooking.

2 tablespoons canola oil

2 cups long-grain rice

1 clove garlic, peeled

3 cups water

1 teaspoon salt

1. Place all the ingredients in a heavy 4-quart saucepan. Bring to a boil over medium-low heat and cook, uncovered, until most of the water has evaporated, about 15 minutes. Reduce the heat to low, cover, and cook until all the water has been absorbed, about 5 minutes.

2. Remove from the heat, fluff with a fork, and discard the garlic. Cover and let sit for 5 minutes before serving.

NOTE **If using converted rice, increase the water to 4 to 4¼ cups.**

ARROZ AMARILLO (Yellow Rice) Add 1 teaspoon *Manteca de Color* (page 331) or sweet paprika, along with ¼ teaspoon ground cumin, if desired.

Arroz Negro con Tocineta y Plátano

BLACK RICE WITH BACON AND PLANTAIN *Serves 8*

I ate this very unusual rice for the first time in the home of Olga Lozano. Olga's mother was visiting, and she prepared this Colombian specialty for a group of friends. It makes a good accompaniment for chicken or wild game.

¼ cup canola oil

1½ cups angel hair pasta broken into
  1-inch pieces

2 cups long-grain rice

4 cups beef broth

1 teaspoon molasses

½ teaspoon salt

1 cup seedless black raisins

1 ripe (yellow) plantain, peeled and cut into
  ½-inch cubes

6 strips bacon, cut into ½-inch pieces

2 hard-cooked eggs, peeled and chopped, for
  garnish

1. In a large skillet with a lid, heat 2 tablespoons of the oil over medium heat. Add the pasta and cook, stirring, until golden. Stir in the rice, beef broth, molasses, and salt. Cover and cook over low heat until most of the water has been absorbed, about 20 minutes. Stir in the raisins, cover, and cook until the rice is tender and dry. Remove from the heat, fluff with a fork, and let sit for 5 minutes.

2. In a medium-size skillet, heat the remaining 2 tablespoons oil over low heat. Add the plantain and cook, stirring, until golden and soft, 3 to 5 minutes. Drain on paper towels, then stir into the rice. In another skillet, cook the bacon over medium heat until crisp. Drain on paper towels.

3. Serve the rice in a heated serving bowl garnished, with the bacon and eggs.

Arroz Blanco Venezolano

VENEZUELAN-STYLE RICE *Serves 4*

This Spanish-style rice includes the Indian peppers for color and flavor. It is the traditional accompaniment for *El Pabellón Criollo* (page 206), but it can also be served with fish or poultry.

1 tablespoon canola oil

1 small onion, finely chopped (about
  ½ cup)

¼ cup seeded and finely chopped red bell
  pepper

1 clove garlic, minced

1½ cups long-grain rice

3 cups water

1 teaspoon salt

1. Heat the oil in a large, heavy saucepan over medium-low heat. Add the onion, bell pepper, and garlic and cook, stirring, until softened, about 5 minutes. Add the rice and cook, stirring constantly, until it has absorbed the oil, about 2 minutes. Add the water and salt and cook, uncovered, until most of the water has been absorbed, about 20 minutes. Reduce the heat to very low, cover, and cook until the rice is tender, about 7 minutes.

2. Remove from the heat and fluff with a fork. Cover and let stand for 5 minutes before serving.

Arroz Brasileiro

BRAZILIAN-STYLE RICE *Serves 6 to 8*

This tasty rice was probably one of the first creole creations, with the Portuguese rice being combined with the native tomato to give it even more flavor and color.

2 tablespoons canola oil

1 medium-size onion, thinly sliced (about 1
  cup)

2 cups long-grain rice

1 medium-size ripe but firm tomato (5 to 6
  ounces), peeled, seeded, and chopped

3 cups hot water

1 teaspoon salt

1. Heat the oil in a heavy 4-quart saucepan over low heat. Add the onion and cook, stirring a few

times, until softened, about 5 minutes. Add the rice and cook, stirring constantly, until the grains are coated with the oil, about 2 minutes. Add the tomato, water, and salt. Cover and simmer until the rice has absorbed all the liquid, about 20 minutes.

2.   Remove from the heat and fluff with a fork. Cover and let stand for 5 minutes before serving.

Arroz con Azafrán

SAFFRON RICE PILAF *Serves 6*

For special occasions, this dish of Spanish origin is the preferred rice to serve, always molded in timbales or 6-ounce Pyrex cups.

> **2 tablespoons unsalted butter**
>
> **⅓ cup minced onion**
>
> **1½ cups converted rice**
>
> **½ teaspoon saffron threads, crumbled and softened in ¼ cup water**
>
> **½ cup dry white wine**
>
> **3 cups chicken broth, heated**

1.   Melt the butter in a heavy 4-quart saucepan over low heat. Add the onion and cook, stirring occasionally, until softened, about 7 minutes. Add the rice and cook for a couple of minutes, stirring, until all grains are coated with butter. Add the saffron and water, wine, and chicken broth and bring to a boil over medium heat. Reduce the heat to low, cover, and cook until all the liquid has been absorbed, about 20 minutes.

2.   Remove from the heat and fluff with a fork. Cover and let stand for 5 minutes before serving.

Arroz con Alcachofas

RICE WITH ARTICHOKES *Serves 4 to 6*

Artichokes, especially in the southern countries of South America, are abundant when in season. They may be prepared boiled, stuffed, as appetizers, in salads, with rice or pasta, or with chicken. Chileans especially are fond of them, preparing them in many different ways. When I was a guest of Howard and Kika Keefe in Santiago, I was treated almost every day to a delicious first course of either artichokes or asparagus—luckily for me, both were in season. Both vegetables were large and beautifully green and fresh.

I like this vegetarian version of rice and artichokes, which can be found in many countries. Sometimes béchamel sauce is used as a binding agent instead of the half-and-half. For convenience, I recommend using frozen artichokes or, if frozen are unavailable, canned, thoroughly rinsed. My daughter Stephanie and her friend Cristin tested this dish for me and adore it to the point that they make it almost every week. Their husbands also rave about it.

> **¼ cup dried porcini mushrooms, soaked in hot water for 30 minutes**
>
> **One 9-ounce package frozen artichoke hearts or one 14-ounce can artichoke hearts**
>
> **2 tablespoons unsalted butter**
>
> **1 medium-size onion, finely chopped (about 1 cup)**
>
> **1 large clove garlic, mashed into a paste with ½ teaspoon salt and ¼ teaspoon freshly ground black pepper**
>
> **1½ cups converted rice**
>
> **3 cups chicken or vegetable broth**
>
> **1 cup half-and-half**
>
> **2 hard-cooked eggs, peeled and chopped**
>
> **¾ cup freshly grated Parmesan cheese**
>
> **¼ cup minced fresh parsley leaves**
>
> **Pimento strips for garnish**

1. Drain the mushrooms and rinse thoroughly, rubbing to remove any leftover sand. Set aside.

2. If using frozen artichokes, cook according to the package directions. Remove the tough outer leaves (they are usually dark green) and chop the artichokes into smaller pieces. Set aside. If using canned artichokes, drain, rinse well, and chop.

3. In a 10-inch skillet with a cover, melt the butter over low heat. Add the onion and mushrooms and cook, stirring a few times, for 5 minutes. Stir in the garlic paste and cook for 1 minute. Add the rice and cook, stirring constantly, for 1 minute. Add the chicken broth and artichokes and bring to a boil over medium heat. Reduce the heat to low, cover, and simmer until all the liquid has been absorbed, about 20 minutes. Remove from the heat, fluff with a fork, cover, and let stand for 5 minutes.

4. Add the half-and-half, eggs, Parmesan, and parsley to the rice and mix well. Season with salt and pepper to taste. Pack the mixture into a well-oiled 6-cup mold. The dish can be prepared to this point up to a day ahead. Let cool, cover with waxed paper and aluminum foil, and refrigerate until needed. Uncover and bring to room temperature before baking.

5. Preheat the oven to 350°F.

6. Cover the mold with aluminum foil and bake until heated through, about 20 minutes. Unmold onto a serving platter and serve right away, garnished with the pimento strips.

Arroz con Coco Cartagenero

CARTAGENA-STYLE RICE WITH COCONUT MILK *Serves 6 to 8*

This rice is very popular on the coast of Colombia, especially in Cartagena, where it is served every night with meat or fish. Sometimes raisins are added.

> **2 cups long-grain rice**
> **One 14-ounce can unsweetened coconut milk mixed with 1½ cups water**
> **1 tablespoon sugar**
> **1 teaspoon salt**

Place all the ingredients in a heavy 4-quart saucepan. Bring to a boil over medium heat, reduce the heat to low, cover, and cook until the rice is tender and dry, about 10 minutes. Remove from the heat and fluff with a fork. Cover and let stand for 5 minutes before serving.

VARIATION There is another version of this recipe in Colombia known as *arroz con coco frito*. One cup thick unsweetened coconut milk is cooked until it turns a deep caramel color and the fat separates out. It is then mixed with 3 cups thin unsweetened coconut milk and sugar to taste and cooked, stirring constantly, until the caramelized milk is completely dissolved. This is used as the base for the rice. Most people add ½ cup raisins before cooking the rice.

Arroz Chino (Chaufa)

CHINESE FRIED RICE *Serves 2 to 4*

This type of rice, better known as *arroz Chaufa*, is typical of the Chinese restaurants found throughout South America. It is one of many specialties that were adopted practically as they came from China. But they also were adapted; the use of ham and shrimp in this dish is very Spanish.

1 cup long-grain rice

1½ cups water

3 tablespoons peanut oil

1 clove garlic, minced

1 teaspoon peeled and minced fresh ginger

4 ounces imported boiled ham, cut into
¼-inch cubes

4 ounces good-quality cooked salad shrimp

2 large eggs, lightly beaten

1 tablespoon canola oil

1 bunch scallions (white part and 1 inch of
the green), sliced ¼ inch thick

1 tablespoon soy sauce

1. Put the rice in a medium-size bowl, add water to cover, and rinse, stirring with your hand. Drain, add more water, and repeat the rinsing until the water comes out clean. Place the drained rice in a medium-size saucepan, add the 1½ cups water, and bring to a boil. Reduce the heat to low, cover, and cook until all the water has been absorbed, about 20 minutes. The grains should be separate and tender. Set aside to cool, then refrigerate for a few hours, preferably overnight. This is the secret of good fried rice.

2. Heat the peanut oil in a wok or large skillet over high heat. Add the garlic and ginger and cook, stirring, for a few seconds, until golden. Remove and discard the garlic. Add the cold rice to the pan and cook, stirring and breaking up any clumps, until all the grains are coated with the oil. Add the ham and shrimp and cook until heated through.

3. Heat a 9-inch skillet over medium heat, add the canola oil, and pour in the eggs, swirling the pan to distribute them evenly over the bottom. Cook until set, flip over, and cook for another minute or so.

4. Remove from the pan, cut into ¼-inch-wide strips, and add to the rice. Sprinkle with the scallions, drizzle with the soy sauce, and stir with a fork. Serve right away.

Pirão de Arroz

RICE FLOUR PUDDING *Serves 6*

Popular in Brazil, *pirãos* are very thick, savory porridges or mushes, like polenta. They are usually served molded and can be enjoyed either hot or at room temperature. For the liquid, you can use water, coconut milk, or the broth from the stew the *pirão* is going to accompany. Rice *pirãos* can be made with rice flour or with rice soaked overnight and cooked to a mush. When made with manioc meal or cornmeal, this same dish is called *angú*. These specialties of African origin are wonderful with seafood or meat dishes that are prepared with a sauce, such as *Bobó de Camarão* (page 270) and *Vatapá de Galinha* (page 181).

2 cups water

½ cup rice flour

½ teaspoon salt

1 cup well-stirred canned unsweetened
coconut milk

1. In a blender, process the water, rice flour, and salt together until well mixed. Transfer to a heavy 2-quart saucepan and cook over low heat, stirring constantly with a wooden spoon, until it comes to a boil. Add the coconut milk and continue to cook, stirring, until the mixture is smooth, thick, and pulls away from the side of the pan. It should be stiff and hold its shape.

2. Lightly oil six 6-ounce molds or a large bread mold and fill with the mixture. Let cool, then unmold and serve.

Quinua Hervida

BASIC BOILED QUINOA

Makes about 3½ cups; 4 servings

The two methods for cooking plain quinoa given here are very simple and can be used for making sweet or savory specialties. If you are not going to use the cooked quinoa right away, store it in a covered container in the refrigerator for up to a couple of days, or freeze it for up to two months. Cooked quinoa is excellent as a breakfast cereal; just reheat it in the microwave and serve with milk and sugar. Raw quinoa can also be toasted to obtain a more intense flavor. Toast for a few minutes in a little butter or oil, stirring constantly, before proceeding with this or other recipes.

> 1 cup quinoa, rinsed (below)
> 1¾ cups water

1. Place the quinoa and water in a 2-quart saucepan and bring to a boil. Cover, reduce the heat to low, and simmer until the quinoa has absorbed all the water, about 12 minutes. For a firmer grain, bring the water to a boil, then add the quinoa.

2. Remove from the heat, fluff with a fork, cover, and let stand for 5 minutes. If the quinoa tastes bitter, rinse with cold water until the bitterness disappears.

VARIATION Cook 1 cup rinsed quinoa in 4 to 6 cups boiling water until the grains are transparent throughout, about 12 minutes. Drain immediately, rinse, cover, and steam dry over low heat for 5 minutes. This yields perfect, separate grains, especially good for salads.

Quinua Graneada

QUINOA PILAF *Serves 6*

This can be served as a side dish with any braised vegetable or beans.

> 2 tablespoons canola oil
> 1 clove garlic, peeled
> 2 tablespoons minced onion
> 1 cup quinoa, rinsed (below)
> 1¾ cups water or chicken broth
> Salt (omit if using chicken broth)

Washing Quinoa

Because not all the saponin (bitter coating) is removed from the quinoa when it is packaged for distribution, it is necessary to thoroughly wash the quinoa before cooking. Some quinoa brands come prewashed, but even those I quickly rinse.

Place the quinoa in a fine-mesh strainer that fits on top of a saucepan. Pick out and discard any impurities. Pour water over the quinoa to fill the saucepan. Rub the quinoa grains until the water becomes sudsy and cloudy. Sudsy water denotes the presence of saponin. Lift the strainer and discard the water. Repeat the process two or three times, until the water stays clear. Now the quinoa is ready to cook.

1. Heat the oil in a heavy 4-quart saucepan over medium heat. Add the garlic and onion and cook, stirring, until softened, about 5 minutes. Add the quinoa and cook, stirring frequently, for 2 minutes, coating it with the oil. Add the water and bring to a boil. Cover, reduce the heat to low, and simmer until all the liquid has been absorbed, about 12 minutes. Season with salt to taste, if using.

2. Remove from the heat, fluff with a fork, and discard the garlic. Cover and let stand for 5 minutes or longer before serving.

QUINUA GRANEADA CON AZAFRAN (Saffron Quinoa Pilaf) Soften ¼ teaspoon crumbled saffron threads in 2 tablespoons warm water. Add this to the water and proceed as directed above.

Kiwicha Hervida

BASIC BOILED AMARANTH *Makes 1½ to 2 cups*

This is the way to prepare amaranth for recipes that call for the cooked grain.

½ **cup amaranth**

1½ **cups water**

Place the amaranth and water in a 2-quart saucepan (preferably nonstick) and bring to a boil. Cover, reduce the heat to low, and simmer, stirring occasionally, until all the water has been absorbed, about 20 minutes. The mixture will look like mush. Remove from the heat, let cool, and use as directed in your recipe.

Guiso de Mote de Trigo

STEWED WHEAT BERRIES *Serves 4*

Guiso de mote, says my friend Beatriz Toso from Santiago, Chile, is a simple dish that needs no recipe. You just make a *sofrito* with onion and garlic, add the wheat berries and enough milk to make a sauce, and *voilà*, you have a very tasty side dish for grilled meat or chicken. Some people add diced cooked potatoes, in which case you need to add more milk. This is very similar to the Peruvian *trigo guisado con queso*, which uses cheese instead of milk and a generous amount of potatoes to provide the energy needed from a main meal.

2 **tablespoons canola oil**

1 **small onion, minced (about ½ cup)**

1 **clove garlic, mashed into a paste with ½ teaspoon salt and ¼ teaspoon freshly ground black pepper**

½ **teaspoon sweet paprika**

¼ **teaspoon dried oregano, crumbled**

2 **cups cooked wheat berries (page 412)**

1 **cup milk, or more if needed**

Heat the oil in a heavy 4-quart saucepan over medium heat. Add the onion and cook, stirring occasionally, until softened, about 5 minutes. Add the garlic paste, paprika, and oregano and cook, stirring constantly, for 1 minute. Add the wheat berries and milk and bring to a boil. Reduce the heat to low and simmer until creamy, about 5 minutes. Add a little more milk if it gets too dry. Taste for salt and pepper and serve hot.

Condimentos

CONDIMENTS

THE SOUTH AMERICAN CUISINE BOASTS a wide variety of condiments—some simple, some complex. Some of these, like the *sofritos* and hot pepper purees, are incorporated during the preparation of the dish. Others, like the hot pepper salsas, are always present on the South American table for the diner to add to his or her own taste. Many European sauces, especially French, have been adopted into the repertoire of the South American cook. White sauce (béchamel), mayonnaise, and tomato sauce, to name just a few, have become part of creole cuisine.

Manteca de Color

ANNATTO LARD OR OIL *Makes ½ to 1 cup*

Appearing under different names, this coloring and flavoring agent is used throughout the Andean countries and parts of Brazil to flavor rice, meat, poultry, and seafood. A small amount imparts a distinctive color and subtle taste to foods. Paprika can be used as a substitute.

The classic way of making this *color* is with *manteca* (lard), because it gives more flavor to the food, but because of dietary restrictions, people also use vegetable shortening or oil.

> **½ cup lard, vegetable shortening, or canola oil, plus ¼ to ½ cup, if reusing the seeds**
>
> **½ cup annatto seeds**

1. Heat the fat in a small, heavy saucepan over low heat. Add the seeds and cook, stirring occasionally, until a deep orange color is obtained, 3 to 5 minutes.

2. Strain the fat through a fine-mesh sieve. This will produce a concentrated annatto lard or oil. Some cooks add another ¼ to ½ cup fat to the seeds (as long as they are not too dark) and repeat the process, cooking again for 2 to 3 minutes. Strain and add to the first batch. Be careful not to burn the seeds, watching closely to remove them from the fat as soon as they turn a deep orange color.

3. *Manteca de color* will keep for several months in a covered jar in the refrigerator. Use as instructed in individual recipes.

Color Chileno

CHILEAN PAPRIKA OIL *Makes about ½ cup*

Similar to *Manteca de Color* (this page), this Chilean oil uses paprika instead of annatto seeds to derive its distinctive color and also includes garlic and hot pepper. It is used in cooking and as a hot pepper sauce to add to finished dishes.

> **½ cup canola oil or lard**
>
> **2 cloves garlic, peeled**
>
> **1 hot pepper, seeded**
>
> **1 tablespoon sweet paprika**

1. Heat the oil in a small saucepan over medium heat. Add the garlic and hot pepper and cook, stirring, until golden. Discard the garlic and pepper.

2. Remove from the heat and stir in the paprika until well blended. Let cool and store in a jar with a tight-fitting lid. This will keep in the refrigerator for several months.

Ají

HOT PEPPER SALSA

JUST AS SALT AND PEPPER appear on most dinner tables in the United States, a bowl of *ají* is found on tables in most South American countries. Just add a little *ají* to soups, stews, meats, or *cebiches* to give a wonderful kick to the food. In the Andean countries, a common sight at fruit stands in the countryside are Indians eating avocado halves filled with *ají*. A side dish of boiled potatoes topped with *ají* is very popular in Ecuador, Peru, and Bolivia. *Ají* is also great for people on a low-salt diet, providing flavor to foods without the added salt. *Ajíes* vary from country to country, and even within countries, but the common denominator is the use of very hot peppers. Use *ají* sparingly.

Ají Molido Fresco

FRESH HOT PEPPER PUREE *Makes about ¹/₄ cup*

This hot pepper puree is called for in many recipes in this book, especially in the *cebiches*. I freeze it in very small containers so that it can be easily thawed when needed. The best varieties of peppers to use are hot red or green finger peppers, which can be found in U.S. supermarkets when they are in season. Alternatively, Andean hot red peppers and *mirasol* (hot yellow) peppers are available frozen or packed in brine in South American groceries. I also like *manzano* peppers for their wonderful flavor; they can be found seasonally. Jalapeños or serranos also can be used. A good substitute for fresh hot pepper puree is habanero hot sauce.

> **10 to 12 hot red or green finger peppers or** *manzano* **peppers**
>
> **2 tablespoons water**
>
> **1 teaspoon salt**

1. Wash the peppers thoroughly in cold water. With a sharp knife, trim the ends and cut them in half lengthwise. With a paring knife, scrape the seeds out and cut the peppers into small pieces.

2. Transfer to a blender, add the water and salt, and process until smooth. Add a little more water, if needed, to make a thick sauce. Transfer to small containers and refrigerate for up to several days or freeze for up to several months.

Ají Molido Seco

DRIED HOT PEPPER PUREE *Makes about ¹/₂ cup*

Peruvian and Bolivian cooks often use dried hot peppers in their specialties. Dried Bolivian or Peruvian peppers are available in South American groceries. A Peruvian paste labeled "yellow hot pepper" is available in jars and is a good substitute for dried hot pepper puree. Some Bolivian and Peruvian shoppers I have met in South American groceries say that they also use bottled or frozen hot peppers instead of the puree for convenience. This puree can be frozen in small containers and used as is or fried, according the recipe you are using it in.

> **12 dried hot yellow or red Bolivian or Peruvian peppers**

1. Cut the peppers in half and remove the seeds. Soak in hot water to cover for 30 minutes. (Some recipes recommend soaking the peppers the day before, but I don't think it is necessary. When they are soft, they are ready.)

2. Remove the stems, place the peppers in a blender, and process with a little of the soaking

water until smooth. Transfer to small containers and refrigerate for up to 1 week or freeze for up to several months.

Aji Criollo

CREOLE HOT PEPPER SALSA *Makes about ¾ cup*

Hot pepper salsas similar to this Ecuadorian version are never missing from the South American table.

> 4 hot red or green finger peppers, 3 to 4 inches long, seeded and chopped (or leave seeds in for an even hotter salsa)
>
> 6 tablespoons water
>
> ½ teaspoon salt
>
> ¼ cup minced scallions (white part only)
>
> 2 tablespoons minced fresh cilantro or parsley leaves

1. Place the hot peppers, 2 tablespoons of the water, and the salt in a blender and process until smooth.
2. Transfer to a small bowl. Add the scallions, cilantro, and remaining 4 tablespoons water and mix well. It is best to use this salsa the same day it is made.

AJI CON CHOCHOS (Hot Pepper Salsa with Lupini Beans) Add 2 tablespoons peeled and chopped bottled lupini beans (page 307), or grind the peeled beans with the hot peppers.

AJI PIQUE (Colombian Hot Pepper Salsa) The small Colombian hot pepper *aji pique* is not available in the United States. I use hot red finger peppers instead. To make the salsa, add ½ small onion, minced (about ¼ cup), 1 teaspoon fresh lemon juice, and 1 teaspoon canola oil in step 2 and proceed as above.

Aji de Tomate de Arbol

TAMARILLO HOT PEPPER SALSA
Makes about 1½ cups

In the last few years, tamarillo salsa has been all the rage in restaurants in Quito, Ecuador. The tamarillo is indigenous to Ecuador and Colombia. It's also called the tree tomato and has a tart taste, ideal for drinks and ice cream. Ecuadorian

Como Limpiar Ajies HOW TO CLEAN HOT PEPPERS

Careful handling of hot peppers is required because of the volatile oils they contain. These oils may burn your skin and eyes. The best way to handle a hot pepper is to wear rubber gloves or surgical gloves, or to use a fork and knife, not touching the pepper at all. If you handle a hot pepper without gloves, do not touch your face or eyes. Wash your hands thoroughly with soap and warm water, or rub them with salt, then rinse with soap and water.

When you wash or rinse the pepper, use cold water. Hold the pepper by the stem. With a sharp knife, make 4 slashes lengthwise. Scrape the seeds out with a knife, then rinse the pepper and cut it into small pieces. Avoid touching the flesh or seeds. Most of the hot pepper's heat is in the seeds and white ribs. Some cooks prefer to leave some or all of the seeds in for a more fiery dish or sauce.

tamarillos have a red skin and orange flesh and seeds and give the salsa a very enticing pale orange color. In the United States, tamarillos have a red skin and orange flesh, but the seeds are red. Unless the seeds are removed, they will give the salsa an unattractive purplish color. At times I have found yellow-skinned tamarillos with yellow flesh and seeds in the United States. They are my choice for preparing this salsa, because the seeds don't have to be removed—just puree the peeled tamarillos and strain through a sieve. If you do remove the seeds, you can use them to make tamarillo juice (see Notes). This salsa can be used as a condiment with any savory dish, just as any other hot pepper salsa would be.

- 2 large ripe but firm yellow or red tamarillos or ½ cup thawed frozen tamarillo pulp (see Notes)
- ¾ cup water
- 4 hot red finger peppers, yellow or red serranos, or jalapeños, seeded
- ¼ cup thinly sliced red onion cut into ½-inch pieces, soaked in hot water for 5 minutes and drained
- 1 tablespoon fresh minced cilantro leaves
- ¼ cup bottled lupini beans, peeled (page 307) and coarsely chopped
- 1 teaspoon canola oil
- ½ teaspoon fresh lemon juice
- ¼ teaspoon salt

1. If you are using fresh tamarillos, blanch in boiling water for 1 minute. Peel, cut in half lengthwise, and remove the seeds with a spoon, if necessary (see headnote). Place the seeded tamarillos or the tamarillo pulp and ½ cup of the water in a blender or food processor and process until smooth. Transfer to a small bowl. Wash the blender or food processor.

2. Coarsely chop the peppers, place in the blender or food processor, add the remaining ¼ cup water, and process until smooth. Transfer to a small bowl. Add 2 tablespoons of the pepper puree to the tamarillo puree. Taste and add more pepper puree, if desired.

3. Add the onion to the tamarillo mixture. Stir in the cilantro, lupini beans, oil, lemon juice, and salt. Taste for salt. It is best to use this salsa the same day it is made.

NOTES To make juice with the seeds, place in a blender along with 1 cup water, 1 tablespoon fresh lemon juice, and sugar to taste. Pulse until the seeds have rendered all their juice. Strain through a fine-mesh strainer and serve over ice.

Frozen tamarillo pulp is available in some Latin American markets.

Salsa Criolla Peruana

PERUVIAN HOT PEPPER ONION SALSA
Makes about 1 cup

This refreshing salsa is the classic accompaniment for *Papas Huancaínas* (page 127), *cebiches*, and many other Peruvian specialties. The Ecuadorian *Cebollas Encurtidas* (page 340) is very similar, without the hot peppers, which are part of many Peruvian specialties.

- 1 medium-size onion, halved and thinly sliced into half-moons (about 1 cup)
- 1 to 2 jalapeños, to your taste, seeded and minced
- 1 large clove garlic (optional), minced
- 2 tablespoons minced fresh cilantro leaves
- Juice of 1 lemon
- ¼ teaspoon salt
- ¼ teaspoon freshly ground black pepper

Rinse the onion in cold water. Drain well and mix with the rest of the ingredients in a small bowl. Cover and refrigerate for up to 1 day.

Llajwa (Salsa de Ají)

BOLIVIAN HOT PEPPER SALSA *Makes about 1 cup*

This salsa is a must on the Bolivian table and comes in various versions. It is always seasoned with a local herb called *quilquiña*, which is available in some Latin American groceries. Parsley is a good substitute.

> 2 hot yellow or red peppers, seeded
> 1 large ripe but firm tomato (about 8 ounces)
> 1 teaspoon dried *quilquiña* or 1 tablespoon chopped fresh parsley leaves
> ½ teaspoon salt
> 1 small onion, finely chopped (about ½ cup)

1. Chop the peppers coarsely. Seed the tomato, reserving the pulp around the seeds and the juices, and chop.

2. In a blender or food processor, process the peppers, tomato, and *quilquiña* until smooth. Transfer to a small bowl.

3. Strain the reserved tomato pulp and juices and add to the salsa along with the salt and onion. Cover and refrigerate. It is best to use this salsa the same day it is made.

Molho de Pimenta e Limão

BRAZILIAN PEPPER AND LIME HOT SAUCE
Makes about ¾ cup

This sauce is made with *malagueta* peppers, which are available only in bottles in the United States. I sometimes substitute very small fresh hot peppers, such as tabasco peppers, when available. This is used to make the sauce served with *feijoada* (bean stew; page 243).

> 4 small fresh or dried hot peppers, seeded and chopped
> 1 small onion, chopped (about ½ cup)
> 1 clove garlic, chopped
> ½ cup fresh lime or lemon juice
> ½ teaspoon salt

Place all the ingredients in a blender and process until smooth. Transfer to a small bowl and let stand for 1 hour at room temperature before serving. This sauce does not keep well because it has a tendency to ferment. It's best to make it the same day you will use it.

MARGARIDA'S HOT SAUCE My Brazilian friend Margarida Nogueira says that Brazilians generally make a simpler version of this sauce when preparing *bobó* (page 270), *vatapá* (page 181), or *feijoada*. Start by crushing about 4 fresh or dried hot peppers with a little olive oil, then add 3 to 4 spoonfuls of the sauce from the main dish. If too thick, add a little hot water. Use only a few drops of this sauce because if it is made with *malagueta* or another very hot pepper, it will have some serious firepower.

Pebre de Cilantro

CHILEAN CILANTRO SALSA *Makes about 1 cup*

Pebres are spicy salsas traditionally served in Chile with grilled meat, seafood, or vegetables. There are many variations. Sometimes only parsley or cilantro is used, other times both. When made with cilantro and parsley, it is called *salsa verde*. Some cooks use paprika and oregano for added flavor. *Pebres* can be made mildly hot or very hot, according to your taste. One medium-size jalapeño will make a mild salsa.

> 2 tablespoons canola or olive oil
>
> 2 tablespoons sherry vinegar or red wine vinegar
>
> 1 clove garlic, mashed into a paste with ¼ teaspoon salt and ¼ teaspoon freshly ground black pepper
>
> ¼ cup water
>
> ¼ cup finely chopped scallions (white part and 1 inch of the green)
>
> 1 cup packed fresh cilantro leaves
>
> 1 to 2 jalapeños or serranos, to your taste, seeded and finely chopped

1. Mix the oil, vinegar, and garlic paste together in a small bowl and beat with a fork until emulsified.

2. Place the water, scallions, cilantro, and jalapeño in a blender and pulse until the scallions and cilantro are minced but not pureed, about 10 seconds. Mix with the vinaigrette.

3. Transfer to a covered jar and let stand for a couple of hours to develop the flavors. Serve in a small bowl with grilled meat, chicken, or seafood.

PEBRE DE CILANTRO CON TOMATES (Chilean Cilantro and Tomato Salsa) Add 1 medium-size ripe but firm tomato (5 to 6 ounces), seeded and finely chopped, with the vinaigrette and proceed as above.

Chancho en Piedra

CHILEAN HOT GREEN PEPPER SALSA *Makes about 1 cup*

The unusual name of this famous salsa comes from *piedra*, a lava stone mortar that is used to crush the ingredients. I love crushing the ingredients with a mortar and pestle, because the aroma is tantalizing, much more so than when using a food processor. Because the tomatoes should be very ripe, this salsa is especially good during the summer months, when it is served with *asados* (grilled meats) instead of salads. It also can be used as a first course, served in individual earthenware bowls, with crispy bread for dipping.

> 2 large cloves garlic, finely chopped
>
> 2 serranos, seeded and chopped
>
> 1 teaspoon sea salt
>
> ½ teaspoon freshly ground black pepper
>
> ½ teaspoon dried oregano
>
> 2 tablespoons chopped fresh cilantro leaves
>
> 2 tablespoons chopped fresh parsley leaves
>
> 2 large very ripe tomatoes (about 1 pound), peeled, seeded, and chopped
>
> 2 tablespoons canola oil
>
> 1 tablespoon red wine vinegar

1. *If using a mortar*: Mash the garlic, serranos, salt, and black pepper into a paste. Add the oregano, cilantro, and parsley and continue to mash until smooth. Add a couple of spoonfuls of the tomatoes and mash. Add the rest of the tomatoes and stir.

If using a blender or food processor: Process the garlic, serranos, salt, black pepper, oregano, cilantro, and parsley together until smooth. Transfer to a bowl and mix in the tomatoes, pressing down with a fork to break up some of the tomatoes.

2. Stir in the oil and vinegar and taste for salt. Like all fresh salsas, this is best used the same day it is made.

Salsa Criolla Argentina

ARGENTINE CREOLE SALSA *Makes about 2 cups*

This salsa should be made a few hours ahead to allow the flavors to develop, but it should be used while still fresh. The longer it sits, the stronger the flavors will become, and it will lose its fresh flavor. This is a classic salsa for *asados* (grilled meats), and there are as many variations as there are cooks. Some feature a combination of wine and vinegar, others have more oil, and some are very simple, with just a few basic ingredients.

- 2 large ripe but firm tomatoes (about 1 pound), peeled, seeded, and finely chopped
- 1 small onion minced (about ½ cup)
- 4 cloves garlic, minced
- ¼ cup minced fresh parsley leaves
- ¼ cup canola oil
- 2 tablespoons red wine vinegar
- ½ teaspoon salt
- ½ teaspoon sweet paprika
- 1 teaspoon dried oregano
- ½ teaspoon freshly ground black pepper
- ¼ teaspoon red pepper flakes, or to taste

Thoroughly mix all the ingredients together in a medium-size bowl. Transfer to a jar with a tight-fitting lid and refrigerate until needed. This salsa is served in a bowl so that diners can add it to taste.

Chimichurri

ARGENTINE PARSLEY SALSA *Makes about 1 cup*

It is impossible to talk about Argentine *asados* (grilled meats) without mentioning *chimichurri*, for it is the indispensable accompaniment. *Chimichurri* recipes are very personal. Although *chim[...]* always made with a lot of parsley, the other [...]ings vary. It also can be made thick, to se[...] bowl at the table to season the meats, or more liquidy, to baste the meats while grilling. The traditional oil used for this salsa is corn oil, but many people now prefer the more flavorful olive oil. Some cooks use half vinegar and half wine—try these different versions and see what appeals to you most. Using dried parsley cuts the preparation time to just a few minutes. *Chimichurri* also goes well with poultry or fish.

- ½ cup boiling water
- ½ teaspoon salt
- ½ cup dried parsley, crumbled
- 4 cloves garlic, minced
- 2 teaspoons dried oregano
- Pinch of dried thyme
- ½ teaspoon freshly ground black pepper
- 1 teaspoon red pepper flakes (preferably Argentine; see Note)
- ¼ cup canola or extra virgin olive oil
- ½ cup red wine vinegar
- Pinch of sugar

Place all the ingredients in a blender and pulse until the mixture is finely chopped. Store in a covered jar in the refrigerator for a few hours or overnight. Shake well before serving.

NOTE Argentine red pepper flakes are milder than American. If using American, use only ¼ teaspoon or to taste.

Sofrito

ONION-BASED SAVORY SAUCE *Makes about 1½ cups*

A *sofrito* is an onion-based flavoring or sauce that is used to season most savory South American specialties. It goes by different names in different countries, the most common being *sofrito*, *refrito*, and *recado*. In Colombia, there are so many regional names that unless you know about them, it is very difficult to understand Colombian recipes, which sometimes call for a specific amount of *sofrito*, *hogado*, *ahogado*, *hogo*, *guiso*, *refrito*, or *riojo*. In Brazil, *sofrito* is called *refogado*, and in Bolivia *ahogado* or *rehogado*. Its origin goes back to the Iberian Peninsula, where hundreds of years ago, a very simple *sofrito* was made by sautéing onions and garlic in olive oil. With the discovery of the Americas, *sofrito* was enriched by the addition of tomatoes and bell peppers, as well as different herbs and spices.

The primary ingredient of any *sofrito*—onions—is the same everywhere. The onions can be minced, coarsely chopped, sliced into rounds, or sliced lengthwise. Preparation of the basic *sofrito* always starts with the sautéing of onions in oil or butter. Garlic, peppers, tomatoes, herbs, or spices may be added, depending on the recipe. Sometimes all the ingredients for a *sofrito* are pureed, then fried in oil until it loses its raw taste. Bolivians believe that the onions should be cooked with salt to soften them. Next come tomatoes and bell peppers, then herbs, and finally salt and black pepper. Hot pepper puree (if using) is added at the end, and the *sofrito* is cooked for a few more minutes. Cooks take pride in preparing a good *sofrito* because they know that it gives character to a dish.

Sofrito is the essential ingredient in soups, stews, braised meats, rice, and other savory specialties. Many cooks prepare the base for the *sofrito*, called *aliño*, in large quantities, to use throughout the week, or they freeze it in small containers for later use.

Annatto (in this case, *manteca de color*) or paprika is used, depending on the recipe. Cooks in the Andean countries and northeastern Brazil most commonly use annatto, whereas those in the southern countries use paprika.

> 2 tablespoons olive oil or canola oil
>
> 1 tablespoon *Manteca de Color* (page 331) or 1 teaspoon sweet paprika

> 1 medium-size onion, finely chopped (about 1 cup)
>
> 2 cloves garlic, mashed into a paste with ½ teaspoon salt and ¼ teaspoon freshly ground black pepper
>
> 1 small green or red bell pepper, seeded and chopped
>
> 2 large ripe but firm tomatoes (about 1 pound), peeled, seeded, and chopped, or two 16-ounce cans pear-shaped tomatoes, drained and chopped (see Note)

Heat the oil in a medium-size, heavy skillet over medium heat. Add the *manteca de color* and onion and cook, stirring occasionally, until the onion is transparent, about 5 minutes. Stir in the garlic paste, bell pepper, and tomatoes. Reduce the heat to low, cover, and cook, stirring occasionally, until the tomatoes have formed a sauce, about 15 minutes. Add water a little at a time if the tomatoes dry out too fast. The finished *sofrito* should have the appearance of a thick sauce.

NOTE In the winter, when tomatoes are not at their best, it is a good idea to add 1 tablespoon tomato paste to enrich the sauce or just use canned tomatoes.

Aliño de la Costa

COASTAL-STYLE SPICE PASTE *Makes about 4 cups*

Aliños or *adobos* are spice mixtures that are usually made with dried spices and herbs. The Venezuelan *aliño criollo* is made with granulated garlic, ground cumin, dried oregano, ground annatto seeds, and salt. In Chile, there is an *aliño* made with oregano, black pepper, salt, and generous amounts of ground cumin. (When freshly made, the scent of cumin permeates the room for days.) And in most countries, some kind of *aliño* that includes each country's favorite spices is available in supermarkets. In Uruguay, for example, the *aliño* for *milanesas* (breaded cutlets), called *ajil*, is very simple, containing only dried parsley and granulated garlic. An *adobo* in

Argentina and Uruguay—a mixture of dried hot peppers and dried herbs such as oregano and parsley—is added to marinades for *asados* (grilled meats) and empanada fillings, among other things. *Aliños* will keep in the refrigerator for at least a week or can be frozen in small containers for up to a month, so they are always made in large quantities. Making *aliños* in a blender is a real timesaver.

In addition to being a condiment on its own, this *aliño* is also a base for *sofrito*. A variety of seasonings can be added, such as ground annatto seeds or paprika, bell peppers, tomatoes, peanut butter, or herbs.

- 8 large cloves garlic, peeled
- 2 medium-size red onions, cut into 1-inch pieces
- 2 medium-size white onions, cut into 1-inch pieces
- 2 leeks (white part and 1 inch of the green), washed well and sliced ½ inch thick
- ½ cup packed fresh parsley leaves
- ½ cup packed fresh cilantro leaves
- 1 teaspoon ground cumin
- 1 teaspoon freshly ground black pepper
- 1 teaspoon salt

In a blender or food processor, with the machine running, drop in the garlic and process until minced. Add the remaining ingredients and process until minced. Transfer to a tightly covered jar and refrigerate for up to 1 week. Or transfer to small containers that hold about 1 cup each and freeze for up to 1 month.

Aliño para Carne de Cerdo

RUB FOR PORK ROAST *Makes enough rub for one 8- to 10-pound pork roast or leg of pork*

This *aliño* can be used on a fresh leg of pork or for any pork roast. It varies not only from country to country but also from cook to cook. Some of the spicing is standard—salt, freshly ground black or white pepper, cayenne, ground annatto or sweet paprika, allspice, oregano, thyme, and lots of garlic. Ground cumin, cinnamon, ground cloves, and nutmeg are also used. Saltpeter is used in Ecuador to give the meat a pink coloring, similar to ham. All of these spices are mixed together with lemon juice and vinegar. In Brazil, wine is used instead of vinegar. The paste is rubbed all over the meat, which is left to marinate overnight.

SPICE MIXTURE
- ¼ cup salt
- ½ teaspoon ground cloves
- 1 teaspoon ground allspice
- ½ teaspoon ground cinnamon or nutmeg
- 4 teaspoons freshly ground black pepper
- 2 teaspoons ground cumin
- 2 tablespoons ground annatto or sweet paprika
- 2 teaspoons saltpeter (optional)

- 1 head garlic, peeled
- ½ cup fresh lemon juice
- ¼ cup white wine vinegar or ½ cup dry white wine
- ¼ cup canola oil

1. To make the spice mixture, combine all the ingredients in a small jar with a tight-fitting cover and store in the cupboard until ready to use.

2. Place the spice mixture in a blender. Add the garlic, lemon juice, vinegar, and oil and process until smooth.

Pesto de Cilantro

CILANTRO PESTO *Makes about ¾ cup*

Pesto is very popular in the southern countries of South America, where a large number of Italian immigrants settled. I freeze this in small containers to use when I need it to flavor soups or pasta dishes (see Note on page 340).

1 cup packed fresh cilantro leaves

⅓ cup packed fresh parsley leaves

⅓ cup extra virgin olive oil

2 tablespoons pine nuts or walnuts

2 cloves garlic, peeled

½ teaspoon salt

¼ teaspoon freshly ground black pepper

¼ cup freshly grated Parmesan cheese

1. Place all the ingredients except the Parmesan in a blender or food processor and process until smooth, scraping down the sides with a rubber spatula to blend evenly. If making pesto for freezing, transfer to small containers, carefully add a layer of olive oil to cover, and freeze. It will keep for up to 6 months. Bring to room temperature before proceeding with the recipe.

2. Pour the mixture into a bowl, add the Parmesan, and mix thoroughly.

NOTE To use with pasta, pesto should be at room temperature. When the pasta is cooked but before it is drained, stir 2 tablespoons (or more) of the hot pasta cooking water into the pesto. Drain the pasta, reserving some of the water, and toss with the pesto, adding 3 tablespoons softened butter. If the pasta is too dry, add more of the hot cooking water, as needed. Serve immediately.

Cebollas Encurtidas

MARINATED ONIONS *Makes about 1 cup*

These delicious onions are popular garnishes in Ecuador and an indispensable part of *cebiches*. They also appear in many recipes in this book.

1 medium-size red onion, halved and sliced lengthwise into paper-thin half-moons

Juice of 1 lemon

½ teaspoon salt

¼ teaspoon freshly ground black pepper

1. Pour hot water over the onion and let stand for 15 minutes, then drain and rinse with cold water.

2. In a small mixing bowl, combine the onion, lemon juice, salt, and pepper. Cover and let stand at room temperature until the onion turns pink, about 3 hours. It is best to make this the day you are going to serve it.

Chutney de Mangas Frescas

FRESH MANGO CHUTNEY *Makes about 5 cups*

Chutneys are not typical Brazilian fare, but are a product of the fusion cuisine that has grown up in this country's sophisticated international cities. Mango chutney is especially good with pork or fowl. It is ideal in the summer, when mangoes are in season. I pack the chutney in pretty canning jars and give them to friends to enjoy with grilled chicken, salmon, turkey, or pork.

2 to 3 large ripe but firm mangoes (12 to 16 ounces each)

1 medium-size onion, minced (about 1 cup)

½ cup seedless black raisins

½ cup seedless golden raisins

Grated zest or julienne of 1 orange

1 small jalapeño, seeded and minced

1¼ cups white wine vinegar

1 cup sugar

1 to 2 teaspoons freshly ground black pepper, to your taste (see Note)

2 teaspoons ground allspice

2 teaspoons peeled and grated or minced fresh ginger

1 teaspoon salt

1 teaspoon curry powder

1. Peel the mangoes, remove the flesh from the seeds, and chop finely. You should have about 3 cups. Place in a medium-size glass bowl and

mix with the onion, raisins, zest, and jalapeño. Set aside.

2.   Place the vinegar and sugar in a large nonreactive saucepan over low heat and cook, stirring to dissolve the sugar, for 5 minutes. Stir in the black pepper, allspice, ginger, salt, and curry powder and simmer for 5 minutes. Add the mango mixture and bring to a boil.

3.   Remove from the heat and let cool completely. Cover and refrigerate for up to a few days.

NOTE Two teaspoons of black pepper will make a very hot chutney.

Mayonesa Clásica

CLASSIC MAYONNAISE *Makes about 1¼ cups*

I can't think of any other dressing that is used more often in the South American kitchen than mayonnaise. It is especially prevalent in the cuisines of the southern countries, where it is used plain or mixed with tomato sauce or green herbs to bind chopped vegetables or seafood for cold salads and to decorate salads and savory *roulades*. Some versions of mayonnaise are great as dips for shrimp or vegetables.

When I was growing up, our mayonnaise was always made at home, and I remember how we loved to watch the tricky process of beating the oil into the eggs. There are two ways to make mayonnaise. One is using just the egg yolk, the other is using the whole egg. Most Latin cooks seem to favor the whole egg version, which is a little lighter. The blender is now commonly used to make mayonnaise. Use the freshest eggs possible to reduce the possibility of salmonella poisoning, which is rare.

1 large egg
½ teaspoon dry or prepared mustard
½ teaspoon salt
¼ teaspoon white pepper
1 tablespoon fresh lemon juice or white or red wine vinegar, or more if needed
½ cup extra virgin olive oil, or more as needed
½ cup canola oil, or more as needed

1.   Break the egg into a blender. Add the mustard, salt, and pepper and process for 1 minute, until the mixture is thick. Add the lemon juice and blend for a few seconds. With the machine running at high speed, add the olive oil in a thin, steady stream. This is the crucial part: do not rush the oil; it has to be poured in very slowly. If the mixture is too thick, add a few drops of lemon juice or vinegar. Add the canola oil in a thin, steady stream. Taste for salt and pepper.

If the mayonnaise separates or fails to thicken, place an egg yolk in a small bowl and, using a wire whisk, beat in the mayonnaise 1 tablespoon at a time.

2.   Transfer the mayonnaise to a tightly covered container and refrigerate for 2 to 3 days.

Salsa Golf

TOMATO-FLAVORED MAYONNAISE
Makes about 1¼ cups

Salsa golf is one the choice dressings for seafood salads, especially if avocado is part of the salad. In Colombia and Venezuela, it is seasoned with cognac or rum. It also is a great sauce for shellfish.

1 cup mayonnaise, store-bought or homemade (this page)
2 tablespoons ketchup
1 tablespoon cognac or rum (optional)
½ teaspoon Worcestershire sauce
Pinch of cayenne pepper
Salt and freshly ground black pepper to taste

1.   Mix all the ingredients together in a small bowl until well blended. Serve cold.

2. If using homemade mayonnaise, this sauce will keep, tightly covered, in the refrigerator for 2 to 3 days. If using store-bought mayonnaise, it will last longer.

Salsa Rosada para Mariscos

PINK MAYONNAISE FOR SHELLFISH
Makes about 1¹/₂ cups

This is a popular condiment for lobster, shrimp, and crabmeat throughout South America. Used mainly to make cold salads or with crab or shrimp to stuff avocados, it also makes a tasty dip for vegetables and whole cooked shrimp.

> 1 cup mayonnaise, store-bought or homemade (page 341)
> 1 tablespoon seeded and minced red bell pepper
> 1 tablespoon seeded and minced green bell pepper
> 1 tablespoon seeded and minced yellow bell pepper
> 1 teaspoon capers, drained
> 2 tablespoons ketchup
> Salt, white pepper, and hot pepper sauce to taste

1. Mix all the ingredients together in a small bowl. Serve cold.

2. If using homemade mayonnaise, this mayonnaise will keep, tightly covered, in the refrigerator for 2 to 3 days. If using store-bought mayonnaise, it will last longer.

Salsa Picante para Pescado

MAYONNAISE WITH HOT PEPPER SAUCE
FOR FISH *Makes about 1¹/₂ cups*

This sauce is ideal for poached fish or served in a small bowl for dipping shrimp.

> 1 cup mayonnaise, store-bought or homemade (page 341)

> ¹/₂ cup ketchup
> 2 teaspoons hot pepper sauce

1. Mix all the ingredients together in a small bowl. Serve cold.

2. If using homemade mayonnaise, this mayonnaise will keep, tightly covered, in the refrigerator for 2 to 3 days. If using store-bought mayonnaise, it will last longer.

Mayonesa Dietética (Sin Huevo)

DIETETIC MAYONNAISE (WITHOUT EGGS)
Makes about 2 cups

This mayonnaise is ideal for chicken, tuna, avocados, and vegetables.

> 1 medium-size boiling potato, peeled and quartered
> 1 large or 2 medium-size carrots, sliced ¹/₄ inch thick
> ¹/₂ cup olive oil or canola oil
> 2 tablespoons sherry vinegar
> 1 heaping teaspoon Dijon mustard
> ¹/₂ teaspoon salt
> ¹/₄ teaspoon white pepper

1. Cook the potatoes and carrots together in boiling salted water to cover until tender, about 20 minutes. Drain, reserving the cooking liquid.

2. Place the vegetables in a blender along with a little of the cooking liquid. Add the oil, vinegar, and mustard and process until smooth, adding more cooking liquid to get the consistency of mayonnaise. Add the salt and white pepper and stir to combine.

3. This mayonnaise will keep, tightly covered, for up to 2 days in the refrigerator. Bring to room temperature before using. If necessary, thin with a little water or oil.

Salsa de Maní

ECUADORIAN PEANUT SAUCE *Makes about 2 cups*

This is the classic sauce for *Llapingachos* (page 300). It is also great on boiled potatoes, yuca, or *ullucos*, as well as many other dishes. In Peru, this sauce is made with a generous amount of *mirasol* peppers and served on potatoes and other specialties.

- 2 tablespoons canola oil
- 1 teaspoon *Manteca de Color* (page 331) or sweet paprika
- ½ cup finely chopped scallions (white part and 1 inch of the green)
- ¼ teaspoon salt
- ¼ teaspoon freshly ground black pepper
- ¼ teaspoon ground cumin
- 1 cup unsalted dry-roasted peanuts pureed with 1½ cups milk
- 2 tablespoons minced fresh cilantro leaves
- Hot pepper sauce
- 2 scallions (white part and 1 inch of the green, minced), or 1 hard-cooked egg, peeled and chopped, for garnish

Heat the oil in a small, heavy skillet over low heat. Add the *manteca de color* and chopped scallions and cook, stirring, for a couple of minutes. Add the salt, pepper, and cumin and cook, stirring constantly, for 15 seconds. Stir in the peanut puree and cilantro, bring to a boil, and cook for 3 minutes, stirring frequently so it doesn't stick to the pan. If it is too thick, add a little more milk or water. The consistency should be like that of very heavy cream. Season with salt and hot pepper sauce to taste. Serve this sauce garnished with the minced scallions or chopped eggs.

Salsa de Pepas de Zambo

PUMPKIN SEED (PEPITA) SAUCE *Makes about 2 cups*

This lovely sauce is more delicate than *Salsa de Maní* (this page) but is used just about the same way. In pre-Hispanic times, the Indians made this sauce without the milk and used wild herbs and hot peppers to season it. Today it is a staple in the provinces of Azuay and Cañar in Ecuador. Cooks prepare this in large quantities and freeze it in small containers to have on hand whenever they need it. It is used as a condiment for tamales, soups, and stews, or as a sauce for boiled potatoes or vegetables, spaghetti, chicken, fish, *Zanahoria Blanca* (page 305), *Llapingachos* (page 300), hominy, and even pig's feet. This sauce is ideal for people who are allergic to peanuts.

- 2 tablespoons canola oil
- 1 teaspoon *Manteca de Color* (page 331) or sweet paprika
- ½ cup finely chopped scallions (white part and 1 inch of the green)
- 1 small clove garlic, mashed into a paste with ¼ teaspoon salt
- 1 cup pumpkin seeds, toasted (page 413)
- 1 cup milk
- Salt
- Hot pepper sauce

1. Heat the oil in a small, heavy saucepan over low heat. Add the *manteca de color*, scallions, and garlic paste and cook for about 15 seconds, stirring.

2. Process the pumpkin seeds and milk in a blender until smooth. Add to the saucepan and cook, stirring frequently, for about 5 minutes. If it is too thick, add up to ½ cup water; the consistency should be like that of heavy cream. Season with salt and hot pepper sauce to taste.

3. If the sauce is not smooth, return it to the blender and process for a few seconds. Serve warm.

Panes

BREADS

THE PRE-COLUMBIAN PEOPLES DID not have a tradition of making bread. The only kind of bread the Spaniards found in what is now Venezuela and Colombia was the *arepa*, a flat, unleavened cornbread. In the tropics, they found cassava bread, made from the bitter cassava (yuca). This is a flat unleavened bread, made by shaping the grated cassava into flat cakes, then slowly cooking them on a griddle. Prepared in different sizes and different thicknesses, this bread is soft when freshly made but hardens when cold. When sun-dried, it can last for years, which made it ideal to take on long trips. The bread could be softened by dipping it in water or broth. This thin cassava bread is now available in one-pound packages in some Caribbean groceries.

When the wives of the Spanish conquistadors started arriving in South America in the sixteenth and seventeenth centuries, they probably experimented with the native flours to make breads using lard, eggs, and dairy products. The cornbread of Paraguay and yuca bread, made from yuca flour and typical of the Andean countries, were probably among their creations. The Spaniards also brought vegetable seeds, wheat, barley, chickpeas, and fava beans with them to the New World. Wheat soon became an important crop and was used to make bread.

Although wheat thrived in Spanish South America, it did not grow well in Brazil. The early Portuguese settlers had to adapt to eating corn and manioc (yuca) in the ways the Indians prepared them. Later, the Portuguese adapted the process of making wheat flour to produce a fine yuca flour, called *polvilho*, and cornstarch. Brazil became one of the largest producers of corn in South America, as well as the largest importer of wheat. (In fact, it was not until the nineteenth century that wheat bread was introduced in Brazil.) Although wheat is now grown in the southern states of Brazil, farmers there cannot grow enough wheat to meet the needs of the Brazilian market.

The wonderful breads that are currently available in South American bakeries are of European origin. They are made either with yeast or baking powder and include French breads (baguettes and smaller loaves), sweet breads (from Spain), dark breads, egg and butter breads, croissants, hard rolls, soft rolls, and the holiday breads, to mention just a few. *Pan de Pascua* (Christmas bread) is a sweet bread made with raisins, candied fruits, and nuts, very much like the European Christmas breads.

Arepas: Comfort Food for the Many

AREPAS ARE A SIMPLE CORNBREAD first made by the Indians of Colombia and Venezuela. They were an important part of the Indians' diet. Over the centuries, the poor people of Colombia and Venezuela continued to prepare *arepas* as an inexpensive, easy-to-make source of nourishment. Today this humble cornbread is a comfort food for rich and poor alike and a heartwarming tribute to simplicity, tradition, versatility, and good taste.

Originally, *arepas* were made from dried corn kernels, which were soaked overnight in water and lime to remove the skins and then cooked, drained, ground, and made into a *masa* (dough). Thanks to modern technology, precooked flour, called *masa al instante* (note that this is different from the Mexican *masa harina*), is now available in most Latin American markets. An instant *masa* can be made by simply mixing this corn flour (either white or yellow) with a little salt and enough hot water to make a stiff dough. The dough is then shaped into flat rounds of varying thicknesses, depending on the intended use, and cooked on a griddle or deep-fried. In pre-Columbian days, *arepas* in Colombia were cooked on top of a *laja*, a special flagstone slab that was heated and brushed with fat. In Venezuela, the Indians used the *aripo*, a cooking utensil from which the name *arepa* was probably derived. *Arepas de chocolo* are made from fresh corn and cooked on top of banana leaves.

Colombian *arepas* are generally thinner than their Venezuelan counterparts. The standard Venezuelan *arepa* looks somewhat like a flat bread roll, crispy on the outside and doughy on the inside. They can be split open and buttered or spread with cream cheese or fresh goat cheese. Made this way, they are served for breakfast or as an accompaniment for grilled fowl, fish, meat stews, or sausages. A popular snack in Colombia consists of *arepas* served with *panela* or brick cheese and fried chorizo. Some cooks also make very thin *arepas*, like Mexican tortillas; these are wonderful just spread with a little butter.

The uses of *arepas* are limited only by the cook's imagination. In Venezuela, the doughy inside is sometimes scooped out and the shell filled with savory mixtures of ground or chopped pork, beef, ham, chicken, seafood, vegetables, or beans. This makes an excellent first course. Venezuelan *mandocas* consist of cheese *arepa* dough shaped into rings and deep-fried. Another Venezuelan specialty is *bollos pelones*—balls of *arepa* dough stuffed with seasoned ground meat, then fried or poached in water and served with tomato sauce. Colombians and Venezuelans also make tasty soups and dumplings using fresh *arepa* dough or leftover *arepas*. And finally, let us not forget *arepitas dulces* (sweet *arepas*), which are served for dessert.

The versatile *arepa* indeed proves that unpretentious foods can be not only satisfying but delicious as well. The recipes for the most popular versions in both countries follow.

Masa de Arepa

BASIC AREPA DOUGH *Makes enough dough for 5 to 10 arepas, depending on the size*

This is the dough used for making basic arepas, or cornbread, and all the variations in this chapter. It is also the basis for dumplings, tamales, and other specialties.

> 1 cup *arepa* flour (page 417)
> ½ teaspoon salt (optional)
> 1½ cups hot water

In a large mixing bowl, combine the flour and salt (if using). Add the water and mix with a wooden spoon or your hands to make a soft dough. Cover with plastic wrap, let stand for 5 minutes, and then knead for about 3 minutes, until smooth. If the dough is too dry, wet your hands and continue kneading and wetting your hands until the dough is soft. (If the dough is too dry, the *arepas* will crack around the edges when you shape them into disks.) The dough is now ready to be shaped into standard *arepas* or to be mixed and kneaded with other ingredients.

Arepa Básica

BASIC CORNBREAD *Makes 5 to 6 Venezuelan* arepas *or 8 to 10 Colombian* arepas

This simple cornbread is used instead of wheat bread by millions of Colombians and Venezuelans, who eat *arepas* for breakfast, lunch, and dinner. It is also a welcome snack, often served with a cup of coffee.

> 1 recipe *Masa de Arepa* (above)
> Butter or cream cheese for serving

1.   Shape the *masa* (dough) into standard Venezuelan *arepas* (3 inches in diameter and ¾ inch thick) or Colombian *arepas* (3 to 4 inches in diameter and ¼ inch thick). Oil or wet your hands lightly and shape the dough into balls the size of golf balls. Place each ball between 2 pieces of waxed paper or plastic wrap and flatten into a circle; shape the edges to form a smooth disk. In Colombia, *arepas* are often made using a small wooden press called a *tostoneras*, a utensil that is also used to flatten disks of cooked plantain to make *patacones*. These presses are available in some Latin American groceries. The *arepas* can be made ahead of time, wrapped tightly in plastic, and refrigerated for up to a couple of days. I've found that it helps to warm the refrigerated *arepas* in a microwave for a few seconds before cooking them, as they get brittle when chilled.

2.   To cook the *arepas*, heat a griddle or cast-iron skillet over medium heat. Grease it lightly with oil and cook the *arepas* on both sides, turning a couple of times, until a crust forms. If the *arepas* are browning too fast, reduce the heat to low. Total cooking time is 10 to 15 minutes.

Colombian *arepas* are ready to be served at this point. Venezuelan *arepas* have to be transferred to ungreased baking sheets and baked in a preheated 350°F oven for 15 minutes. Tap the *arepas* lightly; if they sound hollow, they are ready.

3.   Split the *arepas* in half, slather with butter or cream cheese, and serve immediately.

Arepas de Queso

CORNBREAD WITH CHEESE *Makes 8 to 10* arepas

Arepas de queso are very popular in Colombia, where they are sometimes made like sandwiches with a cheese similar to ricotta. In Venezuela, a variety of cheeses, such as mozzarella and Parmesan, are mixed into the dough. Once shaped into disks, they are fried.

> 1 recipe *Masa de Arepa* (above)
> 1 large egg yolk
> 2 tablespoons unsalted butter, softened

Areperías are very popular restaurants in Venezuela. They specialize in making *arepas* (cornbread) with a variety of fillings, such as egg, cheese, chorizo, or highly seasoned ground meat, as well as all sorts of beverages to go with them. In Colombia, *arepas* are served in many small restaurants that are not as specialized as the *areperías*. It is interesting to note that *areperías* have spread to other countries, such as Ecuador and the United States. *Arepas* can now be found in Miami, New York, and Washington, D.C., as well as in cities on the West Coast.

---

2 ounces Chihuahua, mozzarella, or Muenster cheese, shredded

1. Knead the *masa* (dough) with the egg yolk, butter, and cheese until smooth.

2. Shape the dough into disks measuring 4 inches in diameter and ¼ inch thick, as described in step 1 on page 348. Cook as directed in step 2 on page 348. Serve hot.

Arepas Rellenas con Guiso de Carne

STUFFED AREPAS FROM VENEZUELA
Makes 10 to 12 arepas

This is a very popular stuffing for *arepas*, as well as for empanadas. It can be made a couple of days ahead and refrigerated. Reheat before using.

2 tablespoons vegetable oil

1 teaspoon ground annatto or sweet paprika

1 medium-size onion, minced (about 1 cup)

1 small green bell pepper, seeded and finely chopped

1 clove garlic, minced

2 large ripe but firm tomatoes (about 1 pound), peeled, seeded, and chopped

½ teaspoon ground cumin

¼ teaspoon dried thyme

1 teaspoon salt

¼ teaspoon freshly ground black pepper

8 ounces lean ground beef

8 ounces lean ground pork

8 pimento-stuffed Spanish olives, sliced

1 tablespoon capers, drained

2 recipes *Masa de Arepa* (page 348)

1. Heat the oil in a large, heavy skillet over medium heat. Add the annatto, onion, bell pepper, garlic, tomatoes, cumin, thyme, salt, and black pepper and cook, stirring occasionally, until the tomatoes have formed a thick sauce, about 20 minutes. Add the ground beef and pork and cook, stirring occasionally and breaking up any clumps, for about 10 minutes, until the mixture is dry. Stir in the olives and capers and set aside.

2. Shape the *masa* (dough) into disks measuring 3 inches in diameter and ¾ inch thick, as described in step 1 on page 348. Cook as directed in step 2 on page 348.

3. When done, split the *arepas* in half, scoop out the doughy insides, and fill with the meat sauce. Serve hot.

Arepitas Dulces

SWEET AREPAS *Makes 12* arepas

This is a much-loved sweet snack in Venezuela.

> 1 recipe *Masa de Arepa* (page 348)
>
> ¼ cup firmly packed dark brown sugar
>
> ½ teaspoon anise seeds, crushed
>
> 2 ounces Chihuahua, mozzarella, or Muenster cheese, shredded
>
> Canola oil for frying

1. Knead the *masa* (dough) with the brown sugar, anise, and cheese until evenly distributed.

2. Shape the dough into 12 disks measuring roughly 3 inches in diameter and ¼ inch thick, as described in step 1 on page 348.

3. In an electric fryer, heat about 1 inch of the oil to 350°F. Place several *arepas* at a time in the hot oil, being careful not to crowd them. Gently swish them in the oil to cook evenly. They are done when they rise to the surface. Remove from the oil with tongs or a slotted spoon and drain on paper towels. Serve hot.

VARIATION The dough also can be shaped in the form of a doughnut.

Guaguas de Pan

BREAD DOLLS

Makes about 16 figures, depending on the size

Guaguas de pan and *colada morada* (purple corn and fruit soup) are traditional foods for the Day of the Dead in Ecuador, Peru, and Bolivia. They are among the ritualistic foods combining the traditions of the indigenous peoples and the Spanish colonists. Some historians believe that bread dolls were developed to replace the Indian custom of mummification, because the Spaniards considered this practice barbaric. The Indians adopted the European way of making bread with wheat flour, lard, and yeast and shaped the bread into human forms that represented loved ones who had passed away. Other historians, such as the Quechua researcher Ariruma Kowii, believe that November, called *ayamarka killa*, or month of the dead, was the time the Incas honored their dead. She thinks the bread dolls, which look like mummies, probably date from Inca culture. Because there was no wheat in South America at that time, the bread dolls had to be made with some other kind of flour. To this day, especially in small towns, on November 2, the Indians take bread dolls and *colada morada* to the cemetery to be placed at the graves of deceased loved ones.

Whatever the origin of this custom, making bread dolls has become an important part of the celebration of the Day of the Dead, and an opportunity for families to get together. Our family was no exception, and the memories of this holiday are always with me on the Day of the Dead, wherever I might be. Our aunt Michita was the one with *una buena mano* (a good hand) to make the lightest bread. My mother was the organizer, making sure everything was set up so the children would enjoy the process fully, and my father was always checking that everyone had what they needed. It was a legitimate excuse for the children to get their hands deep into the dough and to play with it, making dolls, horses, donkeys, soldiers, or whatever their imaginations allowed. Coloring of the dough was another matter, because years ago food coloring was not available. Soot from the stove was used to color dough for the eyes, and aniline dyes were used for the rest of the decorations. (Of course, these decorations could not be eaten.) The competition was fierce as to who had the best-looking dolls. When the dolls were baked and the *colada* was ready, it was time to sit at the table and enjoy our creations. It was also time for neighbors to come with their *coladas* for everybody to taste and determine whose was the best.

Unfortunately, the custom of making bread dolls and *colada morada* is disappearing, and these wonderful holiday foods are now purchased in restaurants and markets. What a pity that children are being deprived of the wonderful memories associated with the preparation of these foods.

> 1 package active dry yeast
> ¾ cup warm milk (115°F)
> 1 tablespoon sugar
> 3 cups bread flour or all-purpose flour
> 1 teaspoon salt
> 1 large egg
> 2 large egg yolks
> ½ cup (1 stick) unsalted butter, melted
> Food coloring (optional)
> 1 large egg yolk lightly beaten with 1 tablespoon milk

1. Mix together the yeast, milk, and sugar in a small bowl. Let stand for 10 minutes to proof. (The mixture should bubble; if it doesn't, the yeast is dead and you need to start again with a fresh packet of yeast.)

2. Place 2 cups of the flour and the salt in a food processor. Add the yeast mixture and process for 15 to 20 seconds. Add the egg and egg yolks and process for a few seconds to mix well. Add the remaining 1 cup flour, ¼ cup at a time, processing after each addition until well mixed. If the dough is too soft, add more flour. With the machine running, add the butter through the feed tube in a steady stream and process until a smooth ball forms. Knead the dough on a floured work surface for a couple of minutes. Place in a greased bowl, cover, and let rise in a warm place until doubled in volume, about 1 hour.

3. Punch down the dough and knead it a few times. Shape into dolls or other figures. Part of the dough can be tinted with food coloring for decorations. Place the bread figures on greased baking sheets and let rest in a warm place for 15 minutes.

4. Preheat the oven to 375°F.

5. Brush the figures with the egg yolk mixture and bake on the center oven rack until golden, about 15 minutes. Remove from the oven and transfer to wire racks to cool.

Cuñapés

YUCA FLOUR ROLLS *Makes 36 rolls*

These wonderful little rolls are the specialty of the Andean countries and Brazil. They appear in different shapes and go by different names, but all are essentially the same. In Colombia and Ecuador, they are called *pan de yuca*, in Bolivia *cuñapes*, and in Paraguay *chipás*. They are especially popular in some of the coastal towns, where street vendors sell them fresh out of the oven. Although they can be eaten cold, they are better reheated. I freeze them with great success, and they are a marvelous alternative for people on a wheat-free diet. The rolls may be shaped in a variety of ways, such as rings, ovals, half-moons, or rounds. The kind of cheese used determines the consistency and character of the roll. In South America, the cheese of choice is *queso fresco*, preferably only one to two days old. I have had very good luck with Mexican *queso fresco*, which is sold in all Latin American groceries and is becoming a standard item in most supermarkets. The amount of flour needed for this recipe varies, depending on the freshness of the cheese and the size of the eggs. This recipe comes from Bolivia, where the rolls are usually served for tea or for breakfast, accompanying eggs scrambled with sautéed onions, peppers, and tomatoes. I love to serve them with soup.

> 1 cup yuca flour (page 434), or more if needed
> 1 teaspoon baking powder
> 2 large eggs
> 10 ounces Mexican *queso fresco*, crumbled
> Milk, if needed

1. Place the flour and baking powder in a food processor and pulse 3 or 4 times to mix. Add the

eggs and cheese and process until the dough forms a ball. If the dough is too dry, add milk 1 teaspoon at a time until the dough is soft and easy to shape. If the dough is too moist, add more flour 1 tablespoon at a time.

2. Divide the dough into 4 pieces. Roll each piece into a log 1½ inches in diameter. Cut each log into 9 pieces and roll each piece between the palms of your hands into a ball. Place the balls on a lightly buttered baking sheet and let rest for 30 minutes.

3. Preheat the oven to 375°F.

4. Bake the rolls on the top oven rack until lightly colored, about 20 minutes. Serve warm.

NOTE **To make Colombian** *pan de yuca,* **roll and shape each piece into a U shape.**

Fainá

CHICKPEA PIZZA
Makes one 12-inch pizza; 4 to 6 servings

Genoa was probably where *fainá* originated. Now it is a Uruguayan specialty, found wherever pizza is sold. It is a type of bread made from chickpea flour and baked like a pizza without toppings. The texture of the *fainá* is like a soft bread with a crispy crust. It can be made a couple of hours ahead and kept at room temperature, then reheated in a 350°F for 5 minutes before serving. Sometimes people put a piece of *fainá* on top of a slice of pizza and call it *pizza a caballo* (pizza on a horse). I like to cut it into about two-inch squares and serve it with drinks. This popular specialty can be seasoned with onions and herbs or made with fresh corn and pancetta. Chickpea flour is available in Indian groceries. You will find it labeled as garbanzo flour in Italian markets.

> 1¼ cups chickpea (garbanzo) flour
> ¼ cup all-purpose flour
> 2 cups water

> 1 teaspoon salt
> 3 tablespoons canola oil
> Kosher salt
> White pepper

1. Place the flours, water, 1 teaspoon salt, and 1 tablespoon of the oil in a blender or food processor and process for a few seconds until smooth. Transfer to a medium-size bowl, cover, and refrigerate for at least 2 hours or overnight.

2. Preheat the oven to 425°F. Place a 12-inch pizza pan (not one with removable sides) in the oven to heat.

3. Sprinkle the pan with kosher salt and coat with the remaining 2 tablespoons oil. Spread the batter in the pan and bake on the center oven rack for 20 minutes. Move the pan to the top rack and continue to bake until golden brown, about 5 minutes more.

4. Remove from the oven and sprinkle with white pepper to taste. Let cool for a few minutes, cut into small squares, and serve immediately.

Sopa Paraguaya

PARAGUAYAN CORNBREAD *Serves 8*

The only explanation I have as to why this cornbread is called *sopa* (soup) in Paraguay is that the mixture that goes into the oven is almost soupy. This cornbread is the most popular specialty in Paraguay. It is the traditional dish served at weddings, for holidays, and on special occasions. On Good Friday, especially in rural areas, it is standard fare in every home. It is also great for breakfast with a good cup of coffee. The classic *sopa Paraguaya* does not have fresh corn in it. Some cooks add it for a lighter texture and taste. There is also a version called *sopa Paraguaya rellena,* which is filled with a savory mixture made with meat or chicken. The cheese generally used is *queso fresco.*

1 large onion, chopped (about 1½ cups)

½ cup water

1 teaspoon salt

6 tablespoons (¾ stick) unsalted butter, softened

4 large eggs, separated

5 ounces Mexican *queso fresco*, crumbled

1 cup cooked corn kernels, drained and coarsely chopped in a blender or food processor

1½ cups cornmeal

1 cup buttermilk, or 1 cup milk mixed with 1 tablespoon distilled white vinegar

1. In a small saucepan, combine the onion, water, and salt and bring to the boil. Reduce the heat to medium-low, cover, and simmer for 10 minutes. Set aside to cool.

2. Cream the butter in a large bowl with an electric mixer. While beating, add the egg yolks one at a time, beating well after each addition, then mix in the cheese and corn. Fold in the onions and their cooking liquid. Alternately add the cornmeal and buttermilk, one-third of each at a time.

3. Preheat the oven to 400°F. Generously butter and flour a 2½-quart casserole or rectangular baking pan.

4. In a large bowl, beat the egg whites with an electric mixer (make sure it's washed and well dried) until they hold soft peaks. Carefully fold into the cornmeal mixture. Transfer to the prepared casserole. Bake on the center oven rack until golden brown, about 45 minutes.

5. Remove from the oven and let cool for 5 minutes. Cut into squares and serve. This bread is best eaten right out of the oven, but it is also good reheated and can be frozen. I usually freeze the leftovers and reheat them in the microwave.

Pão de Queijo

YUCA FLOUR AND CHEESE BREAD *Makes 18 rolls*

My friend Teresa Corcao is the owner of Navegador, a popular restaurant in downtown Rio de Janeiro. Among the delights on her menu are many local specialties, including a type of roll that is very popular in Rio. These fabulous rolls are full of flavor, rich, and airy. Teresa gladly shared this recipe with me so that those who might never get to Rio can still enjoy one of this sophisticated town's culinary treasures.

½ cup canola oil or corn oil

½ cup milk

2 large eggs

1¼ cups yuca flour (page 434)

2 heaping tablespoons freshly grated Parmesan cheese

¼ teaspoon salt

2 teaspoons baking powder

1. Preheat the oven to 425°F. Generously butter and flour 2 muffin tins with 1¾-inch cups.

2. Place all the ingredients in a blender or food processor in the order indicated and process until well mixed.

3. Transfer the batter to the prepared tins, filling each cup halfway. Place on a baking sheet and bake on the lower third oven rack until golden, about 20 minutes. Let cool for a few minutes and remove from the tins. Serve warm or at room temperature.

Panqueques de Kiwicha

AMARANTH PANCAKES

Makes twelve 3-inch pancakes; 2 servings

In countries where amaranth is grown, amaranth flour has many uses. It is popular for making nourishing breakfast drinks for children, and it also appears in recipes where we would more commonly expect flour, such as these pancakes. They are light and can be eaten topped with butter and a little syrup, with cooked blueberries sweetened with sugar, or just with honey. They are a treat for the entire family.

¼ cup amaranth flour

½ cup all-purpose flour

¼ teaspoon baking powder

Pinch of salt

1 teaspoon sugar

¼ teaspoon ground cinnamon

1 large egg, lightly beaten

½ cup milk

1 tablespoon canola oil

¼ teaspoon pure vanilla extract

1. In a medium-size bowl, mix together the flours, baking powder, salt, sugar, and cinnamon. In a smaller bowl, combine the egg, milk, oil, and vanilla extract. Pour the egg mixture over the flour mixture and toss with a fork until blended. The batter should be thin.

2. Heat a large skillet or griddle (preferably non-stick) over medium heat. Sprinkle it with a few drops of water, and if the water sizzles, the pan is ready. Pour 1 tablespoon of the batter on the griddle (the batter should spread) and cook until bubbles form on top. Turn and cook for a few seconds on the other side. Serve warm.

NOTE **This recipe can easily be doubled.**

Postres y Dulces

DESSERTS AND SWEETS

BEFORE THE CONQUEST, SOUTH AMERICA'S Indians did not have sugar, and although they did have some natural sweets, they were not familiar with the concept of "dessert." The Indians had honey and some fruit and vegetable sweeteners, and these were used to cook squash and other root vegetables. But mainly South America's natives depended on the sun to sweeten their vegetables. Root vegetables such as *oca* and sweet potatoes, when left in the sun to ripen for a few days before they were roasted or boiled, tasted as if they had been cooked with sugar. But the favorite sweet treat for early people was fresh fruit. South America, with such a varied topography and climate, can grow just about every kind of fruit imaginable. With such a tremendous variety of fruit available, it stands to reason that fruit-based sweets were, and still are, South Americans' favorite desserts. However, the introduction of sugar, as well as European culinary ideas, had a huge impact on the development of sweets and desserts.

In 1502, only two years after first landing in Brazil, the Portuguese brought sugar cane cuttings from the island of Madeira. At that time, sugar was mostly used in Europe as a medicine to cure fatigue, strengthen the heart, and help digestion, among other applications. It was the Portuguese who saw the value of sugar in confections, which originally were made with honey, and they were the ones who industrialized sugar production, making it a large-scale industry.

The best sugar confections were born in the convents of Spain and Portugal. The connection to the convents can still be seen in the unusual names of the sweets that were concocted there, although it is sometimes hard to know which country came up with what first. For example, *tocino del cielo*, or heavenly bacon, supposedly was invented by nuns in a convent in southern Spain. However, this rich, flan-like dessert, made with water, egg yolks, and sugar, is also considered a classic Portuguese sweet, called *toucinho do céu*. *Beijos de freira* (nun's kisses), *cabelos de virgen* (virgin's hair), *fatias de freira* (nun's slices), and *papos de anjo* (angel's bellies) are all old Portuguese sweets. These are just a few examples, with many more confections named after saints, convents, and towns.

This tradition also came to South America, and the production of candies and cakes was closely associated with the convents there. In the middle of the seventeenth century, Spanish nuns began settling in the larger cities of western South America, and over time the convents there became famous for their sweet confections. The nuns raised money for their charities by selling these confections for all kinds of celebrations. Their sweets became easily recognizable at local weddings, anniversaries, christenings, birthdays, and holidays. In Lima, Peru, the nuns at the Convent of the Congregation of the Daughters of the Immaculate Mary still make sweets and cakes dating from colonial times, and their wedding cakes are quite elaborate. The Convent of Santa Clarita in Arequipa, Peru, also was famous for its confections, pastries, and breads, such as *guaguas de pan* (bread dolls). Although the nuns are gone, the building is still there, along with the kitchen and utensils the nuns used to prepare their specialties.

After the sugar plantations were established in Brazil, African cooks in the kitchens of the "Big Houses" of the plantations developed many new, creole-style sweets. They not only adopted the use of sugar and egg yolks but also added peanuts, coconut, and coconut milk, thus creating Brazilian specialties with their own charming names, such as *olhos de mulato* (mulatto's eyes), *olhos de sogra* (mother-in-law's eyes), *bôlo para agradar a sogras* (cake to please mother-in-laws), *delicia de donzela* (maiden's delights), *não toques* (don't touch me), *sonhos* (dreams), and *bem casados* (happily married). Sometimes the mistresses of the plantations had their cooks make these sweets to sell in the market.

The abundance of desserts using egg yolks is due to the practice of clarifying sherry with egg whites, which were also used in working with gold leaf in churches. Custards were the ideal way to use up the leftover yolks.

In addition to custards and flan, the Spanish and Portuguese brought with them rice pudding, fruit compotes, and a variety of specialties that show the Arab influence on the Iberian Peninsula. Soon local cooks started pairing indigenous ingredients with the sugar extracted from sugar cane, using the Hispanics' knowledge of confections and preserving fruits. Native fruits such as strawberries, pineapples, tamarillos, *babacos*, and guavas were used to prepare some of South Americans' favorite desserts: fruit compotes and sweet pastes. Pineapple, coconut, chocolate, and coffee became the basis for flans, custards, and cakes. Squash and sweet potatoes appeared in puddings and soufflés. The French brought their beautiful pastries, which became the staple of pastry shops throughout South America. Baking with puff pastry became a South American tradition.

Brazil has splendid sweets that grace their *festas* (parties). Their classic confections appear not only in pastry and candy shops but also in the streets, sold by strolling vendors. *Cocadas* (coconut confections) and peanut brittle are the most common candies. This is also true for the Andean countries.

And what can I say about *dulce de leche*, the creamy, caramelized-milk sweet that is loved by young and old alike throughout South America. It appears in flans, tortes, ice creams, sauces, and many other specialties. But the favorite way of eating *dulce de leche* is spread on bread or crackers.

Over the years, women across South America kept their recipes closely guarded, passing them on only to their next of kin. Some of these creations were so labor-intensive that they gradually disappeared. Fortunately, however, many sweets from colonial times still survive to satisfy the sweet tooth of millions of South Americans.

Torta de Quinua

QUINOA BARS *Makes 24 bars*

The Incas called quinoa the "mother grain" and revered it for the energy it supplied, which made it possible for them to do sustained hard labor at high altitudes. This recipe was inspired by an Ecuadorian sweet quinoa tamale. In these bars, cinnamon combines with cloves and anise to give these moist, cake-like bars a decided holiday tone. But they are versatile enough to suit any occasion, and stamina seekers, from hikers to woodchoppers, will appreciate the veritable trail mix of nuts and dried fruit. A certain winner; watch them disappear from your serving platter.

> 2 cups water
>
> 1 cup quinoa, rinsed (page 327)
>
> 1 cup firmly packed dark brown sugar
>
> 1 cup rice flour, cornstarch, or all-purpose flour
>
> 1 teaspoon baking powder
>
> ½ teaspoon baking soda
>
> 1 teaspoon ground cinnamon
>
> ½ teaspoon ground cloves
>
> ¼ teaspoon freshly grated nutmeg
>
> 1 teaspoon anise seeds, crushed
>
> ½ cup seedless black or golden raisins
>
> ½ cup coarsely chopped dates or dried apricots
>
> ½ cup chopped walnuts
>
> ½ cup (1 stick) unsalted butter, melted
>
> ½ cup fresh orange juice
>
> 2 teaspoons pure vanilla extract
>
> 3 large eggs, lightly beaten
>
> Confectioners' sugar for dusting (optional)

1. In a medium-size saucepan, bring the water to a boil. Add the quinoa and cook until all the water has been absorbed, about 12 minutes after it comes back to a boil. Remove from the heat and let cool.

2. Preheat the oven to 350°F. Butter and flour a 13 x 9-inch baking pan.

3. In a large mixing bowl, mix together the brown sugar, rice flour, baking powder, baking soda, cinnamon, cloves, nutmeg, anise, raisins, apricots, and walnuts. Add the cooled quinoa, the butter, orange juice, vanilla, and eggs and mix well. Transfer to the prepared baking pan and smooth the top. Bake in the upper third of the oven until a toothpick inserted in the center comes out clean, about 45 minutes.

4. Let cool in the pan, then cut into 24 bars. Serve dusted with confectioners' sugar, if desired.

Cuscuz de Tapioca

TAPIOCA AND COCONUT CAKE
Makes one 8-inch cake; 8 servings

Brazilians love sweets, especially those made with coconut. Tapioca, made from the cassava (yuca) root, is also much loved in Brazil. This cake is pretty standard and is served at teatime with either tea or coffee. It can be served as is or topped with *Molho de Chocolate* (recipe follows). This is a real treat for coconut lovers and a perfect example of creole cooking: the indigenous tapioca mixed with the Portuguese sugar and the African coconut.

> 1 cup grated fresh or frozen unsweetened coconut, plus more for garnish

1 cup quick-cooking tapioca

1 cup milk

½ cup sugar

½ teaspoon salt

1 cup well-stirred canned unsweetened coconut milk

1. In a medium-size mixing bowl, combine the coconut and tapioca.

2. In a 2-quart saucepan, combine the milk, sugar, and salt. Add the coconut milk and bring to a boil, stirring until the sugar has dissolved. Pour over the tapioca mixture, mixing well.

3. Moisten an 8-inch round mold with cold water and pour in the mixture. Cover and let stand at room temperature for at least 4 hours or in the refrigerator overnight.

4. Turn out onto a serving platter, remove the mold, and garnish with coconut.

Molho de Chocolate

CHOCOLATE SAUCE   *Makes about 2 cups*

This is an example of how condensed milk is used to make easy and delicious desserts. This sauce is also wonderful on bananas.

One 14-ounce can sweetened condensed milk

2 tablespoons Dutch-processed unsweetened cocoa powder

1 tablespoon unsalted butter

1 tablespoon water or dark rum

Pinch of salt

Mix together all the ingredients in a small saucepan over low heat. Cook, stirring, until smooth and hot. Let cool and serve at room temperature.

Torta de Batata Doce

SWEET POTATO TORTE

Makes one 9-inch two-layer cake; 12 servings

This wonderfully rich torte is a contribution from my Brazilian friend and colleague Margarida Nogueira. Here the humble sweet potato and walnuts (American ingredients) are combined with European ingredients to produce a decadent, French-inspired torte. The sweet potatoes in the United States are completely different from the South American varieties, which are very starchy. I have also found that there is a difference in moisture content among different varieties of North American sweet potatoes. The best way to cook the sweet potatoes is either in the microwave or in the oven. Do not boil or steam them, because they will absorb too much liquid.

CAKE LAYERS

2 large sweet potatoes (about 1 pound)

5 large eggs, separated

1 cup plus 2 tablespoons sugar

1 teaspoon pure vanilla extract

1½ cups ground walnuts

¼ cup dry bread crumbs

FILLING

½ cup water

1 cup chopped walnuts

3 large egg yolks

6 tablespoons sugar

CHOCOLATE GLAZE

5 ounces good-quality semisweet chocolate

¼ cup (½ stick) unsalted butter, softened

1½ tablespoons light corn syrup

1. To make the cake layers, rinse the potatoes and, without drying them, loosely wrap in paper towels. Microwave on high until they yield to the touch, about 6 minutes. Or wrap the potatoes in

aluminum foil and bake in a preheated 350°F oven until soft to the touch, about 45 minutes. Either way, let the potatoes cool for a few minutes, then peel and puree in a food processor. You need about 1 cup.

2. Preheat the oven to 325°F. Butter two 9-inch round cake pans, then line the bottoms with parchment paper. Butter the parchment paper.

3. In a large mixing bowl, beat the egg yolks and 1 cup of the sugar until light and fluffy. Add the mashed sweet potatoes, vanilla, ground walnuts, and bread crumbs and stir until well mixed.

4. In another large mixing bowl, beat the egg whites with an electric mixer until they form soft peaks, then beat in the remaining 2 tablespoons sugar, 1 tablespoon at a time. Beat until stiff but not dry. Gently fold into the sweet potato mixture. Divide the batter equally between the 2 prepared pans. Bake until lightly browned and pulling away from the sides of the pans, about 40 minutes. Let cool in the pans on wire racks.

5. To make the filling, in a small, heavy saucepan, combine the water and chopped walnuts, bring to a boil, reduce the heat to medium, and simmer for about 5 minutes. In a medium-size mixing bowl, beat the egg yolks and sugar until fluffy. Add to the walnut mixture and cook over low heat, stirring constantly, until thickened, about 5 minutes. Remove from the heat and let cool to lukewarm.

6. To make the glaze, melt the chocolate in the top of a double boiler over simmering water. Add the butter and corn syrup and stir until smooth. Or melt the chocolate in the microwave, then add the butter and corn syrup and microwave for an additional 10 seconds. Stir until smooth. Let cool.

7. Invert one of the cake layers onto a cake stand, remove the pan and parchment paper, place an 8-inch cardboard cake circle on top, and turn over. Spread with the filling. Remove the second cake layer from the pan, remove the parchment, and place on the filling. Spread the glaze over the top and sides.

8. To serve, let the entire cake come to room temperature, then slice with a thin, sharp knife. Use a spatula to transfer pieces to serving plates.

NOTE **This is a rich cake, and I usually serve only small slices. For larger appetites, cut into 8 slices.**

VARIATION For an even more decadent torte, I sometimes use a chocolate *ganache* filling between the layers instead of the walnut filling given above.

Torta de Merengue con Crema de Chirimoyas y Fresas
MERINGUE TORTE FILLED WITH CHERIMOYA AND STRAWBERRY CREAM
Makes one 9-inch two-layer torte; 8 to 10 servings

Although all South Americans enjoy desserts made with meringue, Chileans seem to outdo the rest, making baked meringues for tortes, cakes, pastries, cookies, and other types of sweets. Freshly made unbaked meringue is also very popular throughout South America, and it appears as a filling or *betún* (frosting) for cakes, pies, and *roulades*, or to top fruit desserts. This cake is everybody's favorite, whether it is made with berries alone or, as in this combination, with cherimoya and berries. Feather light, delicious, and lovely to look at, it is a sure winner. Most meringue tortes are very simple—two meringue layers with a fruit cream filling. Chileans have beautiful cherimoyas and use them often in desserts. I have embellished the torte by adding nuts and chocolate.

MERINGUES

4 large egg whites, at room temperature

Pinch of salt

½ cup superfine sugar

1 teaspoon distilled white vinegar or fresh lemon juice

1 teaspoon pure vanilla extract

½ cup granulated sugar

1 cup ground blanched almonds or hazelnuts

1 tablespoon cornstarch

MOCHA GLAZE

4 ounces semisweet chocolate, chopped

2 tablespoons unsalted butter

2 tablespoons strong brewed coffee

FRUIT CREAM FILLING

1 cherimoya (about 1 pound)

1 teaspoon fresh lemon juice

2 tablespoons *pisco* (page 34) or brandy

1 cup hulled and sliced strawberries or whole raspberries

1½ cups whipping cream

1 package Whip It (cream stabilizer; optional)

GARNISHES

Raspberries or chocolate shavings (optional)

Confectioners' sugar

1. Preheat the oven to 350°F. Butter and flour two 9-inch springform pans or cake pans with removable sides. (Or line them with parchment paper.)

2. To make the meringues, in a large mixing bowl, beat the egg whites and salt with an electric mixer on low speed until foamy. Increase the speed to high and beat until the whites form soft peaks. While beating, add the superfine sugar 1 tablespoon at a time and beat until the meringue holds stiff, glossy peaks, about 8 minutes. Beat in the vinegar and vanilla.

3. In a small mixing bowl, mix together the granulated sugar, almonds, and cornstarch and fold into the whipped egg whites. Divide the batter equally between the prepared pans, spreading the mixture evenly. Bake until the meringues are dry, about 30 minutes. Turn off the oven. Remove the sides of the pans and let the meringues cool for about 1 hour in the oven with the door slightly ajar. At this point, the meringues can be removed from the bottoms of the pans and stored in tightly covered tins for a few days, or they may be frozen for a couple of months.

4. To make the glaze, in a small, heavy saucepan over low heat, combine the chocolate, butter, and coffee. Heat, stirring, until melted and smooth. (Or use the microwave oven.) Set aside to cool.

5. To make the filling, cut the cherimoya in half. Using a teaspoon, scrape the flesh into a medium-size mixing bowl. Crush with a fork to loosen the seeds, then pick them out and discard. Toss the flesh with the lemon juice and *pisco*. Rinse the strawberries, dry on paper towels, and mix with the cherimoya.

6. In a large mixing bowl, whip the cream with an electric mixer on low speed. If using the Whip It, sprinkle over the cream and continue to beat until soft peaks form. Increase the speed to high and whip until stiff peaks form. Pour half the cream into another bowl and fold the fruit into the remaining cream.

7. To assemble, place one of the meringues on a serving platter dotted with a little of the whipped cream to secure the meringue in place. Drizzle the glaze over the meringue (do not spread it), then spread the fruit mixture on top. Top with the second meringue. Transfer the remaining whipped cream to a decorating bag fitted with a ¼-inch star tip and pipe 8 to 10 circles around the top edge of the torte. Place a raspberry or

chocolate shaving inside each circle, if desired. Sprinkle the center with the confectioners' sugar. Refrigerate for at least 4 hours or overnight to mellow the meringue.

8. To serve, slice with a thin, sharp knife. Use a spatula to transfer pieces to serving plates.

Pastel de Tres Leches

THREE-MILK CAKE *Serves 16*

Pastel de tres leches is all the rage in Latin American restaurants across the United States. And rightly so, because, when properly done, it is a delicious, moist cake that will catch anyone's fancy. I don't know for sure where this cake originated, but I do know that a Nicaraguan restaurant in Miami was one of the first to offer it. I also have had similar cakes in Mexico. In South America, I have found several versions, some quite different from this. I think this *pastel* is a cousin of the South American *torta de ron* (rum torte). The classic topping for this cake is meringue (see variation). I prefer to use my favorite topping, whipped cream, and berries or berry sauce.

CAKE

6 large eggs, separated

1 cup plus 2 tablespoons sugar

1 teaspoon pure vanilla extract

2 cups sifted all-purpose flour

2 teaspoons baking powder

Pinch of salt

½ cup milk

SOAKING MIXTURE

One 14-ounce can sweetened condensed milk

1 cup half-and-half

1 cup whipping cream

2 tablespoons rum or orange liqueur

1½ cups whipping cream, whipped to stiff peaks

Assorted fresh berries or 1 recipe *Salsa de Frambuesas* (page 400) for garnish (optional)

1. Preheat the oven to 375°F. Butter and flour a 14 x 9 x 2-inch Pyrex baking dish.

2. To make the cake, in a large mixing bowl with an electric mixer, beat the egg yolks until lemon-colored. Add 1 cup of the sugar and continue to beat until the mixture falls from the beaters like ribbons when the beaters are lifted. Beat in the vanilla. Sift together the flour, baking soda, and salt, then fold into the egg yolks, alternating with the milk.

3. In another large mixing bowl, beat the egg whites with the mixer (wash and dry the beaters thoroughly) until they form soft peaks. Beat in the remaining 2 tablespoons sugar, 1 tablespoon at a time, and continue to beat until stiff but not dry. Stir one-fourth of the whites into the batter, then carefully fold in the rest. Turn the batter into the prepared baking dish and bake until the cake is puffed and golden and has begun to show a thin line of shrinkage from the sides of the dish, about 30 minutes. Remove from the oven and let cool in the dish on a wire rack.

4. To make the soaking mixture, place the condensed milk, half-and-half, cream, and rum in a blender and pulse until smooth. With a fork, poke holes in the cake every inch or so. Pour the milk mixture over the cake, making sure every part of the cake gets saturated. Cover with plastic wrap and refrigerate for a few hours or overnight.

5. A couple of hours before serving, either spread the whipped cream on top of the cake or place in a decorating bag fitted with a star tip and pipe rosettes on top, covering it completely. Decorate with the berries, if using, and refrigerate. To

serve, cut into squares. If using the *salsa de frambuesas*, drizzle each square with a little before serving.

MERINGUE TOPPING In a medium-size mixing bowl with an electric mixer, beat 3 large egg whites and a pinch of salt until soft peaks form. Set aside. In a small, heavy saucepan over medium heat, bring ½ cup water and ¾ cup sugar to a boil and cook to the soft ball stage (240°F on a candy thermometer). Add in a thin stream to the whites, beating all the while and continuing to beat until stiff peaks form. Spread on top of the cake and refrigerate until ready to serve.

Torta de Maracujá

PASSION FRUIT TORTE

Makes one 8-inch cake; 10 servings

This has to be the queen of all tortes. I remember the first time I had it in a hotel in Rio de Janeiro. We arrived very late, and the restaurant was not serving dinner anymore, but they had *caipirinhas* (*cachaça* and lime cocktails) and passion fruit torte. After indulging in a couple of *caipirinhas*, I was ready to try the torte. It was love at first bite. I quickly made a sketch of the different layers so that I could reproduce it when I returned to the United States. Here is my interpretation.

1 recipe *Biscochuelo* (page 366)

PASSION FRUIT MOUSSE
  ¼ **cup water**
  1 envelope unflavored gelatin
  ½ **cup plus 2 tablespoons thawed frozen passion fruit pulp**
  ¾ **cup sugar**
  1 cup whipping cream
  3 large egg whites
  ¼ **teaspoon cream of tartar**

WHIPPED CREAM
  1 cup whipping cream
  1 teaspoon Whip It (cream stabilizer)

1 recipe Dessert Syrup (page 401)

ORANGE GLAZE
  ½ **cup fresh orange juice**
  ¾ **teaspoon unflavored gelatin**

1. Carefully slice the *biscochuelo* (sponge cake) horizontally into 2 layers. Set on a cake rack.

2. To make the mousse, pour the water into a small heatproof bowl. Sprinkle the gelatin over the water and let soften for 5 minutes. Heat over simmering water until the gelatin dissolves. In a medium-size mixing bowl, mix together the passion fruit pulp, ½ cup of the sugar, and the dissolved gelatin. Set the bowl in another bowl filled with ice and let sit, stirring occasionally, until it begins to thicken, about 15 minutes.

3. In a large mixing bowl, beat the whipping cream with an electric mixer until soft peaks form. Fold in the thickened passion fruit mixture. In a medium-size mixing bowl, beat the egg whites and cream of tartar together with the mixer (wash and dry the beaters thoroughly) until soft peaks form. Gradually add the remaining ¼ cup sugar and beat until stiff but not dry. Carefully fold into the cream mixture. Cover with plastic wrap and refrigerate.

4. To make the whipped cream, in a medium-size mixing bowl, whip the cream with the mixer (wash and dry the beaters thoroughly) for a few seconds. Sprinkle in the Whip It and continue to beat until shiny, stiff peaks form. Do not overbeat.

5. To assemble the torte, place a cardboard cake circle in an 8-inch springform pan. (This makes it easier to transfer the cake to a serving platter.) Cut a 32-inch-long piece of waxed paper, fold in half lengthwise, and then fold in half again. Use it

to line the inside of the pan (the ring) and secure the end with clear tape. Lightly brush with oil or spray with vegetable cooking spray. Place one of the cake layers cut side up on the cardboard and brush with half of the dessert syrup. Spread three-quarters of the whipped cream on top. Place the other cake layer cut side down on top of the cream. Brush with the remaining dessert syrup. Spread the mousse on top of the cake, tapping the pan on the counter to make sure the mousse is evenly distributed. Cover with plastic wrap and refrigerate until set, about 6 hours or overnight. Cover the remaining whipped cream with plastic wrap and refrigerate.

6. To make the glaze, place 2 tablespoons of the orange juice in a small glass bowl. Sprinkle the gelatin over the juice and let soften for 5 minutes. Heat over simmering water until the gelatin dissolves. Add the remaining orange juice and stir to combine. Set in another bowl filled with ice and let sit, stirring occasionally, until syrupy, about 15 minutes.

7. To finish the cake, carefully remove the ring from the pan. Peel off the waxed paper. Stir the glaze and pour it evenly over the mousse, carefully tilting the cake so that the glaze covers the entire surface. Refrigerate until set, about 30 minutes. If desired, use the remaining whipped cream to decorate the top with rosettes just before serving.

Biscochuelo

SPONGE CAKE *Makes one 9-inch cake; 12 servings*

Biscochuelo is a sponge cake that is widely used not only for making tortes but also to eat as is, topped with confectioners' sugar. It comes in a variety of textures, depending on the cook.

> 3 large eggs, separated
> 1 cup plus 2 tablespoons confectioners' sugar

½ **teaspoon pure vanilla extract**
½ **cup cake flour**

1. Preheat the oven to 375°F. Generously butter and flour a 9-inch springform pan.

2. In a large mixing bowl with an electric mixer, beat the egg yolks until lemon-colored. Add 1 cup of the confectioners' sugar and beat until the mixture is pale yellow and falls from the beaters like ribbons when the beaters are lifted. Beat in the vanilla and carefully fold in the flour.

3. In a medium-size mixing bowl, beat the egg whites with the mixer (wash and dry the beaters thoroughly) until soft peaks form. Add the remaining 2 tablespoons confectioners' sugar, 1 tablespoon at a time, and beat until shiny, stiff peaks form. Stir one-fourth of the egg whites into the yolk mixture, then carefully fold in the rest. Transfer the batter to the prepared pan. Bake on the center oven rack until puffed and lightly colored, about 20 minutes.

4. Remove from the oven and let cool for 10 minutes in the pan on a wire rack. Carefully run a knife around the edge of the pan and remove the cake by turning it out onto the rack. Let cool completely. The cake can be made a couple of days ahead and refrigerated, or it may be frozen for up to a couple of months.

Pastel de Manzanas con Dulce de Leche

APPLE AND WALNUT TART WITH DULCE DE LECHE *Makes one 10- to 11-inch tart; 10 to 12 servings*

Chile is one of the big producers of apples in South America. It also is home to a large number of German immigrants, who brought with them their cakes and pastries. German *kuchens* became some of Chileans' favorite desserts, especially *Apfelkuchen* (apple *kuchen*), of which there are many variations. This is my adaptation of the classic apple *kuchen*. Instead of the custard, I decided to use sweetened condensed milk, which, when baked, turns into one of Chileans' most beloved sweets, *dulce de leche*. Most *kuchens* made with apples include raisins or prunes, but I prefer to use walnuts, because they complement the flavor of *dulce de leche*, while raisins or prunes add more sweetness to something that is already very sweet. I particularly enjoy this tart served slightly warm with a cup of strong black coffee.

> 3 large Golden Delicious or Granny Smith apples (about 1½ pounds)
>
> ½ cup sugar
>
> ½ cup all-purpose flour
>
> 1 teaspoon baking powder
>
> Grated zest of 1 lemon
>
> ½ cup milk
>
> 3 large eggs, lightly beaten
>
> ½ cup coarsely chopped walnuts
>
> One 14-ounce can sweetened condensed milk
>
> 1 teaspoon pure vanilla extract
>
> Ground cinnamon for sprinkling

1. Preheat the oven to 350°F. Generously butter a 10- to 11-inch quiche pan that is at least 1½ inches deep.

2. Peel the apples, then core and cut into slices about ¼ inch thick. Toss with ¼ cup of the sugar.

3. Sift the flour and baking powder together in a large mixing bowl. Add the zest, remaining ¼ cup sugar, the milk, and 1 egg and beat until smooth. Add the apple slices and toss to coat. Transfer to the prepared pan, making sure the apple slices are evenly distributed. Sprinkle the walnuts evenly over the top.

4. In a medium-size mixing bowl, mix together the condensed milk, remaining 2 eggs, and the vanilla. Pour evenly over the apples and sprinkle

with the cinnamon. Bake in the upper third of the oven until set, about 45 minutes.

5. Remove from the oven and let cool. Cut into wedges and serve lukewarm or at room temperature.

Pasta Frola de Membrillo

QUINCE TART *Makes one 10-inch tart; 8 to 10 servings*

Pasta frola (*pasta frolla* in Italian) is a pastry dough brought by Italian immigrants to Argentina and Uruguay. The Italians use this dough to make desserts such as *spongata*, a Christmas cake from Parma, Italy, but it also can be used to make all kinds of pies and tarts, both sweet and savory. Quince was brought to South America by the Spaniards and Portuguese, who used this fruit to make many confections. Their quince preserves and paste are famous and are always part of the sweet table or breakfast table in restaurants. Just walk into a pastry shop in Portugal, and you will find a tremendous assortment of pastries made with quince.

> 1 recipe *Pasta/Masa Frola* (page 368)
>
> One 10-ounce jar quince preserves
>
> 1 teaspoon fresh lemon juice
>
> 2 tablespoons dry vermouth, white wine, or port
>
> 1 large egg lightly beaten with 1 tablespoon water
>
> Vanilla ice cream for serving (optional)

1. Divide the dough into thirds. On a lightly floured surface, roll out two-thirds of the dough to ⅛ inch thick. Carefully roll the dough onto a rolling pin and transfer to a 10-inch tart mold with removable sides. Trim off the excess dough hanging over the edge. Press down on the dough with your index finger to form a scalloped edge and set aside.

2. In a small mixing bowl, mix together the preserves, lemon juice, and vermouth. It helps to warm up the preserves a bit to blend the ingredients well. Transfer to the tart, spreading it evenly.

3. On a lightly floured surface, roll out the remaining dough into a rectangle ⅛ inch thick. Cut lengthwise with a ravioli cutter or knife into ½-inch-wide strips. (If the dough is too soft, refrigerate for 30 minutes.) Carefully transfer the strips to the tart to make a lattice top, placing the strips about 1 inch apart and pinching the ends together with the edge of the bottom crust. Brush the strips with the egg mixture. Refrigerate for 30 minutes.

4. Preheat the oven to 350°F.

5. Bake the tart until the lattice is golden, about 45 minutes. Remove from the oven and let cool completely on a wire rack.

6. To serve, remove from the pan and cut into wedges. A scoop of vanilla ice cream on the side is a welcome addition.

Pasta/Masa Frola
TART DOUGH   *Makes enough dough for 1 tart*

This is the classic dough for tarts in Argentina, used for both sweet and savory tarts.

    2 cups all-purpose flour
    1 tablespoon sugar (see Note)
    1 teaspoon baking powder
    ½ teaspoon salt
    Grated zest of 1 lemon
    ½ cup (1 stick) cold unsalted butter, cut into 8 pieces
    1 large egg plus 1 large egg yolk lightly beaten with 2 tablespoons milk and 1 teaspoon pure vanilla extract

Hand method: In a large bowl, mix together the flour, sugar, baking powder, salt, and zest. Add the butter and blend, using a pastry blender or your fingertips, to make a coarse meal. Add the egg mixture and mix well, adding 1 more tablespoon milk if needed to make a soft dough. Knead a few times, cover with plastic wrap, and let it rest for 30 minutes at room temperature.

Food processor method: Place the flour, sugar, baking powder, salt, and zest in a food processor and pulse 4 times to mix. Add the butter and process until the mixture resembles coarse meal, about 10 seconds. With the machine running, pour the egg mixture through the feed tube and process until the dough comes together almost into a ball. If the dough is too dry, add 1 more tablespoon milk. Do not overprocess, because it will toughen the dough. Cover with plastic wrap and let rest for 30 minutes at room temperature.

NOTE For sweet tarts, you could use ¼ cup sugar instead of 1 tablespoon, if desired. However, I find that the filling provides enough sugar for my taste, so I always use only 1 tablespoon.

Pastas, Galletas, y Confecciones
PASTRIES, COOKIES, AND CONFECTIONS

Pristiños de Noche Buena

CHRISTMAS EVE CRULLERS *Makes 16 crullers*

On Christmas Eve, we look forward to big platters of *pristiños* (crullers) and *buñuelos* (buns). These fritters are the classic Christmas dessert in Ecuador and many other South American countries. Similar fritters, called *picarones* in Peru and *sopapillas* in Chile, are made with yeast instead of baking powder, and the dough is mixed with pureed squash. In Ecuador, the dough also is sometimes made with pureed squash. Variations of this type of fritter can be found throughout South America under different names. It is a European import that went through various transformations, such as the addition of sweet potatoes, squash, or a syrup made with *panela*, depending on the region.

> 2 cups all-purpose flour
>
> ½ teaspoon baking powder
>
> 1 teaspoon sugar
>
> ½ teaspoon salt
>
> ¼ cup (½ stick) unsalted butter or vegetable shortening, softened, and cut into 4 pieces
>
> 3 large eggs, lightly beaten
>
> 1 tablespoon anise liqueur, *aguardiente* (page 34), or rum
>
> Canola oil for frying
>
> 1 recipe *Miel de Panela* (recipe follows) for serving

1.   Place the flour, baking powder, sugar, and salt in a food processor and pulse to combine. Add the butter and pulse until the mixture resembles coarse meal. Add the eggs and liqueur and process until the dough forms a ball. (If preparing by hand, mix together the flour, baking powder, sugar, and salt. Add the butter, eggs, and liqueur and knead until the dough forms bubbles.) Cover with plastic wrap and let rest for 30 minutes at room temperature.

2.   Roll the dough into a cylinder 2 inches in diameter, cut in half, and then cut each half into 8 pieces. On a lightly floured work surface, roll out each piece into a strip measuring about 2 x 6 inches. With scissors, on one side make about 4 diagonal cuts extending about halfway across the strip. Pinch the ends together to form a wreath.

3.   In a large, deep frying pan or electric skillet, heat 1 inch of the oil to 360°F. Drop in 2 or 3 wreaths at a time and fry on both sides until golden, carefully swishing the oil with a large spoon over the wreaths. Transfer to paper towels to drain.

4.   These crullers are best served right away with *miel de panela*. Otherwise, serve at room temperature.

Miel de Panela BROWN SUGAR SYRUP   *Makes about 1 cup*

Miel de panela is a very popular syrup in the Andean countries and is served over various kinds of fritters.

> 1 cup firmly packed dark brown sugar or finely chopped *panela*
>
> ½ cup water
>
> 2 cloves
>
> 1 small cinnamon stick
>
> 2 strips lemon zest

1.   Place all the ingredients in a heavy 4-quart saucepan over low heat and simmer, stirring occasionally, until the mixture forms a thin syrup, about 10 minutes.

2. Strain through a medium-mesh sieve and serve hot. Or let cool and store in the refrigerator for up to several weeks. Reheat before serving.

Aplanchados

FROSTED PUFF PASTRY STRIPS *Makes 36 pastries*

These pastries of French origin are among the most popular in South America. They are made in small sizes for tea and medium and large size for snacks. You'll find them in almost every South American bakery. They are easy to make and will keep well in the refrigerator for a few days or in the freezer for a couple of months. In Montevideo, Uruguay, I had a wonderful version of *aplanchados* called Jesuítas (Jesuits), which had a layer of Swiss cheese and ham, just like a sandwich, along with the sweet topping, reflecting the Basque culinary tradition of mixing sweet and savory.

> 2 large egg whites
>
> 2 cups confectioners' sugar, or more if needed
>
> ½ teaspoon cream of tartar
>
> 1 package Pepperidge Farm frozen puff pastry sheets, thawed

1. Place the egg whites and ½ cup of the confectioners' sugar in a medium-size mixing bowl. Using an electric mixer on medium speed, beat until creamy. Sprinkle in the cream of tartar and add the remaining 1½ cups confectioners' sugar, 1 tablespoon at a time, while still beating. When done, the icing should be the consistency of runny mayonnaise. If too thin, add a little more confectioners' sugar.

2. Gently unfold 1 sheet of the pastry on top of cutting board and trim ⅛ inch from the edges; the pastry is usually dry around the edges, which will prevent rising. Prick with a fork every inch or so, then spread half of the icing on top. With a small, sharp knife, cut the iced pastry into rectangles about 1½ inches wide and 3 inches long, dipping the knife in water as necessary to remove any icing sticking to it. Place the strips on lightly moistened baking sheets. If the icing drips, remove with a small knife, because drippings will prevent the pastry from rising. Repeat with the remaining pastry sheet and icing. Refrigerate for 1 hour.

3. Preheat the oven to 375°F.

4. Bake the strips for about 12 minutes, until the icing is a deep beige. Remove from the baking sheet and let cool on wire racks.

Queijadinhas

BRAZILIAN PARMESAN CHEESE TARTS
Makes 48 tarts

Queijadinhas are just one of the myriad pastries Brazilians make to celebrate any occasion. Many times these tarts are served as appetizers. However, they are sweet and also work well as a snack or sort of a combination dessert and cheese course, perhaps to be enjoyed with an after-dinner drink. Any way you serve them, they are delicious.

CRUST

> 2¾ cups all-purpose flour
>
> ¼ cup (½ stick) unsalted butter, softened
>
> 1 large egg yolk
>
> **Pinch of salt**
>
> ½ cup water

FILLING

> 2¾ cups sugar
>
> 1 cup water
>
> 2 cups finely grated Parmesan cheese
>
> 4 large egg yolks
>
> 4 large eggs

> **Ground cinnamon for sprinkling**

1. To make the crust, in a medium-size mixing bowl, mix together the flour, butter, egg yolk, and salt until well combined. Add the water little by little, stirring until you get a soft dough. Knead for a few minutes, then let rest for 30 minutes at room temperature.

2. To make the filling, combine the sugar and water in a medium-size, heavy saucepan and cook over medium heat until the thread stage (a bit of syrup dropped into cold water will form a thread), 230°F on a candy thermometer. Let cool a bit, then, while still warm, add the Parmesan, egg yolks, and eggs and mix very well.

3. Preheat the oven to 350°F. Butter four 12-cup mini (1¼-inch) muffin tins.

4. Divide the dough into 4 equal portions and roll each into a 1-inch-diameter log. Cut each log into 12 disks. On a lightly floured work surface, roll each disk into a round large enough to fit into the bottom of a muffin cup. Divide the filling equally among the cups and sprinkle a little cinnamon on top. Bake on the center oven rack until golden, about 20 minutes.

5. Let cool in the tins on wire racks for 10 minutes, then run a paring knife around the edges and unmold. Let cool completely on the racks and store in cookie tins. These can be kept refrigerated for a few days or frozen for up to 3 months. Serve at room temperature.

Quindins de Yáyá

COCONUT AND EGG YOLK PETITS FOURS
Makes 24 quindins

These delicious confections are very popular throughout Brazil, where they were created in the "Big Houses" of the plantations in the north. *Yáyá* was the name given by the slaves to the young girls of the "Big Houses," and *quindins de yáyá* were sweets that were made for them. A *quindin* is a very sweet confection that is popular not only for afternoon tea but at any time of the day. In Rio, *quindins* can be found at any snack stand along the boulevards by the sea, as well as in the *confeitarias* (pastry shops).

This version is very easy to prepare. Freshly grated or frozen unsweetened coconut is a must for optimum taste. During baking, the coconut flakes float up in the batter, and the yolk mixture forms a jelly-like layer that drops to the bottom. When turned upside down, the coconut layer is on the bottom and the beautiful, delicate yellow-orange jelly layer on top. Buttering the muffin tins and coating them with sugar is very important; when the sugar melts, it gives the *quindins* a shimmery effect. For a more exotic flavor, use orange-flower water. Other versions use brown sugar instead of granulated sugar, or coconut milk instead of grated coconut.

6 large egg yolks

1 large egg

1 cup sugar, plus more for coating the molds

Pinch of salt

1 cup grated fresh or frozen unsweetened coconut

1 tablespoon unsalted butter, melted

1 teaspoon orange-flower water (optional)

1. In a large glass, ceramic, or plastic mixing bowl, beat the egg yolks, egg, sugar, and salt until well blended. Add the coconut, butter, and orange-flower water (if using) and mix until well blended. Cover with plastic wrap and refrigerate for at least 6 hours or overnight.

2. Preheat the oven to 350°F. Butter two 12-cup mini (1¼-inch) muffin tins and coat the sides and bottoms of the cups with sugar.

3. Stir the batter very well, then fill the cups to within ⅛ inch of the top. Stir the batter often as you fill the cups. Place the tins in a large baking pan with ¼ inch hot water. Bake on the center oven rack until light golden brown, about 45

minutes. A knife inserted in the center should come out clean.

4. Let cool for a few minutes, then, with a tiny icing spatula, loosen the sides of the *quindins*. Remove from the tins with the spatula and place on wire racks to cool completely.

5. Place the cooled *quindins* in paper cups and serve. Store in a single layer in cookie tins. They will keep in the refrigerator for a couple of days or in the freezer for a couple of months.

Alfajores
COOKIES WITH DULCE DE LECHE FILLING
Makes 24 cookies

Alfajores are without a doubt one of the best-known cookies in South America, especially in the southern countries. The dough varies from country to country and cook to cook. The only constant is the *dulce de leche* filling, which also may be spread around the sides of the cookie before it is rolled in coconut. Some *alfajores* are made with just all-purpose flour, while others include a mixture of flour and cornstarch. In the regions where yuca is a staple, these cookies are made with yuca flour.

> ½ cup (1 stick) unsalted butter, softened
>
> ¼ cup confectioners' sugar, plus more for sifting (optional)
>
> 2 large egg yolks
>
> 1 tablespoon grated lemon zest
>
> 2 tablespoons cognac or brandy
>
> 2 cups all-purpose flour, or more if needed
>
> 1 teaspoon baking powder
>
> 1 cup *dulce de leche*, store-bought or homemade (page 390)
>
> Finely grated fresh coconut (optional)

1. In a large mixing bowl, cream together the butter and confectioners' sugar until smooth. Beat in the egg yolks. Add the zest and cognac and mix well. Sift the flour and baking powder together, then mix into the butter mixture to make a dough that is soft but not runny; if it is too soft, add some more flour. Form into a ball, cover with plastic wrap, and refrigerate for 30 minutes.

2. Preheat the oven to 350°F. Grease a large cookie sheet.

3. On a lightly floured work surface, roll the dough out to ⅛ inch thick and cut into 1½-inch rounds. Place on the prepared cookie sheet and bake until set, about 10 minutes; the cookies should not color at all.

4. Remove from the sheet and let cool on wire racks. Spread one cookie with *dulce de leche* and press a second cookie on top. If desired, spread *dulce de leche* around the sides of the cookie and roll in the grated coconut. Or just sift confectioners' sugar on top. Repeat with the remaining cookies and *dulce de leche*. Tightly wrapped, these cookies will keep for a couple of days in the refrigerator or up to 3 months in the freezer.

Suspiros de Café
COFFEE SIGHS *Makes about 30 meringues*

Suspiros are little dry meringues that are very popular in South America. They can be found in just about every bakery, grocery store, and supermarket. Meringues made with coffee flavoring are a Colombian specialty reserved for teas or special occasions. They will keep well for a few days in tins or can be frozen for a couple of months.

> 1 teaspoon coffee liqueur or water
>
> 1 teaspoon pure vanilla extract
>
> 2 teaspoons instant espresso granules
>
> 2 large egg whites, at room temperature
>
> ¼ teaspoon cream of tartar
>
> Pinch of salt

¼ cup superfine sugar

¼ cup superfine sugar sifted with 1 tablespoon cornstarch

1. In a small bowl, mix together the liqueur, vanilla, and espresso, stirring until the espresso is dissolved. Set aside.

2. In a large mixing bowl with an electric mixer on low speed, beat the egg whites until foamy. Add the cream of tartar and salt, increase the speed to high, and beat until the whites have the consistency of mayonnaise. While continuing to beat, add the superfine sugar 1 tablespoon at a time. Beat until the meringue holds stiff, glossy peaks. Beat in the coffee mixture, then carefully fold in the superfine sugar and cornstarch mixture.

3. Preheat the oven to 350°F. Line 2 baking sheets with parchment paper.

4. Transfer the meringue to a decorating bag fitted with a ½-inch tip and pipe 1½-inch mounds on the prepared baking sheets, leaving about 1 inch between them. Place in the oven, immediately reduce the oven temperature to 250°F, and bake for 30 minutes. Turn the heat off and let the meringues dry in the oven, without opening the oven door, for several hours or overnight.

Merenguitos de Maní
LITTLE PEANUT MERINGUES
Makes about 40 meringues

Wonderfully light and crunchy, these meringues are the perfect accompaniment for any fruit-based dessert. They are also made with other ground nuts, such as almonds, walnuts, hazelnuts, and Brazil nuts.

> 3 large egg whites, at room temperature
> ¼ teaspoon cream of tartar
> 1 teaspoon pure vanilla extract

1 cup superfine sugar

8 ounces unsalted dry-roasted peanuts, coarsely ground

1. Preheat the oven to 375°F. Line 2 baking sheets with parchment paper.

2. In a large mixing bowl with an electric mixer on low speed, beat the egg whites until foamy. Add the cream of tartar, increase the speed to high, and beat until stiff but not dry. Beat in the vanilla.

3. In a medium-size mixing bowl, combine the superfine sugar and peanuts. Carefully fold into the beaten egg whites. Using a tablespoon, drop mounds of meringue about 1½ inches in diameter onto the prepared baking sheets, leaving at least 1 inch between. Bake until lightly colored, about 15 minutes. After 10 minutes, switch the baking sheets from the top to the bottom oven rack.

4. Turn off the oven, open the oven door, and let the meringues dry in the oven for 30 minutes. Store in a cookie tin in the refrigerator for up to 1 week or in the freezer up to 3 months.

Docinhos de Nozes
LITTLE WALNUT SWEETS *Makes about 30 balls*

This confection goes back to the convents of South America. It's especially popular in Brazil.

> 2 large egg whites
> Pinch of salt
> One 14-ounce can sweetened condensed milk
> 1 teaspoon unsalted butter
> 4 large egg yolks
> 2½ cups walnuts, ground
> Sugar for coating
> 15 walnut halves, cut in half

1. In a medium-size mixing bowl with an electric mixer, beat the egg whites and salt until soft peaks form.

2. In a 4-quart saucepan, combine the beaten egg whites, condensed milk, butter, egg yolks, and ground walnuts. Cook over medium heat, stirring constantly, until the mixture is smooth and pulls away from the bottom and side of the pan.

3. Turn the mixture onto a buttered platter to cool. Shape into balls about 1 inch in diameter. Roll in the sugar, then top each with a walnut quarter. Place in paper cups and store in cookie tins in the refrigerator for up to 1 week or in the freezer for up to 3 months.

VARIATION These balls can be dipped in chocolate before refrigerating.

Docinhos de Amendoim

PEANUT CROQUETTES *Makes about 40 croquettes*

Peanut confections are very popular in South America, especially in Brazil and the Andean countries. In northern Brazil, these sweets are shaped like the cashew fruit, which looks like an apple. For the stem, they use half a peanut.

> 1 pound skinned peanuts, toasted (page 413), cooled, and finely ground
> 1 cup granulated sugar
> 1 large egg yolk
> 2 teaspoons unsalted butter
> ¼ cup milk
> Pinch of salt
> Coarse sugar for coating

1. In a large, heavy saucepan, combine all the ingredients except the coarse sugar. Cook over medium heat, stirring constantly, until the mixture pulls away from the side of the pan, about 10 minutes.

2. Transfer to a buttered plate and let cool. Shape into 1-inch balls and roll in the coarse sugar. Place in paper cups and store in cookie tins in the refrigerator for up to 1 week or in the freezer for up to 3 months.

Olhos de Sogra

MOTHER-IN-LAW'S EYES *Makes about 40 sweets*

This is one of the many Brazilian sweets with clever names. In a way, they do resemble an eye, but nobody can explain why the African women who ran the kitchens in the "Big Houses" of the plantations gave this name to the confection. It is a wonderful sweet, especially for coconut lovers.

> 1 cup grated fresh or frozen unsweetened coconut
> 1 cup granulated sugar
> 2 large egg yolks
> 1 tablespoon unsalted butter
> ¼ cup milk
> Pinch of salt
> One 12-ounce package bite-size pitted prunes
> Coarse sugar for coating
> Cloves

1. In a heavy 2-quart saucepan, combine the coconut, granulated sugar, egg yolks, butter, milk, and salt. Cook over medium-low heat, stirring constantly, until the mixture starts pulling away from the side of pan, about 10 minutes. Be careful not to overcook, or when it cools, it will crystallize.

2. Transfer to a buttered plate and let cool. Cut a lengthwise slit in one side of a prune. Fill the cavity with about 1 heaping teaspoon of the coconut mixture, shaping the prune so that it looks like an eye. Roll the prune in the coarse sugar and place in a paper cup. Press a clove into the middle of the mixture; this is the pupil of the eye. Repeat with the remaining ingredients. These sweets will stay fresh longer if stored in a candy tin in the freezer. Remove from the freezer 30 minutes before serving.

Pasas Ciruelas con Trufa de Dulce de Leche

PRUNES STUFFED WITH DULCE DE LECHE TRUFFLE *Makes about 40 sweets*

Stuffed prunes or figs are common throughout South America. Colombia has the famous sweets *brevas con arequipe*, figs poached in syrup and stuffed with *dulce de leche*. Argentina has a variety of confections made with figs stuffed with chocolate, raisins, or dried fruits. Because Latin Americans love *dulce de leche* in any shape or form, I have created this fabulous sweet that will certainly please not only Latins but anyone who likes chocolate truffles. *Dulce de leche* is easily made with sweetened condensed milk, or it can be purchased in Latin American markets. The Colombian name for *dulce de leche* is *arequipe*.

- 4 ounces *dulce de leche* or *arequipe*, store-bought or homemade (page 390; see Note)
- 4 ounces good-quality white chocolate, finely chopped
- 2 tablespoons unsalted butter
- 1 tablespoon brandy or dark rum
- One 12-ounce package bite-size pitted prunes
- 1 cup finely chopped walnuts

1. Place the *dulce de leche*, white chocolate, butter, and brandy in the top of a double boiler set over hot water (the water should never touch the top section of the double boiler). Stir until smooth. Transfer to an 8-inch square Pyrex baking dish, spreading it evenly in the dish. Cover with plastic wrap and refrigerate for a couple of hours, until firm.

2. With your thumbs, shape each prune into a cup. Place the prune cups on baking sheets lined with waxed paper. Place the walnuts in a small bowl. With a teaspoon, take about ½ teaspoon of the *dulce de leche* mixture, dip it into the walnuts, roll it into a ball, and then press the ball into a prune cup. Repeat until all the *dulce de leche* mixture, walnuts, and prunes are used. Cover with waxed paper and refrigerate for a couple of hours, until set. Place the sweets in paper cups and store in cookie tins. They will keep in the refrigerator for a few days or in the freezer for a couple of months.

NOTE It is imperative to follow the exact recipe for the *dulce de leche* mixture. The texture and quality of the *dulce de leche* is very important. As a rule, good-quality *dulce de leche* from Argentina or Uruguay or *arequipe* from Colombia is best for this recipe. (San Ignacio *dulce de leche* is firmer than most brands and works well here. It is available in some Argentine markets.) If you are not familiar with *dulce de leche*, the only way to find out whether a particular type will work here is by trial and error. If the chilled mixture is too soft to roll into balls, just return it to the double boiler and melt with 1 more ounce of chocolate. Never let the mixture get hot.

VARIATION For a sinfully delicious truffle, marinate the prunes in ½ cup brandy or rum for about 2 hours, turning them once. Drain well and dry with paper towels before shaping them into cups.

Oritos con Salsa de Caramelo y Maracuyá

NIÑO BANANAS WITH CARAMEL AND PASSION FRUIT SAUCE *Serves 4*

This is a delicious way to serve bananas in any shape or color. They can be baked or sautéed, served warm or at room temperature. Use orange juice or a mixture of passion fruit pulp and orange juice. For flambéing, use rum, brandy, or orange liqueur, or serve plain, with a scoop of vanilla ice cream on the side.

¼ cup sugar

1 tablespoon water

8 *niño* bananas or 4 small bananas

2 tablespoons unsalted butter

¼ cup thawed frozen passion fruit pulp

¼ cup fresh tangerine or orange juice

¼ cup orange liqueur or rum (optional)

Grated fresh or frozen unsweetened coconut, lightly toasted (page 413), or crumbled *amaretti*

Vanilla ice cream for serving

1. In a heavy skillet large enough to hold the bananas, heat the sugar and water over low heat and cook, stirring constantly, until the sugar is completely dissolved. Continue to cook until the syrup turns a light caramel color.

2. Place the bananas in the syrup, then add the butter, passion fruit pulp, and tangerine juice. Cover and cook until the bananas are soft, 4 to 5 minutes, turning them after 2 minutes. The recipe can be prepared up to this point a couple of hours ahead. Cover and set aside at room temperature.

3. To serve, reheat the bananas over low heat, if necessary. If flambéing, add the orange liqueur, let heat, and light with a long match, keeping long hair and dangling sleeves away from the open flame. Let burn for a few seconds, then cover the pan to put out the fire. Remove from the heat.

4. Carefully place 2 *niño* bananas or 1 small banana on each plate. Pour on some of the sauce, sprinkle with the coconut, and serve with a scoop of ice cream on the side.

Ensalada de Frutas Tropicales

TROPICAL FRUIT SALAD *Serves 8*

This fruit salad was a favorite of my family. We had it once a week for dessert and never got tired of it. The chopping takes a little longer than for most salads (cut all the fruit into about ⅜-inch dice), but it is well worth the time, because you get to taste all the fruits at once in each mouthful. I had a wonderful and expensive variation of this salad at the restaurant Chez Panisse in Berkeley, California. The dessert was called Tropical Soup and was basically the same salad served in a soup plate with a lot more juice (passion fruit and tangerine) than my recipe calls for. Passion fruit is very acidic and should never be used alone; always dilute it with water or orange, tangerine, peach, or mango juice.

1½ cups hulled and diced strawberries

Sugar

1 cup peeled and diced pineapple

1½ cups peeled, seeded, and diced papaya or mango

3 kiwifruit, peeled and diced

1 ripe but firm banana, peeled and diced

1 seedless orange, peeled and diced

¾ cup fresh orange juice

⅓ cup dry or sweet white wine

A few drops of pure vanilla extract

1. In a small bowl, toss the strawberries with sugar to taste.

2. In a large bowl, mix together all the fruits.

3. In a small bowl, mix together the orange juice, wine, vanilla, and sugar to taste. Pour over the fruits, mix well with a wooden spoon, and transfer to a nonreactive container. Cover and refrigerate until needed. This salad should be made only a few hours before serving. Serve chilled.

Chirimoya Alegre

CHERIMOYA MARINATED IN ORANGE JUICE
Serves 4

I have never seen cherimoyas more beautiful or larger than the ones I found in Chile. Large bowls of perfectly green and blemish-free cherimoyas can be found in every Chilean home when this delightful fruit is in season. At that time, *chirimoya alegre* is usually served for breakfast or dessert every day. It is so delicious and refreshing that I can never get enough of it. Fortunately, small cherimoyas can now be found in U.S. supermarkets. When ripe, cherimoyas, like avocados, should be firm but yield a little to the touch. If they're too soft, they'll be mushy and brown inside.

2 ripe but firm cherimoyas (at least
  1½ pounds)

Juice of 1 lemon

½ cup fresh orange or tangerine juice

Sugar (optional)

2 tablespoons rum (optional)

Cut the cherimoyas in half. Using a teaspoon, scrape the flesh into a medium-size mixing bowl. With a small knife, cut the flesh into small pieces, removing the seeds. Sprinkle with the lemon juice and toss well. Mix with the orange juice and taste to see if sugar is needed. (Chileans love very sweet desserts and usually sweeten cherimoyas with sugar syrup.) Toss with the rum, if using, refrigerate until well chilled, and serve in stemmed glasses.

Dulce de Cabello de Angel

SPAGHETTI SQUASH PRESERVES *Makes about 2 cups*

Dulces, or preserves, show up on the Latin table at least once a week, and the sweeter the better. This *dulce* is one of the oldest South American sweets. It is made from the most common of all indigenous squash, which goes by different names in different countries. In Ecuador it is called *zambo*, in Colombia *calabaza* and *vitoria*, in Bolivia *lacayote*, in Chile *alcayota*, and in Argentina *cayote*. This squash is very similar to the spaghetti squash found in U.S. markets. It grows in all types of climates in such abundance that, like quinoa, it was once looked down on as "Indian food."

Years ago, in the countryside, where bread ovens were available, the big, ripe squash was baked for several hours, then broken open, and the strands of flesh were removed to prepare sweets flavored with local fruit juices and spices. Chileans add chopped walnuts at the end of the cooking time, and Bolivians add almonds and raisins. This type of *dulce* is served as a dessert, plain or with wedges of brick cheese or a dollop of whipped cream. It is also used as a preserve, to serve for tea or for breakfast or to fill turnovers. Try it as an accompaniment for turkey or ham, or perhaps with Brie cheese.

One 2- to 2¼-pound spaghetti squash

1½ cups pineapple juice

1 cup sugar

1 cinnamon stick

5 allspice berries

1 tablespoon peeled and minced fresh ginger

1. Preheat the oven to 375°F.

2. Pierce the squash with a paring knife in a couple of places and place in a baking pan. Bake for 1 hour, turning it after 30 minutes. When done, it should yield to the touch. Let cool until easy to handle. Cut in half lengthwise, remove the seeds with a spoon, and discard. Pull out the strands of flesh with a spoon or fork.

3. Bring the pineapple juice, sugar, cinnamon, and allspice to a boil in a medium-size nonreactive saucepan, stirring until the sugar dissolves. Reduce the heat to medium-low and simmer for 5 minutes. Remove the cinnamon stick and allspice. Add the ginger and squash, mix well, and simmer, stirring occasionally, until the squash has absorbed most of the liquid, about 30 minutes.

4. Let cool and transfer to a glass jar. This will keep in the refrigerator for a couple of weeks or in the freezer for a couple of months.

Dulce de Guayaba

GUAVA PRESERVES *Makes about 3 cups*

I can't think of any other fruit whose aroma while cooking is more tantalizing than the guava's. The pink variety yields preserves with a beautiful reddish color, which is one of the most popular sweets throughout South America. *Dulce de guayaba* also has the distinction of being the national sweet of Paraguay, where its name in Guarani is *maheê arasá*. It is not known whether South American Indians made this type of preserves using honey or some other sweetener prior to the introduction of

sugar. Today it is made with either granulated sugar or *panela* (molded brown sugar). It is served as a dessert with slices of brick cheese and bread, or it is used as a filling for sweet empanadas and cakes.

2 pounds ripe guavas

1 cup water

2 cups sugar

1. Wash the guavas, then trim off the ends and any bruised spots. Cut in half and place cut side up in a heavy 4-quart saucepan along with the water. Bring to a boil over medium heat, cover, and simmer until softened a bit, about 10 minutes.

2. Using a slotted spoon, transfer to a food processor or blender. Let cool for 15 minutes, then process until smooth, adding a little of the cooking water if the puree is too thick. Pass through a coarse-mesh sieve.

3. Rinse the saucepan, add the puree and sugar, and cook over low heat, uncovered and stirring occasionally, until the bottom of the saucepan can be seen when a wooden spoon is drawn through the mixture, about 20 minutes. Transfer to a glass bowl and let cool. Serve at room temperature. These preserves will keep, covered, in the refrigerator for up to 2 weeks or in the freezer for up to 3 months.

Peras con Salsa de Dulce de Leche

PEARS WITH DULCE DE LECHE SAUCE *Serves 4*

I serve these pears when I need a light dessert. The recipe can be prepared the day before and assembled just before serving.

1½ cups dry red wine

1½ cups water

¾ cup sugar

1 cinnamon stick

1 strip lemon zest

4 medium-size ripe but firm Anjou or Bartlett pears

1 cup *Salsa de Dulce de Leche* (page 401)

8 walnut or pecan halves

1. In a 4-quart enamel or stainless steel saucepan, bring the wine, water, sugar, cinnamon, and zest to a boil. Reduce the heat to medium-low and simmer for 5 minutes.

2. Meanwhile, remove the stems from the pears, cut in half lengthwise, core, and peel. Add to the simmering liquid, cover, and simmer until tender but still firm, about 10 minutes. Using a slotted spoon, transfer to a platter. Remove all but 1 cup of the poaching liquid from the pan (see Note). Reduce what is left in the pan over medium heat to about ½ cup. Set aside.

3. Ladle ¼ cup of the *salsa de dulce de leche* onto each of 4 dessert plates. Place 2 pear halves on the sauce, with the stem ends touching in the center. Pour 1 to 2 teaspoons of the reduced syrup over each pear and top with a walnut half.

NOTE The leftover cooking liquid is similar to *Vino Caliente* (page 47), which is very popular in some South American countries. Let it cool, then refrigerate in a covered jar. Just reheat and enjoy on a cold winter night.

Dulce de Tomate de Arbol

TAMARILLO COMPOTE *Serves 8 to 12*

Tamarillos, also called tree tomatoes, grow in the highlands of South America. This tart, fragrant fruit can be eaten raw, right from the tree, or used in desserts such as this one from Ecuador, where tamarillos are abundant. Tamarillos also make delicious drinks, ice creams, mousses, and salsas, such as *Ají de Tomate de Árbol* (page 333).

12 ripe but firm yellow or red tamarillos

1 cup sugar

2 tablespoons water

1 cinnamon stick

½ teaspoon pure vanilla extract

1. Blanch the tamarillos in boiling water for 10 to 15 seconds. Rinse under cold running water, remove the stems, and peel off the skin. Cut each tamarillo in half. Remove the core and seeds and reserve both (see Note). Rinse the tamarillo halves.

2. Place the tamarillos, sugar, water, and cinnamon in a heavy 4-quart saucepan. Bring to a boil over low heat, shaking the pan often so the fruit doesn't stick to the bottom. Cover and simmer for 5 minutes.

3. Remove from the heat, discard the cinnamon stick, stir in the vanilla, and let cool. Transfer to a jar with a screw top. This will keep in the refrigerator for at least a couple of weeks.

NOTE The cores and seeds can be used to make a tasty juice. Put them in a blender and add the juice of 1 lemon, 3 to 4 cups water, and sugar to taste. Process for a few seconds, strain through a fine-mesh sieve, and refrigerate. Serve chilled.

Doce de Carambola

CARAMBOLA (STAR FRUIT) COMPOTE *Serves 4*

Carambolas are not indigenous to the Americas, but they are now cultivated in South America, especially in Brazil, so they will be showing up in more and more U.S. supermarkets. This is a lovely fruit often used as a garnish for ham, turkey, or chicken. When sliced crosswise, the slices look like stars.

8 large ripe carambolas (star fruit)

¾ cup sugar

1 cup water

Vanilla ice cream for serving (optional)

1. Wash and rinse the carambolas well. With a vegetable peeler, remove the dark fibers on the ridges and trim both ends. With a sharp knife, cut crosswise into ½-inch-thick slices, removing the seeds as they appear.

2. Layer the slices and sugar in a heavy 4-quart casserole. Add the water, cover, and cook over low heat, without stirring, until the fruit is soft, about 20 minutes. Let cool and serve with a scoop of vanilla ice cream, if desired.

Carnival

Carnival originated in Europe, where it has been celebrated since the Middle Ages. The word *carnival* comes from the Italian *carnevale*, which means "removal of meat." The term, as well as the event, is connected to Lent, when Catholics give up eating meat on Fridays. Carnival lasts anywhere from three days to a week and is the last chance to have fun before Lent, which is associated with penance, begins.

Carnival also became a tradition in South America, where it is celebrated in different ways. Perhaps the most spectacular and well known is the Carnival in Rio de Janeiro, as well as that in Bahia, Brazil. People prepare for it the whole year, sometimes spending thousands of dollars to make their costumes. In Uruguay and Barranquilla, Colombia, people start preparing for Carnival after Christmas. One year I happened to be in Barranquilla at Carnival time, and we went to watch the parade of the famous *comparsas* (masquerades with festive singing and dancing groups). We almost drowned in the sea of people. In Uruguay the whole country participates in the *comparsas*, with dancing, singing, drinking, and eating going on for hours.

In Bolivia, the big cities celebrate Carnival with weeklong festivals, but the most famous celebration in Bolivia is the one that takes place in the mining town of Oruro. There is a grand parade of bejeweled cars followed by dance groups, which ends in the local stadium. The stadium is the site of the Diablada, or dance of the devil. After that, the celebration continues for a week, with water fights, music, dancing, and, of course, eating and drinking.

Throughout South America, especially in the Andean countries, Carnival is an important festival that is celebrated with food specialties made just for this occasion, such as corn tamales in northern Argentina and *jucho* in Ecuador. A characteristic of Carnival in some of these countries is water balloon attacks. Children, and sometimes grownups, throw water balloons from their balconies or rooftops onto neighbors, friends, or passersby. It is a game, and most people don't seem to mind getting soaking wet.

Dulce de Frutillas

STRAWBERRY COMPOTE *Serves 4*

Whenever I go back home to Quito, I can count on finding a jar of strawberry compote in the refrigerator. Topped with *crème chantilly* (sweetened whipping cream beaten to soft peaks), it makes an elegant, delicious, easy-to-prepare dessert. This compote is also wonderful served over vanilla ice cream.

1 pound strawberries (see Note)

1¼ cups granulated sugar

1 small cinnamon stick

¼ teaspoon pure vanilla extract, plus a few drops for the cream

½ cup whipping cream

1 tablespoon confectioners' sugar

1. Quickly wash the strawberries under cold running water, hull them, and put in a heavy 4-quart saucepan. With a wooden spoon, toss the strawberries with the granulated sugar, then add the cinnamon. Bring to a boil over low heat, shaking the pan constantly to prevent sticking. Make sure the sugar has dissolved before the strawberries come to a boil. (The strawberries will release liquid as they cook.) Simmer for 2 to 3 minutes; the strawberries should look firm.

2. Remove from the heat and stir in the vanilla. Let cool, then transfer to a jar with a screw top. Refrigerate until needed, up to 2 weeks.

3. In a cold medium-size mixing bowl and using an electric mixer, beat the cream until soft peaks form. Add the confectioners' sugar and a few drops of vanilla.

4. To serve, divide the strawberries among 4 stemmed glasses and top with a dollop of whipped cream.

NOTE **Try to get medium-size strawberries and look for berries that are uniform in size.**

Come y Bebe

EAT AND DRINK

ECUADORIAN CUISINE IS RICH IN this unique category of dessert. These are traditional drinks prepared for specific holidays (such as Carnival) and are redolent with the mixture of native and European spices and fruits. Examples of this type of dessert drink include *champuz*, the Corpus Christi drink made with corn flour, spices, and local fruits such as *naranjilla* (page 427) and *chigualcán*, a fruit indigenous to Ecuador that belongs to the papaya family. There is also the more elaborate *rosero*, which is made with whole hominy instead of corn flour and, in addition to the above-mentioned fruits, also includes strawberries, pineapple, *babaco* (page 418), lemons, and a variety of flavorings, making it the epitome of creole cuisine. *Colada morada*, the ritualistic drink of the Day of the Dead, combines berries and pineapple with blue corn. The origin of these drinks can be traced back to a simple *colada* (soup) prepared by the Quechua that contains corn flour, *panela*, and *capulí* cherries. I have found these drinks, which combine grains and fruits with a light syrup, only in Chile, Colombia, and Ecuador.

Jucho/Cucho

FRUIT AND BARLEY DRINK *Serves 8 to 10*

This version of *jucho* uses sugar, while others use *miel de panela* (brown sugar syrup). Different types of fruit may be used in this beverage, depending on what the cook has available. This drink combines Old World spices introduced into Spain and Portugal by the Arabs, who long controlled these countries, and New World spices, such as allspice, native to the West Indies and Central America, and *ishpingo*, the flower of a cinnamon tree indigenous to Ecuador. *Ishpingo* is sometimes available dried in Ecuadorian groceries, as are dried orange leaves, which can also be found in Mexican markets. Fresh orange leaves sometimes can be found in floral shops, but make sure they haven't been treated with anything.

- 8 cups water
- 1¼ cups sugar
- 2 cinnamon sticks
- 6 cloves
- 4 allspice berries
- 1 *ishpingo* (page 424; optional)
- 2 fresh or dried orange leaves
- 1 stalk lemongrass
- ½ cup barley, rinsed under cold running water until the water runs clear
- 1 small Granny Smith apple, peeled, cored, quartered, and thinly sliced
- 2 large ripe but firm Anjou or Bartlett pears, peeled, cored, and cut into bite-size pieces
- 1 small quince, peeled, cored, and cut into ½-inch cubes
- 2 cups sweet cherries
- 2 large ripe but firm peaches, peeled, pitted, and cut into bite-size pieces

1. In a 4-quart nonreactive saucepan, combine the water, sugar, cinnamon, cloves, allspice, and *ishpingo* (if using). Bring to a boil, reduce the heat to medium-low, and simmer, uncovered, for 15 minutes.

2. Remove from the heat and add the orange leaves and lemongrass. Cover and let stand for 10 minutes. Strain and return the liquid to the saucepan. Add the barley and cook over low heat until the barley is almost tender, about 30 minutes.

3. Add the apple, pears, and quince and simmer until soft, about 10 minutes. Add the cherries and peaches and simmer for 5 minutes more. Taste for sugar.

4. Let cool, then refrigerate. Serve chilled in glasses with spoons. Provide a dish for discarding the cherry pits.

Mote con Huesillos

WHEAT BERRIES WITH DRIED PEACH COMPOTE *Serves 8*

Mote con huesillos is as Chilean as the empanada. It can be found everywhere, alongside soft drinks and fruit juices. It is sold in tall glasses like iced tea, and it is indeed a very refreshing and tasty drink. *Mote con huesillos* can be served as a dessert or a snack.

- 8 dried whole peaches or 16 dried peach halves
- 8 cups water
- 1¼ cups sugar
- 1 cinnamon stick
- 2 strips lemon zest
- 2 strips orange zest
- 1 cup wheat berries, cooked (page 412)

1. Rinse the peaches thoroughly. In a large mixing bowl, combine 6 cups of the water and ½ cup of the sugar. Add the peaches and let soak overnight to enhance their flavor. (This secret was

shared by a man who sold me peaches in Viña del Mar, Chile.)

2. In a 4-quart saucepan, combine the remaining 2 cups water, remaining ¾ cup sugar, the cinnamon, and zests and bring to a boil over medium heat. Add the peaches and their soaking liquid, reduce the heat to low, and simmer until the peaches are soft, about 20 minutes if whole or 10 minutes if halves. Taste for sugar. Discard the cinnamon stick and zest. Let cool and refrigerate.

3. To serve, place 2 heaping tablespoons of wheat berries in each of 8 cocktail glasses. Add 2 peach halves or 1 whole peach and about ½ cup of the syrup. Serve with a teaspoon.

Mazamorra (Colada) Morada

PURPLE CORN AND BERRY SOUP *Serves 12 to 14*

This soup is part of a group of specialties that come under the heading of ritual foods. Its roots go back to the Incas, who would drink a purple liquid at a particular time of the year in some kind of ritual. Since the Indian solar calendar and many Christian holy days often coincided, eventually the rituals and specialties were combined and new creole traditions were born. One of them is the Day of the Dead, which is celebrated on November 2.

On this day, people commemorate the passing of loved ones. Urban people visit cemeteries, bringing flowers and candles to decorate the graves of the departed, but the Indians in the countryside have kept some of their ancient traditions. They believe that during this time of year, because they are spending time with the spirits of their departed loved ones, they should dress in their best clothes and take food to share with the deceased.

Bolivians prepare *tostada*, a drink made with toasted dried corn and barley. After the grains are cooked, they are flavored with spices and sweetened with caramel and honey. On the Day of the Dead, *tostada* is sent as a gift to friends, along with *chicha de maní* (a fermented drink made with peanuts) and little pastries. Bolivians also make bread dolls (page 350) that are beautifully decorated with tinted dough and represent those who have died.

The *mazamorra morada* or *colada morada* (purple soup) in Ecuador is a thick fruit soup traditionally made with blue corn (*maíz morado*) or blue corn flour; blueberries and blackberries; pineapple, *naranjilla*, or guava; and spices. The beautiful purple color is enhanced by the addition of a sprig of purple amaranth. According to some researchers, the soup signifies the animal blood the Incas offered to the gods. In pre-Hispanic times, this soup was probably made with blue corn flour and wild blueberries and flavored with *ishpingo* (the flower of a cinnamon tree), guava, or whatever fruits and flavorings were available. After the Spaniards arrived, the flour was "ripened" by placing it in lukewarm water with crushed *naranjillas* and *panela* and leaving it at room temperature for a couple of days to ferment. Then it was strained and ready to cook. The Peruvian version is thicker than the Ecuadorian, more like a pudding, and uses whole blue corn boiled with pineapple peel for flavor and to give it a deep blue color. This mixture is strained and cooked with sweet potato flour to thicken it, along with a variety of dried fruits that have been previously cooked.

Naranjilla pulp gives this soup a wonderful taste. It is available frozen in Latin American markets. But even without it, the *colada* is delicious. It can be served hot or cold, as a snack or a dessert.

6 cups water

1 cup firmly packed dark brown sugar

½ cup granulated sugar

1 *ishpingo* (page 424; optional), crumbled

4 cinnamon sticks

10 cloves

8 allspice berries

1 stalk lemongrass

2 fresh or dried orange leaves

1 sprig fresh lemon verbena

3 sprigs fresh myrtle (optional)

2 pints blueberries, picked over for stems

1 pint blackberries

1 cup thawed frozen naranjilla pulp
(optional)

2 cups peeled and diced (¼ inch) pineapple

½ cup blue corn flour

2 cups hulled and sliced strawberries

Peeled and finely chopped pineapple and
hulled and finely chopped strawberries for
garnish

1. In a 4-quart saucepan, combine 4 cups of the water, the brown sugar, granulated sugar, *ishpingo* (if using), cinnamon, cloves, and allspice and bring to a boil. Reduce the heat to medium-low and simmer, uncovered, until the cinnamon has given a brown color and distinct taste to the water, about 20 minutes. Add the lemongrass, orange leaves, lemon verbena, and myrtle. Remove from the heat, cover, and let stand for 10 minutes. Strain. It should have a very pronounced taste of the spices and herbs.

2. In another saucepan, combine the blueberries, blackberries, *naranjilla* pulp, and 1 cup of the water and bring to a boil. Reduce the heat to medium-low and simmer for 5 minutes. Remove from the heat and let cool for a few minutes. Puree in a food processor or blender, then strain through a fine-mesh sieve. Mix with the spiced water, add the diced pineapple, and bring back to a boil.

3. In a small mixing bowl, combine the blue corn flour and remaining 1 cup water. Strain through a medium-mesh sieve and pour into the saucepan in a stream, stirring all the time. Simmer over medium-low heat for 5 minutes. The consistency should be a little thicker than that of whipping cream. Add the 2 cups strawberries, bring back to a boil, and remove from the heat. Taste for sugar. Serve either hot or chilled in coffee cups, garnished with the chopped pineapple and chopped strawberries.

Helados

ICE CREAMS AND SHERBETS

THE ICE CREAM INDUSTRY IN South America was born with the introduction of ice in the nineteenth century. In the beginning, ice cream was sold mainly in small shops called *heladerías* in Spanish and *sorveterias* in Portuguese. A variety of ice creams were created, using milk, cream, chocolate, and exotic fruits such as passion fruit, banana passion fruit, *guanábana*, blackberries, and *naranjillas* (which became the favorite).

Before refrigeration, ice cream was made by placing a copper cauldron, called a *paila*, in a large container filled with ice and sprinkled with coarse salt. The ice was sold in large blocks, which had to be broken into small pieces. Once the cauldron was set in the ice, the juice mixture was added, and the long task of turning the cauldron manually began. This had to be done until the ice cream was set. This type of ice cream, called *helados de paila*, is considered superior to commercially produced ice cream and is still available in some small ice cream shops. People who go to resorts on weekends always stop at these establishments for a cone or dish. A couple of years ago, when I was visiting my family in Ecuador, we stopped at a convent on the outskirts of Quito. The nuns had a small ice cream shop where they sold *helados de paila*. They had all the cauldrons with different kinds of ice cream lined up. What a treat it was to order a cone with a couple of scoops of my favorite flavors.

Helados de Leche

VANILLA ICE CREAM *Makes about 1 quart*

Helados de leche is just as popular in South America as ice creams made with exotic tropical fruits. This is especially good when served in combination with fruit-based ice creams. For special dinner parties, serve three scoops of assorted ice creams and garnish with a fruit sauce (pages 399–400).

- 2 cups milk
- 1 cup sugar
- 1 vanilla bean, split lengthwise
- 1 tablespoon cornstarch mixed with 2 tablespoons cold water
- 1 cup whipping cream

1. In a heavy 4-quart saucepan, bring the milk, sugar, and vanilla bean to a boil, stirring until the sugar is dissolved. Reduce the heat to very low and let steep for 15 minutes. Stir in the cornstarch mixture and cook, stirring, until thickened. Add the cream, mix well, and strain through a fine-mesh sieve. Let cool, then refrigerate until thoroughly chilled.

2. Transfer to an ice cream maker and freeze according to the manufacturer's instructions. When done, transfer to a covered container and freeze until completely firm.

Helados de Dulce de Leche

DULCE DE LECHE ICE CREAM *Makes about 1 quart*

Chileans and Argentines are especially fond of desserts made with *dulce de leche*, so it is not surprising that *dulce de leche* ice cream is a favorite in these countries. I had the following version in Buenos Aires; the ice cream had a predominant flavor of burnt caramel, which made it different from most ice creams made with *dulce de leche*. Some French restaurants in the United States are beginning to offer *dulce de leche* ice cream, usually as a filling for *profiteroles*. Some mainstream ice cream makers also are offering it with great success.

- 1 cup *dulce de leche*, store-bought or homemade (page 390)
- 1 cup milk
- ¼ cup sugar
- 1 tablespoon water (optional)
- 1 cup whipping cream
- 1 teaspoon pure vanilla extract
- ½ cup coarsely chopped walnuts, toasted (page 413)

1. Combine the *dulce de leche* and milk in a 2-quart saucepan over low heat, stirring until the *dulce de leche* is completely melted.

2. Place the sugar in a 2-cup Pyrex measuring cup and cook in the microwave on high until it

becomes a dark caramel color, almost to the point of burnt caramel, about 4 minutes. Or place the sugar and water in a small skillet and slowly bring to a boil, stirring until the sugar is dissolved. Cook until the sugar is almost a burnt caramel, about 5 minutes.

3. Pour the caramel immediately into the *dulce de leche* mixture and stir until dissolved. Remove from the heat. Stir in the cream and vanilla and strain through a fine-mesh sieve. Let cool, then refrigerate until thoroughly chilled.

4. Transfer to an ice cream maker and freeze according to the manufacturer's instructions. When done, pour the walnuts through the holes in the cover and process until well mixed. Transfer to a covered container and freeze until completely firm.

Helpful Hints for Making Ice Cream

When making ice cream, there are a few things you need to keep in mind.

1. If the ingredients are chilled, the ice cream will freeze more quickly.
2. Any ice cream mixture that has been heated or cooked should be cooled and thoroughly chilled before processing.
3. If the ice cream doesn't freeze quickly (if it is soft after processing for 20 minutes), it needs more salt. If it freezes too quickly and turns lumpy, it has too much salt and not enough ice. The ice has to be tightly packed.
4. Nuts, fruit, or pieces of chocolate should be added at the end of processing the ice cream.
5. Brandy or liqueur should not be used for flavoring, because alcohol inhibits freezing.
6. Light corn syrup prevents the crystallization of ice cream.
7. Many cooks use eggs or cornstarch to enrich their ice cream. I like to taste the flavor of the fruit and to feel the rich, refreshing taste of the cream. I call for the minimum amount of either cornstarch or eggs in the recipes, mainly to show the technique.

To make ice cream without an ice cream machine, pour the mixture into ice cube trays and freeze until it begins to set. Transfer to a bowl and beat with an electric mixer until smooth. Transfer to a tightly covered container and freeze until hard.

Helados de Coco

COCONUT ICE CREAM *Makes about 1 quart*

Coconut ice cream is a favorite throughout South America, but it is especially popular in Brazil, where it is called *sorvete de côco*.

One 14-ounce can unsweetened coconut milk, well stirred, or one 14-ounce package frozen grated unsweetened coconut, thawed

1 cup milk

½ cup whipping cream

½ cup sugar

¼ cup light corn syrup

½ teaspoon pure coconut or vanilla extract

1 teaspoon grated lime zest

1.   In a blender, combine all the ingredients and process until well mixed.

2.   Transfer to an ice cream maker and freeze according to the manufacturer's instructions. Transfer to a covered container and freeze until completely firm.

Helados de Guanábana

GUANÁBANA ICE CREAM *Makes about 1½ quarts*

Guanábana, or soursop, makes one of the most delicious ice creams. Your guests will enjoy the unusual flavor of this fruit from the tropics of South America.

One 14-ounce package frozen *guanábana* pulp, thawed

2 tablespoons fresh lemon juice

1 cup milk

1 cup whipping cream

¾ cup sugar

⅓ cup light corn syrup

1.   Combine all the ingredients in a large mixing bowl with a whisk or process in a blender until well combined.

2.   Transfer to an ice cream maker and freeze according to the manufacturer's instructions. Transfer to a covered container and freeze until completely firm.

Helados de Mora

ANDEAN BLACKBERRY ICE CREAM
Makes about 2½ pints

The Andean blackberry, or *mora*, is different from the North American variety in flavor. Andean blackberries are used to make one of the most beloved ice creams in the Andean countries. *Mora* pulp is available frozen in some Latin American markets. Blackberry pulp can be used instead, although the flavor will be different.

One 14-ounce package frozen *mora* pulp, thawed

1 cup milk

1 cup whipping cream

1 cup sugar

⅓ cup light corn syrup

1.   Place all the ingredients in a blender and process for a few seconds until well mixed.

2.   Transfer to an ice cream maker and freeze according to the manufacturer's instructions. Transfer to a covered container and freeze until completely firm.

Helados de Tomate de Arbol

TAMARILLO ICE CREAM *Makes about 2½ pints*

Tamarillos make a delicious ice cream. Fresh tamarillos are available in most supermarkets during their season, which begins at the end of the summer. The frozen pulp is available in some Latin American markets and Mexican supermarkets.

8 large ripe but firm yellow or red tamarillos, or one 14-ounce package frozen tamarillo pulp, thawed

¼ cup water

⅔ cup sugar

⅓ cup light corn syrup

1 cup milk

1 cup whipping cream

1. If using fresh tamarillos, blanch in boiling water for 1 minute. Let cool, peel, and rinse to remove the bitter coating left from the skin. Place the fresh tamarillos or the tamarillo pulp in a blender or food processor with the water and process until smooth. Strain through a medium-mesh sieve and mix with the remaining ingredients. Taste for sugar.

2. Transfer to an ice cream maker and freeze according to the manufacturer's instructions. Transfer to a covered container and freeze until completely firm.

Sorvete de Abacate

AVOCADO ICE CREAM *Makes about 1 quart*

Most people are under the misconception that the avocado is a vegetable and used solely as such. In actuality, it is technically a fruit, and many countries, including Venezuela and Brazil, use it in drinks and desserts. For this ice cream, it is important to find top-quality avocados, without blemishes. Sometimes avocados have black fibers and brown spots in their flesh; if this is the case, try to remove them before pureeing. For optimum taste, the avocados should barely yield to the touch.

2 large ripe but firm Hass avocados, peeled and pitted

½ cup sugar

⅓ cup light corn syrup

¼ cup fresh lime juice

1 cup milk

½ cup whipping cream

2 tablespoons dark rum

½ teaspoon pure vanilla extract

Pinch of salt

1. Cut the avocados into 1-inch pieces. Place in a blender with the remaining ingredients and process until very smooth. Taste for sugar.

2. Transfer to an ice cream maker and freeze according to the manufacturer's instructions. Transfer to a covered container and freeze until completely firm.

Helados de Taxo/Curuba (o Maracuyá o Naranjilla)

BANANA PASSION FRUIT (OR PASSION FRUIT OR NARANJILLA) ICE CREAM *Makes about 2½ pints*

In my opinion, the most delicious fruits in South America are banana passion fruit, passion fruit, and *naranjilla*. The first two are members of the Passifloraceae family, and the third one, called *lulo* in Colombia and *naranjilla* in Ecuador, is a member of the Solanacaeae family. Passion fruit, which is also very popular in Brazil, is found in most U.S. supermarkets. The other two are available frozen, in pulp or whole fruit, in some Latin American markets. If using passion fruit or *naranjilla*, increase the amount of sugar to taste, because these fruits are more acidic than banana passion fruit.

One 14-ounce package frozen banana passion fruit pulp, thawed

¾ cup sugar

1 cup milk

1 cup whipping cream

⅓ cup light corn syrup

1. Place all the ingredients in a food processor or blender and process until well mixed. Taste for sugar.

2. Transfer to an ice cream maker and freeze according to the manufacturer's instructions. Transfer to a covered container and freeze until completely firm.

Sorbete o Helados de Mango

MANGO SHERBET OR ICE CREAM
Makes about 1 quart

If you like mangoes, you will love this recipe. The intensity of the mango flavor is enhanced by the addition of lime or lemon juice. Add the cream if you love smooth, rich flavors. Make sure you choose firm mangoes. If they are too soft, they will be difficult to peel and cut into pieces.

> **2 large ripe but firm mangoes, peeled, seeded, and chopped (about 2 cups)**
> ½ **cup sugar**
> ¼ **cup fresh lime or lemon juice**
> ¼ **cup light corn syrup**
> ½ **cup whipping cream (optional; see Note)**

1. Place the mangoes, sugar, and lime juice in a food processor and process until smooth. Strain through a medium-mesh sieve. In a large bowl, mix with the corn syrup and cream (if using). Taste for sugar.

2. Transfer to an ice cream maker and freeze according to the manufacturer's instructions. Transfer to a covered container and freeze until completely firm.

NOTE **For sherbet, do not use the cream.**

Sorbete de Chirimoya

CHERIMOYA SHERBET *Makes about 1½ pints*

Cherimoyas are not as widely available as other fruits in South America, but this is a nice change of pace when they are.

> **Two ripe but firm cherimoyas (about 2 pounds)**
> ¼ **cup fresh lime juice**
> ¾ **cup sugar**
> ¼ **cup light corn syrup**
> **1 cup water**

1. Cut the cherimoyas in half. Using a teaspoon, scrape the flesh into a medium-size bowl. Crush with a fork to loosen the seeds, then pick them out and discard.

2. In a blender or food processor, puree the cherimoya flesh, lime juice, sugar, and corn syrup. Stir in the water and taste for sugar.

3. Transfer to an ice cream maker and freeze according to the manufacturer's instructions. Transfer to a covered container and freeze until completely firm.

Sorbete de Tamarillo

TAMARILLO SHERBET *Makes about 1 pint*

This is found mostly in Ecuador and Colombia, where tamarillos grow abundantly. It is a delicious, fragrant sherbet.

> **8 large ripe but firm yellow or red tamarillos, or one 14-ounce package frozen tamarillo pulp, thawed**
> **1 cup water**
> ¾ **cup sugar**
> ¼ **cup light corn syrup**

1. If using fresh tamarillos, blanch in boiling water for 1 minute. Let cool, peel, and rinse to

remove the bitter coating left from the skin. Place the fresh tamarillos or the tamarillo pulp in a blender or food processor with the water and process until smooth. Strain through a medium-mesh sieve and mix with the remaining ingredients. Taste for sugar.

2. Transfer to an ice cream maker and freeze according to the manufacturer's instructions. Transfer to a covered container and freeze until completely firm.

Helados de Tamarillo y Yogurt

TAMARILLO FROZEN YOGURT *Makes about 2½ pints*

Frozen yogurt is becoming increasingly popular in South America. This recipe yields a creamy texture and a rich flavor.

8 large ripe but firm yellow or red tamarillos, or one 14-ounce package frozen tamarillo pulp, thawed

⅔ cup water

¾ cup sugar

⅓ cup light corn syrup

12 ounces plain yogurt

1. If using fresh tamarillos, blanch in boiling water for 1 minute. Let cool, peel, and rinse to remove the bitter coating left from the skin. Place the fresh tamarillos or the tamarillo pulp in a blender or food processor with the water and process until smooth. Strain through a medium-mesh sieve and mix with the remaining ingredients. Taste for sugar.

2. Transfer to an ice cream maker and freeze according to the manufacturer's instructions. Transfer to a covered container and freeze until completely firm.

Mousses, Budines, Flanes, y Cremas
MOUSSES, PUDDINGS, CUSTARDS, AND CREAMS

Dulce de Leche

CARAMELIZED MILK *Makes about 3 cups*

There are many stories as to the origin of this *invento criollo* (creole invention). One Argentine anecdote that seems not very plausible relates that an African cook simply forgot the sugared milk she was heating on the stove and later found the caramelized milk. It is more likely that the recipe was brought to South America by the Spaniards and Portuguese. Whatever its advent, the fact remains that it became the most popular and beloved sweet in Latin America. Known as *natillas* in Peru, it is usually made with goat's milk and *chancaca* (molded brown sugar), although sometimes cooks use cow's milk. In Chile, it goes by the name *manjar blanco*, in Colombia *arequipe*, and in Mexico *cajeta*. As in Peru, Mexicans make it with goat's milk. In every country, the ingredients are basically the same, but the proportion of milk to sugar may vary. Most Mexican markets in the United States carry *cajeta*, and, increasingly, U.S. supermarkets are carrying *dulce de leche* in the ethnic foods aisle. South American *dulce de leche* or *arequipe* can be found in many specialty shops and in Latin American markets.

When I was growing up in Quito, Ecuador, my favorite after-school snack was *dulce de leche* spread on a freshly baked roll. In Argentina, Uruguay, and Chile, *dulce de leche* is widely used to fill sponge cake rolls, tortes, pastries, crepes, and the famous *alfajores* (page 372). It is simple to make, but the classic method requires constant watching and stirring until the milk is caramelized. The most popular method of making *dulce de leche* for many years was to cook an unopened can of sweetened condensed milk in boiling water in a pressure cooker until caramelized. The problem with this method is the danger of the can exploding, which it often did. A safer method is to bake sweetened condensed milk according the directions given by one manufacturer in the variation below.

4 cups milk

1¼ cups sugar

1 vanilla bean or 1 teaspoon pure vanilla extract

¼ teaspoon baking soda

In a heavy 4-quart saucepan, mix together the milk, sugar, vanilla bean (if using), and baking soda and bring to a boil over medium heat. Reduce the heat to low and simmer, stirring occasionally with a wooden spoon to prevent sticking. As it begins to thicken, stir constantly and cook until caramel-colored and very thick; this will take about 1 hour. If using vanilla extract, add it at this point. Transfer to a jar and store in the refrigerator for up to a few weeks.

VARIATION: Here's how Borden, one manufacturer of sweetened condensed milk, suggests making *dulce de leche*. Pour one 14-ounce can sweetened condensed milk into a pie plate. Cover with aluminum foil, place in a shallow pan of hot water, and bake in a preheated 425°F oven until thick and caramel-colored, about 1 hour. Remove the foil and let cool. Refrigerate before using. Makes about 1 cup.

Crepas con Salsa de Dulce de Leche

CREPES WITH DULCE DE LECHE SAUCE *Serves 4*

Crepes with *dulce de leche* come assembled in different ways, depending on the imagination of the cook. Sometimes the crepes are stacked with *dulce de leche* between the layers and topped with chocolate sauce. Banana slices may be added between the layers. Sometimes the crepes are rolled, folded like an envelope, or, as in this version, folded with the sauce in between and then heated before serving. Whatever the method, they're absolutely delicious.

1 cup *dulce de leche*, store-bought or homemade (page 390)

1 cup whipping cream

2 tablespoons brandy or rum

8 *Crepas* (page 405)

½ cup chopped walnuts or pistachios

1. Place the *dulce de leche* and cream in a small saucepan over low heat. Cook, stirring, until perfectly smooth. Stir in the brandy.

2. Place 1 crepe brown side down on a plate. Spread 1 tablespoon of the sauce over half of it and sprinkle with 1 teaspoon of the walnuts. Fold in half, then fold in half again, and set aside. Repeat with the remaining crepes. The crepes can be assembled up to this point, covered, and refrigerated.

3. Preheat the oven to 350°F. Lightly butter a shallow baking pan.

4. Arrange the crepes in the prepared pan and cover with aluminum foil. Bake for 15 minutes. Meanwhile, heat the remaining sauce over low heat. When the crepes are ready, place 2 crepes on a dessert plate, top with a couple of spoonfuls of sauce, sprinkle with some of the remaining walnuts, and serve immediately.

Arroz con Leche

RICE PUDDING *Serves 6*

Rice pudding is one of the oldest and most popular desserts brought to South America by the Spaniards and Portuguese. Some old-timers used to teach their daughters that to catch a man, they should learn how to make a good *arroz con leche*. There are many versions of this dessert; this is the classic and simplest. Another popular version is similar but has a lot more sauce; the rice is practically swimming in sauce. Some cooks prefer to have a richer sauce and thicken it at the end with egg yolks. The raisins are optional.

> 4 cups whole milk
>
> Pinch of salt
>
> 2 strips lemon zest
>
> One 2-inch-long cinnamon stick
>
> ½ cup Valencia-style short-grain rice (see Note)
>
> ⅓ cup sugar
>
> ¼ cup seedless golden or black raisins (optional)
>
> 2 tablespoons unsalted butter, softened
>
> 1 tablespoons brandy
>
> ½ teaspoon pure vanilla extract
>
> Ground cinnamon for sprinkling

1. In a heavy 4-quart saucepan (preferably non-stick), bring the milk, salt, zest, and cinnamon stick to a boil. Add the rice, reduce the heat to low, and barely simmer, uncovered, for 1 hour, stirring frequently. Stir in the sugar and raisins (if using) and continue to cook, stirring often to prevent sticking, especially once the mixture has thickened, until creamy. The pudding should look very creamy when done.

2. Remove from the heat and discard the zest and cinnamon stick. Stir in the butter, brandy, and vanilla. Serve at room temperature or chilled, with a sprinkling of cinnamon.

NOTE Valencia-style rice is a short, fat grain. Most supermarkets carry it. Risotto rice (arborio rice) can be used instead.

Mungunzá/Canjica

HOMINY AND COCONUT PUDDING *Serves 6*

This very old Brazilian dessert traces its roots to the Tupi-Guaranis. These indigenous people once prepared a simple mush called *acanijic*, which was made with water and cracked dried corn. The name of this ancient mush is reflected in one of the names by which this dessert is currently known, *canjica*. This early concoction is similar to the Colombian and Argentine *mazamorra*, which, under different names, was the basis of the Andean peoples' diets.

In northern Brazil, this pudding is called *mungunzá*, and it is made with cracked dried corn and coconut milk, or a combination of cow's milk and coconut milk. In São Paulo and Minas Gerais, it goes by the name *canjica* and is usually made with cow's milk only, very much like a rice pudding. In some parts of Brazil, it is called *chá-de-burro* (mule's meal). This pudding can also be made with green, or fresh, corn instead of dried corn. When that happens, it is called *canjiquinha de milho verde*. Sometimes crushed peanuts are added. The thickening agent varies with the cook; some use rice flour, others tapioca. The texture can be creamy, like rice pudding, or solid enough to cut into squares, depending on how much thickener is used. Of course, all versions are extremely sweet. I prefer to put very little sugar in the pudding and leave it to the individual to add as much granulated sugar or brown sugar as desired. *Mungunzá* is always prepared for Lent, especially for Good Friday.

This version of *mungunzá* is an old family recipe handed down to the mother of my Brazilian friend Margarida Nogueira, who came from northeastern Brazil. Her recipe uses coconut milk and coconut. Here the coconut is optional. The cracked dried corn can be found in South American groceries under the name *maíz pisado* or *maíz quebrado*. The dish can also be prepared using canned hominy (see Note), which is quicker, though not as traditional, because the hominy is prepared with the whole kernel.

> 1 cup cracked dried white corn (*maíz pisado* or *maíz quebrado*)
>
> 12 cups water
>
> ⅓ cup sugar, plus more for serving (optional)
>
> 1¼ cups well-stirred canned unsweetened coconut milk
>
> 1 cup grated fresh or frozen unsweetened coconut (optional)
>
> 1 teaspoon rose water (optional)
>
> Ground cinnamon for sprinkling
>
> Dark brown sugar for serving (optional)

1. Rinse the corn thoroughly, place in a large bowl, and soak overnight in 6 cups of the water.

2. Drain, put in a heavy casserole (preferably nonstick), and add the remaining 6 cups water. Bring to a boil, reduce the heat to very low, cover, and simmer until the corn is soft and most of the water has been absorbed, about 1 hour. When it begins to thicken, stir often so it doesn't stick to the bottom; this also helps thicken the sauce, making it unnecessary to add a thickening agent at the end.

3. Add the sugar, coconut milk, and grated coconut (if using) and simmer for 15 minutes. The pudding should be very creamy, not dry. Stir in the rose water, if using.

4. Serve warm or cold, sprinkled with the cinnamon. Serve granulated or brown sugar on the side for your guests to add.

NOTE If using hominy, drain two 15-ounce cans white hominy. Put in a casserole, add the sugar and coconut milk, and proceed as directed above.

Pudim de Pão com Côco

COCONUT BREAD PUDDING *Serve 8 to 10*

This classic Brazilian dessert of Portuguese origin shows the African influence with the addition of coconut milk and grated coconut. Brazilians either pass the soaked bread through a sieve or puree it in a blender. The result is a dessert that looks more like a flan than a traditional bread pudding. Some cooks prefer to bake the pudding without the caramel and serve it with caramel sauce. Either way, it is delicious.

> One 8-cup mold coated with caramel (page 415)
>
> 6 slices bakery-quality white bread, crusts trimmed
>
> 2 cups milk
>
> ¼ cup (½ stick) unsalted butter, melted
>
> 6 large eggs, separated
>
> ¾ cup sugar
>
> ¾ cup well-stirred canned unsweetened coconut milk
>
> 2 tablespoons dark rum
>
> 1 cup grated fresh or frozen unsweetened coconut
>
> Pinch of salt

1. Preheat the oven to 375°F. Set the mold aside.

2. Soak the bread in the milk for 30 minutes. Transfer to a blender, add the butter, egg yolks, sugar, coconut milk, and rum and process until smooth. Add the coconut and pulse until blended. Transfer to a large mixing bowl.

3. In another large mixing bowl, beat the egg whites and salt with an electric mixer until stiff, glossy peaks form. Carefully fold into the coconut mixture. Turn into the prepared mold, place in a roasting pan, and add enough hot water to come 2 inches up the side of the mold. Bake until a toothpick inserted in the center comes out clean, about 50 minutes.

4. Remove from the water bath and let cool before unmolding. Loosen the edge of the pudding, place a serving platter on top, and turn over. Cut into wedges and serve at room temperature or chilled.

Esponjosa

EGG WHITE FLAN *Serves 8 to 10*

This very elegant dessert comes from Venezuela. The classic way to serve it is with English custard (a pourable custard sauce that can be made from scratch or using a powdered mix, such as Bird's, often found in the ethnic foods aisle of the supermarket). The best *esponjosa* I ever had was made by a friend who lived in Venezuela for many years. She served it with raspberry sauce and English custard. It was not only delicious but also beautiful, with the white background of the flan and the intermingling of the bright colors of caramel, custard, and berries. A passion fruit or tamarillo sauce is a good alternative to the English custard. I have simplified this dessert by using only raspberry sauce and a mélange of fresh fruits.

> One 8-cup mold coated with caramel (page 415)
>
> 6 large egg whites, at room temperature
>
> Pinch of salt
>
> 1¾ cups superfine sugar
>
> 1 teaspoon fresh lemon juice
>
> 1 recipe *Salsa de Frambuesas* (page 400)
>
> Assorted fruits (such as berries, kiwifruit, mangoes, papayas, and peaches, hulled, peeled, seeded, or pitted and diced, as necessary; see Note)

1. Preheat the oven to 250°F. Set the mold aside.

2. In a large mixing bowl with an electric mixer, beat the egg whites and salt at low speed until foamy. Increase the speed to high and beat until soft peaks form. Beat in 1¼ cups of the superfine sugar, 1 tablespoon at a time, beating constantly. Continue to beat for 8 minutes more.

3. Combine the remaining ½ cup superfine sugar and the lemon juice in a 2-cup Pyrex measuring cup and cook in the microwave on high until golden brown, about 2 minutes. Stir until thickened. (Or combine the sugar and lemon juice in a small saucepan over medium heat and cook, stirring, until golden brown.) Gradually add to the egg whites, beating all the time at low speed for 5 minutes more.

4. Transfer the egg white mixture to the prepared mold and place in a roasting pan half-filled with hot water. Bake until the meringue seems firm when gently shaken, about 1 hour. It should rise a little above the mold.

5. Remove the mold from the hot water bath and place on a wire rack to cool. When cool, refrigerate for least 6 hours or overnight.

6. To unmold, place the mold in a bowl of hot water for 1 minute, run a thin knife around the edge of the meringue, and unmold onto a serving platter. Pour some of the *salsa de frambuesas* around the edge and scatter the fruits on top of the *salsa*.

NOTE **Choose a selection of colorful fruits. For example, blueberries and raspberries always look good together on a plate.**

Flan Clásico

CLASSIC FLAN *Serves 8*

Like paella and gazpacho, flan originated in Spain, but it was overwhelmingly adopted by Latin Americans and is now part of the standard dessert repertoire in all South American countries. South Americans quickly took advantage of indigenous ingredients, incorporating pineapples, mangoes, chocolate, coconut, calabaza, corn, and other fruits and vegetables into the basic recipe. Among the favorites is a flan made with sweetened condensed milk and orange juice. For me, that version is a little too heavy and sweet. The recipe here is a superb flan that started with my mother's recipe and ended with some refinement from the restaurant O'Xeito in Madrid. Chef Ramón was gracious enough to share with me his secret—steeping a vanilla bean, cinnamon stick, and orange and lemon zest in the milk, then adding a shot of cognac or brandy afterward. He sometimes adds a scoop of ice cream to further enrich the flavor of the flan.

> **One 8-cup mold coated with caramel (page 415)**
>
> **4 cups milk**
>
> **1 vanilla bean or 1½ teaspoons pure vanilla extract**
>
> **2 strips orange zest**
>
> **2 strips lemon zest**
>
> **One 2-inch-long cinnamon stick**
>
> **5 large eggs**
>
> **5 large egg yolks**
>
> **¾ cup sugar**
>
> **2 tablespoons cognac or brandy**

1. Preheat the oven to 325°F. Set the mold aside.

2. In a medium-size, heavy saucepan, bring the milk to a simmer. Add the vanilla bean (if using), zests, and cinnamon. Let steep for 20 minutes at a temperature below a simmer.

3. In a large mixing bowl, beat together the eggs, egg yolks, and sugar until well mixed. Add the hot milk in a stream, beating all the time with a wire whisk. Add the cognac and vanilla extract (if using). Remove any froth that forms on the surface.

4. Strain the mixture through a medium-mesh sieve into the prepared mold. Set the mold in a roasting pan half-filled with hot water and lay a piece of aluminum foil over the top. Bake in the lower third of the oven until a knife inserted in the center comes out clean, about 45 minutes.

5. To serve warm, let the custard settle for 30 minutes, then run a knife around the edge of the custard and turn out onto a serving platter. Cut into pieces.

To serve cold, let cool to room temperature, then refrigerate for at least 6 hours or overnight. To unmold, place the mold in a bowl of hot water for 1 minute and proceed as directed above.

Flan de Chocolate

CHOCOLATE CUSTARD *Serves 8*

This dessert combines two favorite indigenous American ingredients—chocolate and vanilla—with some Old World contributions.

> **One 8-cup mold coated with caramel (page 415)**
>
> **4 cups whole milk**
>
> **¼ cup Dutch-processed unsweetened cocoa powder**
>
> **1 tablespoon instant espresso granules**
>
> **1 cinnamon stick**
>
> **2 strips orange zest**
>
> **1 ounce unsweetened chocolate, finely chopped**
>
> **8 large eggs**
>
> **¾ cup sugar**
>
> **2 tablespoons coffee liqueur**
>
> **2 teaspoons pure vanilla extract**

1. Preheat the oven to 325°F. Set the mold aside.

2. In a heavy 4-quart saucepan, bring the milk, cocoa, espresso, cinnamon, and zest to a simmer, beating with a wire whisk until the cocoa has been incorporated. Remove from the heat, add the chocolate, and stir until melted. Let stand for 5 minutes.

3. In a large mixing bowl with a wire whisk, beat the eggs, sugar, coffee liqueur, and vanilla until well mixed. Pour the hot milk into the mixture in a stream, beating constantly. Remove the froth that forms on the surface.

4. Strain the mixture through a medium-mesh sieve into the prepared mold. Set the mold in a roasting pan half-filled with hot water and lay a piece of aluminum foil over the top. Bake on the center oven rack until a knife inserted in the center comes out clean, about 45 minutes.

5. To serve warm, let the custard settle for 30 minutes, then run a knife around the edge of the custard and turn out onto a serving platter. Cut into pieces.

To serve cold, let cool to room temperature, then refrigerate for a few hours. To unmold, set the mold in a bowl of hot water for 1 minute and proceed as directed above.

Crema de Aguacate con Jengibre

AVOCADO CREAM WITH GINGER *Serves 6 to 8*

Most people don't associate avocado with desserts. Venezuelans and Brazilians prepare not only *crema de aguacate* (called *creme de abacate* in Brazil) but also avocado ice cream. Rum and port wine are favorite flavorings. Another version of this cream uses only lime juice, sugar, and rum—no milk or whipping cream.

>   3 ripe but firm Hass avocados
>   ½ cup confectioners' sugar
>   2 tablespoons fresh lemon juice
>   ¼ cup dark rum
>   1 cup whipping cream, whipped to stiff peaks
>   4 pieces crystallized ginger (see Note), finely chopped

1. Peel and pit the avocados. In a medium-size mixing bowl, mash the avocados, then mix in the confectioners' sugar, lemon juice, and rum. Fold in half of the whipped cream.

2. Divide the mixture evenly between 6 to 8 stemmed glasses, cover with Saran wrap, and refrigerate.

3. To serve, top with a dollop of whipped cream and sprinkle with the crystallized ginger.

NOTE **Crystallized ginger is available in many grocery stores, specialty stores, and spice shops.**

Creme de Mamão com Cassis

PAPAYA CREAM WITH CASSIS *Serves 4*

The first time I tasted this splendid dessert was in Florianópolis, a beautiful resort in southern Brazil. I was thrilled to find out how easy it is to make it. A perfect dessert for the busy hostess, it will be a hit even with people who don't care for papaya. Sometimes I make it with mango, which results in a stronger-flavored dessert. Get the best brand of vanilla ice cream, chop the fruit ahead of time, cover with Saran wrap, and, just before serving, blend the ingredients in a blender or food processor.

>   2 cups peeled, seeded, and chopped papaya
>   4 scoops vanilla ice cream
>   ¼ cup cassis

Put the papaya and ice cream in a blender or food processor and process until creamy. Divide the cream among 4 stemmed glasses and swirl about 1 tablespoon of cassis on top of each. Serve immediately.

Bananas con Mousse de Duraznos

BANANAS WITH PEACH MOUSSE *Serves 6*

Variations of this exquisite dessert are common throughout South America. It is sometimes made simply with bananas topped with a mixture of stiffly beaten egg whites, which are folded together with whipped cream. Any kind of fruit puree can be used.

> 4 ripe but firm bananas
>
> 2 tablespoons fresh lemon juice
>
> ¼ cup curaçao
>
> ½ cup finely chopped nuts (such as walnuts, Brazil nuts, hazelnuts, or pecans)
>
> 1 cup peeled, pitted, and sliced (¼ inch thick) ripe peaches
>
> ½ cup whipping cream, whipped to stiff peaks
>
> 2 large egg whites
>
> 3 tablespoons sugar
>
> Sliced peaches, tossed with fresh lemon juice, or chopped nuts for garnish

1. Peel the bananas and slice into ¼-inch-thick rounds. In a medium-size mixing bowl, toss the bananas with the lemon juice and curaçao. Transfer to a 6-cup glass dish. Top evenly with the nuts.

2. Place the 1 cup peaches in a blender or a food processor and process until smooth. Fold into the whipped cream. In a medium-size mixing bowl with an electric mixer, whip the egg whites until soft peaks form. Beat in the sugar 1 tablespoon at a time. Fold the peach mixture into the egg whites. Spread on top of the nuts and bananas. Cover with plastic wrap and refrigerate until needed. This is best if made only a couple of hours ahead.

3. To serve, divide the mixture between 6 stemmed glasses or dessert dishes. Spoon some of the liquid that collects on the bottom of the glass dish on top of each dessert. Garnish with sliced peaches or chopped nuts.

Mousse de Mango

MANGO MOUSSE *Serves 8*

This heavenly mousse will quickly become your favorite dessert. It is made throughout South America, whether mangoes are grown in the region or not. You can also make this with peaches, nectarines, or fresh apricots.

> 1 envelope unflavored gelatin
>
> ¼ cup fresh orange juice or water
>
> 2 large ripe but firm mangoes, peeled, seeded, and chopped (about 2 cups)
>
> ¾ cup granulated sugar
>
> 2 tablespoons rum or orange liqueur
>
> 1 cup whipping cream
>
> 2 large egg whites
>
> ¼ teaspoon cream of tartar
>
> 2 tablespoons confectioners' sugar
>
> 1 recipe *Salsa de Frambuesas* (page 400) or *Salsa de Maracuyá* (page 400)

1. In a small Pyrex bowl, sprinkle the gelatin over the orange juice and let soften for 5 minutes. Set the bowl in a small saucepan with 1 inch of simmering water and heat until the gelatin is completely dissolved.

2. Place the mangoes in a blender or food processor and process until smooth. Add the granulated sugar, rum, and dissolved gelatin and process again until smooth. Strain through a medium-mesh sieve.

3. In a medium-size mixing bowl with an electric mixer, whip the cream until soft peaks form. Fold into the mango mixture. Refrigerate until slightly thickened, about 30 minutes.

4. In a small mixing bowl, beat the egg whites with the cream of tartar until soft peaks form. While beating, add the confectioners' sugar 1 tablespoon at a time and beat until stiff peaks form. Fold into the chilled mango mixture.

5. Transfer to a glass serving bowl, cover with plastic wrap, and refrigerate for 6 hours or overnight. This mousse freezes very well for up to a couple of months; thaw in the refrigerator overnight.

6. To serve, scoop spoonfuls of the mousse into dessert glasses and top with the fruit *salsa*.

Paté de Curuba (Taxo)

BANANA PASSION FRUIT PÂTÉ *Serves 4*

The recipe for this unusual and perfectly delicious dessert was given to me by a dear Colombian friend, Margarita Patmore. She told me to serve it with poached prunes and their syrup. However, the flavor of banana passion fruit is so special that I do not want any other strong flavor to interfere with it. Instead, I serve with raspberry or blackberry sauce and garnished with additional berries. This way, I achieve a dramatic contrast of the salmon color of the *pâté* and the color of the berries.

> 1 envelope plus ⅓ teaspoon unflavored gelatin
>
> 2 tablespoons water
>
> 1 cup thawed frozen banana passion fruit pulp
>
> ½ cup sugar
>
> 1 cup whipping cream
>
> 1 recipe *Salsa de Moras* (page 400)
>
> ½ pint raspberries for garnish

1. In a small Pyrex cup, sprinkle the gelatin over the water and let soften for about 5 minutes. Place the cup in a small saucepan with 1 inch of simmering water and heat until the gelatin is completely dissolved.

2. In another small saucepan, combine the banana passion fruit pulp and sugar and bring to a boil. Cook, stirring occasionally, until the sugar is dissolved. Remove from the heat, add the gelatin mixture, and stir until well blended. Transfer to a blender, add the cream, and process until smooth, about 5 seconds. Taste for sugar.

3. Lightly oil four 6-ounce molds, then divide the cream among them. Let cool, cover with plastic wrap, and refrigerate until set, about 6 hours or overnight.

4. To unmold, dip each mold in a bowl of hot water for about 4 seconds, then invert onto a dessert plate. Top with a couple of spoonfuls of the *salsa de moras* and garnish with the raspberries.

Paté de Mango y Maracuyá

MANGO AND PASSION FRUIT PÂTÉ *Serves 8*

This is one of the most delicious desserts made with mangoes. Summertime is when these heavenly fruits are at their peak, although fortunately mangoes are now available all year round. This type of dessert is popular throughout South America, with many variations. It can be made ahead and kept frozen for a couple of months. During mango season, I take advantage of their abundance and make a couple of *pâtés* to keep in the freezer. They come in handy when I am invited to a potluck dinner and need to have a superb dessert ready to go.

> 2 medium-size ripe but firm mangoes, peeled, seeded, and diced (about 2 cups)
>
> ½ cup thawed frozen passion fruit pulp (see Note)
>
> 1 envelope plus ¼ teaspoon unflavored gelatin
>
> 2 tablespoons water
>
> 1 cup whipping cream
>
> ½ cup sugar

4 ounces cream cheese, cubed

½ teaspoon pure vanilla extract

***Salsa de Frambuesas o Moras* (page 400)**

GARNISHES
Fresh berries
Peeled, seeded, and diced (¼ inch) mangoes
Fresh mint leaves

1. Place the mangoes and passion fruit pulp in a blender or food processor and process until smooth. Pass through a medium-mesh sieve and return to the blender or food processor.

2. In a small heatproof bowl or Pyrex cup, sprinkle the gelatin over the water and let soften for about 5 minutes. Place the bowl in a small saucepan with 1 inch of simmering water and heat until the gelatin is completely dissolved.

3. In a medium-size, heavy saucepan, heat the cream and sugar almost to the boiling point and remove from the heat. Add the gelatin mixture and stir until well incorporated. Add the cream cheese and stir until most of it has melted. Add the cream mixture and vanilla to the mango mixture and process until smooth. Taste for sugar. Pulse 3 or 4 times to deflate the mixture. Transfer to a 9 x 5-inch loaf pan or 8 individual molds sprayed lightly with vegetable cooking spray. Refrigerate until set, at least 6 hours or overnight. This dessert freezes very well for up to a couple of months. Thaw overnight in the refrigerator before serving.

4. To unmold, loosen the edge of the *pâté* with a paring knife. Dip the pan (or molds) into a bowl of hot water for 4 to 5 seconds, place a serving dish (or dessert plates) rinsed with cold water on top, and invert. Spoon some of the fruit *salsa* around the *pâté*. Scatter the berries and diced mango pieces on the sauce. Scatter the mint leaves on top of the *pâté*.

NOTE **If passion fruit pulp is not available, use fresh orange or tangerine juice instead.**

Salsas para Postres
SAUCES FOR DESSERTS

T HE FOLLOWING SAUCES ARE IDEAL for all molded desserts, poached fruits, egg white flans, or ice creams.

Salsa de Chocolate y Frambuesa

CHOCOLATE TRUFFLE SAUCE
WITH RASPBERRY LIQUEUR *Makes about 2½ cups*

Since a new wave of elegant, international foods is reaching South America, I thought it was fitting that I contribute this recipe that I developed. This absolutely delicious sauce has turned out to be a hit with everybody who has tried it. Pour it over poached pears, cream puffs, or ice cream. It's also delicious over bananas, strawberries, or kiwifruit. The wonderful thing is that it freezes very well and is ideal to take as a hostess gift.

1 cup whipping cream

1 ounce unsweetened chocolate, cut into small pieces

8 ounces good quality semi-sweet chocolate

1 teaspoon instant espresso granules

½ cup seedless raspberry jam

2 tablespoons raspberry liqueur

1 tablespoon cognac or brandy

1. In a 2-quart saucepan, bring the cream almost to a boil. Remove from the heat, add the chocolate and espresso, and stir until completely melted.

2. In a small saucepan, warm the raspberry jam over low heat and stir until smooth. Mix with the chocolate mixture, then stir in the raspberry liqueur until smooth. Let cool to lukewarm, then transfer to a jar with a tight-fitting lid.

3. This sauce will keep in the refrigerator for 2 weeks or in the freezer for 2 months. To reheat, place the jar in a saucepan of hot water until warmed through, or microwave on low until melted. Let cool to lukewarm before serving.

Salsa de Maracuyá

PASSION FRUIT SAUCE *Makes about 1½ cups*

This versatile sauce is easy to prepare and should be made just before serving.

> ¼ cup thawed frozen passion fruit pulp
> 2 tablespoons fresh orange juice
> 1 cup whipping cream
> ⅓ cup sugar

Put all the ingredients in a blender and process until smooth and thickened. Taste for sugar.

Salsa de Tomate de Arbol

TAMARILLO SAUCE *Makes about 1 cup*

Tamarillo sauce is excellent to serve with ice cream or, as in the southern provinces of Ecuador, with ham or pork.

> 4 large ripe but firm yellow or red tamarillos (see Note) or 1 cup thawed frozen tamarillo pulp
> ¼ cup sugar
> 1 teaspoon cornstarch mixed with 2 tablespoons cold water (optional)

1. If using fresh tamarillos, blanch in boiling water for 1 minute. Let cool, peel, and rinse to remove the bitter coating left from the skin. Place in a blender or food processor with the sugar and process until smooth. Strain through a medium-mesh sieve and transfer to a tightly covered jar.

If using frozen pulp, just mix with the sugar in a small saucepan and bring to a boil over medium heat. Stir in the cornstarch mixture and simmer for a couple of minutes. Let cool, then transfer to a tightly covered jar.

2. This sauce will keep in the refrigerator for a couple of days or in the freezer for a couple of months.

NOTE Yellow tamarillos will result in an orange sauce. Red tamarillos will produce a reddish sauce with a hint of purple.

Salsa de Frambuesas o Moras

RASPBERRY OR BLACKBERRY SAUCE *Makes about 1 cup*

This is my favorite sauce for mousses, fruit *pâtés*, and ice creams.

> ½ pint raspberries or blackberries, or a combination
> 2 tablespoons sugar
> Fresh orange juice, if needed
> 1 tablespoon orange, cherry, or raspberry liqueur

In a blender or food processor, process the berries and sugar until smooth. Strain through a fine-mesh sieve. If too thick, add a little orange juice. Stir in the liqueur. Transfer to a tightly covered jar and refrigerate for a couple of days or freeze for a couple of months.

Salsa de Dulce de Leche

DULCE DE LECHE SAUCE *Makes about 2 cups*

This is the ideal sauce for crepes and poached pears.

> 1 cup *dulce de leche*, store-bought or homemade (page 390)
>
> 1 cup whipping cream
>
> 2 tablespoons brandy or rum

In a small saucepan over medium heat, combine the *dulce de leche* and cream. Cook, stirring constantly, until smooth and completely heated through. Remove from the heat and stir in the brandy. Serve warm.

Dessert Syrup *Makes about 1/2 cup*

This syrup sometimes is used to brush on cake layers to enhance the flavor of tortes.

> ¼ cup water
>
> ¼ cup sugar
>
> 2 tablespoons rum

In a small saucepan, combine the water and sugar and bring to a boil over medium heat. Cook, stirring, until the sugar is dissolved. Remove from the heat and let cool. Stir in the rum and use immediately.

Básicos

BASICS

FOLLOWING ARE THE ESSENTIAL METHODS and guidelines that underlie many of the recipes in this book. From stocks and sauces to working with unfamiliar vegetables, this section is filled with useful information. As you go through the cookbook, you will often see references to items in this chapter. This is the foundation of *la cocina Latina*.

Consejos y Secretos de la Cocina Latina
ADVICE AND SECRETS FROM THE LATIN KITCHEN

It always amazed me how people without much education knew so many *secretos de la cocina* that even people who went to cooking schools didn't know. Not long ago, my friend Teresa Corcao told me her cook's secret for reheating black beans (see below). For a long time, such secrets were jealously guarded. Fortunately, more and more of them are becoming available, thanks to the increase in cookbook publishing. Here are some of the most useful secrets.

1. To enhance the flavor of foods, add a pinch of salt to sweets and a pinch of sugar to savory foods.
2. To remove the bitter taste of onions, slice or chop the onions, put them in a colander, and rinse them with lots of hot or cold water.
3. To avoid the bad smell of cauliflower when cooking, add 1 teaspoon salt and 1 teaspoon sugar to the cooking water, or put a slice of bread on top of the cauliflower. To keep the cauliflower white, add a little lemon juice to the cooking water.
4. Everything that grows underground should be cooked covered, and everything that grows above the ground should be cooked uncovered.
5. Some cooks believe that salt should always be added at the end of the cooking time.
6. Always cook potatoes in boiling salted water, covered.
7. To prevent a green plantain from getting black after peeling, rub with half a lemon, let stand for five minutes, rinse, and use. This removes the substance that can turn a dish containing plantains gray.
8. To remove the bitterness from tamarillos, peel and soak in cold water for five minutes, then rinse under running water.
9. A frying pan should be heated before adding butter or oil. This prevents the food from sticking to the pan.
10. Never cook quinoa with salt, because salt keeps the grains from bursting open.
11. To prevent avocados from turning brown after peeling, cover tightly with Saran wrap.
12. Never boil avocados, because they turn bitter.
13. When reheating black beans, add hot water. Adding cold water will cause the beans to lose their color and turn brownish.
14. To clean metal, mix equal amounts of salt and vinegar.
15. To remove wine stains, soak in salted water for 2 hours, then rinse and launder as usual.

Crepas

CREPES *Makes about eighteen 6-inch crepes*

These crepes can be used for savory or sweet dishes. They can be prepared ahead and frozen.

1¼ cups all-purpose flour

¼ teaspoon salt

4 large eggs

1½ cups milk

3 tablespoons clarified butter or canola oil, plus more for brushing

1. Place all the ingredients in a blender or food processor and process until smooth, scraping down the sides of the container with a rubber spatula after blending for a few seconds. Let rest for 30 minutes at room temperature.

2. Heat a 6-inch crepe pan over high heat until very hot (a drop of water should sizzle on the surface). Brush the pan with some of the clarified butter. Remove from the heat and ladle 2 tablespoons of batter into the center, quickly rotating/swirling the pan so that the batter runs out to the edge and coats the bottom thinly and evenly. Return to the heat and cook until the bottom is golden brown, about 30 seconds. With a metal spatula, flip the crepe over and cook for 10 seconds. After cooking a few crepes, you may need to brush the pan with more butter.

3. You can use the crepes immediately or let cool, wrap in plastic and then in aluminum foil, and either refrigerate for up to 2 days or freeze. If refrigerated, reheat wrapped in aluminum foil in a preheated 300°F oven for 10 minutes. If frozen, thaw overnight in the refrigerator, then reheat as described. Never use cold crepes in a recipe, because they have a tendency to break.

CREPAS CON ALBAHACA (Basil Crepes)
To the plain crepe batter, add 12 large fresh basil leaves, coarsely chopped. Pulse the blender until the leaves are finely chopped and well mixed into the batter. Proceed as directed above.

Salsa Blanca

MEDIUM WHITE SAUCE (BÉCHAMEL)
Makes about 2 cups

This is the most common sauce found throughout South America. The ingredients make it clear that it was a gift from Europe. This sauce is used more often in Chile, Argentina, and Uruguay than in the northern Andean countries.

2 tablespoons unsalted butter

3 tablespoons all-purpose flour

2 cups hot milk

¼ teaspoon salt

¼ teaspoon white pepper

Pinch of freshly grated nutmeg

Pinch of sugar

1. Melt the butter in a medium-size, heavy saucepan over low heat. Add the flour and cook, stirring constantly, until bubbling, about 2 minutes. Do not let it color. Remove from the heat and, using a whisk, beat in the milk until smooth. Return to the heat and add the salt, pepper, nutmeg, and sugar. Cook, stirring constantly, until the sauce comes to a boil and thickens. Reduce the heat to low and simmer for a couple of minutes.

2. Remove from the heat. Place a round of waxed paper on the surface of the sauce to prevent the formation of a skin. If not using immediately, let cool, then refrigerate until needed. The sauce can be prepared a couple of days ahead and refrigerated, or it may be frozen for up to 1 month. To use the sauce, reheat, adding milk 1 tablespoon at a time to get the desired consis-

tency. If the sauce is lumpy, strain through a fine-mesh sieve.

VARIATIONS To make a lighter sauce, use only 2 tablespoons flour or thin the finished sauce with additional milk.

To make *velouté* sauce, use chicken broth instead of milk.

Salsa de Tomate

TOMATO SAUCE *Makes about 2 cups*

Tomatoes were a gift of the Americas to the world, but they had to travel to Italy to return transformed into the wonderful and versatile sauces that we all enjoy today.

>   2 tablespoons olive oil
>
>   2 large cloves garlic, lightly crushed, or 1 small onion, chopped (about ½ cup)
>
>   2 pounds very ripe plum tomatoes, peeled and chopped, or one 28-ounce can Italian-style peeled plum tomatoes, chopped, with juices
>
>   ¼ teaspoon freshly ground black pepper
>
>   8 fresh basil leaves, torn into pieces, or 1 teaspoon dried basil
>
>   Pinch of red pepper flakes
>
>   ½ cup dry red or white wine (optional)
>
>   ½ teaspoon salt (optional)
>
>   ½ teaspoon sugar

1. Heat the oil in a large, heavy casserole over low heat. If using the garlic, cook until browned on both sides, pressing on it with a wooden spoon; discard. If using the onion, cook, stirring, until transparent, about 3 minutes. Add the tomatoes, black pepper, basil, red pepper, and wine (if using), and cook, uncovered and stirring occasionally, until the sauce thickens to the desired consistency, about 30 minutes. If the sauce begins to dry out before the tomatoes are cooked, add a little water. Add the salt (if using)

and sugar and simmer for a couple of minutes. (If using canned tomatoes, the sauce might not need additional salt.)

2. Pass through a food mill. If the sauce is too thin, return to the pan and simmer for a few minutes; if too thick, add a little water and simmer to heat through. Store in a tightly covered container for a couple of days in the refrigerator or a couple of months in the freezer.

Salsa de Choclo

FRESH CORN SAUCE *Makes about 2 cups*

This unassuming corn sauce is a delight to the taste buds and shows yet another way in which South Americans love corn. Fresh corn sauce is made in many South American countries. It is excellent on eggs, steamed broccoli, cauliflower, vegetable puddings, fish, poultry, and even meat. In Brazil, I had it served over steak. For a smoother consistency, put the sauce through a medium-mesh sieve. For a fancier sauce, add a pinch of saffron.

>   1 tablespoon unsalted butter
>
>   1 tablespoon minced scallions (white part only)
>
>   2 cups fresh or thawed frozen corn kernels
>
>   ¾ cup milk, or more if needed
>
>   ¼ teaspoon salt
>
>   Pinch of white pepper
>
>   Pinch of saffron threads (optional), crumbled
>
>   2 tablespoons whipping cream (optional)
>
>   Sweet paprika or minced fresh basil leaves for garnish

1. Melt the butter in a medium-size, heavy skillet over medium heat. Add the scallions and cook for a few seconds.

2. In a food processor or blender, process the corn with some of the milk until smooth. Add the rest of the milk and process for a few seconds.

Add the puree to the skillet along with the salt, pepper, and saffron (if using). Cook, stirring constantly, for a few minutes, adding more milk if needed to make a medium-thick sauce. Add the cream, if using. Stir for a few seconds, taste for salt and pepper, and remove from the heat. This sauce is usually served garnished with paprika or minced basil.

Pechugas de Pollo Hervidas

POACHED CHICKEN BREASTS
Makes about 4 cups chopped chicken

The best way to poach chicken breasts is with the skin on and bones in. Done this way, the meat is juicier and perfectly white. If you must use boneless breasts, cut the poaching time to 10 to 15 minutes, depending on their size. Always reserve the poaching liquid to be used in the recipe or as a base for soup.

- 2 whole bone-in chicken breasts (about 2 pounds), split
- 1 medium-size onion, peeled
- 1 medium-size carrot, peeled
- 1 celery stalk with leaves
- 1 bay leaf
- 4 cups chicken broth
- 2 cups water

1. Place all the ingredients in a 4-quart saucepan. The liquid should cover all the solids by 1 inch; add more water, if needed. Bring to a boil over medium heat, skimming off the froth as it rises to the surface. Reduce the heat to low, partially cover, and cook until the juices run clear when a breast is pierced with a fork, about 20 minutes. Remove from the heat but let the breasts stay in the broth for 30 minutes.

2. Remove the breasts from the broth. When cool enough to handle, remove the skin and bones and discard. Strain the broth and reserve for another use. Wrap the breasts in plastic and refrigerate until needed.

Lengua Hervida

BOILED TONGUE
Beef tongue serves 6; veal tongue serves 3 to 4

This is the basic procedure for any recipe that calls for cooked tongue, whether it is beef or veal tongue (see Note).

- 1 beef tongue (3 to 4 pounds)
- 1 medium-size onion, peeled
- 1 celery stalk with leaves
- 1 clove garlic, peeled
- 2 sprigs fresh parsley
- 1 bay leaf
- 1 teaspoon salt

1. Rinse the tongue thoroughly and place in a large casserole along with all the remaining ingredients and enough water to cover everything by 1 inch. Bring to a boil over medium heat, skimming off the froth as it rises to the surface. Reduce the heat to low, cover, and simmer until tender (a fork can be inserted into the thickest part), about 3 hours.

2. Transfer to a cutting board and let stand until just cool enough to handle—the skin will come off easily when hot or warm, but not when cold. Remove all the skin and any small bones and gristle. Cut on the diagonal into ¼-inch-thick slices, cutting toward the tip and the hump. Strain the broth and reserve for another use.

NOTE Veal tongue usually weighs 1½ to 2 pounds. Place it in a 4-quart saucepan and proceed as directed above. The cooking time will be about 1 hour.

Calamares

SQUID *Serves 2*

Squid are very versatile. South Americans love them simply deep-fried or in stews, rice dishes, salads, or *cebiches*.

> 8 ounces cleaned squid (see Note)
> 2 cups water
> ½ teaspoon salt

Rinse the squid thoroughly. Cut the tentacles in half if large; otherwise, leave whole. Slice the body into ¼- to ½-inch-thick rings, depending on the recipe. Bring the water and salt to a boil in a 4-quart saucepan. Add the squid and cook until it turns white, about 45 seconds—the water won't have time to return to a boil. (Longer cooking will toughen the squid, and it will need to be cooked for about 45 minutes to retenderize it.) Drain thoroughly.

The squid can also be sautéed in olive oil flavored with 1 clove garlic for a few seconds over high heat until it turns milky white and curls. Again, the longer you cook it, the tougher it will get.

NOTE If you are not certain whether the squid has been cleaned, ask the fish merchant. He or she will either do it for you or give you instructions for doing it yourself. (It is not difficult.) You do not want to cook squid that has not been cleaned.

Pulpo

OCTOPUS *Serves 2*

Small octopus is widely available fresh or frozen and is more tender than larger octopus. It also takes less time to cook.

> 8 ounces octopus (preferably baby octopus), cleaned

> 1 medium-size onion, peeled
> 4 black peppercorns
> 6 cloves garlic, peeled
> 1 teaspoon salt

1. Place all the ingredients in a 4-quart saucepan and add water to cover everything by 2 inches. Cook over low heat, uncovered, for 45 minutes. Remove from the heat and let cool in the cooking liquid.

2. Drain and cut into small pieces. Refrigerate until needed. Prepared this way, octopus can be used in soups, stews, *cebiches*, and all kinds of recipes that call for an assortment of shellfish.

Mejillones y Almejas

MUSSELS AND CLAMS *Serves 2*

Mussels and clams are very much a part of South American cuisine. They are commonly eaten steamed and in *cebiches*, soups and stews, rice dishes, and salads.

> 1 pound mussels or clams
> ¼ cup dry white wine
> 1 tablespoon olive oil

1. Rinse the mussels or clams thoroughly and, using a vegetable brush, scrub to remove any sand or grit. Pull the beards from the mussels. Sometimes it is necessary to soak crustaceans in several changes of water to remove all the grit. Discard any clams or mussels that will not close.

2. Put the wine and oil in a large frying pan. Add the clams or mussels and bring to a boil over high heat. Cover and cook until the clams or mussels open, 3 to 5 minutes; discard any that do not open. Drain, reserving the broth. Strain the broth and keep for another use.

Concha Prieta

BLACK CLAMS

Black clams are indigenous to Peru and Ecuador and are used in *cebiches* and rice dishes. They are available frozen or canned in Latin American groceries in the United States.

Wash the clams thoroughly in several changes of water. Place in a casserole with ¼ cup water and steam until they open. Transfer to a bowl. Let cool for a few minutes and remove the meat from the shells. Strain the broth through cheesecloth and reserve. Pull off the black skins and cut each clam into 4 pieces. Return to the bowl with the clam broth. The clams are now ready to use in other recipes.

Colas de Langosta

LOBSTER TAILS

Plunge 8-ounce frozen lobster tails into boiling salted water, cover tightly, and cook over medium heat until the water returns to a boil. Reduce the heat to low and simmer for about 7 minutes. Cook thawed lobster tails the same way, but simmer for only 5 minutes. Drain and let cool. Cut the membrane under the tail and remove the flesh.

To broil lobster tails, insert a sharp knife between the hard upper shell and the soft membrane underneath. Cut down each side and remove the membrane. Crack the shell with your hands so that the tail lies lay flat during broiling. Place the tails flesh side up in a broiler pan. Brush with melted butter and lemon juice. Broil 5 inches from the heat until the flesh is creamy white and opaque, 3 to 5 minutes.

Camarones

SHRIMP

To shell shrimp, make a shallow incision along the back with a sharp paring knife. Remove the shell, leaving it on the tail if the recipe requires it; otherwise, remove the tail shell. With your fingers, pull out the black "vein" that runs down the middle of the back (just below the surface), then rinse. My favorite way to remove the shell and the vein all at once is by using a nifty gadget called shrimp scissors. If you cook a lot of shrimp, this gadget is worth buying.

To cook shrimp, bring a pot of water along with 1 scallion (white part and 1 inch of the green) to a boil. Add the shrimp and cook until they turn pink and begin to curl. This takes only a few seconds for small shrimp, slightly longer for large. Do not overcook. Drain in a colander and rinse with cold water (this makes the shrimp's texture "crisp").

Caldo de Pescado

FISH STOCK *Makes about 6 cups*

This stock is easy to prepare. Just remember to order the head and trimmings ahead of time, because they are not always available. The stock can be made a day ahead and kept refrigerated. It also freezes well for up to a couple of months.

> 1½ pounds heads, bones, and trimmings of any white fish (such as *corvina*, flounder, or sole)
>
> 1 medium-size onion, quartered
>
> 1 leek (white part and 1 inch of the green), washed well and quartered
>
> 4 cloves garlic, lightly crushed
>
> 1 medium-size carrot, peeled
>
> 6 sprigs fresh parsley
>
> 2 sprigs fresh thyme or ¼ teaspoon dried thyme
>
> 1 bay leaf
>
> 10 black peppercorns
>
> 6 cups water
>
> ½ cup dry white wine

1. Place all the ingredients in a large casserole and bring to boil over medium heat, skimming off the froth as it rises to the surface. Reduce the heat to low, partially cover, and simmer for 20 minutes.

2. Strain the stock through a fine-mesh sieve. Do not press on the solids. Let the stock cool. Store in a tightly covered container in the refrigerator or freezer.

Caldo de Cáscaras de Camarones

SHRIMP SHELL BROTH *Makes about 3 cups*

There are two ways of making shrimp shell broth.

The first one is quite simple and is used mainly to flavor rice dishes: Cook shrimp shells and 1 clove garlic in water to cover in a saucepan over medium

heat for 10 minutes. Strain through a fine-mesh sieve. If the recipe requires, put the shells and liquid in a blender, process until coarsely chopped, and strain through a fine-mesh sieve.

The second method, which follows, is a little more elaborate and is used in some Bahian recipes.

> 4 cups water
>
> Shrimp shells
>
> 1 medium-size onion, quartered
>
> 1 clove garlic, peeled
>
> 2 small carrots, peeled
>
> 1 sprig fresh parsley
>
> 1 bay leaf

Put all the ingredients in a 4-quart saucepan. Bring to a boil, reduce the heat, and simmer for 20 minutes. Strain, discarding the solids. Let cool, then refrigerate until needed. Store in a tightly covered container in the refrigerator for 1 day or freeze for up to 2 months.

Como Pelar y Cocinar Yuca

HOW TO PEEL AND COOK YUCA *Serves 4*

Yuca is a staple in many South American homes, especially in the coastal towns of the Andes and the tropics. Often it is used as a substitute for potatoes.

> 1 pound trimmed fresh yuca or frozen yuca
>
> 1 teaspoon fresh lemon juice

If using fresh yuca, you need to buy about 1½ pounds because of the trimming that has to be done. To peel, cut crosswise into 2- to 3-inch pieces. With a sharp paring knife, cut lengthwise through the bark and the pink skin under the bark. Place the knife under the skin to loosen it and pull off the skin and bark. Rinse the yuca and place in cold water so it doesn't discolor.

To cook, place fresh or frozen yuca in a 4-quart saucepan. Add salted cold water to cover by

2 inches and the lemon juice. Bring to a boil over medium heat, reduce the heat to low, cover, and simmer for 20 minutes. At this time, start testing with a fork; if it goes in easily, the yuca is done. The cooking time for each piece may vary. Using a slotted spoon, transfer to a colander, drain, and let cool. When cool enough to handle, cut in half lengthwise and, using a paring knife, remove the fibrous cord in the center.

Como Limpiar Cebolla Puerro
HOW TO CLEAN LEEKS

Wash each leek thoroughly. Cut off all but 1 inch of the green. (Reserve and freeze the rest of the green to use in soups, if desired.) With a sharp knife, cut a cross in both ends of the leek; usually 2 inches long is enough. Rinse under cold running water, opening the ends so all the sand is removed.

Como Cocinar Acelgas
HOW TO COOK SWISS CHARD

Wash the Swiss chard thoroughly and remove any bruised spots. With a small knife, remove the middle rib and cut into ½-inch pieces. Set aside. Cut the leaves into ½-inch-wide strips. Bring a large saucepan of salted water to a boil. Add the diced ribs, cover, and cook for 3 minutes. Add the leaves, cover, and cook for 3 minutes. Drain and rinse with cold water. Squeeze all the water out of the leaves.

Como Cocinar Espinaca
HOW TO COOK SPINACH

Wash spinach leaves thoroughly in several changes of water. Remove the tough stems and place the wet leaves in a large saucepan with ¼ teaspoon salt. Cover and cook over low heat for about 5 minutes, stirring once. Spinach is done when it is reduced in volume and the leaves are bright green. Drain and rinse with cold water. Squeeze all the water out of the leaves. Chop, if the recipe calls for it.

Como Asar Pimientos
HOW TO ROAST BELL PEPPERS

Wash the peppers. Place in a single layer on a baking sheet and broil 6 inches from the heat, turning them with tongs as they blister. Once they are black all around, transfer to a paper or plastic bag, close the bag, and let stand for 30 minutes. (This helps steam the skin off the peppers.) Remove the core and peel off the skin. Roasted peppers freeze very well in zippered-top plastic bags. Use the same procedure if you want to roast hot peppers.

Como Pelar Tomates
HOW TO PEEL TOMATOES

Wash the tomatoes and dip them in boiling water for 15 seconds. With tongs, transfer to a bowl filled with cold water. With a small knife, remove the core and peel off the skin. To seed, cut the tomatoes in half crosswise and squeeze out the seeds.

Como Preparar Chochos Secos
HOW TO PREPARE DRIED LUPINI BEANS

Lupini beans are bitter, because of the alkaloids they contain, so dried beans have to be soaked for a long time before they are edible. Soak ¼ cup dried beans in 2 quarts water for 1 day. Drain, then blanch in 2 quarts boiling water for 5 minutes. Drain and soak in 2 quarts water for 5 days, changing the water 2 or 3 times each day, until the bitterness has disappeared. Drain, add fresh water to cover and ½ teaspoon salt, and store in the refrigerator until ready to use. They will keep for several days.

Como Cocinar Trigo
HOW TO COOK WHEAT BERRIES

Rinse the wheat berries in a strainer under cold running water until the water runs clear. In a 4-quart saucepan, soak in water to cover overnight. Place the pan over medium heat and bring to a boil. Reduce the heat to low and simmer, uncovered, until tender, about 50 minutes. The berries will be slightly chewy, even when fully cooked. Drain, rinse, let cool, and use as directed in the recipe.

Although precooked wheat berries are not available in the United States now, they may be soon. To cook them, place in a saucepan with water to cover by 2 inches and bring to a boil over medium heat. Reduce the heat and simmer, uncovered, for 3 to 5 minutes. Remove from the heat and let stand for 10 minutes. Drain, rinse, let cool, and use as directed in the recipe.

Como Remojar Frejoles Secos
HOW TO SOAK DRIED BEANS

There are two methods of soaking beans. One is to soak them overnight; the other is the quick-soak method. For both methods, thoroughly wash and pick over the beans. For the first method, soak the beans overnight in plenty of water, then cook in the same water (for better flavor) or fresh water (for less intestinal disturbance). For the quick-soak method, put the beans in a large saucepan with water that is at least double the volume of the beans. Bring to a boil and cook, uncovered, over medium heat for 2 to 3 minutes. Remove the pan from the heat, cover, and let soak for 2 hours. The beans are now ready to cook.

Huevos Duros
HARD-COOKED EGGS

The eggs should be at room temperature before cooking; this keeps them from cracking. Place in a saucepan large enough to hold them in a single layer and add salted water to cover by 1 inch. Bring to a boil, cover, remove from the heat, and let stand for 20 minutes. Alternatively, leave uncovered and boil gently for 15 minutes. Drain and rinse under cold running water until cool. Remove the shells right away (the salt in the water makes it easier to remove the shells). I usually remove the shells under cold running water, as they come off more easily that way.

HUEVOS DE CODORNIZ (Hard-Cooked Quail Eggs) Cook as above, except reduce the standing time to 10 minutes.

Croutons   *Makes about 2 cups*

Croutons are a nice addition to cream soups and a good way to use up leftover bread.

>   **6 slices day-old homemade bread or French bread**
>   **¼ cup olive oil**

Preheat the oven to 350°F. Remove the crusts from bread. Cut the bread into ½-inch cubes. Heat the oil in a large skillet over low heat and add the bread cubes. Toss to coat with the oil. Transfer to a jellyroll pan and bake until golden, about 10 minutes. Let cool on a plate lined with paper towels.

Migas de Pan
BREAD CRUMBS

Remove the crust from any good-quality day-old bread. French, Italian, and bakery white bread are good choices. Cut the bread into cubes and process in a blender or food processor.

Como Pelar Avellanas y Almendras
HOW TO PEEL HAZELNUTS AND ALMONDS

To peel hazelnuts: Spread in a single layer in a baking pan and toast in a preheated 350°F oven for 12 to 15 minutes. The skins should blister. Wrap the hot nuts in a clean kitchen towel and steam for about 15 minutes. Rub the nuts in the towel to remove the skins, then let cool.

To peel whole almonds: Bring about 2 cups water to a boil in a 2-quart saucepan. Add 1 cup almonds. When, after 15 to 20 seconds, they start to rise to the top, drain and rinse under cold running water. Start popping the almonds out of their skins. Spread the blanched almonds in a single layer on a jellyroll pan and let dry for a few hours. If they are still moist, dry in a preheated 300°F oven for a few minutes.

Store the nuts in a zippered-top plastic bag in the refrigerator.

Como Tostar Nueces y Semillas
HOW TO TOAST NUTS AND SEEDS

Nuts and seeds can be toasted in a dry, heavy skillet over low heat, stirring until lightly browned. Some nuts and seeds burn quickly, so watch carefully once they start browning. A safer way is to spread the nuts on a jellyroll pan and bake in a preheated 350°F for about 10 minutes. Pumpkin seeds, sesame seeds, and coconut can be done the same way; watch closely after 5 minutes.

Como Preparar un Coco Fresco
HOW TO PREPARE A COCONUT

The coconuts sold in supermarkets usually have the husks already removed. Check to see that the shell has no cracks and shake to find out whether it has any liquid—old coconuts are almost dry inside. The best are always the heaviest for their size.

To extract the liquid, pierce 2 of the 3 "eyes" with a screwdriver, hammering until it goes through the shell. (One "eye" will always be softer than the others.) Pour out the liquid, strain, and reserve. This liquid is known as coconut water. It is used in some recipes, such as Coconut Milk (recipe follows), and is a refreshing drink.

To remove the meat, bake the coconut in a preheated 350°F for 10 minutes. Put the warm coconut in a paper bag and hammer it until it cracks. Remove the meat from the shell. If you are going to grate the coconut, use a sharp paring knife to cut the brown skin off the white meat. Use a blender or food processor for grating. One coconut yields about 2 cups grated coconut.

Leche de Coco

COCONUT MILK

Prepare the coconut as directed in the previous recipe. To extract the milk, there is no need to remove the brown skin. Cut the meat into small pieces and put in a blender. Add the coconut water and 1 cup boiling water or milk. Process until finely chopped, then strain through damp cheesecloth, pressing hard to extract as much liquid as possible. This is called thick coconut milk, of which you should get about 1½ cups. Repeat the process 2 more times to obtain thin coconut milk, which is less rich.

Packaged desiccated unsweetened coconut can be used to extract thin milk only. Two cups of desiccated coconut will yield the same amount of coconut milk as 1 fresh coconut. Use milk instead of water and coconut water and proceed as above.

Coconut milk should be refrigerated until needed. Its shelf life is only a couple of days.

Beurre Manié

Beurre manié is a paste made with butter and flour and is used to thicken sauces, especially in French cooking.

¼ cup (½ stick) unsalted butter, softened
¼ cup all-purpose flour

In a small bowl, cream together the butter and flour until well blended. Freeze in 1-tablespoon amounts. When needed, simply add 1 tablespoon of the frozen paste to ¾ cup hot liquid, stir until it is dissolved, and cook until thickened. If a thicker sauce is needed, add more *beurre manié* until you get the desired consistency.

Brown Coloring   *Makes about ½ cup*

Brown coloring is used to give sauces a dark, rich color.

½ cup sugar
2 tablespoons water
2 tablespoons boiling water
1 teaspoon canola oil
Red food coloring (optional)

In a small saucepan over low heat, bring the sugar and 2 tablespoons water to a boil, swirling the pan occasionally until the sugar melts. Cook until the syrup caramelizes and turns a burnt brown color. The sugar will lose its sweetness when it is burnt. Add the boiling water, holding a lid over the pan to prevent splatters, then stir until well blended. Mix in the canola oil and a couple of drops of red food coloring, if desired. Let cool and transfer to a bottle with a tight-fitting lid. It will keep indefinitely at room temperature. Add 1 teaspoon at a time to stews, soups, gravies, or sauces.

NOTE **There are some products on the market that are used for coloring sauces and gravies, but they are flavored. If I need to give a little color to a sauce and I don't have any homemade brown coloring, I use soy sauce instead.**

Como Caramelizar Moldes

HOW TO CARAMELIZE MOLDS

Makes enough caramel to coat 1 large mold or 12 small molds

There are two methods of making caramel: the classic stovetop method and the microwave method. The microwave method is definitely easier. When working with caramel, wear gloves as a precaution against burns. The most commonly used molds are 6-cup cylindrical or rectangular molds, 3 to 4 inches deep, and individual 6- or 8-ounce molds. For large molds, pour all the caramel into the mold at once. For small molds, pour about a spoonful of caramel in each and swirl quickly. If the caramel thickens before finishing all the molds, reheat for a few seconds.

¾ **cup sugar**

2 tablespoons water

Stovetop method: In a small, heavy saucepan or skillet, bring the water and sugar to a boil, swirling the pan occasionally until the sugar melts. Cook over low heat until the syrup turns a caramel color. Immediately pour the caramel into the mold(s) and turn it in all directions to coat the bottom and as much of the sides as possible.

Microwave method: Place the sugar and water in a 2-cup Pyrex measuring cup, cover with waxed paper, and microwave on high for about 4 minutes. (The time will vary depending on the microwave.) If the caramel is too light, microwave at 30-seconds intervals until it is a dark, rich brown. Immediately coat the mold(s) as directed above.

A Glossary of South American Ingredients

Achiote See Annatto.

Achira (*Canna edulis*), also called edible canna, is a member of the same genus as the canna lily. It looks much like a canna lily but has larger leaves and smaller flowers. It grows in temperate and tropical climates throughout most of South America. Scientists believe that *achira* was one of the first plants to be domesticated in the Andean region. The leaves are used to wrap different types of food, such as fish and tamales. The roots are edible and have a sweet flavor and a floury texture. They can be eaten raw or cooked, or they can be made into a starch that is used in the preparation of delicate pastries, bread, and drinks. *Achira* is widely used in Ecuador and Peru. The Indians boil the roots, then peel and serve them instead of bread with *agua de panela* (brown sugar tea).

Ahipa (*Pachyrhizus ahipa*) is a leguminous plant grown for its roots, which can weigh more than two pounds. It is cultivated in only a few places in southern Ecuador, Peru, and Bolivia. The succulent flesh is white and crisp and can be eaten raw or cooked. When cooked, it retains its crispness. It is a close relative of *jícama* and can be used in the same way. It is not available in the United States.

Allspice is the berry of the *pimienta de Jamaica* tree (*Pimenta dioica*), an evergreen that is indigenous to the New World and that was first encountered by the Spaniards in Jamaica. It is called allspice because it tastes much like a blend of cloves, cinnamon, and nutmeg. It is used mainly in ground form to flavor baked products and desserts (especially fruit pies and cakes, fruit compotes, mincemeat, and steamed puddings), as well as to season meat, seafood, poultry, *pâtés*, and sausages. Its flavor is also essential in the preparation of pickles, *escabeches*, and relishes.

Annatto, or *achiote*, is the red-orange seed of a tropical tree (*Bixa orellana*). Called *urucú* or *urucum* in Brazil, it is the basis for *manteca de color* (annatto lard or oil) and is also used as a flavoring in rice dishes, soups, and stews. A small amount imparts a subtle but distinctive color and taste to foods. Annatto seeds were very much appreciated by the Andean Indians, who used them in barter with the Amazonian Indians. Even the Incas were fond of these valuable seeds and bartered to obtain them. Annatto seeds grow only in the tropics.

There are many nonculinary uses for annatto as well. It is used as a coloring agent in the Caribbean and parts of Latin America. At the time of the conquest, some Amazonian tribes used it as a cosmetic to paint their hair, faces, and bodies. The Brazilian Indians painted their bodies with this orange-red coloring to protect themselves from the sun and mosquitoes while fishing and hunting. The paint also was used (and still is) to protect against evil spirits. Some Indian tribes, such as the Colorados of Ecuador, dye their hair red most of the time or before taking part in ceremonies such as funeral dances. The Tupis painted their newborns red to protect them against evil spirits. The seeds were also used to color wool for the manufacture of textiles after sheep were introduced by the Spaniards. As medicine, a tincture of annatto seeds is supposed to help treat epilepsy, dysentery, and burns.

Annatto seeds are available in the United States at spice shops and Latin American groceries. Annatto also may be found in powdered form. Sweet paprika can be used as a substitute in cooking.

Arepa Flour (not to be confused with the Mexican *masa harina*) is a precooked corn flour used to make *arepas* and tamales in Colombia and Venezuela. It has a grainy texture and comes in two varieties, white and yellow. It is also called *masarepa*, *harina precocida*, and *masa al instante*. It is available in one-, two-, and five-pound bags at most Latin American groceries and some ethnic markets.

Arrowroot (*Maranta arundinacea*), also called *araruta*, is the flour made from the tuber of the same name. Brazilian Indians believed that *araruta* neutralized the poison used by their enemies. Almost pure starch, arrowroot is used for thickening sauces and in cakes, cookies, and desserts.

Avocado (*Persea americana*, *P. drymifolia*), called *aguacate* or *palta* in Spanish, has been widely used in Latin America since the time of the Aztecs, Mayas, and Incas. Botanically a fruit, the avocado is usually used as if it were a vegetable. Once peeled, avocados oxidize quickly, turning brown; tossing them with an acid such as lemon juice will slow this process. Although avocados can be added to hot soups or sauces, they should never be cooked because they become bitter. Avocados come in different colors and sizes. The best is the Hass variety, which has an oval shape and knobby green skin that turns black when the fruit is ripe. California avocados are similar in size but have a smooth green skin and a slightly sweet taste. Florida avocados are very large and have a smooth, light green skin, a more watery texture, and a slightly sweet taste. (This type of avocado originally came from the West Indies, where it was called alligator pear and was served for dessert.) Avocados will ripen at room temperature in three to four days. When fully ripe, the flesh should yield slightly to pressure, but it should still feel slightly firm to the touch.

Avocados are rich in proteins and vitamins and, now that they are grown in California, are quite popular in the United States. They are also popular in Europe, where they are imported mainly from Israel. In ancient times, the natives of Latin America used them for skin care, and if you can stand to buy an avocado and not eat it, the rich oils and nutrients do, in fact, make for an excellent facial mask.

To peel an avocado, cut it in half lengthwise, going around the pit, then separate the halves (a slight rotating of the halves may help) and remove the pit. If the recipe calls for chopped or mashed avocado, you can scoop out the flesh with a spoon. If avocado is to be used sliced, cut it into sections and, using a paring knife, pull off the skin. To store cut avocado, wrap tightly in Saran wrap to prevent air from turning the avocado brown. (Saran is the only brand that stops avocados from turning brown.)

Babaco (*Carica pentagona*) is a member of the papaya family. It looks like a papaya but is smaller in diameter and has a tougher skin. It is harvested when it is mostly green. When ripe, it turns yellow and develops a delicious aroma. (To ripen it, put it in a sunny window.) The fruit has delicate white flesh and seeds that are reminiscent of those of passion fruit. To prepare *babaco*, remove the skin with a paring knife and cut the fruit in half lengthwise. Remove the seeds with a spoon and reserve. Cut the pulp into pieces as needed for your recipe. Press the reserved seeds through a sieve and add the juice to the fruit. A little orange juice intensifies the taste of *babaco*. If making *babaco* juice, add the seeds for extra flavor. Until recently, this fragrant fruit was cultivated only in the temperate climates of Ecuador. Now it is also grown in New Zealand. Occasionally, it is available in the United States in Latin American specialty stores. There is no substitute.

Bacalao is dried, salted codfish. Introduced by Spanish and Portuguese settlers, it is very popular in Latin America, especially during Lent. It is available in the United States in some Latin American, Oriental, and Italian markets. The whiter the *bacalao* is, the better the quality. Soak it in cold water overnight in the refrigerator, changing the water a couple of times, before using.

Badea (*Passiflora quadrangularis*) is a tropical fruit that has an oval shape and grows about a foot long. The skin is light green, and the pulp can be white or light green, similar to the flesh of a soft melon, with seeds in the center that resemble those of passion fruit. It is used to make drinks, ice creams, and sweets. Prepare *badea* just as you would *babaco* (see above). The only place you can find this fruit in the United States is in Miami.

Bananas (*Musa sapientium*) were first introduced to the Americas in 1516 by Tomás de Berlanga, discoverer of the Galápagos Islands and later bishop of Panama. He brought them from West Africa, where they had been cultivated for centuries. Bananas come in two major categories: eating bananas and cooking bananas, or plantains. Bananas come in many sizes, degrees of sweetness, and colors. In addition to the familiar yellow banana, many supermarkets in the United States now carry red bananas, which are about five inches long and one and a half inches in diameter. Their flesh is pink and delicate. Also increasingly available in the United States are *niño* bananas, the smallest of all bananas. They are yellow and have flesh similar to that of common bananas, but more delicate, almost silky. Eating bananas can be used for cooking when they are green.

Banana Leaves are used as wrappers for foods that require steaming, such as tamales, imparting a distinctive flavor to the foods. Now available in Latin American grocery stores, they come frozen in one-pound packages.

Banana Passion Fruit (*Passiflora mollissima*) is called *taxo* in Ecuador, *curuba* in Colombia, and *tumbo* in Bolivia and also grows in some areas of Peru, Venezuela, and Brazil. It has an oval shape and measures one and a half to two inches in diameter and three to four inches long. The skin is smooth and thick and ranges in color from light green to very pale yellow. Banana passion fruit should be used when almost white, or it will be extremely tart. When fresh, it should feel firm to the touch and have no wrinkles. The pulp is bright orange, similar to that of passion fruit, to which it is related. The seeds are tart, with a tinge of sweetness. Banana passion fruit can be eaten raw but is usually made into delicious drinks, ice creams, and desserts. The seeds are scooped out and prepared the same way as those of passion fruit. The whole fruit is sold frozen, but I prefer to buy the frozen pulp; both are available in South American groceries.

Brazil Nuts (*Bertholletia excelsa*) grow on large trees along the Amazon River in Brazil. The nuts are protected inside a thick, spherical, dark brown capsule that can weigh more than four pounds. These nuts are large, with a triangular shape, and are encased in a tough shell that is hard to remove. There are anywhere from 14 to 24 nuts in each capsule. Brazil nuts are rich in protein—there is as much protein in two nuts as in one egg. They are available with or without the shells in supermarkets.

Breadfruit (*Artocarpus communis*) is cultivated mainly in Brazil and the Caribbean. It looks like a melon with bumpy green scales, weighs two to four pounds, and is used primarily as a vegetable. The taste of breadfruit varies with the degree of ripeness. When green, it is like a raw potato. When partially ripened, it resembles eggplant and has the sticky consistency of a ripe plantain. When fully ripe, it has the texture of soft Brie. Breadfruit is never eaten raw and is cooked like potatoes. It is available in some Caribbean markets, stored in water, and it does not keep well. (You can keep it for only a day or two in the refrigerator.) A good fruit should feel firm to the touch, not spongy.

Cape Gooseberry (*Physalis peruviana*) is native to the Andes but is also found in other places around the world. The fruit is about the size of a cherry and is wrapped in a waxy husk very similar to that of a tomatillo. The skin is similar in texture to that of a cherry, but with a lime green or yellow color when ripe. The dense pulp is full of tiny seeds and tastes sweet, with a faint acidity. To eat, remove the husk and rinse. In South America, cape gooseberries are used mainly as a fruit or to make preserves. They are sometimes available in the United States in Latin American markets under the name *uvilla* or *uchuva*, both of which mean "little grape."

Carambola (*Averrhoa carambola*), a native of Asia, was introduced into northern Brazil around 1800. Today it is cultivated throughout the tropics of the Americas. The carambola tree is a beautiful ornamental that is covered with small violet blossoms edged in white during flowering season. The carambola fruit, sometimes marketed as star fruit, is unusual and attractive. It looks waxy and almost translucent. It has five protruding edges, and when cut in a cross section, the slices show a perfect five-pointed star, which makes it useful for decoration. The color varies from light green to yellow, depending on the degree of ripeness. It is eaten as is when ripe, without peeling, and is usually sweet. When green, it is rather acidic and astringent and is used to make jellies, preserves, pickles, juices, ices, and cocktails. The juice of the carambola is also used in South America to remove rust stains on clothing and metal objects. You can find carambolas in some U.S. supermarkets and South American groceries.

Cashews (*Anacardium occidentale*) are native to Central and South America, particularly the northern and northeastern coastal areas of Brazil. The name derives from the Tupi Indian word *acaiu*, which means "nut that produces itself." The cashew produces two edible parts—the cashew fruit and the nut, which grows outside the fruit. The nut, which is the seed of the cashew, is the more commonly seen and more important of the two. Roasted cashew nuts are readily available and widely enjoyed across the United States. The fruit contains a refreshing, aromatic, and astringent juice that can be very sweet or sour and is used as a basis for many popular drinks in Brazil. In regions where the cashew grows, the fruit is also used in jams and jellies, and even in a dried form, which resembles a tough prune. It is rich in vitamins A and C. It can be round or oval, which is why the cashew fruit is often referred to as a cashew pear or cashew apple. The color ranges from yellow to red. This fruit supports a small bean-shaped seed, which is the nut. The nut has two shells, a glassy outer shell and a dark, hard inner shell. Between the two is a caustic oil that can raise blisters on human skin. This oil has many uses in industry because of its insulating and protective properties. The fruit and the attached nut are available frozen in some Latin American groceries. To eat, defrost, then extract the juice of the fruit and discard the nut. Or roast the nut before eating. (The nut must be roasted to remove the shell. However, cashew oil easily catches fire, so be careful if you try to roast it.)

Cherimoya (*Annona cherimola*) has been grown in the highlands of Ecuador, Peru, and Chile for centuries and was prized by the Incas. It also has been grown in California for the past 100 years. It has a roundish shape, with a thick green-yellow skin and projecting scales. The cherimoyas available in the United States weigh an average of one pound; those available in South America are generally larger. The delicious white flesh has a custard-like texture and envelops several shiny black seeds. When ripe, a cherimoya should be fairly firm to the touch but yield a little when pressed with the thumb. If it's hard, ripen at room temperature for a few days. It can be refrigerated for several days after ripening. To eat, cut the cherimoya in half and scoop out the flesh with a teaspoon. Crush the flesh with a fork to loosen the seeds, then pick them out and discard.

Chicharrón, or fried pork rind, is a byproduct of making lard. It is available packaged in U.S. supermarkets, but the quality is not as good as homemade, which can be found in Latin American groceries. Colombians and Venezuelans use *chicharrónes* when preparing *arepas*, beans, and other specialties.

Chiles See Peppers.

Choclo is fresh corn on the cob. The term is used primarily in Peru, Bolivia, and Ecuador.

Chorizo, the famous sausage from Spain, is very popular throughout Latin America. The Mexican variety is different from the Spanish and cannot be used as a substitute. Spanish chorizo is made with pork, spices, and generous amounts of paprika and is usually air-dried. Its spicy flavor is hard to imitate, but a good Hungarian sausage could be used instead. Mexican chorizo is also made with pork, but the spices are different: herbs, dark red chili powder, and a little vinegar. Because Mexican chorizo is not usually cured or dried, the texture is crumbly.

Chuchoca is corn that is boiled and then sun-dried for two to three days. This is a very old way to preserve corn in Chile and also in Peru, where the dried corn is called *chochoca*, and in Ecuador, where it is called *chuchuca*. Coarsely ground, it is used to thicken stews or to make sauces for potatoes. Polenta can be used as a substitute, even though the corn used in polenta is not cooked, only dried.

Cilantro (*Coriandrum sativum*) is a member of the parsley family and an essential ingredient in many Indian, Mediterranean, and Middle Eastern dishes, as well as in Latin American cooking, particularly Mexican, Andean, and Brazilian. It works well in many soups, salads, and meat and fish dishes. The fresh leaves have a very assertive flavor, sort of citrusy, and a very short shelf life. Use the leaves and top stems; discard the tough bottom stems. To increase cilantro's shelf life, try to get branches that have roots, put them in a jar with a little water, and cover with a plastic bag. Some people puree the cilantro without the roots and freeze it in ice cube trays to use in soups, stews, and other dishes. In dried form, cilantro leaves lose all their flavor. Also see Coriander seeds.

Cinnamon, Mexican (*Cinnamomum zeylanicum*), is also known as Ceylon cinnamon (for the island where it originated). It is a multi-layered, milder type of cinnamon than the cassia cinnamon (*Cinnamomum verum*) commonly available in grocery stores, with a softer, thinner texture. The two are not inter-changeable, but either kind can be used for the recipes in this book.

Coca (*Erythroxylon coca*). It is unfortunate that we know about coca leaves only through the deadly cocaine. Coca has been a part of life for the Indians of the highlands of Peru and Bolivia for 4,000 years. Coca leaves have a mild anesthetic effect when chewed and help numb pain, cold, and hunger. Early miners could not have survived the arduous work without coca leaves. Coca is also very effective in suppressing or relieving the effects of *soroche*, an altitude sickness that often affects newcomers who are unaccustomed to the high altitudes of the Andes. When I was in Cuzco, I saw the difference coca tea could make. We were served it as soon as we checked into our hotel. The next day, we met a gentleman from Texas who had not been given the tea, and he had been terribly ill all night. The natives also believe that the plant has magical qualities. Coca is part of Indian mythology and is believed to have been the only plant to survive a storm caused by an angry local god. Coca leaves are sold on the streets of Peru and Bolivia.

Cochayuyo is a seaweed found along the coast of Chile and is very important in the Chilean diet. It grows in long green strands attached to rocks and is harvested at low tide. It comes in flat pieces called *trolas* and tubular shapes. *Cochayuyo* is folded in small bundles and dried in the sun. It is sold in packages of four bundles tied together, and Chilean recipes call for it in number of bundles.

To cook *cochayuyo*, first soak it overnight in vinegar and water to cover, then drain and scrape it with the back of a knife to remove the gelatin attached to the surface. Wipe clean with a kitchen towel and cut into pieces to fit in a four-quart saucepan. Cover with water, add 1 tablespoon vinegar, and simmer until tender, about 30 minutes. *Cochayuyo* should be cooked *al dente* for optimum taste. The vinegar softens it, so test after 20 minutes so as not to overcook. Drain, rinse thoroughly, and cut into half-inch squares.

Once cooked, *cochayuyo* has a firm texture that resembles that of meat. Therefore, it can be used in almost any recipe that calls for chopped or ground meat. It is not available in the United States, but because of its nutritional value, especially for vegetarians, I believe that it will be sold sooner or later in health food stores.

Coconut (*Cocos nucifera*). Although we do not know precisely where the coconut palm originated (likely somewhere in Indonesia or the Pacific islands), we do know that coconuts arrived in Bahia, Brazil, in 1553 and from there spread throughout South America. The coconut palm is considered the most useful of all the palms. Coconuts grow in clusters and are used for a great many applications, both industrially and in home kitchens. Coconut is available fresh and dehydrated (shredded) in all supermarkets. Grated frozen coconut is available in some Latin American and Oriental groceries. The dehydrated shredded coconut most commonly found in U.S. supermarkets is sweetened. Unsweetened coconut is harder to find but is usually available frozen in specialty food markets and health food stores. The meat of one fresh coconut equals about two cups grated coconut. See page 413 for information on working with coconuts.

Coconut Milk is the unsweetened milk extracted from the grated coconut. To find out how to extract the milk from a coconut, see page 414. Coconut milk is available frozen or canned in some Oriental and Latin American groceries. Make sure to stir well before measuring.

Coriander Seeds are small, brownish beige seeds used for flavoring breads, pastries, curries, pickles, and other recipes. In Mexico, they are used to make *colaciones*, which are traditional for the Christmas *posadas* (processions commemorating Mary and Joseph's journey to Bethlehem). *Colaciones* are coriander seeds dipped in sugar and dyed different colors.

Cornhusks are very important in Latin American cuisine, where they are mainly used fresh to wrap tamales. In Mexico, cooks use dried cornhusks to wrap their tamales. The dried husks have to be soaked in hot water before using. In the United States, they are available in one-pound packages in Latin American groceries and many supermarkets. They keep indefinitely.

Cumin (*Cuminum cyminum*) is native to the Mediterranean region. It is the dried, yellowish brown seed of a plant belonging to the parsley family. Strongly aromatic, with an earthy flavor, it has been used throughout the world since ancient times. It is an essential ingredient in chili powder and curry powder, as well as in many South American specialties. Available whole or ground, cumin is used commercially to prepare meats, sausages, pickles, stews, and cheeses, but also goes well with rice, beans, poultry, soups, and bread. Use it sparingly, as its flavor is aggressive. Cumin seed looks somewhat like caraway seed, and the two are sometimes confused.

Cuy See Guinea pig.

Dendê (palm oil) is obtained from the oil palm (*Elaeis guineensis*), which originated in central Africa. The small, clustered fruit of this palm goes through a variety of colors (yellow, rust, and red) before finally turning black when ripe. Palm oil is extracted from the pulp of the fruit and is used extensively in the Bahian cooking of Brazil. Its nutty flavor and deep orange-yellow color lend a special touch to foods. Some cooks would not dream of preparing certain dishes without it. There is no substitute. *Dendê* may be available at specialty stores or international markets. If not, you can use olive oil instead. The taste will not be the same, but the dish will still be delicious.

Feijoa (*Feijoa sellowiana*) is a subtropical fruit native to the grasslands of southern Brazil and part of Paraguay and Uruguay. In Brazil, it is also called *goiaba serrana* (mountain guava), and it is a close relative of the guava. It has an oval shape and is about two inches long. It has a thin green skin and semisoft, juicy, cream-colored flesh with tiny seeds in the center. The taste is reminiscent of pineapple, which is why it is also called pineapple guava. It can be eaten fresh or made into desserts. When the fruit is ready to eat, it is fragrant and feels soft to the touch, like a slightly soft plum. Let it ripen at room temperature. Once ripened, it can be stored in the refrigerator for a couple of days. Peel before using. You can find *feijoa* in U.S. supermarkets.

Figs (*Ficus carica*) originated in Asia and became very popular in the Mediterranean countries. The Spaniards and Portuguese introduced them to South America. Fresh figs are very fragile and for that reason are difficult to transport to market. Nevertheless, they are showing up more frequently in supermarkets, even though the season is very short. When available, they should be consumed right away. Dried figs are used in a variety of confections throughout South America.

Granadilla (*Passiflora ligularis*) is a tropical fruit that belongs to the passion fruit family. It is the largest and sweetest member of that family. The shell is smooth and bright yellow. It is usually eaten fresh—just cut the fruit in half and scoop out the pulp. Eat seeds and all.

Guaba (not to be confused with guava—see below) is a fruit (*Inga* species) indigenous to some of the Andean countries and Brazil. There are two varieties: the mountain variety has small pods about 6 inches long and is called *guaba*; the coastal variety has very large, tough pods and is called *pacay* or *guaba de la costa*. In Brazil, it is called *ingá-cipó*. The pods have a row of black seeds covered with a delicious, sweet, spongy, white substance, which is the edible part. As far as I can tell, this is not available in the United States, although you might find it in Miami.

Guanábana (*Annona muricata*), also known as soursop, originated in Central America. It is similar in appearance to the cherimoya, though much larger in size, with an average weight of two to 10 pounds. Some fruits actually weigh as much as 20 pounds. The *guanábana* is considered the most fragrant and important of all the tropical fruits of the Anonaceae family. The flesh is more acidic than that of the cherimoya, which makes it ideal for sorbets, ice creams, and other desserts. It is rarely eaten as a fruit out of hand. The frozen pulp is available in Latin American markets.

Guaraná is the fruit of a Brazilian plant (*Paullinia cupana*) that is a vine when growing in the forest and a creeper when growing in open, sunny places. The plant has bright green leaves and small fruits that grow in bunches. When the fruit is ripe, it opens up, disclosing a white flesh with a large black seed, resembling the human eye. The Sateré-Maué Indians were the first to cultivate this plant and to discover the technique for processing the seeds, which are painstakingly made into a paste that is then shaped into rods called *guaraná* loaves. These loaves are smoked for two months, after which then they can be grated and mixed with water to make a very refreshing drink. *Guaraná* is a powerful stimulant, containing more caffeine than coffee or tea. It is also used for medicinal purposes and may be made into a syrup, powder, or capsules. A *guaraná* carbonated soft drink is available in Latin American groceries.

Guava (*Psidium guajava*) originated in tropical America. It is one of the most cherished fruits in South America, where about 150 species can be found. In Brazil, the famous *goiabada* (guava paste or jam) is the most popular dessert. The average guava is the size of a large plum. It can be round or oval and has a yellowish to light green skin. The abundant pulp comes in colors that range from cream to orange or bright salmon. The small, hard seeds in the center have to be removed. The salmon-colored flesh is used to make the beloved *dulce de guayaba* (guava preserves), fruit compotes, and drinks. When ripe, the guava is very sweet and can be eaten out of hand, skin and all. It also can be peeled, seeded, and cooked. Few fruits smell better while cooking. Guavas are available fresh in Latin American groceries and some supermarkets when in season. Guava paste and guava halves preserved in syrup are available in most supermarkets.

Guinea Pigs are called *cuy* or *curi* in the Andean countries. They are vegetarian rodents that are raised for food in Indian homes. *Cuyes* can be roasted, stewed, fried, or grilled. They are very popular in Peru, Ecuador, and southern Colombia and are available frozen in the United States in some Latin American supermarkets.

Hearts of Palm are the tender, ivory-colored buds of a particular palm tree that is a member of the Arecaceae family. They are used in elegant salads, *cebiches*, and soups or served as a vegetable with chicken or seafood. They are available canned in most supermarkets. Once opened, they can be stored in their own juice in a glass jar in the refrigerator for up to a week.

Huacatay (*Chenopodium ambrosioides*) is an herb of the marigold family that is also known as *paico*. It is indigenous to Peru and used to flavor many sauces and dishes. It has a very pungent taste, and there is no substitute. *Huacatay* is available in some Latin American markets, dried or as a paste.

Ishpingo is the dried flower of an Ecuadorian tree (*Ocotea quixos*) and is similar in taste to cinnamon. *Ishpingo* is used to flavor some drinks and desserts, just like cinnamon. You may be able to find it in some Ecuadorian groceries.

Lard When the Spanish brought pigs to South America, they also brought the widespread use of lard. The butchering of pigs provided generous amounts of pig fat, which, once rendered, could be stored for a few months and used for frying and to make *sofritos*, tamales, and pastries. In recent years, because of concerns about cholesterol, lard has gradually been replaced by vegetable oil and margarine or butter. (Actually, lard contains less cholesterol than butter.) Many cooks still used lard, but some combine half lard and half butter to retain some of the wonderful flavor lard imparts to foods. I have used mainly butter and oil in my recipes, largely because it is hard to find lard that has not been hydrogenated and really good-quality lard must be made at home.

Limes (*Citrus aurantifolia*) are used extensively in Latin America, primarily as juice, and appear in everything from *cebiches* to drinks. Frequently used interchangeably with lemons, Latin American limes are typically different in appearance from American limes but similar in taste. There is also a sweet lime that is larger than the other varieties and is eaten like an orange.

Lingüiça is a Brazilian garlic pork sausage of Portuguese origin that is available both cured and fresh. It is available in Latin American groceries. Polish sausage can be used instead.

Longaniza is a popular pork sausage from Spain that is frequently used in Latin American cooking. Polish smoked sausage can be substituted.

Luche is a seaweed that grows on rocks close to Chilean beaches and can be picked by hand at low tide. It is bright green when fresh but turns black when dried in the sun. It is sold in round bundles that have to be separated, thoroughly rinsed to remove the sand, and soaked in lukewarm water before cooking. Very popular in southern Chile, *luche* can be made into *budines* (custards), casseroles, and omelets. It is not available in the United States.

Lucuma (*Pouteria lucuma, Lukuma bifera, Lucuma obovata*) is a fruit that is native to southern Ecuador, Peru, and Chile. It is called *lucuma* in Chile and *lugma* in Ecuador and Peru. This fruit grows on large, beautiful trees that have leaves similar to those of the magnolia. It is about three inches in diameter, with smooth, dark green or bronze-yellow skin. The yellow flesh is hard, not juicy, with a butterscotch flavor that cannot be reproduced artificially. One variety has a large, brilliant brown seed in the center, and another has three seeds. *Lucuma* can weigh up to two pounds and can be eaten raw, but it is used mainly in milk shakes, ice creams, and desserts, especially in Chile, where the fruit is very popular. It is also made into a starch that is used for making fine cookies and cakes and can be stored in airtight containers for years. *Lucuma* is not available in the United States.

Malanga is an edible tuber and the most popular form of *cocoyam*, a general name applied to several species of the genus *Xanthosoma*. It is grown and used in the tropics of the Americas and is an important food in the Caribbean islands and in Venezuela. A rough brown skin covers cream-colored flesh. *Malanga* can be cooked like and used in place of potatoes. Some supermarkets and Latin American groceries carry it.

Mamey (*Mammea americana*) is a tropical fruit that is indigenous to Mexico through the northern regions of South America. It is round, is five to six inches in diameter, and has coarse brown skin. The hard yellow flesh has a wonderful aroma and is used mainly to make ice creams, drinks, compotes, and desserts. When ripe, the fruit falls from the tree. It has large seeds that are used to make an insecticide. The frozen pulp is available in some Latin American markets.

Mamey Zapote (*Calocarpun sapota*) is similar in outward appearance to *mamey*, but it has either a creamy pink or salmon-orange flesh with a grainy texture. It is very sweet and has a large pit. It is used to make drinks, ice creams, compotes, and creamy sweets.

Mango (*Magnifera indica*) is often called the "king of the fruits" because of its delicious, fragrant, juicy, sweet flesh when fully ripe. It is native to Asia, where it has been cultivated for at least 5,000 years. The Portuguese first brought mangoes to Africa and then to America in the 1700s. The mango tree is known for its longevity and abundant fruit. Mangoes come in many sizes and colors. It is believed that there are more than 500 species of mangoes worldwide.

Mangoes are cultivated in Florida and in Central and South America and are available throughout the year. The season for Florida mangoes starts in May and lasts through the summer. Most mangoes weigh three-quarters to one pound. A one-pound mango yields about one cup of flesh. Although unripe (green) mangoes are sometimes prepared as a vegetable and in India are used for mango chutney, the mango's predominant use is as a fresh fruit and in the preparation of a variety of desserts.

To select a mango, pick one that has a smooth skin—part green, part red—and that feels firm but yields just a little to the touch. These are ideal for salads or other uses where firm pieces of mango are desired. If a mango has a slightly wrinkled skin, it is too ripe for dicing but okay for eating, as long as it doesn't taste sour. (A sour taste means the mango has started to ferment.) The best way to judge a mango is to sniff the stem end; it should smell sweet and fresh. Brown spots and softness denote overripeness. Green mangoes will ripen at room temperature; you can then refrigerate them until needed. (They will keep for a few days in the refrigerator.) The easiest way to prepare a mango is to cut the flesh away from both sides of the flat stone, following the contours of the stone with your knife. Then cut the flesh into sections and remove the skin.

Manteca de Color See Annatto.

Maté is a caffeinated "tea" leaf that is indigenous to South America. For more information, see page 47.

Medlar There are two fruits called medlar, or *níspero*. One type (*Achras sapota*) belongs to the Sapotaceae family, originated in the American tropics, and can be found from Florida to Brazil. It is a small, oval fruit with rough brown skin and reddish pulp containing small black seeds. It has a sweet, pleasant taste and is consumed as is (it must be peeled) or used in desserts, sorbets, and ice creams. The seeds are used to treat urinary problems. The second type (*Eriobotrya japonica*), called Japanese medlar, or *níspero del Japón*, belongs to the Rosaceae family. The fruit, which grows in bunches, is orange, looks like a small quince, and has one or two black seeds, which are poisonous. The pulp is very hard and juicy and the fruit has to be very ripe before it can be made into jams or jellies. It has a semi-acid taste. Japanese medlar is not available in the United States, except perhaps from farms growing heirloom produce.

Milk, Condensed and Evaporated It would be impossible to write a book about Latin American cuisine without mentioning canned sweetened condensed milk. This sweet, thick, caramel-flavored milk is widely used in desserts of all kinds, such as flans, puddings, and a variety of confections. Above all, it can be used to make the classic South American sweet *dulce de leche* (page 390). Sweetened condensed milk is available under different brand names in 14-ounce cans. It also comes in light and skim milk forms. The storage life of an unopened can is about a year. Once opened, it will keep, tightly covered and refrigerated, for about a week.

Evaporated milk also is widely used in South America and is much more versatile than sweetened condensed milk. It is used to prepare all types of foods, both savory and sweet. My theory is that because whipping cream was not widely available many years ago due to lack of refrigeration, people turned to canned milk instead. Evaporated milk is simply whole milk that has been reduced by removing 60 percent of the water. To return it to its original volume, the rule of thumb is to add one can of water for each can of milk.

Mint is one of the oldest herbs, though not indigenous to South America, with a long history as both a seasoning and a medicine. Spearmint is preferred in South America, where it is used in teas, jellies, chutneys, soups, salads, and desserts.

Naranjilla (*Solanum quitoence*) was called "little orange" by the Spaniards because of its similarity in color and shape to oranges. It grows in the foothills of the Andes in Colombia, Ecuador, and Peru, where the Amazon basin starts. It has a tough, smooth, yellowish orange skin that is covered with brown hairs, which can easily be removed with a kitchen towel. The pulp, which has many tiny yellow-green seeds, produces delicious juice. This sweet-tart fruit can be eaten out of hand, but it is mainly used to make juices, sorbets, and ice creams. The whole fruit is available frozen or canned in some Latin American markets. The canned variety has a strong metallic taste that makes it unappealing. The pulp is available frozen in 14-ounce packages.

Oca (*Oxalis tuberosa*) is a small tuber native to the Andean highlands. It has an oval, elongated shape and a floury texture. Colors range from white to yellow to reddish. It is the most important root crop in South America after the potato and is a staple of the Indians living from Venezuela to northern Argentina. There are two varieties: sweet, which can be eaten raw, cooked, or sun-dried (called *caui* in Quechua), and bitter, which is freeze-dried for long storage. Fresh *oca* is usually boiled and served with a syrup made with *panela*. *Oca* is not available in the United States.

Olives, Black The most popular South American black olives (*Olea europaea*) are Alfonso olives, which are brine-cured, ripe olives. Grown in Peru, they are packed in brine for shipping, although sometimes they are bottled in olive oil.

Onions (*Allium cepa*) are indispensable in South American cooking. It would be impossible to prepare many dishes without onions. The most common varieties are yellow, white, and red. In some countries, scallions (green onions) are used in many specialties. Pearl onions are also used for pickling or *escabeches*. Always rinse cut onions in hot water or soak in cold water for a few minutes to get rid of the pungent taste.

Orange, Sour (*Citrus aurantia*) is known as *naranja agria* in Latin America. The tart juice of this species of orange, also called bitter orange, is widely used in *cebiches* and meat marinades. The frozen fruit is available in Latin American groceries. To substitute, use two-thirds cup orange juice and one-third cup lemon or lime juice per one cup sour orange juice.

Orange-Flower Water, brought to South American by the Spaniards, is distilled from orange-blossom petals and used to flavor desserts. It is available in some U.S. supermarkets and Middle Eastern groceries.

Palillo is an indigenous herb that is widely used in the cooking of Peru and Bolivia. The leaves are dried and ground, and it gives foods, such as *Papas Huancaínas* (page 127), an intense yellow color. *Palillo* is available in some South American markets. Turmeric is a good substitute.

Palm Oil See Dendê.

Panela, Chancaca, Raspadura This Latin American unrefined brown sugar tastes like molasses and comes molded in different shapes. It is widely used in the preparation of sweets and desserts. Recently, *panela* has become available in cubes and in granulated form. Dark brown sugar can be used instead of *panela*, but keep in mind that *panela* is not as sweet as brown sugar. The Mexican *piloncillo* is a good substitute. It is available in many U.S. supermarkets and Mexican groceries.

Papaya (*Carica papaya*) is a fruit that enchanted Columbus on his first visit to the New World. Widely used in Latin America, it is usually eaten fresh or in fruit salads and refreshing drinks. It is becoming more popular and available in the United States and is sold in supermarkets. Papaya leaves have been used by Indians for centuries to tenderize meat. The same enzyme found in the leaves, papain, is found in unripe papayas and is used commercially in the production of meat tenderizers. Unripe papaya is also used as a squash-like vegetable in Latin America. Peel and remove the seeds before using papaya.

Papaya, Chilean and Colombian This fruit looks like a small regular papaya but is a different species, *Carica goudotiana*. It is called *papayuela* in Colombia. There are about 20 varieties of this fruit, none of which can be eaten raw. This papaya is usually candied or used in compotes. It is not available in the United States.

Passion Fruit (*Passiflora edulis*) has an intense tropical fragrance that is hard to match. Its potent flavor makes it ideal to use in various desserts. Passion fruit juice should never be used full strength because it causes diarrhea. Native to Brazil, passion fruit is now grown in Australia, New Zealand, Hawaii, Central America, Florida, and California. There are many varieties of passion fruit. The purple kind found in the United States is about the size of an egg and has a firm shell casing that is smooth when underripe. It takes a few days to ripen at room temperature, becoming wrinkled as it does. The South American varieties are larger and are mostly yellow. They also wrinkle when ripe. Once ripe, passion fruit can be stored in the refrigerator for a few days or frozen whole. I prefer to extract the juice and freeze it in a jar. The best way to extract the juice is to cut the fruit in half with a knife, holding the fruit above of a bowl to save the juice that comes out when the knife is inserted, then scoop out the seeds with a teaspoon. Place the seeds and juice in a blender and pulse until the pulp has been removed from the seeds. Do not overprocess, or the seeds will be pulverized. Strain the juice through a fine-mesh nonmetallic sieve. The average yield is one tablespoon of juice per fruit. The frozen pulp can be found in some Latin American markets.

Pepino (*Solanum muricatum*). Native to Ecuador, Peru, and Chile, this refreshing fruit, called *cachun* in Quechua, comes in a variety of sizes and shapes: some are round, some are egg-shaped, and others resemble an eggplant. Sizes range from that of an egg to that of a medium-size eggplant. The golden skin is smooth and leathery with violet stripes. *Pepinos* have a juicy, fragrant, sweet, cream-colored flesh, somewhat like that of a melon, with a few seeds in the middle. The fruit is usually peeled before eating. *Pepinos* are eaten only out of hand. They are now grown in Australia and New Zealand and are available during winter and spring in many supermarkets. The *pepinos* available in the United States are rather small, weighing maybe half a pound, and have an oval shape that comes to a point at one end. When ripe, *pepinos* should feel firm to the touch, yielding just a little. Long storage destroys the quality of *pepinos*.

Peppercorns, Pink These small berries are indigenous to Peru and Ecuador but are also found in Brazil. They are the fruit of the mulli tree (*Shinus molle*), a pungent-smelling tree with drooping branches. Mulli trees grow in the valleys of the Andes. In precolonial times, this tree was widely used as fuel, and the berries were used in the preparation of foods and medicines. In fact, Juan de Velasco, in *Historia del Reino de Quito*, writes that the tree was "an entire pharmacy" that was used to cure "a thousand illnesses." The Incas used the berries to make aromatic drinks and also added them to *chicha de jora* (a fermented corn drink) to improve its taste and accelerate fermentation. They also used them to make drinks to cure urinary problems. Pink peppercorns, which are often used in combination with white and black peppercorns (to which they are not related), are now being grown in California.

Peppers come in a wide variety of colors and sizes and can be sweet or hot, with heat ranging from mild to blinding. They have become hugely popular all over the world and are so much a part of some Asian and African cuisines that it is hard to believe they are not indigenous to those regions. They were first cultivated in Mexico about 9,000 years ago, and archaeological diggings in Peru show that they had been domesticated there by about 2500 B.C.

Peppers are called *chiles* in Mexico and *ajíes* in South America. In English, the term *chile* is generally reserved to describe hot peppers. In Spanish, however, all peppers are called *chiles*, while hot peppers are called *ajíes*, although in some South American countries, bell peppers also are called *ajíes*.

There are numerous species of *ajíes* in South America, many of which are still wild and were used by the Indians as condiments, vegetables, and medicines, as well as in rituals. The Incas required that hot peppers be included in the tribute paid to them, and they made sure the estate warehouses always had *ajíes*.

There are five cultivated species of the genus *Capsicum*, with hundreds of variations. Varieties of the species *Capsicum annuum* were first cultivated in Mexico and Central America. The other cultivated species are native to South America. In addition, about 20 wild species have been identified in South America. Following are the most commonly used varieties in South America.

Andean ají (ají de montaña) is widely cultivated in Ecuador, Peru, Bolivia, Argentina, and Brazil. It appears to have originated in central Bolivia, where most of the varieties of hot peppers are found. It has a shiny skin and a finger-like shape, and it measures about three inches long and one inch wide, tapering to a point at one end. These peppers can be red, orange, purple, or green. They are very fragrant and very hot and are available packed in brine under the name *ají entero* (whole hot red peppers) in Ecuadorian and South American groceries. I refer to them as finger peppers in the recipes in this book.

Ají cacho de cabra is a fresh red pepper that is long, thin, and very hot. It is used in Chile to make hot pepper sauces.

Ají verde is a milder variety with a thicker flesh and a waxy, lime green skin. It is used to make condiments in Chile, such as the *pebre* sauces.

Habanero is considered to be the hottest pepper available, similar to the Scotch bonnet. The Amazon basin is the home of the largest variety of *habanero* peppers. *Habaneros* can be found in most supermarkets and Caribbean specialty stores. They also come in jars preserved in brine or vinegar.

Jalapeño is a green pepper that comes from Mexico and now is being grown in South America. I like to use it in salads and to garnish *cebiches*. It is medium hot, but once the seeds and white veins are removed, it is rather mild and adds a wonderful zest to foods. The size can vary, ranging from two inches long and one inch wide to much larger, but all taper to a rather round point. The flesh is thick and juicy. *Jalapeños* are commonly available in U.S. supermarkets.

Serrano is a slender hot green pepper from Mexico that is usually about one and a half inches long.

Rocoto is a widely cultivated pepper in the Andes. It has a thick flesh, similar to that of a bell pepper, and sometimes gets as large as a bell pepper. It is hotter than some other *ajíes*. When ripe, it has a shiny skin and can be bright yellow, brown, orange, or red. A favorite way to prepare *rocotos* is stuffed with meat. In some areas, this pepper is called *rocoto-manzana* or *locoto*. One variety of *rocoto* is elongated and very hot. The Peruvian *rocoto* used for stuffing is available frozen in some South American groceries. The Mexican *manzano* pepper, though much hotter, is a good substitute.

Aji mirasol, also called *ají amarillo*, is one of the most common and beloved Peruvian and Bolivian hot peppers. It is widely used by Peruvians in many specialties, such as hot pepper sauces, because it provides a lot of heat and a beautiful yellow color. Fresh yellow peppers come in jars, packed in water. *Ají mirasol* is also available dried, in powder and paste, both of which are quite hot but very handy to have in the refrigerator. One teaspoon will give a lift to your dish; if you want more heat, add more to taste. All of these forms are available in some South American markets. *Ají panca*, or *ají colorado*, is a red variety that is similar to *ají mirasol* but a little milder.

Aji limo is a very small, elongated hot pepper indigenous to Peru and Bolivia, where it is called *aribibi*. It comes in red and green varieties and is used mainly for salsas.

Aji chivato is a tiny, very hot Colombian pepper with a round shape. It is used to make salsas.

Malagueta is a small green, yellow, or red pepper from Brazil. It is about one inch long and one-quarter inch wide. It is extremely hot and an essential ingredient in the Bahian kitchen. This pepper should not be confused with the African *melegueta*, also called grains of paradise, which is a ginger and related to cardamom. *Malagueta* peppers come preserved in jars or as a table sauce and can be found in Latin American markets. They are not available fresh in the United States. Tabasco sauce can be used as a substitute.

Pimenta-de-cheiro is a small, round Brazilian pepper about three-quarters inch in diameter. Generally yellow, it is very fragrant and mildly hot. This pepper is indigenous to the Amazon and widely used in the cuisine of Pará, in northern Brazil. It is the pepper used to make *molho de pimenta ao tucupi*. You can sometimes find it in supermarkets.

Pimenta cheirosa is a small, mild, very flavorful green pepper found along the Amazon. It is used in different specialties where a milder pepper is called for.

Pimenta muripi is a mild pepper that turns yellow when ripe. It is widely used in the Amazon.

Persimmon (*Diospyros kaki*) originated in China but is fairly common in Chile, where it is usually known as *kaki*. It is generally eaten out of hand. The beautiful, flaming orange color of the skin is echoed in the pulp, which has an almost jelly-like consistency and is extremely sweet when fully ripe. However, persimmons can be a little astringent when underripe. When ripe, the skin yields slightly to the touch. This is widely available in the United States in season.

Pirarucu is one of the most important species of fish inhabiting the Amazon River and its tributaries. It is considered the *bacalhau Brasilero* (codfish of Brazil). Used fresh and dried, it has a delicious white flesh and can weigh more than 200 pounds. It is not available in the United States.

Plantains See Bananas.

Pomegranates (*Punica granatum*) are among the oldest fruits known to man, probably originating in Persia. Though not widely used in South America, they are now grown in many Latin American countries. The fruit is the size of a large orange. The hard reddish skin breaks away to reveal beautiful, shimmering, jewel-like, red seeds (actually, they are pale seeds encased in clear membranes filled with brilliant red juice). The seeds are separated into compartments by a tougher pale membrane. They are crisp and edible, though most people prefer to suck the juice and discard the seeds. The seeds can be removed either by peeling the fruit and scraping them away from the pale membrane or by cutting the fruit in half and scooping the seeds out with a teaspoon. Extract the juice by pressing the seeds in a sieve or pulsing them in a blender (do not pulverize). Pomegranates will keep very well in the refrigerator for up to three months, and both the seeds and the whole fruit freeze very well. The seeds make a beautiful garnish for salads or desserts. Pomegranates are widely available in U.S. supermarkets in November and December.

Prickly Pear (*Opuntia* species) is among the most important desert plants in the Americas. The prickly "pears" that give the cactus its name are the fleshy, thorny fruits. They are called *tunas* in South America and grow at the top of the upper pads. They range in color from yellow-green to pink to dark purple. The skin is covered with spots of prickly fuzz that can get into your hands, so wear rubber gloves when handling. To remove the flesh, trim off the ends of the pears, cut in half lengthwise, and peel off the entire skin—it comes off easily. The flesh is full of large, edible seeds that some people find offensive; remove them if you wish. The fruit is usually eaten fresh and uncooked. You can find prickly pears in most U.S. supermarkets and Latin American groceries.

In South America, Central America, and Mexico, this cactus takes on another dimension—that of host. The cochineal insect (*Dactylopius coccus*), which produces a red dye that has been widely used for centuries, infests the prickly pear cactus. The dye, called cochineal, is produced in many areas of South America. The desert south of Lima, Peru, where hardly any plant can survive, is the ideal home for the prickly pear cactus, making Peru one of the largest producers of cochineal in South America. Traditionally, Peruvians used the vivid red dye to color wool for clothing. Today it is used worldwide to color cosmetics, clothing, foods, and drinks.

Pumpkin Seeds, also called pepitas, are the hulled seeds of squashes belonging to the *Cucurbitaceae* family. They are either toasted and eaten like peanuts or are ground to make sauces. They are available hulled or unhulled in supermarkets, Mexican groceries, and specialty food shops.

Purslane (*Portulaca oleracea*) is a vegetable that was cultivated in Europe and the Americas at the time of the conquest. It was widely used by the Incas. Purslane is sometimes considered a weed. It usually grows next to tomatoes. The leaves and tender shoots are edible and have a tart flavor. Purslane is used as a vegetable or added to stews, soups, and salads. It is available in the United States at the end of the summer in ethnic groceries. Rinse thoroughly, like spinach, and store between paper towels in a plastic bag. It will last for a few days in the refrigerator. Cook in boiling water for five to eight minutes.

Quesos (Cheeses). For hundreds of years, *queso blanco* or *queso fresco* (white cheese) was the cheese all South Americans used to make their specialties. It was, and still is, used almost every day, especially in the Andean countries. This cheese is a fresh, moist, lightly salted, unripened cheese made from cow's milk. It comes mainly in two varieties, depending on the age of the cheese. One, called *quesillo*, is used the same day it is made or within a few days. It is very refreshing, reminiscent of ricotta cheese, but unlike ricotta, it has been molded and can be cut into thick slices. It is available in some Mexican groceries. For crumbling, I substitute Mexican *queso fresco*.

The other type of *queso blanco*, called *queso de mesa*, is firmer because after it is placed in the mold, it is pressed and left to mature for a couple of weeks. I have found that this type of cheese can be replaced by brick, *panela*, Chihuahua, mozzarella, or Muenster. In some South American countries, *queso blanco* comes in various degrees of maturation, ranging from the ricotta type to the hard cheese. As for the names, almost every country has a different name—a nightmare for anyone doing research on the foods of South America.

Next in popularity in South America is Parmesan cheese. *Queso de cabra* (goat cheese) has always been used in the areas where sheep are raised. Edam, Gouda, and Swiss cheese are popular in Venezuela and the southern countries, where large numbers of Europeans settled. Mozzarella and provolone are much more prevalent than white cheese in the areas settled by Italian immigrants.

The assortment of cheeses in South American supermarkets today is overwhelming. I think that white cheese is gradually going to disappear (at least among the wealthy) and be replaced by European-type cheeses as South Americans start experimenting with international cuisine and adopt new cheeses to use in their creole recipes.

Quince (*Cydonia oblonga*) is an aromatic fruit brought to the Americas by the Spaniards and Portuguese. Depending on the variety, it can have the shape of an apple or a Bartlett pear (it is related to both; all three are members of the rose family). The skin is sometimes smooth and sometimes covered with fuzz; it usually has a golden color. The hard flesh is an ivory color that turns a pale pink-orange when cooked. It is rarely eaten raw because it is quite tart. It should be peeled and cored before cooking. In South America, quinces are used in stews, desserts, and various confections, such as marmalades and quince paste. Quinces are available in U.S. supermarkets in the fall and winter. They should be handled with care because they bruise easily. If stored in a cool place, they will last for months. To store, wrap them individually in plastic wrap and make sure they don't touch one another.

Quince Paste is a confection made with quince and sugar and either molded into bars or packed in round tins. It is available in Latin American groceries. Quince paste is usually served sliced with pieces of brick cheese.

Rose Water is a flavoring used mainly in the preparation of desserts. Brought over by the Spaniards, it is the extract of roses mixed with distilled water. It can be found in most Latin American and Middle Eastern groceries and some supermarkets.

Saffron (*Crocus sativus*) is the king of spices, largely because it commands an incredibly high price. It takes more than 200,000 stigmas of a specific type of crocus to make one pound of saffron. Each stigma has to be picked by hand and then dried. Fortunately, very little saffron is needed in cooking, as it takes only a few strands soaked in a little water to give food a pleasant yellow color and an exotic flavor that is hard to describe. Saffron powder, also rather expensive, should be avoided because it tends to give just the color without the flavor. Saffron is the indispensable ingredient in *paella* and is used in other rice dishes, soups, and curries, as well as in some bakery products. Do not confuse it with Mexican saffron, which is entirely different from Spanish saffron. Mexican saffron is an herb that gives color but not flavor.

Shrimp, Dried These are tiny shrimp that have been salted and dried. Dried shrimp are widely used in Bahian cooking and some Peruvian specialties. They come in two varieties, either with the head and shell on or peeled. Dried shrimp are usually ground before using and can be found in Chinese and Latin American markets.

Sofrito is the uniting element of the diverse cuisines of South America. This onion-based flavoring or sauce has many regional variations, which can include garlic, peppers, tomatoes, and diverse herbs and seasonings. For more information, see page 337.

Tamarillo (*Cyphomandra betacea*), also called tree tomato, belongs to the nightshade family. This fruit is native to South America and is very popular in Ecuador and Colombia. The tamarillo is the size of a large plum tomato, with a smooth, tough skin similar to that of an eggplant—which is why it is called eggplant fruit in southern Ecuador. Tamarillos are bright red or yellow in color. The red variety has orange flesh with two whorls of purple seeds embedded in the flesh. The yellow variety has orange flesh and seeds. The flesh is tart and fragrant, ideal for making ice creams, compotes, mousses, and fruit drinks. To peel, just drop them into boiling water for a few seconds, rinse with cold water, and peel. Then soak the fruit for a few seconds in cold water and rinse to remove the bitter coating. If the seeds need to be removed, cut the fruit in half lengthwise and scoop them out with a teaspoon. Tamarillos are available fresh in U.S. supermarkets in early fall, and frozen pulp can be found in some Latin American markets.

Tamarind (*Tamarindus indica*) originated in either Africa or Asia, but the Spaniards brought it to the Americas in the 1600s. This tart fruit is widely used in some Latin American cuisines to make refreshing drinks, sauces for meat and fowl, and some desserts. Tamarind pods are three to four inches long, crack easily, and house up to 12 large, flat seeds surrounded by a soft brownish pulp. Stored in a cool, dark place, they will keep indefinitely. Tamarind is also made into a paste. Tamarind pods are available in many U.S. supermarkets, and the frozen pulp and tamarind paste are available in some Latin American and Asian groceries. To extract the juice from the pods, soak them in water to cover for 30 minutes. Remove the seeds, place the pulp and half a cup of the soaking water in a blender, and puree. Pass through a medium-mesh sieve and discard the solids.

Tapioca is a starch extracted mostly from bitter cassava (yuca) roots. When a flour made from the roots, called yuca flour (or *polvilho* in Brazil), is heated in big iron pans, it is transformed into little balls that are called tapioca. In Brazil, it is used to prepare couscous, cream soups, and puddings.

Tucupi is a condiment used in the Amazon region of Brazil. It is the indispensable ingredient in the preparation of *tucupi* duck. *Tucupi* is the liquid extracted from bitter cassava (yuca) when preparing manioc meal. This liquid is then boiled with *jambú* leaves, chicory, garlic, and *malagueta* pepper. *Tucupi* is not available in the United States.

Vanilla (*Vanilla planifolia*) is a native of Mexico and a member of the orchid family. The vanilla bean is black and looks like a skinny string bean, with hundreds of tiny black seeds inside. The beans have to be cured by a complex process before they can be used. They can be made into vanilla extract or kept whole. Whole beans can be used to flavor liquids, much as a whole cinnamon stick might be used—to add flavor but not to be eaten. They also may be soaked and used to make desserts. After soaking, the bean is often cut lengthwise so that the tiny seeds can be scraped out and added to the soaking liquid.

Yuca Flour is made from the bitter cassava (yuca). It has a texture similar to that of cornstarch and can be found in most Latin American markets. It comes packaged in one-pound boxes under the name tapioca starch or *almidón de yuca*. In Brazil, it goes by the name *polvilho*. There are two kinds of *polvilho*—*polvilho doce* (which is drier) and *polvilho azedo* (which is fresh). This very delicate flour is the deposit left after the cassava has been grated, pressed, and washed. It is used to make breads, cookies, cakes, and tapioca.

Zapote (*Matisia cordata*) looks like *mamey*, but it has beautiful orange or reddish flesh, which is wrapped around three to five seeds. It has a fibrous texture and is eaten fresh or in fruit juices or ice creams. *Zapote* is native to some areas of the Amazon, from Brazil to Colombia and Peru. It can sometimes be found in the United States in ethnic groceries.

A Dictionary of South American Ingredients

Note: The Spanish names are in roman. The Portuguese names are in boldface. (A) = Aymara; (G) = Guarani; (M) = Mapuche; (Q) = Quechua; (AI) = other South American Indian.

ENGLISH	SPANISH/INDIAN/ PORTUGUESE	SCIENTIFIC NAMES
Achira	Achira	*Canna edulis*
	Atsera	
Achogcha (also called caigua)	Achoccha	*Cyclanthera pedata*
	Achogcha	
	Caigua	
	Chayotero	
	Pepino Andino	
	Pepino de Rellenar	
	Accoccha, achogcha (Q)	
	Caigua (Q)	
Agave	Penco negro	*Agave americana*
	Chahuar, yana chahuar (Q)	

ENGLISH	SPANISH/INDIAN/ PORTUGUESE	SCIENTIFIC NAMES
Ahipa	Achipa	*Pachyrhizus ahipa*
	Ahipa	
	Ajipa	
	Ajipa, asipa (Q)	
	Villu, huitoto (A)	
	Ahipa	
Allspice	Guyabita	*Pimenta dioica*
	Pimienta de chapa	
	Pimienta de Jamaica	
	Pimienta de malagueta	
	Pimienta de olor	
	Pimienta de Tabasco	
	Pimienta dulce	
	Pimienta gorda	
	Pimenta da Jamaica	

ENGLISH	SPANISH/INDIAN/ PORTUGUESE	SCIENTIFIC NAMES	ENGLISH	SPANISH/INDIAN/ PORTUGUESE	SCIENTIFIC NAMES
Almond	Alloza	*Prunus dulcis*	Arracacha	Apio	*Arracacia esculenta,*
	Almendra		(also called	Apio criollo	*Arracacia xanthorriza*
	Amêndoa		white carrot)	Arracacha	
Amaranth	Amaranto	*Amaranthus caudatus,*		Racacha	
	Ataco	*Amaranthus quitensis*		Zanahoria blanca	
	Coyolito			Lakachu (A)	
	Huauti			Laqachu, rakkacha (Q)	
	Kiwicha			**Batata cenoura**	
	Quihuicha			**Mandoquinha**	
	Sangorache		Arrowroot	Chuño	*Maranta arundinacea*
	Trigo inca			Arruruz	
	Kiwicha, quihuicha (Q)			**Araruta**	
	Qamasa (A)		Artichoke	Alcachofa	*Cynara scolymus*
	Sankurachi (Q)			Alcaucil	
	Amaranto			**Alcachofra**	
Anise	Anís	*Pimpinella anisum*	Asparagus	Espárragos	*Asparagus officinalis*
	Matalauva			**Aspergo**	
	Pimpinela		Avocado	Aguacali	*Persea americana,*
	Anís			Aguacate	*Persea drymifolia*
Annatto, ground	Achiote molido			Chuchu	
	Colorau			Pagua	
Annatto seeds	Achiote	*Bixa orellana*		Palta	
	Bija			Palto	
	Bijol			Palta (Q)	
	Mantur			**Abacate**	
	Manzana		Babaco	Babaco	*Carica pentagona*
	Onoto		Bacon	Chulla	
	Semilla de anato			Entrecijo	
	Mantur (Q)			Grasa	
	Urucú			Lardo	
	Urucum			Loncha	
Appetizer	Aperitivo			Lonja	
	Entrada			Merceo	
	Aperitivo			Panceta	
Apple	Manzana	*Malus* spp.		Pelas	
	Poma			Tocineta	
	Maçã			Tocino	
Apricot	Albaricoque	*Prunus armeniaca*		**Toucinho defumado**	
	Chabacano		Badea	Badea	*Passiflora quadrangularis*
	Damasco		Baking powder	Levadura en polvo	
	Abricó			Polvo de hornear	
	Damasco			Royal	
				Fermento em pó	
			Baking soda	Bicarbonato de soda	
				Soda de hornear	
				Bicarbonato de sódio	

ENGLISH	SPANISH/INDIAN/ PORTUGUESE	SCIENTIFIC NAMES	ENGLISH	SPANISH/INDIAN/ PORTUGUESE	SCIENTIFIC NAMES
Banana	Banana	*Musa sapientium*	Bean, Lupini	Chocho	*Lupinus mutabilis*
	Cambur		Bean, Pinto	Fríjol	
	Guineo		Bean, String	Alubia	*Phaseolus vulgaris*
	Plátano		or Green	Bajoca	
	Plátano de seda			Caucha	
	Banano			Chaucha	
Banana,	Guineíto niño	*Musa sapientium*		Ejote	
Niño	Guineo de oro			Habichuela	
	Orito			Judía verde	
Banana, Red	Guineo morado	*Musa sapientium*		Porotito	
	Plátano rosado			Poroto verde	
Banana	Hojas de plátano			Vainita	
leaves	**Folha de banana**		Bean, White	Alubias	
Banana	Curuba	*Passiflora mollissima*		Fríjol blanco	
passion fruit	Curuba quiteña			Habichuela blanca	
	Churuba			Judía	
	Purush		Beans	Alubias	*Phaseolus vulgaris*
	Tacso			Ayocotes	
	Taxo			Caraotas	
	Tumbo			Frejoles	
	Tacsu, tagsu, tausu (Q)			Fríjoles	
	Maracuyá suspiro			Frisol	
Barley	Alcacer	*Hordeum vulgare*		Guandú	
	Cebada			Habichuela	
	Cevada			Judías	
Barnacle	Percebe	*Lepas anatifera*		Porotos	
Basil	Alabeja	*Ocimum basilicum*		Poroto, purutu (Q)	
	Albahaca			**Feijão**	
	Alfabega		Beef	Carne de res	
	Manjericão			**Carne de boi ou de vaca**	
Bay leaf	Hoja de laurel	*Laurus nobilis*	Bottom	Bola	
	Louro		round	Boliche	
Bean, Black	Caraota negra		roast	Punta de ganso	
	Fríjol negro			Salón	
	Freijão preto		Brisket	Estomaguillo	
Bean,	Poroto granado			Pecho	
Cranberry			Chuck	Espalda	
Bean, Fava	Faba	*Vicia faba*	roast	Posta negra	
(also called	Fava			Pulpa de solomo abierto	
broad bean)	Haba		Eye of	Gansillo	
	Fava		round	Lechón	
Bean, Kidney	Habichuela colorada			Muchacho redondo	
Bean, Lima	Fríjol de manteca	*Phaseolus lunatus,*	Fillet	Lomo	
	Fríjol payar	*Phaseolus limensis*	Flank	Buche	
	Haba de Lima		steak	Faldilla	
	Pallar			Ganso	
	Torta			Malaya	
	Pallar (Q)				

ENGLISH	SPANISH/INDIAN/PORTUGUESE	SCIENTIFIC NAMES	ENGLISH	SPANISH/INDIAN/PORTUGUESE	SCIENTIFIC NAMES
Loin	Lomillo		Breadfruit	Árbol de pan	*Artocarpus communis*
Round	Babilla			Pana	
Rump	Cadera			Panapén	
roast	Punta trasero			**Fanta pão**	
Shank	Garrón		Brine	Salmuera	
	Lagarto			**Salmoura**	
T-bone	Bife de costilla		Broccoli	Brecoli	*Brassica oleracea*
Tenderloin	Filete			Brocoli	
	Lomito			Broculi	
	Lomo			**Brócolis**	
Beef jerky	Carne seca		Butter	Manteca	
(dried	Cecina			Mantequilla	
meat)	Charque			**Manteiga**	
	Charqui		Cabbage	Berza sin rizar	*Brassica* spp.
	Machaca			Col	
	Tasajo			Repollo	
	Ch'arki (Q)			Taioba	
	Carne seca			Tallo	
Beer	Cerveza			**Repollo**	
	Cerveja		Cabbage,	Berza morada	*Brassica oleracea*
Beet	Betabel	*Beta vulgaris*	Red	Col morada	
	Betarraga			Lombarda	
	Betarrave			Repollo morado	
	Remolacha		Cacao	Cacao	*Theobroma cacao*
	Beterraba			Cacáho, kakao, mirricumba (AI)	
Biscuit	Galleta			**Cacau**	
	Sequilho		Cactus fruit (see Prickly pear)		
Blackberry	Mora	*Rubus glaucus*	Caigua (see Achogcha)		
of the Andes	Mora de Castilla		Cake	Biscocho	
	Zarzamora			Cake	
	Ccjari-cjari (Q)			Pastel	
	Amora preta			Ponque	
Blood	Morcilla			Torta	
sausage	Moronga			**Bola, torta**	
	Morulla		Calabaza	Abóbora	*Cucurbita pepo* var.,
	Chouriço			Ahuyama	*Cucurbita maxima* var.
Blueberry of	Mortiño	*Vaccinium*		Andahí	
the Andes	Macha-macha, chivacu, congama (AI)	*floribundum*		Ayote	
Boldo	Boldo	*Peumus boldus*		Bule	
Brains	Sesos			Calabaza	
Brazil nut	Nuez del Brazil	*Bertholletia excelsa*		Cidracayote	
	Ouriço			Hoco	
	Pará nut			Lacayote	
	Castanha do Pará			Zapallo	
Bread	Miga de pan			Yuví (AI)	
crumbs	Pan rallado			**Abóbora**	
	Farinha de pao				
	Farinha de rosca				

ENGLISH	SPANISH/INDIAN/ PORTUGUESE	SCIENTIFIC NAMES	ENGLISH	SPANISH/INDIAN/ PORTUGUESE	SCIENTIFIC NAMES
Canapés	Bocas		Celeriac	Apio	*Apium graveolens*
	Bocadillos		(also called celery root)		var. *dulce*
	Canapés		Celery	Apio	*Apium graveolens*
Canihua (see Kaniwa)				Ersmirnio	
Cantaloupe	Melón	*Cucumis melo*		Panul	
Cape	Cereza del Perú	*Physalis peruviana*		Perejil macedonio	
gooseberry	Chuchuva			**Aipo**	
	Topotopo		Celery root (see Celeriac)		
	Uchuva		Chamburo	Chamburo	*Carica chrysopetala*
	Uvilla			Toronchi	
	Topopo (Q)		Chamomile	Albarillo	*Matricaria recutita*
	Uchuva, cuchuva (A)			Camomila	
	Batetesta			Manzanilla	
	Groselha do Peru			**Camomila**	
Capers	Alcaparras	*Capparris spinosa*	Chayote	Alcayote	*Sechium edule*
Capulí	Capulí	*Prunus capuli*	(also called	Apupu	
cherry	Murmumtu, Ussum (Q)		mango	Chayote	
Carambola	Carambola	*Averrhoa carambola*	squash,	Chayotli	
(also called			vegetable	Chilhuacán	
star fruit)			pear, and	Cho-cho	
Carrot	Azahorio	*Daucus carota*	vegetable	Chu-chu	
	Caraota		squash)	Cidracayote	
	Carota			Cidrayota	
	Zanahoria			Cidrayote	
	Zanahoria amarilla			Espinosos	
	Cenoura			Guisayote	
Carrot, White (see Arracacha)				Guisquil	
Cashew	Acajú	*Anacardium*		Hisquil	
	Anacardo	*occidentale*		Pataste	
	Cajuil			Tallote	
	Marañón			Tayote	
	Merey			Zapallo	
	Pajuil			**Xuxu**	
	Caju		Cheese	Queso	
	Castanha de caju			**Queijo**	
Cassava	Aipín	*Manihot esculenta*	Cherimoya	Chirimorriñon	*Annona cherimola*
	Mandioca		(also called	Chirimoya	
	Manioc		sweetsop)	Fruta de conde	
	Yuca			Chirimuyu, masa (Q)	
	Mandi'ó (G)			Pa'tanaca, chichivilla, jaéch (AI)	
	Mandioca			Yuructira (A)	
	Manihot			**Cherimólia**	
Catfish	Bagre	*Arius jordani*		**Fruta do conde**	
	Jurupoca		Cherry	Cereza	*Prunus* spp.
	Surubí			Guinda	
	Surubim			**Cereja**	
Cauliflower	Coliflor	*Brassica oleracea*	Chervil	Cerafolio	*Anthriscus cerefolium*
	Couve-flor			Perifollo	

ENGLISH	SPANISH/INDIAN/ PORTUGUESE	SCIENTIFIC NAMES	ENGLISH	SPANISH/INDIAN/ PORTUGUESE	SCIENTIFIC NAMES
Chestnut	Castaña	*Castanea sativa*	Cod, Salt	Bacalao	
	Marrona			**Bacalhau**	
	Castanha		Coffee	Café	
Chicken	Pollo			**Café**	
	Frango		Collard	Berza	*Brassica* var.
Chicken breast	Pechuga de pollo		greens	**Couve**	
Chickpea	Arvejón	*Cicer arietinum*	Cookie	Galleta dulce	
(also called garbanzo)	Ceci			**Biscoito, Bolacha**	
	Cícero		Coriander (see Cilantro)		
	Chícharo		Coriander seed	Semilla de culantro	
	Garbanzo		Corn	Cenacle	*Zea mays*
	Grão de bico			Chalo	
Chilguacán	Jigacho	*Carica candamarcensis*		Chilote	
	Siglalón			Choclo	
Chives	Cebollinos	*Allium schoenoprasum*		Chocolo	
	Ciboulet			Elote	
	Cibullete			Jojote	
	Cebolinho			Maíz	
Chorizo	Chorizo			Maíz tierno	
	Chouriço			Maíz verde	
Cilantro	Chillangua	*Coriandrum sativum*		Abatí (G)	
(also called fresh coriander)	Chirara			Sara, zara (Q)	
	Cilantro			**Milho verde**	
	Coriandro		Cornhusk	Amero	
	Corindro			Chala	
	Culantro			Cutul	
	Coentro			Hoja de milpa	
Cinnamon	Canela	*Cinnamomum verum*		Panca	
	Canela		Cornish hen	Pollito	
Cinnamon, Mexican	Canela	*Cinnamomum zeylanicum*	Cornmeal	Chuchoca	
			(also called corn flour)	Harina de maíz	
Cinnamon flower (see Ishpingo)				Hu'ití (G)	
Citrón	Cidra	*Citrus medica*		**Fubá**	
Clam	Almeja	*Tapes decussata*	Corn on	Choclo	
	Chirca		the cob	Coronta	
	Amêijoa			Mazorca de maíz tierno	
Clam, Chilean	Macha	*Mesodesma donacium*		Tuzas	
				Abatiky (G)	
Cloves	Clavo de olor	*Syzygium aromaticum*		Api (A, Q)	
	Cravo-da-Índia			**Espiga**	
Coconut	Coco	*Cocos nucifera*	Cornstarch	Almidón de maíz	
	Coco			Chuño	
Cod, Fresh	Abadejo			Fécula de maíz	
	Bacalao			Maicena	
	Bacalhao			**Maisena**	
	Mojito		Crab, Blue	Jaiba	*Callinectes sapidus*
	Reyezuelo		Crab, King	Centollo	*Maia squinado*

ENGLISH	SPANISH/INDIAN/ PORTUGUESE	SCIENTIFIC NAMES
Crab, Land	Cangrejo	*Ucides occidentalis*
Crab, Rock	Pangora	*Cancer pagurus*
	Caraguejo	
Cracker	Galleta	
	Bolacha	
Cranberry	Arándano	*Vaccinium macrocarpon*
Crayfish	Cangrejo de río	*Astacus fluviatilis*
Cream	Crema	
	Grasa de leche	
	Nata	
	Creme	
	Nata	
Cream,	Cacuja	
Whipping	Crema	
	Natas	
	Natillas	
	Nata	
Cream of	Cremor tártaro	
tartar		
Cucumber	Cohombrillo	*Cucumis sativus*
	Cohombro	
	Pepino	
	Pepino	
Cumin	Comino	*Cuminum cyminum*
	Cominho	
Cumin seed	Alcaeavea	
	Comino	
	Hummel	
Currant	Grosella	*Ribes* spp.
	Pasa de corinto	
	Uva de corinto	
Curry	Curri	
powder	Polvo curry	
	Caril	
Custard	Flan	
	Leche asada	
	Creme	
	Flã	
Date	Dátil	*Phoenix* spp.
	Datil	
Dendê (also	Aceite de palma	*Elaeis guineensis*
called palm	**Dendê**	
oil)		
Dessert	Postre	
	Sobremesa	
Dill	Eneldo	*Anethum graveolens*

ENGLISH	SPANISH/INDIAN/ PORTUGUESE	SCIENTIFIC NAMES
Dolphin	Delfín	
	Delfim	
	Golfinho	
Duck	Pato	
	Pato	
Eel	Anguila	
	Enguia	
Egg	Huevo	
	Ovo	
Eggplant	Berenjena	*Solanum* spp.
	Chicha	
	Chichigua	
	Chirimora	
	Huistomate	
	Pepino morado	
	Berinjela	
Endive	Chicoria	*Cichorium endivia*
	Endivia	
	Escarola	
	Pascueta	
	Endivia	
Feijoa	Feijoa	*Feijoa sellowiana*
	Feijoa	
Fig	Breva	*Ficus carica*
	Higo	
	Figo	
Filbert (see Hazelnut)		
Fish	Pescado	
	Peixe	
Flounder	Lenguado del Pacífico	*Paralichtys woolmani*
Flour	Harina	
	Farinha	
	Farinha de trigo	
Fruit	Fruta	
	Fruta	
Garbanzo (see Chickpea)		
Garlic, Fresh	Ajo	*Allium sativum*
	Alho	
Garlic,	Ajo en polvo	
Granulated		
Gelatin	Gelatina	
	Gelatina	
Gelatin,	Colapez	
Unflavored	Gelatina sin sabor	
	Grenetina	
	Plantillas	
	Gelatina	
	Gelatina en folha	

ENGLISH	SPANISH/INDIAN/ PORTUGUESE	SCIENTIFIC NAMES	ENGLISH	SPANISH/INDIAN/ PORTUGUESE	SCIENTIFIC NAMES
Gherkin	Gohombrillo	*Cucumis sativus*	Guava	Guayaba	*Psidium guajava*
	Pepinillo			Guayabo	
	Pepino de sal			Arasá (G)	
Ginger	Gengibre	*Zingiber officinalis*		Savintu, sahuintu (Q)	
	Jengibre			**Goiaba**	
	Kión		Guinea pig	Cobayo	*Cavia porcellus*
	Gengibre			Conejillo de Indias	
Goat	Cabra			Conejo silvestre	
	Chivo			Curi	
	Bode			Cuy	
	Cabra			Cuye	
Goose	Ganso		Hake	Merluza	
	Ganso		Ham	Jamón	
Granadilla	Granadilla	*Passiflora ligularis*	Hazelnut	Avellana	*Corylus avellana*
	Granadilla común		(also called	**Avelã**	
	Granadilla de mate		filbert)		
	Granadilla tripona		Heart	Corazón	
	Tintin, ccjoto (Q)			**Coração**	
Grape	Uva	*Vitis vinifera*	Hearts of	Palmitos	*Arecaceae*
	Uva		palm	Chunta (Q)	
Grapefruit	Cidro	*Citrus paradisi*		**Palmitos**	
	Pamplemusa		Hominy	Mote	
	Pomelo			Patasca	
	Toronja		Honey	Miel de abeja	
	Toronja			**Mel**	
Grouper	Mero	Serranidae	Hors	Abrebocas	
(also called			d'oeuvres	Bocadillos	
sea bass)				Bocaditos	
Guaba	Guaba	*Inga edulis,*		Botanas	
(also called	Guaba de la costa	*Inga feuillei,*		Copetíns	
pacay)	Guama	*Inga pachicarpa*		Entremeses	
	Ingá			Pasapalos	
	Pacae			Picadas	
	Pacay			Picoteos	
	Paqay			**Salgadinhos**	
	Pa'qay, paccai (Q)		Horseradish	Rábano picante	*Armoracia rusticana*
	Pa'qaya (A)			Raíz fuerte	
	Ingá cipó			Raíz picante	
	Rabo de mico			**Rábano picante**	
Guanábana	Guanábana	*Annona muricata*	Hot dog	Perro caliente	
(also called	Jachali guanábana		Huacatay	Huacatay	*Chenopodium ambrosioides*
soursop)	Masasamba (Q)			Paico	
	Graviola			Payco	
	Jaca de Pará			Té de México	
Guaraná	Guaraná	*Paullinia cupana*	Innards	Achuras	
				Interiores	
				Órganos	

ENGLISH	SPANISH/INDIAN/ PORTUGUESE	SCIENTIFIC NAMES	ENGLISH	SPANISH/INDIAN/ PORTUGUESE	SCIENTIFIC NAMES
Ishpingo (also called cinnamon flower)	Flor de canela Ishpingo	*Ocotea quixos*	Lemon balm	Cidronela Melisa Toronjil **Bálsamo**	*Melissa officinalis*
Jam	Mermelada		Lemongrass	Hierba luisa	*Cymbopogon citratus*
Jelly	Jalea **Geléia**		Lemon verbena	Cedrón	*Lippia citriodora*
Jerusalem artichoke	Alcachofa de Jerusalen Aleachofra Topinambur	*Helianthus tuberosus*	Lentil	Lenteja **Lentilha**	*Lens culinaris*
Jícama	Jícama	*Pachyrhizus erosus*	Lettuce	Lechuga **Alface**	*Lactuca sativa*
Juice	Jugo **Suco**		Lime	Lima Limón pequeño	*Citrus aurantifolia*
Juniper berry	Nebrina **Zimbro**	*Juniperus communis*		Limón sútil **Limão-doce**	
Kale	Guita **Couve**	*Brassica oleracea*	Liver	Hígado **Figado**	
Kaniwa (also called canihua)	Cañigua Cañihua Cañiwa Kañiwa Cuchi-quinoa, kañiwa (Q) Iswalla hupa, ahara hupa, cañahua (A)	*Chenopodium palladicaule*	Lobster	Bogavante Cabrajo Langosta **Lagosta**	
			Longaniza	Longaniza	
Ketchup	Salsa de tomate		Lucuma	Lucmo Lúcuma	*Pouteria lucuma,* *Lukuma bifera,*
Kid	Cabrito Chivito **Criança**			Lugma Rukma Aguaí, aguay (G) Lucma (A) Lugma (Q)	*Lucuma obovata*
Kidney	Riñón **Rim**		Lupini bean	Altramuz Chocho	*Lupinus mutabilis*
Kiwifruit	Apterix Kiwi	*Actinidia deliciosa*		Tarwi Chuchus muti, tarhui (Q) Tauri (A) **Tremoço**	
Lamb	Borrego Cordero **Cordeiro**		Mace	Mace Macia	*Myristica fragrans*
Lard	Manteca **Gordura** **Lardo**			Macis	
Leek	Ajo porro Cebolla puerro Poro Porro Puerro **Alho-porro**	*Allium porrum*	Mackerel	Berdela Caballa Escombro Macarela Pintado **Cavala**	*Scomber japonicus*
Lemon	Acitrón Citrón Limón Limón grande Limón real **Limão**	*Citrus limon*	Malanga (also called yautia)	Cocoyam Tannia Tannier Yautía	*Xanthosoma* spp.

ENGLISH	SPANISH/INDIAN/PORTUGUESE	SCIENTIFIC NAMES	ENGLISH	SPANISH/INDIAN/PORTUGUESE	SCIENTIFIC NAMES
Mamey	Mamey	*Mammea americana*	Muffin	Mollete	
Mamey zapote	Mamey	*Calocarpun sapota*		**Bolinho doce**	
			Mullet	Lisa	*Mugil cephalus*
Mandarin	Mandarina	*Citrus reticulata*	Mushroom	Callampas	*Agaricus* spp.
	Naranja china			Champiñón	
Mango	Mango	*Mangifera indica*		Hongo	
	Mangó			Seta	
	Manga			**Cogumelo, champinhon**	
Mango squash (see Chayote)			Mussel	Cholga	*Mytilus edulis*
Manioc				Cholgua	
Manioc meal	**Farinha de mandioca**			Chorito	
Marjoram	Marjorama	*Origanum* spp.		Choro	
	Merjorana			Choto	
Mashua	Añú	*Tropaealum tuberosum*		Mejillón	
	Mashua			Sururú	
	Añu, apiñu, yanaoca, ysaño (Q)		Mustard	Jenabé	*Brassica* spp.
	Isau, issanu, kkayacha (A)			Mostaza	
Maté	Maté	*Ilex paraguariensis*		Mostazo	
(also called Paraguay tea)	Yerba mate			**Mustarda**	
			Mutton	Carnero	
Mayonnaise	Mahonesa			**Carneiro**	
	Mayonesa		Myrtle	Arrayán	*Eugenia* spp.
	Maionese		Ñame (also called yam)	Aje	*Dioscorea alata*
Meat	Carne			Mapuey	
	So'ó (G)			Ñame	
	Carne			Yampi	
Meat, Ground	Carne molida			**Inhame**	
			Naranjilla	Lulo	*Solanum quitoence*
Medlar	Chico zapote	*Achras sapota*		Lulun	
	Níspero			Naranjilla	
	Zapatillo			Quito orange	
	Zapote			Lulu, puscolulu, pushsuc-lulum (Q)	
Medlar, Japanese	Níspero del Japón	*Eriobotrya japonica*		Lulu (AI)	
Melon	Melón	*Cucumis melo*	Nectarine	Nectareo	*Prunus* spp.
	Melão			Nectarino	
Melon pear (see Pepino)			Noodles	Fideos	
Milk	Leche			**Talharim**	
	Kamby (G)		Nut	Nuez	
	Leite			**Castahna**	
Millet	Mijo	*Panicum miliaceum*		**Nos**	
	Millo		Nutmeg	Nuez moscada	*Myristica fragans*
	Painço		Oats	Avena	*Avena sativa*
Mineral water	Agua mineral			Dulzaina	
	Água mineral			Poema pastoril	
Molasses	Melado			Zampona	
	Tintura de panela			**Aveia**	

ENGLISH	SPANISH/INDIAN/ PORTUGUESE	SCIENTIFIC NAMES	ENGLISH	SPANISH/INDIAN/ PORTUGUESE	SCIENTIFIC NAMES
Oca	Ciuba	*Oxalis tuberosa*	Palm oil (see Dendê)		
	Ibia		Panela (see Sugar, Molded Brown)		
	Oca		Papaya	Fruta bomba	*Carica papaya*
	Quiba			Lechosa	
	Apiña, apilla, kawi (A)			Mamao	
	Uca, oca, occa, o'qa, okka (Q)			Mamón	
Octopus	Pulpo	*Eledone cirrosa*		Papaw	
	Polvo, octópode			Papaya	
Oil	Aceite			Pawpaw	
	Oleo			**Mamão**	
	Azeite		Papaya,	Chilacuán	*Carica goudotiana*
Okra	Angú	*Hibiscus esculentus*	Chilean and	Papaya de montaña	
	Bamias		Colombian	Papaya silvestre	
	Candia			Papayote	
	Chicombó			Papayuela	
	Chimbombó		Paprika	Ají de color	*Capsicum tetragonum*
	Guingambó			Ají dulce	
	Majagua			Pimentón	
	Molondrones			Pimentón molido	
	Quimbombó			Pimentón rojo dulce	
	Quingombó			**Páprica**	
	Yerba de culebra		Paraguay tea (see Maté)		
	Quiabo		Parsley	Perejil	*Pretroselinum hortense*
Olive	Aceituna	*Olea europaea*		**Salsa**	
	Oliva		Parsnip	Chirivía	*Pastinaca sativa*
	Azeitona			Pastinaca	
Omelet	Tortilla		Partridge	Perdíz	
Onion	Cebolla	*Allium cepa*		**Perdiz**	
	Cebola		Passion fruit	Ceibey	*Passiflora edulis*
Onion, Green (see Scallion)				Curcuba	
Onion, Red	Cebolla morada	*Allium cepa*		Granadilla	
	Cebolla paiteña			Maracuyá	
Orange	China	*Citrus sinensis*		Parcha	
	Naranja			Parchita	
	Naranja dulce			**Maracujá**	
	Laranja		Pea, Green	Allgarroba	*Pisum sativum*
Orange, Sour (also called bitter orange)	Naranja agria	*Citrus aurantia*		Alverja	
				Arverja	
				Chícharo	
Oregano	Orégano	*Origanum vulgare*		Guisante	
Oxtail	Rabo			Petit pois	
	Cauda			**Ervilha**	
	Rabo		Pea, Pigeon	Gandules	*Cajanus cajan*
Oyster	Ostra	*Ostrea edulis*		Goongoo	
	Venera		Peas, Dried	Alverjitas secas	
	Vieira			Arverjión	
	Ostra			Chícharo seco	
Pacay (see Guaba)				Guisante seco	

ENGLISH	SPANISH/INDIAN/PORTUGUESE	SCIENTIFIC NAMES	ENGLISH	SPANISH/INDIAN/PORTUGUESE	SCIENTIFIC NAMES
Peach	Durazno	*Prunus persica*	Pepper, Red Bell	Ají dulce	*Capsicum annuum* var.
	Melocotón			Ají rojo	
	Pêssego			Chile morrón	
Peanut	Cacahuate	*Arachis hypogaea*		Chiltona	
	Cacahuey			Conguito	
	Maní			Morrón	
	Inchic (Q)			Peperrone	
	Manduví (G)			Pimiento rojo	
	Torale, nússe (AI)			**Pimentão vermelho**	
	Amendoim		Pepper, Rocoto	Rocoto	*Capsicum pubescens*
Peanut butter	Mantequilla de maní		Pepper, White	Pimienta blanca	
Pear	Pera	*Pyrus communis*	Pepper, Yellow Bell	Pimienta amarilla	*Capsicum* spp.
	Pêra				
Pecan	Nuez	*Carya illinoiensis*	Peppercorn, Pink	Molle	*Shinus molle*
	Nuez cáscara de papel			Mulli (Q)	
	Nuez encarcelada			**Pimenta rosa**	
	Pacana		Peppermint	Hierbabuena	*Mentha piperita*
Pepino (also called melon pear)	Pepino	*Solanum muricatum*		Menta	
	Pepino dulce		Pepperoni	Pepperoni	
	Cachum, xachum (Q)			**Salaminho**	
	Kachan, kachuma (A)		Persimmon	Kaki	*Diospyros kaki*
Pepper, Black	Pimienta negra	*Piper nigrum*		Kaqui	
	Pimenta-do-reino			Maqui	
Pepper, Cayenne	Pimentón	*Capsicum annuum*	Pheasant	Faisán	
	Pimienta de cayena			**Faisão**	
	Pimienta roja		Pigeon, Wild	Torcaza	
Pepper, Green bell	Ají	*Capsicum* spp.	Pimento	Pimiento morrón	
	Chile		Pineapple	Anana	*Ananas comosus*
	Pimiento			Piña	
	Pimiento verde			Acupalla (Q)	
	Pimentão verde			Chula, chiguila, chui (AI)	
Pepper, Habanero	Habanero	*Capsicum chinense*		**Abacaxi**	
			Pine nut	Piñón	*Pinus pinea*
Pepper, Hot	Ají	*Capsicum baccatum*	Pistachio	Pistacho	*Pistacia vera*
	Chile		Pitaya	Pithaya	*Hylocereus undatus,*
	Guindilla			Pithaya de cardón	*Hylocereus triangularis*
	Pimentón				
	Pimiento		Plantain	Plátano	*Musa paradisiaca*
	Uchu (A, Q)			Plátano hartón	
	Pimenta			Plátano macho	
Pepper, Malagueta	Malagueta	*Capsicum annuum*	Plantain, Ripe	Amarillo	
	Pimenta malagueta			Maduro	
Pepper, Mirasol	Mirasol		Plum	Ciruela	*Prunus* spp.
				Claudia	
Pepper, Panca	Panca			Pruna	
				Ameixa	

ENGLISH	SPANISH/INDIAN/ PORTUGUESE	SCIENTIFIC NAMES	ENGLISH	SPANISH/INDIAN/ PORTUGUESE	SCIENTIFIC NAMES
Pomegranate	Granada	*Punica granatum*	Quail	Codorníz	
	Roma			**Codorna**	
Popcorn	Canguil		Quilquiña	Quilquiña	
	Maíz reventado		Quince	Membrillo	*Cydonia oblonga*
	Palomitas de maíz			**Marmelo**	
	Pipoca		Quinoa	Arroz del Perú	*Chenopodium quinoa*
Porgy	Pargo			Chancas	
Pork	Cebón			Dalma	
	Cerdo			Hupa	
	Chancho			Jupa	
	Coche			Kiuna	
	Cochino			Quinua	
	Cocho			Suba	
	Cuchi			Trigo Inca	
	Marrano			Triguillo	
	Puerco			Kinua, parca, quinua (Q)	
	Tunco			Quinhua (M)	
	Kuré (G)			Suba, pasca (AI)	
	Carne de porco			Supha, jopa, jupha, aara (A)	
Potato, Black	Papa negra	*Solanum tuberosum*		**Arroz miúdo do Perú**	
Potato, Sweet	(see Sweet Potato)			**Espinafre do Perú**	
Potato,	Papa	*Solanum tuberosum*	Rabbit	Conejo	
White	Patata			**Coelho**	
	Accsu, acshu (Q)		Radish	Rabanito	*Raphanus sativus*
	Batata			Rábano	
Potato,	Papa amarilla	*Solanum tuberosum*		**Rabanete**	
Yellow	Papa criolla		Raisin	Pasa	
Potatoes,	Chullurqa			Pasa de uva	
Dried	Chuño			Uva seca	
	Papa seca			**Passa**	
	Tunta (A)		Raspberry	Frambuesa	*Rubus idaeus*
Prickly pear	Jiotilla	*Opuntia* spp.		Sanguesa	
(also called	Tuna			**Framboesa**	
cactus fruit)			Red snapper	Huachinango	*Lutjanus peru*
Prune	Ciruela	*Spondia purpurea*		Pargo	
	Ciruela pasa		Rice	Arroz	*Oriza sativa*
	Guindón			Casula	
	Jocote			Macho	
	Xocotl			Kamby (G)	
	Ameixa seca			**Arroz**	
Puff pastry	Masa de ojaldre		Rosemary	Romero	*Rosmarinus officinalis*
Pumpkin	Calabaza	*Cucurbitaceae*	Rose water	Agua de azahares	
	Zapallo			Aguanafa	
	Abóbora		Rue	Ruda	*Ruta graveolens*
Pumpkin	Aiguaxte		Rye	Centeno	*Secale cereale*
seeds	Pepitas		Saffron	Azafrán	*Crocus sativus*
	Pepitoria			Brin	
Purslane	Verdolaga	*Portulaca oleracea*		Croco	
				Açafrão	

ENGLISH	SPANISH/INDIAN/ PORTUGUESE	SCIENTIFIC NAMES	ENGLISH	SPANISH/INDIAN/ PORTUGUESE	SCIENTIFIC NAMES
Sage	Hierba salvia **Salva**	*Salvia officinalis*	Shrimp	Camarón Cambaro Chacalín Gamba Quisquilla **Camarão**	
Salad	Ensalada **Salada**				
Salmon	Salmón **Salmão**	*Oncorhyncus* spp.			
Salsify	Salsifís	*Scorzonera hispanica*	Shrimp, Dried	Camarón seco	
Salt	Sal		Sierra	Sierra	*Scombridae*
Saltpeter	Nitro Salitre Tesquite		Snail	Caracole	
			Sole	Lenguado Lenguana	
Sapodilla	Sapodilla	*Manilkara zapota*	Sorrel	Acedera	*Rumex* spp.
Sapote, Black	Sapote negro	*Diospyros digyna*	Soup	Sopa **Sopa**	
Sapote, White	Sapote blanco	*Casimiroa edulis*	Soursop (see Guanábana)		
Sapote, Yellow	Mamey	*Pouteria mammosa*	Soy sauce	Salsa de soja Salsa soya Sillao	
Sardine	Sardina **Sardhina**	*Sardinopus* spp.	Spaghetti	Tallarines	
Sausage	Salchicha **Lingüiça**		Spearmint	Menta del Castillo Menta verde	*Menta viridis*
Scallion (also called green onion)	Cebolla blanca Cebolla china Cebolla en rama Cebolla junca Cebolla larga Cebolla verde Cebollín **Cebolinha**	*Allium cepa*	Spinach	Espinaca **Spinafre**	*Spinacia oleracea*
			Squab	Pichón	
			Squash, Spaghetti	Calabaza	*Cucurbita pepo*
			Squash, Winter	Calabaza Zapallo **Abobora**	*Cucurbitaceae*
Scallop	Conchita Vieira **Vieira**		Squash flower	Flor de calabaza	
Sea bass (see Grouper)			Squid	Calamar Chipirón Sipia **Lula**	*Loligo vulgaris*
Sea bream	Besugo				
Sea snail	Loco	*Concholepas concholepas*	Star anise	Anís estrellado	*Illicium verum*
Sesame seed	Ajonjolí Gergelim Sésamo **Sésamo**	*Sesamum indicum*	Star apple	Caimito Caimo	*Chrysophyllum cainito*
			Star fruit (see Carambola)		
Shallot	Ascalonia Chalote Escaloña **Cebolinha branca**	*Allium cepa*	Strawberry	Fresa Fresón Frutilla Madroneillo Lahueñ (wild) (M) Quellghen (cultivated) (M) **Morango**	*Fragaria chiloenses, Fragaria vesca*
Shark	Cazón				
Shortening	Manteca vegetal				

ENGLISH	SPANISH/INDIAN/ PORTUGUESE	SCIENTIFIC NAMES	ENGLISH	SPANISH/INDIAN/ PORTUGUESE	SCIENTIFIC NAMES
Sugar, Brown	Azúcar morena		Syrup	Jarabe	
	Azúcar rubia			Miel	
	Azúcar prieta fina			**Mel**	
	Açúcar mascavo			**Xarope**	
Sugar, Confectioners'	Azúcar flor		Tamarillo (also called tree tomato)	Tomate de árbol	*Cyphomandra betacea*
	Azúcar glas			Tomate dulce	
	Azúcar impalpable				
	Azúcar molida		Tamarind	Tamarindo	*Tamarindus indica*
	Azúcar pulverizada			**Tamarindo**	
Sugar, Granulated	Azúcar		Tangerine	Mandarina	*Citrus reticulata*
	Azúca (G)			Naranja china	
	Açúcar			**Tangerina**	
Sugar, Molded Brown (also called panela)	Azúcar negra		Tapioca	Mandioca	*Manihot esculenta*
	Chancaca			Tapioca	
	Moscabado			**Tapioca**	
	Panela		Taro	Taro	*Colocasia esculenta*
	Panocha		Tarragon	Estragón	*Artemisia dracunculus*
	Papelón			**Estragão**	
	Piloncillo		Tea	Té	*Thea sinensis*
	Raspadura			**Chá**	
Sugar cane	Caña de azúcar	*Saccharom officinarum*	Thyme	Tomillo	*Thymus vulgaris*
	Caña de miel			**Tomilho**	
	Cana de açúcar		Tofu	Queso de soya	
Sunflower seeds	Semillas de girasol	*Helianthus annuus*	Tomato	Jitomate	*Lycopersicon esculentum*
	Girassol			Jitomate de bola	
Sweetbreads	Blanca			Jitomate guaje (plum)	
	Landra			Tomate encarnado	
	Lechecillas			Tomate rojo	
	Mollejas			Tomatl	
Sweet potato	Achin	*Ipomoea batatas*		Xitomatl	
	Apicho			**Tomate**	
	Batata		Tongue	Lengua	
	Boniato			**Lingua**	
	Buniato		Tree tomato (see Tamarillo)		
	Camote		Tripe	Callos	
	Camotli			Guatita	
	Cumar			Librillo	
	Monato			Mondongo	
	Moniato			Panza	
	Nanqui			Tiras	
	Patata dulce			Tripa	
	Iety (G)			Vientre	
	Batata-doce		Trout	Trucha	
Sweetsop (see Cherimoya)			Tuna	Atún	
Swiss chard	Acelga	*Beta vulgaris*		Bonito	
	Chard			Tuna	
Swordfish	Pez espada	*Xiphias gladius*	Tuna, Albacore	Albacora	
	Espadarte				

ENGLISH	SPANISH/INDIAN/PORTUGUESE	SCIENTIFIC NAMES	ENGLISH	SPANISH/INDIAN/PORTUGUESE	SCIENTIFIC NAMES
Turbot	Rodaballo		Walnut,	Nogal	*Juglans cinerea*
Turkey	Chompipe	*Maleagris mexicana*	English	Nuez	
	Cuchimpe			Nuez de Castilla	
	Guajalote			Nuez de nogal	
	Guanajo			**Noz**	
	Mulito		Watercress	Berro	*Nasturtium officinalis*
	Pavito			Cresón	
	Pavo			**Agriao**	
	Pisco		Watermelon	Cayote	*Citrullus vulgaris*
	Peru			Patilla	
Turmeric	Azafrán de las Indias	*Curcuma longa*		Sandía	
	Curcuma			**Melancia**	
Turnip	Colinabo	*Brassica rapa,*	Wheat	Trigo	*Tricum aestivum,*
	Coyocho	*Brassica napus*		**Trigo**	*Tricum durum*
	Nabo		Wild rice	Arroz silvestre	*Zizania aquatica*
	Papa nabo		Worcester-	Salsa inglesa	
	Nabo		shire sauce		
Turnip	Berza	*Brassica rapa,*	Yacon	Yacón	*Polymnia sonchifolia*
greens	Grelos	*Brassica napus*		Llakuma	
Turtle	Tortuga		Yam (see Ñame)		
	Tartaruja		Yautia (see Malanga)		
Turtledove	Pichón		Yeast	Levadura	
	Rola			**Fermento**	
Ulluco	Cubio	*Ullucus tuberosus*	Yuca (see Cassava)		
	Melloco		Yuca flour	Almidón de yuca	
	Olloco			Yuca-harina	
	Papalisa			**Polvilho**	
	Ulluco		Zambo	Alcayota	*Cucurbita pepo*
Vanilla	Vainilla	*Vanilla planifolia*		Calabaza	*Cucurbita ficifolia*
	Baunilha			Cayote	
Veal	Becerra			Lacayote	
	Mamón			Vitoria	
	Ternera			**Chila**	
	Vitella			**Gila**	
Vegetable pear, vegetable squash (see Chayote)			Zapote	Zapote	*Matisia cordata*
Venison	Venado			**Sapota-do-solimões**	
	Venison		Zucchini	Calabacín	*Cucurbita pepo*
	Veado			Calabacita tierna	
Vinegar	Vinagre			Chaucha	
	Vinagre			Guicoyitos	
Walnut,	Nuez	*Juglans nigra*		Suquini	
Black	Tocte			Zapallito italiano	
	Togte			Zucchini	

Sources

American Roland Food Corporation
71 West 23rd Street
New York, NY 10010
Phone: 800-221-4030
www.rolandfood.com
One-pound packages of whole-grain,
prewashed organic quinoa.

Bob's Red Mill
5209 Southeast International Way
Milwaukie, OR 97222
Phone: 800-349-2173
Fax: 503-653-1339
www.bobsredmill.com
Whole-grain quinoa in 26-ounce packages
and quinoa flour in 22-ounce packages.

Buenos Aires Liquor & Deli
3100 North Cicero Avenue
Chicago, IL 60641
Phone: 773-685-4241
Fax: 773-685-4428
www.buenosairesdeli.com
South American products, especially from
Peru, Argentina, and Brazil.

Catalina's Super Market
1070 North Western Avenue
Los Angeles, CA 90029
Phone: 323-464-1064
Fax: 323-464-3411
www.miseta.com/catalinas.htm
South American products, especially from
Argentina and Peru.

Coisa Nossa
47 West 46th Street
New York, NY 10036
Phone: 212-719-4779
Products from Brazil.

Condor
2349 North Milwaukee Avenue
Chicago, IL 60647
Phone: 773-252-5112
Fax: 773-252-5610
Large selection of Ecuadorian products.

Continental Gourmet
12921 South Prairie Avenue
Hawthorne, CA 90250
Phone: 310-676-5444
South American products, especially from
Argentina and Brazil, and fresh cuts of meat
for *parrilladas*.

Dean & DeLuca
2526 East 36th Street North Circle
Wichita, KS 67219
Phone: 877-826-9246
Fax: 800-781-4050
www.deandeluca.com
Many South American products.

Frieda's
4465 Corporate Center Drive
Los Alamitos, CA 90720
Phone: 800-241-1771
www.friedas.com
Assorted Andean potatoes, dried and fresh
hot peppers from Peru, cornhusks and
banana leaves, calabaza, *chayote*, and all
kinds of dried beans.

Gotham Wines & Liquors
2519 Broadway
New York, NY 10025
Phone: 212-932-0990
Good selection of South American wines
and spirits.

Inca Organics (Wholesalers)
P.O. Box 61-8154
Chicago, IL 60661
Phone: 312-575-9880
Fax: 312-575-9881
www.incaorganics.com

International Market
365 Somerville Avenue
Somerville, MA 02143
Phone: 617-776-1880
Products from Brazil.

Joe's Food & Liquor
3626 West Lawrence Avenue
Chicago, IL 60625
Phone: 773-478-1078
Large selection of products from Colombia,
Venezuela, Ecuador, and Peru.

Kitchen/Market
218 Eighth Avenue
New York, NY 10011
Phone: 212-243-4433 or 888-HOT-4433
www.kitchenmarket.com
Variety of hot peppers from Peru, dried
potatoes (*chuño blanco* and *negro*), and *chuño*
flour.

Liborio Markets
171 South Hudson Avenue
Pasadena, CA 91101
Phone: 626-564-1100
Fax: 626-564-1150
www.liborio.com
Many South American products.

Melissa's/World Variety Produce, Inc.
P.O. Box 21127
Los Angeles, CA 90021
Phone: 800-468-7111
            323-588-0151
Fax: 323-585-4738
www.melissas.com
Assorted Andean potatoes, blue potatoes,
and a variety of South American produce.

El Mercado Food Mart
3767 North Southport
Chicago, IL 60613
Phone: 773-477-5020
All kinds of South American meats.
Products from Argentina, Brazil, Ecuador,
and Peru.

Pepe's Food & Liquor
2333 North Western Avenue
Chicago, IL 60647
Phone: 773-278-8756
Fax: 773-278-8865
Products from Brazil, including *cachaça, carne
seca, chouriço*, and canned corn.

La Única Food Mart
1515 West Devon
Chicago, IL 60660
Phone: 773-274-7788
Many products from Spain and South
America.

White Mountain Farm
8890 Lane 4 North
Mosca, CO 81146
Phone: 800-364-3019
www.whitemountainfarm.com
Organically grown quinoa and a variety
of specialty potatoes (blue, fingerling, and
others).

Ethnic Markets
These are a good source for fresh peas and
fava beans, a variety of greens and vegetables, tropical fruits, frozen rabbit, and quail.

Mexican Markets
Mexican groceries are a good source for
fresh cheese, chorizo, cornhusks, and frozen
banana leaves. In large Mexican supermarkets, it is possible to find *cecina* (dried
meat), which is similar to the South
American *charqui*, as well as many of the
frozen tropical fruit pulps used in this book.

Middle Eastern Meat Markets
These are a good source for baby lamb and
goat, rabbit, frozen wild birds, and variety
meats.

Oriental Markets
Large Oriental supermarkets carry a variety
of items used in South American cuisine,
including unsweetened coconut milk; frozen
squid, baby octopus, wild birds, and rabbit;
fresh tripe; and a variety of other meats and
vegetables.

Selected Bibliography

Acosta, Joseph de. *Historia Natural de las Indias*. México-Buenos Aires: Fondo de Cultura Económica,1962.

Aguirre Achá, Aída Gainsborg v. de. *La Cocina en Bolivia*. La Paz: Cooperativa de Artes Gráficas E. Burrillo, 1968.

Andrade, Margarette de. *Brazilian Cookery*. Rio de Janeiro: A Casa do Livro Eldorado, 1985.

Andrews, Jean. *Peppers: The Domesticated Capsicums*. Austin: University of Texas Press, 1984.

Anunciato, Ofélia Ramos. *Ofélia e a Coziha Brasileira*. São Paulo: Melhoramentos de São Paulo, 1980.

Aquino, Josefina Velila de. *Comida Paraguaya*. 1964. Reprint, Asunción: RP Ediciones, 1993.

Arciniegas, Germán. *América in Europe*. Orlando, Fla.: Harcourt Brace Jovanovich, 1986.

Arguiñando, Karlos. *Karlos Arguiñando en tu Cocina*. Madrid: Editorial Debate, 1998.

Arias Alzate, Eugenio. *Plantas Medicinales*. Medellín: 1985.

Arias Alzate, Eugenio. *Recetario para el Hogar*. Colombia.

Aris, Pepita. *Spanish Cooking*. Secaucus, N.J.: Chartwell Books, 1993.

Barría, Juana. *El Otro Oro de América*. Buenos Aires: Editorial Albatros SACI, 1992.

Bernstein, Harry. *Venezuela and Colombia*. Englewood Cliff: Prentice Hall, N.J., 1964.

Berreteaga, Choly. *Berreteaga Express*. Buenos Aires: Editorial Atlántida, 1994.

Berreteaga, Choly. *La Cocina de Nuestra Tierra*. Buenos Aires: Editorial Atlántida, 1991.

Berroterán, Juana. *La Cocina Venezolana*. Caracas: Talleres Gráficos EDUVEN, 1986.

Bianchini, Francesco, and F. Corbeta. *The Fruits of the Earth*. London: Bloomsbury Books, 1988.

Bosisio, Arturo. *Culinária Amazônica: O sabor da natureza*. Rio de Janeiro: Editora Senac Nacional, 2000.

Botafogo, Dolores. *The Art of Brazilian Cookery*. New York: Hippocrene Books, 1993.

Bravo Walker, Mariana. *Cocina Popular*. Santiago de Chile: Editora Zig-Zag, 1990.

Carrión, Benjamín. *Atahualpa*. Guayaquil: Ediciones Noticia, 1939.

Castillo, Bernal Díaz. *Historia de la Conquista de Nueva España*. México: Editoria Porrúa, SA, 1986.

Centro Cultural Afro-Ecuatoriano. *El Negro en la Historia del Ecuador y del Sur de Colombia*. Quito: Ediciones Abya-Yala, 1988.

Chapellín P., María. *El Libro de Tía María II*. Caracas: Distribuídora Continental, SA, 1963.

Cieza de León, Pedro. *La Crónica del Perú*. Lima: Peisa, 1988.

Círculo de Lectores, SA. *El Gran Libro de La Cocina Ecuatoriana*. Quito.

Círculo de Lectores, SA. *El Menú Diario Ecuatoriano*. Bogotá: 1992.

Círculo de Lectores, SA. *Gran Libro de la Cocina Colombiana*. Colombia, 1985.

Círculo de Lectores, SA. *La Cocina Colombiana*. Vol. 2. Colombia.

Claudia Cozinha (Rio de Janeiro), June/July 2001.

Club "La Orquídea." *El Placer de Comer*. La Paz: Editorial "Los Amigos del Libro," 1986.

Cobo, Bernabé. *Historia del Nuevo Mundo*. Sevilla: Bustos Tavera, 1892.

Cobos, Carmela Ordoñez de. *Cocina Moderna*. Cuenca: Talleres Gráficas "MS," 1958.

Coe, Sophie D. *America's First Cuisines*. Austin: University of Texas Press, 1994.

Coe, Sophie D., and Michael D. Coe. *The True History of Chocolate*. London: Thames and Hudson, 1996.

Conniff, Michael L., and Thomas J. Davis. *Africans in the Americas*. New York: St. Martin's Press, 1994.

Corona, Laurel. *Peru*. San Diego: Lucent Books, 1949.

Crespo, Eulalia Vintimilla de. *Viejos Secretos de la Cocina Cuencana*. Cuenca: 1993.

Davidson, Alan. *Fruit*. New York: Simon and Schuster, 1991.

Davidson, Alan. *The Oxford Companion to Food*. Oxford University Press, 1999.

DeWitt, Dave, Mary Jane Wilan, and Melissa Stock. *Flavors of Africa Cookbook: Spicy African Cooking*. Rocklin, Calif.: Prima Publishing, 1998.

Díaz, Bernal. *The Conquest of New Spain*. Harmondsworth: Penguin Books, 1963.

Doña Juanita. *Cocina Traditional del Ecuador*. Quito: Promotora Cultural Popular, 1984.

Doña Juanita. *Lo Mejor de la Cocina Latinoamericana*. Quito: Promotora Cultural Popular, 1985.

Dor-Ner, Zvi. *Columbus and the Age of Discovery*. New York. William Morrow, 1991.

Editora Lima. *Comidas Típicas del Perú*. Lima: Editora Lima, SA, 1988.

El Comercio (Reportajes). *Finados*. Quito: El Comercio, 1999.

Espinosa, Ismael. *Lo que se Come en Chile*. Santiago de Chile: Ismael Espinosa SA, 1988.

Estrella, Eduardo. *El Pan de América*. Quito: Ediciones Abya-Yala, 1988.

Feibleman, Peter S. *The Cooking of Spain and Portugal*. New York: Time-Life Books, 1969.

Fernandes, Caloca. *Viagem Gastronômica a Través do Brasil*. São Paulo: Editora Senac São Paulo, 2000.

Freyre, Gilberto. *The Masters and the Slaves*. New York: Alfred A. Knopf, 1956.

Gandulfo, Petrona C. de. *El Libro de Doña Petrona*. Buenos Aires: Talleres Gráficos de la Cía. Gral. Fabril Financiera SA, 1959.

González Suárez, Federico. *Historia General de la Republica del Ecuador*. Guayaquil: Cromograf SA.

Harris, Jessica B. *The Africa Cookbook*. New York: Simon and Schuster, 1998.

Harris, Jessica B. *Tasting Brazil*. New York: Macmillan, 1992.

Hartmann, Armando A. *El Libro de Oro de los Peces y Mariscos*. Quito: Impreseñal Cia., 1993.

Hémala, María Rosa García de. *María Rosa y su Cocina*. Guayaquil: Artes Gráficas Senefelder, 1990.

Imprenta Editores. *ABC de la Cocina*. Lima: Imprenta Editores Tipo-Offset.

Imprenta Editores. *Cocina China "Chifa."* Lima: Imprenta Editores Tipo-Offset, 1986.

Jermyn, Leslie. *Paraguay*. New York: Marshall Cavendish, 2000.

Jermyn, Leslie. *Uruguay*. New York: Marshall Cavendish, 1999.

Leandro, Acheele. *Cocina Venezolana para Gente Joven*. Caracas: Refolit C.A.

León, Ramón David. *Geografía Gastronómica Venezolana*. Caracas: Editorial Promo Print, 1984.

Leonard, Jonathan Norton. *Latin American Cooking*. New York: Time-Life Books, 1968.

Loveman, Brian. *Chile: The Legacy of Hispanic Capitalism*. New York: Oxford University Press, 1988.

Manjón, Maite. *The Gastronomy of Spain and Portugal*. New York: Prentice Hall, 1990.

Marín Vivado, Roberto. *Chilenos Cocinando a la Chilena*. Santiago: Max Besser Leiva, 1997.

Marsland, William D., and Amy L. Marsland. *Venezuela Through Its History*. Binghamton, N.Y.: Vail-Ballou Press, 1954.

Misia-Peta. *Cocina Oriental Chifa*. Lima: Editorial Mercurio SA, 1987.

Misia-Peta. *Nueva Cocina Peruana*. Lima: Editorial Mercurio SA, 1988.

Misia-Peta. *Pescados y Mariscos*. Lima: Editorial Mercurio SA, 1988.

Morales, Albert Ronald. *Frutoterapia*. Santa Fe de Bogotá: Ecoe Ediciones, 1999.

Murgueytio, Reinaldo. *Yachay-Huasi*. Quito: Editorial Escuela Central Técnica, 1945.

National Research Council. *Lost Crops of the Incas*. Washington, D.C.: National Academy Press, 1990.

Ordoñes, Delia Crespo de. *Cocinemos con Kristy*. Quito: Artes Gráficas, 1969.

Ortins, Patuleia Ana. *Portuguese Homestyle Cooking*. Northampton, Mass.: Interlink Publishing Group, 2001.

Ortiz, Elisabeth Lambert. *The Book of Latin American Cooking*. New York: Alfred A. Knopf, 1979.

Oviedo, Gonzalo Fernandez. *Natural History of the West Indies*. Chapel Hill: University of North Carolina Press, 1959.

Pateman, Robert. *Bolivia*. New York: Marshall Cavendish, 1979.

Paz Lagarrigue, María. *Recetas de Las Rengifo*. 17th ed. Santiago de Chile: Editora Zig-Zag, 1986.

Pazos B. Julio. *Recetas Criollas*. Quito: Editorial El Conejo, 1991.

Pirolo, Ketty de. *Cocina Práctica y Económica*. Buenos Aires: Ediciones Lidiun, 1990.

Post, Laurens van der. *African Cooking*. New York: Time-Life Books, 1970.

Publicación de la Revista Hogar. *Lo Mejor de la Cocina Criolla*. Guayaquil: 1993.

Riett, Riordan, and Richard Scott Sacks. *Paraguay: The Personalist Legacy*. Boulder, Colo.: Westview Press, 1991.

Rios, R. *Moderna Cocina Peruana*. Lima: Editorial Navarrete, 1985.

Rojas-Lombardi, Felipe. *The Art of South American Cooking*. New York: HarperCollins, 1991.

Sahagún, Fray Bernardino de. *Historia General de Nueva España*. Vols. 1 and 2. Madrid: Alianza Editorial, SA, 1988.

Sanabria, Ana Marlene Cañipa de, ed. *Recetas de Comida Regional Boliviana*. Vols. 1 and 2. La Paz: Empresa Editora PROINSA.

Scannone, Armando. *Mi Cocina II*. 9th ed. Caracas: Impresos Altamira, 2001.

Schurz, William Lytle. *Latin America*. New York: E. P. Dutton, 1964.

Sertima, Ivan van. *They Came Before Columbus*. New York: Random House, 1976.

Silva, Silvestre. *Fruit in Brazil*. São Paulo: Empresa das Artes, 1996.

Skidmore, Thomas E., and Peter Smith. *Modern Latin America*. New York: Oxford University Press, 1984.

Smith, Andrew F. *The Tomato in America*. Columbia: University of South Carolina Press, 1994.

Smithsonian Institution Quincentenary Symposium. *Good as Gold*. Washington, D.C.: Smithsonian National Museum of American History, 1991.

Sokolov, Raymond. *Why We Eat What We Eat*. New York: Summit Books, 1991.

Stanbury Aguirre, Jorge, and Jonathan Cavanagh. *Great Peruvian Recipes*. Lima, Peru: Peru Reporting, 1997.

Sternberg, Rabbi Robert. *The Sephardic Kitchen*. New York: HarperCollins, 1996.

Super, John C. *Food, Conquest, and Colonization in Sixteen-Century Spanish America*. Albuquerque: University of New Mexico Press, 1988.

Tannahill, Reay. *Food in History*. New York: Stein and Day, 1984.

Tapia, Mario E., and Ana de la Torre. *La mujer Campesina y las Semillas Andinas*. Lima: Fredy's Publicaciones y Servicios, 1993.

Varese, Juan Antonio. *Las Recetas del "Valiza."* Uruguay: Editorial Fin de Siglo, 1994.

Vázquez Prego, Alfredo. *Así Cocinamos los Argentinos*. Buenos Aires: Editorial El Ateneo, 1979.

Vega, Garcilaso de la. *Comentarios Reales*. 1609. Reprint, México: Editorial Porrúa, SA, 1984.

Velasco, Emilia de, and Carola G. de Muzevich. *Cocina Tradicional Boliviana*. La Paz: Editorial los Amigos del Libro, 1988.

Velasco, Juan de. *Historia del Reino de Quito*. Vols. 1 and 2. Quito: Ediciones de Ultimas Noticias, Editora "El Comercio," 1789.

Viard, Michel. *Fruits and Vegetables of the World*. Ann Arbor, Mich.: Longmeadow Press, 1995.

Viola, Herman J., and Carolyn Margolis. *Seeds of Change*. Washington, D.C.: Smithsonian Institution, 1991.

Vokral, Edita V. *Qoñi-Chiri*. Quito: Ediciones Abya-Yala, 1991.

Weatherford, Jack. *Indian Givers*. New York: Crown Publishers, 1988.

Weinstein, Martin. *Uruguay: Democracy at the Crossroads*. Boulder, Colo.: Westview Press, 1988.

Werlich, David P. *Peru: A Short History*. Carbondale: Southern Illinois University Press, 1978.

White, Alan. *Hierbas del Ecuador*. Quito: Ediciones Libri-Mundi, 1985.

Winn, Peter. *Americas*. New York: Pantheon Books, 1992.

Index

Bean(s) *(cont.)*
lupini, preparing, 411–12
Lupini, Watercress, and
Avocado Salad, 169–70
Spicy Mashed Chickpeas, 309
and Spinach, Veal Tongue
with, 238
Stewed Lentils, 310–11
Tuna with Onion and Hot
Pepper Salsa, 167
Vegetable Salad with
Vinaigrette Dressing, 175
and Vegetable Stew, 281–82
Venezuelan Shredded Beef
with Rice and, 206–7
with Walnuts and Hot
Peppers, 309–10
Béchamel (Medium White
Sauce), 405–6
Beef. *See also* Veal
Andean Meat and Vegetable
Soup with Chuño Negro,
142–43
Argentine Hominy and Bean
Soup, 140–41
Baked Turnovers, 103–4
Black Beans with Smoked and
Fresh Meats, 244–46
Boiled Tongue, 407
Braised, 203–4
Braised Oxtails with Sausage,
207
Chilean Corn Torte, 208–9
Cow's Feet Soup, 142
Dried, with Rice, 211–12
Filling, Yuca Pie with, 209–10
and Ham, Achoghas/Caiguas
Stuffed with, 246–47
and Ham, Pasta Torte with,
246
Heart, Skewered, 125–26
with Manioc Meal and Ripe
Plantains, 210–11
Oxtail Stew with Watercress,
208

Rolled Flank Steak, 205–6
Salad Greens with Meat,
167–68
Seasoned Ground, with
Potatoes and Onion Sauce,
212–13
Shredded, with Rice and
Beans, Venezuelan, 206–7
Stew with Vegetables and
Fruit, Uruguayan, 204–5
Stuffed Arepas from
Venezuela, 349
Tongue with Raisin Sauce,
238–39
Venezuelan Turnovers,
111–12
and Yuca Patties, 214
Berenjena a la Vinagreta, 75–76
Berenjena Escabechada, 76
Berry(ies). *See also*
Strawberry(ies)
Andean Blackberry Ice
Cream, 387
Blackberry Sauce, 400
and Purple Corn Soup,
383–84
Raspberry Sauce, 400
Beurre Manié, 414
Beverages. *See also* Cocktails;
Milk Shakes
Brazilian Coffee, 52
Champagne Punch with
Passion Fruit Juice, 39
Cinnamon Tea, 47
Corn Drink, 43
Fruit and Barley Drink, 382
Fruit Drink, 44
Hot Chocolate Brazilian Style,
51
Hot Chocolate with Coconut
Milk, 50–51
Hot Chocolate with Milk for
Eleven O'Clock, 50
Hot Quinoa Drink, 48
Hot Wine Drink, 47

maté, about, 55
prepared with bitter yuca,
53–54
prepared with toasted flours,
52–53
Ripe Plantain and Milk Drink,
48
Rum Punch, 38
spirits, types of, 34
Tamarind Drink, 44
tea, types of, 54–56
Wheat Berries with Dried
Peach Compote, 382–83
wine, types of, 40–41
Wine Punch, 38
Wine Punch with Port, 39
Biche de Pescado, 151
Biscochuelo, 366
*Biscoitinhos de Castanha com
Pimenta*, 115
Black Beans, 308–9
and Corn, Quinoa Salad with,
163–64
with Smoked and Fresh
Meats, 244–46
Blackberry, Andean, Ice Cream,
387
Blackberry Sauce, 400
Black Clam Cebiche, 70–71
black clams, preparing, 409
Bobó de Camarão, 270–71
Bocados de Quinua, 122
Bolinhos de Bacalhua, 123–24
Bolitas de Mandioca, 122
Bolivian Chicken Turnovers,
108–9
Bolivian Hot Pepper Salsa, 335
Bolivian Humita, 91
Bolivian Pisco Cocktail, 35
Boronia, 291
Brains, Calf's, and Mushrooms,
Crepes Filled with, 239–40
Brazilian Chicken Soup with
Rice, 148
Brazilian Coffee, 52